# WITHOUT HESITATION

# WITHOUT HESITATION

The Odyssey of an American Warrior

*General* (RET.) Hugh Shelton

*14th Chairman, Joint Chiefs of Staff*

with *RONALD LEVINSON*

and *MALCOLM McCONNELL*

St. Martin's Griffin
New York

www.stmartins.com

The Library of Congress has cataloged the hardcover edition as follows:

Shelton, Henry H.
    Without hesitation : the odyssey of an American warrior / Hugh Shelton with Ronald Levinson and Malcolm McConnell.—1st ed.
        p. cm.
    Includes index.
    ISBN 978-0-312-59905-8
    1. Shelton, Henry H.   2. Generals—United States—Biography.   3. United States. Army—Biography.   4. U.S. Special Operations Command—Biography.   5. United States. Joint Chiefs of Staff—Biography.   6. United States—History, Military—20th century.   7. United States—History, Military—21st century.   8. United States—Military policy.   I. Levinson, Ronald.   II. McConnell, Malcolm.   III. Title.
    E840.5.S474A3 2010
    355.0092—dc22
    [B]

2010037249

ISBN 978-0-312-60457-8 (trade paperback)

First St. Martin's Griffin Edition: September 2011

10  9  8  7  6  5  4  3  2  1

*Dedicated to Carolyn, who was with me every step*

*of the journey, and to our sons, Jon, Jeff, and Mark,*

*whose sacrifices made it possible*

# CONTENTS

## Part III: AFTER THE FALL

# ACKNOWLEDGMENTS

In acknowledging all those without whose inspiration, encouragement, and persistence this book would not have been written, first and foremost are my coauthors, Ron Levinson, who provided insistence, dedication, and hard work, and Malcolm McConnell, whose contributions were in spite of having to battle personal challenges simultaneously; Marc Resnick, our editor at St. Martin's Press, whose guidance, understanding, and professionalism were indispensible; and Doug Grad, my literary agent, whose expertise and knowledge led to finding the very best publisher. Without these four individuals it would not have happened. And to Cheryl and Mitch Marovitz, a special thanks for their great hospitality and the use of their home for many meetings.

I have been privileged to be associated with many great people, from presidents to privates, who inspired, supported, and assisted me along the way. To the millions of men and women in our armed forces, thank you for your outstanding support and performance. There is no one who can compare with you. I literally stood on the shoulders of giants; so many that it is impossible to list them all, but I would be remiss if I did not mention Charlie Speed, Ben and Will Godwin, Lucille Anderson, Charlie Lockhart, John Caldwell, Bill Friday, Walter "Buse" Tully, Arne Eliasson, "Doc" Simpson, Jerry Esterson, Doug Coulter, Bob Moberg, Harold Stanley, Dan Schungle, Jarold Hutchison, Jim McElroy, Ken Lewis, Ken Acousti, Dean Schnoor, Bill Marr, Jim Tucker, Bill Old, John and Chuck Lemoyne, Dick Malvesti, Tom Groppel, Frank Audrain, Francis Donovan, Victor Robertson, Monte Hess, Terry Scott, Edwin Kennedy, Harry Brooks, Bob Edwards, Bill Shackelford, Carmen Cavezza, Bob Elton, John Otjen, George Close, Denny Leach, Ralph Pryor, Bill Carpenter, Lee Mortenson,

Jim Townes, Orville Windham, Dick Cavazos, Ed Trobaugh, Linc Jones, Charlie Otstott, Bill Kail, Glenn Marsh, Peter Boylan, J. D. Smith, Bobby Porter, Bill McBride, Keith Kellogg, William "Buck" Kernan, Jack Hook, Bob Frusha, CSM Denny, Corinna Clouston, Mark Erwin, Ralph Newman, Paul Cerjan, Sherm Williford, Jack Keane, Terry Roche, Mike Plummer, Sonny Moore, Jack Nix, Felix Acosta, Mike Byron, Marie Allen, Jim Lindsey, Carl Stiner, Gary Luck, Tony Zinni, Binnie Peay, Bill Mason, Ron Adams, Doug Brown, Charlie Holland, Pete Schoomaker, Ray Smith, Jim McCombs, Andy Serrano, Mark "Ranger" Jones, Richard LaQuesta, Kay Leonard, Benny Suggs, John Campbell, Burke Garrett, Tony Peterson, Suzanne Giesemann, Carolyn Petrina, Randy Buhidar, Marty Dempsey, Dave Petraeus, Doug Lute, Bill Caldwell, Steve Pietropaoli, Denny Klauer, T. McCreary, Phil Strub, Bonnie Goff, Frank Angelo, Marshall McCants, Kris Cicio, Scott Fry, Marty Dempsey, Dave Weisman, Joe Ralston, Dick Myers, Vern Clarke, Ric Shinseki, Tom Fargo, Denny Reimer, Gordon Sullivan, H. T. Johnson, Bob Riscassi, Ann Dunwoody, Carl Vuono, P. D. Miller, Mike Ryan, Jay Johnson, Pete Pace, Russ Honore, Walt Slocombe, John Hamre, Rudy DeLeon, John Shalikashvili, Bill Crowe, Tom Kelly, John Abizaid, Stan McChrystal, Dell Dailey, Jim Steinbrenner, Sandy Berger, Don Kerrick, Lew Merletti, Brian Stafford, Louie Freeh, Bob Mueller, Jim Hunt, Bob Etheridge, Mike McIntyre, Bruce Willingham, Bill Shippey, Walter Jones, Sue Myrick, Jesse Helms, Ike Skelton, John Warner, Carl Levin, Strom Thurmond, Trent Lott, Hillary Clinton, George Tenet, Colin Powell, Bill Perry, Bill Cohen, and Presidents Bill Clinton and G. W. Bush. Several others I cannot mention due to the nature of their assignments, but they know who they are and how much I valued their support.

Members of the Fourth Estate whom I am indebted to are numerous but first and foremost are Tom Brokaw and Bradley Graham, whose friendship I truly value and whose integrity is unquestionable. Others to whom I am indebted include Jack McWethy, Barbara Starr, David Martin, Bob Schieffer, Cokie Roberts, Sam Donaldson, Tim Russert, Larry King, and Jamie McIntyre.

Since retiring in 2001, I have worked with a number of outstanding values-based leaders and individuals who have also truly inspired me. These include Ross Perot, August Busch III, Ed Whittaker, Chuck Knight, Billy Payne, Bill White, Tom and Bill O'Gara, Chip Lennon, Joe Kampf, Matthew Szulik, Jim Whitehurst, Connie Stevens, Erskine Bowles, Mike Davis, Debbie Reno, Ambassador Jim Jones, John Britt, Rob Jones, John Marselle, Jim Forese, Vilma Martinez, Joyce Roche, Pat Stokes, Ed Gore,

August Busch IV, Stephen Ondra, Ed Carney, Marc Fath, Darryl Smith, Dave Wolfe, Barry Goss, Jim Hunt, Tom O'Brien, and John Jacobs.

Recovery from a fall that left me paralyzed and doomed to "never walk again or be able to use my hands" was made possible by God, ably assisted by the superb team at Walter Reed Army Medical Center. A big thanks to Hal Timboe, Kevin Kiley, Geoff Ling, Avery Davis, the staff of Ward 72, Mary Maniscalco-Theberge, Rick Rickley, Zack "Ironman" Solomon, Lynn Lowe, Chuck Quick, Dave Polly, and the world's finest neurosurgeon and a great leader, Jim Ecklund. To Jim and the staff that cared for me during my eighty-three days as a patient, you are the best and I offer you my heartfelt thanks.

The data in this book has come primarily from memory. If there are errors, they are errors of omission versus commission. Events are described to the best of my recollection, and in a few instances I have changed the names.

Finally, I have been blessed with a loving family. While God has been my copilot, Carolyn has been my pillar of strength and my greatest inspiration. My parents, Hugh and Sarah "Patsy" Shelton, made me the man I am. Carolyn's parents, James and Annie Bell Johnson, were always there for us. My sister, Sarah, and her husband, Jim, my brothers David and Ben and their wives, Claudette and Susan, have been constant sources of strength. Our three sons, Jon, Jeff, and Mark, remain my greatest pride and joy. Jon, Anne, Cassie, Heather and Hannah, Jeff, Savannah, Sam, Ben, Mark, Aylan, and Henry provide the greatest joys of life.

As I have learned over and over, faith, family, and friends are indeed the greatest treasures of life.

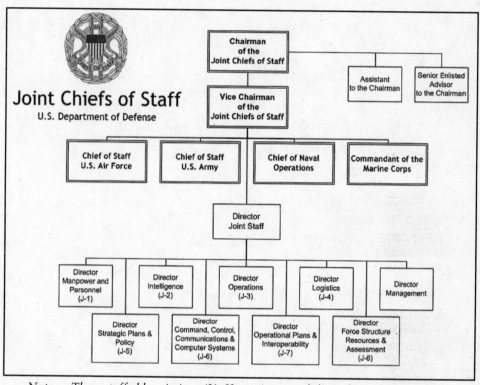

**Joint Chiefs of Staff**

U.S. Department of Defense

Chairman of the Joint Chiefs of Staff

Assistant to the Chairman

Senior Enlisted Advisor to the Chairman

Vice Chairman of the Joint Chiefs of Staff

Chief of Staff U.S. Air Force

Chief of Staff U.S. Army

Chief of Naval Operations

Commandant of the Marine Corps

Director Joint Staff

Director Manpower and Personnel (J-1)

Director Intelligence (J-2)

Director Operations (J-3)

Director Logistics (J-4)

Director Management

Director Strategic Plans & Policy (J-5)

Director Command, Control, Communications & Computer Systems (J-6)

Director Operational Plans & Interoperability (J-7)

Director Force Structure Resources & Assessment (J-8)

*Note — These staff abbreviations (J1, J2, etc.) are used throughout the book.*

With this honor comes the awesome responsibility of ensuring that our own forces remain trained, ready, and equipped to deal with the threats and dangers of today, as well as an uncertain future.

This is a responsibility that I accept *without hesitation or reservation*.

*—General Hugh Shelton,*
*upon nomination for Chairman, July 17, 1997*

# WITHOUT HESITATION

# Prologue

# BREATHLESS

8:33 A.M. March 23, 2002, Fairfax, Virginia

I'd been poisoned in Vietnam and ambushed in Haiti; instituted the war plan for invading Afghanistan and knighted by the Queen; attacked by the Vice President and prevented a high-ranking Cabinet official from precipitating global war by deliberately shooting down an American airplane—so the last scenario I could have imagined for my own death was falling off a ladder while trimming a tree in my backyard. Yet, that's exactly where I found myself on the morning of March 23, when I slammed headfirst onto the ground.

I was completely paralyzed from the neck down and unable to breathe . . . oxygen nearly depleted . . . starting to lose consciousness . . . powerless to do anything about it. . . .

My mind flashed through snippets of the incredible "ride" that constituted my life.

October 1997

Early on in my days as Chairman of the Joint Chiefs of Staff, we had small, weekly White House breakfasts in National Security Advisor Sandy Berger's office that included me, Sandy, Bill Cohen (Secretary of Defense), Madeleine Albright (Secretary of State), George Tenet (head of the CIA), Leon Firth (VP chief of staff for security), Bill Richardson (ambassador to the U.N.), and a few other senior administration officials. These were informal sessions where we would gather around Berger's table and talk about concerns over coffee and breakfast served by the White House dining facility. It was a comfortable setting that encouraged brainstorming of potential options on a variety of issues of the day.

During that time we had U-2 aircraft on reconnaissance sorties over Iraq. These planes were designed to fly at extremely high speeds and altitudes (over seventy thousand feet) both for pilot safety and to avoid detection.

At one of my very first breakfasts, while Berger and Cohen were engaged in a sidebar discussion down at one end of the table and Tenet and Richardson were preoccupied in another, one of the Cabinet members present leaned over to me and said, "Hugh, I know I shouldn't even be asking you this, but what we really need in order to go in and take out Saddam is a precipitous event—something that would make us look good in the eyes of the world. *Could you have one of our U-2s fly low enough—and slow enough—so as to guarantee that Saddam could shoot it down?*"

The hair on the back of my neck bristled, my teeth clenched, and my fists tightened. I was so mad I was about to explode. I looked across the table, thinking about the pilot in the U-2 and responded, "Of course we can . . ." which prompted a big smile on the official's face.

"You can?" was the excited reply.

"Why, of course we can," I countered. "Just as soon as we get *your* ass qualified to fly it, I will have it flown just as low and slow as you want to go."

The official reeled back and immediately the smile disappeared. "I knew I should not have asked that. . . ."

"No, you should not have," I strongly agreed, still shocked at the disrespect and sheer audacity of the question. "Remember, there is one of our great Americans flying that U-2, and you are asking me to intentionally send him or her to their death for an opportunity to kick Saddam. The last time I checked, we don't operate like that here in America."

I left the room that day but I never forgot it. I went back and I shared it with the Joint Chiefs—not revealing who the official was—but nonetheless getting into how it had played out. "You may not think those types of things still happen in Washington, but trust me—they do, and I've just been exposed to it. Keep your antennas up and *do not ever fall into it.*"

* * *

Looking back on the thirty-four years of my career that led up to my appointment as Chairman, I felt comfortable with the man I saw in the mirror. I had earned a solid reputation as an honest, straightforward role model for integrity, ethics, and selflessness—a leader whose moral character was beyond reproach. Now, as I proudly stepped into my position as highest-ranking military officer in all of the United States Armed Forces—the principal military adviser to the President and the National Security Council—I was excited to serve as a living example to the three million-plus men and women of our armed forces that it really is possible to rise to the top of one's profession through character-based leadership and without its being at the expense of others.

But what was I stepping into behind the heavily fortified walls of the Pentagon's inner circle? Would subsequent White House gatherings attempt to drag me into more revolting conspiracies? I'd had bosses who asked me to steal for them, others to access and falsify their records. I'd seen my share of cowards and relieved them of duty. But never in those thirty-four years had I seen—or even imagined—anything that came close to a senior Cabinet member suggesting I be party to killing one of our great airmen in hopes of starting a war. Was this typical of what really went on at the highest levels of the United States government, the country I had passionately devoted my life to serve?


If my first few weeks as Chairman were any indication of the challenges the next four years would bring, I would have countless opportunities to call upon those principles deeply ingrained within me as a young boy in a small North Carolina town called Speed.

# Part I
# UP THE RANKS

*We make war that we may live in peace.*
—ARISTOTLE

# Chapter One

# THE BEGINNING

January 1942–July 1963

Mapleton Farm was two miles north of Speed, a small North Carolina coastal plains town of about eighty people with a cluster of white frame houses shaded by tall old oaks and elms. The tracks of the Atlantic Coast Line ran through town. There was the post office, the train station, three stores, and the Speed Baptist and Episcopal churches.

My grandfather, Benjamin Franklin Shelton, developed a farm of over one thousand acres. He was one of the state's first "master farmers," recognized for introducing modern agricultural techniques, especially for breeding quality Hereford cattle. Ben Shelton and his family did well on their farm, but the Depression hit them hard. Grandfather died on August 30, 1931. He had three sons and two daughters. My uncle Henry Gray Shelton (who later went on to become a state senator) borrowed money to save the farm and provide a home for my grandmother and his fourteen-year-old brother, my father, Hugh Shelton.

Hugh would marry my mother, Sarah Laughlin, in January 1939. From the very beginning Mother was known as "Patsy," since she'd been born on St. Patrick's Day and lived at 1107 St. Patrick Street. Mother was a graduate of Eastern Carolina Teachers College and taught first grade at Speed Elementary School. She also played the organ at Speed Baptist Church—in fact she played it for more than sixty years, until she died on February 16, 2006, at the age of eighty-nine. My parents lived on Mapleton Farm, across Route 122 from the main house of my grandmother and my uncle Henry Gray. I was my parents' first child, born on January 2, 1942, less than a month after the attack on Pearl Harbor. My father and Uncle Henry were exempt from military duty due to their essential farm work.

But both my maternal uncles, Buddy and Cham Laughlin, served in the Army in World War II. Like most of their generation, they didn't dwell on their experiences, but just quietly got on with their lives once they came home.

My younger brother, David, was born in 1944, my sister, Sarah, in 1949, and the youngest, Ben, in 1956. It was a good thing we had a large family because there was always plenty of work to go around. We raised corn, tobacco, soybeans, millet, peanuts, and cotton, in addition to mowing pastures and cutting silage for the registered Hereford herd of around two hundred head.

One of my earliest memories, when I was about three-years-old, is of helping my grandmother "Mammy" Shelton feed her chickens. A speckled rooster must have seen me as a threat to his brood because he flew up, pecking at my head.

"Mammy!" I yelled.

She grabbed the rooster and wrung its neck, then dropped the flapping body to the ground, where it jumped and rolled for almost a minute.

"Can't have *that* kind of chicken around here, Hugh," Mammy said.

Sunday after church we had stewed chicken with dumplings.


My maternal grandfather was the Edgecombe County Manager and he worked at the old courthouse. Mother used to tell how I would accompany him for quick trips to work, and we would have great times together. For the most part I was very well behaved, but on one of those trips I decided to exert my independence. I was four at the time.

Granddaddy pulled up to the front of the courthouse and parked, taking the same spot as always. "Now you stay here in the car, Hugh, and Granddaddy will be right back."

"Okay," I said. Then I slid across to the driver's side and had no trouble occupying myself playing with the knobs, buttons, and that great big steering wheel. I'd looked out the open window at the busy town square and pretend that I was driving the car. It was so much fun . . . for about five minutes. Then I got bored. To this four-year-old, it looked a lot more interesting on the *other* side of that window than it did on my side. So I opened that heavy car door and left to explore.

I crossed the street and walked around a bit, and eventually entered Mr. George Howard Fountain's office. "I'm looking for my granddaddy," I said, gazing up at the man behind the desk.

"What's his name?" he asked.

"Granddaddy," I replied.

"Any idea where he works?"

"At the courthouse," I said, turning and pointing through the big plate-glass window.

"Well, let's go over and find him," the man said, taking my hand with a warm smile so typical of Tarboro in the 1940s.

Needless to say, Granddaddy was surprised, although not upset. I was the apple of his eye. On the way home he would stop and pick up *The New York Times*; he read it out loud to me and my brother David from the time I was two. I seemed engrossed, Mother would say. Since that time period included the war years, maybe those early newspaper sessions with Granddaddy explain my fascination with the military.

I also remember as a small child holding Daddy's big hand as we walked among the placid, deep-chested cattle with their dark reddish orange coats and white heads, chests, and feet. The herd was stocky and fat by today's standards, and it produced top-quality, well-marbled beef.

At about age nine, I started helping grind millet and corn-stalk silage, which we loaded onto a clanking conveyor belt into tall, cylindrical brick silos and two underground silage pits. This was a late-summer job, done before school started after Labor Day. The fermenting silage radiated heat and a sweet-sour smell. Grinding silage was tough, unpleasant work.

One summer morning I was pitching chopped silage onto the conveyer belt and my sweaty face and neck were itchy with flecks of stalk. The sun pounded down and the humidity was about 90 percent. I was thirsty—*real* thirsty. A big thermos of cold water sat in the shade of the tractor. I lowered my pitchfork and gazed at the thermos. Then I saw Daddy watching me under the brim of his cap. He didn't say a word. That wasn't necessary. The message was clear: we drank water when we took a break, once an hour and at lunch. I lifted the pitchfork and got back to work.

We also raised pigs for ham, bacon, and fresh pork. Every October, the adults would slaughter several hogs, then hoist them on a block-and-tackle to bleed out. They'd deep-fry strips of skin into cracklings and then wash the ropy white lengths of small intestines and cook them into chitterlings. To put it mildly, that produced a rather unique odor. I'm proud of my southern heritage, but to this day I cannot eat chitterlings.

Hunting was good on the farm; rabbits, squirrels, and deer were plentiful. My daddy taught me to shoot when I was seven, first with a .22, then, when I was about twelve, with my own 20-gauge shotgun, and later with a family heirloom Parker 10-gauge double barrel that kicked so hard it almost knocked me over. Years later, during infantry training, the skills of marksmanship and silent stalking became second nature to me, but they had been recreation for me as a young kid hunting on the farm.

———

I began raising Hereford steers as a 4-H project when I was nine and continued until I was seventeen and a senior in high school. Each year I had the responsibility of raising a young steer calf, taking the animal soon after it was castrated. The steer barn was three-quarters of a mile through woods, pasture, and over a stream from our house. My brother David and I walked to the barn twice every day in the summer heat and freezing winter rain to feed, wash, and curry our steers and trim their hooves.

The April livestock shows where cattle were judged on their condition and appearance were the high point of the 4-H year. My parents bought me a black leather silver-studded steer halter to show my calf. When the auction was over, I replaced that fancy halter with one made of rope before the steer was taken away to slaughter. Like other farm kids, I learned to be kind to animals but not unduly sentimental about their fate.

The steers were quite small in the beginning but grew rapidly during the year. Once I took on steers as a 4-H project, I acquired what city people might have seen as an unusual maturity for a child. One of the greatest lessons I learned was that the animal was my responsibility. I could ask for advice, but no one else would do the work.

The 4-H club in Edgecombe County, as elsewhere in rural America, was a wholesome focus of activity for young people. We took very seriously the 4-H pledge to dedicate our Heads to clearer thinking, our Hearts to greater loyalty, our Hands to larger service, and our Health to better living. Farming was a family-centered way of life; 4-H prepared boys and girls for a future in agriculture.

But 4-H also honed organizational skills valuable off the farm, particularly the ability to speak in front of other people at a very young age. It's no coincidence that I have felt comfortable with public speaking since I was a boy.

When I was twelve, I joined the county 4-H livestock judging team with three other boys. We practiced under the supervision of the county agricultural agent, Charlie Lockhart, who critiqued our ability. Usually our team would visit a neighboring farm and be shown a group of four cattle we had never seen before. Individual team members would have to rate each cow or steer, writing its rank in a small notebook before declaring.

One fall day we judged Hereford steers on a farm south of Tarboro. When it came time to declare, I held up my notebook and did my best to speak confidently. But I was certainly aware of Charlie Lockhart and the three other boys. "I place number four first," I said, using the proper judging formula. "I place number three second. I place number one third. And I place number two fourth."

Then Charlie came forward and spoke in a kind, quiet tone. "Hugh, do you really think number four is fuller in the loin than number three? Let's look at them again."

*What am I missing?* I thought. Then Charlie took the time to show the whole team. As always, he was patient and thorough.

This was excellent training for later life: I learned to gain from constructive criticism, and because of Charlie's respectful demeanor, I learned how to give it most effectively, too. Throughout my career I would encounter great leaders who reflected Charlie's manner, and many others not so great who had missed that lesson.

———

At Speed Elementary School, I was so bored in second grade that I cried because my mother, who had been my first-grade teacher, had already taught me the alphabet, numbers, and cursive writing at home. Fortunately, I was able to skip third grade and move right on to fourth, which, combined with 4-H projects, made life challenging again.

Rural Edgecombe County was a great place to live in the 1950s. There were no drugs and no alcohol problems. Crime was almost nonexistent. In summer, unlocked screen doors caught the breeze.

Schools reinforced home values. Every morning we had a short prayer, followed by the Pledge of Allegiance. There were rules, and we followed them. If we did not, what's now called corporal punishment (which we knew as paddling) was the quick and certain outcome.

I made it a point to be good and avoid being paddled. I knew that if I was bad I'd get my rear whacked both at school and at home by Daddy, who was an old-fashioned disciplinarian. One day in lunch line, Ray, the kid in front of me, began stomping his feet and the noise echoed loudly on the pine-plank floor.

Mrs. Hart, the teacher in charge of the lunchroom that day, strode up. "Hugh Shelton, you stop that racket."

As soon as she turned her back, Ray grinned and began stomping again.

Mrs. Hart marched back and shook her finger at me. "Didn't you hear what I said, Hugh?"

"Mrs. Hart," I said, trying to explain, "I wasn't stomping my feet."

Lying was bad. Trying to cover up the original offense was even worse. Punishment came fast: a solid whack to my backside. Ray grinned again, but the matter was closed. Although there was no justice that day, I didn't complain. I was learning to accept the hand I was dealt and make the best of it. But I never stood in line near Ray again.

That was far from the end of my troubles at school, thanks to a bully named Arnold—the playground tyrant who picked on everybody. Up through seventh grade, I was smaller than him. But by eighth grade I had shot up six inches and had long arms, strong from farm work. One day on the playground during a recess baseball game Arnold swaggered up and pushed me hard in the chest. I'd never been in a fight, but I wasn't going to let this guy continue intimidating the school. My reach now exceeded his by several inches, so I got under his flailing arms and proceeded to use him as a punching bag, bloodying his nose and swelling his left eye. Unknown to either of us, up in the schoolhouse, the principal, Mittie Spencer, my mother, and several other teachers watched me pound Arnold to the grass and continue until he cried uncle. They couldn't have been happier. Finally somebody had paid Arnold in the only currency he understood.

I never saw him bully anyone again.

———

I met Carolyn Johnson when I was starting fifth grade and she was in fourth. Carolyn was tall for her age with blond hair and striking blue eyes. There was an immediate spark of attraction.

She was one of six children and, like me, had grown up on a farm. Her father, James Johnson, owned and drove an eighteen-wheeler, and her family had moved from Tarboro to Speed that summer. The Johnsons were a great family and a joy to be around.

Carolyn and I began to date in the fall of 1958, when I was in eleventh grade at North Edgecombe High School. That was before I had a driver's license, so we went on a triple date to a drive-in movie with Berry Lane Anderson and Bobby Joyner and their girlfriends. We saw the new Alfred Hitchcock thriller, *Vertigo,* with Jimmy Stewart and Kim Novak. I don't remember much about the movie, but I do remember thinking that Carolyn was prettier than any Hollywood star. After that, we began to date regularly.

My family always had three or four horses on the farm. The one that I usually rode was a white gelding named Silver. He was wild, loved to rear up, and had a very tough mouth on the bit. I often rode him two miles into Speed to visit Carolyn and watch television with her family. They all enjoyed *I Love Lucy* and *Ted Mack's Amateur Hour.* I preferred Chuck Connors in *The Rifleman* because he was a tough farmer defending his rights, although I thought it odd that he never did any real farm work. I sure could have used all that free time away from the barn and plowing to chase bandits and renegades.

Once, riding Silver back to the farm after watching *Gunsmoke* at Carolyn's house, I started him galloping. His mane was flying when the right rein snapped. I had trained him to neck rein and could guide his direction but could not slow him down. "Whoa" did not work with that horse. Silver was at a dead run all the way to the farm; like all horses, he was eager to get home. He turned off the highway and onto the dirt road leading to the barn. Unfortunately, the gate was closed. Silver skidded to a stop but I kept going right over the gate.

In hindsight, I suppose this was good training for all the parachute-landing falls I later made in the Army, but I sure didn't feel any value in it at the time. I was bruised, battered, and had the wind knocked out of me. Even worse, my good jeans and shirt were torn and dirty. "Okay, horse, you want to run, we'll run." I tied a light line to the right rein and ran Silver up and down a plowed field until he was completely winded. I felt bad about that when Silver died the next day.

––––––––

I rode the school bus for years, but when I turned sixteen, during my junior year, I completed bus driver training and became a bus driver. That eighteen dollars per month sure came in handy. The bus sat out in my yard and I got up very early every morning to start my route picking up the other kids. It was fun at first, but then I became somewhat frustrated because they had a governor on those buses so we couldn't drive them more than thirty-two or thirty-three miles per hour. That was unless a certain mechanically inclined sixteen-year-old could figure out how to loosen the vacuum hose underneath, and then that baby could fly all the way up to thirty-five miles per hour. It wasn't legal, but it wasn't exactly number one on the sheriff's list of punishable offenses. My comfort level with anything mechanical would continue to serve me well in the years to come.

In addition to driving the bus, I continued to work on the farm, meticulously completing my morning and afternoon chores all week. After the noon bell rang on Saturday at the farm, I went to my job at Edward and Eleanor Leggett's store in Hobgood and worked for eight more hours, from 2:00 P.M. to 10:00 P.M., for a grand total of $2.75, no Social Security deducted. That was my money to date Carolyn, including gas for Mother's 1957 Ford, movies, and Cokes. All the profits from my 4-H steer sales went into savings for college.

North Edgecombe High School in Leggett, North Carolina, was a small school of about ninety students, sixteen of whom were in my graduating class. This gave all the kids a chance to participate in school plays, glee club, or sports. I chose sports.

We didn't have a football team because it was too expensive and there weren't enough players. But I played first base on the baseball team and was the starting center on the basketball team: I was six foot four by my sophomore year. We called our basketball court in the narrow gym the "cracker box" because the collapsible stands came right to the sideline and the old wooden backboards abutted brick walls, protected only by thin hanging mats. Knowing up front how bad an idea it was to charge in on lay-ups or dive for rebounds was what I always thought of as a real home-court advantage.

My mother drove me home from practice four afternoons a week and to the Friday games until I had my license. Our team's record averaged five hundred since we always lost to bigger schools. My opposing center on the

Tarboro team was Bill Hull. He was just as tall as me and a great athlete; he went on to play for the Dallas Cowboys. But I enjoyed the challenge of competing with him.

———

There is a very proud military tradition throughout North Carolina, and in Edgecombe County in particular. A large bronze statue of a Confederate soldier stood on the Tarboro Common. One of the most historic homes in town was The Grove, built by Thomas Blount, a plantation owner who fought as a young officer in the Revolutionary War. The Grove was later owned by Colonel Louis Wilson, who served in the Mexican War, and by Colonel John Bridgers, the Confederate commander of Fort Macon in the War between the States (my grandmother Laughlin always used that term instead of Civil War.)

North Carolinians were known as tar heels because they dug their heels in and did not retreat during the War between the States; one version of several of the epithet's origin concerned the 1864 Battle of Petersburg as Robert E. Lee's half-starved Army of Northern Virginia fell back before Grant's superior force. General Lee was overheard to say of North Carolina troops, "There they stand, as if they have tar on their heels." The Twenty-sixth North Carolina Regiment was one of the most heroic of the war and was virtually wiped out at Gettysburg during Pickett's Charge: of the approximately 800 men in the unit, 708 were killed, wounded, or reported missing in action. But they penetrated the Union lines near the heavily defended redoubt called The Angle before they were blown apart with double-charged canister shot and massed musketry.

We had a book on General Lee at home, and I was very impressed by the dignified strength of his death mask. I still have a picture of General Lee hanging in my home today.

———

I had always wanted to graduate from North Carolina State in Raleigh: four of my uncles and my father had attended State. I also wanted to study aeronautical engineering and build jet planes and spacecraft, but in spite of the fact that I pulled mostly As throughout high school (without working very hard), my math SATs were not good enough. Also, my father preferred that I attend a smaller school nearby, Campbell College.

But even then, my stubborn streak was developing: "If I can't go to State, Daddy, I won't go anywhere."

My parents relented. I would go to State. But I still had to do something about math. So I took a summer tutorial in algebra, calculus, trigonometry, and geometry from my high school math teacher, Mrs. Lucille Anderson. This was tough, especially with my farm chores and the job at the Hobgood store, but Mrs. Anderson and I struggled through those courses together. I think she learned as much if not more than I did through those courses. Another valuable lesson learned: hard work paid off. I was accepted as a freshman majoring in engineering—but those straight As were a thing of the past.

The North Carolina State University campus in Raleigh was pleasant, with redbrick buildings and handsome shade trees. A train track runs through the campus. The huge William Reynolds Coliseum was the venue of the Dixie Classic Atlantic Coast Conference basketball tournament. Some folks joked that there were two state religions in North Carolina: the Southern Baptist Church and basketball, and I loved playing basketball more than eating. Good thing, since we called the central dining room in my old brick dorm "Ptomaine Hall."

My actual classes were a shock. Nothing at rural North Edgecombe High School had prepared me for the rigors of university engineering.

On the first day of Mathematics for Engineers, the professor, Mrs. Bryant, turned to us and said in a calm tone, "Open your books to chapter five, page sixty-two. I'm sure you all covered the material in the first four chapters in high school." That was easy for *her* to say. There was no way my North Edgecombe geometry and algebra courses had prepared me for what I saw when I flipped open the textbook.

I stared at the dense columns of calculus problems and felt a flush of embarrassed anxiety. I was completely lost. Mrs. Bryant glanced around the room and thank God she looked past me and called on a guy seated two rows behind me. Maybe she already knew he'd gone to Myers Park High School in Charlotte. "Mr. Steinberg, please go to the board and solve problem twenty-two."

He carried his book to the blackboard. "It'll take me a minute to derive a formula to solve it," he said.

David Steinberg patiently worked through the equation and reached his solution in precise symbols at the bottom of the board. To me he might just as well have been writing Chinese.

"You've just earned an A for the whole course," Mrs. Bryant said. "I suggest you take a more advanced class."

I was way out of my depth in this class and I would soon find out that the same proved true in chemistry. The professor lectured for six weeks straight without assigning a single problem; they were all at the back of the book, if we chose to look at them on our own time. The first exam, however, was made up entirely of those problems without one question covering anything he had talked about in class.

By midterm of my freshman year things were looking pretty grim—with one major exception: basketball. I had grown up hearing Daddy and Uncle Ben swap tales about Dick Dickey and Ronnie Shavlik, who later went on to play for the Knicks. In high school I loved listening to Wolfpack games on the radio and I'd think to myself, *If Lou Pucillo can play*

*like that at five feet nine inches, I sure as hell could do some damage at
six feet five.* My enthusiasm and motivation to play under that huge red-
and-white banner translated into a performance that I was proud of, and
it came down to the final three selection slots on the team when the coach
called me into his office.

"Hugh, we've reviewed your current academic standing and it appears
you've got Fs on the horizon in at least three of your courses," he said.
"That would put you on academic probation and you would be suspended
from the team." My heart sank. "Now, perhaps if you'd switch majors to
something easier to handle, like recreation and park administration . . ."
He continued, but I was no longer hearing his words.

I appreciated his attempts to keep me on the team, but as much as I
loved basketball, I knew that my parents expected me to graduate with a
degree in a field we believed would benefit my future. Between my heavy
eighteen-hour course load and my three hours of practice each afternoon,
by the time I trudged back into the dorm I was exhausted—far too fatigued
to study.

I felt deep disappointment in myself and responsibility toward my parents. We were not a wealthy family and there were younger kids at home.
I was determined not to let my folks down. It was my stubborn pride and
overconfidence that had brought me here, and I was still determined to
succeed academically. "Thanks, coach," I said. "But I came to State to get
an education, not to play basketball."

As the coach had predicted, I was put on academic probation, and I
knew that somehow I had to turn things around. I didn't have to be hit over
the head to realize that given my current challenges in advanced math, continuing to pursue a degree in aeronautical engineering would be like rear-
ranging the deck chairs on the *Titanic*—it would take a great deal of work
and I'd look good going through the exercise, but in the end it just wouldn't
matter. I had to find alternatives.

———

One of the guys in my dorm was a textile-technology major. As I was looking over his textbooks, he told me how great the courses were. They combined theoretical physics and practical chemistry, the characteristics of
fabrics with plant design and management. "This is the kind of major you
would really like, Hugh," he said.

I agreed, so at midyear I transferred over to textiles, and I was able to
start raising my grade point average back up. I found textiles very exciting
and I loved what I was doing—which was probably half the battle right
there. I was intrigued by the process of how to make a loom come out with
just the right type of cloth, and I looked forward not only to the classes
but to using the skills after graduation, too.

Since I still had that little issue of academic probation, I took a few courses in summer school and fortunately was able to zip through them with an A and a B; so I was off academic probation and things were looking up.

Clearly appreciative of how hard I had worked to turn things around, my daddy gave me a 1950 Studebaker, one of those bullet-in-the-nose jobs: six cylinders, overdrive. I would drive the ninety miles from Raleigh to Speed to see Carolyn just as often as I could—spending a few hours with her and her family watching television and then turning right around and driving another ninety miles back again. It was a good thing that gas cost only thirty-one cents a gallon back then, and I was also fortunate that the Studebaker was ahead of its time and got twenty-six miles per gallon.

During the summer between my freshman and sophomore years, I worked in the shipping department at Mayo Knitting Mills in Tarboro. Columbus Mayo, the owner, and his sons, Ben and Lum Jr., were great bosses. I became fascinated with the process of making socks. The machinery was ingenious, the workers and foremen resourceful. This was my first exposure to complex work off the farm. Textiles were practically North Carolina's state industry in the early 1960s, and I was definitely interested in the profession. I saw a bright future in this work and made official my transfer from engineering to a textiles major when I returned to school.

———

Because North Carolina State was a land-grant school, two years of Reserve Officer Training Corps (ROTC) were mandatory for all able-bodied male students. I became fascinated with military history during the weekly lectures and took pride in wearing the traditional olive-drab-and-khaki uniform, and in formation marching. There were around twenty-five hundred cadets in the ROTC brigade. Regular Army NCOs, several master sergeant Korean War veterans, were our instructors during twice-weekly close-order drills with heavy, wooden-stocked M-1 rifles. This was the first time I'd encountered the Army's noncommissioned officers. They were quietly competent professionals who worked patiently and encouraged us to do well.

My friend Jack Jordan belonged to the Pershing Rifles and suggested I try out for the elite ROTC drill-competition unit.

*If I'm going to be a cadet,* I figured, *I may as well be the best.*

As always, I enjoyed the challenge and worked hard on my uniform, military bearing, and knowledge of military science and history. Senior cadets tested the other candidates and me. I found that 4-H had given me confidence to face the process of elimination. I made the cut. The best thing about the Pershing Rifles was traveling to other universities to compete. The rippling smack of the rifle butts on asphalt during precision drill maneuvers, where two parallel ranks of cadets tossed their rifles in a tumbling blur of polished stocks, were the high points of these competitions.

As my second mandatory ROTC year was ending, I had to decide if I wanted to continue. I enjoyed the training and learned that they would pay me a whopping $27.50 a month (big bucks for a kid from Speed, North Carolina back then), but taking the next two years would entail a two-year active-duty obligation as a commissioned officer. This was a decision I had to discuss with Carolyn.

After high school, Carolyn could not afford college and instead had gone to work as a keypunch operator for Carolina Telephone Company in Tarboro. As soon as the company acquired their first two computers, she was chosen to operate one of them. Special glassed-in rooms were built for them. We had already decided by the end of my sophomore year to marry when I graduated, but we hadn't announced a formal engagement. We were in love, but neither of us had a firm idea of what the next few years would bring or a clear idea of what Army life would be like for a young couple.

But Carolyn trusted my judgment and stood beside me as she would continue to do in the years to follow, my closest confidante and greatest sounding board. "Whatever you want is fine with me," she had said after helping me work through the pros and cons of this important decision. Later that day I signed the papers to continue into advanced ROTC.

———

My last two years at State were fascinating. The professors were gifted teachers, and I gained a true sense of accomplishment as I acquired the complex business and technical skills needed to be a manager in the textile industry.

That summer I went to ROTC training camp at Fort Bragg, which provided my first real glimpse of elite army troops, the legendary parachute infantry regiments of the 82nd Airborne Division. These young men had pride in themselves, their units, and their country. As we sweated through our physical training (PT) before breakfast, the troopers of the 82nd Airborne would double-time past our barracks, their spit-shined jump boots gleaming. They were sharp, squared-away soldiers.

"Airborne, Airborne, all the way," they chanted.

During that summer camp, we got the chance to "jump" from the mock aircraft practice structure mounted thirty-four feet high and slide down the slanted cable in a parachute harness. A few of the guys around me in the boxy plywood structure looked queasy at the prospect of stepping out the door three stories above the raked gravel, feet and knees together, chin and helmet brim tucked down, hands at the sides of the dummy reserve-chute chest pack. I guess they had no intention of ever going airborne and just looked forward to doing their minimum two years as "straight-leg" lieutenants.

But as I exited the practice structure and dropped eight feet before the springy bounce of the mock reserve chute opening, I felt an adrenaline surge. *This is great!* I slid down the cable yelling, "Airborne!" Trotting back to climb the tower ladder again, I was already hoping to go airborne on active duty.

That summer camp drew me closer to the Army. Running in the cool morning with my fellow cadets, I felt the camaraderie of being a soldier. That feeling returned each sunset as retreat sounded and we stood at attention to salute the colors, and again when taps sounded across the base at night.

I had earlier thought that the Quartermaster Corps (which entailed clothing and equipping army units) would be the best choice of branches to prepare me for a career in the textile industry; but now I leaned toward the infantry, where I would learn to lead soldiers. In my senior year, I had to make my branch choice and listed quartermaster first, infantry second. I was appointed to infantry.

Then, in May, the Department of the Army list was posted in the North Carolina State ROTC building. "The following individuals will report . . ." I was ordered to Infantry Officer Basic Course, Fort Benning, Georgia, and I was elated.

———

That spring, textile-industry recruiters had come to campus. All the major companies were there: Burlington, J. P. Stevens, and Riegel Textile Corporation. I had heard that Riegel was the best company in America, so I signed up for an interview and flew to Greenville, South Carolina, en route to Ware Shoals, a company town and site of one of the largest textile mills in the country.

The company took me to lunch at a white antebellum mansion. The polished oak table and waiters in white jackets and black bow ties evoked Tara in *Gone with the Wind*. All the important men from the southern executive offices were there to size me up. Again, my experience in 4-H and Pershing Rifles gave me confidence. I spent several hours talking with Jim Morrow, the personnel director, who drove me back to the airport.

"Hugh," he said with a grin, "although I'm not supposed to discuss your prospects, I have no doubt you'll be getting an offer, one of the best we can make."

"Sir, I have to remind the company that I have a two-year military obligation."

"We're willing to wait," Morrow said.

The letter with a job offer came in a few days. I called Jim Morrow and said, "I'll be signing the contract."

Riegel's Ware Shoals operation was a huge, "complete" mill: bales of raw cotton arrived by train and truck on one side of the plant, and finished textiles were shipped from the other side of the five-story brick building. Trucks drove away with pallets full of boxed diapers, flannel baby clothing, and camouflage military material. I looked forward to starting work in two years. But first I had my military obligation.

————

June 1, 1963, was a proud day for my parents. It had not been easy on them and I knew that; they had struggled hard to put their oldest child through college, but they had done it. There were two ceremonies that day, one my bachelor's degree commencement, and the other my commissioning oath, which I took with several hundred other new second lieutenants. I swore to support and defend the Constitution of the United States against all enemies foreign and domestic and to bear "true faith and allegiance to the same . . ."

As I look back, I realize that these were the years that most significantly impacted the man I had become. School plays and 4-H had fostered poise and comfort in public speaking, and even that eighth-grade fight with Arnold had helped forge my resolve to stand up for what is right, no matter the obstacles. At home, in church, at school—I had been surrounded by fabulous role models who were a part of what Tom Brokaw refers to as the "greatest generation"—and it was growing up in this environment that had instilled my sense of character, integrity, and ethics. My father had taught me right from wrong and blessed me with a solid moral compass; and, in her own way, my loving mother had shown me what it meant to be a great leader.

I would have a chance to go home for about three weeks before I was due to report to Fort Benning for my initial entry duty, and I savored every minute of that time with Carolyn and our families.

When Chancellor Caldwell signaled the conclusion of the ceremonies, hundreds of caps went flying skyward and I could not have been happier. I was now a North Carolina State University graduate and an officer in the United States Army. Life was good.

**8:34 A.M., March 23, 2002, Fairfax, Virginia**

Lying paralyzed on the freezing ground, I was completely aware that if my breath did not return within seconds, I'd lose consciousness and in short order my brain cells would start to die from oxygen deprivation. In under four minutes I would be dead. But despite almost superhuman attempts to will my lungs to gasp, their unresponsiveness was suffocating me to death just as surely as if I'd been under water or in the airless vacuum of space.

Only three hours earlier, I'd been absorbed in the same predawn five-mile run that had started every day since I'd joined the military some thirty-eight years earlier, and had I not known better I might have believed that my thoughts during that run had tempted the fates.

Having just turned sixty a few months earlier, I thought to myself that if this was what it felt like to be sixty, I had no clue what everyone was bitching about because I felt great. Other than a few aches from more than 450 parachute jumps, I felt as strong and healthy and mentally sharp as I had twenty years earlier, and I was elated with my new corporate opportunities and speaking engagements and even somewhat curious about my new gig as a "consultant" for NBC News. I cranked it up a notch as I ran past Robinson High School and thought to myself that life couldn't be much better; I was truly blessed.

I went in, showered, and around 7:30 A.M. or so I sat down with a fresh cup of coffee and scanned the morning Washington Post. The country was still on edge post-9/11, and I read that just the day before, the Delta terminal at LaGuardia had been evacuated because of some terrorist threat. First-class postage would be jumping three cents to thirty-seven cents, supposedly to cover the cost of new security measures as well as to recoup some of the expenses incurred as a result of last fall's anthrax contamination. Finally, the first annual D.C. Marathon would be held the following day, and I wondered why I hadn't signed up for it—but in any event, the way the traffic would be tied up in the District, staying in and doing work around the house would be a much better idea. It was therapy for me anyway, something I have always enjoyed.

I looked out the window and saw the hundred-year-old oak tree that I had trimmed the preceding weekend and took pride in how much better it looked. Getting out there to finish a couple of smaller trees in an hour or so would be a great start to my weekend.

There were really only a few small limbs on one of the trees that needed trimming, so I grabbed my small, twelve-inch electric Remington chain saw and ran the extension cord from the back of my house, then propped my thirty-two-foot extension ladder against the tree and climbed up to attack the limbs. The Remington sliced through a three-inch limb like a warm knife through butter, but instead of falling to the side as I expected, a dead branch broke away from above and drove it straight down into the ladder, which twisted away from the tree and left me on a direct collision course with the four-foot chain-link fence immediately beneath me. I tossed the saw to the left, out of harm's way, and quickly snapped my ankles together to avoid being impaled between my legs on the fence. It was a decent plan, had my toes not caught the top of the fence, causing me to jackknife upside down and slam headfirst into the ground.

There was no pain, but as I attempted to move my arms to get up, they remained motionless. Worse yet, I was unable to breathe. I fought for air and thought, What a way to go.

I closed my eyes and left it in God's good hands.

*Chapter Two*

# THE FORMATIVE YEARS

July 1963–December 1966

I arrived at Fort Benning for the two months of the Infantry Officer Basic Course on a hot afternoon in July 1963. My ROTC training had prepared me for the technical side of being a soldier, but I had a long way to go as far as acclimating myself to the full spectrum of Army culture. I knew how to keep my uniform, field equipment, and rifle ready for inspection. The training cadre, which once more included Korean War NCOs with combat experience, sent us on patrols through the chigger-infested piney woods, kept us on the firing ranges through one-hundred-degree days, and sent us off on long field marches carrying full field packs laden with spare ammo and bivouac gear. But, despite the baking summer heat and the pressure the instructors kept up day and night, I thrived. Becoming a soldier was even more satisfying than I had expected.

By September, I was a fully qualified second lieutenant of infantry in the Army of the United States. I wanted to excel, and that meant becoming an airborne ranger.

Before I completed Officer Basic, I had managed to be accepted at a September class in ranger school, but that bubble was soon to burst when the cadre adviser came in with some devastating news. "Lieutenant Shelton, I just got the results of your medical exam and I'm afraid you're unfit for airborne or ranger school," he said after pulling me aside from the group.

NOTE—Throughout the book, chapters will open with insignia of my rank at the time.

"There is obviously some mistake," I shot back, confident that my lean, muscular frame was in excellent condition.

"You're color-blind, no mistake about it. That makes you unfit to be a ranger or go airborne."

I was beside myself. I knew I had a touch of color blindness but certainly not enough to impair my abilities in any significant way. "That's totally unacceptable," I said. "You've got to grant me a waiver or something, because if I don't get into one of those two schools I will be counting the hours until my obligation is up and I can get out of the Army."

"No such thing as a waiver, sorry," he responded. "But I might be able to convince them to let you retake the test."

That was all I needed. Three days later I was back at Martin Army Hospital, sitting in front of an optometrist. He pulled out the same book that had been used to test me the first time. He flipped through fourteen pages that showed numbers, letters, or, if you were color-blind, nothing but a series of colored dots. When we finished, he said, "You're very close, but . . ." He stopped and reached for a shoe box that had seen better days. Opening it up, he continued, "I'm going to do things a little differently this time. I'm going to throw four pieces of yarn on the table, then snatch them away quickly. Tell me their colors as fast as you can."

"Red, green, blue . . ." I announced as quickly as they hit the table. He went on with half-a-dozen more, and I had no trouble identifying them correctly.

"Last one," he said, reaching into the box. "You get this and you're good to go."

He threw out the last one, which obviously was white.

"Black," I said confidently, just to screw with him. I thought he was going to jump out of his chair. He looked at me with big eyes and I started laughing. Fortunately, he had a sense of humor.

"Get the hell out of here," he smiled. "And good luck with the school."

I completed the basic course and drove seven hundred miles back to Speed to see Carolyn, on cloud nine the entire trip. I took five days' leave before ranger school and I had big plans to make the best of them.

---

Carolyn and I were married at Speed Baptist Church on September 15, 1963. There was a soaking downpour that day with water two to three inches deep in the churchyard. Charlie Speed, one of the town's leading citizens, carried Carolyn from the car into the church to keep her wedding dress above the mud, ruining his best shoes in the process. Every time we managed to get back to Speed, he mentioned that day and those shoes.

My parents had helped us buy a new 1963 red Chevrolet Impala. For our one-night honeymoon, we drove south to a motel on I-95, then returned the next day to pack the car for the trip to Fort Benning.

Our efficiency unit in the Camilla Apartments near the main gate of Fort Benning was small but comfortable. Carolyn thought the pink metal bed was cute. I, on the other hand, thought it was . . . pink. And short— way too short for my six feet five inches. The first order of business (once I got settled) would be to disassemble it and get rid of the footboard, then wire a couple of ammo cans to the frame so that my legs could hang off the end without the whole thing collapsing. Most of the tenants were lieuten- ants and captains attending Army schools or assigned to the 2nd Infantry Division, which was based at Fort Benning at the time (although now it's in Korea)—and I've always wondered what they must have thought when they saw me carrying those ammo cans into the place. Even with all the challenges, this was our first home together and as such was very special.

Since we had reached Columbus during duty hours, I decided to drive to the post and get the signing-in out of the way so I could come back and get the new place in order for Carolyn before I had to report back for ranger school in two days. We still needed light bulbs, bathroom tissue, and such— and there were a few mechanical things that needed tweaking, as is usually the case when you move into a new place. Although it was no palace (to say the least), I wanted to make our first home as comfortable as possible for my new wife, especially since I would be deserting her in forty-eight short hours. "Let me get this out of the way and I'll be back in about an hour," I promised Carolyn, grabbing the car keys and giving her a quick kiss on the way out. I also planned to stop at the hardware store on the way back to make some copies of our apartment and car keys since we only had one set.

Once inside the fenced-in ranger compound, I signed in and approached the staff duty NCO, a lean, hard-eyed sergeant first class who had given me the paperwork. "I start the course on Monday and I'd like to verify I've got the time right. We're due at 0630?" I asked.

"Ranger, as of now you *are* in the course," he snarled. "You will get your ass over to that barracks and get the *hell* with the program. Now get out of that uniform and take your rank off." I had heard that in ranger school every student had to strip off his rank so that no one could tell if the student next to him was a buck sergeant or a major.

"But you don't understand," I tried to clarify. "I don't actually start for two more days and I've got to get back to my wife. We just got mar- ried, she's alone and I've got the checkbook, the car, and all of our keys."

"That will not be a problem," he said. "Just say the word and I will gladly remove your ass from the class, in which case I don't give a flying fuck where you go. If you are not out of my face and on your way to that barracks within five seconds I will remove your name anyway." It wouldn't have mattered to him if my house had been on fire. He had control of me, and if I wanted to stay in the class I would have to accept it. I'd learned that lesson back in second grade with Mrs. Hart in the lunch line.

I did as instructed and stayed there the rest of that day and throughout that night. There were no phones in the barracks or any of the other areas we were allowed to access, and I could not get my mind off my young wife, who was alone without any food or supplies or the car, wondering what could possibly have happened to me. Although there was a 7-Eleven four blocks away from the apartment, it was a terrible way to start what I had so expected to be a grinding yet worthwhile experience at ranger school—but so far there was not one thing worthwhile about it. After tossing and turning in my bunk that entire first night, the next morning I went back to the office and insisted on seeing the TAC (tactical) officer.

"Sir, my wife is all alone. When I left yesterday, I told her I'd be right back. She needs the car and keys."

The captain scowled at my obvious incompetence. "You've got two hours, max. Now move."

When I arrived at the apartment I found Carolyn in tears, all alone in a strange town where she didn't know a soul. That was one of those times that we would look back on through the years and tell each other that if our marriage could survive a start like that, it could probably survive anything.

The lesson I learned from this, which I drew on throughout my Army career, was always to give soldiers the chance to settle their families before beginning duty. If a soldier is preoccupied with family worries, he's worthless to his unit.

———

The two months of ranger school were divided into three phases held at Fort Benning, in the Appalachians of northern Georgia, and in the Florida swamps.

During the Benning phase, there was always a lot of attrition, as less-qualified candidates could not deliver the physical and mental endurance required of a ranger. We were kept busy twenty hours a day, being trained to lead in combat, and combat is a stern master. So the course watchword was—and remains—"No Excuses."

I was fortunate in having just completed the Infantry Officer Basic Course because I was in excellent physical shape. And I certainly needed every bit of strength and stamina I could muster to pass the increasingly difficult PT tests the instructors threw at us.

During the confidence-building stage early in the course we practiced hand-to-hand combat in the sandy training pit. A tough staff sergeant named Mize taught us how to disarm a man lunging at you with a knife. The technique was simple and brutally efficient: kick the knife wielder's body, flip him over your hip, then stamp on his knife arm.

I stabbed at my training partner with the sheathed K-bar combat knife; not wanting to hurt me, he faked a real kick—not exactly what the sergeant had in mind.

"Ranger," Sergeant Mize bellowed, "when I say kick, you damn well kick. If you can't handle that, just pack up your gear 'cause there's no place in the rangers for wimps."

"Yes, Sergeant," the soldier replied.

"Let me show you," Mize said. "You rush me with the knife." I rushed at Sergeant Mize, thrusting the K-bar.

He disarmed me as he threw me down into the sawdust pit and delivered a vicious kick, hitting me right in the groin. I collapsed in agony and could not get back to my feet. I had to be half carried to the barracks. Within an hour, my scrotum had swollen to three times its normal size and was discolored like bad fruit.

Later that morning, I hobbled in to see the tactical officer. "Sir, I'm not going to be able to make the run this afternoon."

"Ranger," the captain said flatly, "if you can't run, you're out of the course."

I had come smack up against the No Excuses doctrine, meant to prepare rangers for combat. Here, students lived by the old adage "more sweat in training, less blood in combat." Since I could not train, I faced being cut in the first phase, something I had never expected.

Then the tactical officer offered a possible solution: "If you're dropped for medical reasons, you can rejoin the course later."

After a medical exam, the doctor recommended a medical waiver and said that I would be out of commission for about two weeks.

As would happen so often during my ascent through the ranks, even this seemed to happen for a reason, turning out to be a key piece of the puzzle that would forge my career path. Returning to my unit, I received word from the TAC officer that someone had just dropped off the waiting list for the upcoming class at airborne school. Would I be interested in filling that slot? The class was scheduled to begin in a little over two weeks.

———

Jump school was held on a sprawling Fort Benning compound dominated by the three 250-foot girders of the "Coney Island" practice towers, from which students make their first descent under an actual parachute canopy.

As with the officer-basic and ranger-school cadre, the "black hat" instructors in jump school were demanding and prone to order a trainee to deliver "twenty-five real ones" (push-ups) for every perceived infraction.

Airborne school lasted three weeks. We began each day with an intense PT session and double-timed everywhere. Instruction was concentrated and moved quickly from theory to practice. At the ground-level mock door, we learned how to exit the aircraft in the proper position.

"You people don't want to go out that door like rag dolls," an instructor told us, explaining that arms and legs flailing in the one-hundred-knot prop blast could send you "ass over teakettle" and throw your tumbling body through the parachute's deploying suspension lines to cause a malfunction; and dropping at an altitude of 1,250 feet left little time to activate your reserve chute.

Correct exit position required being tucked tight, feet and legs pressed together, elbows in, hands on the sides of the reserve, and chin down. The black hats liked to tell stories of men who hadn't kept their heads down and had been strangled by the chute-opening static line anchored to the cable inside the plane. You also had to make sure your eyes were open, not that anybody would be out there to check up on you. It wasn't that they were worried about your missing that spectacular view; if your eyes were frozen shut with fear, you would be unable to see a malfunction and could be dead within seconds. That got my attention.

By the end of week one, most of us could properly exit the mock door and thirty-four-foot tower. We endured the "swing landing trainer," where we hung from parachute harnesses that suspended us in the air and swung back and forth over a sawdust pit. Suddenly, the instructor would release you and you had to make a proper parachute-landing fall. When done properly, you hit with feet and knees together but relaxed, like human shock absorbers, and rolled onto the calf, buttocks, and push-up muscles. Those who could not master these simple skills were cut from the course. Because of my height I had to duck to exit the doors and I knew the black hats had their eyes on me; I had previously been told by a black hat that I was too tall for airborne. But I had been this tall since high school and had learned how to move fluidly on that little cracker-box basketball court in the school gym. I may not have stuck with the basketball at North Carolina State, but there was no way I was leaving airborne without my jump wings.

The second week was tower training, where we honed the individual skills we'd learned in ground week. First came mass-exit practice from the aircraft mockups. The purpose of the airborne was to put as many troops on the ground—in cohesive units—as quickly as possible. That required delivering multiple planeloads of men—"chalks"—to a drop zone very quickly. In fact, drop-zone length was measured not in feet or meters but in seconds, the time it took the aircraft to pass overhead. All that week we double-timed from one training apparatus to the next. The instructors were tough and many students thought it was harassment, but it wasn't—it was just good, solid training, and I loved it.

We also practiced on the 250-foot tower. Just like the old Coney Island attraction, these gantries were topped with protruding arms that held the chute mechanisms. Our fully deployed T-10 parachute canopy was attached to a circular hoist frame and winched up before the instructors tripped a release and we floated down.

As I rose rapidly to the top of the tower, I had the chance to judge if there was any hidden acrophobia lurking inside me. Nope. I enjoyed the view, although maybe not so much the sight of a few classmates whose stomachs didn't quite agree with the descent. I had reached the top and it was my turn; the canopy release tripped and as I was floating down I had only one thought: *This is* great, *get me up there again.*

At the start of jump-training week, the instructors taught us malfunction procedures. The T-10 parachute was a big improvement over the post–World War II T-7, in which the static line tore open the main-chute backpack and jerked the canopy out. That system left the partially filled canopy flapping in the slipstream as the pleated suspension lines deployed. Malfunctions were common with the old T-7. But the T-10 canopy was packed in a cotton deployment bag that did not open until the suspension lines and double risers connected to the harness shoulders had been pulled from the backpack and stretched taut. Still, there could be malfunctions with the new chutes, and our lives literally depended on knowing instinctively how to deal with them.

The instructors taught us the traditional technique of counting after exiting the door, "one thousand . . . two thousand . . . three thousand . . ." If you didn't feel the shock of your chute's opening—actually more of a harsh elastic jolt with the T-10—by the count of five, you were to look up to check your canopy. No canopy, a twisted "cigarette roll," or a line forming a giant "Mae West" brassiere meant that you had a malfunction and immediately had to pull the rip cord of the smaller reserve-chute chest pack and toss the folded canopy clear of the mess above.

Our first real jump was scheduled for the next morning and it was a big deal. Many of our wives, including Carolyn, would travel to the Fryar Field drop zone (DZ) to observe this important milestone. Everybody in the classroom listened intently to our prejump briefing and studied the diagrams with obvious concentration.

At breakfast, some of the guys looked a little pale and couldn't even finish a glass of juice or a cup of coffee. Others couldn't keep down what little they had consumed. I ate well that morning: scrambled eggs, bacon, toast, and a bowl of oatmeal.

We drew our chutes in the big shed at Lawson Army Airfield, and the riggers and jumpmasters very carefully inspected the backpacks, reserves, and harness snaps. While we filed out to the squat, twin-engine C-123 planes and lifted off for the short flight to Fryar DZ, Carolyn took her seat in the drop zone bleachers along with the other wives and some personnel from the school. She happened to be seated next to an Army chaplain. "Related to one of the jumpers?" he asked, making small talk until the jumps began.

"Yes, it's my husband's very first jump," she shared, with a combination of excitement and trepidation.

"I'm sure he'll do great," the chaplain reassured.

It was a beautiful fall Georgia morning, with bright sun and a few puffy white clouds. As the plane banked and the engine roar softened, I already felt exhilarated. Standing at the open door aft on the port side of the cabin, the jumpmaster looked us over and then raised both open hands in a lifting motion.

"Stand up," he yelled.

We rose from the sling seats and stood on the vibrating aluminum deck.

"Hook up."

We snapped our static-line clips to the overhead cable and inserted the safety pins.

"Check static lines . . ."

The ritual sequence of orders continued through "Equipment Check" and "Move Up to the Door."

Earlier I had told Carolyn that I would jump second to last, but on the way to the aircraft, the jumpmaster switched the order and I was now the second to go; Carolyn would have absolutely no idea that it was me jumping second, but there was nothing I could do about that now. Already I could see over the helmet of the guy ahead of me, out the open door of the aircraft. The groves of tiny pine trees below gave way to fields of wilted grass. That was our drop zone. At the door, the light snapped from red to green.

"Go!" the jumpmaster shouted, tapping the first man's helmet.

He stepped out the door and disappeared beneath the edge of the fuselage. I was at the door and felt the tap.

My exit position wasn't 100 percent because I felt one boot toe above the other. Still, the drop into the rush of sunny slipstream was electrifying.

"One thousand . . . two thousand . . ." I felt my main canopy tugging at my harness three seconds out of the plane. Excited as I was, the training paid off, and it's a damn good thing it did. At "four thousand," I remembered to look up to make sure I had a full canopy with no blown panels. Instead of the wide circle of a good chute, I was shocked to see the dreaded cigarette roll whipping back and forth. Glancing down, I saw the ground rushing toward me.

From the bleachers, the spectators were horrified at the sight of this poor soldier plummeting to the earth. The chaplain beside Carolyn yelled, "We've got a trooper in trouble," then: "Everybody turn away!" The airborne-school cadre screamed into their bullhorns, skyward, "Pull your reserve! Pull your reserve!" But I was falling like a brick, far too preoccupied to hear them.

Recognizing what had happened, I snapped my boots together, tucked my chin into my chest, grasped my reserve with my left hand, and pulled the rip cord handle with my right—just like we had been trained to do in the event of such an emergency.

In a heartbeat the green nylon spilled out, and I reached down to throw out more folds until suddenly the rushing wind caught the reserve and the small canopy exploded open, cracking like a shotgun and jerking me violently to what seemed a sudden stop. I looked down again. The brown grass of the DZ could not have been more than one hundred feet below my toes and I had little time to think, since the much smaller reserve chute dropped me so much faster than the main canopy. I hit the ground so hard that my fillings rattled. But I was safe. For a minute, I just lay there, letting the adrenaline settle. Then I smiled. Excellent. One down, four to go.

When I dragged myself stiffly to my feet, the black hats were all over me. One buck sergeant said, "Well done, trooper." Another barked, "Leave your chute right where it is and you go get on the truck to get yourself another one." The main chute would be thoroughly inspected to determine if the malfunction had been the result of the rigger's error or if there had been a flaw in the equipment itself.

Before I knew it they had me back at Lawson Field, buckling on another parachute to go back up for my second jump. No way did they intend to let me worry all night about that malfunction. The old adage "if the horse throws you, get right back on" applied here. What the black hats didn't know was that I'd been thrown off the horse before and that had never deterred me.

An hour later, I descended to the DZ again, this time under a good main canopy and with a lot less drama.


At home that evening Carolyn asked, "Who was the poor guy who almost died out there today? His wife must have been scared to death."

"You really don't want to know," I answered.

She stared at me with a stricken expression when I explained that it had been me. But I quickly added, "I've already jumped again, and everything worked perfectly."

Maybe the black hats had wanted to reassure my wife as much as me when they had me make that second jump immediately. At any rate, their technique was successful on both fronts, and Carolyn was learning under fire what being an army wife was all about.

By the end of the week I had made my required jumps, the fourth at night and the fifth with full combat gear. On Friday morning I stood with my class on Eubanks Field for the graduation ceremony. Carolyn pinned on the silver wings of my Army-Parachutist Badge. I was halfway to meeting my goal of becoming an airborne ranger.

———

After jump school I stayed at Fort Benning as a platoon leader in the 1st Battalion, 38th Infantry, 2nd Infantry Division. I liked the assignment and found that I really enjoyed leading troops. Once more I was impressed by the quality of the NCOs—soldiers who really ran the platoon and just let a young lieutenant like me think I was in charge until I absorbed enough of their leadership skills to take over. I must have been a quick learner because my platoon of forty-odd men was soon scoring high on all the battalion training tests: marksmanship with small arms and heavier weapons, day and night patrolling, and land-navigation problems. Following my sergeants' example, I spent a lot more time with my troops than I did with my wife—great for troop morale, not so great for the wife stranded at home.

In April 1964, I was notified that there was an opening in the next ranger class, so I could pick up where I'd left off and resume training. "Count me in," I told my company commander, Captain Larry Bennet, who had called me with the news. This time I would make it my business to be prepared for whatever stray kicks might be launched in my direction. This meant that Carolyn would be alone for the nine weeks that the course would last, but by now she had a job and we were settled.

———

In the new course I was teamed with a British ranger buddy, Lieutenant (pronounced *Leff*tenant) Jeremy Mackenzie. Jerry was a Sandhurst officer who had already seen combat against communist guerrillas in Malaya and was competing for Great Britain in the upcoming Olympics. (The Royal Military Academy, Sandhurst, in Surrey is where all officers in the British Army are trained.)

At first I found Jerry somewhat arrogant, very "British," and almost anti-American. Bear in mind that at that point I had never traveled outside the United States, and what I took for anti-American prejudice was really nothing more than a huge pride he had in his own great country. In the years to come I would gain a deep appreciation for our important British allies, and their students, but in 1964 I had not yet come to this realization.

I would soon see that Jerry was both tough and smart, which was important because if one man made a mistake, both were punished, and this usually meant push-ups, running with heavy rucksacks, being deprived of a meal, or standing guard while the rest of the class snatched a quick hour's sleep. Jerry's biggest challenge was with American accents and GI slang. He and I would go on to become the only ranger buddy team where both men made four-star rank. To this day Carolyn and I remain good friends with Jerry and his wife, Liz, and I'm sure they still find my Caro-

lina drawl challenging to understand. (General Sir John Jeremy Mackenzie became Deputy Supreme Allied Commander Europe and Aide-de-Camp
General to the Queen.)

The Fort Benning phase of ranger school was meant to sort out the weakest students, and the water-survival test was a damn fine way of doing so.
It was harsh. Students had to step blindfolded from a diving board wearing full combat gear and holding their rifles diagonally across their chests
at port arms, and when they hit the water they would sink like lead bricks.
When they finally kicked to the surface, gasping for air, they had to have
their rifles in the same position or be dropped from the course. Some men
instinctively dropped their rifles and tried to stay afloat, while others pan-
icked completely and ripped off their helmets and packs. This was truly
"separating the men from the boys" early on in training.

Sleep deprivation combined with grueling physical-endurance sessions
past the point of exhaustion were interspersed with mental-acuity problems such as knot tying, night patrolling, and ground navigation. Those
who couldn't hack it were out. Once again it was No Excuses.

The second phase was mountain training near Dahlonega, Georgia. We
climbed sheer rock cliffs, rappelled, and slogged up and down the Appalachians day and night, lugging seventy-pound rucksacks. This wasn't just
another toughening-up exercise. In combat, rangers often had to fight
in steep terrain. Probably the most famous such attack was the assault
that the 2nd Ranger Battalion made on D-Day 1944, scaling the vertical
limestone face of Pointe du Hoc near Omaha Beach to destroy German
artillery reported to be dug into concrete pillboxes. The enemy had moved
the guns inland, but the outnumbered rangers destroyed them with ther-
mite grenades and then fell back to defend the empty German fortifications
on the cliff tops against fierce counterattacks. Those were the rangers we
were training to emulate.

The swamp phase of ranger school was held at an old satellite field of Eglin Air Force Base, Florida. We called this swamp "LA" (Lower Alabama)
because it was just too damn cold to be Florida. Constantly soaked and
shivering, we waded through streams and paddled inflatable rubber raid-
ing crafts on the rivers among the tangled roots and trees. When we
patrolled the thickets, we were snagged by wait-a-minute vines, our fatigues and flesh ripped by thorns. Cypress knees or "dammit" stumps in
the watery swamp kept our shins black-and-blue. If a man complained to
the instructors, he was dropped from the course. Some nights were so

pitch black that the only things I saw were the two dim cat-eye reflectors of luminous tape on the back of the patrol cap of the man in front of me.

We were constantly harassed by OPFOR (opposing force) "aggressors" from a special unit at Fort Benning who were hell-bent on "killing" or capturing as many ranger students as they could. We averaged one or two hours of sleep every twenty-four and one meal a day. Jerry and I would share a cold can of C-ration ham and lima beans or turkey loaf, savoring each greasy spoonful of the feast. The little cans of fruit cocktail or pears were nectar. Some days, if we were extremely fortunate, we got to make a canteen cup of tepid powdered coffee and actually drink it before the instructors or the OPFOR pounced on us.

But often the food was more primitive. One day, a "partisan" gave our four-man patrol a live chicken. I thought back to Mammy Shelton's red rooster as we wrung the chicken's neck, plucked the feathers, and searched for dry wood. Once we got a small fire burning, we started to boil the bird. But the chicken was only half cooked when the OPFOR attacked, throwing smoke grenades and firing blanks through the cypress swamp. We grabbed the half-cooked chicken from the pot, ripped it apart, and wolfed down bloody chunks as we ran.

The students in my class averaged about a thirty-pound weight loss by the time we graduated. We were so gaunt when we got back to Benning from the Florida phase that some of our wives didn't even recognize us.

My class had about a 70 percent dropout rate, and only fifty students graduated. We looked like old men, even though our true ages ranged from early twenties to midthirties. The one thing we all had in common at the end of those nine weeks was that we were all rangers.

The Army calls ranger school the best small-unit leadership training in the world. I believe it is *the best available leadership training,* period. Students learned both to lead and to follow. We could be voted out by our classmates ("peered out") for not following orders quickly and accurately, as well as by instructors. One of the great lessons of ranger school was how to work as a team and never to let a single-point failure (a vulnerable link in the chain) jeopardize the overall mission. This reflected the eighteenth-century edict of the original ranger, Colonel William Rogers, "Don't forget nothing."

———

When I returned to the 1st Battalion, 38th Infantry Regiment of the 2nd Infantry Division, I was assigned as the scout platoon leader. This was duty that I thoroughly enjoyed because it made use of the skills I'd just learned in ranger school, such as night patrolling, deep reconnaissance, and ambush.

Our battalion became part of the new 11th Air Assault Division, a test unit for the concept of helicopter-borne airmobile forces headed by Major General Harry Kinnard. (Kinnard was the original source of the famous

"Nuts" reply to the German demand for surrender during the 1944 Battle of the Bulge.)

We trained hard, first at the company, then at the battalion, then all the way up to the full division level, deploying hundreds and eventually thousands of troops by UH-1 Huey and CH-47 Chinook helicopters with wide twin main rotors. This all culminated in a huge field training exercise, Air Assault II, during which we engaged the best of the 82nd and 101st Airborne Divisions in South Carolina. The exercise validated the air-assault concept.

One of my missions was to secure a landing zone for the rest of the battalion to come in on, and that LZ was at Harmony Church.

I briefed my platoon that there would be four aircraft transporting us, and I assigned who was to board which one. At the predetermined time, four UH-1 Huey helicopters made their sweeping arcs and touched down for us to board, and we sprinted out to our assigned choppers.

There were twenty-eight of us, seven assigned to each helo. I ran to board chopper two along with my radio-telephone operator (RTO), who had been assigned to the same bird. As I started to jump in, a voice from the pilot's seat cut through the roar of the rotor blades: "You can't get on here, I've got a weak engine. This thing doesn't have enough power. Go get on one of the other birds so we can take you both to Harmony Church."

I turned to Campbell, my radio operator, and shouted over the ear-splitting whirl of the rotors, "You go jump on the third bird and I'm right behind you." Within seconds we were at helo number three.

"I can only take one of you," the pilot shouted. "Got a full house in here already."

"Campbell, you jump on here and I'll get on the fourth one. We'll meet up at the church," I said.

"Will do, sir," he yelled back as he jumped on, the turbo shaft accelerating and the aircraft shooting skyward. I ran to the fourth bird and boarded with no problem, and we lifted off to join the formation to Fort Benning's Harmony Church.

Moments earlier the skies had been fairly clear, but visibility quickly diminished and we hit a fog bank. I put on a headset to hear what was going on. "Juliet One to Two, Three, and Four, let's take it easy and just follow the road for nav," crackled the voice over the chopper's radio.

Suddenly it was like somebody had thrown a white sheet in front of us. The fog was completely blinding. "Slow turn to the left, we've got to get out of this fog," I heard over the radio. "Nice and easy, slow turn to the left." I could feel the aircraft making the slow turn, and I was just looking out the open door and waiting to see that we had broken through. The moment it did, *helo three banked into helo two* and together they exploded in a tremendous ball of fire—the wreckage plummeting to the earth, rotors still spinning but helos in a dozen separate pieces. Right before my eyes, I saw half of my platoon killed instantly, including my RTO—whom I had just sent to his death by instructing him to board helo three.

The two remaining birds—mine and helo one—flew back and landed at Kelly Hill, out by the road that runs from the main post to Harmony Church, our assigned landing zone.

The pilots got out and ran to each other. I joined them. "Have you notified the emergency crews?" I asked.

"They're on the way, but I doubt if anyone could have survived that," the first pilot said.

"Roger that, but we've got to get those crews there just in case," I said, satisfied that first responders had been dispatched. But I still had a mission in progress. "Okay," I said, gathering my remaining members, pulling them into a huddle. "Get out your maps, men. We are missing half now, so we have to reassign who is doing what to secure this thing." I started going through troop-leading procedures to get them all squared away to secure the same LZ, and they were responding professionally to my calm command of the situation—highly respectable on their part considering what had just occurred, but a great lesson in leadership.

All of a sudden a big guy, Lieutenant Colonel Arne Eliasson, the battalion commander, came striding up and asked, "What are you doing?"

I said, "Colonel, I think I've just lost half of my platoon; I've got to get this mission reassigned to these men so that we can get on with it."

He had big crocodile tears running down his face as he said, "The mission is over. You've lost half your platoon. We're stopping this whole exercise right now." I thought to myself, *Man, we're getting ready to deploy to Vietnam; you're going to have to learn to deal with this. The mission won't stop because you lose two planeloads of troops.* But we stopped, and I will be the first one to tell you that it was a terrible thing.

Between my men and the UH-1 crews, we lost a total of twenty-one people that day. We had a memorial service, but it was closed casket since everyone was burned well beyond recognition. It was a bad scene, but out of that I learned that *you've got to be prepared to press on even when you lose people.* In a real battle we sure wouldn't stop to rewind the tape when things went wrong. If we did, it wouldn't be half the troops that were dead, it would be all of us.

––––––

Shortly thereafter, in a ceremony in June 1965, we assembled on the parade field across from The Infantry School at Fort Benning to retire the colors of the 11th Air Assault Division and unfurl the colors of the new division, the 1st Cavalry (Airmobile). On the freshly mowed grass parade ground, we stood in a mass formation in our green dress uniforms, looking extremely sharp, while Major General Harry Kinnard "trooped the line" by making a slow, low-flying pass in his Huey before getting out and saluting all the troops. It was an extremely class act by General Kinnard.

Above the chopper's thump and whine, the division band cut loose with a rousing rendition of the old 7th Cavalry tune "Gary Owen." Fortunately I was an officer, so I was standing right up front as the helo edged by, close enough to look the general in the eye as he sat right there in the front seat. The only problem was that it had rained the day before and the helicopter rotor wash blew up clouds of wet grass clippings, which plastered the front ranks from head to toe. We were so proud, no one cared. Morale and esprit de corps were about as high as they could get. I turned around to savor the significance of this momentous event and took a moment to reflect: *Hugh, note to self: inspirational idea but don't ever try it on a freshly mowed field the day after it rains.*

Everyone realized that the division would be heading to Vietnam soon, and we all thought the Vietcong would meet its match with the new air cav. At that point in history, no one among us on that sunny parade ground had every heard of a wide gully of scrub jungle and elephant grass in the Central Highlands of South Vietnam called Ia Drang Valley.

———

My two-year enlistment was almost over but it had been a *great* run. Both my battalion commander, Lieutenant Colonel Arne Eliasson (a decorated Korean War combat helicopter pilot), and my company commander, Captain Buse Tully, made repeated appeals for me to reenlist. I was certainly tempted to stay with the division but I'd given Riegel Textile Corporation my word.

Captain Tully was a real role model for me. He demanded that things be done right and was a big believer in exceeding expectations and taking pride in a job well done. Buse, by then a major, was killed by enemy mortar fire in March 1969, but the leadership principles I learned from him stayed with me and helped me to become the man I am today.

———

In Ware Shoals, South Carolina, Carolyn and I rented a house from an elderly couple named Estes, and I began the nine-month management-trainee course. We understood that my hours would be long, so Carolyn and I agreed to get a puppy to keep her company when I was away at work. We checked around and ended up selecting a real ball of fire, a beautiful German shepherd we named Trooper. I had sold the 1963 Impala and picked up a '62 red Corvette convertible; it was the start of a longstanding love affair I've had with Corvettes—but not the only one that would start in Ware Shoals.

I have always loved music, but up 'til then I had never played an instrument; it was high time to correct that. One weekend about a month into training, I dropped by Sears and gave careful consideration to the racks of instruments lining the walls. I wanted something I could pick up easily and enjoy with Carolyn for fun and relaxation. A young salesman guided me over to a simple yet stylish Stella six-string guitar. The combination of the high action and the steel strings killed my fingers, but I persevered and really grew to enjoy it. I was a big fan of Johnny Cash before most people had any idea who he was, and I also enjoyed Peter, Paul and Mary. The first two songs I learned to play were "Folsom Prison Blues," by Cash, and "Blowing in the Wind." Throughout the years, as we traveled from location to location, that Stella—and a collection of others I would acquire through the years—would travel with us and serve as a great source of peace and calm. At the time I bought it, it was more fun than calm, since Trooper felt compelled to join in and "sing along" just as soon as I began.

At work, my training was divided into three-week segments, beginning at the "card" room of the gray mill, where raw cotton entered the plant.

Working for Captain Tully, I had learned to write proper Army reports, neat, concise, and complete. So I typed my Riegel trainee reports on onionskin, while the other trainees scrawled theirs like schoolboys, on lined paper torn from notebooks.

One day Rip Hardeman, the general manager, sent for the five trainees. "I got you all in here," he said, "because you need to understand something. You're not just being trained, you're being evaluated. I am looking for the man who will eventually replace me." He held up a particularly messy trainee report on rumpled notepad paper that had words crossed out and misspelled. "I don't think you appreciate our standards." Then he held up my neatly typed report. "This is a professional presentation. That's all. Let's get with it."

After that session, my fellow trainees were chagrined. "Who the hell wrote that typed-up job?"

"I did. That's the way I was taught to write reports in the Army."

After about three months of training, Vice President Jim Lindsey gave me a small white swatch of woven cotton fabric. "I want you to research this and design me a gray mill that can produce products like this. I'm taking you off the regular training course. You've got three months for the project."

I fingered the cloth. *I've been here before,* I thought. My last course at North Carolina State had been mill design.

Later that day I went to see Mr. Lindsey. "Can someone lend me an electric typewriter?"

I got a brand-new IBM Selectric.

Visiting the plant lab that weekend, I used a microscope to study the weave dimensions and the bleach and dye properties of the sample. Then I dragged out my old textile-technology textbooks and course notes. Working nights and weekends, three weeks later, I was finished.

"Mr. Lindsey," I said, "I've completed the report."

Lindsey was obviously skeptical. He flipped through the pages and began to tap out figures on his hand-cranked Burroughs adding machine, frowning more as he studied the paper scroll. The figures made sense. "Okay, Hugh, we'll get back to you."

Within days, word spread that Hugh Shelton had been able to design a new product line in only three weeks.

I was immediately taken off the training program and promoted to technical superintendent of spinning, working for Barney Mabrey, the superintendent and a sergeant major in the Army Reserve. We shared an office, and I learned a lot from Barney. He was a great boss who took the time to coach, train, and mentor me.

---

I also joined the Army Reserve, the 108th Training Regiment in Honea Path, South Carolina, an ordnance unit where all the NCOs were skilled mechanics from car dealerships. I was a platoon leader and taught combat skills, which they thoroughly enjoyed. But at summer camp at Fort Jackson, I realized how much I missed the Army because I hadn't made a parachute jump in months.

I also missed the camaraderie I had within my unit—a unit that was now deployed and making vital contributions. Almost immediately upon arrival in Vietnam the 1st Cavalry found itself in combat. That was *my* unit and those were my buddies fighting, which we had trained side by side to do for more than two years. But instead of fighting in the Ia Drang Valley of the Central Highlands, I was being trained as a junior executive for the Riegel Textile Corporation in Ware Shoals, South Carolina. I was getting letters from friends I had served with who were now in Vietnam, some scrawled on cardboard ripped from C-ration cartons, others caked in mud from the trenches in which they'd been written. With almost every letter came an update on the officers and NCOs who had become casualties. It was heart-wrenching to read of some of my best friends and close acquaintances who had either been killed or had suffered disabling wounds, like Staff Sergeant Russell, my platoon sergeant at Fort Benning.

One evening after work, I broached the problem with Carolyn. "This job is okay," I said. "The people at Riegel are great to me, and the money is certainly good. But you just can't duplicate the camaraderie of working with troops. What would you think if I applied for a regular-army commission and returned to active duty?"

The war in Vietnam was constantly on my mind, and every evening TV news broadcasts showed graphic footage of American soldiers on the ground, fighting and dying. Carolyn and I understood what my reentering the Army on a regular commission would entail. Since I had completed my active-duty obligation I did not have to fight this war—but if I chose to reenter the Army, I would be sure to see combat in Vietnam.

Compounding the difficulty of my decision was some great news we had recently received—Carolyn was pregnant with our first child. As always, however, she supported me. "I know you won't be happy staying home if the men you've served with are over there."

I went to a local recruiter, but at first the sergeant couldn't figure out any way for me to reenter the service with a regular-army commission. I pushed, and finally, together, we worked our way through the extensive paperwork required for my return to the Army. And then I waited.

Months went by and the perfect storm was gathering. Riegel was considering me for a great assignment and Burlington Industries had made job overtures to me—yet the Army's decision was still dragging on.

I wrote directly to the Department of the Army, in Washington, but received no response.

Then one day a Western Union employee wearing what looked like an old-fashioned railroad conductor's cap came into my office asking for "Lieutenant Shelton." Barney Mabrey pointed at me. The telegram was several pages long, thick with army acronyms and abbreviations. *You are hereby directed to report to Fort Bragg for twelve weeks of Special Forces training en route to 5SFGP RVN.*

I handed Mabrey the telegram, and he immediately called Rip Hardeman. Together, they lobbied hard to do whatever it would take to keep me at Riegel. "We'll double your salary if that's what it takes to keep you," Mr. Hardeman said.

"Sir, it's not about money. It's really a calling that I feel, and I want to return to the Army—it's what I want to do with my life."

"Then God bless you, son. You've always got a place here if you change your mind."


By this point Carolyn was eight months pregnant and I was due to report to Fort Bragg in four days. We discussed the pros and cons of her moving to Fort Bragg with me and decided that between the long hours I'd be spending in Special Forces training and my rapidly approaching deployment to Vietnam, it would make far more sense for her to move in with

```
NNNNCBC4 7CBB529 TBA2610GA526
RR RUCBC                                              609419
DE RUWPOG 426A 2562125                    cSWLAN
ZNR UUUUU                                  dotion  (61)
R 1313082 SEP 66                          ary - sws
                                               MPD
FM CO USARCPC DA FTBENHARRISON IND
TO RUWTPSA/1LT HENRY H SHELTON PO BOX 35 WARE SHOALS SC
INFO RUCBC/CG JFKCEN FOR SP WARFARE FTBRAGG NC
RUEPDA/USADATCOM
RUCBEA/CO 7TH DPU EDGEWOOD ARSENAL MD
BT
        UNCLAS 5637
        SUBJ   ACTIVE DUTY
        IN REPLY REFER TO RCPAP
        IN REPLY REFER TO RCPAP
        DEPT OF ARMY LETTER ORDER A-09-266 DATED 12 SEP 66 ORDERS YOU
TO ACTIVE DUTY. YOU ARE ASSIGNED TO 5TH SPECIAL FORCES GROUP (ABN)
APO SF 96240 SN 05319031 ALLOCATION FEB 226E MOS 31542 WITH APPROX
8 WEEKS TEMPORARY DUTY (TDY) ENROUTE AT JFK CENTER FOR SPECIAL WARFARE
FT BRAGG, NC TO ATTEND SPECIAL FORCES OFFICER COURSE (24 OCT - 17 DEC
66) REPORTING 21 SEPTEMBER 1966 EDCSA 19 SEP 66, TO BE UTILIZED BY
CO JFK CENTER PENDING START OF CLASS. YOU WILL PROCEED TO TDY
STATION IN SUFFICIENT TIME TO REPORT ON DATE SPECIFIED. PERMANENT
CHANGE OF STATION. TRAVEL BY PRIVATELY OWNED CONPEYANCE, COMMERCIAL
AIRCRAFT, RAIL OR BUS AUTHORIZED. ORDERS FORWARDED TDY STATION, THIS
```

*September 12, 1966 telegram ordering me to active duty at Ft. Bragg for Special Forces training.*

her parents back in Speed, where she'd spend the year while I was overseas. I knew she would be in great hands, and her parents couldn't have been more thrilled that they would have a grandchild in the house.

——————

One of the more frustrating things that happened after I first reported for duty involved six brand-new uniforms that I had purchased and taken to a local tailor to have all my patches sewn on. In those days they were all very bright: the Airborne wings were white, the captains' bars were white, and the "U.S. Army" was a very bright gold on black tape. Shortly after I'd spent sixty dollars to have all those patches sewn on, I reported to the office, very proud of myself and feeling great in that new uniform.

I couldn't have been there more than fifteen minutes before the boss came out and announced that the Army had just changed the regulation and now everyone was required to wear subdued rank (black letters on olive-drab green), the theory being that the bright lettering stood out too much to enemy snipers. He gave us one week to get that taken care of.

So the following morning I carried all those fatigues back down to the tailor and plopped down another sixty dollars (which was a lot of money in those days) to have the bright patches ripped off and the subdued ones sewn on instead. I went back to work the following day and felt pretty good when I looked around and saw that I was the only one who had taken care of the new patches so far.

I barely had time to fill up my coffee cup before the boss stepped out and announced that the commanding general of Special Warfare Center had decided that Special Forces would continue to wear the bright white for the foreseeable future. So I went back and spent another sixty dollars getting the muted patches ripped off and the bright white sewn back on. I had no doubt that the tailor would enjoy a great summer vacation compliments of me and my $180 worth of patch repairs. While I was not averse to the rigors of deadly combat, I had far less patience for chickenshit like this.


When my course actually started, I was pleased to see that the John F. Kennedy School of Special Warfare offered practical, hands-on training surrounding unconventional warfare and guerrilla warfare behind enemy lines—perfect for Vietnam.

We were trained on the "A-Team" principle, by which a small group of American specialists would serve as "force multipliers" for irregular local troops. Most A-Teams had twelve members, each of whom had a specialty but was cross-trained in the combat skills of his teammates. Our team had an Army major as commander assisted by an executive officer, a senior NCO team sergeant, heavy- and light-weapons NCOs, a senior and junior commo (communications) NCO, a senior and junior medic, a demolitions man, an intelligence officer and his NCO assistant, and a psychological-warfare (PSYOPS) officer.

Unlike ranger training, which stresses platoon or company-size patrolling and assaults and defense on the conventional battlefield, Special Forces were trained to operate in much smaller units, often from isolated bases where indigenous irregular troops comprised the bulk of our strength. We learned to gain the confidence of these foreign guerrillas by demonstrating an understanding of their culture and leading through example. We were taught that most of our fighting manpower would come from the Civilian Irregular Defense Groups (CIDG), often non-Vietnamese ethnic warriors of the Montagnard tribes in the Central Highlands. They held Saigon and Hanoi in equal contempt, but respected Americans—and our willingness to reciprocate that respect. The "Yards" viewed the firepower of our artillery and aircraft with awe.

———————

At Fort Bragg, the instructors expected us to pay attention, to learn fast, and to demonstrate what we had learned. Three months was not much time to prepare for combat; however, we were all airborne, many were ranger qualified, and most were experienced infantrymen. But as Special Forces soldiers we had an even more demanding challenge: not only did we personally have to master complex land navigation and ambushing—as well as breaking enemy counterambushes—at night and in dense mountain forests, but we had to be prepared to teach those skills to "native" guerrillas.

At the same time, we were required to learn as much as possible about a wide variety of weapons: our AR-15 rifles and .45-caliber pistols as well as World War II vintage M-1 Garand rifles, the smaller .30-caliber carbines, and heavier Browning Automatic Rifles that were issued to the Civilian Irregular Defense Group (CIDG) Vietnamese who fought with us. The weapons men in our teams had to master these arms *as well as* the 60-mm, 81-mm, and big 4.2-inch mortars.

Our demolitions specialists had to be completely familiar (and comfortable) with C-4 plastic explosives and defensive claymore mines, which were diabolically effective weapons that sprayed a cloud of spherical steel balls across a sixty-degree arc when the mine was detonated. The lethal effect reached at least one hundred meters, so there was a good reason why the business end of the mine was clearly marked, FRONT TOWARD ENEMY.

As if this weapons training weren't challenging enough, the instructors expected us to be experienced with enemy AK-47 and SKS rifles, rocket-propelled grenades (RPGs), and 57-mm recoilless rifles.

———————

Once the instructors considered us ready, we prepared for our final and most demanding field exercise in western North Carolina. We were ordered to jump in at night to link up with a "guerrilla-chief" and his allies, then organize "guerrilla bands" and carry out strikes without being detected by the "enemy," played by local citizen "role players" the Army hired to capture us.

Our team leader was a major from the Quartermaster Branch named Kaufman, who had the makings of an excellent combat-arms officer, so we bonded into a tight, unified team. For this exercise, I was chosen as the intelligence specialist, something I considered a great challenge that I looked forward to tackling.

We were scheduled to jump in about 11:00 P.M. for a middle-of-the-night insertion near Rockingham, east of Charlotte, North Carolina, and had been given the whole day off so that we could rest up and prepare. Our final prejump briefing was set for 6:00 P.M., with TOT (time on target) estimated for midnight.

At around five o'clock in the morning my phone rang; it was Carolyn's father. "I just took Carolyn to the hospital," he said quite calmly. "She's already had the baby. It's a boy and they're both doing well."

"I'm on my way," I said, beaming with pride for this new little son I couldn't wait to meet. I was sure that I'd have plenty of time to make it up and back before the jump.

I quickly changed clothes and headed over to check in with my supervisors, more a formality than anything else since I was sure they wouldn't have a problem with my hopping two hours north to the hospital in Tarboro.

I reported in to the colonel in the Special Warfare Center. "Sir, Lieutenant Shelton reporting. My wife's just given birth and she's in the hospital only two hours north of here. Since I don't have anything to do for the rest of the day, with your permission I'd like to go up for a quick visit and I'll be back by noon."

I will never forget his answer, particularly since it reminded me so much of that son of a bitch ranger sergeant who wouldn't let me go back to give Carolyn the car keys when I showed up two days early. "Lieutenant, you are in this course to train. If it's your decision to leave the post, you feel free and go right ahead, but you're out of the course."

To this day I don't understand what short-sighted morons like that are hoping to achieve. I certainly couldn't throw in the towel at that point, and the facts were that as much as I wanted to see Carolyn and my son, they were both okay and her parents were there.

I called Carolyn and explained the situation. She wasn't happy about it and understood that I wasn't, either. So much for celebrating with my wife what should have been one of the happiest days of my life (although of course I was thankful and grateful that they were both in good health). We had already decided that if the baby was a boy we would name him Jonathan Hugh Shelton and call him Jon. Now he would be twelve days old before I got to hold him, and although he wouldn't miss me, I would certainly miss him.

We jumped in that night and the exercise lasted around the clock for the next twelve days . . . and I had one series of thoughts dominating everything else: *I wonder how Jon is doing, wonder what he looks like, wonder how Carolyn is.*

I learned a great lesson out of that: *You have to treat people right,* need to do the proper thing, and as you rise in rank, *never forget what it's like down at the bottom.* As the Golden Rule says, "Do unto others as you would have them do unto you." I was a young lieutenant without a lot of money and my wife was in the hospital with a new baby, yet the colonel couldn't allow me to go up and visit her for two hours and come right back—when there was absolutely nothing scheduled for us during that time.

———

Flying into the training area that night proved to be an interesting experience. As we approached the drop zone in a blacked-out C-123, Major Kaufman, the jumpmaster, positioned me in the door first. I stood there, whipped by the prop blast, feeling the engine vibration throb up though the soles of my boots. We were supposed to be jumping at one thousand feet—low, but close to actual combat conditions.

I was staring into the blackness outside the door when I saw the faint glint of a river. We'd spent hours studying the terrain in that area so we didn't need anyone to help navigate to the DZ. There was no river in our drop zone.

"Stand in the door," Major Kaufman shouted.

As I stared down intently, I had no doubt that I was looking at the Pee Dee River. I'd spent too many hours studying maps and aerial recon photos to be in doubt.

The green jump light came on, but I backed away from the door. The major was trying to push me, yelling, "Go, go, *go!*"

"A river, a river!" I shouted back. Finally he leaned out and saw the faint moonlit reflection of the river. So we flew back to Pope Air Force Base and Fort Bragg. After landing, the pilot conceded that he might have become "a little bit disoriented" up front. Then he flat-out admitted that he'd been in the wrong place.

The Air Force announced that they were going to give us a new crew to fly the mission, which helped to restore our confidence to a certain degree. Around two o'clock in the morning we took off again to fly back to the drop zone.

Major Kaufman was still the jumpmaster and he assured us that there would be no confusion this time. The drop zone would be marked by a smoke pot placed on a pasture by our partisan guerrilla chief, and even though this dim glow would be the plane's only guiding light, he was sure there'd be no problem picking it up. Wrong. We approached the DZ and it was obvious that the major could not see a damn thing out there, let alone the smoke pot. He leaned way out the door and strained to catch sight of it. Finally he ducked back into the noisy cabin and shouted, "Okay, come on up and stand in the door."

I shifted my rucksack and stood up in the door. It was dark as soot outside: the moon had already set and there was nothing to see. The green light blinked on and Major Kaufman tapped me on the butt. I jumped, and as soon as I was out, the chute deployed. I had my feet and knees together because it was so black that I couldn't see anything.

Then suddenly I saw a tree line on the horizon, but I was already *below* treetop level, *damn!* Instinct kicked in and I immediately prepared for a parachute-landing fall and BAM!—I crashed into the ground, banged up pretty hard but all pieces intact, no broken bones. The rest of the team were smacking down around me, some shaken up but only one real injury: Major Kaufman had reportedly broken his legs.

After the exercise, we learned that we had exited the aircraft somewhere between four hundred and five hundred feet instead of one thousand. Apparently, prior to takeoff the crew had failed to set their altimeter correctly—the first thing any student pilot learns before his first flight. Five hundred feet was lower than the D-Day drop into Normandy.

After all was said and done, we felt pretty good that we had made a combat jump without even knowing it. Except for Major Kaufman, that is. We really didn't know how he felt, since they had carried him off to the hospital.

———

With Major Kaufman gone, we got a new detachment commander, and I moved up to be the radio-telephone operator (RTO) and took over all his equipment. That was the way things were in Special Forces: each man had to be capable of doing every job of his team members, including communications, intelligence, weapons, and field medicine. With our team intact again, we pressed on.

Even though this was not Indochina—hickory and red oak trees instead of jungle and rain forest—this exercise was realistic training in how to operate in enemy-controlled territory. The local dry-cleaning guy—part of our partisan team—drove his truck down to a designated spot at night on the road and picked up the demolitions team. I went with them as both security overwatch and commo man. The dry cleaner dropped us off at a bridge we'd been ordered to blow up and we dismounted as he was still rolling. We planted our explosive charges—actually dummy charges rigged just like the real thing. The umpires would award us credit for a blown bridge if the charges were rigged and placed correctly, and the aggressor force would be denied use of the bridge.

This was a tremendous training experience for unconventional warfare—exhausting and nerve-racking to be sure—but it turned out to be so realistic that it was often easy to believe we were in an actual war zone.

At the end of the twelve long but thoroughly satisfying days, I finally graduated. The morning before the ceremony, we did our daily run at dawn. Now when we chanted cadence, the words had real meaning:

"Airborne . . . Ranger . . . Green Beret . . .
This is the way we start our day."
I could now wear the coveted Green Beret with pride.

––––––––

I drove north on I-95 substantially faster than the law allows to see my wife and new son at Carolyn's parents' house where they would continue to live while I was in Vietnam. It would be good practice for many years later when I would race down I-395 toward the Pentagon at similar needle-pinning speeds. During those times I would be responsible for overseeing international incidents. On this day, I looked forward to holding my son, Jon, since because of that Colonel's decision at Fort Bragg, I was unable to do so when he was born. I'll never forget my feeling of awe as I held him for the first time.

As Christmas approached, I had leave and the three of us stayed with my mother and daddy, Patsy and Hugh. They had moved into a new house in 1964 and had plenty of room to accommodate us. This was where we enjoyed the company of both families for the holidays.

But even as I unwound, eating fried chicken, barbecue, and desserts from my family's kitchen, we were always aware that the time was fast approaching for me to leave for Vietnam. As we relished our first Christmas with our new son, Carolyn and I knew that these moments together would be our last for a year, and potentially forever.

Now I stood at the tiny baby's crib (the same crib I had slept in as a baby) in the soft glow of the Christmas lights, feeling myself divided by the quiet rural night outside the windows and images of glaring trip flares and blinding illumination rounds in the jungle mountains of Vietnam.

Because I had to report for duty with the 5th Special Forces Group in Nha Trang, on the coast of central South Vietnam, on January 2, I had to begin the flight halfway around world on Friday, December 30. My parents drove Carolyn, me, and baby Jon up to Raleigh, where I would catch a flight to San Francisco. In the echoing airport terminal, I saw tears in my daddy's eyes for the first time as the flight was called. Carolyn's lips were trembling as we kissed goodbye, and I realized that the coming year was going to be a lot harder on my family than it would be on me.

And I was off to war.

**8:34 A.M. March 23, 2002, Fairfax, Virginia**

*S*uddenly, *God intervened, and as instantly as my lungs were shut down, they ballooned to life and I gasped for air—still not able to move anything else, but I could not have been more grateful. While my blood reoxygenated, I focused on thanking God for restoring my breath.*

*Being able to breathe certainly beat the alternative, but however you sliced it, I was still in bad shape. I was on my left side and, strangely, still felt no pain—I didn't feel anything beneath my chin, and that was a lot more worrisome than any pain could have been. I thought of Christopher Reeve, who had been paralyzed for life after suffering a similar fall while riding in Culpeper, Virginia, not an hour away down I-66. There was no doubt in my mind that I, too, had injured my spine. I also knew that if there was any chance of recovery, I'd need medical attention fast, since once the injured cells died, they could never be brought back to life.*

*But Carolyn was inside, busy with her morning chores with the TV on in the background—and with the windows closed and the furnace blasting, there was no way she could have heard any meek cries for help I might have been able to make. I was on the ground across the fence, in our next-door neighbor's yard, so her spotting me was unlikely. For somebody who prided himself on living life with multiple redundancies to eliminate the chances of single point failure, my lack of viable options was incredibly frustrating. "Help," I tried to call out, hoping that somebody would hear me. But about all I could muster was little more than a whisper, and there didn't seem to be anyone within earshot on that cold morning anyway. I waited about five minutes to regain my strength to call out again, and this time it was somewhat louder. "Help," I called again, then again every five minutes or so. "I need help, anyone—please—help." And on it went, over and over again, but suddenly it appeared that Fairfax had become a ghost town.*

## Chapter Three

# JAR OF EARS

The staff treated me royally in the downtown San Francisco hotel where I spent my last night in the States. Elsewhere, the antiwar movement was heating up, but not here, not yet.

We flew from Oakland in a chartered Pan American 707, the flight known as the Freedom Bird returning with troops who'd completed their tours of duty in the war zone. Although I had made multiple jumps out of the twin-engine C-123 transport plane, this was my first flight in an aircraft as big, fast, and plush as the Pan Am Boeing 707. I was impressed that each seat had its very own overhead light and adjustable air vent, and there were drop-down tables in the backs of every seat in front of us. I felt energized when those four powerful jet engines kicked in and pinned me against the upholstered seat during takeoff.

At that time, I could never have imagined that one day I would become a four-star general and by virtue of my command, the same armed forces that was shuttling me and some two hundred fellow soldiers across the Pacific would be providing me with a VIP version of this identical aircraft (along with a crew of eighteen) for carrying out my duties as commander in chief, U.S. Special Operations Command.

My first glimpse of Vietnam was a vivid green mosaic of coastal rice paddies and muddy rivers pouring into a milky blue sea. From our high altitude, everything below looked peaceful. But then the pilots made an unnaturally steep decent into Tan Son Nhut Air Base outside Saigon to avoid enemy ground fire. I was on the wrong side of the plane to see the city, but I spotted the clumps of thatch houses with rusty sheet-metal roofs near the sprawling headquarters of the U.S. Military Assistance Command, Vietnam (MACV).

When the crew opened the plane's doors, the cabin was flooded with the smell of stale mildew, diesel, and jet exhaust. I had grown up working through stifling summers on the farm, so heat didn't bother me too much. But I had never experienced the sheer *weight* of the tropical sun out on the tarmac.

Olive-drab school buses with chain-link grenade screens on the windows carried us over to a big billeting area on the base. We slept in barracks with rows of double bunks and screened windows with sun shutters. Most of the guys I'd flown over with were waiting for their unit assignments. Six lieutenants and I already had orders to report to the 5th Group in Nha Trang, so on the second day an NCO from the downtown Saigon detachment drove us to headquarters, a big white-brick building.

I was amazed by the traffic in central Saigon: shoe box Renault taxis laying down smoke screens as they swerved recklessly through the congestion. Lambretta motor scooter "trucks" piled with heaping loads of bamboo poultry cages and bales of produce braked and sped ahead. Tinny car horns were incessant. Every inch of the pavement was jammed with sputtering swarms of Japanese motorbikes. When you threw in the endless clots of cyclo pedicabs, it was easy to understand why the city's streets were so dangerous, even discounting the ever-present threat of Vietcong grenades, about which we'd been warned.

On the shaded patios inside the walled enclosure of the city's Special Forces headquarters, the din fell away and it was almost possible to forget the chaos on the street. The interior of the building had chandeliers and was tastefully decorated in the French colonial style. There were neatly rolled mosquito nets over the bunks.

*This place is pretty nice,* I thought, remembering some of the rickety old barracks I'd slept in during ranger school. Here, Saigonese cooks served excellent meals—either Vietnamese cuisine or French-American.

We stayed there for a couple of days, going through what they called Initial Orientation, which was basically just a fancy name for a bunch of long, drawn-out briefings.

We then climbed aboard a twin-engine C-7 Caribou transport out at Tan Son Nhut and flew up the coast to the 5th Special Forces Group in Nha Trang. The flight was far more peaceful than my next encounter with a C-7 would be. We passed over the orange laterite-mud scars of fire support bases and saw dust trails of armored personnel carriers and military truck convoys. Inland from the white beaches and tangled mangrove swamps, the green rice paddies spread in scattered patterns among thatched villages surrounded by lychee and banana groves. As the droning plane banked, the sun glinted off the muddy duck and fish ponds below.

Away to the west, the ground rose toward the Central Highlands, and scrub jungle gave way to towering triple-canopy forest. That was where the multiple branches of the Ho Chi Minh Trail infiltration route spilled thousands of North Vietnamese reinforcements into the South each month. People read about the Vietcong guerrillas back in the States, but those insurgents were actually under the control of the North Vietnamese Army (NVA). It was near the exit points of the Trail infiltration system that the U.S. Special Forces had established many of its A-Team camps—to serve as a kind of human trip wire that would alert Saigon to the presence of enemy troops.

Inland, afternoon clouds were puffing above the dark shadows of the mountains. It was up there that the 1st Cav, my old unit from Fort Benning, had been bloodied during their first big engagement with the NVA in 1965 in the Ia Drang Valley.

Those mountains were the north–south spine of Indochina, both a cultural and a geographical divide. Ethnic Vietnamese rice farmers lived in the lowland countryside and villages. Montagnard tribes lived in the mountains. The triple-canopy forests of the high country hid the Trail system: networks of mud roads, bamboo bridges, and concrete culverts strong enough to support truck convoys and the passage of regiments and even divisions of enemy troops.

One of the main assignments of the small Special Forces A-Teams was to man camps near this Trail spiderweb—so that our artillery and airpower could be used effectively against them. Obviously, the NVA hated these camps for the damage they were inflicting, and had placed their annihilation high on their list of objectives.

Serving on an A-Team would be exciting work, I thought as the plane descended toward the coast.

———

Nha Trang was a big base outside a pleasant coastal city with long, curving white beaches. The headquarters of the 5th Special Forces Group itself was a neat building of smooth hardwood planking with the ubiquitous corrugated roof, sun shutters, and stacked sandbags protecting the lower walls. The long, black headquarters sign was framed on the left by an emblazoned Special Forces "arrowhead" and on the right by the yellow and red diagonal slashes of the 5th Special Forces Group flash (mistaken by some to signify the identical colors of the South Vietnamese flag).

I was among seven new lieutenants reporting to the group adjutant in the headquarters conference room to be briefed on how the unit assignments would be made. The headquarters map showed dozens of isolated A-Team bases spread across South Vietnam's four tactical zones: I Corps in the north, II Corps, which included the Central Highlands, III Corps from Saigon out to the Cambodian border, and IV Corps in the swampy Mekong Delta, which had been a hotbed of Vietcong activity for years.

The adjutant asked if any of us had a preference. Having always been a good swimmer who loved the water, I answered, "I'd like to serve in IV Corps, sir."

We wrote our choices on a form, and he dismissed us. That night we headed over to the Officers' Club. The bar was upstairs and the dining room was at ground level. Again, I was amazed at the luxury: linen tablecloths, whirring fans overhead, and waiters in spotless white dinner jackets.

I commented on all this to one of the base officers. "We've been here since 1959," he said. "So this isn't something we started yesterday."

Dinner was great—fresh jumbo prawns and Australian filet steak—but I kept wondering, *Is this really Vietnam?* It was not at all how I'd pictured the war zone. Then we went upstairs to see Martha Raye perform. She put on quite a show, wisecracking and belting Broadway show tunes. One of her routines spoofed her long string of marriages, sung to the tune of "I'm Just a Girl Who Can't Say No" from *Oklahoma*. Listening, I was still wondering, *When I am* really *going to get to Vietnam?*

It didn't take long to find out. Leaving the O-Club, we spun around to see a gaudy string of parachute flares floating several kilometers to the west. The flares' magnesium dazzle was followed by streams of candy-red 7.62-mm minigun tracers looping down from an unseen, slow-flying aircraft. After several seconds, we heard the rasping buzz of those guns. Every fifth round was a tracer, but from here, the fire looked like an unbroken torrent from the sky to the ground.

"Spooky," one of the lieutenants said, referring to the nickname for the AC-47 gunship, a modified workhorse DC-3 troop plane that carried three multibarrel, electrically driven machine guns. Used primarily for close air support, Spooky's presence indicated that troops were in trouble.

The tracers stopped, but the chalky-white flares continued to drift down as the Spooky orbited above the firebase that had called for air support. Then we heard the dry thump of artillery from that base, firing as the Vietcong fell back.

Despite the holiday dinner of prawns and steak—and Martha Raye in a Santa Claus hat—we had obviously arrived in the war zone. It was January 2, 1967, and this was one hell of a way to celebrate my twenty-fifth birthday.

---

The next day, the adjutant called us back in. "Okay, I've got your assignments." He started through his list and then called out, "Lieutenant Shelton, you're going to Project Delta."

Back at Fort Bragg, Project Delta had a reputation as an assignment where you died fairly quickly. It was the long-range-reconnaissance arm of the MACV commander, General William Westmoreland. Delta operated "behind the lines," as if there were any clear lines of battle in this war, or at least in those remote areas where the Army of the Republic of Vietnam (ARVN) or our conventional forces did not operate. The unit's mission was to identify where the North Vietnamese were infiltrating off the branches of the main axis of the Ho Chi Minh Trail. Delta went in light, usually two Americans and two or four tough ARVN Special Forces, the *Lượng Đặc Biệt Quân Lực Việt Nam Cộng Hòa* or LLDB.

Because long-range radios were too heavy, teams relied on small line-of-sight sets that could reach our U-1A Otter aircraft orbiting high overhead to relay messages. Once the enemy was located moving beneath the jungle or triple-canopy rain forest roof, a Project Delta team could call in air strikes with fighter bombers or lumbering B-52 strategic bombers. (If this sounds familiar it's because it is almost identical to one of the more-talked-about missions of our current-day "Delta Force"—when, during Operation Desert Storm, they radioed in for air strikes after identifying Scud missile sites from well inside Iraq. It is no coincidence that today's elite counterterrorist team bears the same name as my assigned Project Delta team in Vietnam.) When radio propagation was better at night, we could send and receive brief Morse code messages, using a long wire antenna strung between tree trunks.

If possible, a team might also direct airmobile forces from the ARVN Airborne–Ranger battalion assigned to Project Delta against enemy units. Because the teams were hurting the NVA so badly, the enemy made blunting the Delta effort a priority.

Project Delta was a top-secret operation that had its own compound adjacent to the 5th Group headquarters. Ethnic Chinese Nung guards in their distinctive black-and-green tiger-stripe jungle fatigues guarded the barbed-wire enclosure around the clock.

"Sir," I told the adjutant, "I meant IV Corps, not Project Delta."

"I know what you meant," he said. "But you're going to Delta."

"Yes, sir. I got it," I replied, wondering why in the hell he had asked us what we preferred in the first place. It turned out that the six other lieutenants were also headed to Delta. We learned that just prior to our arrival, MACV headquarters had received a badly flawed Delta reconnaissance report that identified major enemy activity in a specific area, but when a larger reaction force had been dispatched to follow up, it had found nothing. MACV Saigon felt it was possible that the team's integrity had failed or that they might have simply been slacking off to avoid their hazardous mission. Either way, Saigon decided that instead of having NCOs head the teams, lieutenants would command each one to improve the chances of better reporting.

Joining Project Delta with the other new lieutenants was a real test of our leadership skills because the unit already had thirty-two senior NCOs whom we'd be supplanting as team leaders. These were hard-core, well-trained, seasoned guys to whom the gold bar of an untested second lieutenant meant nothing. One of the NCOs had been in Project Delta forty months and had seen it all, including lots of new lieutenants carried to Graves Registration in black rubber body bags.

Long-range reconnaissance was our mission, so we had our own dedicated aviation element—six UH-1 Huey transport helicopters and four Huey gunships. We had a priority code that could instantly divert aircraft anywhere in Vietnam to strike targets we'd identified. We even had our own combat air controllers guiding operations from overhead, and dedicated spotter planes to direct the fighter-bombers. At the time, Delta was headed by Lieutenant Colonel John Hayes, whose executive officer was Major John Assente.

They ordered the new lieutenants to attend yet another series of orientation briefings, these much more intense than those we'd received in Saigon. There were a lot of techniques to master, including transmitting and receiving Morse code. Morse code might be our sole link when we were far from base and needed to report—or call for urgent extraction at first light—so we had to learn how to send at least three words per minute and accurately receive up to ten words per minute.

There would be a lot more to learn, and our lives would depend on how fast we could learn it, but I was highly motivated and thrilled to be a part of such a vital mission—until the day Colonel Hayes called me into his office.

"Shelton," he said. "I'm thinking about pulling you out of Delta and sending you back to 5th Group."

I was stunned. *Have I screwed up already?*

"You're just too damn tall," he explained. "If we put you out there with the Vietnamese it would be suicide. You'll stand out head-and-shoulders above them and almost impossible to disguise. The NVA will immediately spot you as an American and that'll be the end of it."

"I accept that risk," I said. I was six foot five and there was no way to shrink. "But I'd still like to do it. Delta is a great outfit," I said. "And I'd really like to be a member of it."

"I'll consider your request overnight" was all he said before dismissing me.

The next day, he told me I could stay. So I rejoined the other lieutenants and we got to work learning the practical details of Project Delta. Since they needed to get us out there as quickly as possible, our timetable was condensed and training far more concentrated than any I had experienced to date.

On a typical mission, we would "ingress" along carefully preplanned

routes and "egress" on others, just in case the enemy had tracked our helicopters on the way in and set up ambushes. These routes involved coldly
serious planning on which we were briefed in great detail. A typical flight
would consist of four UH-1 Huey "slicks"—troop-carrier helicopters
with two door gunners—and two Huey gunships armed with either M-60
machine guns or multibarrel miniguns plus 2.75-inch rocket pods protruding from each side of the hull. The flight of four Huey slicks would
overfly the landing zone (LZ) with only one UH-1 landing or hovering, so
the team could jump off while the others were providing a distraction.
The flight was timed to set down at sundown—often after several false
landings elsewhere to confuse the enemy: carefully planned and well-
executed deception, a classic Special Operations tactic.

Once on the ground, the Delta team would immediately depart the
area and establish a small defensive perimeter, while the four Huey slicks
and two gunships headed back to the base camp. This was similar to our
Special Forces qualification course at Fort Bragg during which a "friendly
guerrilla" would use his dry cleaning truck as a cover vehicle to disguise
our drop-off.

The difference, of course, was that the enemy in North Carolina did
not shoot at us with live ammunition.

We studied aerial recon photos and matched them to our maps, memo-
rizing key landmarks in this hostile enemy territory—rivers, hills or mountains, clearings, bluffs—anything unique about the locale that we could
use for positioning and navigation. This was 1967 and there was no such
thing as GPS, just our preparation and proficiency at mental cartography.
Instant identification of specific evacuation sites and pickup points (both
primary and alternate) was crucial, and it was just as important that the
crew of our assigned aircraft also knew the plan intimately. Everybody
went to the briefings and everybody went to the brief backs—pilots, boots
on the ground, it didn't make a difference. We were a team—a team on
the ground who operated hand in glove with a team in the air. They put
us in. They took us out. Our lives depended on them.

One of the Hueys' extraction devices was the jungle penetrator, a yel-
lowish orange bullet-shaped steel seat with three folded petals, each big
enough for one full-size American or two average ARVN troops to strad-
dle. A hovering Huey would drop the penetrator on a winch cable down
through the forest canopy and hoist us up through the branches to the
open doorway of the aircraft.

The ingress-egress plan (with all of its backups and redundancies) was
an excellent concept—but it would require thorough preparation and fine-
tuned coordination.

There was no ramping up to speed since our first trip would take us
right into the middle of a heavy infiltration area directly on the border of
South Vietnam and North Vietnam. We would jump off from a base near

an old A-Team camp in the A Shau Valley south of Khe Sanh near the mountainous border with Laos. As a team leader on my initial operation, I really wanted this to go like clockwork. I certainly did not want to screw anything up, since doing so most likely would result in either injury or death and I sure as hell didn't want that for either my team *or* myself. Still, this was damn exciting stuff and I was champing at the bit for my first mission.

It was at this point that Major Assente called two other lieutenants and me to the conference room. It was a top-secret facility with soundproof walls that had been electronically swept for bugs. The major closed and locked the thick door, then stared silently at the three of us before he spoke. The man to my right was Doug Coulter, a Harvard graduate who'd earned a commission and then gone through Special Forces training, determined to be the best recon-platoon leader in the Army. He studied hard, worked hard, and he was very, very good. We all looked up to him and aspired to be like him.

The other was Willis (Bill) Larrabee, another sharp, dedicated young officer.

"Okay," Major Assente said flatly. "Take a good look at the guy on your left and the guy on your right." We followed his order. "Memorize what they look like because six weeks from now two of you will be dead. That's our track record here—only one out of three survives his tour with Delta. I just want you to know the score and get yourself right with God, because that's the way it is."

That scared the daylights out of all three of us. *That's too bad about my two buddies here,* I thought.

———

Our team of two Americans and four ARVN Special Forces deployed north to the old A-Team camp on the edge of the A Shau Valley, the main North Vietnamese infiltration route into I Corps. Sergeant First Class Orville "Robbie" Robinette was my second-in-command, chosen because he was a veteran of many Delta missions and because we were both big enough to carry the other guy if he was wounded. Army aviator Captain Bob Moberg, another veteran of numerous operations, commanded the Hueys. A wiry little LLDB lieutenant led the four Vietnamese Special Forces.

As the Hueys were refueling, I had the team triple-check the radios and all their equipment. We wore ARVN Ranger green-and-black tiger-stripe camouflage jungle fatigues. Our lightweight .223-caliber CAR-15 rifles had short barrels and collapsible stocks, but the rest of our gear was standard—and heavy—M1911 .45-caliber semiautomatic pistols, machetes, fragmentation and smoke grenades, first-aid pouches, ponchos, pen flares, and extra radio batteries. With spare ammunition and water, our basic loads topped seventy pounds, which didn't leave much room for food—so, like other Americans on recon teams, I shoved a few packages of long-range patrol rations into empty corners of my rucksack. Ammunition, radio batteries, and water were more important than food, and it was better to forgo a balanced diet for a few days than to break our backs.

The string of helicopters lifted off in the early evening and flew southwest toward the dark clouds rising above the ridges. About five miles from the primary LZ, our helicopter dropped down to treetop level and moved in front of the other, higher helos in this carefully orchestrated aerial dance of deception. The flight commander vectored us toward the LZ and suddenly it came into view: a narrow clearing where elephant grass was overgrowing what had once been a Montagnard dry paddy rice field. Our six-man team jumped off in a flash as the other aircraft passed overhead. In a heartbeat Captain Moberg eased back on his cyclic and powered up to rejoin the formation—our collective hope was that the noise of the three passing aircraft successfully masked our landing.

No such luck. The flat crack of small-arms fire exploded from the tree line about two hundred meters down the slope to our left, and distinctive hot green tracers slashed overhead. This was the first time I had been shot at in anger and my heart was pounding through my chest. So much for an undetected ingress.

"Let's go," I called. "Move. Follow me."

But as we plunged into the waist-high grass, one of the LLDB troopers began to cough loudly—a deep, rattling hack. He continued to gasp and cough as we ran. Down the mountainside, NVA soldiers were shouting back and forth and even shining flashlights in the deepening gloom.

On the first brief pause to catch our wind, I used the small VHF radio to contact the Otter orbiting high overhead. "Contact," I said softly into the device, holding down the transmit button. "We are proceeding to E and E."

I could only hope that the escape-and-evasion training we'd planned would work. We changed direction several times and even plunged back downslope, attempting to throw off our pursuers. But as full darkness descended, the shrill Vietnamese cries seemed to be getting even closer. Thank God I didn't hear the yipping of the tracker dogs that the NVA sometimes used.

Late into the night we moved up the slope, away from the enemy voices and flashlights. Shortly before dawn, we threw ourselves, exhausted, into a clump of bushes and formed a small perimeter, feet toward the center, heads and weapons facing out. As we lay there, tired, winded, and feeling the anxiety brought about by the nearby enemy troops, the LLDB trooper continued his noisy, incessant cough.

I grabbed the Vietnamese lieutenant's arm and clamped his biceps hard. *"Trung Úy,"* I hissed, calling him by rank. "If you don't keep him quiet, he'll get us *all* killed."

"I do it," the lieutenant whispered back.

At first light, as the birds began their harsh songs in the canopy high overhead, we again heard Vietnamese shouts down the mountainside, clos-ing toward us, and we started moving rapidly.

All day we were on the move. When we stopped to sip water, the last of our supply, the enemy voices echoed toward us through the tall pillars of the tropical hardwoods. Although the forest floor was clear of entangl-ing vines and brush, we still had to run through an ankle-deep carpet of dry leaves that had drifted down from the canopy, the cleated soles of our jungle boots crunching loudly as we staggered ahead.

Finally, after sunset that second night, we no longer heard the NVA or saw their flashlights. But by this time we were completely out of water. My lips and tongue were sticky, as if I'd been sucking cough medicine; and still the ARVN Special Forces man coughed, his hacking rasp even louder than before.

Robinette and I rotated on watch, each pulling a two-hour period on guard while the other slept. When I woke for my rotation just before mid-night I realized that the Vietnamese trooper had finally stopped coughing. *It's about time,* I thought. As we prepared to move out before dawn, I discovered the reason why the man was so quiet. His face was cold, dead. I concluded that to protect the lives of the rest of us, his lieutenant had either strangled or smothered him. In the brutal logic of the long war that the ARVN Special Forces were fighting, this act had been necessary. Had the NVA captured us, we would have been tortured, possibly beyond en-durance to resist, forced to divulge critical information, and then exe-cuted when we were no longer useful. Each of us had been told up front that if we had a cold, cough, or anything like that, we would not go on a mission because we would jeopardize the whole team. The ARVN soldier had disregarded that edict and ended up paying the ultimate price for it. I marked the site on my map and we moved on.

That morning, the NVA began chasing us again, but this time we man-aged to evade them. Even so, we had long since run out of water, and by the end of that long day things were looking bleak. Exacerbating the situ-ation was the triple-canopy jungle overhead, which made it virtually im-possible for us to be picked up with the enemy so near. We had to get to our alternate pickup zone, so once more I jutted east toward that location.

As with all Special Forces troopers, I had been trained in basic first aid, and a part of that involved recognizing signs of severe dehydration—it was clear that we were rapidly approaching that point. Our skin was shriveling and bouts of intermittent dizziness had started to plague us all. I searched for *anything* from which I could extract precious fluid to pre-vent our falling prey to hypovolemic shock or kidney failure, but there

was nothing. All we could do was forge ahead and pray that we reached
that alternate site before our bodies succumbed.

In moving toward our alternate pickup zone, we stumbled onto a
North Vietnamese base camp that still had rows of green NVA pith helmets on the ground next to cooking fires with glowing coals, indicating
that the NVA troops had to be somewhere in the area. This was a bivouac
for at least a battalion of four hundred men. And now there were only five
of us. There had to be water there, but was it worth it?

I took a moment to mark the camp's location on my map and then we
got the hell out of there—these men were going to return at any second.
As we moved down the faint game trail, I suddenly heard a rustling noise
emanating from the brush directly ahead and looked up to see a huge
Bengal tiger trotting toward us. I flipped the selector switch of my CAR-
15 from SAFE to AUTO and raised the weapon. The big cat stopped about
ten feet away, sank into a crouch, and studied us with yellow eyes, the tip
of his striped tail switching nervously. Although not normally a threat to
humans, I had heard that wild animals in war zones like this were known
to cultivate appetites for human flesh after consuming the bodies of casualties that were yet to be buried. If I fired now, I could probably kill the
tiger before he sprang. But every NVA soldier in the area would hear the
burst and be on us in minutes.

Was it better to let the tiger kill us fast or let the NVA do it slowly?

The tiger finally snorted and spun away in another direction. God was
on our side. We moved off quickly to get out of the area, but I wanted to
find an appropriate area where I could get our long-range communications set up so that I could call in an air strike on that NVA base camp.
This was a tricky situation. On the one hand, we needed to hit that camp
*soon* because obviously the NVA troops would be coming back to retrieve
their gear and spend the night. On the other, we couldn't make much
noise moving again, knowing that the enemy was all around us.

We hadn't gone more than another forty or fifty meters when there
was a sudden crashing overhead. I reeled down into a crouch and again
my right thumb instinctively moved my CAR-15 selector switch to AUTO. I
slowly raised my head to investigate. *Sniper? Ambush?*

A big, dark-furred ape swung through the branches. As I watched him
disappear in the canopy, my heart thudded hard against my ribs. "What
the hell was *that?*" I whispered to Robinette.

"Beats the shit outta me, sir," he said with a strained grin. "Orang-
utan maybe."

My breath was coming in dry gasps, which only worsened the thirst.
We had to keep moving, but I felt too shaky to continue immediately. The
dehydration had almost overpowered us. We'd been out of water for more
than a day and a half. My lips and tongue felt like I'd been gobbling cotton candy at a county fair. This thirst was far worse than any I'd ever

suffered while loading chopped silage onto the conveyor belt in the North Carolina summer heat. I felt like every cell in my body was dehydrated, and my tongue was swollen.

We finally reached a small clearing on a high ridge and flopped down into our perimeter. One of the Vietnamese team members reached into his rucksack and pulled out a red can of Coke and a can of beer. What the hell had he been waiting for? He opened both the foaming Coke and warm beer and offered them to Robinette and me. Robinette took the Coke and each of us took a long swallow, as the Vietnamese team members consumed the beer. But the Coke instantly turned into sticky liquid, sealing our lips and pallets. If anything, our thirst grew worse.

Suddenly, the sun glare above the canopy darkened and thunder rumbled nearby. Rain began to pelt down through the branches, wetting our faces and drenching our salt-crusted uniforms. Soon it was pouring down on us. We rolled ponchos into crude funnels and caught enough rain to refill our canteens, but only after we'd sucked down so much that we were bloated.

That night we rigged the antenna wire and tapped out a Morse message, identifying the NVA base camp as a potential B-52 target and requesting pickup at the nearest extraction point. It took us most of the next morning to reach that location—a small, cleared area among the trees, with daylight filtering down to the forest floor. There were just enough breaks in the canopy for our pilot, Captain Moberg, to drop the jungle penetrator. We waited tensely in our defensive perimeter until we heard the distinctive whop-whop of the Huey's two-bladed rotor.

On the small VHF radio, I asked Moberg if he wanted me to pop a smoke grenade or send up some pen flares to guide him.

"Negative," he said calmly. "Just talk me in by my sound."

That was a good decision: if he'd been able to see our smoke, so would any nearby NVA.

Moberg held a hover while his crew chief manned the winch to send down the penetrator. The orange bullet-shaped penetrator bounced among the branches until the cable reached its full 165-foot length. The metal seat swayed there, six feet off the ground, so high that I was the only member of the team who could even grab it. With the free-hanging penetrator comes the risk of deadly high-voltage static-electricity shock, so we propped a long branch on the ground and wedged it between the metal seats, hoping that it would ground any electrical charge. This worked, so when I grabbed the steel penetrator with my naked, grimy hand, I wasn't shocked.

I hoisted up the three Vietnamese, one at a time. The winch whirred and the men rose into the canopy. When Moberg dropped the penetrator again, I dropped on all fours so that Sergeant Robinette could stand on my back and grip the sling straps.

"Back up!" I yelled to Moberg's slick.

As Robinette disappeared into the canopy, I heard the deep, pounding blast of AK-47s firing at the helicopter. I was all alone and the enemy was close and getting even closer, their 7.62-mm high-power rounds ripping up the foliage all around me—but it wasn't the foliage I was worried about. I threw down my rucksack and stuffed my map and radio inside my shirt, then slung my CAR-15 across my back and clung hard to the swaying orange metal as the cable hauled me up.

But even without my heavy rucksack, my weight added too much load and made it almost impossible for the packed Huey to hold hover, and the aircraft's rotors seemed unable to generate sufficient lift. As the penetrator jerked up through the branches, Moberg fought hard to maintain control. He had lost altitude and his rotors were literally cutting out the tops of the trees. His left-door gunner was blasting machine-gun fire at the enemy tracers but the Huey was losing the battle. It seemed to stagger, then sink.

*Get the fuck out of the trees, Bob,* I pleaded in desperation.

The green NVA tracers slashed up from the gloom below. Moberg's slick was still wobbling on the edge of control but the crew chief kept the winch turning and I continued to rise, feeling all the while like I had a huge bull's-eye painted on my back. I finally reached the right landing skid and threw my arm around it as someone leaned out and gripped my shoulder.

I looked forward and saw Bob Moberg's face as he sat in the command pilot's seat. He was smiling widely, but his eyes were brimming with tears as he fought the bucking collective and cyclic controls, the Huey still on the edge of a stall with this tremendous load. More enemy fire snapped around us and I was hanging down from the chopper, completely exposed. Bob applied maximum power and rotor torque, and the helicopter slowly rose out of the doughnut of chopped treetops that the slick had slashed from the canopy. To this day I cannot imagine how a barrage of gunfire like that missed me and the Huey, but at that point I was more concerned with hanging on for dear life, since gunfire wasn't the only thing that could have prevented me from ever seeing Carolyn or Jon again. The chopper rolled left down the mountain slope toward Khe Sanh, with me still dangling from the bird with my arm life-locked on to that skid and the sounds of enemy gunfire fading away. En route back, the crew chief, firmly attached to the aircraft with his "monkey strap," leaned down and assisted me back inside.

When we landed, Moberg slapped his arm around me and said, "You had me worried, big guy."

I thanked him profusely for his heroic actions. "Better change those rotor blades," I said, only half jokingly.

"Plenty more where they came from," he replied, somewhat stoically.

*But talk about going above and beyond,* I thought, wondering how many other lives Captain Bob Moberg had saved with his selfless courage and almost superhuman piloting skills. I knew they didn't make them any better than Bob Moberg.

---

We did that type of operation day in and day out for months. Despite Saigon's plans, experienced NCOs continued to command many Project Delta recon teams, and from my observation their reporting was always deadly accurate. The veteran sergeants were the real backbone of Delta.

Most of the new young lieutenants entering the program certainly rose to the occasion, and those who didn't tended to be few and far between. But some of them slipped by, like a coward I'll call Harold West. This loser was so terrified, he refused to get off the helicopter—and I gave him three separate chances. On the third day I told him, "You are a lieutenant in the United States Army and as an officer you're supposed to set a good example. If you don't get off that helicopter when it touches down, I will have you relieved of duty as a coward." He said *no problem,* but for the third straight day, as soon as the helo touched down, he cowered back and froze up—just wouldn't get off. I relieved him and forwarded a scathing OER (Officer Efficiency Report), noting that he was relieved for cowardice. Turned out he got a job as an adjutant in another unit, and since one of the adjutant's responsibilities is to receive and pass along these OERs, I concluded that he must have intercepted his own and just threw it in the trash. Somehow he stayed off the radar screen long enough for his yellow-bellied ass to retire as a colonel—but I'd be shocked if the entirety of that career wasn't spent hidden away in some meaningless office.

In spite of anomalies like that, our teams continued to take the fight to the enemy no matter the risk. Delta teams were giving U.S. taxpayers a big bang for their buck since the "punch" we delivered was much heavier than our small numbers would indicate.

I gained tremendous respect for the NCOs and aviators assigned to Project Delta and to the dedication they displayed in carrying out the mission. Occasionally we lost helicopter crews but only because they refused to stop trying to extract teams on the ground regardless of the lethal risk to themselves. The same dedication was embedded in the teams on the ground. We had two great NCOs—Sergeants First Class Willie Stark and Pete Bott—who went down fighting right up on the North Vietnamese border, refusing to let the helicopter come in and try to get them out because they knew the choppers could never make it out with the enemy completely surrounding them. That kind of bravery was not rare among the men of Project Delta.

---

Carolyn wrote to me daily and I tried to do the same, when circumstances permitted. Since this was long before e-mail and I didn't have access to a telephone that could call the United States, this was our only means of staying in touch. "Mail call" was a big event. Sometimes a mailbag would arrive in the unit containing an accumulation of four to seven letters from Carolyn. Her mail was like nectar from heaven. It was the only way I had to hear about baby Jon and his development and be reassured that Carolyn was coping with my absence and living with her parents. Her letters included all the details of her daily life in Speed, including information about my parents, whom she saw several times a week. Sadly, in that same batch was some news that Carolyn had considered withholding until my return—but that was not what we were about. We shared the bad as well as the good, and this letter revealed that Trooper, our two-year-old German shepherd, had been struck and killed by a passing motorist.

———

In March 1967, I was promoted to captain. One night our reconnaissance-platoon leader, another captain, was playing poker with Colonel Hayes up in our forward operating base near the Demilitarized Zone along the border with North Vietnam (which, ironically, was one of the heaviest *militarized* zones on planet Earth) and a great deal of money was in play. Hayes had already lost a large sum to his young subordinate but this final hand was his chance to turn things around. "I call," he said confidently, exposing his ten-high full house.

The captain shook his head. "Not your night, sir," he gloated, slapping down a full house of his own, taking the hand with queens high. He raked in the cash and called it a night.

The next day they went out to put in a recon team, but for whatever reason they put them in the wrong place—right in the middle of an enemy stronghold. The team got surrounded and ultimately we lost them, every man. The captain was immediately relieved of duty and Hayes called me in and said that I was taking command. There was no, "Do you want the job?" It was, "Shelton, you've got the platoon."

Since I would now be overseeing fifteen Delta teams, I would go out on fewer actual missions than I would have liked, but I would be more involved with wider intelligence and making sure the teams went into the right LZs. I did that job for about two months with Major Assente as my new commander, following Lieutenant Colonel Hayes's return to the United States.

Late one afternoon I was going over the following day's assignments with Major Assente when Lieutenant Colonel Eleazar Parmly IV burst into our Delta headquarters. Brigadier General S. L. A. Marshall once described Parmly as "one of the most outspoken Army officers extant," and he didn't pull any punches this time, either.

"I've got to have the best lieutenant or captain that you've got," Parmly brusquely told Assente. "I just had to relieve a detachment commander for psychological reasons, and his executive officer was killed."

Everybody in the tent was listening. This was not a good situation.

"Detachment A-104 at Ha Thanh is basically leaderless right now," the colonel added. "The camp's in southern I Corps, up against the Highlands, west of Quang Ngai, and they need a new commander. Who have you got?"

That was bad country, a stronghold of enemy resistance dating back to the first Indochina war against the French. Whoever went up there would have his hands full. Not surprising that in conditions so punishing, some just couldn't handle it and would basically implode psychologically. I wondered how many other commanders they had gone through.

"Well," Assente said, "the best captain I've got is standing right here in front of you, but he . . ."

"You can stop right there," the colonel said. "Shelton, pack your bags. You're coming with me."

I looked at Assente but found no relief there.

I ran back over to my tent and packed my rucksack, barely having time to extend a few quick goodbyes to friends I might never see again—friends whose very lives we had entrusted in one another's. "Let's go," shouted Colonel Parmly from the UH-1 as the rotors started to spin. I jumped on board and we lifted off, making a gentle arc toward the south; we flew straight to Ha Thanh, the dark jungle mountains looming ahead.

This definitely did not look like good country.

————

The UH-1 banked steeply as we approached the Special Forces camp. Ha Thanh looked like a sculpted oval turtleback of treeless laterite terraces carved by big bulldozers. There was a perimeter of barbed-wire entanglements and, along the crest, a jumbled line of low buildings with rusty corrugated-metal roofs. Circular sandbagged mortar and heavy-machine-gun pits were placed unevenly behind the barbed wire.

Once in the camp, the colonel quickly introduced me to Sergeant First Class James Flood. As team sergeant, Flood had been the ranking survivor in the A-104 detachment before I arrived.

Lieutenant Colonel Parmly seemed eager to be out of there before the afternoon clouds thickened. "Okay, Shelton, you've got it," he said. "You're on your own. Good luck." And with that he flew off to Da Nang, where his C-Team headquarters was located.

Sergeant Flood led me to the commander's bunker near the wide-roofed team house that doubled as the intel room.

"Let me show you around the rest of the camp," he said as I dumped my gear. We made the short tour, with Flood pointing out the obvious, including the muddy weapons pits and commo bunker with split and sagging sandbags. The whole camp looked run-down, shabby, as if nobody gave a damn about either the look or the strength of our fortifications. That should have been the responsibility of the detachment commander, the executive officer (XO), or the team sergeant; but in this case the commander had lost it and been medevaced, the XO was lying dead someplace out in the jungle, and Flood didn't appear to give much of a damn about anything.

"I've got something else to show you, Captain," he said with a glint in his eye, finally displaying some enthusiasm about something.

He led me down into the musty dimness of his own bunker. "Wanna see something, sir?" he asked hauntingly.

Flood hefted a wide-mouth jar that had probably come from a Da Nang mess hall. The jar was stuffed with shriveled human ears, all left ears—probably about a hundred of them.

"I've been here around six months," he said. "And this is what I collect. It helps keep track of how many slopes we kill."

It was then that I smelled the rank odor of alcohol on his breath. "How about a drink, Captain?" he offered, swaying drunk in the late afternoon. He reached for a bottle.

This man was not fit to be a team leader. It was hard to believe that he wore a Special Forces uniform or was a member of the United States Army. *Slopes . . .* Did this bigot think that his racist attitude would bolster loyalty among the CIDG Montagnards and the Vietnamese Special Forces who lived and fought beside us?

*The situation is way worse than I thought.* "Put that damn bottle away and get rid of that fucking jar—now." He pulled back his rocking head and squinted at me in horror, like I was the one who didn't get it. And I was livid. "In fact, pack up your shit. You are not fit to be a team sergeant and I'm relieving you. You're damn lucky I don't recommend a court-martial, but if you don't move your sorry ass right now that's exactly what I'll do."

At first he seemed inclined to dispute my order, but when he saw the rage in my eyes staring down at him, he thought better of it.

I radioed 5th Group to request a helicopter in the morning to remove Flood from the camp. "I've got to get rid of this guy. He's committed multiple war crimes and on top of that it appeared obvious to me that he was drinking on duty."

Then I found Sergeant First Class Jim Dupe, the team medic. "You may be a medic," I said, "but as of now you're the new team sergeant." He nodded. This was a Special Forces A-Team and we were cross-trained to do all the jobs.

"First thing," I told him, "no more alcohol in this detachment. People can drink when they go on R and R in Da Nang. We're here to fight, not party." Dupe got the message and I got the impression that he was relieved to see that the new kid in town meant business—and that the new kid was committed to turning around this detachment.

\* \* \*

At dawn, ARVN Special Forces Lieutenant Dat and I led a company of Montagnards out into the jungle hills to locate and recover the XO's body—but not before I shared an admonition. We would be heading directly back to where the team had been ambushed, to where the indigenous troops had seen the XO fall. It was feasible that NVA soldiers were still in wait, ready for a reprise of their attack. I didn't know how my team had approached their prior missions, but from that point forward I wanted them focused and vigilant.

Lieutenant Dat was a little guy around five feet tall who weighed about ninety pounds, but he was strong and fearless. He conveyed my warning to the Montagnards and we forged ahead.

It didn't take long for us to find the American lieutenant; the stench of death was overpowering as we drew near the ambush site. The XO had been sprawled on the jungle floor in the premonsoon heat for several days and it was not a pretty sight. Maggots were feeding on his decaying body as it lay in the exact spot where it had fallen just days before, but the enemy had cut off his head and placed it neatly on the center of his chest.

The message was obvious: *You cut off ears, we cut off heads.*

The tough little Yards rolled the body tightly in a poncho and slung it beneath a length of bamboo. We got back to camp just as the Huey from Da Nang was kicking up stinging dust, about to lift off with Flood on board.

I waved at the pilot to cut the engine. "Get your ass over here and help lift him inside," I ordered Flood, referring to the XO's remains.

His face was pale with an obvious hangover. But he followed my order.

---

Jim Dupe proved to be an outstanding team sergeant, cool in a firefight and very concerned with the needs of the approximately six hundred Vietnamese and Montagnard troops living in the Ha Thanh camp or its outposts. Like myself, he did not consider them "slopes."

There were two companies of Vietnamese and four companies of Montagnards in the camp—at least that was the official roster. Sometimes getting them assembled for an accurate head count was difficult at best, since their concept of time and date was different from ours.

Out beyond the barbed wire, I found that the ARVN troops were adequate, depending on who led them—but the Montagnard troops were *superb.* We were only advisers to our Vietnamese Special Forces counterparts in the camp; officially the LLDB commanded the Montagnards and the ARVN troops. But that wasn't how the Montagnards saw things. They always looked to the Americans for leadership, and when the shooting began they turned to me for their orders. "What do *you* want us to do, Daiwie [Captain]?"

* * *

Lieutenant Colonel Dan Schungel now commanded the C-Team in Da Nang, our higher headquarters. He was a tattooed veteran with several combat tours in Vietnam who looked more like a tough sergeant major than a field-grade officer. Schungel devised what he called the "hit parade," a ranking of the nine A-Team camps in I Corps in terms of which one was the most vulnerable to attack and had the highest probability of being overrun. When I arrived in June 1967, Ha Thanh was number one, and it remained on the top of the chart throughout my command.

The Ha Thanh camp sat astride a major enemy infiltration route and required a "layer defense"—barbed wire and mines, machine guns and mortars, and heavily reinforced bunkers—plus constant patrolling, if we were going to survive. The NVA and their allies, the Vietcong, badly wanted free control of this valley, so that they could gather food and "patriotic" taxes from the villagers between the Highlands to the west and Quang Ngai City on the coast. We stood in their way, and by the look of the present state of defenses around the camp, it was sheer luck rather than physical obstacles that had been its protector.

My first priority when I took over the camp was to rebuild its defenses, which were in a horrific state. From a military standpoint, the camp was virtually a ruin. A lot of the barbed wire was rusted, sagging, and so thin in places that a determined enemy could have beaten through it with a stout bamboo club—and there was no shortage of bamboo in the area. Many of our claymore mines were facing the wrong direction, which meant that had they been detonated, the seven hundred steel balls of shrapnel would have fired at *us* at the rate of four thousand feet per second instead of at the enemy. I would think that even an illiterate moron could understand that when the device has FRONT TOWARD ENEMY written all across its front, you would face that side toward the enemy. Between the mines aimed back at us, the lack of functional detonation cables on others, and the sheer corrosion that rendered others inoperable, it was evident that this camp was completely vulnerable to enemy attack. Add to that a complete lack of red-and-white-striped aiming stakes that were needed to lay down accurate fire from our 81-mm mortars, and you had a disastrous situation that put our lives at risk on a nightly basis.

I had to make sure the camp could withstand the big assault when they came at us—and this assault was inevitable.

I gathered my men and started rebuilding, with the young NCOs completely behind me. For too long they'd seen the camp's standards slide toward disaster.

We all rolled up our sleeves and chipped in, every day, as a team. If we weren't out on patrol, we were in hard labor back at the camp, and we *did* work hard. Every minute I was back from patrol I would be either grabbing a few hours sleep or out there in the sun, swinging a pickax or a shovel with my teammates.

New barbed-wire defenses were high on our priority list so I flew into Da Nang and came back with tons of loosely coiled concertina wire and tighter rolls to be staked down ankle-high as tangle-foot. Huge twin-rotor CH-47 Chinook cargo helicopters flew in with bulging sling loads of even more barbed wire, thick, rough-hewn timbers, steel rebar, and sacks of ready mix concrete.

Once the barbed wire, claymores, and trip flares had been replaced, we set to work on the new command bunker, right up on top of the camp mound. This was our nerve center, an obvious target for the NVA—either the enemy observing us from the nearby mountains or the "invisible" Vietcong spies coming and going every day through the camp gates. We built a solid box of reinforced concrete with a thick roof strengthened with additional timbers and heaped layers of fresh sandbags.

The Navy's Seabee construction chief petty officer who flew out to inspect our work was impressed. "Captain," he said, pointing to the command bunker, "this baby could take a direct hit from a seven-hundred-fifty-pound bomb." While I appreciated his optimism, I hoped it would never be tested.

At the end of several backbreaking weeks of labor in the sweltering pre-monsoon weather, I believed we had accomplished as much as we could—enough that I could feel at least adequately safe when I turned in at night.

But there was one last refinement. Providing accurate close-air-support directions at night had been a problem for decades. The difficulty had two critical elements: where was the friendly force and where was the enemy? We approached the problem by building a large, swiveling wooden arrow and mounting it on the roof of the command bunker. Then we attached big cans filled with oil-and-gas-soaked rags to the arrow. The principle was to point that arrow toward the main enemy force as soon as they attacked—and then give the F-4 Phantom fighter-bombers, A1-E Skyraiders, or Spooky gunships the estimated distance in meters from the pointed end of the arrow to the attacking force. That is where the fighters or gunships were to place their bombs or fires.

The system was primitive but it worked. After a couple of practice runs, the supporting aviators learned exactly how close they could place their ordnance without endangering the camp. And we became confident that Ha Thanh would have reliable air support, even on the darkest monsoon night.

But we couldn't depend solely on fighter-bombers or AC-47 Spooky gunships. We had to know if the NVA or Vietcong were trying to slip around behind the camp, east toward Quang Ngai. So for this we kept a minimum of two patrols out of the camp at all times.

Now it was time to get down to the business at hand. Our job was to disrupt the enemy forces attempting to infiltrate the South and to deny them access to the population and resources in the valley. To do this, we had to patrol our assigned area, which normally meant two companies outside the camp operating in two different areas. We always left the camp in the dead of night so that the enemy, with their network of observers, would not know in which direction the patrol had gone.

We also worked with the local Vietnamese district chief to provide security for the people living in the valley floor, as well as medical assistance and foodstuffs as necessary.

---

One of my most important functions as team leader was to maintain an excellent relationship with the indigenous Montagnard population. To that end, I became close with the village chief and would periodically meet with him in his village. In theory, this was enemy-controlled territory, but even the NVA knew better than to mess with the Yards on their own turf—and trigger a blood feud in the process. The Montagnard people had lived in these rain-forest mountains for centuries and could severely disrupt infiltration routes from the North, should they have chosen to do so.

The chief's village was typical: several large, thatched longhouse communal dwellings standing on short hardwood legs, surrounded by smaller coops and granaries. Squat potbellied pigs slept, grunting occasionally, in the shade beneath the houses. As we sat on tiny carved stools (with my long legs jutting out awkwardly), the chief presented his family and the village elders, wizened men prematurely aged by years of hard work and poor diet.

ARVN Lieutenant Dat translated my words into Vietnamese—which a few of the villagers seemed to understand—and the chief's words back to me in broken English.

Sometimes the chief would actually join me when I went to the village to bargain with the local farmers to buy a cow to feed the Montagnard soldiers. Often the farmer would start by asking the equivalent of more than one thousand dollars U.S. for a single cow, and by the time we finished haggling I would've bought the cow for around fifty dollars or so. In theory, the chief was there to help me get a good price, but I really think he just enjoyed watching me negotiate. Each time money changed hands, he would break out in a deep belly laugh and Lieutenant Dat would translate the same phrase each and every time: *Mr. Captain Shelton, you are the toughest I have ever seen.*

Every thirty days the tribe would have a ceremony in the village, and they took this very seriously. My men knew that anyone who was not out on patrol was expected to attend. The ceremony would start with the chief putting a bamboo rope around the neck of a sacrificial water buffalo and tying the animal to a tall stake with about a twelve-foot bamboo cord. Then two Montagnards dressed in loincloths would approach the animal and start jabbing him with spears to get him running around the pole. With each pass they would lunge with the spear until the beast was bleeding so profusely that he would fall to the ground.

At this point the drama kicked in and the locals would wait with bated breath to see which way the huge animal would fall. If he fell toward the village when he died, the villagers would erupt in a big cheer, since it signified good luck for the next thirty days. If he fell away from it, there were looks of horror in anticipation of the trouble that would soon follow.

In either event, the highlight for the tribe occurred the moment the animal hit the ground. It was then that a tribesman would run out and sever the bull's throat. Using old rusty beer cans, Coke cans—any kind of cans—they would then catch the hot gushing blood and pass it around for everyone to enjoy. Our Special Forces teams were expected to drink right along with the locals or risk gravely insulting the tribe, and the potential repercussions of that could be devastating.

The chief would normally invite me to be right by his side, so you know he'd be checking to make sure that I didn't leave a drop—and it seemed that they went out of their way to make sure my can was filled all the way to the top.

I personally had one extra step I injected into the monthly ritual—popping two tetracycline tablets the morning before the event and two as soon as I got back to the camp. Not only did it preclude my getting sick from the rusty cans and buffalo blood, but I was about the only team member who remained perfectly healthy for my entire deployment.

A few months before I left, the ceremony was conducted slightly differently. Instead of the buffalo ritual, this time it started out with the chief inviting me to join him for a little more rice wine than had been customary, and he also invited a young Montagnard woman of about twenty or twenty-one to come over and join us. She wore her finest skirt of striped homespun cloth and chunky copper bracelets on both plump wrists and ankles, and seemed somewhat embarrassed as she glanced quickly in my direction. A slight trickle of betel-nut juice ran down her lip.

About ten minutes into it, the chief got all excited and started firing off something to the translator, all the while gesturing to the newly constructed longhouse behind him.

The translator nodded and turned to me. "Our chief wants you to understand that he is presenting this beautiful girl to you as your wife and this new house that has been built is yours and hers to live in." It was his way of thanking me for protecting the tribe from the NVA.

This knocked me off my feet and instinctively I glanced at the "wife" I had just been presented, who smiled a big smile with even more red betel-nut juice running from her mouth down her chin. This was my cue to thank him profusely for the great honor and his generosity and to explain to him that I had already been married for four years and in fact already had a son, so as a Christian I could not have another wife and could not accept his kind offer.

Of course I did it as tactfully and politely as I could, but I left that celebration quicker than I'd ever left one before, and to my knowledge I never saw that girl again. For that matter, I don't recall ever having rice wine again, either.

———

On August 3, 1967, the district chief came about a stone's throw away from being crushed to death when a U.S. C-7A Caribou aircraft was shot down by friendly fire and crashed into his compound, which was contiguous to our Special Forces camp.

The Army had commenced Operation Hood River the day before, and for the next ten days the 1st Brigade, 101st Airborne Division would conduct operations to find, fix, and destroy VC and NVA forces in the western portion of Base Area 121 (between Ha Thanh and Quang Ngai City) in coordination with ARVN (Army of the Republic of Vietnam), ROK (Republic of Korea), and CIDG (Civilian Irregular Defense Group, such as the Montagnards) forces.

Leading the operation was Brigadier General Salve H. Matheson, a highly decorated war hero who participated in the D-Day invasion of Normandy and the seizure of Hitler's Eagle's Nest, and whose experiences would later be made famous in Stephen Ambrose's 1992 book *Band of Brothers*.

In addition to small-unit actions, saturation patrols, and night ambushes, the operation would be supplemented by artillery support provided by the 11th and 320th artilleries (C Battery, 2nd Battalion) of the 101st Airborne, which would also be celebrating the firing of their one-hundred-thousandth artillery round in Vietnam.

My detachment was not involved in this operation—at least we were not supposed to be.

I was in the team house when I heard the thunderous blast of a 105-mm "arty" round, which in and of itself was not of note, given that they'd been firing on and off since Operation Hood River had begun the day before. What grabbed my attention was the unmistakable overhead engine whine that immediately followed—some aircraft was in big trouble.

I ran outside to see an Air Force C-7A flying erratically in a downward arc heading directly toward the Montagnard district chief's compound on the north end of my camp. The vertical stabilizer had been blasted off and was on its own track toward the village. I knew that aircraft—it had been an Army plane and part of the 11th Air Assault Division with me at Fort

HIROMICHI MINE

*C-7A Crashing into Montagnard district chief's compound at north end of my camp, Ha Thahn, Vietnam.*

Benning, but it had subsequently been transferred to the Air Force over a "roles and missions" issue. As I ran full speed out the front gate of our camp and down the dirt road leading to the little village of Ha Thanh, the plane rotated upside down and crashed into the compound.

Turning into the village, I could already see (and smell) that the fuel tank had ruptured and highly flammable aviation fuel was flowing freely and creating a potentially explosive pool around the wreckage. A portion of the rear had blown off, so I was able to crawl into the sheered fuselage to try to get the crew out before the plane burst into flames. Climbing over the debris and artillery rounds that the C-7A had been in the process of delivering to our camp's dirt runway, I was able to get close enough to the front to determine that both pilots were dead, still belted into their seats and upside down in the cockpit but crushed almost beyond recognition. The crew chief in the back was still alive but barely—a mere bowl of jelly, with almost every bone broken.

I looked out the torn side of the aircraft and saw the pool of fuel expanding as if being fed from a fire hose, and to my utter disbelief I saw a guy walking toward it chomping on a lit cigar.

"Get rid of that cigar, you dumb son of a bitch!" I screamed, hoping to catch him before a stray ash drifted down onto the fuel.

I pulled out the crew chief (Technical Sergeant Zane Aubry Carter), but by then he, too, had died. Later I learned that Captain Alan Hendrickson and Captain John Dudley Wiley were on final approach to the tiny airstrip just outside our base when the 101st artillery gunner was cleared to fire his howitzer at the enemy, completely unaware that the aircraft was headed directly into his line of fire.

Of course I didn't know it when I called him a dumb son of a bitch, but the cigar chomper turned out to be Brigadier General Matheson, who had arrived that morning to oversee the operation as well as to celebrate with the 101st unit when they fired their one-hundred-thousandth round in Vietnam. As it played out, there was nothing to celebrate. We all mourned the loss of a great crew as we set about to recover and evacuate their bodies.

———

Back on our base, our hard work was paying off. We did a good job of keeping the North Vietnamese and the Vietcong from using our valley as a major infiltration route. Our constant patrolling forced them back up into the rougher high terrain, which kept them out of the villages, away from the food those settlements could provide.

We became a real impediment to the enemy. As Colonel Schungel had predicted, Ha Thanh remained right at the top of the hit parade. But when the enemy tried to attack our camp, we called down rockets, napalm, or mortar fire. We eventually obtained a 105-mm howitzer to shore up our defenses.

This cheered up the team, instilling in them a sense of professional pride. They were dedicated and hardworking NCOs—motivated, physically fit, and very well trained in their areas of expertise, whatever they might be, weapons, commo, demolitions, or intelligence.

———

We often sent out company-size patrols with more than one hundred Montagnards and ARVN troops. The most dramatic was when the monsoon arrived and the rains came down almost every afternoon.

On October 16, 1967, intell reported that an NVA field hospital with Chinese medics and military advisers had been set up in the high country southeast of Ha Thanh. Our mission was to locate and eliminate this NVA facility.

The team's assistant medic, Sergeant M. Thornton, and I led the Montagnards for two days, sweeping the trails and villages, searching for signs of the enemy. Around midnight on the second day, as a light rain started to fall, we were moving up a hill with thin to moderate jungle vegetation when suddenly we came under intense fire from what appeared to be the summit of the hill. The NVA was firing both machine guns and AK-47 assault rifles.

"Move out!" I yelled to Thornton as I lunged up the slope. "Let's keep them moving."

Getting pinned down here by a plunging crossfire would be a disaster because if the enemy had machine guns, they no doubt also had mortars, and the mortars would be devastating to our force. Thornton and I dashed among the Yards, rallying them to follow us, and they did so without regard for the vicious torrent of enemy crossfire.

Preoccupied with maneuvering my men, I didn't see the multiple rows of sharpened bamboo punji stakes set at shallow angles and half hidden by branches as well as the darkness of night. A punji stake ripped into my left-calf muscle, bounced off the shinbone, and exited the other side of my leg. The pain was excruciating. I actually saw pinwheeling stars as I writhed in agony, pinned like a trapped animal against the wet slope.

In addition, punji stakes were usually smeared with human or animal excrement, which increased the rapid onset of infection. Still, my job was to provide leadership and motivation to the Montagnards, and the contract never said that the job ended upon injury.

I snatched out my heavy-bladed K-bar knife, which I kept razor sharp and carried on my web belt, and hacked off the stake at the ground end. I then pulled the rest of the stake out of my leg and continued up the hill with the Montagnards. They were doing well, staying low, laying down covering fire as they maneuvered and throwing grenades when they got into range of the enemy guns. The NVA knew the Yards' reputation as cruel, relentless fighters, and that no doubt played a major role in the enemy's retreat. By the time we reached the crest, we found mounds of brass shell casings and some body bandages. But the enemy had pulled back, dragging their dead and wounded with them.

The lower left leg of my fatigues was shredded and blood soaked, but Sergeant Thornton applied a tight pressure bandage.

"Captain," he said, "we gotta call for a Dustoff chopper. That wound looks nasty."

I'd seen the ripped, blood-crusted flesh in the shielded glow of Thornton's flashlight. It *was* a bad wound . . . but I didn't believe it was life-threatening. And I wasn't about to risk the lives of a medevac helicopter crew or the team lieutenant who'd have to fly up from Ha Thanh to replace me.

The pain washed over me in hot spasms and Thornton continued his appeals for me to relent and call for help. I tried to will myself to retain consciousness as my head started to spin, but I finally realized that regardless of my brain's telling my body to respond, it wasn't going to happen—I had to relent to Thornton's pleas for a medevac.

It was first light when the Huey Dustoff made a skilled landing in our ridge-top perimeter, the fog having thinned just enough for sufficient visibility. I had at most thirty seconds to brief my replacement before we lifted off.

Less than an hour later I was in surgery at the Da Nang hospital, praying that in the short term they would clean out whatever infection might already have set in.

As the doctors debrided the wound, my mind drifted elsewhere. From a young age I've always felt comfortable making decisions, and I suppose that's just part of being a good leader. Some come easy, like relieving that drunk sergeant when I first got to the camp, and severing the punji stick to get the hell out of Dodge. Others are not so easy, and I was up against one of those at that moment.

I've already mentioned how those letters from Carolyn were my lifeblood, my inspiration—my nine-thousand-mile driving force—and I had no doubt that mine were the same to her. So as I lay there with the nurses applying thick layers of bandage to my leg, my first thought was, *Damn, do I tell Carolyn about this or not?* On the one hand, we'd always been open and honest with each other; on the other, why scare her when there was absolutely nothing she could do but worry? And what would I say? *Tough day, honey—a poisoned spear pierced my calf and I'm back at the Da Nang hospital. How's Jon doing today?*

As luck would have it, the doctor stepped in and the decision (and the letter) would have to wait. "Good news, Captain. I'm declaring you fit for light duty back at your base, so long as team medics check the wound daily and keep it well bandaged." That was music to my ears.

While I waited to be released, I asked for some paper and a pencil and began to write. *"Dearest Carolyn, you are not going to believe this but . . ."*

———

As my Vietnam tour progressed, beyond the scope of my immediate team, I observed a growing lack of professionalism in the Special Forces officer corps. The 5th Group was now recruiting young lieutenants and captains who had not even been to the qualification course back at Fort Bragg. Instead, they had agreed to pull an extra six months in Vietnam and were issued Green Berets and assigned to Special Forces. We were losing everything that went with being a member of what had begun as an elite body of troops, and the caliber of the organization began to decay. They were cutting corners, getting by with minimum effort, and hanging out drinking in team houses and telling inflated war stories—but they were no longer made of the same material as the original heroic Green Berets whom I had always held in such high regard, and certainly no longer exemplified the qualities of leadership to which I wanted to aspire. I found this incredibly depressing—so much so that by the end of my tour I had decided that I no longer wanted to be a career Special Forces officer.

———

I turned over the A-Team and Ha Thanh camp to Captain Bob Gesregan in late December 1967, then departed for my outprocessing down at C-Team headquarters in Da Nang.

While much of this consisted of bureaucratic red tape, there was one element that I took very seriously since it directly affected our mission and the lives of those I had just left—my intelligence debriefing. It was there that I would systematically talk the intelligence people through all the pertinent updates on the situation in Ha Thanh's area of operations.

"There seems to be a lot more movement down the trail," I reported, heading over to a large map board that occupied almost the entire length of the wall. I pointed out the specific areas. "Something is definitely brewing, particularly in here . . . and also over here."

The intell people didn't seem to pay much attention. One nodded and snuffed out his cigarette but didn't say much. The other shot a quick smile and said, "Okay, thanks." It came across more dismissive than polite; he appeared to just want to get on with whatever he had been doing.

The following day, while I was preparing to depart for home, I happened to run into a couple of team NCOs who had been down in Da Nang overnight. They told me that in the four days that I had been gone, security at the camp had already gone to hell in a hand basket. There was no longer an American team member on duty around the clock, and the constant patrol pressure that I had been so stringent about enforcing had completely broken down.

———

But the problems would not be mine to face. In two days, I caught the chartered Pan Am 707 Freedom Bird from Tan Son Nhut. Scrunched up in the jet's narrow seat in January 1968 was much the same as the flight out had been the year before. But this time, we lost a day instead of gained one crossing the international date line, and there were no champagne toasts to usher in the New Year.

As much as it seemed like I had been away from Carolyn and my family for a decade, I couldn't believe that a whole year had flown by since Major Assente had first instilled the fear of God in us with his forewarning that only one of us three lieutenants would make it out alive. Fortunately, the major's prediction proved wrong. Doug Coulter survived and went on to have a distinguished academic career, eventually teaching at the University of Beijing, and Bill Larrabee lived to retire as a colonel.

* * *

The mood in the San Francisco Bay Area had certainly changed. Soldiers were no longer treated with respect on the street. Although I was big enough that none of the long-haired young men challenged me physically, a few foul-mouthed girls in soiled peasant blouses cussed me out. The antiwar movement was building to an alarming level of pressure, and the country's mind-set had spun a 180 while I'd been gone.

Waiting at O'Hare for my Piedmont flight to Raleigh, I bought a copy of the *Chicago Tribune* and I could not believe what I saw. Right there on the front page was a big picture of U.S. soldiers fighting at my camp at Ha Thanh. The accompanying article detailed how the camp had been "overrun" by North Vietnamese Regulars and how the surviving Special Forces team members had been pushed back to seek refuge inside the thickly sandbagged walls of the latrine.

Bob Gesregan, my replacement, had been wounded and medevaced out.

*I hope Carolyn doesn't see this before I get home,* I thought.

9:25 A.M., March 23, 2002, Fairfax, Virginia

*U*ntil around 9:30 A.M. that Saturday morning, I had never been a fan of smoking. Neither Carolyn nor I had ever smoked, and my dad was such a heavy smoker that he developed emphysema and lung cancer and eventually died of a heart attack. But had it not been for the R.J. Reynolds Tobacco Company, I'm not sure that I'd be here to tell this story.

I had continued calling out for close to an hour, when a neighbor living in a house behind ours stepped out onto her porch for a smoke, and finally she heard me. "Who's calling?" she asked, looking all around to pinpoint the source of the cries.

"Please help me, I've fallen and I can't move. I'm here by this tree." She immediately climbed over the fence and ran to help.

"I need you to knock on my door and get my wife. Tell her I'm badly injured and need her to call 911," I said. An instant later, Carolyn ran out the door and knelt down beside me, her cordless phone in hand. Seeing my condition, she knew better than to try to move me. "You've got to get the paramedics here right away, Carolyn. I can't move and I've got to get to a hospital fast."

The real question was unspoken: Could they get me there fast enough?

*Chapter Four*

# BIRTH UNDER FIRE

January 1968–December 1969

**B**eing home was wonderful, of course. Carolyn and I held hands in the backseat of my parents' car as they drove us to Speed. But now there was a third person seated between us, a little guy in a corduroy jacket who peered up at me quizzically and babbled to Carolyn, "Da-da?" Jon was now fourteen months old.

The family had shown Jon lots of pictures of me, but he must not have associated the pictures of the suntanned soldier with a real person. I was almost as shy with him as he was with me, but I knew that would change for both of us with time.

Home on the Shelton Farm was just as I remembered it, hardwood and pine forests, delicious scents rising in the chill winter air; Carolyn, and now Jon, beside me as I softly strummed "If I Had a Hammer" on the Stella six-string. Dancing circles around our feet like a tiny wind-up toy gone mad was our latest addition to the family, another German shepherd pup, whom we called Stryker.

Driving slowly through the small towns, I fought down the instinct to watch for snipers and booby traps. I was out of Vietnam; the war was behind me. I had survived.

———

My holiday leave passed too quickly and it was soon time to get back to work. If I was going to be a career officer, I needed a meaningful assignment, one that reflected my combat experience. My top preference was to command a rifle company of the 82nd Airborne at Fort Bragg, since even though I'd led a Special Forces detachment and an indigenous Vietnam force much larger than company strength, commanding a company of American riflemen was considered a traditional stepping stone in a regular officer's career. The last thing I wanted was to be shoved into some second-tier position that would later come back to haunt me in the form of a forced early retirement because I had not followed a desirable career path, and you can't get any better than commanding a company at the 82nd Airborne.

Unfortunately, the Army's Military Personnel Center disagreed, and they were adamant: "You don't need the 82nd. The Army needs you down at Fort Jackson to command a company there." Fort Jackson is a *training* center, so I was disappointed, to say the least. Not only was I concerned that this might jeopardize any chance of a long-term Army career (should I choose to go that route), but commanding trainees with only a few weeks in uniform was a far cry from having my own rifle company in the sharpest unit in the world.

When I got off that call, Carolyn could see that I was not a happy camper. We talked it out and, as always, she turned the lemon into lemonade. "At least we'll only be a five-hour drive from the family," she said, without even mentioning the *real* positive—that, unlike the past year, the three of us would be living *together* again.

We packed up and headed for my new assignment at Fort Jackson's 3rd Advanced Individual Training (AIT) Brigade. Located within the wide city limits of Columbia, South Carolina, the post was the Army's most active "port of entry" for recruits; and with the military draft at its height, this was a very active time period.

Everybody assigned to Vietnam was sent to the 3rd Brigade to go through training oriented specifically to Vietnam—practical skills with a curriculum based on the hard lessons learned by Vietnam veterans who had been there, done that. Geared to guerilla warfare and how to fight enemy irregulars, the training covered how to conduct search-and-cordon, search-and-destroy sweeps, how to search caves and remote wooded areas, and how to detect and disarm booby traps—essential skills that would save lives.

Although I wasn't exactly doing back flips at the turn my career was taking, at least I felt that by commanding a company at Fort Jackson I would play a part in one of the finest training regimens the Army could possibly have created, and I fervently believed that the Army owed the new recruits training that would provide their best chance of survival.

————

When I reached Fort Jackson, the NVA–Vietcong Tet offensive exploded across South Vietnam, with enemy forces attacking every provincial capital and major population center. There was plenty of grist for the news media to grind, especially when Vietcong sappers blasted a hole in the wall of the

American embassy in Saigon and almost fought their way into the chancery building itself before being repulsed. It seemed that the enemy was everywhere, attacking U.S. and ARVN bases, ambushing relief convoys, overrunning isolated outposts. The remote Marine combat base at Khe Sanh in the misty mountains of northern I Corps was besieged for weeks, and the old citadel of the imperial capital of Hue was captured by NVA regulars.

This only added more fuel to the antiwar, antidraft protests on America's campuses and streets.

Just back from a fact-finding trip to Vietnam in late February, legendary CBS anchorman Walter Cronkite commented, "Who won and who lost the great Tet offensive against the cities? I'm not sure. The Vietcong did not win by a knockout, but neither did we. The referees of history may make it a draw. . . . It seems now more certain than ever that the bloody experience of Vietnam is to end in a stalemate."

When President Lyndon Johnson heard the remarks, he said, "That's it. If I've lost Cronkite, I've lost middle America."

Johnson chose not to run for reelection.

The national mood was bleak.

———

When I reported for duty at the 3rd AIT Brigade, I felt slapped in the face as I learned that I would have to wait to get my company command. Although I had been promoted to captain only nine months earlier, at Fort Jackson I was considered a "senior" captain and consequently would be assigned to a staff position (which was normally filled by a major) instead of getting the command.

I was assigned to be battalion executive officer (XO) to Major Jarold Hutchinson, a tremendous leader and a great mentor, a fine role model in every respect. I worked for Hutchinson for more than four months, with me reminding him almost every other day that I was in line for a company and him telling me how valuable I was as his executive officer.

What I got instead was another staff position, the brigade S4 (logistics officer) for Colonel Richard T. Saint-Sauver. The job actually turned out to an interesting experience and I walked away having learned two valuable lessons that would play out over and over again: First, *you don't always get to pick your assignments.* But more important, I discovered that *if you apply yourself and do the best possible job, good things will happen in the end.*

Our year at Fort Jackson passed quickly and it became clear that I was never going to be given command of a rifle company there, so it was time to move on. I called the Military Personnel Center and was told that I was being considered for an assignment with the 2nd Infantry Division in South Korea.

"You have got to be kidding me," I retorted. "There hasn't been any real fighting there in over fifteen years." I wanted to command soldiers actually engaged with the enemy so that I could pass on what I had learned from a year of combat in Vietnam. In fact, if I had to leave my family for another year, I would *prefer* going back to Vietnam, where the action was.

So, once more, Carolyn and I sat down and had a calm and sober discussion. We had recently bought our first boat and were so enjoying spending quality family time together, getting up to Lake Murray whenever we could. We did a lot of waterskiing and Jon loved being in the boat. Even though he wasn't quite two years old, I could tell that he was as much of a water rat as his dad, and I looked forward to getting a fishing rod into his tiny hands just as soon as I could teach him to hold on. Yet, I also felt a sense of duty to the planeloads of young GIs leaving the States each day for Vietnam.

"You do what you think is best," was Carolyn's heartfelt advice, offering her complete support, as always.

———

My orders to report to Vietnam for my second tour came fast, and I was ordered to report to MACV headquarters at Tan Son Nhut Air Base for an unspecified assignment to an infantry unit no later than January 1. We had spent barely eleven months at Fort Jackson, yet it was already time to call the movers, pack up our household goods for storage, and head back to Speed, where Carolyn and Jon would stay with her parents while I deployed.

Christmas, as usual, was a joyous time, but it was tempered by almost everyone coming down with the flu—that, and Walter Cronkite bringing the battlefield into our living room every night, as if we needed another blunt reminder of my imminent departure back to a deadly war zone that seemed to be escalating by the hour. A phone call informing me that Captain Jim Hansard, my best friend from my days at Fort Benning, had been killed in Vietnam added to the gloom. Carolyn and I had been close to him and his wife, Mary Jane, and their young son, Jimmy. My parents were beside themselves over my heading back over there.

I could not bear the thought of having another tearful goodbye at the airport, so while everyone was still asleep, I gently kissed Carolyn and Jon on their foreheads—both of them still burning up with fever—and quietly left my parents' home. Outside, I met my younger brother, David, who would drive me to Raleigh to catch my flight to San Francisco. We were all still sick, but I was hoping my fever would subside by the time I arrived in Vietnam.

Carolyn's condition had not improved, so the week following my departure she went to the doctor for treatment. Although I wouldn't learn about it for weeks, she was given the great news that she was pregnant.

———

Once again I ushered in the New Year on the long flight, and, as in the past, we celebrated twice. When I stepped off the airplane I had been gone one year. But when the humidity and the scent of mildew washed over me as they rolled back the door, it felt like I had left just yesterday. I did, however, notice lines of machine-gun rounds and mortar fragments in the airport buildings, reminders of the Tet offensive.

At MACV headquarters the personnel officers passed out the standard wish list of where we would like to go, and I couldn't help but wonder if, unlike the last time, they might actually give some consideration to my request. I requested the 173rd Airborne Brigade, a legendary outfit that in November 1967 had fought one of the epic battles of the war on Hill 875, near Dak To in the Central Highlands. The Americans slashed through the jungle to the mountaintop to engage what intelligence had estimated to be an NVA company of between one hundred and two hundred men dug in east of the main axis of the Ho Chi Minh Trail. That "company" turned out to be a *regiment* of two thousand. In the four-day fight that followed, the Americans were badly mauled, but they held their ground and called in airstrikes that forced the enemy to abandon their bunkers and trench lines and retreat into Cambodia.

That was the kind of unit I was looking for. As an added bonus, the 173rd had a great-looking patch: a wing with a red sword beneath the airborne tab. I told the personnel guy, "Give me the 173rd."

He opened a file cabinet, shuffled through some papers, and scribbled something onto mine. Then with a quick thump of a rubber stamp onto my orders, he looked up and said, "You got it."

The following day I climbed aboard a Huey and flew north to the 4th Battalion near An Khe. Also on board was another captain who'd just arrived from the States, a guy named Bill Marr, who would instantly become a lifelong friend. We flew in trail formation behind four other helicopters loaded with troops, and the separation between the tail rotors and the main rotors of the aircraft could not have been more than a foot—it was insane. At that rate, both Marr and I gave it a fifty-fifty chance that we would even make it to the base alive.

As soon as we landed, I reported it to the battalion officer who picked us up. "Somebody needs to counsel those aviators," I said. "They're going to kill themselves and a lot of troops." He thought it was funny and shrugged. It turned out that this was by design and SOP for these skilled aviators. The distinctive whup-whup of the Hueys' rotors could be heard

for miles in this flat country, but if a group of choppers flew low and fast
in a single clump, they stood a better chance at evading enemy gunners—
providing that the passengers didn't die of heart failure.

Marr and I reported to the commander of the 4th Battalion, Lieutenant
Colonel Sandy Weyand—who would go on to become a three-star general,
but you'd never have guessed it by the way he looked. He dragged out of
his bunker with what appeared to be a three-day growth of beard and eyes
sunken with fatigue. "What do you guys want to do?" he asked. "We have
a couple of openings. I've got the assistant S3 [operations] and the battalion S2 [intelligence] open. Which job do you want?"

"I don't care, sir," Marr said.

"Colonel," I said, "wherever you think I can best serve you."

"Doesn't matter, you tell me," Weyand said. Obviously he had bigger
fish to fry at that moment. "You don't need to decide today. Better get
yourselves dug in over there and we'll talk about it later."

Marr and I dumped our rucksacks, found a shovel, and dug a fox
hole. This was around two o'clock in the afternoon, and by four we were
getting slammed with a massive mortar attack, rounds of whistling 82-
mm mortars exploding all around us like Fourth of July rockets gone
astray.

While we hunkered down and waited out the barrage, Bill and I discussed our assignment preferences. "You know," I said, "I'd just as soon
be the battalion 2 if you want the assistant 3 job." To be the S2 intelligence officer meant I could be independent and develop my own way of
thinking and procedures. I liked intell and had learned a lot about the field
during my first Special Forces tour, both in Project Delta and commanding the detachment at Ha Thanh.

We saw Colonel Weyand again the next morning. He had apparently
located his razor but looked even more haggard.

"I'd like to be the S2," I told him.

"Okay, you got it."

And with that I became the intelligence officer of the 4th Battalion,
503rd Infantry (Airborne), and reported directly to the colonel—which
was fine by me. Working for me would be a gruff, crusty senior intell
master sergeant named Giddens. He and I instantly hit it off; I appreciated his experience as well as his direct, no-bullshit approach, and he respected my record as a combat leader. We'd make a good team.

Marr, on the other hand, went over to work for a guy named Ken
Wright, who, in my opinion, turned out to be one of the worst leaders I
have ever encountered.

Shortly thereafter, Lieutenant Colonel Weyand was replaced by the
former 173rd Brigade S3, Lieutenant Colonel Dan Schneider. It was obvious from day one that Lieutenant Colonel Schneider had a wealth of experience and liked to have all the facts before making a decision.

* * *

Over the next few weeks I charged into my new position and started trying some innovative things. I had heard from the brigade S2 that they had trained dogs to sniff out booby traps, which were a big problem in our area—in fact, that had been one of the key challenges that was weighing so heavily on Colonel Schneider. I pushed and found out that some of these dogs were available to us.

One night following an intell brief I recommended to Colonel Schneider that, with his permission, I would like to bring out three of these dogs and put one with each of our three line companies. It could yield dramatic dividends and there didn't appear to be any downside.

"That's a great idea," the colonel said. "Go ahead and pursue it."

After the colonel left, we sat around for a while in the briefing tent, and then I walked outside. It was dark, and suddenly a figure appeared beside me. It was Bill Marr's boss, Major Wright. "Captain, you *will* remember that I am the S3 of this battalion, so don't you ever make a recommendation like that to the colonel without clearing it with me first. That should have been my recommendation, not yours. You got that?"

"Well, sir," I said, "the way I see it, as long as the battalion's well served by it, it doesn't make any difference who made it."

As he huffed away, I called after him in an even tone, "Major, let me remind you that I am a primary staff officer in this battalion just like you, and as such I make my recommendations directly to the colonel, not to you." I never had any more trouble with Major Wright, even though I was a captain.

About a week later, the colonel returned from a meeting in An Khe. He had met with the Korean division commander to which our battalion was attached and learned of an upcoming op in which we were to participate.

"They're going to do a thirteen-battalion search-and-cordon operation around this particular area," he announced, sweeping his hand across the map to indicate an area just to our north in the Central Highlands—an area known to be a haven for the NVA. The operation envisioned surrounding, or "cordoning off," the area, and then each battalion searching their assigned area starting at the outside of the perimeter and working toward the center. "And they've given us our choice as to which slice of the pie we want. I'll have to tell him tomorrow which one of the thirteen sectors we chose."

He looked right past Major Wright and spoke to me. "Hugh, it's your call. By morning let me know which sector we should take."

This was a tremendous opportunity and exemplified what intelligence was all about. I remembered the practical problems I'd solved as a trainee at the Riegel Textile Corporation. Finding answers to complex problems was basically the same whether it involved designing a textile mill or creating an intelligence plan for an infantry battalion, and I would have to be as imaginative and resourceful with this. The difference was that young soldiers didn't die if you screwed up in the textile business.

I grabbed Giddens and we went out to the S2 "office," a windowless steel Conex shipping container with a row of secret files down one wall, and I hoped that within them would be the golden nugget that would allow me to identify which of those thirteen "segments" would contain the biggest concentration of enemy soldiers—which is what the op was all about.

We opened the files and found hundreds of maps and after-action reviews and data reports of all types, but if that gold mine was to be found, I'd have to have some idea what to look for. It was about 7:00 P.M. when it hit me. I remembered area study maps I'd seen at MACV headquarters and that's what we needed. We flipped back through unit logs and scanned incident reports—checked out enemy-contact reports and analyzed where those contacts had originated. We also had overhead-imagery reports—the secret data secured by our U-2s and SR-71 spy planes. We were hunting for *patterns*—some commonality and consistency that would tie everything together.

Giddens and I sat there all night long and plotted all this data. I suggested we break it down into specific *types* of intelligence data and plot each type on separate, clear-acetate overlay—one for voice intercepts, one for the overhead reconnaissance, etc.

By the next morning we had a map with six completed transparent overlays that we would stack over one another. When we did so, what we found was staggering. There were three or four overlapping areas about the size of a quarter that 90 percent of the data fell into. That told me that without question there was enemy activity concentrated in those locations.

At the morning briefing, Colonel Schneider said, "Okay, it's time to decide which segment we want."

Major Wright quickly hopped up and approached the map. "Colonel," he said, "I've done a detailed analysis of this so let me show you which area we ought to take." Then, with an almost laughable dramatic flair, he pointed to a certain area. "It's right here. That's where the water is and that's where we'll find the enemy."

The colonel looked at him and sighed, "Thanks, Major Wright, but I was asking the S2. Hugh?"

I stepped up to the map. "Sir, if you'll bear with me just a second, I want to show you what we have. First of all, here is where we've had numerous HUMINT (HUMan INTelligence refers to intelligence gathering by interpersonal contact as opposed to electronic means) hits in the area." I hung up that overlay. "And here's where we've had electronic intercepts," and I hung up that overlay. "And here is where the . . ."

I went right through all six overlays, and each time another was added, the overlapping patterns grew—an obvious, *objective* indication of exactly where we would be most likely to encounter the heaviest concentration of enemy troops. The entire staff was enthralled with the process and the results—all but Major Wright, who was mortified and angry. What he should have been was *thankful,* since Colonel Schneider had saved him from making a complete horse's ass out of himself. My S2 patterns showed that our battalion should choose the sector exactly *opposite* the one he had pointed to.

Bill Marr was sitting behind the S3 and he was trying to stifle a smile. The colonel was ecstatic. "Great work, Hugh. That's where we're going." And with that he was off for headquarters, taking with him a couple of NCOs as his "horse holders" to carry the big map board and its overlays for his presentation. He was obviously ecstatic when he left.

————

Normally I would have been elated, but within the first two hours of the operation we had two company commanders killed. Like that battle near Dak To, with the aid of my intell, we had "stumbled upon" an enemy stronghold of enormous proportion—a full NVA regiment (approximately two thousand soldiers), and our battalion was up to its earlobes and underequipped to handle an element of this size.

We did what we could, and pushed against them with combined infantry and carefully targeted artillery. Our larger force tried to the block the fleeing enemy remnants. Because this was populated rice-farming country, we couldn't call in air strikes for fear of killing civilians. The old saying about jamming a stick into a hornets' nest certainly applied, and the operation was turning into a bloody mess. It was all just a function of the *number* of NVA troops. As I listened to the tactical radio net and heard the earsplitting impacts of 105-mm and 155-mm artillery shells, I felt increasingly bad about the operation I had helped plan.

Putting this into perspective, what Giddens and I had done via our all-nighter with overlays was to manually institute algorithms and data-mining techniques that in the years to come would become the foundation for intelligence-gathering computer systems still in use at the CIA, NSA, and DIA. It involved the same principles we're using today to track the Taliban in Afghanistan, and it's how we tracked down Saddam inside that spider hole outside of Tikrit.

For me, that experience as intelligence officer taught me valuable lessons in the importance of outside-the-box thinking from both strategic and tactical perspectives—but now it was time to move on. I still wanted that company command of my own.

————

"Hugh," the colonel told me one morning, "you're getting Charlie Company."

All I said was "Thank you, sir," but he could tell that I was ready to do about a dozen backflips. The colonel had actually given me the command ahead of some others who literally had volunteered to stay for a second tour to have a command in the 173rd. My misfortune at Fort Jackson of not getting a company turned out to be a godsend when I reached the 173rd. My new first sergeant was named Sizemore; he'd been in country about three years and had forgotten more than most junior officers would ever learn. Sizemore really ran a top-notch company from the command post at LZ North English, which was just to the north of LZ English, where the brigade headquarters was located. The old Army refrain "In the Rear with the Beer, and the Sergeant Major, and the Gear" did *not* apply to Sizemore. He had seen a lot of combat and always made sure the troops' needs were met.

After I met with First Sergeant Sizemore, I went straight out to the field to join the company. My place was with the troops and I wanted to be known as a leader who leads from the front. It's where the action is, it's where I could observe what was going on, and, most important, it's where I could best inspire my troops by asking them to do only those things that they see I am perfectly willing—and able—to do myself.


I found that there were some outstanding officers and NCOs in the 173rd, but the troops were a mixed bag. While there were some fine soldiers, many others missed the mark. They were not true combat troops, and they needed a great deal of motivation and hands-on leadership.

The challenge began at the squad level with a mixture of both regular army and draftee sergeants, and often I couldn't even differentiate between the two. One problem was the so-called Shake and Bake sergeant program the Army had instituted. It allowed a draftee to become a three-stripe (E-5) NCO squad leader after passing a very truncated eight-week training course and it really degraded the promotion standards. Thank Defense Secretary Robert McNamara for that one; along with another one of his "great" ideas, to lower educational and physical fitness standards to expand the pool of potential draftees.

Many of the troops caught up in this were poorly educated members of inner-city racial minorities who were usually shunted to the infantry. Others had been accepted on "moral waivers"—petty criminals who had been given a choice between jail and the Army. But in the middle of all of that we had college graduates and good people who have gone on to become CEOs of major corporations. But there was no doubt that the average was way below where it needed to be in order to fight a protracted war.

Out in the field, I found that many NCOs had retained what I considered a Korean War mentality: we were fighting a conventional army that we could expect to attack us in a standard manner—rather than having to weed them out of the villages and dig them out of the jungle. We needed lots of small-unit ambushes instead of setting up one big ambush to detect a North Korean battalion trying to move through our lines. In this war, we had to be out day and night trying to catch them in groups of three or four. We had to spread squads through a wide area, tied in by radio to air support and artillery. Then, when a squad did make contact, we could quickly augment it with reinforcements. These were skills I had observed new recruits being taught at Fort Jackson, but these guys had never gone through that course.

One of my first orders of business was to change the size of our patrols. Instead of taking out whole forty-man platoons, which were almost impossible to conceal, I ordered my company to search for the enemy using eight- to nine-man rifle squads. Sifting with a finer-mesh net was a better tactic, but I had to train the NCOs in this technique.

---

The battalion was part of the overall pacification mission, patrolling the area to keep the Vietcong and the NVA out; and working with the local people as they rebuilt their war-damaged schools and farm buildings and repaired their churches and clinics so that their lives could return to normal. We provided timber, cement, and roofing tiles. I even wrote to my church in Speed, North Carolina, and they collected and sent huge amounts of young-kids' clothing. We all found this work very satisfying and achieved some degree of success.

But there was still a war going on. One night we set up our command post on the edge of a big rice paddy. We dug in with sandbags and claymores, and M-60 machine guns were placed to cover a wide arc. Around 2:00 A.M., we came under intense fire from one of our pacification-program villages across the paddy—it had obviously been infiltrated by the enemy and they had spotted our position. I called for gunship support.

As they came thumping low over the tree line to our right front, I provided fire-support directions—and key to those instructions was a warning that I personally conveyed to the flight leader: "Be advised the gunfire is coming from *the edge of a pacification village,* so you're going to have to be very careful about where you put your own fire. There are civilians all over that village."

I heard the choppers approaching fast. "Tango Charlie, confirm you copy," I said into the radio handset. "Be careful with your suppressing fire. We have a pacification village packed with civilians."

The lead pilot came on the air. "Roger," he said. "I've got a pacification program of my own." Then he swooped in and let go with 2.75-inch rockets into the edge of the village from which we were receiving the fire. Houses caught fire and we could see figures running around in flames as that Huey cut loose with its minigun. It was a horrible scene. But the enemy ground fire stopped, and we didn't get another round shot at us out of that village.

When we went in to check at dawn, we found that the situation was not as bad as it had looked in the night. Unfortunately, two local civilians had been killed and three others wounded, but it could have been much worse.

———

My airborne-infantry rifle company was now assigned to an area of operations west of LZ North English. It was a fertile rice-growing valley with steep mountainous terrain on both sides. It was known as a Vietcong-controlled area, which was of significance to them because of its ability to supply both rice for their subsistence and piasters to fund their other activities. Our job was to extend the influence of the central government by providing a safe and secure environment for the villagers in the valley and denying the Vietcong access. It was a daunting task for the 160-man rifle company under my command. We patrolled during the day and occupied a number of ambush sites at night.

When our interpreters questioned the villagers regarding Vietcong activities, it was always the same answer: "I don't know." It was incredibly frustrating.

I awoke that morning, looked down at my Seiko watch, and noted the date: June 6—D-Day. It would prove ironic. By 0730 I had brushed my teeth and shaved, using water from my canteen, and was on the move with about a thirty-man patrol headed up the valley. The villagers were already in their rice paddies tending their crops as the hot sun beat down on us. The steel pots and heavy protective vests we wore added to our discomfort. Weeks earlier, battalion had mandated that we wear the vests due to the extraordinary number of casualties our battalion had been receiving from booby traps or IEDs. The Vietcong had become professionals at using unexploded U.S. munitions—primarily artillery and mortar rounds and hand grenades—combining them with rudely fabricated pressure devices or trip wires to produce an even greater number of casualties. My company had suffered sixty-five casualties in the past thirty days. It was taking its toll and I had lost a lot of good men. This day would be no exception.

A single shot rang out. One of my finest soldiers, positioned two men in front of me, screamed in agony as he went down, grabbing his leg. I hollered, "Medic!" as I rushed forward, hitting the ground next to him. The front of his leg was bleeding profusely. "Get Lieutenant Smith on the line," I screamed at my radio telephone operator. Smith was up ahead but out of sight and I needed to have him start maneuvering the forces immediately since the sniper obviously had us in sight.

Two more shots rang out and impacted nearby. I rolled the injured soldier onto his side to check for an exit wound. There wasn't one. "Make that a *Priority Alpha* medevac," I screamed at the battalion RTO, indicating the highest priority.

"Captain, they say they've got other medevacs under way and want to know if we can lower the priority since it's a single gunshot wound to the leg," the RTO called out a few seconds later.

"No!" I screamed emphatically. "It's an *Alpha*—I can't find an exit wound." By now the soldier had started to lose consciousness. He was sweating profusely, although it was hard to tell if it was from heat or if he was going into shock.

The medic arrived and took over my direct pressure application as he commenced treatment. "Captain, we're running out of time."

I ripped away the handset and called for the battalion S3, "Major Houston, I need that medevac *now*." The tone of my voice reinforced the urgency.

"It's on the way," he responded, as I heard the thump, thump, thump of the medevac helicopter rotor blades in the distance.

I turned back to the medic. The look of hopelessness on his face said it all. "Sir, it's too late. He's gone."

Later, we would learn that the bullet had struck the femur and then traveled through his body and caused extensive internal injuries that resulted in death. We loaded his lifeless body onto the medevac. There would be time for grieving and an appropriate memorial service in his honor later, but right now we had to keep moving.

It was approaching noon and we were now traveling along the edge of the mountains on the west side of the valley parallel to the rice paddies. Suddenly, an individual emerged on the far side of the rice paddies. He (or she) was dressed in typical black PJs, wearing a conical straw hat and carrying a distinctive shoulder pack—almost like a purse. Slung over the other shoulder was what appeared to be a 7.62-mm SKS rifle.

The word went up and down my file to freeze. The individual was now moving along the rice-paddy dikes headed in our direction but was still a few hundred meters away. At about seventy-five meters, I leaned in to my translator. "Tell him to freeze, tell him we want to talk to him," I said.

My translator stood and yelled, *"Dư'ng lại. Chúng tôi muốn nói chuyện vòi ban."* Instantaneously, the individual turned and started running away as fast as he could. He had about two hundred meters to go to escape into the distant wood line, and our translator continued to attempt to get him to stop. *"Dư'ng lại. Dư'ng lại. Dư'ng lại hoặc chúng tôi sẽ bắn."* He was completely disregarding our instructions, and in this area you did not run from guys with guns, or you died trying.

Before he disappeared into the woods, I yelled, "Fire!"

Instantly, around twenty riflemen commenced firing at the individual, who by now had run out of his Ho Chi Minh sandals and was rapidly closing on the wood line. Bullets were striking all around him but he was unscathed. I was getting concerned that he would escape. I brought my CAR-15 up to my shoulder. Not known for its accuracy because of its much shorter barrel, it was all I had, so it would have to do. There was a brief lull in the fire, and I squeezed the trigger just as if I were shooting squirrels back on the farm in Speed. The individual went flying ass over teakettle and then lay still.

"Damn good shooting, Captain," hollered my RTO.

We cautiously approached the lifeless body. The individual turned out to be the VC tax collector. The shoulder pack was filled with a treasure trove of information showing which villagers had paid in rice, piasters, or both. With it, we would finally be able to crack their infrastructure in a way that we had been unable to before. It was an incredible intelligence boon, and, as an added bonus, we secured another gun. It's probably never a good day to be a tax collector, but I doubt if most days are this bad.

Our jubilation was short-lived. We had moved to the north end of our assigned area and turned to travel down the other side of the valley en route back to our base. It was now about 2:00 P.M. and the sun was blistering hot. Leading our formation was Duke, a German shepard trained in Saigon to detect booby traps. One of my accomplishments as the battalion S2 had been to get one of these specially trained canines assigned to each company.

By this time, Duke had been credited with detecting over a dozen booby traps, saving countless lives and preventing even more devastating injuries. I moved up closer to the head of the column, behind Staff Sergeant Jefferies (name changed to protect the family's privacy). Jefferies came from Southeast Missouri. Tough and smart, he was one of my finest NCOs. Suddenly, the column stopped moving. I looked at my map and saw that we should have been approaching a stream. Word quickly filtered back that Duke had alerted. Staff Sergeant Jefferies started moving to the front while I knelt down and reached back to grab the handset and give battalion an update.

The blast from the explosion was deafening and it completely knocked me over. I jumped up and charged toward the detonation. The scene was out of a horror show. Staff Sergeant Jefferies had both legs and one arm blown off but was till trying to walk. He died minutes later. Both Duke and his handler were dead, killed instantly by the blast. Another soldier lay unconscious (he would live), and another lost an arm by traumatic amputation. That soldier later told us what had happened.

Duke had alerted at the streambed, in which the water was about ten inches deep. The handler came forward but found nothing, so he tried to coax Duke into going across the stream. Duke would not budge; instead, he stood firm in the alert position. The handler became impatient and plunged into the water, hitting an underwater trip wire that ignited a 175-mm-round booby trap.

By the time we completed the medevac and returned to base camp, night had fallen and another patrol was already leaving to establish an ambush site. *Perhaps they can even the score,* I thought.

A year later, while in the Infantry Officer Advanced Course at Fort Benning, I received a request from Staff Sergeant Jefferies's father to visit with me. We arranged a date and he flew in from Cape Girardeau. I picked him up at the Columbus airport and we drove to a nearby restaurant to have lunch.

"Barry's mom and I are not doing so good, Captain," he explained, trying to keep it together as his bloodshot eyes moistened. "He's our only child, and when they brought him home they had already sealed up his casket. They wouldn't even let us see his body." He took a sip of coffee and tried to fight back his emotions. "I don't know if it'll help anything, but maybe if we hear how he died—hear the extent of his injuries and hear the honest truth on whether or not he suffered—maybe we could get some kind of closure, if there ever is such a thing."

"First of all, I can tell you that your son was one of my very finest soldiers, and he had a reputation as one of our finest NCOs. He died a hero in every sense of the word," I said with complete conviction, and that part was true. "Now I'll tell you something else that I want you to remember: no, he did not suffer. He went quickly and with absolutely no pain."

Between the time I picked him up and put him back on his return flight around 5:00 P.M., he had asked at least a half-a-dozen times about how badly his son had been injured. I knew it was bad enough that I would have to live with that memory and I also knew that there'd be nothing gained by inflicting that kind of torture on his loving parents.

I pulled up to the front of the Columbus airport and got out to shake hands with Mr. Jefferies.

"Captain, I can't thank you enough for taking the time to meet me and tell me . . ." and that was it. Suddenly overcome with emotion, he started sobbing uncontrollably. Although Vietnam was starting to draw down, it was obvious that many of the emotional scars would never heal.

A month or so after the situation with Duke and Staff Sergeant Jefferies, we were operating in yet another area that had a lot of well-placed booby traps that had been causing a lot of casualties. A week earlier, one had killed an excellent young lieutenant named Browning, and I had just been sent his replacement from the battalion staff, a guy named Ken Lorbin. He arrived just as I was briefing all the lieutenants on a routine local-area sweep we were about to commence.

When I got to Lorbin's platoon, I moved in his direction and looked him straight in the eye. "Right in the middle of your area of operation there is a schoolhouse, and there is an excellent chance that that schoolhouse is booby trapped. In fact, the only reason you are here is because your predecessor was leading a patrol in that area and he wandered too close to the entrance and triggered the trap. It killed him and wounded six others. You will stay away from that school. You got that straight, Lieutenant?" I asked.

"Roger, sir. Understand." He nodded.

"Just stay the hell away from there." I repeated. "It's just bait for these guys."

The operation kicked off and not two hours later I got an emergency call for a medevac. It was Lorbin. "Where are you?" I asked.

"At the school," he answered. "And besides me I've got five others seriously injured."

"You stupid son of a bitch!" I shouted into the handset, completely losing it. "I'm going to see your ass court-martialed."

We got the medevac en route and I took off running like hell to get to this guy before he was taken away. Unknown to me, the new battalion commander, Lieutenant Colonel Ken Acousti, was flying overhead and heard everything that was going on.

By the time I arrived I had just missed the medevacs; I could see them flying away with Lorbin and the others, and I was pissed.

"Uh, sir, do you copy?" I heard Lorbin whine over the radio.

"You damn well better be using that chopper's radio," I screamed, searching in vain for the radio unit that Lorbin was supposed to have left behind.

"No sir, that's another problem. Took off with it by mistake." In one of the all-time world-class examples of supreme stupidity, he flew off with our radio, leaving the entire platoon without one.

"You are the sorriest son of a bitch I have ever known and you *will* be thrown out of the Army," I hollered back.

A short while later, the battalion commander landed and came over to me. "Hugh, who is that that you were talking to a while ago? You were really upset." I told him the whole story. Bottom line, Colonel Acousti agreed with me and forwarded the court-martial orders up the chain of command through Japan, where Lorbin had been evacuated to—but other than the fact that he had been treated and made a full recovery, we never heard another word about him.

One would think that would be the end of it, but some twenty years later I had just gotten my first star and was working at the Pentagon, and whom do I see striding down the corridor but Lorbin, still in the Army but then a lieutenant colonel, rounding out a lackluster career as another anonymous pencil-pusher in some tiny cubicle. My best guess is that some commander who was far removed from the battlefield probably felt sorry for him because he had been injured and ripped up the court-martial papers. Happens all the time.

---

On August 5, at the steamy height of the monsoon season, I led the company on a sweep out from our forward base camp, searching for an NVA unit that was reported to have recently entered the area. For a couple of days the battalion had encountered booby traps and sniper fire that seemed better coordinated than the harassment a local-force Vietcong unit could mount, so we knew that a larger enemy element had to be somewhere close.

I was maneuvering my troops around a big rice paddy, with one platoon on the raised mud dike and another trailing us to the right. As always, I went out on these sweeps because I refused to be stuck back at base camp, where I couldn't see the situation. My radio telephone operator (RTO), who humped the company's short-range PRC-77, stayed close beside me.

Suddenly, out of the clear blue, we got lambasted with machine-gun fire coming from the brush to our left. One of the first rounds hit my RTO in the face, entering above his lip and exiting behind his jaw. He immediately went down and I dropped down beside him; I grabbed his radio so I could call the rear to have them send in gunships and send them fast. Meanwhile, I had my small short-range radio and was simultaneously hollering into it to reach the other platoon so that I could maneuver them over to my side of the paddy—and all the while I was being fired upon, with steady streams of high-caliber automatic gunfire coming at me from multiple locations. My problem was that every time I keyed that little radio, First Sergeant Sizemore, back in the rear, would overpower my signal by simultaneously transmitting over his longer-range, more-powerful VRC-46 radio. As I clutched the handset, all I could hear over the roar of the enemy machine guns and the bullets chopping into the mud edge of the dike above my head was Sizemore's voice.

"Sir," he was saying, "got some exciting news for you. Red Cross reports you have a new son. His name is Jeffrey Michael Shelton, and he's twenty inches long and weighs seven pounds."

I kept hollering, "Get off the radio . . . Get off the radio!" But he couldn't hear me because I was lying flat and my antenna was too low. The bullets were whizzing by, kicking up chunks of mud all around me. I needed a medevac for my RTO, whose face, it appeared, had been blown off; I needed to maneuver my other platoon to have them take out the enemy position; and I desperately needed a gunship before we all died.

"Sir, did you hear the good news? Your wife just delivered—"

"Get off the damn frequency!" I screamed into the handset, but the first sergeant (miles to the rear) still could not hear me as I lay flat on the ground with machine-gun fire striking all around me. Sizemore went through the birth announcement three more times before he finally gave up.

All the while, there was just one thought going through my mind the entire time I was lying there: *I am never going to get to see this son; I am going to be killed right here because I can't get Sizemore off the damn frequency.*

Ultimately he stopped, and I was able to communicate. We got the other platoon moving and drove the NVA out of their tree line using both platoons to fire and maneuver. I never did get through to the gunships, but fortunately we reached the medevacs. My RTO was medevaced and later recovered and resumed his duties with me in the field. Thanks to the surgeons, he looked none the worse for wear.

As we were evacuating our wounded, I told the lieutenants, "Hey, I just got notified I have a new baby boy." Years later, Jeff would become a top aviator for the Night Stalkers, the Army's premier Special Operations aviation unit; and Carolyn and I have never stopped kidding him that from that very first day he did everything with a flourish.

That was the end of my command of Charlie Company.

———

One day the battalion commander came out to see me. "Hugh, I'm jerking you out of the field tomorrow." Major Houston, our terrific S3 who had replaced the unlamented Major Wright, had a family emergency and was headed back to the States on compassionate leave. "You're coming up to be the acting S3 while he's gone."

For two months I was the acting battalion S3. It was a great experience, and I tried to contribute the most important tactical experience I'd learned as a company commander.

Although I had not stopped to consider it, I was becoming a much more well-rounded soldier. I had served as a brigade S4, battalion XO, S2, and now S3—*all positions that would serve me well as my career progressed.*

Major Houston came back and resumed his job as the S3—at about the same time as the command of Delta Company, or "Dog Company" as it was derisively known, came open. The commander was going to be gone for a month, so the colonel turned to me. "How'd you like to get another command?"

"Throw me in that briar patch," I said. "I'm happy to go take it."

I went back out to find a challenging unit that was sorely in need of good leadership. This company had long been regarded as the wild bunch of the battalion, and when I arrived it was not a good scene.

They were plagued by a combination of lethargy and lack of discipline. Our base camp was fired on almost nightly, but the troops could never even locate the enemy. Many of the men felt that they were risking their lives for nothing, that we could never defeat the VC or NVA, so why bother?

First and foremost for me was to *motivate* them. No point in teaching skills if they refused to use them. This was one of those times when the best motivation became making them aware that if they didn't get off their asses and learn these skills, *they were going to die*. The enemy didn't care about what these guys did or did not believe in; they just wanted to kill them. So it was important that they learned never to rest at night without first placing effective patterns of claymore mines—and to make sure the men on guard stayed awake and didn't smoke after dark. We had received some of the first truly functional human sensors that were both acoustic as well as seismic, and we placed them in key positions along a trail that ran near the company's base camp, which we suspected was used by the enemy. During daylight, we registered and adjusted our supporting artillery until it would hit right on the trail midway between the sensors we had placed there. Then, for the next several nights, we waited.

About the third night, our sensors suddenly activated. Enemy troops were on the move out there. I waited fifteen seconds and then called for TOT (time on target)—all the rounds landing at once. The 105-mm howitzer shells came crashing down in one catastrophic, overlapping wave. The next day, we went out and found seven Vietcong bodies with weapons right on that site. Dog Company's outlook skyrocketed after that. When the company commander returned, he found morale at an all-time high.

And mine was also high because my second tour in Vietnam was almost over. It was time to catch the Freedom Bird out of Saigon, back to the States, back to Carolyn and our growing family.

———

I arrived back on U.S. soil in Oakland in the early morning of Christmas Eve 1969. Commercial flights were packed, so I'd have to race to San Francisco Airport in order to catch one to the East Coast if I was going to arrive home before Christmas. A bus was provided to shuttle us from Oakland to San Francisco, but at the rate the driver was loading the bags, I'd have been lucky to make it there by the *following* Christmas. Grabbing my bags, I spotted a single taxi and made a beeline for it—*almost* making it before three other soldiers hopped in and took off—then it screeched to a halt about twenty yards up the road.

"Headed to SFO, Captain?" one of the soldiers asked, sticking his head out the open window. A heartbeat later we were racing over the Bay Bridge on a spectacular Sunday morning, thanks to the benevolence of my brothers in arms.

In the early-morning hours of Christmas Eve day the airport was practically deserted, yet when I checked with three airlines, all their flights were booked. Discouraged and dejected, I passed a USO office and stopped in to grab a cup of coffee, wondering how in the hell I was going to make it to Speed by Christmas. A lady from the USO approached me and asked if she could be of assistance. I responded politely, "Not unless you can get me a flight to Raleigh, North Carolina."

Surprisingly, she said, "Give me a minute." I overheard her telling someone about a soldier badly in need of a flight to the East Coast, and something about Vietnam. Then she called out, "If you can be at the Eastern Airlines departure desk in ten minutes, they can get you on a fight to Raleigh that connects through Chicago."

I hollered "thanks" and took off at a dead run to the departure area.


It was a cold Christmas Day, 1969, when the Boeing 727 touched down on the runway at Raleigh-Durham Airport. Carolyn, Jon, and my new son, Jeff, were there to meet me, along with my parents, sister Sarah, and brother Ben. It could not have been a more perfect day or a more joyous homecoming. Although Carolyn and I had seen each other six months earlier in Hawaii, it seemed like years had passed. I was overjoyed as I held Jon, now two, and together we talked to baby Jeff.


Suddenly, Vietnam seemed light-years away.

**9:45 A.M., March 23, 2002, Fairfax, Virginia**

*he Fairfax County rescue ambulance raced along Guinea Road en
route to Inova Fairfax Hospital, which had recently been rated the
top hospital in northern Virginia. Perhaps the strangest sensation for me
was my feeling of total helplessness as I lay flat on my back strapped to a
backboard, a cervical collar restricting my field of vision to the pale
taupe vinyl of the ambulance's ceiling, but I knew Carolyn was right up
front; she had tried to get in the back with me but was told it was against
regulations. In more than 450 parachute jumps from as high as thirty
thousand feet, I had always felt the master of my own destiny—including
the very first jump, when my main shoot failed to open—but not so now
as we screeched to a halt and the rear doors burst open with a rush of
sunlight, and I was urgently yet gingerly transported into Inova's emergency room. "Probable spinal injury," reported the EMT as he handed
me off to the waiting team of doctors. I still had no feeling beneath my
neck, and in my mind there was nothing "probable" about it.*

## Chapter Five

# NEVER BELLY DANCE
# DRUNK WITH YOUR
# BOSS'S WIFE

January 1970–June 1977

If Carolyn had not sent me out to the store for milk and eggs, most likely I would not have seen the incredible news. I was standing in an interminably long checkout line at the Piggly Wiggly just up the road from a small but comfortable rental house we had just moved into on Blueridge Drive in Columbus, Georgia—just a couple of miles outside Fort Benning's main gate. While my patience was growing shorter, the line was not.

"How the hell long does it take to ring up a damn Snickers bar?" asked the portly sergeant first class immediately in front of me, still three spots back from the register—more a statement than a question.

"I can feel your pain." I smiled back at him, grabbing an *Army Times* off the rack, yet dreading what I might find if the company commander back in Vietnam had let Dog Company fall apart again after I'd left.

When I got to page six, I could not believe my eyes—it was one of those times when I really had to do a double take, because I just couldn't believe it was true . . . and I could not wait to get back home to show it to Carolyn.

———

Before leaving Vietnam, I'd received orders to enter the Infantry Officer Advanced Course (IOAC) at Fort Benning, Georgia in late January 1970. This nine-month school was a rite of passage for any infantry-branch officer seeking higher command or staff responsibility; and as much as I was looking forward to moving to Georgia and learning valuable new skills that were essential to becoming a well-rounded soldier, that did not come close to the joy I felt in anticipation of spending my first three weeks back from Vietnam on leave getting to know my two sons back in Speed, North Carolina. Those three weeks provided an important transition from the ultra-tense, life and death, "switched-on" state of readiness I'd required back in Vietnam, to the calm, more relaxed demeanor I would take on in my role of husband, father, and student once we moved to Columbus and I'd begin my IOAC classes.

We spent those three weeks at my parents' home, where we helped around the house, visited with relatives, and just enjoyed being a family again. I cannot imagine how Carolyn managed on her own through nine months of pregnancy and Jeff's birth, all with a healthy, energetic three-year-old who demanded so much of her attention. Thank God for Carolyn's parents, who once again stepped in like guardian angels and provided a warm home and plenty of support the entire time I was overseas.

Carolyn's letters had been a godsend, and for the entire year I was in Vietnam they had been the sole mechanism for me to track the progress of her pregnancy and Jon's development. But they paled in comparison to the joy I felt at being together and experiencing it firsthand.

On Sunday it felt so good to put on my suit, pack everyone into my 1968 Pontiac GTO, and go to Speed Baptist Church—the place where Carolyn and I had said our vows five years earlier—where we would attend services together as a family. Between Carolyn, Jon, Jeff (five months old and cradled in Carolyn's arms), my parents, my brothers, David and Ben, and sister, Sarah, and her husband, Jim Balkcum, with their girls Jennifer and Kristen, and Carolyn's sisters, Linda and Janie, along with Janie's husband, Perry, and their four girls, Beth, Lynne, Gina, and Crystal, the Shelton/Johnson clan took up nearly three rows. Actually, Mother didn't take up any room in our row—she was front and center, feet pumping and fingers dancing over the keyboard of the same church organ she would play for sixty-three years. During my teens I was the appointed youth minister at church, and at sixteen I gave my very first sermon (which I still have buried in one of the many boxes I hope to sort through "someday"). As soon as I finished, Mother (seated at the organ right beside me) hit that first long chord of *Amazing Grace*; and I don't think I ever saw her sit any taller or play with any more pride and joy.

That Sunday was a special day. I was surrounded by family and

*Mother played the organ at Speed Baptist Church for sixty-three years.*

friends, and I felt so grateful that I had made it home safely to be reunitied with those I loved.

I have always felt a deep connection to that little white church—and for that matter, to God—but for me, religion is a private thing and the choice of each individual. I've tried to live a principled life of honesty, character, and integrity—a life that glorifies God—but I never felt it was my place to push my religion on others. I'd rather live in a way that sets an example.

Besides being a frequent guest speaker at prayer breakfasts on National Prayer Day and actively supporting chaplains throughout my career, I've thoroughly enjoyed the opportunities I've had to learn about other religions I greatly respect. Whether it was through one-on-one discussions with Prime Minister Ehud Barak of Israel (both in Jerusalem and at the Pentagon) or visits to Yad Vashem, time within the Temple of Buddhist Virtue in Beijing or at Raghadan Palace with my close friend King Abdullah II of Jordan—the important concepts I've picked up along the way have made me a better man. I'm a strong believer that a sound religious base well-centered around a morality as simple as the Golden Rule can be a worthwhile compass by which to navigate through life's many challenges.

Those three weeks flew by faster than a pack of dogs on a three-legged cat, and once again Carolyn and I found ourselves packing up the '68 GTO and hitching on our 1968 Glastron eighteen-foot boat in preparation for our second move to Fort Benning, Georgia. But this time we'd need more room than that tiny efficiency apartment with the pink bed with ammo cans to support this young lieutenant's feet, and instead of swapping wedding stories from the day before, we'd end our days with Carolyn filling me in on all the amazing achievements our two young boys had accomplished during the day.

———

When I returned home from the market in Columbus, I could not wait to show Carolyn the *Army Times*. I burst through the door almost waving the paper. "You're not going to believe this!" I yelled.

Carolyn hurried in from the boys' bedroom and at that moment did not exactly share my enthusiasm. In a loud whisper, she said, "Shhhh. It took me an hour to get the boys settled down for the night. What has you so excited?"

Whoops. Having been back from Vietnam for only a few weeks, I still hadn't totally gotten the drill down pat—*when the kids are asleep, I've got to take it down a few decibels.* "Sorry," I said, clearly nailed. "But I remembered the milk and eggs."

"And bread, right? You mean you remembered the milk, eggs, and bread?"

I just shook my head; I suppose I'd gotten distracted at the store. "At least I made it home this time," I said with a smile, referring to my stranding her, alone and in tears, the last time we arrived at Fort Benning and I left our tiny apartment for a quick "grocery run" six years earlier.

"Don't think that didn't cross my mind, as long as you were gone," she shot right back with a dance in her eyes, trying hard to keep a straight face. "Let's see what you've got."

I showed her the paper and its prominent headline: OVER 4000 CAPTAINS SELECTED FOR PROMOTION TO MAJOR. Then, flipping to the list itself, I showed her one of the very last names: *Henry H. Shelton*. She could not have been more excited.

Since I had been a captain for only two years, neither of us dreamed I would even be in the "zone of consideration" for promotion. And I wasn't—in the "primary zone." Army promotions are regulated by a very specific set of rules, conditions that must be met before a candidate can be considered for promotion. The two most important are "time in service"—that's the total length of time served, from the very first day—and then there's "minimum time in grade," which refers to how long one has held a given rank. Beyond that, there's usually an estimated time around which one can expect to be promoted, but that becomes subjective at that point.

### U.S. Army Officer Promotions

| Promote to: | | Time in Service | Minimum Time in Grade Required by Law |
|---|---|---|---|
| O-2 | 2nd Lieutenant | 18 months | 18 months |
| O-3 | Captain | 4 years | 2 years |
| O-4 | Major | 10 years | 3 years |
| O-5 | Lieutenant Colonel | 16 years | 3 years |
| O-6 | Colonel | 22 years | 3 years |

If one is passed over and *not* promoted during a specified window, that person is forced to leave the service, in some cases short of retirement eligibility. The standard window is called the "primary zone," and this is the time period in which most promotions occur. The secondary zone is designed to allow the *accelerated* promotion of outstanding officers who have demonstrated performance and indicated potential clearly superior to those who otherwise would be promoted—i.e., officers the selection board feels should be promoted ahead of their contemporaries. This is called being promoted "below the zone" and it's an honor reserved for only a select few. The list indicated that I had been selected below the zone for early promotion to major. I was just about the last name on there (around 4,190 out of 4,195) but nonetheless, there I was. Since they promote sequentially, I would have to wait until they promoted the 4,189 ahead of me, but until that time I would be called a "captain promotable" and be allowed to fill positions normally occupied by full majors, albeit at a captain's salary—a pretty good deal for the Army. This would be the first of three early promotions I would receive.

Little did I know at that point that it would be *five years* before I would pin on the major's gold leaf. Vietnam was winding down and so was the speed of promotions.

The three-week leave could not have been any better, and when I reported in to IOAC as "Captain Promotable" Shelton I felt invigorated—completely recharged and eager to take on my next challenge. But with the country at war, there were more captains and majors scheduled for the course than there were openings for students, so I snowbirded with the school's airborne department for four months and would not be allowed to enter the course officially until May 1970.

Carolyn was happy with this as it meant we would be here four extra months before we would have to move again, and this arrangement was fine with me, since I got the chance to "observe" airborne-training procedures and rack up extra jumps by participating in mass troop drops, day and night from both low and medium altitudes. The more I jumped, the more I loved it, and I knew that somehow my future would include Airborne.

What I never could have imagined was that one day many years down the road I'd personally accompany the former President of the United States on a celebratory birthday jump.

In May, classes finally began, and I became totally immersed in the intense coursework. We learned to calculate the destructive potential of fire support, of both "air" (close tactical bombing dropped by fighter-bombers) and "arty" (105-mm and 155-mm howitzers), and land navigation, both day and night, in any weather. Precise map reading became literally a matter of life and death. None of this was easy, but having already mastered ranger school and qualified for Special Forces gave me a leg up.

Time was marching by with very little letup in pace. The summer's highlight occurred on August 5—or actually the following weekend—when we celebrated Jeff's first birthday. Carolyn had befriended a number of other moms with young children in the neighborhood, and we had a full house to witness Jon blowing out Jeff's single candle. She had made two chocolate cakes, one of which was a small, personal size just for the birthday boy, and by the time the last "thanks for having us" was uttered and we closed the front door, there was not a crumb of either of Carolyn's delicious

DEPARTMENT OF DEFENSE

*Former President George H. W. Bush celebrates his seventy-fifth birthday by jumping with me and the U.S. Army Golden Knights parachute team.*

chocolate birthday cakes to be found (except all over both Jon's and Jeff's faces).

By year's end (about seven months into the IOAC course), I was selected to attend a highly specialized "Prefix Five" course that taught the intricacies of tactical nuclear-weapon target selection, and how to employ those weapons to achieve the desired destruction objective. Using complex formulas that took into account factors such as yield (what size explosive, measured in kilotons or megatons—a ten-kiloton bomb would have the explosive power of ten thousand tons of TNT), altitude, environmental conditions, and other considerations, our calculations would determine what was required to penetrate earth (in the case of killing troops hiding in caves), to destroy specific structures (wood, cement, steel, etc.), or to start fires in selected areas without taking out entire forests or towns.

We learned how nuclear energy transferred to its surrounding medium in the form of direct blast and both thermal and nuclear radiation, and how to factor this into our calculations. It was all very complicated, but with good reason since you didn't want to take out half of China with a blast intended for a block of aircraft plants outside Hanoi. (No, to my knowledge we had no plans to nuke Hanoi—at least none that I was involved in. Just making a point.) There were only twenty-five of us in the class, and between the early morning start times, full days of classes, and nightly study halls from seven to ten, I was not seeing much of Carolyn and the boys—but even so, it beat the heck out of letters from nine thousand miles away.

There were weekly tests that we had to pass or we were out—lots of math and lots of formulas to memorize. It was in that class that I met Frank Akers, a brilliant guy who would go on to become Brigadier General Frank Akers—and he would become very instrumental in pulling the plug on a near suicide mission I became aware of years later in Desert Storm. I really wanted Frank to be my study partner, but he had no time for that.

"Come on, Hugh, don't you get enough of that crap in class? Study halls are for wimps," Frank would scoff. While the rest of us came to class haggard and drained after burning the midnight oil at the books, Frank would stroll in refreshed, energetic, well rested—and as much as we all really liked him, we couldn't wait for the test scores to be posted because it was obvious that his indifferent attitude toward study would finally catch up with him. On the big day when grades were posted, we all crammed around the outer hallway bulletin board in anxious anticipation, almost as curious to see how badly Frank had tanked as much as to check out our own scores. I was thrilled to see that I had passed with flying colors, yet not flying quite as high as Frank; he scored 100 percent on every test. (I wonder if I would have studied even harder had I known that eighteen years down the road, I would be the Pentagon general coordinating our nuclear strikes and actually turning the key to launch the nuclear missiles.)

It was a great course that gave me added skills that were considered highly desirable at the time.

———

During the Prefix Five course I was contacted by a major from the Military Personnel Center who asked me what I'd like to do next. Getting a call like that in the Army was about as common as having Ed McMahon drop by to present you with the Publishers Clearing House sweepstakes check—it was like winning the lottery. Basically they were telling me that the world was in my hands and I could choose wherever I wanted to go. We agreed that I'd give him my answer the following day because first I wanted to discuss it with the world's greatest sounding board and career counselor. That night, after playing with the boys and enjoying Jon's extremely creative list of reasons why he preferred to stay up and play instead of going to sleep, Carolyn and I collapsed onto the sofa to discuss it. It was a short discussion. We both said it at the same time: ranger instructor.

"Ever since ranger school you've always looked up to those guys," she said.

"With my experience in Vietnam, I really think I could do some good . . . instill in these students the same principles, tactics, and techniques I had to fix when I was over there. I believe it could save a lot of lives."

"Nobody could set a better example, Hugh," my biggest supporter proffered. "You walk the walk."

\* \* \*

The following day I called the major to inform him that I would consider it an honor to be assigned as a ranger instructor. "Excellent, Captain," he replied. "Any preference as to which phase?"

There were three phases of ranger school, "basic" at Fort Benning, Georgia; "mountain" phase in Dahlonega, Georgia; and the Florida phase down at Camp James E. Rudder, located at Eglin Air Force Base just east of Pensacola. "Yes, sir, I do have a preference—a strong one. With my experience in Vietnam, I believe I would be of great value in the 'Swamp-and-jungle' phase in Florida."

"That will not be a problem, Captain—looks like a perfect fit. Just see Major Ionides there at the infantry school and he will cut the official orders."

"Thank you, sir," I said, replacing the receiver and hightailing it over to meet with Ionides upstairs in building five (Infantry Hall), the same building where all our IOAC and Prefix Five courses were conducted. I don't know why I couldn't have just called him since the meeting was more a formality than anything else; but rules are rules, so I did as requested and was in and out of there in under five minutes.

"Ranger instructor, Florida phase. Got it," Ionides acknowledged.

I was elated, and it was another perfect example of how my concentrating on doing the very best job I could at the moment, combined with doing whatever I could to fully prepare myself for whatever the future might bring, paid big dividends. No master plan, no politicizing, and no manipulation. Just do a great job and be prepared for tomorrow. In the course of my career I've seen a number of others who did not share this philosophy.

In my very first assignment, I worked with a young second lieutenant named Watson. From day number one he had a clearly defined goal: *I'm going to be Chief of Staff of the Army,* he would tell everyone. I don't believe he ever made it to first lieutenant.

Wes Clark was another one with ambition. He made it clear that he wanted to go all the way to the top, and would seek out assignments with the highest level of visibility instead of other, more-important considerations. That's fine if it works for him, but it's something I've just never been interested in—and as far as I was concerned, life could not have been any better.

The time had come once again to load up the GTO and the boat with the boys, a diaper bag, and a bunch of toys—but this time it would be a quick four-hour drive southwest into the tangled cypress wastes of Eglin Air Force Base, Florida . . . still fondly known as "Lower Alabama." At one and three years of age, the boys were getting an early taste of military life in the form of moving—there would be many more to come.

---

I have always liked to be around water—even murky swamp water crawling with copperheads and alligators—and the new position also allowed me to stay connected to the Special Operations arena, if only as an instructor at this point. (Organizationally, ranger school is under TRADOC, the U.S. Army Training and Doctrine Command, not Special Operations Command, but it still serves as a solid foundation and valuable combat-leadership resource for the great men and women of the 75th Ranger Regiment.) Looking back, assignments like this helped me gain a greater understanding of the Special Ops organization, an added edge of particular value when I became a four-star general and commander in chief of the entire U.S. Special Operations Command—the component command under which the rangers functioned.

Shortly after I arrived, I crossed paths with an interesting character treading to the HQ building like a man on a mission. Head shaved and massive muscles threatening to burst through his jumpsuit, he carried a parachute under one arm and had a crazy grin on his face. "Damn fine way to start the day," he beamed as he passed. I snapped to attention and saluted, once I saw he bore the lieutenant colonel leaves.

"I see you met the boss," said a voice from behind. "I'm Troy Shirley."

I turned around and saluted the major. "Captain Hugh Shelton, sir. Just arrived."

"I'm the S3, Hugh. We've heard all about you. And that was Colonel Tucker; he's never met a jump he didn't like. You'll find he's got some kind of superhearing—doesn't matter what he's doing, if he hears a helo coming in, he'll grab his jump gear and take off for the airfield. The man is addicted to free fall, but you'll like him; he's a dynamic leader and takes care of his people. Let's get you settled in."

Troy took me on a short tour and eventually officially introduced me to the eccentric camp commander I had passed earlier, Lieutenant Colonel James Tucker. It was no wonder that Tucker's upper arms looked like watermelons; in the corner of his office he kept a bench press with what looked like five-hundred-pound weights. As I settled in, I would totally concur with Troy's observation: Colonel Tucker was inspiring—a complete wild man, but a great leader. Between the commander and U.S.

Marine Corps Major Shirley, I already felt confident that I had made the right choice; this was going to be a great assignment.

Walking out of the office, we passed another major who appeared extremely busy trying to appear extremely busy behind his desk; he didn't even bother to look up as I passed. Once outside, Troy glanced conspiratorially in my direction and whispered, "That was Major Knox, the XO. And in case you're wondering, he was not voted Mr. Congeniality in high school."

Major Dean Knox was an oddball, a bitter dork who found it difficult to stand upright with the giant chip on his shoulder. He was detached and not well liked by the instructors, but he had one saving grace: a unique talent of boiling cypress stumps and carving them out with personalized ranger logos he would present as gifts to departing instructors. We called them "dammit stumps" since "dammit" was the first thing we would yell after tripping over those damn stumps at night in the swamps.

The camp itself was ideal for our mission. The terrain was much like Vietnam; teeming with swampland, slash pines, and scrub oaks—the perfect venue to duplicate the Republic of Vietnam, and that's exactly where most of these students would be heading upon graduation. We set up "Vietcong" villages and peppered them with "Vietcong" guerrilla units; our goal was to make everything as realistic as possible within the confines of safety and common sense. *Train as you fight* had been drilled into us, and this was a perfect opportunity to put that concept into action now that I was the trainer.

Ranger school was far from a traditional classroom situation. We trained out in the field, in rigorous, real-life conditions. Sure, there were specific topics that entailed specialized instructions—like reptile education taught by the "Snake Man," a real character who taught which snakes were venomous and which were safe, and how to catch and handle both types. But you'd never find the Snake Man behind a desk projecting pictures on some overhead projector. His classroom was the swampland, and he was fairly easy to identify: he'd be the one with his pet twenty-foot python wrapped around his arms or holding a poisonous diamondback rattlesnake. It was highly recommended not to sleep through his class.

Since I was already a captain promotable, I instantly became one of the three "committee chiefs"—meaning I had nine instructors working under me, and each of these was either a captain or a senior sergeant. The other two committee chiefs were majors.

I was issued my ranger-instructor cap, walking stick, and very realistic-looking rubber M1911 .45-caliber pistol and I went about doing my job the best that I knew how.

In addition to scheduling, managing, and evaluating my instructors, I also pulled my share of the instructional mission-oriented patrols we called "walks," and I would grade the students on how well they had planned and executed their missions under conditions of extreme mental and physical stress. We pushed them to the limit, but then showed them that their *actual* capabilities far exceeded any preconceived limits they may have had.

The officers (young captains) and the NCO corps that instructed there were about as good as they came; they were outstanding—and there was no question that I picked up every bit as much as I taught just from watching and listening to the NCOs, many of whom had seen far more combat than I had, and they were eager to share those valuable experiences.

In about my third month, two significant events happened. The first was the departure of the commander, Lieutenant Colonel Tucker, who was replaced by an older gentleman who was the exact opposite of Tucker. Lieutenant Colonel William D. Old came out of the budgeting group of Training and Doctrine Command. Although his style would be much more low-key, Colonel Old was also highly respected and we were fortunate to have him as our new commander.

Just a short while after Lieutenant Commander Old arrived, Major Troy Shirley received word that he was being transferred, which left Colonel Old the responsibility of finding a replacement S3—probably the second-most-important position in the camp—and Troy would be a tough act to follow. In addition to running the entire training operation, the S3 would be responsible for securing all our outside assets—Air Force airplanes, navy ships, Coast Guard cutters, and helicopters from both the Army and Marines. Even though it wasn't officially recognized as such, it really was a joint assignment involving every branch of the U.S. military—a tremendous experience but an enormous amount of work.

Colonel Old had his work cut out for him. There were a number of excellent majors from whom to choose, and it would take time for him to interview them all. In the interim, the senior ops NCO would be keeping the department in check—but that entailed way too much work for one man, even considering how extraordinary Sergeant First Class Donovan was.

I was almost finished evaluating my instructors' lane grades when I got a call from Major Knox. "The colonel wants to see you," he said, with all the enthusiasm of a dead fish. I presumed he was upset because the colonel had called me instead of him to help screen potential applicants. Knox was such a downer, he would look at a doughnut and see only the hole.

"You wanted to see me, sir?" I asked, knocking on the side of Lieutenant Commander Old's open door.

"Hugh, yes, come in. About this S3 opening . . ." he began as I stepped in and closed the door behind me.

"Yes, sir, I'm a step ahead of you on that one. I took the liberty of putting together a list of the top—"

"I don't want a list," he interrupted. "I want you to be my S3."

It wasn't often that I found myself speechless, but at that moment I was. For him to bypass all the majors and select a captain promotable for the position was a staggering show of faith. Of course, I felt 100 percent up to the task and had complete confidence in my ability—it's just that I was shocked. Had I known Lieutenant Commander Old better at that point, I might not have been so surprised, since later I would see that he never shied away from following his gut even if it meant going against the grain.

After bringing in a new major to take over my committee, Colonel Old allowed me to make whatever changes were needed to keep the operation running smoothly. He became a great role model and I give him credit for helping me to understand that an effective leader is not a hands-on micromanager; in fact, the freer the rein you give your people, generally speaking, the more they will excel—as long as you've clearly communicated your objectives and expectations, and surrounded yourself with good, independent thinkers who are not afraid to speak up. Although I've never really had a mentor, Bill Old was about as close to that as anyone had been.

Once again, this created a situation where my job responsibility had me functioning *above* officers who were technically higher in rank than I—and some were not happy about it. But if anyone was concerned about the rank situation, that became *their* problem, not mine. I never relished being in those positions where my superiors actually became my subordinates, but neither did I shy away from them.

One thing we were always trying to do at the ranger camp was come up with innovative training techniques to make the process as practical from a real-world perspective as possible. To that end, Colonel Old and I flew to New Orleans to coordinate the use of a Coast Guard cutter as part of a Florida ranger-camp program.

We met with the Coast Guard admiral and were successful in securing a 210-foot cutter for our exercises. The admiral was excited to make this a part of his training and would use it to hone his corp's ability to rendezvous with our rubber boats at sea, pick us up, and then proceed to a designated drop-off point. From the colonel's perspective, it offered a unique opportunity to give our ranger students an exciting, practical experience, and from my personal perspective, it was a great opportunity to meet with the admiral and see firsthand how my commander "negotiated" for assets like that.

We finished our business and Colonel Old decided that it would be good to walk down Bourbon Street while we were in town, since neither of us had ever been to New Orleans before. We were both in our green Army uniforms with ribbons and black berets that we wore as ranger instructors, and our jump boots—and we were just proud as punch. Still, this was 1972, and we were right in the middle of some pretty heated public controversies over Vietnam, and there was a great deal of anti-U.S. sentiment out there. "Are you sure you want to go to Bourbon Street, sir?" I asked the colonel.

"What are you worried about, Hugh? Are you forgetting we're rangers? Thought rangers were supposed to be tough," he responded.

He was the boss, so I figured, why not? We started walking down Bourbon Street and it was a rowdy scene, just like I imagined it would be—with makeshift stands selling Hurricanes and giant beers, and carnival beads flying down from second-story balconies in exchange for females exposing a quick flash of their breasts, and crazy costumes of all types.

Suddenly, out of the clear, came a young man dressed in a priest's outfit—with a long black robe and high white collar. He stepped right in front of Colonel Old's face and spit out, "You're a baby killer. How do you like killing babies?"

To his credit, Colonel Old kept right on walking and looking straight ahead, not paying any attention to the man. This troublemaker did not like being ignored, so he came back and made more disparaging remarks to the colonel.

Still, the colonel just proceeded on up the street, figuring this piece of garbage wasn't worth his effort. While at first the "priest" had had enough, next thing we knew he was back and screaming, "You are both killers. That's right—both of you." By that point I was getting angrier and angrier and my blood started to boil. He didn't want to tangle with me, but he had no problem going back and yelling at Colonel Old again, this time much louder. That's when I lost it. I turned, grabbed him, and slammed him into a brick wall, where his head bashed hard against it and just bounced off.

I lifted him up off the sidewalk and pinned him against the wall. "You ignorant sack of shit," I said, about an inch from his face. "That is a colonel in the United States Army and if you ever do anything like that again, you will die. You will not insult him and you will not make any comments making light of him fighting to keep your sorry, worthless ass free—'cause if you do I will kill you as dead as a doornail." I slammed him into the wall again and then let him go.

I must have knocked the breath out of him because he just sank down to the pavement. In hindsight I suppose I'm lucky to be here today because I probably could have killed him, but he was okay and got up and ran off in another direction. I turned to see how Colonel Old was doing, but he was gone. Then I glanced up and saw him a half block up the street, still walking and looking straight ahead. It was the strangest thing, he never mentioned a word about it and it was like it never happened.

All things considered, it turned out to be a great trip. We got our Coast Guard cutter, and since that day I have never been in another fight in my life. In fact, other than the one altercation with the class bully in eighth grade, I had never been in one before that, either.

Back at camp, I didn't dread the heat or the humidity as much as I did the uncertainty about my future. I'd been awaiting word on my next assignment but hadn't heard a thing. I wanted to make at least one final field exercise, since word of my departure could come at any time. The exercises, or FTXs, were arduous, demanding experiences. For the students, the twelve-day outings constituted their final exam, of sorts. They'd be allowed one 1,200-calorie field ration per day and allowed only two hours of sleep per night. During this entire time, they would be required to plan and execute critical missions that pushed them to the extreme. Weight loss of over twenty pounds was not uncommon, nor were cases of chilblains, cellulitis, tissue tears, pulled muscles, and dehydration.

On about the eighth or ninth day, hallucinations would start to set in. This was not merely a possibility, it was a given. I've seen students poking others in the chest because they thought they were cigarette machines, and it was common for these starving students to mob the catering truck that stopped in the middle of the road. Of course, the truck was just a hallucination, and in reality there wasn't even a road. We were in the middle of the swampland. Students would ask us why we carried firearms and we'd tell them, "Those swamps are packed with alligators and sometimes they don't observe the Keep Out signs we post at night. The guns are to protect your sorry ass in case one wants dessert." The gators were real, but they seldom came anywhere close. The guns were rubber. (Personally, I always hoped they looked as real to the alligators as they did to the students.)

As instructors we would stay out for thirty-six to forty-eight hours straight, then be relieved, but we wouldn't see our beds for another ten to twelve hours after we'd completed our reports. As S3 I could have skipped the FTX and just done the nine-to-five thing in my office, but that has never been my style and it wasn't the example I wanted to set. Early on I had been taught to *lead from the front,* and it's a principle I would always live by throughout my career.

One night, one of the students approached me, very concerned about something. Previously I had read his records and knew him to be a good man, with excellent grades (both peer and instructor). He had just received orders to report to Vietnam following ranger camp. "What's your question, ranger?" I asked.

"Sir, what do you feel after you've pulled the trigger and killed a man?" he asked, knowing he would personally have to deal with this very shortly.

"Recoil, ranger," I quipped back without delay, and his eyes widened as if to ask, *Are you really that heartless an SOB?* Of course, I would go on to answer him in an honest manner, and I fully understand that my response sounds totally cold and inappropriate—but as much as this sounds like a casual father/son fireside chat, I was his instructor and my goal was to teach him skills and techniques that would keep him and his fellow soldiers alive, and I had learned that there was a certain way to do this. Had I begun with some soft, sensitive response on how I understood that the man I killed was a fellow child of God or something similar, I can guarantee you that student would be having that conversation with God directly, because if he paused to think about that kind of thing, he would be the one on the receiving end of the gunshot.

"To answer your question honestly," I began, "I will tell you about the first NVA soldier I encountered face-to-face, because prior to that I had participated in ambushes that killed enemy forces, and directed artillery and helicopter gunships onto enemy positions that resulted in killing enemy soldiers, but those had an impersonal, distant quality to them." Not only was this student glued to my every word, but others had gathered around— these were questions they wanted to ask but felt too macho to verbalize.

"My first face-to-face encounter occurred while on patrol as a Special Forces captain, and as I rounded a thicket of bamboo, approaching me was an NVA lieutenant. My CAR-15 was at the ready, my thumb on the AUTO/SEMIAUTO selector switch and my finger on the trigger. The lieutenant had his AK-47 slung over his shoulder, something we are all taught never to do, and for good reason." Instinctively, the student nodded, having had that drilled into him from day one.

I continued. "We looked eye-to-eye for what seemed like two seconds. His eyes widened as he frantically tried to bring his weapon to the firing position. Mine was already in position. My thumb switched to automatic and my finger pulled the trigger. In a split second he was dead, hit by four rounds of 5.56-mm ammunition in the chest and head. I crouched down and waited for his unit to open fire, but instead they had turned and rapidly moved away. I searched his body for documents and found a small plastic bag that contained a picture of him and apparently his wife and two children. Another victim of war, another family whose husband/father would not be coming home."

"But how did you feel, sir? I mean . . . his poor kids . . ."

"I felt remorse for his family," I explained. "But none for him. It had been him or me, and I had a wife and son that I very much wanted to go home to. There would be no need for psychological counseling. I felt great having survived my first face-to-face encounter. It was killing for survival and I was ready to do it many more times if that was what it took to return home to my wife and son. As it turned out, it was. I was somewhat fortunate that first time, since the soldier stupidly had his rifle slung over his shoulder. That would not be the case in future confrontations, so let me tell you this . . . the time to do whatever 'thinking about it' you have to do is now, and I mean right now, because when you graduate this class you damn well better be running on instinct. If you delay for one millisecond out there in the field, your wife will be presented with a brand-new, perfectly folded American flag, compliments of the honor guard that just lowered your casket into the ground. Now you better get some sleep."

"Yes, sir. Thank you, sir," he said, damn near asleep before the words were out of his mouth.

I was going on forty-eight hours without sleep myself, so it was time for me to head back to the office to write it all up. Eight more hours of paperwork before I could hop on my motorcycle and speed home to that pillow.

As I sat behind my desk, both assigning grades and reviewing grades the other instructors had submitted, I thought about how I had handled that student's question. I had been honest, sincere, and open, and helping others by sharing my personal experiences was exactly the reason I was so intent on becoming a ranger instructor. Whatever my next assignment would be, I felt satisfied with what I had accomplished in this one.

"What the hell are you still doing here?" I looked up and saw Lieutenant Colonel Old standing in the doorway. Although it was barely past noon, the colonel knew how long I had been without sleep, and how long I had been away from Carolyn, Jon, and Jeff. "Hugh, c'mon, you've been out there for going on three days now. Go on home."

"You know the drill, sir. Gotta finish these grades."

He walked in and closed my door. "Hugh, you're a hard worker and nobody does a better job, but I'm going to be blunt. Those grades are going to be there in the morning, but before you know it—your kids will not be. You are working yourself to death in this job."

"Oh, I don't think I'm that bad, sir," I said sheepishly, and with a touch of defensiveness.

He reached down and picked up a framed photo I kept on my desk; it was one of my favorites—of Carolyn, Jon, and Jeff. As he stared at the picture, he continued. "I've got two kids myself, one's in his second year at college, and my daughter takes off for her first year in a few weeks. I look back on my life and just ask myself where did all that time go. They're both out of the nest and I didn't spend nearly enough time with them. I keep having this recurring dream—more like a nightmare, I suppose. In it my daughter is about to get married, and I'm walking her down the aisle. When we get to the front, I lift up her veil to kiss her goodbye, but instead she extends her hand to shake mine, and she says, 'It's really nice to meet you, sir, and I can't tell you how much I appreciate you dropping by.' I don't want to see you fall into that same trap, being gone so much your kids don't even know who you are. But to be perfectly honest with you—at the rate you're going, I think you may be even worse than I was." He looked across my desk and smiled at the perfectly aligned stacks of completed reports—*case in point.* "The Army doesn't give medals for missing your kid's first step, or Little League games."

"Sir, that's one medal I have no interest in getting," I said without hesitation.

"I know you don't. But the thing to watch out for is the *one more time* syndrome. I know you love those kids. But the night before the CG is due to drop by and you tell yourself, 'Just this one time I've got to stay late because it's so important'—or when you're about to walk out that door and you get word the Coast Guard got deployed and you've got no boats for the next morning's exercise—those are the ones that'll sneak up on you."

"Sir, somebody's got to handle those situations."

"I'm just sayin', Hugh. Now get the hell out of here."

"Will do, Colonel. If I don't, I have no doubt you'll bring me up on charges of insubordination." He smiled and turned to leave. There was merit—if not downright wisdom—in his words.

"And, sir," I said as he turned into the hallway, "message received loud and clear. Thank you."

"I hope you're a better listener than I was at your age. . . . Take care, Hugh." He turned and walked away—a good and decent man who was well respected by his command, yet for the first time I saw an inner sadness based on choices he wished he had made differently along the way.


I wrapped my filthy fatigues around my Honda 450 and the powerful 444-cc dual overhead cams exploded to life. The harsh Florida sun was not kind to the "candy gold" finish; its beautiful luster had already started to fade.

Racing the twenty-three miles to our small duplex house on Eglin main, the wind ripped into my scorched skin—and it felt great. Somewhat reminiscent of a free fall's descent, paradoxically it felt both exhilarating and calming at the same time. It had been a day for valuable lessons, and I could only hope that the ranger student took as much from mine as I had from Bill Old's.

In the coming weeks and months I would enjoy immersing myself in my sons' early development, to the extent that my job allowed. But as the years went on and I ascended up the ranks, the positions I had became so demanding that I do look back with a sense of regret that's probably shared by most individuals who reach the top of their professions—that I did not have the time to spend with Carolyn and my great sons that I would have liked to. For the next thirty years, Colonel Old's words would haunt me; but on the flip side, there were many nights when I found myself about to make some very realistic assessment as to why it was necessary for me to stay and work late rather than meet Carolyn and the boys for some prearranged family event—and then Bill Old's words would come to mind, and I'd end up locking the files in my safe and heading home early to meet them. I just wish there had been more of them.

Sympathetic to the fact that I would need to collapse as soon as I got home, Carolyn had taken the boys out for a few hours. She knew that with Daddy having been gone for three days, Jon would want to play with me as soon as he saw me; and even though my mind would have desired the same thing, my body would need the sleep.

Less than five minutes after stepping from the shower, I was in a deep sleep; it was time to make up for the past sixty-plus hours without any.

I'd been asleep for about an hour when the phone started ringing off the hook, and with Carolyn still out, I had to answer it.

"Shelton, who in the name of Christ do you know? You've been selected to attend the Air Command and Staff College at Maxwell Air Force Base and *it's just not right.*" It was Major Knox, and the son of a bitch was fully aware that I had just gone to sleep. What's more, his tone was angry, accusatory.

"Major, I have no idea what you're talking about," I said groggily.

"I want to know how the hell you managed that. I've got three years in grade and I still haven't been to Command and Staff, and you're not even wearing your major leaves yet."

He was now being downright nasty, and in truth I had no clue how or why I had been selected. As a captain promotable, it was a great honor and showed that I had caught the attention of someone. This was the *Air*

*Force* version of the Army's Command and General Staff College, where about 60 to 70 percent of the Army *majors* were selected to attend. It was a pretty sure bet that if you weren't selected for Command and Staff, you were not going to be promoted from major to lieutenant colonel, so elimination from the service could be right around the corner. In my case, I assume somebody picked up on the fact that I was a captain functioning as the S3—not an everyday occurrence.

It had been a terrific eighteen months at ranger school. I left there feeling that I had imparted a lot of knowledge to a good number of students, and helped boost their confidence and develop their maturity in a way that would serve them well as they headed for Vietnam or other deployments. I was thrilled by what *I* had learned through the exceptional—yet polar-opposite—leadership styles of Lieutenant Colonels Tucker and Old. Finally, having served as the S3, I had taken an important step toward my next major goal of becoming a battalion commander.

———

It was a blistering August afternoon when we pulled into Montgomery, Alabama—capital of the state and home to Governor George Wallace, who had recently been shot. Now paralyzed and restricted to a wheelchair for the rest of his life, he still had no qualms taking out the political ad we had just passed. It showed a cute white girl surrounded by seven black boys, and the slogan read WAKE UP ALABAMA. BLACKS VOW TO TAKE OVER ALABAMA. Unbelievable, but that was the state of affairs in 1972, when Carolyn, Jon, Jeff, and I arrived at our new home on Devonshire Drive in Montgomery. Turbulent, violent times.

These were tough times for the country, and I was about to begin what would play out as the most challenging year of my professional life. The Air Force didn't have quarters on base for students, so we were forced to rent in the local community. On the bright side, we were directly across the street from another Army officer, Major Glenn Marsh (who would go on to become a three-star general). It turned out that Glenn was also in Montgomery for Air Force Command and Staff, so we carpooled together every day and eventually became close friends.

With my background in the Army, attending an Air Force school with predominantly Air Force officers on an Air Force base initially felt like I'd been dropped into a foreign country. I was ready to work hard. And, I soon learned, I would not be disappointed in that regard.

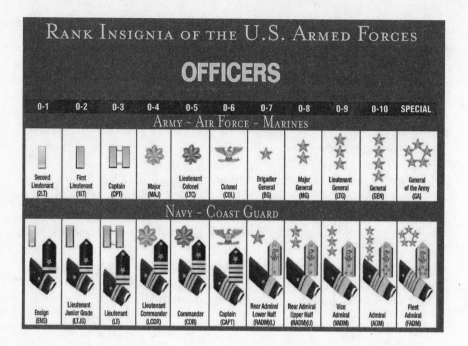

RANK INSIGNIA OF THE U.S. ARMED FORCES

## OFFICERS

| 0-1 | 0-2 | 0-3 | 0-4 | 0-5 | 0-6 | 0-7 | 0-8 | 0-9 | 0-10 | SPECIAL |
|-----|-----|-----|-----|-----|-----|-----|-----|-----|------|---------|

ARMY – AIR FORCE – MARINES

| Second Lieutenant (2LT) | First Lieutenant (1LT) | Captain (CPT) | Major (MAJ) | Lieutenant Colonel (LTC) | Colonel (COL) | Brigadier General (BG) | Major General (MG) | Lieutenant General (LTG) | General (GEN) | General of the Army (GA) |

NAVY – COAST GUARD

| Ensign (ENS) | Lieutenant Junior Grade (LTJG) | Lieutenant (LT) | Lieutenant Commander (LCDR) | Commander (CDR) | Captain (CAPT) | Rear Admiral Lower Half (RADM)(L) | Rear Admiral Upper Half (RADM)(U) | Vice Admiral (VADM) | Admiral (ADM) | Fleet Admiral (FADM) |

This was long before the concept of joint warfare had been introduced, so there really were a number of differences between the various service branches.

"Just be glad it's not a Navy school," Glenn would joke. "You tell me why they call captains 'lieutenant' and colonels 'captains,'" referring to the somewhat confusing difference in ranks between Army and Navy officers. (See chart above.)

Glenn and I would kid about it, but the truth was that there really were cultural differences between the services. We started to see some of that in school, with junior officers calling more senior officers by their first names instead of their ranks—but it would really play out before my eyes when I became Chairman, and the Joint Chiefs would each represent a different service branch.

In many respects, the *differences* constitute major assets and contribute to why the Joint Chiefs are such a valuable strategic and tactical sounding board. The Navy guy would certainly not be expected to step to the table and deliver in-depth analyses of air operations, any more than the Air Force Chief would be the one to approach for the most thorough understanding of submarines.

But beyond these tremendous advantages, in certain instances the cultural differences became problematic. Generally speaking, I have found that Marines tend to be very gung-ho, very confident, and have no problem suggesting that almost anything and everything is possible. Semper

Fi. Well, that briefs well, but it's a very dangerous position to be in if the reality is that their enthusiasm extends far beyond their actual capabilities, and I have seen this over and over again.

I have found that in many cases, the Air Force culture seemed to lean more toward an almost blind acceptance of a superior's position, without questioning that position quite as much as most Army officers were prone to. It's subtle, but all these things would play out in dramatic fashion after I retired and my successor would be an Air Force Chairman, who would be followed by a Marine Chairman. More on that later.

The first phase of the class was fairly easy since it covered general topics like geopolitics; but later, when it transitioned to the strategy, tactics, and logistics of air power, I found it much more challenging, since I had never previously been exposed to it. For example, I'd never thought much about the complexity of aerial refueling or locating dispersed fighter-bomber bases overseas—but these were topics we covered in detail. Math became a series of calculations involving tracks, anchor points, and rendezvous times—all new terminology that we would have to learn before even trying to tackle the math part of it. It was a challenge in the beginning, with many of the new concepts sounding like Greek to me. Here's a taste of what we were hit with on our first day of "midair refueling":

> The track from the ARIP to the ARCP should be along a TACAN/ VORTAC radial and within 100 NM of the station. Tanker may, with ARTCC approval, proceed to the exit/reentry fix, execute a left turn and refuel southeast bound to the ARCP, but only between the hours of 1630-2359Z. The basic types of rendezvous procedures are the point parallel (PP) and enroute (ENRT). All other procedures are modifications of the basic types, such as fighter-turn-on (FTO), and GCI, which is radar vector/control.

Nor had I considered the significant role the reserve component played in meeting the Air Force's manpower requirements. Not many Army officers were injected into a position like this where they had to assimilate information from the perspective of a totally different branch of the service (in this case, the Air Force)—but I recognized that the chance to learn the intricate ways of another service offered a unique opportunity that I'd be wise to exploit as fully as possible.

Not only would successfully completing the Air Command and Staff College be a major achievement for an Army Infantry officer, but acquiring a firsthand knowledge of Air Force weapons and how best to use them would open a window of insight that remained closed to most of my Army peers. These were skills that would put me in good stead as we transitioned into a joint military, and they would become extraordinarily valuable years down the road when I became Chairman—and in particular during my private meetings with the President in which an Air Force adviser might not be present. Some of these involved our pursuit of a terrorist we referred to as UBL—short for Usama bin Laden. (Most American government agencies including the CIA, FBI, as well as the Department of Defense and the President, use either Usama bin Laden or UBL instead of the more common spelling, Osama.)

Many people don't realize that UBL was an incredibly hot topic in the E Ring and the White House long before 9/11, and we were all exceedingly frustrated that he continued to elude us—none more so than President Clinton himself. There were many occasions when we would discuss various kill or capture possibilities, along with Secretary of Defense Bill Cohen, National Security Advisor Sandy Berger, CIA Director George Tenet, and others.

During the 9/11 hearings, President Clinton told the commission that our frustration became so palpable, at one time he had proposed to me, *You know, Hugh, it would scare the shit out of al-Qaeda if suddenly a bunch of black ninjas rappelled out of helicopters into the middle of their camp.* Secretary Cohen explained that the question remained how to get the "ninjas" into and out of the theater of operations—and what he was referring to involved some of the very concepts I had picked up at Air Command and Staff—and these were discussions I would frequently have with the President, Secretary of Defense, National Security Council, and others within both the Clinton and the Bush administrations.

Just for the sake of argument, let's say that the camp the ninjas are going to rappel into is 1,000 miles into Afghanistan from the Arabian Sea—and I pick the Arabian Sea because in this hypothetical we're going to fly them from an aircraft carrier we've got standing by in the area. If it's a Delta operation, we often use Little Birds—small, highly maneuverable MH-6 helicopters that have platforms on the outside where the operators often sit, so that they can hop right off. But an MH-6 has only a sixty-two-gallon fuel tank, and that will get you only 232 miles, and it's not capable of in-flight refueling, so that's out.

How about a UH-60, a Black Hawk? Sure, that might work, but that goes only 373 miles and has a ceiling of ten thousand feet, so for safety we may want to go higher, so let's talk about a Pave Low, an MH-53. Still, it's going only 630 miles, so we are definitely going to need some in-flight refueling. Now we're talking about bringing in the tankers, maybe some MC-130P Combat Shadows to gas up a few times. If they come in, we're going to need more planes for command and control, not to mention communications jamming—probably some MC-130H airplanes, and we damn well better have CSAR (combat search and rescue) teams standing by on their helos in case something goes wrong, because if they don't get in *immediately,* it could get very messy very fast and those ninjas just might not make it out at all.

The bottom line is that this single helicopter of ninjas we want to swoop right in has suddenly grown to hundreds of individuals and a number of aircraft and support—and that's not even getting into the State Department end of things. We're damn well not going to fly over Iran, so we need to get overflight clearance from Pakistan, perhaps.

I will get into all this later when I talk about my days as Chairman, but I bring it up now to point out how exceptionally valuable this Air Force tactical training would become for me down the road, paying off big time when I became the principal military adviser to the President and the National Security Council. When I look back on how my career played out, I am amazed at how many times assignments such as this—which at the time might have seemed like wastes of time or divergences from my intended path of assuming a command—ended up not only falling into place but doing so in such a way that they could not have been more perfectly targeted for the position of Chairman had they been designed with that in mind.

———

The Army wanted me to get a master's degree and, to that end, offered me the opportunity to attend Auburn University while I was at Maxwell. Although my first instinct was that there was little value in taking time out of my Army career to attend graduate school, I eventually decided it was an excellent opportunity to get an advanced degree that would serve me well, even though the hours of study would be a killer.

I signed up to attend night courses for a political science master's program at Auburn, and unfortunately it kicked in the week that we started the most intensive phase of the Air Force program. I set specific goals for myself: I wanted all As at Auburn and to be in at least the top third of the class at Maxwell. For one thing, I had been sitting in the classroom in my Army uniform, and I wanted to represent the Army well. Additionally—and I know this might sound strange—my parents had always valued education and I knew they would both be extremely proud to hear that I had earned an advanced degree, particularly if I could do so with straight As.

For that to happen, I would have to burn the candle at both ends—going directly from Command and Staff to the Auburn course and getting home at 10:00 P.M. every night. Following a quick check-in on the sleeping boys and a way-too-short debrief with Carolyn, I would study until at least 1:00 A.M., and all day on the weekends. Then I'd get up at 4:00 A.M. and head right back to the books; and head back to school and continue what became a vicious cycle. My real challenge was finding quality time to spend with the boys. Jon was in first grade and already doing very well at football, so I tried to make time to throw the ball with him whenever I could. He was a natural and would go on to play every year through high school.

My thesis explored a concept that was twenty years ahead of its time: I analyzed the possibility of merging the Army Pathfinder program with the Air Force Combat Controllers, a joint operation if there ever was one.

To be candid, the time requirements caused this to become one of the worst years of my life, and I was able to complete it as effectively as I did only because of Carolyn. As always, she was extremely supportive and did way more than her fair share without a single word of complaint.

When all was said and done, I made it through the year and learned a great deal at Air Command and Staff. I finished well up in the class and did get straight As at Auburn. To top it off, my marriage survived it—so in hindsight, I suppose it turned out to be a good year after all.

———

In summer of 1973 I was notified that I would be transferring to the 2nd Brigade of the 25th Infantry Division stationed in Hawaii. Both Carolyn and I were thrilled, at least until I got my letter of welcome from my new brigade commander, Colonel Lucien E. Bolduc Jr., who informed me that I was going to be his brigade S1 (a personnel job) instead of the XO or S3 (Head of Operations) job I had hoped for. Carolyn knew that "I'd rather have a sister in a whorehouse than a brother who was an S1," so I wrote Colonel Bolduc back and thanked him profusely, told him how very much I was looking forward to working for him, and went on to suggest that he reconsider since I really was hoping for either the XO or S3 slot. *Sir, I promise you would not be disappointed; and between my enthusiasm for both of these important positions, my organizational skills, and my great attention to detail, you could not ask for anyone who would bring more to the table,* I wrote.

I give him credit for a prompt reply, but it was not the most eloquent correspondence I had ever received. Scribbled almost illegibly by hand on a sheet of brigade letterhead was one line: *You will be the S1.*

Carolyn looked up at me and just shook her head, an unspoken *What have we gotten ourselves into?*

I shrugged. "On the bright side, at least the man seems to know what he wants." She cracked up, and we both knew that we had no other choice at that point, so why not make the best of it? How bad could Hawaii be?

Several weeks later, the big Pan Am jet circled above Oahu and began its descent to Hickam Field. A few of our friends had warned us that some of their kids—particularly those around Jeff's age or younger—became apprehensive during their first flight, troubled by their ears popping and anxious as the plane hit pockets of turbulence. Our kids must have missed that memo, because they *loved* it. Actually, Jon (seven years old) was preoccupied with drawing and playing with his action figures, but Jeff was taking everything in, and loving every minute of it. He was fascinated by the way the plane went right through the clouds; and then as we descended beneath them, he beamed upon seeing the lush green volcanic slopes and creamy white surf rolling in to the beach of his new island home. It's no wonder that many years later he would become one of the Army's finest aviators.

Riding in from the airport to Schofield Barracks felt more like a vacation than a new assignment. We were all enthralled by the endless rows of pineapples, brightly colored birds, and old produce trucks rattling along the narrow highway.

*This is going to be a great assignment after all,* I thought.

There's a great deal to be said for optimism and approaching challenges with a positive attitude, and I tried my best to do so. But when I arrived at 2nd Brigade headquarters in one of the four blockish stucco buildings made famous in the film *From Here to Eternity,* I found the situation even worse than I had imagined. Racial tensions were high throughout the division, and violent demonstrations among the troops were not uncommon.

Making matters worse was Colonel Bolduc himself; he turned out to be a real tyrant whose joy in life seemed to be thrashing his people in public. It was painful to watch him time after time berate his executive officer, Lieutenant Colonel Marx, in front of the troops and Marx's subordinates. The shabby, disrespectful manner in which Bolduc treated his people was a leadership lesson I would never forget. At times he would be right in the middle of ripping some poor guy apart—and then if a lady walked in, a switch would flip in his brain and he would instantly turn into this charismatic bon vivant, smiling and literally kissing the back of her hand—a custom he picked up during his time attending the French military academy in Paris. You would think he was quite the Francophile, but he detested France and anything having to do with it. Working for this dual personality was quite a challenge.

Occupying the S3 position that I wanted was an older major I'll call Ted Dunlap. He had taken the test for his Expert Infantry Badge two years in a row and failed both years. This is a very demanding test comprised of twelve stations, and everything had to be done to precision. On his third and final attempt, Dunlap successfully completed the first eleven stations and all he had to do to pass was complete the "live grenade" exercise—which consisted of his getting down on his stomach, himself, and going through a set procedure to throw a hand grenade into a circle target about twenty yards away. He threw the first two and completely missed the circle, and then he had only one grenade left. *If he makes this one, he walks away with the badge,* I thought. So he came up, reared back, threw the grenade, and it actually hit the pole directly in the middle of the target—a perfect throw that could not have been better. He jumped up cocky as can be and was full of himself—after three years, he'd finally passed. The evaluator smiled and said, "Great throw, Major. Too bad you forgot to pull the pin on the grenade." Three tries, three failures—so no Expert Badge for Major Dunlap. When I heard about this, it pissed me off even more that there I was in this S1 slot when a screw-up like that had the coveted S3 position.

In spite of the fact that I was still the S1 (and working for a temperamental madman), Carolyn, the boys, and I were loving our time on Oahu. Before we left the mainland a friend had told me that there were two things I had to do immediately upon arriving in Hawaii, and the second one was to sign up for a scuba dive.

"What's the first one?" I asked.

"Put your bags down," my friend replied. That was great advice, and I was smart enough to heed it. Shortly after we arrived, I linked up with a crusty former UDT (Navy SEAL Underwater Demolition Team) dive instructor named Kerwin. I'm sure he had some sadist DNA, but he really knew his stuff. He damn near killed a number of people, but in his mind, as long as he didn't cross that threshold, he was good. He'd take me out to a crystal-clear spot just off Hunauma Bay, where we'd dive a full sixty feet down—that's the limit for the first certification for open-water dives. Once down there, he would yank off my regulator and I'd have to free ascend from sixty feet. He couldn't have cared less if I sucked water, he just assumed that I could be resuscitated if necessary.

Truth is, he saved my life by teaching me how to handle dicey situations I got myself into long after I got my card, but it was something I really enjoyed—especially getting out there with my diving buddy, Major Bill Marr. Bill and I would swim out to a good diving depth and stay under water until our tanks were depleted. We would collect shells under water while Carolyn and the boys played on the beach. Life was good.

About nine months into my assignment, we got some *great* news. Not only was Colonel Bolduc being transferred out, but of all the places in the world, he was ordered to report to Paris to become the U.S. defense attaché to France. Considering his total disdain for the French, I thought it poetic justice that he would most likely serve out his career in an environment he so detested. (As for his career playing out in La Ville-Lumière, that never happened. Instead, he was promoted to major general and retired in 1981 as commander of Fort Jackson and the U.S. Army Training Center.)

Our new brigade commander was Colonel Victor M. Robertson, who turned out to be the exact opposite of Bolduc—an inspirational guy to work for. When I introduced myself I wasn't shy about sharing my desire to transition to that S3 slot, even though *nobody could be doing a finer job than Major Dunlap*—or so I told him. Despite how much I wanted that job, stabbing somebody else in the back to get it has never been my style, and even as inept an S3 as Dunlap was, I was not going to play dirty to get the position.

Colonel Robertson's wife, Lois, had been a reporter for the *Chicago Tribune* and she was really a great lady—poised, charismatic, great bearing—and Colonel Robertson wanted me to work with her to put together a brigade party, a top-notch formal affair. She envisioned a big round head table where the generals would sit, and the focal point would be an ornate silver candelabrum that had been handed down from her great-grandmother—an irreplaceable, treasured family heirloom.

The night came around and we had put together one hell of an elaborate affair—the officers were all seated with their wives, and we had skits and performances and specialty acts, one of which featured "The Amazing Zabata"—the headquarters company executive-officer's wife, who was a Turkish belly dancer. Just after dinner she hit the stage and wowed the officers and their wives with her act. Building to her finale, she ignited a big torch and started twirling it, then balanced it on her nose as she did her belly dance.

The whole room was applauding and everyone was having a great time. Suddenly, somebody jumped up from a table in the back and stumbled to the front—clearly inebriated—and grabbed the candelabrum, which held a dozen burning candles. He danced his way to the center of the room in full dress uniform and attempted to mimic Zabata by doing his own belly dance. It was Major Dunlap, the S3 who had forgotten to pull the pin on his hand grenade.

He was about as good at belly dancing as he was at taking the test for his Expert Infantry Badge. The crowd watched as he waltzed about the floor with the magnificent candelabrum held high. Laughter erupted and got even louder as he attempted to balance the heirloom on his nose. Suddenly the magnificent silver relic fell to the floor and broke into pieces. The crowd was laughing somewhat nervously . . . *except* for the head table, where Lois Robertson was sobbing uncontrollably. Colonel Robertson tried his best to console her, but it was no use. He went to the floor and tried to gather the pieces, but the crowd didn't give up; laughter still filled the room. I quickly jumped up and started helping the colonel retrieve the scattered pieces.

Lois Robertson looked like she was on the verge of passing out as I accompanied the couple out to their car. "Don't worry, honey," said Colonel Robertson, still trying in vain to comfort his wife. "We'll get it to a silversmith to repair it."

With the condition that piece was in, that comment was almost funnier than anything else—I was thinking to myself that the last silversmith who could repair that candelabrum had probably died a century ago.

The next day it was announced that that Major Dunlap was retiring from the Army unexpectedly, and effective immediately the new S3 would be Captain (promotable) Hugh Shelton. Major Dunlap became a laughingstock and I became the new S3.

This became another situation when my position outweighed my rank (i.e., as captain I would be commanding certain soldiers who were higher in rank than I, since the S3 position is usually held by a major). It was one of those times when you couldn't believe what just happened. On one hand, you felt like laughing, but when you thought about this guy flushing his twenty-year career down the toilet with one dumb act, there was really nothing funny about it.

In March 1974, after four years of being on the early-promotions list, I finally received word that it was official—I had been promoted to major and could pin on the leaf. For the moment, my rank was equivalent to my position, but that wouldn't last for long . . . my next two promotions would come early, "below the zone," and again I'd be put in positions that outweighed my rank.

The division trained hard and we were out in the field all the time—real soldiering. It was one field-training exercise after the other, with at least one long one on the big island of Hawaii each year. Hard work but good, challenging fun.

This was a high-visibility job in which I designed and implemented many of the exercises. One was called Operation Quick Strike, and it was all-encompassing. We started out with a real dose of showmanship when I had my assistant S3 design a logo for the presentation. Sergeant First Class Bishop was an animator at Disney before entering the Army, and the Quick Strike logo and charts he put together were magnificent. From the first time the commanders laid eyes on that, they loved the whole exercise. I had never seen anything like it, and it was something I would never forget.

One night, there was a race riot in the brigade quad where the troops had formed around one of the battalion buildings and were threatening to burn the barracks down.

This was soon after the military draft was abolished, and the American military had shifted to an all-volunteer force in 1973. After years of racial tension among draftees during the Vietnam War, the move was well justified. Now the soldiers entering the Army would serve because they wanted to serve their country, in addition to having stable employment, good pay, and the respect of their countrymen.

But the troops rioting in the Schofield quad that night were mostly hold-over draftees, no doubt many of whom resented the opportunities offered to the incoming volunteers. This was a reminder, as if any were needed, that the long ordeal of the Vietnam War had wrung the soul of the American military. For some reason, the 25th Infantry Division seemed especially afflicted.

Our division commander was Major General Harry Brooks, himself an African American. Brooks had joined the Army as a private and had quickly risen to sergeant. Eventually he was noticed because of his base-ball prowess, then was invited to OCS (Officer Candidates School) and climbed through the ranks of a very segregated Army, becoming only the sixth African American general in U.S. Army history. Another future Chairman, Colin Powell, was one of his subordinates.

On the night of the riots, General Brooks came to the quad and, following a great deal of "negotiation," persuaded the riotous troops to behave and return to their building. Brooks was a persuasive leader with a natural way with people, so it was fortunate that he was there that night.

As far as I was concerned, everything was going fine when out of the blue, in July 1975, I got a call from division headquarters saying that they wanted to bring me up to HQ to be their officer-management guy. I did not want to do that; I still wanted a battalion XO job. But they said, "No, you really need to come do this. We need help and we need it badly; we need you right now." So I went from S1 to S3 and then to G1, which was the same officer-management position as S1 only at a higher level—the Division level (with the G signifying the position was on the commanding generals staff.)

I went up to Division and I could not have scripted a better career move. Once again, it turned out to be a blessing. I learned the personnel system backward and forward and made great contacts in the personnel centers in Washington, D.C. I became expert at the intricacies of the officer MOS (military occupation specialty) and made repeated briefs to Major General Brooks (the division commander) and the two Brigadier General Assistant Division Commanders on proposed officers and changes. I got to know the record of every officer in the division, and along with this bright young captain who worked for me—Captain Bill Sharp—kept tabs on the personnel details of more than fifteen thousand troops in our 25th Infantry Division.

By this point I was working closely with Major General Brooks, and, like others before me, I found inspiration in his vibrant style. He had a sign on the wall behind his desk, and on one hand it was motivational; on the other, it would prove to be his demise. The sign read, "YOU TELL ME THAT IT CAN'T BE DONE, I KNOW THAT IS NOT TRUE. THE TRUTH IS IT CAN BE DONE, BUT IT CAN'T BE DONE BY YOU." What it really said was, "Give it your best shot before you go tell your boss you can't do it."

The fact is, in the real world not everything *can* be done—at least in ways that are ethical, moral, and within the law. In those cases, subordinates must be free—and in fact, encouraged—to confide in the boss and explain the reality. They have to be willing to share bad news and be up front about potential risks associated with certain choices. But that sign said otherwise. It gave the message that *under no circumstances do I want to hear excuses, just do it however you can.* On a couple of occasions subordinates were flat-out afraid to confide in General Brooks, so they kept their thoughts to themselves and neglected to point out to him potential problems within his orders. It is my opinion that it cost him his third star, and this powerful leader was forced to retire as a two-star.

* * *

After three years in Hawaii, we were hard-pressed to imagine anywhere topping the tropical paradise. Between the fantastic climate, the great diving, the excellent housing, and the superb elementary schools on the installation, my entire family was loving it. Carolyn had taken up tennis, and we even got the boys a dog—the cutest little world-class Doberman pup you could ever imagine; we named him Sentry. (Our last dog, Stryker, was on indefinite vacation with my parents, since he had become overly protective of Jon and too aggressive with Jon's friends.) And I had even bolstered my confidence and tried something I had not attempted before—or would again.

Although I have never had any trouble jumping out of airplanes, speaking in front of groups (no matter the size or rank of the audience), or immersing myself in the thicket of enemy gunfire and bombs—I had always left public music performances to my mother to enjoy every week at church—at least until one magnificent Sunday morning on the island of Oahu. Before leaving Montgomery I splurged and purchased my first Martin guitar, and I could not resist the temptation to put it through its paces when asked to play in the main post chapel at Schofield Barracks. The church provided the perfect acoustical setting. So much for "nerves"—they were nonexistent as I sat in front of the congregation, gazed down at Carolyn and the boys eagerly anticipating what Dad could do—and from the very first chord I became completely absorbed in a sound I can only describe as heavenly . . . and one I attribute far more to the engineering gurus at the Martin Guitar Company than I do to any musical prowess on my part. But it was another great Sunday that I will never forget.

All I needed to make our Hawaiian experience a complete grand slam was a job as battalion XO, and if that would come through, it would justify our being able to stay on the island for another year.

The fates were good to me, and I would close out my time at Schofield Barracks as the XO of the 14th Infantry Battalion. Another West Point graduate, Colonel Ed Trobaugh, who later became a two-star general and commander of the 82nd Airborne Division, was commander of the 2nd Brigade. He came to me and said, "Hugh, I'd like to have you come down and be the XO of the 14th Infantry." That got my attention, and there was no way I would consider passing up an opportunity like that.

The 14th Infantry Battalion, the Golden Dragons, was commanded by Lieutenant Colonel Bob Edwards, who had been one of the commanders in the Ia Drang Valley made famous in *We Were Soldiers Once . . . and Young*. He was a tremendous guy with a great family. My time as XO gave me a chance to coach and mentor some of the young lieutenants in the battalion, and to help the company commanders in any way that I could. It was an exciting and very enjoyable period.

Overall, my tour in Hawaii had been very pleasurable, not only for me but for Carolyn and the boys. I would be leaving as an experienced battalion executive officer and an experienced brigade S3, two key positions that are highly prized when one is under consideration for battalion commander.

I received my orders and learned that I would be heading for the Military Personnel Center as a professional development officer, where my new challenges would include not only officer placements but navigating the overcrowded highways of Washington, D.C., and an even more turbulent housing market.

**11:15 A.M., March 23, 2002, Inova Fairfax Hospital**

In the hour since I had been rushed into Inova's emergency room the pace had slowed considerably. Carolyn remained at my side until I was taken away for my MRI, at which time she stepped out in hopes of reaching Hal Timboe, a former neighbor who had recently been promoted to major general and assumed command of Walter Reed Army Medical Center. As always, Carolyn was three steps ahead of the game and wanted to ensure that she handled everything correctly from the TriCare HMO perspective; she was fully aware that no matter how you sliced it, I was in bad shape. This promised to be a long and expensive endeavor. We had both heard horror stories about patients being declined benefits because they neglected to dot some i or cross some t.

She also called Jon, whom Anne, his wife, was dropping off at the airport for a Secret Service assignment. "I'll be right over," Jon told his mom, ready to drop everything to be at my side.

"Dad's in good hands, so you go ahead with your trip and you can call for an update when you land," she told him. "But don't bother calling the hospital—they've checked him in as John Doe to avoid publicity."

"Okay, Mom. Anne and the girls are heading your way," he said, "and please leave word on my voice mail if anything changes."

"I sure will," she said reassuringly, completely unaware of how very dire the situation was about to become.

I was still strapped flat on my back but was able to make out half-a-dozen doctors pouring over my MRI. Their grim demeanor did little to bolster my confidence, and neither did the words I was about to hear from one of them.

"General, I have seen many cases almost identical to yours, and I am going to put it to you straight. . . . You are never going to walk again, and it is highly doubtful that you will ever regain any use of your hands. My hope is that sometime down the road—way down the road—you might be able to move your fingertips enough to operate the toggles on an electric wheelchair, but we can't even guarantee that."

I rolled my eyes in the direction of the voice that had just given me the very grim prognosis. "Your name isn't God, is it?" I asked.

"No, sir, it is not," the doctor responded.

"Then we'll see about that," I snapped back at him.

\* \* \*

*I have often found that when somebody tells me I can't do something, I will fight that much harder to prove him wrong; and that was certainly the case with this doctor's completely inappropriate prediction. His dismal prognosis actually bolstered my confidence, as if he'd thrown down the gauntlet to fire me up. As I lay there unable to move, I felt 100 percent certain that I would battle back.*

What I didn't know at the time was that nobody in the history of recorded medicine had ever recovered from a spinal injury such as mine.

*Chapter Six* ✤

# THE UNDERTAKER

June 1977–July 1987

Finding a house in the D.C. area proved to be an even worse nightmare than I had anticipated. I was due to begin work at the Army Military Personnel Center (MILPERCEN) in less than a week, but considering the cost of living, inflation, and extraordinarily high interest rates, finding a place within our price range was not looking good. We had forty thousand dollars budgeted for the home, but we soon learned that a decent place would cost us seventy thousand—a lot of money in 1977—and that's what we paid for a nice home out in Kings Park West. It was farther out than we had originally intended, but these were quality homes in a sprawling subdivision, and Fairfax County had a great school system. So we settled into our four-bedroom, two-story colonial home on Swinton Drive in Fairfax, Virginia.

————

When I reported to my new assignment on Monday, I found an extremely empathetic boss in Colonel Ostrowidski, the chief of the division at the personnel center. He understood the trauma associated with moving into Washington because he owned a home in the same subdivision and knew what it meant to have every spare penny of your pay going into a house payment.

"I've got some exciting news that might dampen the blow," he said. "Tomorrow morning the promotion list will be announced and you're on it. You just came out below the zone for lieutenant colonel so you are no longer a major."

What a great way to start the new job, and totally unexpected. That made twice in a row that I had been chosen for that select below-the-zone early promotion—and timing could not have been any better since I was due to close on the new house the following day. (Even though the raise would not take effect until the promotion actually became official, at least we knew that it was coming.)

Later, I met with Colonel Charlie Johnson, Chief of Majors Division. "Since one of the factors we evaluate in the personnel files is a soldier's physical conditioning, I like to encourage the same here in the office. A bunch of us get together for an hour or so every day during lunch and head on over to Bolling Air Force Base or the old Coast Guard station for a nice run. We'd love to have you join us." What a great way to run the office—and I had found a number of commanders who were less than agreeable to far less.

"Sir, you will *not* have to do any arm twisting on that. I look forward to getting out there with you."

"Excellent. The only other order of business is something you're not going to be thrilled about, and I'm almost embarrassed to bring it up," he said, and I was thinking, *Okay, here it comes. . . .* "In one of the worst Army decisions since Custer attacked at Little Bighorn, the U.S. Army decided to rent this entire building from Mr. Hoffman, but let Hoffman keep the parking concession. So what I'm saying is you have to pay to park here. We can either deduct it from your paycheck or you can pay direct, doesn't matter."

That caught my attention. I wish I would have brought Mr. Hoffman along to negotiate my house deal for me.


My initial assignment was as the professional development officer, where I took calls from majors all over the world who were in the Infantry or Aviation branches and advised them in terms of what they needed to do to develop their careers and to maximize their chances of promotion and command selection.

We would screen thousands of individual personnel files and analyze each one, then communicate to the individual what steps should be taken to become branch-qualified for promotion. Civilians rarely understand the complexity involved in a successful military career. Every officer efficiency report (OER) is prepared and reviewed by tiers of leadership in order to reduce the chance that personal animosity might play a role and to ensure that the officer's performance is accurately recorded.

But officers' advancement went beyond the OER system. They had to have "military bearing," look like fit soldiers proud to wear their country's uniform. So we identified people who might have been overweight and told them, "Given your current height and weight and the photograph in your file, you're probably not going to be selected unless you correct that."

It was a highly rewarding job in which I met a lot of good people and worked with a tremendous group of officers. There were eighteen majors assigned to my division, all the pick of the litter. Many of them went on to do some great things for the Army.

Lieutenant Colonel Carl Cavezza came in to replace Colonel Charlie Johnson as my boss. Cavezza would go on to become a three-star. Above him was Brigadier General Robert M. Elton, who would go on to become a three-star and Deputy Chief of Staff of the Army in Charge of Personnel (DCSPERS). General Elton and I would cross paths over and over throughout my career. Our first in-depth interaction came as a result of complaints he was getting from an irate division commander at Fort Lewis.

"Hugh, pack your bags," General Elton said, after he called me to report to his office. "General Cavazos [not to be confused with Lieutenant Commander *Cavezza*, in our office] has a bug up his ass about something he thinks we're screwing up on, so I want you to fly out there with me to the 9th I.D. [Infantry Division] in Seattle and see if we can make him happy."

"Any idea what the problem is, sir?" I asked, hoping to get something that would help me to prepare.

"The way he feels about this office, I'm sure we'll get an earful," he said, shaking his head as if this was not the first time.

"To be blunt, for some reason you guys have decided to use me and Fort Lewis as a goddamn dumping ground for your deadwood colonels. I've got a list of all these homesteaders [individuals who try to stay in the same place] and I want them the hell moved." General Elton and I were sitting across a conference table from an irate two-star, and even though he had said "you guys," he was looking directly at General Elton. At that moment it hit me where I had seen him before, and it had been under very different circumstances.

It was 1965 and I was a first lieutenant in the reserves, and during one of my command-information classes at Fort Jackson, my instructor played a film clip of Peter, Paul and Mary singing "This Land Is Your Land, This Land Is My Land," intercut with various shots of America and soldiers; it was well done and extremely touching. While I was standing at the rear of the class watching the clip, I noticed that the active duty senior evaluator for our summer camp, a lieutenant colonel, had come in and was standing directly next to me. I really didn't pay much attention until the clip was almost finished, but when I glanced over at him at that point I was surprised—and, I have to admit, greatly touched—that he was crying, and tears were running down his face. That's how much the film meant to him, and in my mind, that's how much he cared about our great country and the soldiers risking their lives for it. Before he left I was able to make out his name, and it was Cavazos—the same officer who was now a two-star reaming out my boss. (I would later learn that General Cavazos was a legend, a war hero who was the first Hispanic American to become a Brigadier General, and would go on to become the first Hispanic to become a four-star—not to mention one of the greatest bosses I ever had.)

He had just rattled off the names of a number of colonels he believed had long since outlived their value to the Army and was launching another barrage at General Elton. "So am I going to get more damn MILPERCEN double-talk or do you think maybe you can do something about it this time, General?"

"General, that's exactly why I brought Major Shelton along. Although I will be very much on top of it, you will not find a better man to make it happen." Strong words from my boss to the two-star, and they were certainly words that motivated me to make sure that it did happen. As soon as we left the meeting, I was on the phone back to MILPERCEN to start the process.

Even though the meeting had become heated, it was a great learning experience for me, and it would be one of many lessons I would learn from Bob Elton. Because of the time difference, we decided to spend the night and fly back to D.C. the following morning. This worked for me, as long as I got back in time to take the boys trick-or-treating, since it was Halloween.

The trek from house to house on Swinton and up around Wycliff and Eland yielded Jon (wearing his football uniform, of course) and Jeff (Darth Vader from the new *Star Wars* film that had taken the country by storm) enough candy to finance their dentist's next three vacations; but the real shocker came after the boys turned in.

"How do you like my costume?" asked Carolyn. I looked her up and down, and the thing was—she wasn't wearing a costume. Weird. So naturally, like any husband, I figured there was *something* I was supposed to notice, so I went down the mental checklist. Hair? No, that hadn't changed. Weight loss? Well, if anything she might have put on a half pound or so, but I wasn't about to mention that. Finally, I gave up.

"You know what? I do, I really think it's . . . fantastic," I said.

"It's a good thing you always tell the truth, because you're a *terrible* liar," she said, laughing. "I thought it would be fun for me to go as a pregnant woman. We're going to have another baby, Hugh." My mouth about hit the floor but I could not have asked for any better news. We hugged, and even Sentry did his best to come over and join the celebration. Only three years old, he was already having terrible problems with a degenerative back disorder—but it was great that he seemed as excited as I was about our ever-growing family.

* * *

A few days later, I got another great surprise. I was appointed Chief of Assignments, where I had eighteen majors working for me and we made every major's assignment anywhere in the world for the entire U.S. Army—that's 14,000 assignments. I was "frocked" to the rank of lieutenant colonel, which is another way of saying I was allowed to pin on the rank but would not actually be paid as a lieutenant colonel until my promotion number came up almost a year later. This was one of the easiest assignments I've ever had, and it was completely due to the dedicated, talented staff I had working for me.

The winter passed, and we were fortunate that it was a mild one. I returned to the office on Tuesday, May 30, 1978, after a three-day Memorial Day holiday weekend spent entirely with Carolyn and the boys. With the new baby due in a week, she was appreciative to have had the help.

The morning flew by and I was well out the door for our noontime run when Cherri, the executive assistant to Colonel Cavezza, called out, "You've got a phone call from your wife." The guys were already en route to the car, so I said, "Tell her I'll call her back after the run," but then I remembered that she was in her ninth month of pregnancy, so I decided I'd better take the call. "Hey, Cherri, never mind. Have her hang on, I'll be right there."

"You'd better come right home, I need to go to the hospital now," Carolyn said, almost before I picked up the phone. I ran outside so fast I actually got to my car before any of the others got to theirs. "The baby's coming!" I yelled to them out the window as I peeled away at breakneck speed.

In no time I spun around the corner from Wycliff onto Swinton Drive and fishtailed into my driveway. Carolyn was already standing there, suitcase in hand, and was in the car almost before the wheels had stopped turning; I slipped it into Reverse and was in and out faster than a Formula One pit stop.

"Hurry, Hugh," Carolyn pleaded. "These contractions are almost nonstop and they are strong. Please—hurry."

"Do you think an F-15 could go any faster?" I shot back, pretty proud of the way I was navigating the lunchtime traffic.

Carolyn is usually calm under any circumstance, but as I approached the I-95 entrance ramp, either she was in a great deal of pain or about to deliver right there on my leather seats—maybe both. "Hugh, I'm not kidding, we're not even on the highway yet. You're going to have to drive faster." The speedometer needle was already almost pinned.

"Don't worry, the highway entrance is just up ahead, but I'm going to make a very quick stop at McDonald's here first—not a big order," I said, then joked as if I were turning into the into the lot as we passed it.

"Henry Hugh Shelton, you are not funny," she said. But I sure thought I was.

"I can do the drive-up window if you'd prefer. . . ." Somehow I don't think at that moment she was appreciative of my sense of humor, but I was just so thrilled to finally be there with her to experience this incredible life event after having missed the births of both Jon and Jeff—something I feel bad about to this day.

Fortunately we did make it to the Fort Belvoir, Virginia, hospital in time, although not by much. I walked Carolyn into the emergency room, but by the time I got back in there after parking the car, I was already being summoned to don a gown and prepare to enter the delivery room. That would have really been something if I went O for three and she delivered while I was parking, but fortunately that was not the case.

When I entered, Carolyn was pushing and biting her lip in pain. The doctor, who turned out to be one she'd never seen before—along with incredibly patient and understanding nurses—gave her encouragement while I felt like a fifth wheel—totally helpless. As the baby started to crown and the doctor was so instrumental in helping to bring a new life into the world, I thought to myself, *Now that guy's got an interesting job* . . . not a job that I'd want to do, but it was amazing nonetheless. Just a moment later he confirmed what I could actually see for myself: "It's a boy."

He was a precious, eight-pound, two-ounce boy and we would name him Mark Phillip. I could not have been more elated. Better yet, he was healthy and Carolyn was doing great. It was one of the most joyous days of my life, but once again I sadly remembered that I had missed two other glorious days, when Jon and Jeff were born. As I drove Carolyn and Mark home the next day, I silently thanked God that Carolyn's mother and father had been there by her side on both those occasions.

———

In conjunction with my hardworking team, Major assignment-satisfaction percentages were off the charts; in the case of a Leavenworth graduating class, 100 percent of the nine hundred graduates reported being satisfied with their assignments. Lesson learned: work hard to make the system work rather than let the system work you. It was one I would come back to throughout my career.

I completed my job as the chief of assignments and it was announced that as a lieutenant colonel I would become a battalion commander and have the opportunity to lead a 600–750-person battalion; even though at that point I had no idea where that command might be. Still, I will never forget the day I saw my name on that list; it was a real professional milestone.

————

The Army does offer you choices as to where you would like to go next—at least they like you to think you have a choice. Every time I submitted my personal wish list, I repeated the same place for choices one, two, and three: *82nd Airborne Division.* You would think they would get the point, but it seemed that the more I wanted the 82nd, the farther it slipped away.

One day, Colonel Denny Leach—a friend who worked down the hall and handled lieutenant colonels and colonels—came into my office and closed the door.

"Hugh, it hasn't been released yet but I have some great news for you."

I brightened right up. I was finally going to the 82nd Airborne.

"You're going to command a battalion in the 9th Infantry Division at Fort Lewis, Washington." *So much for the 82nd*, I thought as he beamed and waited for my reaction. "What do you think?" Fort Lewis was a large post south of Seattle, an area many considered ideal.

I've always felt bad about my response: "Colonel, it beats a kick in the teeth." It was as though I begrudged hitting a double because I didn't hit a home run. Part of my reaction was due to the location. After four years in Hawaii, we had so enjoyed being back on the East Coast, near our families, but Fort Lewis would take us all the way out to the West Coast. Still, the bottom line was that I was getting my command, and, even better, an *infantry* command—and I couldn't have been any happier about that. Battalion command is an important milestone in a combat officer's career, as few advance to senior rank without first having led a battalion.

————

It was the summer of 1979, and I spent the next week painting the Fairfax house and getting it into tiptop shape so we could put it on the rental market and hope for the best. I must have done a pretty good job of it, since my next-door neighbor saw the end result and rented it himself.

We packed up the three boys (now ages twelve, nine, and one), lifted Sentry into the car (his back had gotten so bad he could no longer jump into the car on his own), and embarked on our three-thousand-mile cross-country journey from one Washington to the other. It was not one of our better trips. We only had seven days before I was due at my job and Mark did not nap well in the car. While at home the one-year-old would easily fall asleep just as soon as Carolyn put him into his crib, but that was far from the case in a car packed with four talkative family-members.

A few sightseeing stops became welcome reliefs. We piled out of the car and stretched our legs amidst the beautiful Black Hills of South Dakota where we viewed the majestic Mount Rushmore. The following day we explored the Little Bighorn Battlefield, where General Custer and 263 U.S. Army soldiers died fighting thousands of Lakota and Cheyenne warriors. We enjoyed them both, although probably not as much as everyone enjoyed my announcement that we had finally arrived at Fort Lewis.

———

I reported in to the 9th Division commanding general—my new boss— who turned out to be none other than Major General Dick Cavazos—the same one I had seen crying over the Peter, Paul and Mary film clip; and subsequently met when he declared war on the two "personnel pukes" (General Elton and me) who "flew out to give him more lip service about his

## Current Level of Command

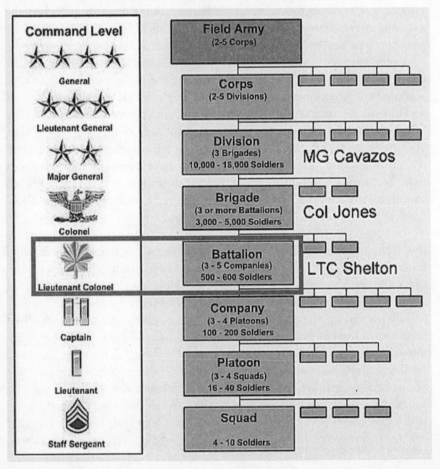

deadwood colonels." *Maybe he'll think differently now that I'm a member of his team,* I tried to convince myself as he stared me down from the other side of his desk.

The truth is that Dick Cavazos was a great soldier and a fascinating man. Coming from a large Hispanic family of Texas ranch workers, rumor had it that his father was the foreman of the famous King Ranch. After earning his commission through ROTC, he won the second-highest decoration for valor, the Distinguished Service Cross, in Korea in 1953. In Vietnam in 1967, he won a second DSC.

As I sat across from him over his sprawling desk, he looked me over coldly—it was hard to tell if it was with contempt or just plain disregard. "What makes you think working in the personnel business back in Washington qualifies you to command an infantry battalion?"

I assured him that I had not been in MILPERCEN all my life; in fact I had been there for less than two years. I was ready to go—ready to prove myself to him and ready to learn from a great leader and a great war fighter, such as he was known to be. Both statements were completely true and neither was an attempt to brown-nose the new boss. He could see that I was sincere, and from that moment on, he and I had a productive discussion that led to an exceptional history together.

He talked about colonels who would buy expensive Gore-Tex boots and all kinds of custom recreational equipment and they would be out in the field feeling warm and fuzzy while the troops would be freezing to death in their rain-soaked field jackets because they couldn't afford to buy the newest civilian gear.

"Always dress like the troops do," he told me. "That way you'll know what their level of pain is."

Great advice that I would take to heart, and I'm sure it came from some personal experiences in Korea or Vietnam. If that was any indication of what it was going to be like working for this man, it would be an amazing experience, I thought. Happily, that was only the first of countless pieces of wisdom he would share. General Cavazos was a great teacher and a great mentor.

"Tomorrow when you take command of the 3rd Battalion, you will bear the distinction of leading the worst battalion in the 9th Infantry Division—maybe even the worst in the entire history of the division. They've got the worst reenlistment rate and are in dire need of effective leadership. You're going into a terrible state of affairs, and frankly, I doubt if anyone could turn it around."

"I accept your challenge, General."

\* \* \*

The following morning was one of the most memorable of my life, and neither Carolyn nor I will ever forget how it unfolded on the parade field of the 9th Infantry Division at Fort Lewis. We had just moved into our beautiful quarters—a thirty-five-hundred-square-foot two-story brick house with a nice office, spectacular Tacoma green lawn, and a playground right out front for all the neighborhood children—and driven over to the field for the festivities. The division band played for hundreds of eager spectators, and Carolyn and the boys took their seats front and center. The brigade commander passed the colors and I proudly stepped up to receive the battalion flag from outgoing commander D. A. Miller. By doing so, I had officially become battalion commander of the "Go Devils," the 3rd Battalion of the 60th Infantry Brigade—and I was 100 percent confident that whatever "challenges" the battalion may have faced before my arrival, I would face them head-on and turn them into a highly respected, top-notch fighting component. I don't know what Miller had done to piss off the general, but it must have been something. When the ceremony was finished, rather than the general presenting the outgoing commander his going-away gift, as is the tradition, he had instructed his driver to hand it to Miller.

Following the ceremony, I made my rounds, starting with Brigadier General Ed Trobaugh, with whom I'd served as battalion XO in Hawaii. Now the assistant division commander for operations, Trobaugh had a slightly higher opinion of the Go Devils. Maybe things weren't so bad after all.

I then met the brigade commander, Colonel Lincoln Jones—and that meeting was about as comfortable as tap-dancing through a minefield while blindfolded. Not thirty seconds after meeting the man, he handed me a file and said, "Really great to meet you, Colonel—and I hear you just came in from personnel. That's my private personnel file and I'd really appreciate your taking a look and giving me your honest assessment of what you think my chances are of becoming a general." I felt like I had just been handed the poison apple and I sure as hell wasn't going to bite into it. The last thing I was about to do was critique my boss's file. He continued, "Be assured this is just between us, off the record, and you can tell it like it is; if there are problems, I want to hear about them."

"Sir," I said as I handed him back the file without opening it, "I can assure you that you are very highly regarded back in Washington and I have no doubt that you will make general. I don't need to see your file to know that."

I'm not sure he knew what to make of me at that moment—whether he thought I was blowing him off or whether he believed me. Either way, he seemed satisfied—and later on, he did make general.

General Cavazos—being the great coach and mentor that he was—frequently joined us in the field; and each and every time, he would take interest and observe how I was handling myself as a young battalion commander. When there were things he felt I could have accomplished more effectively, he would kneel down in the sand, get out a stick, and say something to the effect of, "I watched what you did and you did great. I like your plan, but let me show you an alternate approach that you might want to think about the next time." Here was this highly respected, highly decorated two-star general who consistently took the time to get out there and mentor this young lieutenant colonel. He would sketch it out with no bluster and no hectoring—just soldier-to-soldier. He was a wonderful role model whom I've attempted to emulate in many ways.

Next, I went down to my battalion and discovered that we had lieutenants—not captains—serving as company commanders. That was very odd. Plus, the sergeant major—a good man who had been awarded the Medal of Honor—had physical problems that precluded his participation in any physical activities with the battalion: he couldn't run with them, oversee their field exercises: he couldn't run with them or oversee their final exercises—couldn't really do much of anything of a physical nature.

The one bright point was the S3, a dynamic captain filling a major's position, Lee Mortenson. "You know, Lee, I think we've got some real potential here," I told him. "Our leaders are a little inexperienced and we need a good, solid NCO corps, but we've got a lot to work with." The following morning I would see why Lee had looked at me as though I were crazy to think that our motley group showed potential. What I saw was a scene I could never have imagined and not one I would ever care to repeat.

I had set up an early morning four-mile battalion run in which all seven hundred soldiers would run in unison, grouped by company, with me leading the pack beside the battalion colors and staff, and then dropping back to run beside the various companies. The division standard was four miles in thirty-six minutes, and in my mind there was no reason why any of them should not have been able to handle that pace. As it turned out, most of the senior NCOs fell out early, but those who did stick it out presented an even more appalling situation.

Instead of inspiring their companies with motivational cadences, a number of the senior noncommissioned officers led their companies in anti-Army, anti-U.S.-military chants—things like "Hell no, we won't go" and "Screw the Army." I was horrified. At first I felt sick to my stomach, but by the time I got back to the battalion I was spitting nails.

"I want you to get me the name of every NCO that led any kind of a derogatory chant," I told the command sergeant major. "And while you're at it, you tell them I already took down five names and those five better be on that list or I'll know they're lying to me—and let's just say that I don't take to that kindly."

"Yes, sir," he said with a sharp salute before leaving to secure the names.

A short while later he returned with eighteen names—each of which I subsequently read to my adjutant. "I will not put up with what I witnessed out there this morning and I don't ever want to hear it again," I told him while handing over the eighteen files. "Before the close of business today, I want 'bar to reenlistment' papers drawn up on every one of these noncommissioned officers. If they don't like the Army, the Army doesn't like them. And then I want you to notify their company commanders that I want to see them up here before they go home, and before they release their companies for the evening." He looked at me somewhat puzzled, like he had never heard of such an outrageous request. "Are you not understanding me? Because if you are, get with it."

At 4:00 P.M. he came back and announced that he had completed the task, and by 4:30 I had met with each company commander personally; I put the fear of God into them on how this was no longer going to be an organization consisting of rabbles that could do whatever they wanted without regard for what was right. Then I instructed them to find each of the eighteen NCOs and personally administer the bars to reenlistment. By 6:00 P.M. they all reported that they had done so, and I left them with an admonition to spread the word: "From this moment on we are conducting business around here as *professionals*. The bad apples will no longer cause the good soldiers to leave the army because I am going to identify the duds and send their asses packing. The good soldiers will have a great reason to re-up. This is *the new 3-60* and this is how it's going to be." That message reverberated loud and clear.

I felt like I had earned my pay that first day on the job and looked forward to getting home to our beautiful new quarters and spending the evening with the family. I picked up the phone to let Carolyn know I'd be home shortly. "One day down, five hundred forty-five left to go." I told her, referring to the eighteen-month assignment that was standard at that time (later it would be extended to two years). "I'm on my way."

"See you soon," she replied, but I could tell there was something off in her voice.

When I walked in I was flooded with the indescribable aroma of the finest meal known to mankind, thanks to Carolyn at the helm. While she tended to the feast in the kitchen, I reached down and lifted Mark from the playpen and yelled hi to the boys in the family room. Jon was glued to the TV (which appeared to be cranked up to one hundred decibels) but Jeff raced in and seemed almost ready to burst with his news. "Daddy," he said sadly, pointing to the corner of the kitchen. "It's Sentry. He feels real bad."

I quickly glanced at Carolyn, who almost imperceptibly shook her head to indicate that things did not look good. Holding Mark in my left arm, I knelt down beside our five-year-old pet and reached over to stroke him gently—but before I got anywhere close he let out a wincing yelp of pain, followed by long, tortured whines. Mark became frightened and started to cry in my arms, and by this time Jon had come in to see what was going on. "Guys, Sentry's back has gotten really bad and he's in a tremendous amount of pain . . ." I explained, attempting to prepare them for the inevitable.

The next day, during lunch while Jon and Jeff were in school, I went home and carried Sentry to the car for his last ride to the vet.

When I returned home that evening, Carolyn and I sat on the same sofa that had accompanied us from Florida to Hawaii to Montgomery to Virginia and now to Fort Lewis, and we had a discussion with the boys about pets, life and death, moving from city to city, and most important, about the overriding constant that would always weave it all together—family.

It was one helluva start to my time as battalion commander, but another one of those times when I felt especially blessed. I was surrounded by loved ones and embarking on a job where I could really make a difference.

———

About a week into my command, General Cavazos gathered all twenty-six battalion commanders together to discuss retention—which battalions were getting the most reenlistments, and which the least. The way it was handled by General Cavazos, you did *not* want to be anywhere near the bottom of that list. He never mentioned anything about the top battalions; instead he just focused on the bottom three, and specifically the one on the bottom.

When he stepped up to speak you could hear a pin drop; each and every one of the twenty-six commanders was silently praying, *Please, God, whatever you do, don't let me be last.* Twenty-five of them would have their prayers answered.

"All right, here we go," he said, seeming almost eager to mortify the unfortunate loser at the bottom. "Hearty congratulations to numbers one through twenty-five. The big loser award goes to the battalion with the absolute worst—and in this instance a particularly pathetic—reenlistment percentage. The *3-60 Infantry, the Go Devils*. Shelton, you're from MILP-ERCEN. Do you think you can turn this around?"

It was my first reenlistment meeting at the division and my battalion's retention rate was dead last; it was beyond humiliating. I wasn't used to being on the bottom in anything. But it sure provided a motivation for me to do something about it.


At the end of the week, the general called me about another matter. He had selected my battalion to be a part of the OPFOR element in an up-coming Joint Readiness Training Exercise to take place at the Yakima Training Center, a six-hundred-square-mile Army training ground sepa-rated from Fort Lewis by Mount Rainier. OPFOR stands for "opposing force," and in the case of Army war games, it's generally considered to be the "bad guys." While it may sound like an honor to bear such a distinc-tion, I was well aware that such a role was usually reserved for the worst battalions so that the BLUFOR (blue force)—the "good guys"—had the best chance of winning. Cavazos viewed my 3rd Battalion as the 1962 Mets against Mickey Mantle and the mighty '61 Yankees. Okay, I ac-cepted that—but that didn't mean I couldn't do everything in my power to pull off an upset.

I was to be teamed up with another battalion coming in from the 7th Division at Fort Ord, California. Our combined force of fifteen hundred soldiers would take on more than five thousand soldiers that comprised the eight battalions that would form the BLUFOR.


Since I'd been there barely a week, my first step was to get my guys into the field and shake them out—see what they were made of. Were they really as bad as Cavazos thought they were? I called in the company com-manders.

"On Monday we will head out to the South Rainier training area and spend three days practicing various actions—attacks, night infils, and such—then on Thursday afternoon we will commence with a Battalion in the Defense."

South Rainier is a very desolate area, and very remote. As for the Bat-talion in the Defense, I knew it was General Cavazos's pet exercise—the one demonstration that would instantly reveal just how good—or bad—a battalion really was. It's a timed exercise to test how well a battalion sets up its defenses in twelve hours—meaning that within twelve hours you had better be completely dug in and camouflaged, with fields of fire prepared and range cards made out; it's everything you need to do to have an effective, integrated defense prepared—and a great way to get a feel for that battalion's capabilities.

We departed for the training area on one of the ugliest days I had ever seen, with nonstop downpours that blackened the skies and numbed the skin it was so cold. To my utter surprise, the battalion wasn't half bad during Monday's attack exercises, and they were even better during Tuesday's night infiltrations. *We really might have a chance to win this thing,* I began to think.

By Wednesday the rain had still not let up—not unusual for Washington State in April. I started the timer and twelve hours later I would "walk the line" to see how well they had done.

At about 10:30 A.M. I started walking the line and it was a *disaster.* I told them what was wrong and gave them an hour to fix it. Noon rolled around and it was no better. "Guess what?" I said to the company commanders. "We are going to stay in the field another day, and we are going to get it right." This continued over and over again all the way until Saturday, and I was fully aware that by then I was running into their weekend, but I couldn't have cared less. We would do it to standard before we left. That was the price they were paying for not getting it right to start with. By 3:00 P.M. Saturday they finally passed—but just barely, and it was time to head back.

"But, sir, where are the buses positioned?" asked one of the company commanders.

"I'm so glad you asked that," I told him. "The buses are now back at Fort Lewis. They were positioned right here on Thursday, when we were supposed to go back. They even stayed an extra day until Friday. But it's now Saturday and there are no more buses, so we will make a forced march [faster than a standard "road march"] back the thirty miles, and we will march straight through the night, and through the rain, and through whatever the hell else it takes to get back there, and we will take one short break an hour for you to change socks and check feet. Now, does anyone else have any questions about buses?"

And the march back began, along with heavy mortars to carry, and machine guns, and soaking-wet clothing—it was a mess, but it was important training and was essential that they understood the importance of the mission.

As the sun rose we approached the base garrison area, and they were about the most bedraggled troops I had ever seen. They looked like the devil himself, but eventually they made it back. We went back out the following week and somehow, magically, they got it absolutely perfect the first time. Funny how that works.

Something even stranger occurred the first Monday after we got back. I went into the office to find everyone walking on eggshells because their feet were so sore, and mine were no better. To my utter amazement, the enlistment sergeant ran in and announced to me that already that day (and it was not even noon) ten soldiers had dropped by his office and signed up to reenlist. Between my aggressive response to the anti-Army chants and what played out during that field training, they could see that the standards were substantially higher than the prior week, and they were proud to be a part of those higher standards. Three weeks later, when the reenlistment stats came out, we had gone from dead last all the way to first place, the absolute highest percentage of reenlistments of any of the battalions.

When Operation Brave Shield rolled around, it was played out at both Yakima Training Center and Fort Lewis. At Fort Lewis, it was my battalion teamed up with one from Fort Ord, against the entire 3rd Brigade, 9th Division, who were commanded by Colonel Clyde Tate. The first thing I did—and this was even before the exercise began—was to have my S2 (intelligence officer) infiltrate Colonel Tate's office after hours and "borrow" his official command portrait, which was framed and mounted on the wall of his office. We took the portrait, copied it, and turned it into a very realistic-looking old-time western wanted poster that said WANTED—CRAZY CLYDE. We mounted those posters all over Fort Lewis. He didn't think it was funny but we all sure did. I figured if it's two against eight and there was such a great chance of our going down in flames, we might as well have fun in the process.

It was a raw, rainy night when the exercises rolled around and the "games" were set to begin—and these were realistic exercises involving thousands of soldiers and pieces of equipment spread over hundreds of square miles at Yakima.

Rather than face that mighty BLUFOR head-on and see how fast we could get annihilated, I suggested a very bold move called a "night infiltration"—something we had been rehearsing for weeks. One of the most difficult infantry maneuvers, it involves ascertaining exactly where the enemy is positioned and sneaking past their defenses and right through their lines without getting shot—then reassembling in their rear area to attack from behind.

When I suggested this, the brigade commander from Fort Ord's 7th

Division (who would be my boss for the exercise), thought I was nuts. "We can't do that," he initially complained. But after conferring with his own battalion commander, Lieutenant Colonel Dave Meade, he finally went along with it.

We started our move at about 10:00 P.M., and by midnight it was raining like the devil, with temperatures that had to be approaching the freezing mark. Still, my battalion's plan was on track. Then, much to my dismay, I heard a radio call from the other battalion commander: "My troops have had it. I have to pull them back and reassemble. We've kind of fallen apart over here."

It was an amazing call. The conditions were just too tough for them, and apparently they assumed that they were too difficult for us, too. Well, the hell with that. We proceeded anyway. And damned if we didn't end up successfully infiltrating the BLUFOR lines. By around four in the morning I received word that all my companies had reassembled as coherent units *behind* the enemy lines and were ready to attack their assigned objectives— BLUFOR battalion command posts and the main brigade command post.

By dawn, the 3-60 Infantry owned all the BLUFOR mortars and three of their command posts. My one battalion—the very guys who a week earlier didn't seem to know what the hell they were doing—effectively executed an almost impossibly difficult infantry maneuver, and we ended up winning the whole damn "war" the first night.

I thought it was great fun. General Cavazos did not. Although he couldn't have been more pleased with our performance, he was irate with Colonel Tate for allowing such a thing to happen. It's too bad, because Tate was a good guy and, in truth, an excellent commander—but the general no longer saw it that way. In time he pulled back, but during that week he came exceedingly close to relieving Tate from duty. So as not to add insult to injury, I had my S2 sneak back into his office to return the command portrait to its place on the wall, but this time the S2 was nailed—captured by Colonel Tate himself.

"I've got your S2," the colonel said with glee when he called me.

"That's quite all right, Colonel," I replied. "You can go ahead and keep him, the exercise is over and I don't really care much for the man anyway," I said with a smile. Five minutes later the S2 showed up back at our office, pleased as punch at the way it had all played out.

A few days later, at the outbrief for the exercise, General Cavazos publically singled out 3-60 for their outstanding performance in front of numerous visiting generals and commanders from all over the division. Our reputation was starting to improve.

———

Things continued to improve and our reenlistment numbers remained high. We had not given one waiver for reenlisting, nor did we in any way lower our standards. In fact, we continued to *raise* those standards. Even though had I started out with a firm hand, I made sure to supplement it with a great deal of honest, objective, sincere positive reinforcement.

I started a breakfast program for those within ninety days of reenlisting who were recommended by their first sergeants and the company commanders. During those breakfasts, I would talk about the great service that this Army provided to the nation and the role each of them played, often quoting Rudyard Kipling about the archetypal British soldier, Tommy Adkins: ". . . For it's Tommy this, an' Tommy that, an' 'Chuck him out, the brute.' But it's 'Saviour of 'is country' when the guns begin to shoot . . ." The troops loved it. Before long they were asking, "Who's been invited to the breakfast?" It became a big deal.

———

I've always believed that publicly rewarding the good guys is a fundamental principle in effective leadership, so I held monthly awards formations at the end of every payday and called several men per company up in front of the battalion to receive certificates of merit or other awards. We made up our own certificates and had them professionally printed. Word quickly spread that it was far more fun to be a good guy in 3-60 than it was to be a troublemaker.

———

On the other hand, I continued to crack the whip, particularly in matters that involved AWOL (absent without leave), insubordination, and drug-abuse cases. I was harsh because I had to keep the rot from spreading.

Much to my delight, I became known as "The Undertaker" as word of my actions became more and more exaggerated—finally reaching the point where rumor had it that if I found you incorrigibly unsuited for service, you would be called to my office, and by the time I was finished with you they would have to carry you out feet first because I would "bury your ass." I became the equivalent of an Old West hanging judge, and the 3-60 became the top battalion in the division.

———

Commanding that battalion turned out to be a great experience, with lots of ups and downs along the way. General Cavazos would eventually move on, and General Howie Stone came in to take his place.

General Stone offered me the chance to become his G3 (operations officer) which was a great compliment since the G3 position was highly sought after and an important addition to have on one's résumé; one normally reserved for War College graduates. For about two seconds I was tempted to take it, but then I declined. I had unfinished business with my own battalion.

Two years later, I did move up to G3, after I'd had the chance to mold the battalion to my full satisfaction. By that time General Bob Elton had taken over as division commander, so it was another opportunity to work under a boss I both knew and respected. Between June 1981 and June 1982, we were known as the Army's High Technology Test Bed (HTTB), in essence the real-life equivalent of James Bond's Q-branch. We tested all the new equipment and gadgets and developed the tactics and doctrine for the new High Technology Light Division (HTLD) concept—which stressed high mobility and maneuverability. It was important work that entailed reconfiguring the way divisions fought and changed the configuration of battalions.

We came up with entirely new concepts on how to fight using fast attack vehicles, artillery, and aviation (such as the new AH-64 Apache attack helicopter armed with wire-guided TOW [Tube-launched, Optically-tracked, Wire command-link guided] antitank missiles); and we experimented with drones (remotely piloted vehicles and robotics)—very innovative ideas at the time.

Our basic principle was: *hit the enemy hard, back off, and come in from a different direction, constantly pounding him throughout.* These were entirely new tactics for the Army. Since this was a special project directly for the Chief of Staff of the Army, we were able to bypass the normal seven-to-ten-year Army procurement cycle and acquire this equipment almost instantaneously.

I spent one weekend helping to write a new manual on how to fight an infantry battalion in a high-technology air–ground battle to be tested in an upcoming live-fire exercise. While I felt confident that my input contained some innovative suggestions, I was fully aware that it was only a piece of a much bigger picture. But on Monday morning, when I gave my contribution to the assistant division commander—now *Brigadier General* Lincoln Jones—he was so happy he about did a backflip. I was thinking, *Man, this is just one guy's thoughts on how you fight a new light division.* I didn't think it was that big a deal, but I couldn't complain that the boss felt so strongly otherwise.

Although it was rewarding in some ways, the truth is that it was a nightmare job. Not only were we charged with testing all this high-tech equipment, but the Army never relieved us from our original obligation to be armed, trained, and fully ready to fight. And as much as I respected General Elton and considered him a great boss, I was getting zero feedback from him and had no idea whether he felt I was a good G3 or a lousy G3; he just let me do my job, one long day after another.

It taught me an important lesson for the future: take the time to praise people when deserved and, whether positive or negative—provide them with feedback. Rewarding people, especially when they've been working long hours with demanding assignments, would keep them motivated and pressing on—resulting in even greater effort.

It was only through General Elton's wife that I eventually learned his opinion of my performance. One Friday evening at a friend's promotion party, I was just about to leave when Marilyn Elton approached me. "Hugh, just a minute, I need to talk to you. Bob told me something at the table the other morning I thought you would like to hear."

"Yes, ma'am?"

"Bob said, 'Marilyn, you know I used to think I was a pretty hot division G3, but I tell you, I didn't know what a good G3 was until I saw Hugh Shelton in action. He is *really* good.'"

"Thank you very much for sharing that with me," I said sincerely. It was the first feedback I had received in eight months of long days and weekend work. Even though it was only secondhand, it beat hearing nothing by a long shot. General Elton was a brilliant guy, but impossible to read. It was one of many valuable lessons, both good and bad, that I learned from the leaders I worked for.

———

During that same period, I learned that I was going to attend the Industrial College of the Armed Forces (ICAF), which many considered a second-tier school for a combat arms officer. When General Elton read that I had been slated to attend ICAF instead of the highly regarded National War College, he almost became unglued. He picked up the phone without any prompting from me and called the assignment people at MILPERCEN, and the next thing I knew they were telling me the assignment had been amended and I was going to the National War College. Another valuable lesson learned: take care of the people who work for you.

———

Once again, we packed our belongings and loaded up the cars, but just as I locked the front door and turned to leave, I heard the phone ringing inside.

"Hugh, why don't you just let it ring?" Carolyn said from the car, already set to leave. I thought about it—and then I unlocked the door and grabbed the phone. It was Charlie Otstott, the Chief of Staff, who wanted to see me right away.

"Sir, your timing couldn't be much worse. We're all packed and ready to fly. In fact, Carolyn's waiting for me in the car."

"I understand that, Hugh, but this is extremely important—you know I wouldn't ask you, otherwise." Charlie Otstott (who retired as a Lieutenant General Charles Otstott, Deputy Chairman, NATO Military Committee), was another no-nonsense boss and a brilliant individual that I had worked for.

I hustled down to the office while the family waited in the car, wondering what could be so urgent, particularly since I had already turned over the command. When I walked into Colonel Otstott's office, he had this wall-to-wall smile on his face and extended his hand. "Congratulations, Colonel," he said. "I couldn't let you go without personally giving you the great news. You've been selected below the zone for O6 [full colonel], two years early, I might add." It could not have been a more perfect way to end this important chapter in my life, and this would be the third straight time that I was recognized for early promotion.

———

We left Fort Lewis in the summer of 1982 and headed right back to where we came from, our house on Swinton Drive in Fairfax, Virginia. This time, instead of taking the northern route across the U.S. as we had done on the way out, we took the southern one and enjoyed a relaxed trip with lots of laughs and special times. Mark was older, of course, and we took more time to enjoy the sights. Jon had recently gotten his driver's permit, so he drove the Volkswagen most of the way, with Carolyn riding with him; while Jeff, Mark, and I were in the Grand Prix, pulling the boat. I figured if I could handle driving that old "souped up" school bus at sixteen years of age, Jon would have no trouble with the VW, and to nobody's surprise, he did a great job. We camped every other night, and I made sure that one of those nights was at the Grand Canyon. The boys absolutely loved it, and this trip was one of those truly special times that Carolyn and I would always treasure.

We finally arrived back in Fairfax, and it felt almost like going home because this was the first time the boys remembered ever moving back to the same place.

The National War College proved to be a great break from a good number of years in fairly stressful environments with a lot of hard jobs back to back. Fort McNair, a Civil War–era post on Anacostia River, was a friendly place in a wonderful setting, with wide, well-shaded lawns and athletic fields.

It felt nice to be back on the East Coast where all our family lived, and unlike the past few assignments, the hours were regular at the War College.

The school also had an intramural sports program and I ended up running track and playing basketball in a tough "over thirty" league, and I still have the scars to prove it. Of course there was a fierce competition between the various war colleges, and I loved every second of it. We beat Army that year, and I scored the winning shot right at the buzzer in spite of the fact that an Army general on the sidelines pulled me aside and said, "Shelton, if NWC wins this one, your Army career is toast." (As long as he smiled when he said it, I figured I would go ahead and take the shot.)

The National War College was especially great preparation for Chairman in that it was a 100 percent *joint* program that had all the services and many civilian agencies represented. I'd already gotten good exposure to the Air Force, but now I was going to meet peers from the Marine Corps as well as the Navy. There was a wide breadth of subjects and visiting speakers, made richer because the school was located in Washington. Everybody from the President to visiting foreign dignitaries would come to the National War College.

The curriculum was superb, with the scope of case studies and war games instrumental in developing us as strategic thinkers. And we weren't just *military* officers anymore because now members of the interagency organizations studied beside us. My group included CIA officers, FBI special agents, and analysts from the Library of Congress. I learned a great deal from these people, who viewed national security from their own perspectives.

The case study my team conducted would prove incredibly valuable during my time at the Pentagon, and remain so today. It analyzed what it would take to win a war against Iran using the Rapid Deployment Joint Task Force (RDJTF) that was headquartered at MacDill in Tampa and headed by General Bob "Barbed Wire" Kingston. We studied all challenges surrounding a war fighting through the rugged the Zagros Mountains. We clearly saw the formidable task that would be in front of U.S. forces in this scenario. To this day, I have an appreciation for the difference in fighting in Iraq as opposed to the Zagros Mountains in Iran.

———

That year at the National War College was satisfying in every way. It culminated with graduation in the summer of 1983. My follow-on assignment was initially to command a brigade at the 2nd Infantry Division in Korea—but it was to be an unaccompanied tour, which meant being away from the family for thirteen months.

* * *

Because I had about a ninety-day period of time before my departure for Korea, I went to work for the DCSPER (Deputy Chief of Staff, Personnel) of the army in the Pentagon, running a special analytical project that dealt with the manpower needs of the National Guard and the army reserve. It was a detailed and stressful task, overseen by a fair but demanding taskmaster, General "Mad Max" Thurman, also a North Carolina State graduate, who would later lead Southern Command and command the U.S. invasion of Panama.

The reserve-manpower job dragged on into October 1983, keeping me at the Pentagon and prolonging my departure for Korea. Jon was entering his senior year in high school, and Carolyn appreciated having me around.

It was a frustrating project that entailed long hours and volumes of in-depth research, but the real problem was that the numbers were just not adding up to the figures that General John Wickham, the Army Chief of Staff, had provided to the Congress when pressed for an answer during testimony a few weeks earlier. Something was very wrong, and the deadline for my presentation to General Thurman was rapidly approaching. Then late one night in mid-October, while I was on a flight back from the West Coast—out of the clear blue it hit me. One of the individuals working on the project had made an incorrect assumption regarding a formula, and once we corrected that, everything fell into place beautifully.


The following week I was to meet with General Thurman and present to him a detailed PowerPoint briefing that consisted of 172 slides laying out all the details. My boss, Colonel Jack Wheeler (who went on to become a Major General and Commander of the U.S. Army Recruiting Command) was terrified of General Thurman, and he had warned me up front to sail through the slides like lightning, because Thurman was an incredibly quick study who hated wasting time. While I started the day of our meeting with a nice breakfast of bacon and eggs, it's doubtful that Thurman had any breakfast since he was known to eat briefers alive, and according to Colonel Wheeler, I would most likely be his main course.

From the moment I commenced the briefing I felt completely at ease, flying through the slides as I had been instructed to do. Unlike so many others I've encountered throughout my career, I have always felt perfectly comfortable with public speaking, no matter the audience. As far as briefing four-stars, my feeling was that they were very smart people who knew their business—so as long as I knew mine (which I did) and walked in adequately prepared, what was there to be concerned about?

General Thurman was attentive and focused. He probed, questioned, and demanded detailed answers. Colonel Wheeler was visibly nervous and perspiration was literally dripping down his face. At one point General Thurman looked disturbed, upset by something I'd said.

"Hold on there," he interrupted, as Colonel Wheeler nearly had a stroke. "Why are you assuming a retirement age of sixty-two? That assumption has the potential of invalidating every one of your findings."

"Sir, that is an excellent question and I'm glad you asked it," I began, resisting the temptation to call the paramedics just in case Colonel Wheeler passed out. "I assumed the age of sixty-two based on the presentation you made to Congress just last week where *you* made a number of compelling arguments why sixty-two is the age that should be used—and I agree with your proposal."

He thought about it for a moment, then nodded his head. "Good answer. Carry on."

Finally, he stood up and smiled. "Great brief, Colonel." Then he left the office and my boss slumped in his chair. He would live to see another day and I was ecstatic, if for no other reason than that I could finally put that project to bed.

"Hugh, how long would it take you to drive to Fort Bragg?"

*Fort Bragg,* I thought. The 82nd Airborne. "General," I answered, "I can be there in six hours and two minutes if I stop for lunch, six hours flat-out if I don't."

"We've had a brigade come open down there and they need a brigade commander right away. I'm diverting you from the 2nd Infantry Division in Korea to the 82nd Airborne at Fort Bragg. Now I know how excited you were about eating all that kimchi, but do you think you can handle that?"

It was General Bob Elton—my boss—who was now the Army's Deputy Chief of Staff for Personnel; he'd been my commander while I was his division G3 and while assigned to the Military Personnel Center. General Elton himself had been a brigade commander in the 82nd and he loved that division. What's more, he knew how I felt about it.

After enthusiastically assuring him that I could handle it upside down with my hands tied behind my back, I raced home and broke the great

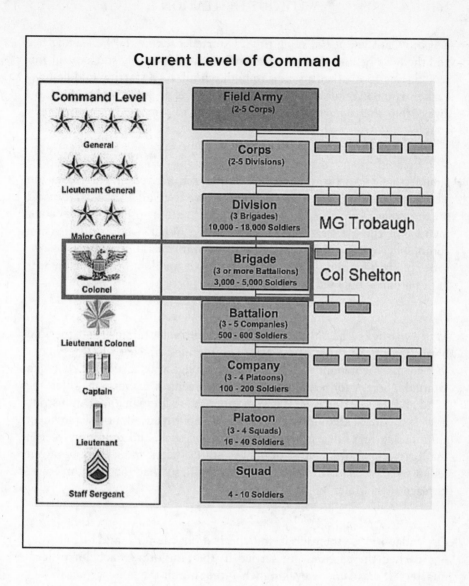

# Current Level of Command

## Command Level

General

Lieutenant General

Major General

Colonel

Lieutenant Colonel

Captain

Lieutenant

Staff Sergeant

**Field Army**
(2-5 Corps)

**Corps**
(2-5 Divisions)

**Division**
(3 Brigades)
10,000 - 18,000 Soldiers

MG Trobaugh

**Brigade**
(3 or more Battalions)
3,000 - 5,000 Soldiers

Col Shelton

**Battalion**
(3 - 5 Companies)
500 - 600 Soldiers

**Company**
(3 - 4 Platoons)
100 - 200 Soldiers

**Platoon**
(3 - 4 Squads)
16 - 40 Soldiers

**Squad**
4 - 10 Soldiers

news to Carolyn; at the same time, I started packing. I'd be leaving her and the boys behind since the academic year had already started and Jon was playing football as a senior in high school. As a starting middle line-backer who had made it as a walk-on, there was no way I was pulling him away from there, but they'd be coming out to join me as soon as they could.

I made that trip in way under six hours, and arrived at Fort Bragg on Thursday morning. Just a few hours later, we were all on the parade field for the change-of-command ceremony and it became official—I was com-mander of the 1st Brigade, 82nd Airborne. What's more, the division commander was Ed Trobaugh, now a two-star general. He'd been my bri-gade commander in the 25th Division, and we got along very well. He was hard but fair—my kind of leader.

My new brigade had three parachute infantry battalions, and the first battallion of the three (the 1-504, commanded by Keith Kellogg, later to become Lieutenant General Keith Kellogg) was scheduled to go to Granada, Spain, for a major NATO reinforcement exercise in which the 82nd had the starring role. We were supposed to jump in and demonstrate how fast America could respond with a rapid transatlantic deployment culminating in a full battalion jump right on time, and right on target in the Iberian Peninsula. Most of my key staff officers and a number of our senior sergeants had already deployed to Spain, so I had the "backup crew" in place at the time.

On Friday I made the rounds and checked out the staff, and on Saturday I unpacked the car and got settled in the temporary bachelor-officers quarters. It was Sunday evening when the shit hit the fan.

"Colonel Shelton? Report to the N+2 room immediately," instructed the alert officer on the phone. When you get a call like that, you don't wait 'til the inning is over and leave at the commercial—that call means get your ass over there double time because the stopwatch has begun the count-down.

At the 82nd, "N-hour" stands for "notification hour"—and in a rapid-deployment environment like the 82nd, it means you have exactly *eigh-teen hours* until wheels are up and that first plane takes off in a deployment of up *to sixteen thousand* troops nonstop, one airplane after the other, *including* the time to prepare all the vehicles for air drop, heavy rigging for load-up, securing all the equipment, loading ammunition, weighing every item per Air Force specifications, and about a thousand other events that take place in a finely detailed sequence—because, most likely, an invasion is imminent.

What's more, just the day before, there had been a rotation that put my brigade as the "push brigade," meaning it was my responsibility to orchestrate the entire division deployment before I deployed myself. Under any circumstance it's an enormous undertaking, but when you just arrived a few days earlier and your entire staff is already deployed more than five thousand miles away—it certainly can be described as a real oh-shit moment.

In addition to myself, the five other brigade-level commanders, along with the commanding general and the two assistant division commanders under him, were all scrambling to get to that secure, fortified N+2 briefing room at division headquarters, named after a former 82nd Airborne Division commander, Matthew Ridgway, of WWII and Korean War fame. We'd learn who the enemy was, what the targets were, and which of our many pre-determined configurations would be utilized.


"Gentleman," General Trobaugh began, "we are about to commence Operation Urgent Fury, the invasion of the island of Grenada [not to be confused with Granada, Spain, where the NATO exercise was to take place]. Radical leftists have overthrown the constitutional government, massacred its leaders, and basically seized the island hostage. Their real muscle is a large contingent of Cuban construction 'workers'—in reality, armed combat engineers building a big international airport at Point Salinas.

To complicate matters, there are eight hundred American medical students at St. George's on the island. President Reagan has authorized military action to free the students and eliminate the radical government."

And with that, we were off and running—quite literally, in my case. I had eighteen hours to do whatever it took to get that first in a long line of airplanes off the ground and on its way. In the 82nd, the fact that my staff was deployed elsewhere was not an obstacle for the troops. The battalions were filled with staff and senior sergeants who had served in the division most of their careers. They were real self-starters. The organization was a well-greased machine where everybody knew his job—and his or her boss's job in most cases and was motivated to do it—no butt-kicking required.

I went back to my brigade headquarters where my key leaders and staff were already assembled. The S3 and I gave a very quick update on where we were and who had to do what, and we started to work. The brigade

S4, NCO Master Sergeant Whitman, was magnificent. My S3, Major Mark Keegan, knew his stuff backward and forward, so the flow out was flawless.

When I drove past Pope Air Force Base that morning, there were two C-141s sitting peacefully on the tarmac. In just a few short hours, it was completely packed with hundreds of them.

My one concern had to do with the standard rotation order, since it would take Kellogg's 1-504 Battalion and send them to Grenada rather than the NATO exercise in Spain, for which they had been trained. I called General Trobaugh to make the decision.

"Screw the NATO exercise, Hugh. We've got a real-life damn invasion going on down here. When they're up, let 'em go," he said. Still, I had just returned from enough time at the Pentagon to know that it wasn't that easy. There could be real political implications of a U.S. no-show in Spain, no matter the reason. Of course I understood that it wasn't my call, it was the general's . . . but if I could just buy a little more time . . .

I decided to make an unprecedented change in the standard battalion order of deployment and swap the 1st 504 Battalion with the 2nd 508 (2-508), meaning the "NATO battalion" would be the very last to deploy— just in case a last-minute change was made. I was fully authorized to do it, and it wasn't negating the general's order—it was more a "creative" approach to buying as much time as possible.

As it happened, not ten minutes after the 2-508 took off for Urgent Fury, I received a frantic call from General Trobaugh.

"Hugh, we have got this situation covered so please tell me you have not yet deployed that battalion that was intended for Spain."

"General, they were about to head your way, but no, sir, they have not yet taken off."

"Great," he said, almost shouting into the phone. "The big boys wanna show the Russians that we're Americans, and we don't have any problem flying transatlantic for a perfect drop on target, just because of some pissant little invasion on some island. Let's show them what we're made of."

"Roger that, sir—I couldn't agree with you more." And that's exactly what we did. The deployment for Operation Urgent Fury could not have gone any smoother, and the 1-504 were heroes in Granada, Spain . . . well, all but one slight mishap.

In Spain, the drop zone in the Iberian Peninsula was getting rain for the first time in six years. And the rain pounded down, and the plowed sunflower fields got wetter and wetter and even *wetter,* so finally by the time they dropped, the heavy-load platforms sank into the mud right on up to the vehicle level and they couldn't get them out. The vehicles were stuck there in the muck, and then the sun came out and the mud started drying. They brought in a couple of big twin-rotor Chinooks and tried pulling them out, but then the choppers' slings snapped. They finally threw that out as a bad idea. Otherwise, everything worked according to plan and we got kudos for the push-out.

I, on the other hand, spent the whole time sitting back at Fort Bragg, initially with Keith Kellogg and Jerry Metcalf and General J. D. Smith, who was the assistant division commander for support. We all wished we were down in Grenada, but it was not meant to be. Some days you're the windshield, some days you're the bug, and on that Sunday in October 1983, we were definitely the bug.

--------

In early December, I received a call from Carolyn with great news. Jon had completed his last football game and had come home saying he was ready to move to Fort Bragg. I signed for quarters on post and accepted delivery of our household goods. Carolyn and the boys arrived just a few days before Christmas and I could not have asked for a better Christmas present than that. They were thrilled when they entered the living room to find a beautiful, fully decorated Christmas tree—the first I had ever put up and decorated on my own. I gave Carolyn about five minutes to settle in before I broke the news that in a little over a week, we would be hosting about three hundred people at our home for a New Year's Day celebration. Typical of Carolyn, she took it in stride and didn't bat an eye.

By New Year's Day, the downstairs was completely unpacked—with pictures hung and knickknacks, figurines, and mementos perfectly placed—it looked like a perfectly decorated model home. Thankfully, none of the guests ventured *upstairs*.

It was a joyous, festive event that went off without a hitch—thanks to the hard work and amazing help of Carolyn's sister, Janie, her husband Perry, and my sister Sarah, who stepped in to help cook, serve, and clean. Our families have done so much to support us through the years and we could not be more grateful.

On March 10, I called home to see how my parents were doing; but I could tell something was wrong. Daddy had been a heavy smoker for years and eventually developed emphysema, then lung cancer, followed by a mild heart attack. In recent months he had not been doing well. Although it was 8 P.M., I told Carolyn we'd better go home. We arrived to find Daddy resting but having trouble breathing. I called for the rescue squad, which arrived in minutes. The trip to the hospital seemed like an eternity but was only twenty minutes away. A short while later, the doctor explained that he had died of heart failure.

On a cold and rainy March day, we held his funeral in Speed at the same white church where Carolyn and I got married. Following the service, we buried him at the cemetery immediately contiguous to Carolyn's parents' back yard—the same one where we would bury Mother twenty-two years later.

---

My command philosophy had been consistent from the time I was a captain right on up to lieutenant colonel and colonel (and then on up to division and corps commands). First, you must be prepared to carry out the mission the higher headquarters expects of you. You must be trained and ready and equipped to do the job, and if you're not, you'd better tell your boss what the shortcomings are. That's been reinforced time and time again as people have been called on to carry out actions and not been up to the task and then either failed or were chastised for not having performed to the standard expected of them. Never confuse enthusiasm with capability.

That was certainly true when I was a brigade commander in the 82nd. I always believed it was incumbent upon me to let people know ahead of time what challenges they faced and what I viewed as shortfalls in their capabilities if they weren't fixed.

The second lesson I learned was, people, people, *people*. They were the wind beneath the wings of the organization. If you take care of them, they will take care of you. If you take the time to praise them, they will respond to that praise. If you offer constructive criticism, they will also respond. If they don't, after coaching and teaching, you fire them.

Leaders must take the time to coach, mentor, and teach. When you're a colonel approaching forty, you think you know everything you should know about leading or commanding a brigade. And if you become a two-star general and a division commander you think there's probably not much more to learn. But everyone's doing it for the first time, so you learn a lot. The division commander can coach and teach brigade commanders because they've been there before.

It's a ladder built on trust and mutual support.

Readiness and taking care of people are the foundation upon which everything else is built. The rest is secondary.

Taking care of people also means supporting soldiers' families. In the 82nd, the roots of the family-support system sprang from the 508th Infantry. Ralph Newman and his wife, Vivian, set up a great family-support system for their battalion. No family had to feel isolated when the husband—or the wife—deployed. When the unit returned from Grenada, the system worked so well that we briefed the division, recommending that it become the standard system for the 82nd. And the next thing you knew, the division was briefing this family-support-group concept at the FORSCOM (U.S. Army Forces Command) Commanders' Conference. It quickly spread across the army. But it all went straight back to Vivian and Ralph Newman, the 508th Infantry, and Operation Urgent Fury.

Truly professional NCOs were the glue that held the 82nd Airborne together. The division had a cadre of NCOs who had spent their lives in uniform in the 82nd. I had a first sergeant who had been a private in the same company but was now the senior NCO.

I learned what a great asset the NCO corps is, and that if you cultivate it, you create true military power. Those guys knew all the drills and a lot of history. They knew about the 82nd fifty years before in Sicily, Salerno, and those bloody Dutch bridges. They weren't just rehearsing for war games; they were upholding a proud tradition. They were, and are, our secret weapon.

Beyond working with those professional soldiers, one of my greatest pleasures in commanding that brigade was the chance to jump almost as often as I wanted to. I knew the troops enjoyed having their colonel jump with them, but for me, jumping was an even greater pleasure. The C-141 Starlifter gave us the legs to cross oceans. We jumped in Egypt, in Europe, in Central America—and all over the East Coast. We jumped at night, during the day, sometimes several times a day. To me, swinging beneath a parachute canopy was a form of relaxation that erased the pressures and detailed work piling up on my desk at headquarters. I was the commander of an airborne infantry brigade, an honor I never thought I would achieve.


As my two-year command assignment came to an end, thoughts of retiring while on a high note crossed my mind—and those thoughts lasted for about thirty seconds. As I walked into my office in early September 1985 with sand in my boots, having just gotten off a long flight from Cairo, where we had participated in an airborne assault on Exercise Bright Star, my phone was ringing. It was Major General Bill Carpenter, now commander of the newly activated 10th Mountain Division (Light Infantry); this time, instead of offering me Hawaii he was asking if I would like to be his division Chief of Staff stationed at Fort Drum, New York, in virtual wilderness near Lake Ontario just below the Canadian border. At the time I didn't know where Fort Drum was, but I knew it was a chance to continue to serve with troops and to work for one of the army's greatest leaders.

"Sign me up, sir," I responded.

Jon was now a student at East Carolina University—so he would remain at college. But the rest of the family would embark on a new chapter in their lives.

————

We decided that Carolyn, Jeff, and Mark would drive to Fort Drum so that the boys would be there before the school year started, and I would join them in October, when I relinquished command of the brigade. This would ensure that Jeff would have his final two years of school in the same high school.

Once I finally did arrive, it was obvious that we had a tremendous task in front of us. We had an opportunity that few have ever had—to build a new installation from the ground up—and even though the conditions were anything but optimal, we had no excuse for not getting it right.

Late afternoon on Thanksgiving Day, the first big flakes of snow started to fall on Fort Drum. It didn't stop snowing until my birthday, January 2. More than twelve feet of snow had accumulated on level surfaces, without drifts. That was our introduction to Fort Drum—a very hardy climate with temperatures that dropped to the minus-forties, and you wondered why in the world anyone would ever put a light division in that kind of place where the roads were covered with ice and snow six months out of the year. It was, in fact, Congressional pressure to improve the economy in upstate New York. Now our job was to make that division a reality, and provide an installation perfectly suited for the extreme conditions.

The first troops started to arrive to form the new battalions of the 10th Mountain Division. Most had to be housed in run-down World War II wooden buildings—but soon there would be families flooding in behind those soldiers—an interesting dilemma, since there was very little family housing and the surrounding communities had very limited available housing, and that was mostly substandard. Our immediate concern was where we were going to house all these people in the fast-approaching subarctic winter.

Step one: design innovative plans and get them approved. General Carpenter wisely decided to form "working groups" to analyze needs, since he had learned from experience that one size doesn't necessarily fit all. The groups would include individuals who were living in barracks or who had lived in barracks most of their careers—they had certain specialized needs that would have to be considered. The climate obviously created many concerns, so another working group would include first sergeants who had been serving in the North Country for a number of years and knew firsthand the unique challenges posed by the area's severe weather.

Great recommendations started to emerge from day one. One recommendation was the addition of a large storage area for the combat equipment a soldier needs close at hand in the event of a deployment. It sounds simple, and it is—but it's something that had never been anticipated in the past.

Other ideas included large mudrooms built in each barracks because in this climate, the troops would need an area to remove all the snow and mud they'd been traipsing through before entering the living area.

We surveyed both male and female troops and determined that they both preferred nice showers to bathtubs in their rooms, so we modified the plans accordingly—bathtubs out, showers in.

The bottom line was that housing was designed to be troop-friendly and unit-friendly. It wasn't just another rubber-stamp U.S. army cutout that might work well at Fort Huachuca, Arizona, but not in the North Country, with everything we had to deal with. Everything was customized, everything designed to be user-friendly.

Suddenly, contractors from all over the country started arriving, and ground was cleared and bricks and mortar started going up. It was very exciting to watch it happen.

The strange thing was, in spite of all this activity, the local population did not believe it was really taking place. They had heard talk of this so many times in the past, and been promised it so many times in the past, they simply did not believe that this time was any different, even after construction began.

Clearly we needed their support, so we offered helicopter tours for the key civilian leaders. They could now fly over Fort Drum and see Caterpillars and John Deere equipment removing earth and clearing trees, and it took seeing this, firsthand, for them to truly believe it.

We had to become innovative on so many fronts and encountered regulatory obstacles at many turns. It was only because of the righteous mind-set of Bill Carpenter that we were able to navigate this bureaucratic minefield. Bill was a guy who believed in doing what was right and taking care of the troops, and he wasn't about to let some pencil-pusher obstruct his path.

When the DAIG (Deputy Assistant Inspector General) came up and said, "You can't run buses back and forth to bring family members in—that violates Army regulations," he wouldn't sit there and argue with them, because you know how far that would have gotten him. Instead, he listened carefully, soaked in all the information very attentively, thanked the inspector for making the trip all the way out there—especially considering the ghastly climatic conditions; then, after the inspector had departed, Bill basically said, "The hell with you. I'm doing it anyway. What are you going to do, fire me?" That was his attitude and I loved it. We've got to take care of our people and that's all he was trying to do—protect them and lobby on their behalf. In his mind—and mine, as well—if you don't understand that, you're in the wrong business. So we continued to do whatever we needed to do. We didn't intentionally violate the law or regulations, but if a regulation didn't support doing what was obviously the right thing, we did it anyway. To my knowledge, those installations are still standing, and no one ever said a word about any of it. It was a great time.

I instituted what was known as the Chief's physical training or PT program. We did PT five days a week, no matter the weather. When the weather was a challenge, we would dress appropriately. Early on in my tenure, the G2 (intelligence officer) came in and said, "Chief, I need to tell you it is projected to be minus-ten degrees tomorrow."

I said, "Okay." And he stood there. I looked up and said, "What's the problem?"

He said, "Chief, it's predicted to be minus-ten degrees at PT time tomorrow."

I said, "Well, good, let's get the word out. Everybody dress appropriately, we don't want to hurt anybody." And that kind of set the tone. If you dressed appropriately, the weather was not a problem. Let's face it, we were not based in Palm Springs, so the chance was we'd wake up to some pretty crappy weather, but if we'd waited around for seventy-two-degree sunshine to do PT, we'd have had a base filled with overweight heart-attack candidates completely incapable of deploying.

So the PT program continued and it bonded us in the North Country; it just kind of pulled everybody together. I became the enemy, not the weather and not the division or the CG. It was the Chief and his damned PT program that he wouldn't let go of—and that was perfectly fine with me.

As the months went on, we continued to make great progress and were pretty upbeat about it, then on February 21, 1987, we received word that we knew would be coming, yet could never really be fully prepared to receive. After having been hospitalized for some time, Carolyn's mother had died. She'd had a stroke when we were in Hawaii and her health continued to deteriorate as she had several more. She was the glue that bound all her family together and one of the most patient, calm people I've ever known. Of course, we all made it back to Tarboro for her funeral.

––––––

One day I was summoned to the CG's office to take a call from Carolyn. *That was strange,* I thought, but I went down to Carpenter's office for the call.

"Take it in here, Hugh," called the general from his inner office. When I entered, he was holding up the headset and had a big smile on his face. *What the hell is this all about?* I wondered.

I took the phone and said hello, then Carolyn responded, "Congratulations, General."

"What in the world are you talking about?"

Then Carpenter started talking. "You've made the list, Hugh. I just wanted Carolyn to be the one to tell you that you've been promoted to general."

It was a great day and one of my fondest memories of serving at Fort Drum. But also among the fondest was working for Bill Carpenter. He was a great man who believed in doing what was right and taking care of the troops. They don't get any better, and after being so profoundly affected by his advocacy for the well-being of the troops, I told myself that it was an area that I, too, would try to impact as I joined the rank of general officer.

————

The promotion ceremony took place on the old Fort Drum main post parade field, and it was packed. The senior commanders and their wives were present, along with local civilian friends we had made during our two years at Fort Drum. The command elements of all the units at Fort Drum unfurled their colors and the band played Army marching music. My two brothers, David and Ben, and of course Mother, made the twelve-hour drive from North Carolina to experience the big event firsthand. Jon, Jeff, and Mark were present, wearing matching blue blazers; and with Carolyn's red dress, the Shelton family looked very patriotic.

Major General Bill Carpenter would preside over the ceremony, but for now Bill and I stood to the side in a holding area while the crowd took their seats and formations assembled. It was Bill who had earlier sent me to Hawaii for four years of valuable troop duty and then provided the opportunity for me to serve in the most pivotal assignment in my selection for brigadier general—his division Chief of Staff.

Bill also sat on the Army Brigadier General Selection Board, which had selected me. To say that I was indebted to him for my promotion would be the understatement of the century. His wife, Toni, whom Carolyn and I had grown to love, was also present.

A number of generals had told me that no other promotion ceremony would stand out any greater or hold more significance than this one—the time an officer receives his or her first star. I fully understood that only in subsequent promotions to two, three, and four stars. While each would be both poignant and meaningful, none would compare to the depth of emotion I was about to experience on that day; and it was yet another time that I made a conscious decision to savor the moment and etch it into my mind.

The time had arrived and we snapped to attention as the honor guard brought the Army and division colors front and center, then we marched onto the field. Carolyn, Jon, Jeff, Mark, and Mother were escorted onto

*Carolyn, Mother, Jon, Jeff, and Mark (far right, and today 6 feet 6½) participate in the ceremony as Major General Bill Carpenter presents me with my first general officer star on the parade field of Fort Drum, New York.*

the field and assumed their predetermined positions, with Carolyn directly on my right, and Mother on my left; the boys lined up in descending order of height behind her. Major General Carpenter stood directly in front of me and the narrator read the Army orders announcing my promotion to brigadier general: "Attention to orders! The President of the United States, acting upon the recommendation of the Secretary of the Army, has placed special trust and confidence in the . . ." Carolyn pinned the star on one collar while Mother pinned it on the other. Jon pinned it on the helmet and placed it on my head, while Jeff and Mark handed me the general officer pistol belt that is authorized to be worn only by general officers. I felt enormous pride at having achieved this milestone and afforded the opportunity to continue to make improvements in the system that I had grown up with yet realized needed fixing. I was also elated that I would still be in a position where I could contribute.

Having Carolyn, our three sons, both brothers, and my seventy-year-old mother present made it all the more special. Several times that day I thought of my father, who had died two years earlier, and how proud he would have been.

\* \* \*

I'd been prepared for my assignment to the 10th Mountain Division to be my last tour in the army before retiring with a total of twenty-four years on active duty. Now all that had changed. Promotion to general officer was one of the hardest "gates" through which an officer had to pass. I had to put aside thoughts of retirement in my mid-forties and explore what my future held as a general officer.

Like so many of my peers, I realized how indebted I was to the troops with whom I had served over the years and to the mentors who got me where was. I now stood on their shoulders: Captain Buse Tully, Lieutenant Colonel Dan Shungle, Generals Dick Cavazos, Ed Trobaugh, and, of course, Bill Carpenter.

I could only hope that I would measure up to the task. To be very candid, I had never expected to make the cut to brigadier. I wasn't a politician who sought out positions that you typically associate with being promoted to general. I just enjoyed being out with the soldiers, in the field, and giving it my best shot every day and not worrying about what came next.

Later, when I went back to Fort Bragg, people would ask, "When you were attending ROTC summer camp, did you ever dream that you might come back to Fort Bragg as the corps commander, as the commander of Fort Bragg?"

"Are you kidding?" I would respond. "I never dreamed I'd even make it through summer camp, much less come back as a general officer."

I never had any real ambitions to keep climbing up to the next rung. I did believe that you owed it to yourself and to the troops to try to prepare yourself in the event that something else came along that would allow you to make another contribution. But if it didn't come along, that was fine with me, too; I would serve until my services were no longer required and then move on to the next phase of my life—and I knew that whatever that entailed, it would be centered around my faith, family, and friends, just as it always had been.

I now recognized that moving into the general-officer ranks, I might have an opportunity to correct some of the things that I'd found wrong along the way, or have a chance to make a much greater impact than I had been able to make as a lieutenant colonel or colonel in terms of making the Army better. Greater responsibility came with the turf, and I viewed the promotion as an opportunity in that regard.

But I had no idea what my next assignment would be. At my new rank, I could be a headquarters staff officer or an assistant division commander in a combat-arms unit. By definition, general officers were in fact qualified to serve in almost any kind of assignment, which was one reason you stopped wearing your branch insignia on your uniform lapel.

\* \* \*

For several months, I was in limbo, waiting to learn. Then I got my orders: Deputy Director of Operations (J3) at the National Military Command Center, the critical nerve center of the Pentagon. Not only would I be in charge of monitoring and coordinating every U.S. military operation worldwide, I would also be in charge of our nuclear watch.

**12:49 P.M., March 23, 2002, Inova Fairfax E.R.**

I felt like I was in a scene from M*A*S*H. As Carolyn filled me in on her conversations with Jon and Hal Timboe, two men burst into the E.R. in casual attire and headed for the nursing station.

As soon as Hal had heard about the extent of my injuries, Carolyn explained, he'd insisted on sending over his chiefs of neurosurgery and spinal surgery, Colonel (Doctor) Jim Ecklund and Colonel (Doctor) Dave Polly, each top in his field.

I glanced at the two individuals, who reminded me of Hawkeye and Trapper John, and saw them scrutinizing the results of my MRI. They approached and introduced themselves. "Colonels Ecklund and Polly, sir. I apologize for the outfits but that's what you get for pulling us in on a Saturday."

As time went on I would find that they normally worked seven days per week and would prove themselves to be lifesavers in more ways than one; they were literally two of the finest in their fields.

"We've got to get you to Walter Reed right away," Ecklund said.

"There's a military medical-evacuation helicopter on alert at Bolling but Inova already has a bird on the pad with flight clearance to Walter Reed," Polly said. "It will save a good twenty minutes—and those twenty minutes are crucial."

I knew I was in trouble but Polly's urgency definitely caught my attention. In a heartbeat I found myself transferred onto another gurney and rushed down a long hallway and into a waiting elevator. Before I knew it, the ground fell away and the helicopter banked northeast for the short skip over eastern Virginia and D.C. to Walter Reed Army Medical Center. Had I been able to turn my head and look out the window, I might have seen the White House to the south. Instead, I found myself reflecting on the many White House meetings I had participated in over the past four years—and the magnitude of my assignments even before that.

## Chapter Seven ★

# DOOMSDAY WATCH

July 1987—June 1988

It was just past 2:00 A.M. when the computer-synthesized voice crackled to life and repeated, "*Missiles inbound, missiles inbound.*" My CRT flashed "MISSILE WARNING," then dissolved to a computer-generated map of the Eastern Seaboard, where a number of ballistic trajectories sprang to life. I spun around and grabbed the red notebook labeled TOP SECRET, then sailed through my checklist almost by rote.

August 1, 1987. Margaret Thatcher had recently swept a landslide election to lock in her third term as British prime minister, President Reagan was back in D.C. after visiting Berlin, where he had challenged Soviet Premier Gorbachev to "tear down this wall," ABC News chief Middle East correspondent Charles Glass was still being held hostage by Hezbollah kidnappers in Beirut, and I was settling in to my very first job as general—Deputy Director of Operations (DDO) in the office of the J3—a long name signifying that I was in charge of the nuclear watch, and at that moment *the system was indicating there were incoming ballistic missiles rocketing toward Washington, D.C.*

My "office" was an impenetrable vault deep inside the Pentagon's National Military Command Center (NMCC), with secure 24/7 links to the President, direct contact with U.S. missile-tracking stations worldwide, a safe containing nuclear codes behind my desk, and the key to initiate a nuclear launch at my fingertips.

I had been trained on how to walk the President through deploying the nuclear device and on how to carry out whatever nuclear strike he ordered. My job was to initiate the conference call that said "we have missiles incoming" and report the predicted impact at a particular time and place and present the President with specific, predetermined options in terms of how we could respond. At the time, these responses were consolidated into a highly classified document called the SIOP (single integrated operational plan), put together by our J34 (nuclear planning group) based on conceptual objectives outlined by the President along with operational considerations delineated by the Secretary of Defense and the Joint Chiefs of Staff. (As of 2008, OPLAN 8010 replaced the SIOP with smaller and more flexible strike plans that include strike objectives beyond just Russia and China.)

"We have a strategic missile launch with predicted RV (reentry vehicle) entry into BMEW fan (ballistic missile early warning system area of coverage) in two minutes, predicted impact in eight minutes," reported the NCO monitoring our missile-defense network from his highly secured station in the EAC (Emergency Action Cell) only a few rooms away—my cue to commence an immediate Missile-Warning Conference.

While my Assistant DDO was patching in commanders of NORAD (North American Aerospace Defense Command), STRATCOM (United States Strategic Command, which has the deployable assets—the bombers, etcetera), and the Secretary of Defense, I was being connected to the President's military aide, one of five whose primary responsibility was to shadow the President at all times with the "football," a forty-pound black-leather-covered titanium briefcase that contains the nuclear-retaliatory options and a small laminated card of presidential authorization codes. Within seconds I would be speaking with the President and informing him of the attack—or, in this case, I would be in contact with a *role player* assuming the part of the President—since I was in the middle of one of our frequent Night Blue *exercises*.

Had this been a real-life situation in which NORAD was notifying me that they were tracking inbound missiles from the Atlantic where the Soviet fleet patrolled their nuclear submarines, those Russian missiles could have reached Washington, D.C. within eight minutes—eight minutes for me to notify the President, exchange the authentication codes, and transmit the launch message authorizing our nuclear forces to exercise whatever option had been selected by the President.

In addition to my frequent Night Blue exercises, in conjunction with STRATCOM we would run quarterly large-scale operational assessments we called Polo Hat—very realistic scenarios that would involve every link in the global chain, from sensors through command centers, logistics through communication, primary through alternate sites, with redundant fail-safe mechanisms in place at multiple points along the way. Our guiding philosophy was—and still is—practice, then practice again. Maintaining positive control of our nuclear forces and ensuring uninterrupted secure connectivity between the Secretary of Defense and strategic and theater forces was an unforgiving area in which there was no tolerance for error; the consequences were just far too great—and as Deputy Director of Operations I was at the hub of this undertaking.

In contrast to the scale of our mission, the fortified office itself looked rather simple, about the size of a medium-size corporate conference room. My desk and that of my deputy, Air Force Colonel Kurt Anderson (a highly decorated F-15 command pilot who went on to become a major general commanding the 19th Air Force at Randolph Air Force Base, Texas) were on a slightly elevated platform that overlooked a conference table and three large wall-mounted TV monitors topped by a row of digital clocks that were set to display local times in whatever hot spots we were monitoring at that moment. The table bore nameplates for the President, Secretary of Defense, Chairman, and J3 (Joint Staff Director of Operations), along with other high ranking government officials who would often assemble there to monitor key operations and manage various crises.

When I was DDO (and subsequently Chairman), the NMCC was just a short jog down Corridor 9 from the Chairman's office, both of which were on the main level of the Pentagon (referred to as Level 2 even though there are four levels beneath it) and occupied a large space between the B and C rings (the Chairman's office was on the outer E Ring). It truly was the most secure facility in the building, providing HEMP protection (hardened against high-altitude electromagnetic pulses that might radiate from nuclear blasts) and exceeding the security requirements of CIA directive DCID 6/9, which governs the construction and operation of SCIFs (Sensitive Compartmented Information Facilities)—meaning that specific physical construction barriers, access controls, and alarm monitoring would allow for the discussion of Top-Secret information throughout the center.

In addition to being cleared past an armed sentry with an authorized access log controlling entry to the NMCC itself, entrance to each office could be gained only via proper use of a current electronic ID card, cypher lock, and physical combination locks on each door. Offices were frequently swept for electronic eavesdropping devices, and walls were both soundproofed and constructed to block any outside attempts at intercepting communications. Air vents were padlocked, and in the old NMCC we even had "elevator music" constantly playing in the background to serve as white noise in case anybody did try to listen in. (In the new NMCC facility, which moved to the basement in April 2005, thankfully they eliminated that awful background music, so today's DDOs no longer have to endure driving home with Toto playing over and over in their heads.)

The video feeds for the wall displays would vary depending on the mission at hand. At the push of a button we could pull up air-traffic feeds depicting every flight over U.S. airspace, or zoom it in to a single plane that might be sending a distress signal or squawking the silent transponder code alerting us that they were being hijacked.

For sensitive missions we might be using Blue Force Tracker and viewing computerized graphic representations of our troops' locations as they moved anywhere around the globe. Trackers with unique identification codes would be secured to vehicles or placed inside soldiers' rucksacks.

Just a few years later we'd start phasing in unmanned remotely piloted reconnaissance ARLs (Aerial Reconnaissance Low)—fixed-wing birds that circle over a site and send back live video images relayed through satellites. During those days, the SR-71 Blackbird and U-2s were our primary airborne assets. Today, it could be a Predator or one of the more sophisticated aircrafts that literally allow you to watch a team on the ground executing a hostage rescue, for example. And of course that leads to the big concern that we are going to be giving "rudder orders" right out of the White House someday—too much tactical control from the top brass thousands of miles away. I've already watched that happen several times, but never have I injected myself into the middle of a field commander's operation.

Although we didn't have it when I was DDO, they've now got a system called Land Warrior that takes it a step farther and attaches cameras and tiny computer screens to a soldier's helmet that he can view through an eyepiece. Maps, enemy positions—it's all right there, and that, too, can be transmitted live via satellite relay to those screens in the DDO's office. In essence, today's DDO (and commanders) can see the exact point of view of a Land Warrior–equipped soldier—kind of like a real-life first-person shooter video game, only the lives at stake are real.

Land Warrior was quite a success with the 4th Battalion, 9th Infantry Regiment in Iraq, and it's currently being used in Afghanistan by the 5th Stryker Brigade Combat Team, 2nd Infantry Division. But it comes with a great deal of baggage, too—and a tremendous temptation for abuse by wannabe tacticians in cushy chairs at the Pentagon or other remote sites. While remotely piloting ARLs from the safety of a trailer outside CIA headquarters in Virginia or a virtual cockpit at March Air Force Base in Riverside, California makes sense, interfering with tactical boots-on-the-ground battlefield decisions from thousands of miles away could cost lives.

\* \* \*

In the case of a strategic-missile alert, whatever else was being depicted on the main video monitor would instantly be preempted by the early-warning radar sites and missile-tracking satellites so that we could provide the President an immediate situational awareness.

As for that third screen on the wall, I can't remember a single night when it wasn't tuned to CNN, which would often alert us to some international crisis even before our own intelligence services. The last time I was in there it was showing MSNBC, but whatever the channel, we always found value in keeping one of the broadcast or cable news channels up and running to keep us even more in touch with the "outside world."

Just outside my office but within the NMCC complex was a team of thirty or so representatives of all the major intell agencies in Washington—CIA, DIA, NSA—all reporting to me, along with a number of others on the ops side. I had a translator fluent in Russian assigned to the communications team since the strategic-arms talks demanded that the link between Moscow and the United States was always manned—an important piece of the threat-reduction initiative at that time.

Behind the scenes were banks of computers that constituted the Worldwide Military Command and Control System (WWMCCS), which tied together the Pentagon, satellites that detected missile launches and nuclear explosions, the White House, NORAD, Looking Glass (an airborne command post that circled our skies twenty-four hours a day from February 3, 1961, through July 24, 1990, and still stands at the ready on airborne strip alert) and all the combatant commanders' headquarters worldwide.

WWMCCS, which has now been replaced by the more advanced Global Command and Control System (GCCS), linked us all together into one big net in case we had a preemptive-strike launch by another nation against the United States. It was the system that allowed us to provide tactical warning and attack assessment (TW/AA) data to the watch team in that Emergency Actions Room behind me, and instantly convene the secure missile conference call and transmit the subsequent data via a jam-resistant secure communication (JRSC) circuit.

In addition to our strategic-watch component, as DDO I was also in charge of monitoring every U.S. military operation worldwide—the intent being that no matter the time or day, there would always be at least one general on top of the situation.

\* \* \*

My final responsibility as DDO was to monitor and record every phone call the Principles (President, Vice President, SecDef, Chairman, J3) made through the NMCC, which was the preponderance of their calls since the center functioned as the primary crisis-communication hub for the entire military. It might be a call routed by the White House out to the Pacific to reach a senator who was on some remote island or the Vice President calling from *Air Force Two*—but if it came in through the NMCC switchboard, it was monitored and recorded by the DDO.

Although call monitoring remains a key function to this day, the actual recording itself lasted for only my first eleven months or so, until one day an incident occurred and a judge ruled that the tapes in the National Military Command Center could be used as evidence in a court case. Later that day, we received orders that the recorders were to be turned off, and to my knowledge they remain off to this day.

Our protocol called for me to join the call in a listening mode only. The purpose was to be on top of any military actions that needed to get rolling right away, because at this level we were talking about crucial actions that more often than not were of an extremely time-sensitive nature where every minute lost could have dire consequences.

If the President told the Secretary of Defense or Chairman, *I want you to reinforce our ships in the Persian Gulf by moving those elements that are currently off the coast of Africa to join the fleet in the Persian Gulf*, just as soon as that call ended, I was on the phone to CENTCOM saying, *Very shortly you are going to get an order to move them so you might want to go ahead and issue a warning order and maybe even start moving because the order is coming.*

By the time the Chairman would walk in the next morning, we would have prepared for him a movement order (a SecDef DEPORD, or deployment order) for him to approve prior to the J33 (Director of Current Operations) walking it up to the Secretary of Defense, but because of our early intervention, the wheels for that operation would already be well in motion.

It was a very different assignment for me. It was shift work, something I was not accustomed to and would be quite happy never to do again. There were three eight-hour shifts a day, and I would work for six days straight, then be off for three. When my eight hours were up there was another shift that came in to take my place. Sometimes I would work a day shift, sometimes late night, it made no difference to me—I still felt like a nine-to-fiver. I had been used to working twelve to thirteen hours a

day for many years, with seventeen- or eighteen-hour workdays not uncommon, and the requirement that I completely switch off whatever operation I'd be in the midst of the moment that shift would end is something
I found extremely frustrating. At the end of my shift, when the next
brigadier came in and said, "I've got the controls," it was time for me to
pack up, outbrief, and head home, because there was not one thing I was
allowed to take out of there with me; I turned it all over to the next guy
and got out of his way.

It was exactly the *opposite* of one general we would encounter no matter which shift we were working, Brigadier General Craig Boyce, who was
the continuity between the five of us DDOs. Craig was a sharp officer and
as J33 he worked directly for the J3 and was charged with overseeing
*every* current operation of *every* branch of the military. What that meant
was that if a current op was in progress, Craig had to be there. It doesn't
take a rocket scientist to do those numbers—he basically *lived* in the Pentagon. As DDO, it was just the opposite for me—eight hours, and it was
time for me to hang it up.

You might think that given the importance of our mission, our support team would have been the cream of the crop, but this was 1987 and
Goldwater-Nichols had not yet been fully implemented (the Goldwater-
Nichols Department of Defense Reorganization Act created sweeping
changes to the military-command structure), so this meant that some of
the teams were "competent," at best. I was fortunate in that Kurt was a
top deputy, and I had the same good fortune with my ops officer, Army
Lieutenant Colonel Colie McDevitt, who sat in a cubicle just outside
where we sat. He was a very sharp lieutenant colonel with a lot of experience. For whatever reason, he had been passed over for promotion multiple
times but he did a great job for us. By the following year, Goldwater-
Nichols had been fully implemented and all the services would be fighting
for these valuable joint spots, so the intense competition really raised the
bar on the level of personnel throughout the whole NMCC, and that
same high standard is still evident today.


It almost goes without saying that when one pursues a military career,
constant moves are pretty much part of the package, but that doesn't
make it any easier. Carolyn has this little wooden plaque hanging in our
kitchen that's in the shape of a house, and under it she has added a little
wooden heart for each time we moved. Each has the place we moved to
written on it. When I retired, that house had *twenty-three* hearts dangling from it. Can you imagine, as a kid, having to move that many
times? Sometimes the moves were easy, but with others, timing was such
that we just knew that one of the children was going to have a real hard

time. I had the feeling that this move back to D.C. would be one of those times.

While Jon was away at East Carolina University, Jeff was about to graduate from Carthage High School (about eight miles outside Fort Drum, New York) and was comfortable in a serious two-year relationship with his girlfriend, Heather Roche, the daughter of a friend, Army Colonel Terry Roche and his wife, Marie. Mark was looking forward to starting fourth grade with the friends he had been with for two years.

The one saving grace was that we had held on to our house on Swinton Drive in Fairfax, Virginia, both for an investment and in case we ever moved back to the D.C. area. That familiar turf would bring at least a bit of solace to this latest geographic upheaval. With Jon already away in college and Jeff graduating and leaving for college soon, Mark would be the only child still living at home. While he was still in elementary school, we thought he would adapt pretty easily, and we knew the school he'd be going into was excellent. Jeff was a standout football player, and before we left Fort Drum he had caught the eye of my old boss, General Bill Carpenter. Carpenter had been an all-American at West Point in both lacrosse and football and, like Jeff, was a top wide receiver himself, known as the "Lonesome End" based on Army coach Red Blaik's innovative formation that set him clear across the field at the far end of the line of scrimmage. Carpenter was so impressed by Jeff's play that he took it upon himself to send Jeff's game tapes to the Air Force Academy, and they recruited him. The last thing we ever thought Jeff would do was join the service, so we couldn't have been more surprised when he decided to accept the Air Force offer and pack up for Colorado Springs to play football for them as a wide receiver.

On one hand, he was excited, but at the same time here we were in the middle of another move and he was about to go halfway across the country to school and leave his girlfriend of two years behind—so basically his home as he knew it was disappearing.

Before starting the new job in Washington, I was able to arrange for a week off so that we could spend some quality family time together at one of our favorite spots, Emerald Isle, North Carolina, at the beach. We joined my mother, brothers, sister, and their families there for a week each summer. Neither Jon nor Mark had started his school year yet, so we were thrilled to have the time with them, but unfortunately Jeff had to be in Colorado Springs that very week, so on our way out of Fort Drum, we stopped off in Syracuse to put him on a plane.

Carolyn and I waited while he checked in at the airport, then walked with him to the security checkpoint where we would say our goodbyes and send him on his way, but before that I pulled him aside for a private father–son chat in which I tried to prep him for what I knew would be a challenging start. I told him that the academy was known for its rigorous first few weeks, but if he could just stick with it through the first month or two, things would ease up substantially, and I knew that he would do great and love it there. But as soon as he stepped on that plane, Carolyn and I looked at each other; these were far from the best conditions in which to be going off to any college but especially one of the service academies.

We were still at the beach when the calls started coming in—the first from his football coach, a fine individual who really wanted Jeff to succeed. "General," he began, "Jeff is homesick as hell and he wants to throw in the towel. We've just started hell week but if he can clear that hurdle I know he'll love it here—and do great. But I need you to talk to him." It couldn't have been more than twenty minutes later when the phone rang again, and this time it was the offensive coach calling with the same plea: *won't I please talk to Jeff?* By the end of that day I'd probably had three or four calls from various coaches telling me how much they wanted Jeff on the team, and wouldn't I please talk to him? I told them all that *yes, I will talk to him and I will try to convince him that this is really worthwhile, but the bottom line is that it has to be his decision.* If he didn't want to stay, I wasn't going to push him.

I did talk to Jeff, but he was adamant that he did not want to stay there, and in spite of my best efforts, there was no convincing him otherwise. Two days later he was on a plane headed back to D.C., where he lived at home and got a job working at Hechinger's Hardware in Burke, Virginia, not three miles from our home. Meanwhile, he applied for a four year ROTC scholarship (which in many respects is harder to get into than the Air Force Academy) and damned if he didn't get that. So, the following semester, he went to my alma mater, North Carolina State University, and was happy as could be as he embarked upon a path that would eventually lead him into the Army as a ranger-qualified Special Operations aviator.

As Jeff got settled into North Carolina State University, things started heating up at the Pentagon, particularly in the Persian Gulf region. In May, the guided-missile frigate USS *Stark* was fired upon by an Iraqi warplane, and although Iraq contended that the Exocet missile strike was a mistake, it was no mistake that Iran had decided to destroy any Kuwaiti oil tanker attempting passage through the five-hundred-mile run between the Gulf of Oman and ports of Kuwait. Kuwait looked to the Reagan administration for help, and that help came through in the form of Operation Ernest Will, the world's largest maritime convoy operation since World War II.

\* \* \*

I have to admit, even though I had become a general officer, there were a few times during my stint as DDO that certain situations almost intimidated me. One of these occurred at around 2100 hours (9:00 P.M.), when I received a call from Atlantic Command that one of our submarines operating off the coast of Key West had sunk with about sixty U.S. sailors onboard. Although lack of breathable air could ultimately be an issue, at that time the air-purification and CO2-scrubber systems were still functioning, even as the sub was disabled and resting on the ocean floor. There was great concern about getting that submarine back to the surface for a variety of reasons, and Atlantic Command was already initiating submarine-rescue procedures. While our primary concern was, of course, the lives of the sailors, there were also very serious security issues since these subs contained highly classified material, if not the weapons themselves—all of which had to be safeguarded against falling into enemy hands.

Behind my DDO station was a set of notebooks that covered virtually any potential scenario—checklists outlining specific procedures and protocols that had to be followed. Immediately upon receiving the call, I swung around and cracked open the book that dealt with issues of this nature, and my ADDO, Colonel Kurt Anderson, did the same. First we had to take care of the notifications. I would start at the top of the list, and Kurt would start at the middle and work down.

My first call was to Admiral William J. Crowe, the Chairman of the Joint Chiefs of Staff; it was common knowledge that Admiral Crowe was a renowned submariner. While I didn't believe that I would be waking him at that time, I certainly understood that this was not the kind of news one looks forward to at any time.

It barely rang once before I heard the Chairman's deep, gravelly voice, in a tone that left no doubt he was all business: "Admiral Crowe."

"Mr. Chairman," I began. "We have a submarine that has sunk off the coast of Key West and it's on the floor in 120 feet of water." I had no doubt that my voice revealed the adrenaline rush I felt at moments like this as I proceeded to give him the name and hull number of the sub, realizing that he knew every sub's hull number like the back of his hand. "As for the crew—"

He cut me off and barked, "That is a nuclear submarine. Have they contained the reactor?"

With that, I gulped. Normally an admiral knows a lot more about submarines than a general, and that is especially the case with *this* admiral, but the fact is that I had already checked *Jane's* (the consummate bible of submarines) and it indicated that this particular ship was *not* a nuclear submarine.

So I said, "Mr. Chairman, that is a diesel, not a nuclear sub."

"General, you better check your facts. That is a nuclear submarine," he fired right back, with absolutely no uncertainty. With anybody else I might have questioned this, but Admiral Crowe was extremely intelligent and arguably the foremost authority on submarines, so I figured that in this case that "bible" must have it wrong.

"I will double check on that, sir, and I will get right back to you," I volleyed back, and then disconnected to make three or four other calls to get the word out in a hurry. I called Atlantic Command and asked for the data. They immediately came back and verified that it was a *diesel* submarine. I confirmed the hull number again, as well as the depth, and after making sure that every fact that I had was correct, I called Admiral Crowe back again and said, "Admiral, I have checked again with *Jane's,* and I have checked with Atlantic Command. Both state that it is a diesel submarine and Atlantic Command confirms that it sank in 120 feet of water. So, sir, those are the facts as they are being reported."

"Thank you, General," he said, followed immediately by a loud click. End of message. I looked down and saw that I had been sweating profusely. The next day the sailors were rescued and the submarine was recovered. That episode reinforced my belief that when you know for a fact that you are right, you don't back down. That's not to be confused with exceeding your authority, but when your job is to present the facts the way they are, you do so accurately and with confidence, regardless of what the other party wants to hear and irrespective of the other party's position or level of authority. That lesson would come in handy years later when I would have frequent interplay with the President and the Secretary of Defense.

Besides having listened in on all those top-level phone conversations, I observed much of it playing out at the conference table right there in front of my desk. I saw everything from combatant commanders being relieved of their duties down to multiple fast-moving actions in which my ability to get things moving quickly may have saved the day by virtue of the time it bought to get the decision implemented.

That went on for about a year. Since we had two sons in college, Carolyn started working as an administrative assistant at Longs Plumbing Contracting, but I had more time on my hands than I knew what to do with, although needless to say that was a tremendous learning experience about how things work at the top. The plus was that I could spend more time with Mark, who had settled in well and was playing basketball during the winter, football in the fall, and baseball in the summer. We'd also gotten him a dog, a cocker spaniel that he had immediately named Charlie. Charlie lived for thirteen years and made many moves with us.

* * *

At the end of my one-year time, I was beginning to wonder what was going to happen next. (You normally served only one year as a DDO because they realized that repetitive shift changes and time changes would leave you with jet lag half the time.) The first call I got was from General James Lindsay, the first commander of SOCOM (U.S. Special Operations Command), who wanted me to take over the Washington office of SOCOM. He needed help with budgeting, legislative affairs, etc., in the D.C. area. Since there was a requirement that I spend two years in an officially recognized *joint* assignment (assignments that involve more than one branch of the service, and for some idiotic reason SOCOM was not considered a joint assignment at the time), he got his wrist slapped for even approaching me. From my perspective, I should have been able to slide right over there because of all I had done that should have counted as joint time, but that wasn't the way it was viewed by the powers that be. Since I was serving on the Joint Staff and working for the Chairman of the Joint Chiefs, until my mandatory two-year joint tour was completed, the Director of the Joint Staff would have to agree to release me in order for the Army to move me to another assignment.

Shortly thereafter, I received inquiries from GOMO (General Officer Management Office, the group responsible for making general-officer assignments) asking me if I would be interested in a job as the assistant division commander of the 82nd Airborne. Needless to say, I was thrilled to death and I immediately said yes.

That celebration lasted only about a week, until I got call informing me that this was not going to happen, either, for the very same reason—it was not considered a joint assignment and I needed my two years of joint time.

Then one night about thirteen months into my tour as a DDO, Brigadier General Craig Boyce came in and sat down in front of my desk. He said he had some great news for me, and by his excitement, it looked to me like he could barely contain himself. As I've mentioned, all five DDOs had kidded about how Craig (as J33) would inevitably be called in to handle an operation no matter which shift we were working. It was a thankless job and the hours were just incredible; he was on call literally 24/7 and it was about as non-family-friendly a job as you can get.

Leaning on the back of a chair turned backward in front of my desk, Craig looked up at me and said conspiratorially, "Hugh, you've got to keep this under your hat, but tomorrow morning Lieutenant General Tom Kelly is going to call you in and tell you that you will be replacing me as the new J33. Can you believe it?"

Needless to say, my reaction was one of disbelief (if not horror) instead of the exhilaration that Craig was expecting. "Aren't you excited about it?" he asked like a kid in a candy store.

"It beats a punch in the eye with a sharp stick," I threw back at him. "But not by much." I was not happy—far from it. I was thinking, *Oh, man, here we go again, I am now being thrown into the fire.*

But maybe he was wrong; maybe that great assignment at the 82nd would come through after all. I figured I would find out one way or the other the following morning, but I will tell you one thing: that was one night that I did not sleep a wink.

Inside the trauma center, I was surrounded by a focused team of medical professionals checking my vitals and hooking me up to all kinds of sensors and intravenous drips of medicines and nutrients when in walked Dr. Ecklund and Dr. Polly. "What the hell did you two fly over in?" I asked them, perplexed that they'd made it over nearly as quickly as I had in the helicopter.

"I would tell you, but then I'd have to kill you," Polly deadpanned.

"The goal is for you not to," I shot right back, as they stepped aside to confer with a group of others.


Somehow, time slipped away from me. By then, Carolyn had also arrived. Anne (Jon's wife)—along with Cassie, Hannah, and Heather (three of my grandchildren)—had driven Carolyn home to pick up her car, and Carolyn had already made it back from Fairfax to Walter Reed.

"Charlie sends his best," Carolyn reported—referring to our cocker spaniel. "He'll be vacationing with Jon and Anne until we get back home."

"I'll bet the girls will love that," I said, just as Colonel Ecklund approached with my MRI and a small, flexible medical model of the spine.

Referring to the MRI, he explained, "The good news is there is no fracture to either the spinal column or the neck bones. But you do have a substantial buildup of calcium deposits throughout the cervical spine, and a cervical stenosis—a narrowing of the passageway through which the spinal cord runs—both most likely caused by repeated prior trauma to the area."

"Hundreds of parachute jumps might have something to do with that," Carolyn volunteered.

"It's not the jump, it's the landing," I corrected her. She just rolled her eyes and shook her head, but this would be our dynamic throughout the ordeal—maintaining our sense of humor while fully cognizant of the life-or-death enormity of the situation.

"We see it a lot in paratroopers, and it predisposes you to further injury," Ecklund explained. He then used the model to elucidate the physiology of the vertebrae and spinal cord. "You have what we call 'central cord syndrome,' an acute cervical-spinal-cord injury that's usually caused by a traumatic hyperextension—and that's most likely what happened when you hit the ground: your head snapped way back and hyperextended the spine—kind of like a whiplash, only much worse.

*"The impact compressed the outer part of your vertebral arch—what we call the 'laminae'—against the spinal cord itself, and that's where the paralysis comes in."*

*"So the obvious question is how you go about repairing it,"* I said, not even considering the possibility that the earlier doctor's prognosis was correct—that there was no viable repair.

*"Eventually, surgery,"* he said. *"But it all depends on how many of those cells have already died. Once they're gone, they can't be brought back. What we can—and will—do is create the absolute optimum environment for healing."*


*In my mind there was far more significance in what he didn't say than what he did. He never said I couldn't walk again and for that matter never said I couldn't make a total recovery—so, from my perspective, he left the door open. My next request would be to a higher power, and all I asked from him was that He please give me something to work with—anything— and if He did that, I pledged to give 200 percent to overcome the barriers.*

*Jim Ecklund's decision to leave my sense of hope intact at that early stage—even though he was fully aware of how infinitesimally small a chance there was for a recovery—was one of many actions he would make that typified his great leadership.*

## Chapter Eight ★

# THE MOST EXCITING JOB IN THE PENTAGON

**June 1988–July 1989**

"Guess I should have mentioned that," I said to Carolyn, who had called me at the Pentagon to ask if I knew anything about three soldiers coming by to drill holes through our bedroom wall.

Apparently I neglected to tell her about the JCS (Joint Chiefs of Staff) communications team that would be completely rewiring the phone system in our home on Swinton Drive in Fairfax, Virginia—installing a bank of secure telephones encrypted to the Top-Secret level.

A few days earlier, just as Craig Boyce had predicted, Director of Operations (J3) Lieutenant General Tom Kelly had called me into his second-floor D Ring Pentagon office and announced that I would be replacing Craig as his new J33—Director of Current Operations for the Joint Staff. As much as I had hoped for the assignment at the 82nd, I would soon learn that Lieutenant General Kelly had selected me for the most exciting job in the building—one that would position me squarely in the middle of every hot spot around the world and afford me an exceedingly high level of visibility. Although visibility did not bother me, I was certainly not looking for it.

If you asked me which job best prepared me to be the Chairman, there's no question that it was the J33. The on-the-job training was indispensable and I was at the hands of the master, Admiral Bill Crowe, who was Chairman at the time. Army General Tom Kelly was the J3 (Director of Operations) and between the two of them I had a front-row seat to soak in their fifty-five years of combined experience. They were both blunt and direct, but, as the public would see when General Kelly conducted his Pentagon press briefings during Desert Storm, he had an incredible wit and a unique way of spinning a phrase. When asked about the status of the war, he quipped, "Iraq went from being the fourth-largest army in the world to the second-largest army in Iraq in 100 hours." A.few weeks later he was asked whether sending B-52 bombers to attack a single Scud-missile site was comparable to killing a fly with a sledgehammer, he replied, "My own personal opinion is that's a delightful way to kill a fly."

It wouldn't be long before I would become Chairman and would be the one in front of the cameras, briefing the press beside Bill Cohen and Donald Rumsfeld; and I attribute so much of how I handled those sessions to the techniques that I picked up firsthand from Admiral Crowe and General Kelly.

As J33 I would be directly responsible to Lieutenant General Kelly, who in turn reported to Admiral Crowe. The J3 directorate was responsible for synchronizing and monitoring worldwide military operations and activities, moving military forces, and conducting operational briefings to the national leadership, and served as the operational link between the war-fighting commanders in chief and the National Command Authority (President and Secretary of Defense).

Every current operation fell under the J33 including wars in progress, time-sensitive Special Operations (Top-Secret JSOC [Joint Special Operations Command] actions or otherwise), humanitarian missions, training exercises—you name it. Army, Navy, Marine, joint—it didn't matter, if it was a current operation, it was my responsibility and Lieutenant General Kelly expected me to be on top of it. (The only exception to that were nuclear-related incidents such as missile conference calls. Nuclear matters fell under the J34.)

The logistics involved in running an organization made up of more than 2.5 million individuals (active plus reserve military) with an annual budget of more than $650 billion were almost inconceivable. Yet, even with an operation this immense, each and every troop that left the United States to go into another country required a deployment order, and that order had to be approved by the Secretary of Defense. These orders fell under my scope of responsibility. Lieutenant General Kelly expected me to have the orders correctly prepared in a way that kept everything moving, with the completed paperwork right there in front of him without somebody having to hassle him for it.

For example, if somebody called in and said they needed to move SEAL Team Six into Abidjan or needed to bring the USS *Stout* guided-missile destroyer into the Gulf of Aden, I'd be the one who had to cut that deployment order. Then, often I had to hand-walk it to the Chairman and in many cases right into the SecDef's office. I think my record for getting a deployment order out from the time we got the request through to the time the Secretary of Defense approved it was about an hour. The Pentagon might be lethargic and bureaucratic in some areas, like acquisition and procurement, but when it came to meeting the combatant commanders' requirements on time-sensitive operations, we could move with lightning speed.

The request could come in from one of the combatant commanders anywhere in the world. The President would not have to sign off on every one since the SecDef had authority on most of them, *but,* if it involved a combat operation or something involving flying bullets—then yes, the President would have to sign off on it, too. Many times the Chairman would accompany the SecDef to meet with the President, and if the issue had already been discussed with the National Security Council, it would be a rather straightforward process for the President to approve it.

Where it gets even more involved is that, generally speaking, these requests for deployment orders don't just come out of the blue. Even in the case of crises, deployment orders are often preceded by Warning Orders, then Planning Orders, then Alert Orders—and followed by Execute Orders and Operation Orders (OPORDS). If it sounds involved, it's because *it is,* especially since these orders are not merely one-line memos to *move this asset there* . . . the template alone for a standard Warning Order is eleven pages long, encompassing a detailed matrix of operational needs and considerations.

Fortunately, Goldwater-Nichols had been fully instituted by now, so I had a great staff working for me—really the cream of the crop who were getting these joint assignments. In fact, the services were beginning to push their frontrunners to be nominees for the various joint positions because of the Goldwater-Nichols requirement to be "joint qualified" prior to promotion to flag rank (general or admiral).

———

It was Saturday, July 2, 1988, and I returned home from my first day "flying solo" as J33 (after about a week of overlap with Brigadier General Craig Boyce to get up to speed) and was looking forward to a relaxing Fourth of July weekend with Carolyn and the boys.

Jon, now majoring in criminal justice at East Carolina University, was home for the summer and working as an intern with the Park Police in D.C. Jeff had completed his first term at North Carolina State, where he was also enrolled in the Army ROTC program. D.C. always had a nice fireworks display, so I considered catching that, or maybe inviting some friends over to join us for a picnic at some point over the long holiday weekend.

The Joint Chiefs of Staff commo team had done a bang-up job of setting up the new communications system in my bedroom. Unlike the local cable-TV company, which had left cable clippings and tiny mounds of sawdust near the floorboards, there was no trace of the secure wires the JCS guys had hidden beneath my baseboards. Besides my regular house phones, on the dresser beside my chest of drawers I now had a red phone that was connected directly to the NMCC switchboard—a hotline, so to speak—fully encrypted with no intermediary—and the STU-III, which was the "standard" device that allowed anyone on the system to securely communicate with me from anywhere in the world. The NSA had cleared both for communication through the Top-Secret classification level. A short while later I would be getting a fourth phone, the older STU-II device, which would provide for instant hotline secure communication with any of the combatant commanders. The STU-II had a big box of electrical circuitry attached to it, and man did that thing put off heat. On the positive side, our electric bills during the winter months were dramatically lower since, despite those biting-cold D.C. blizzards, we seldom had to run the heat at night—not with that communications "furnace" right next to the bed. The hot, humid summer nights were not so pleasant.

While it could take more than forty-five minutes for me to drive from home to the Pentagon in traffic, I've been known to make it in under fifteen when some middle-of-the-night crisis would necessitate my hitting well over ninety miles per hour on the long, almost straight I-395 Henry G. Shirley Memorial Highway. One of the greatest perks I've ever received came with the J33 job—a premium Pentagon parking spot immediately next to where the limos parked, so I could go flying into the Pentagon, race down the ramp, park right next to the River Entrance, and run inside and up the stairwell to my office. It was that fast, but it had to be. Neither the Chairman, the J3, the Secretary of Defense, nor the President was going to wait around for me to show up, and in the case of a current operation, I *had* to be there to get the ball rolling.


That very first night as I climbed into bed and turned off the light, Carolyn only halfway joked that she sure hoped that "thing" wouldn't go off in the middle of night or it would probably wake half the families in Fairfax. It's true that it had one *loud* ringer that was sure to rattle your fillings; they had tested it earlier that day and she had easily heard it all the way downstairs in the kitchen—they wanted to make damn sure it would be impossible to sleep through an incoming call. I chided her for jinxing us (joking, of course) since now that she had made the comment, it was sure to sound just as soon as we fell asleep. The truth is that you didn't really even need the ringer. About a second before the bell sounded, a bright red light would start to flash, and that would always wake me even before the sound.

Sure enough, at about 2:00 A.M. I saw a red light flashing out of the corner of my eye and then the bell started to clang. I answered and it was the DDO telling me that an Iran Air civilian jetliner had just been shot down and indications were that one of our ships had done the shooting. I commented that I'd be right there, even as I started moving toward my clothes.

I had laid out my clothing similar to the way a fireman does—so I slid into my Army-green trousers, grabbed my short-sleeve shirt and cap on the way out of the bedroom, slipped into my shoes as I sailed out the front door, fired up the engine on my Corvette, and I was racing through the subdivision less than five minutes after that STU-III's red light started to blink. Unfortunately, I did not have a siren or flashing red emergency lights, so I'd just hope that some policeman would pull me over when I soared past him at close to one hundred miles per hour (his escort would be a big help), but of course that only happens when you don't want to be stopped. It never did.

I arrived at the NMCC about five minutes before Secretary of Defense Frank Carlucci and Admiral Crowe. Secretary Carlucci was an interesting personality—past deputy director of the CIA and most recently national security advisor to President Reagan; while at Princeton he was roommates with another individual who would cross my path—Donald Rumsfeld.

The watch team had briefed me very quickly, so I shared what I knew and got them both up to speed as we all assembled around the conference table beneath the three TV monitors in front of the DDO's desk. I didn't even give it a thought that this was my first time on the "other side" of the DDO desk with the ops group down in front. By this point, J3 Lieutenant General Tom Kelly and his deputy, Rear Admiral Robert J. "Barney" Kelly, had also arrived. When the J3 was present for duty (as he was that night), Rear Admiral Kelly stayed in the background/office. When it was a Navy incident, he often tried to protect the Navy's interest—not to cover it up but to put as positive a spin on it as he could and, when possible, let the Navy investigate their own.

Following a short burst of static, we heard the voice of Rear Admiral Anthony Less on the overhead speaker system. The Joint Task Force–Middle East commander was giving us a situation report from the JTF flagship, the USS *Coronado,* and from all reports, the situation was ugly.

"USS *Vincennes* was taking fire from a small craft in the Strait of Hormuz when NSA alerted them of two Iranian F-14s preparing to take off from Bandar Abass [Iran]," the JTF commander reported. "They initiated CCIR (Commander's Critical Information Requirement) and picked up an airborne target departing Bandar Abass that was vectored directly towards them. After not receiving responses to multiple radio inquiries, the captain ordered two SM2-MR missiles fired at the target and at least one of those missiles was successful in striking it." There was a brief surge of static, then the admiral continued: "Indications are that what they struck was an Iran Air passenger flight."

"How bad is it, Tony?" Carlucci asked.

"Bodies are starting to surface along with civilian life vests and pieces of the aircraft."

The Secretary of Defense was kind of shaking his head in disbelief, and the Chairman's first words were something to the effect of, *I don't believe this, how could we have done this?*

Slowly but surely it all started to be pieced together, and you could see how it had happened. It was a terrible mistake, but it was a mistake. . . . The bottom line is that Iran Air flight 655 took off at the exact time the F-14s would have taken off and flew what the ship's crew believed to be the same flight pattern as the F-14s would have flown had they been on a hostile path toward the ship. In the radar clutter, the ship's commander thought they were being attacked by Iranian F-14s, and made the split-second decision to fire the missiles, since they had no idea that the Airbus had even taken off. What they hit was a civilian airline carrying 290 people to Dubai.

Secretary Carlucci notified President Reagan, and I thought, *What a first night on the job as J33*. But the truth is, it was a fairly typical example of what would consume my life for the next twelve months; but I could not have asked for a more exciting position, or one in which I could possibly have learned more.

———

Fortunately, not everything played out at night, and I was able to ease into some semblance of "routine" business hours (notwithstanding periodic middle-of-the-night interruptions from the STU-III). Normally, I would pull out of my driveway at about 5:00 A.M., which would put me into that parking space somewhere around 5:30 A.M. I would begin by dropping by the DDO's office for their NMCC briefing, then pick up the intell updates, which would cover additional incidents that had transpired through the night. Then my own team would come in, and after they had independently gone through their own intell briefs they would bring me up to speed on those. At around 8:00 A.M. I would attend Lieutenant General Kelly's J3 briefing, where I would be expected to brief him and Admiral Tuttle, the J6 (commo) on everything. We would go around the horn so General Kelly had a complete feel for what was happening, then he assigned whatever action items he wanted to give us and we would head back to our offices to begin our day in earnest at about 8:30 A.M.

———

Just a couple of months after I started as J33, one night at about 3:00 A.M. the red light went off and it was the DDO telling me that an SR-71 Blackbird off the coast of China had just experienced a flameout (complete loss of engine power) and its two-man crew was going down.

Needless to say, with the Blackbird it was a highly sensitive mission. It was part of our joint reconnaissance program, and each mission had to have presidential approval. We did this joint-reconnaissance plan monthly and it was basically using all our reconnaissance assets—submarines as well as aircraft that have intell capability—and getting presidential approval over certain routes that are highly sensitive. The SR-71 with the flameout was on one of those missions. The information they had on board was highly sensitive, as was the airplane itself—so there was no way that either could be allowed to fall into enemy hands, and the pilot was calling us from just off the coast of China. Bottom line, if it went down it would become a recovery operation.

Fully aware that he had to land at some "friendly" airfield, the pilot reported that he thought he could glide all the way to the Philippines and land safely at Luzon. Since the SR-71 was a long-range, supersonic aircraft capable of flying at Mach 3.2, it was possible that he had enough airspeed for the extended glide.

By that time I had become adept at slipping into my uniform and jumping into my shoes on the way out my front door, then gunning the Corvette through my subdivision and racing north on I-395 to the

*SR-71 Blackbird*

DEPARTMENT OF DEFENSE

Pentagon—and that night it felt like I was approaching the Blackbird's Mach 3. The whole trip I was going over that flight path in my mind. I knew that route well, and that pilot must have been one incredible optimist because gliding with no power for that great a distance to Luzon was a long shot.

The DDO had already notified the J3 who decided not to come in, instead leaving it in my hands to take care of—ditto the Chairman. I checked in with DDO the and learned that so far the plane was still in the air. He went on to fill me in on certain other alerts and notifications he had made—all predetermined and specified in those briefing notebooks behind him—because there are some individuals whom you would never have thought would have had to be notified, but on a sensitive mission like this, they would, since they were actually operating under certain covers. As I learned during my time as DDO, the rule was that you followed your book and didn't second-guess any of those notifications.

I arrived at the Pentagon to find the pilot in communication with our joint reconnaissance center, which was located contiguous to the NMCC. I listened to a couple of the transmissions and was surprised to hear the pilot still sounding confident that he could make it, given his high altitude and speed at the time of flameout. He was over the Spratly Islands, midway between Vietnam and Malaysia and still heading toward the Philippines. I made a call to the command center in the Pacific to alert them that there might be problems with a SR-71 and I suggested that they have some of their ships in that area set course for the Philippines just in case. They reported having a couple within fifty or seventy-five miles and agreed to start them steaming toward Luzon.

It was beginning to look good and the pilot was still sounding confident when suddenly we got a report that he did *not* make it—he was down in the water. Fortunately, he fell short by only about a mile, and both he and his recon officer were able to get out safely before the plane started sinking in about forty feet of water. A Philippine fishing boat witnessed the whole thing and powered over to pick up the crew, even though by then the Navy ship was only a mile or so away.

The Navy ship dropped anchor right over the SR-71 and provided the appropriate security until the recovery team arrived and retrieved the aircraft along with its sensitive data.

Situations like this became the rule rather than the exception; it was something like that every day.

———

Early in my tenure as J33, we were running Operation Ernest Will missions in the Persian Gulf, and it was not unusual for the Iranians to fire at our ships and claim that we were in their waters instead of international waters—and every morning Chairman Bill Crowe would expect me to brief him personally on what had transpired in the Gulf the night before. I could not have asked for a finer mentor than Chairman Crowe, and I knew that he would be supportive of my using those briefing sessions to coach, train, and mentor some of the young officers I had working for me.

I had interns, normally lieutenants or captains (or their equivalents in the Navy) who would be working in JCS to get a flavor for how the system worked, and on occasion I would use them to brief the Chairman—I wanted them to learn. I would go in with them and would be fully responsible for knowing the information, but the intern would do the actual brief. I would rehearse them first and warn them that Admiral Crowe was not always the most patient individual, particularly if they did not know their stuff. I reminded them that he was a brilliant sailor and that because he served in the Persian Gulf, he knew every marker out there—it was truly unbelievable that he could remember all of them in such detail. My advice to them was clear—be prepared or he would blast them out of the office. I am happy to report that there were no casualties, but I always respected the admiral for allowing—even encouraging—me to use his high-level briefing sessions as learning tools for young officers. I'm sure it was an experience that they have never forgotten.

---

At some point after the Iranians had fired at one of our ships, the decision was made to retaliate with multiple air strikes to hit a couple of their big ships that operated out of Bandar Abbas. We looked at various options, including sending in SEAL teams to blow up their ships or seal their harbors, but eventually we elected just to use the air strikes on the ships and use the SEALs to take down one of the oil platforms they were operating from—and from which they had fired at us in the past. We carried out both the SEAL assault and the air strikes. The SecDef joined the Chairman, J3, and me to monitor the situation live from the DDO's office. Prior to our arrival, they had patched in Admiral Less, who was coordinating the operation from his command ship in the Gulf. Once the op got under way, we pretty much just sat there and monitored it, although we did communicate back and forth with the admiral.

One of the pilots reported that he had identified a ship that was supposedly hit but was still functional and steaming back to Bandar Abbas. He requested permission to strike it again and sink it, as was the original intention.

Secretary Carlucci asked for confirmation that it was, for certain, the Iranian ship that we had intended to sink, and the pilot replied that he knew it was the ship because he had flown by so low he'd read the hull number off its side. The pilot reiterated, *Request permission to strike the ship.*

Carlucci looked at me and asked, "What do you think?"

"Sink it, sir," I replied.

He looked at Admiral Crowe, and Crowe volunteered, "It wouldn't hurt to hit it again but we have already hit it once and it appears to be disabled, so . . ."

Carlucci turned to the DDO and said, "Get me the President," then he stepped behind the desk to pick up the phone. A few words were exchanged and he hung up. "Okay, let's don't hit it again. It's disabled, so let her go."

The following morning we analyzed the satellite imaging and determined that the ship had made it safely back into port; it had not been disabled. I was asked to meet Secretary Carlucci at 7:00 A.M. outside the Pentagon gym, where he had his early-morning workout, and ride with him over to the White House, where he was to brief the President on the results of the operation. I had all the photos and intell reports that documented what had or had not been damaged—and I boiled it all down into a one-page talking paper so that he could read it on the way over.

At exactly 7:00 A.M. he came out of the gym, and we got into his limo for the short trip to the White House. En route he scanned my summary page and flipped through the recon photos. When he got to the picture of the ship back in port, he looked at me and said, "Well, I guess I screwed up on this one, didn't I?" And without even thinking, I said, "Yes, sir, you did." And almost before the words were out of my mouth, I thought, *My God, I am a brigadier and I just told the Secretary of Defense that he just screwed up.* I was greatly relieved when he didn't seem to mind and actually appeared to agree with me.

———

One of the most exciting things I did as J33 was something that fell into my lap by default—an area not usually handled by the current ops officer. Due to a situation I can only describe as political in-fighting, I became the military counterterrorism representative to the National Security Council. Headed by Ambassador Jerry Bremer, this was really a deputy-level job— one that was way above my pay grade. Every Thursday we would have meetings at the White House that would include the Deputy Director of the FBI, the Deputy Director of the CIA, Ambassador Bremer from the State Department, the Assistant Secretary of Defense for Special Operations and Low-intensity Conflicts (ASD/SOLIC), and I represented the Chairman.

These were important meetings on many levels—the attendees were high level, and the issues were key. Lieutenant General Kelly, my boss, wanted to attend, as did the special Assistant to the Chairman, Vice Admiral Jonathan T. Howe (who was the equivalent rank as Lieutenant General Kelly). As this conflict escalated, the Director of the Joint Staff, Lieutenant General Bob Riscassi, made the decision that I would be the one to attend, as long as I would immediately report back to them (individually) as soon as the meeting was over.

The meetings would last about an hour and a half. We discussed the terrorists we were tracking at that time, which ones we had sufficient actionable intell on to snatch, and what assets would be needed to do it. I was a highly valued member of the team since I had the ability to provide assets that could move quickly. On more than one occasion, I had to provide them a C-141 or other asset at the very last minute for some time-sensitive counterterrorist op.

Immediately following the meeting, I would go back to the Pentagon and separately debrief three people. First would be the director of the Joint Staff—three-star Lieutenant General Riscassi and later USAF Lieutenant General H. T. Johnson—then the J3 (Lieutenant General Kelly), and then finally Admiral Howe. All separately.

These weekly meetings greatly expanded my knowledge of the counter-terrorism arena and established my position in a new network of high-level contacts who would be worth their weight in gold when I became Chairman. Working in the interagency and speaking on behalf of the Department of Defense in terms of what we could and could not do was a tremendous experience—as was watching firsthand how deftly Ambassador Bremer navigated his way through these meetings. I learned how essential it was to see what was important in the minds of other governmental agencies that weren't necessarily directly lined up with the priorities of the Defense Department, and how, if you wanted to sell a program, you would have to make sure that you worked it in such a way that they would either accept it or, if not totally buy into it, at least agree to live with it. Those weekly meetings gave me thirteen months of tremendous experience that I would later fall back on repeatedly when I became the Chairman.

---

Finally, there was one function I took on as J33 that I had never even heard existed: I became the sole clearinghouse for classified documents that might be used by FBI double agents who were spies for various countries around the world. The agents wanted to use these documents in double-agent sting operations, where anything less than compete authenticity could blow one's cover and potentially blow entire operations that might have been many years in the making. Still, we weren't just going to turn over Top-Secret material that could cause grave danger to our national security. Somebody had to decide what was safe to turn over and what wasn't. That somebody was me.

It might have been a classified manual associated with a jet engine that had certain specifications that in the hands of the wrong people could have divulged vulnerabilities, or internal reports on a new missile system that would have allowed the enemy to gain insight into how to detect or defeat it—whatever it was, I was the one to get it, review it, and make whatever undetectable changes were necessary to protect the integrity of the information without tipping off the individual that it had been sanitized. The responsibility that I felt was palpable.

On my very first day, three documents came to me that were classified as Top-Secret. My predecessor had warned me that this was to be my sole responsibility and nobody else even wanted to know about it, including my boss. That got my attention. Still, I did not feel comfortable taking a classified document and knowingly turning it over to the "other side," so I took this thick document up to the J3, Lieutenant General Kelly, and I started to ask him for direction. "Sir," I began, lifting up the classified packet, "I've got this document that the FBI wants cleared to use for our double agent—" Before I could get out another word, Kelly cut me off and said, *Get out of here. You are the clearing authority, not me, and I don't want to know anything about it.*

Like the Nike commercial, he said, "Just do it."

As I walked back to my office, I thought, *Boy, if this ever blows up . . .* This carried with it by far the most anxiety of anything I had to do as J33, having to turn over certain material that might have been stamped TOP SECRET to a Russian agent, or Chinese agent—I knew it had to be done, and I did it—but I was never happy about it.

———

From my daily contact with all the CINCs (combatant commanders) to those I would interact with at all levels of the Pentagon, this was a great job that allowed me to get to know all kinds of people. It grew into an incredible network of valuable contacts—and friends—far greater than most brigadiers would be fortunate enough to have at this point. Even though it was the most demanding job I had ever had, I left the job with mixed emotions since I knew I was leaving the epicenter of the armed forces.

7:15 P.M., March 23, 2002, Walter Reed Intensive Care Unit

I *want to introduce you to Major Jeremy Blanchard, head of the ICU, and Major Geoff Ling. Geoff just returned from a medical fellowship in advanced spinal injuries at Johns Hopkins," Ecklund said, indicating Ling in the small group of physicians and interns that appeared to have become his entourage.*

*"You'll forgive me if I don't shake your hand," I said to the young neurologist. He smiled, totally in sync with my dry wit; several others just looked at me in horror.*

*"We brought Geoff in to discuss an experimental new procedure," explained Polly. "It is extremely risky but worth consideration—quick consideration—as it's a now-or-never kind of thing."*

*"Research on animals shows a great deal of potential," Ling began, and I could almost hear Carolyn take a big gulp at the infancy of this dangerous procedure—as she debated whether I really should be adding "human guinea pig" to my bio. We listened intently as Geoff presented us with a more specialized perspective on the physiology behind paralysis and spinal-cord injuries, expanding upon Ecklund's comments about the impossibility of bringing dead cells back to life. "Once that stage is reached, regaining feeling and movement become physical impossibilities," Ling said firmly.*

Hope was one thing, but scientific reality was another; and my MRI revealed that I was precariously close to crossing that threshold. That explained their mad rush to transport me to Walter Reed. Geoff took us through the new procedure, which involved boosting one's blood pressure to a dangerously high level within the first few hours after the trauma. The theory was that the increased pressure would force elevated concentrations of oxygen into the damaged cells, potentially forestalling cellular death and allowing for their eventual regrowth. There would be no immediate indication of success or failure, but the procedure did provide a slim chance that some feeling and movement might eventually be restored.

"Let's hear the fun part," I said, understanding that the downside could be great.

"The procedure involves keeping the blood pressure elevated for six to seven hours. And we're talking off-the-charts levels to have any chance of forcing enough oxygen into those cells. At these levels, the risk of massive stroke or heart attack is very real."

\* \* \*

I had never experienced any heart-related problems and felt confident that my fitness contributed to a strong and healthy cardio system—still, it was clear that this entailed a great risk with a slight chance of success. There was a huge possibility that I would die on the table during the seven hours.

"Why don't you take some time to discuss it with Mrs. Shelton," suggested Ling. "Take all the time you need. I'll be back in thirty seconds." He gave me a slight smile and stepped away.


Carolyn left the decision entirely up to me, offering her complete support, as always.

"The game favors the bold; let's do it," I told her, using my own personal variation of Virgil's famous quote, "Fortune favors the brave."

"I knew you would say that," she said calmly, as if we'd just decided to repaint the living room. Typical Carolyn, the voice of total calm in the midst of any storm. Although I couldn't feel it, she had been squeezing my hand the entire time.

## Chapter Nine ★

# A STORM ON
# THE HORIZON

It was a hot, muggy July day, but I could not have been happier. I had just become assistant commander of the world's only air assault division, and I was now an integral part of it. Based at Fort Campbell, Kentucky, the 101st Airborne (Air Assault) had the capability of inserting a four-thousand-soldier combined task force with more than thirty-five AH-64 Apache attack helicopters a hundred miles behind enemy lines. When you add in the AH-1 Cobras (armed with TOW missiles), UH-60 Black Hawks, and the heavy-lifting CH-47 Chinooks, the 101st was normally equipped with more than two hundred helicopters—far more than any other Army division. It was quite a force multiplier, and one that would soon be called upon in some of the most challenging conditions imaginable when we deployed to the Middle East to take on Saddam Hussein. My job would be to get to Saudi Arabia first, and coordinate the incredible undertaking of receiving almost twenty thousand troops and all the equipment and supplies that come with them.

But first, it was time to welcome my new boss. Major General Teddy Allen was about to turn over the 101st to its new commander, Major General Binnie Peay—and I had been charged with orchestrating the event.

I was in the Humvee with Major General Allen and Lieutenant General Carl Stiner (the corps commander) and together we rounded the corner to inspect the troops, and they could not have looked any sharper. We stepped out for the massive pass-in-review and were smacked in the face with the one-hundred-plus temperature that blistering Kentucky afternoon. Little did I know that it would feel like a meat locker compared to what I'd be hit with in the Middle East in a few short months. Major General Peay joined us for the pass-in-review, in which sixteen thousand members of the 101st paraded in front of us in perfect synchronicity. General Stiner and Major General Peay could not have been more impressed.

Major General Allen was a good man—an aviation pioneer—but I would also relate very well to the new commander, Major General Peay. Our philosophies were hand and glove, and I was delighted to have the opportunity to be there to assist him in the field. He was a big believer in taking care of people, too, although his style was a bit more unforgiving than mine when battalions didn't measure up—and until we completed the task of turning things around over the next few months, many didn't.

I tried to be tactful and make constructive comments at the appropriate forum, pulling the battalion commander behind the scenes whenever I could. *Okay, let's sit down here in the tent or the office and talk about the challenges we've got in addition to the great things that I saw.* He tended to be a lot less merciful, leaving more than one battalion commander shell-shocked and wondering what type of ordnance they had just been blasted by.

On August 2, 1990, Saddam Hussein ordered his Iraqi troops to invade Kuwait with the intention of annexing the country. Following an international outcry, the United Nations passed a number of resolutions that ultimately led to operations Desert Shield and Desert Storm, intended to expel the invading Iraqi forces from Kuwait. The United States, along with a coalition of thirty-three other countries, began with an extensive air campaign consisting of more than one hundred thousand sorties that dropped more than 885,000 tons of bombs.

After that, it was time for the ground campaign, which is where we came in. I would leave for Saudi Arabia on the first plane out, well ahead of the rest of the division, so that I could select (and secure) a location for the base camp—most likely near the King Fahd Airport in Saudi Arabia. Then I'd set the wheels in motion to receive the almost twenty thousand troops of the entire 101st Airborne Division (Air Assault), which would be closing fast on my tail within five to ten days. Once they arrived, our mission would be to establish a forward command post near the border of Iraq; then delay, impede, and attrite an Iraqi force if they decided to attack again.

At this point Carolyn and Mark (who had recently turned twelve) were living with me at Fort Campbell; Jeff was a student at North Carolina State University, having received a four-year ROTC scholarship; and Jon had graduated from East Carolina University and was now living near Atlanta, where he worked as a police officer and was engaged to his future wife, Anne. We were all looking forward to their upcoming wedding in October—but since I had just received word that it was time to go, sadly, it appeared that I would miss it.

We left Fort Campbell on August 17, 1990, and it was late morning when we landed in Saudi Arabia. The instant I stepped off the aircraft ramp, I felt like I had stepped into a blast furnace—I'm not talking "uncomfortably hot," but a wind so cruel that it literally felt like it seared my skin when it slammed into my face. It would not ease up and I would never get used to it—but that *did* become an important consideration when determining the needs of the division.

While the rest of the team stood by to help Lieutenant Colonel Dick Cody (Apache battalion commander) off-load the Apaches, I immediately got on with the task of trying to ascertain where we would locate and house the thousands of "Screaming Eagles" who would be arriving within a few short days.

I linked up with JSOC in hopes of utilizing the impressive new airport-terminal building, but they refused to give it up. That left only a nearby water-treatment plant, but it was totally insufficient for the men, women, and equipment that had to be housed in short order. I finally ended up persuading JSOC to give me part of the airport parking facility—not ideal by any means, but it would have to do. This had already become considerably more complicated than it should have been, and I had to move more swiftly if I was going to pull it off prior to the division's arrival. To expedite matters, I linked up with the logistics commander, Lieutenant General Gus Pagonis, and told him that I was going to need tents—*lots of tents*, and a workforce to erect them fast. Having a place where the division could escape the deadly rays of the sun was not a convenience, it was a lifesaving necessity. General Pagonis promised to help.

I called the commanding general back at Fort Campbell and he asked what I considered a very astute question: "What can you tell me that would help us get better prepared back here?"

I said, "Tell the troops how hot it's going to be—it's like standing in a boiler room in hell. Tell them to go home and get their wife's hair dryer, turn it on high, and hold it right to their face and start breathing. That's what they will feel when they step off the aircraft and it will not let up. It is extremely hot, probably a hundred twenty degrees—so they're going to have to be hydrated and prepared for heat."

* * *

Pagonis came through not only with the tents but by contracting third-country nationals to put them up—and it was just in the knick of time. The tents went up as the planes started coming in. Troops were off-loading by the hundreds, then thousands, and I was sweating blood because some days we would literally get just enough tents erected for the troops to move into before the next plane came in. Once the flow started, it came fast. That's what the 101st is all about. Fast and efficient, and eighteen thousand strong at the time. I needed to set up areas for aviation, motor pools, troop-living areas, and dining-facility areas, just to name a few. It was like setting up a fully functioning city within a matter of days, but we pulled it off. I will forever be indebted to my assistant, Major (now Lieutenant General) Keith Huber. While I worked hard, Keith worked *tirelessly* to make it happen.

In the meantime we had to concentrate on force protection and contingency plans in terms of what would we do if we were attacked, and how we could best prevent those attacks in the first place. These were all lessons I had learned early on as a young captain in Vietnam, and they were every bit as important on this side of the world.


The division closed rapidly and it seemed we were always only one airplane load ahead in getting the tents erected, which also provided shade for the troops and helped protect them from the blistering sun and 120-degree heat.

As the base camp swiftly expanded, the corps directed the 101st to relieve the 82nd Airborne Division at FOB Essex, a forward operating base along Tapline Road, near An Nuayriyah—a strategic location in the event that the Iraqis headed for either Dhahran or Riyadh. It involved moving both an infantry and an aviation brigade (each brigade contained approximately twenty-five hundred troops plus support elements, which equals about six thousand total troops) north approximately one hundred miles, and included setting up a tactical command post. Noticing the logistical similarities between this location and the Belgian city of Bastogne, where the 101st fought the great World War II Battle of the Bulge, we renamed this site FOB Bastogne in their honor. This command post allowed us to command and control these forward deployed assets, which also included key logistical units. I was given the task of moving forward and being prepared to fight the forward elements to delay, destroy, and impede the Iraqi forces if they elected to come south.

I was elated since it placed me in a position to practice the skills I had learned and refined all my career. It would also place me in a position to kill as many Iraqis as possible while preserving the lives of those entrusted to my care.

The division forward command post was established in an old ARAMCO (Arabian-American Oil Company) building. The floor of the deserted building was covered in eighteen inches of sand and a large colony of bats "hung out" in one room. We shoveled out the sand, named the bat room the "Gotham Room" and quickly set up the command post. Knowing that Saddam could attack at any moment added impetus to our efforts and served as an excellent motivator.

From then until we attacked in February, we honed our war-fighting skills, frequently displacing the command post using our command-and-control helicopter until it became second nature. We were good and we knew it. Major Keith Huber, who had accompanied me north and was now my operations officer, was relentless in demanding perfection. Speed, efficiency, and effectiveness were our standards.

The hard work ultimately paid huge dividends. When the Desert Storm attack commenced, the division main remained in the rear as the division commander, Major General Peay, came forward and joined us in the tactical command post (TAC CP). He was so impressed with the operation that the huge division main command post never came forward.

---

We had just been advised that G-day, the day upon which the ground invasion would begin, was only four days off. It would be February 24, 1991, and our mission was immense.

*We were about to pull off the largest air assault in history.*

It was a rather bold plan by the corps to quickly move forward right along the Euphrates River and show Saddam that we were capable of moving just as quickly right on into Baghdad—and that he was in an untenable position because all the Iraqi forces in between Kuwait and the river would have been bypassed, overrun, or we'd be behind them.

It was a long haul for the 101st because it meant that when using a combination of "Lindbergh" UH-60s and the CH-47s, we would have to move massive quantities of fuel ahead since the helicopters were going to require refueling in order to turn around and fly back. The CH-47s could lift the necessary equipment and fuel to allow us to establish "forward area refueling and rearming points" (FARPs) in the middle of the night.

With the FARPs in place, we could then operate almost at will in that area and insert the 1st Infantry Brigade to secure the FARP area, the division tactical command post, and establish a forward operating base. The choppers would then insert the division's 3rd Brigade right along the Euphrates.

My role was to make recommendations regarding the tactical employment of the brigade and for the division, and look closely at how we would execute this plan—looking for any loopholes or shortfalls or anything at all that might go awry. I would look for the greatest risk areas and see what kinds of sequels or contingency plans we had if that happened—I would anticipate the worst and always ensure that we were prepared for it.

Then we would practice—real-time practices with the actual personnel, aircraft, and other equipment. We practiced the actual distances in another part of the desert to make sure the plan was completely feasible and we hadn't overlooked anything. This went on for months.

As we were in the desert preparing for the invasion, in October 1990, Jon and Anne were married (they had offered to postpone the date but since I had no idea how long I would be deployed, I wouldn't hear of that)—and of course I was the only family member missing. I still regret that I couldn't be a part of that special day. It's another example of how sacrifices are a part of a soldier's life and the lives of his or her family.

Finally, after months in the hot, harsh desert, it was time to go. The troops were angry—angry with Saddam for his actions, but also with what those actions had cost them in terms of time away from their families and time they had spent in the desert under these conditions.

Four days before the main assault, we had sent reconnaissance aircrafts (including Apaches, each armed with eighteen deadly Hellfire missiles) along the border to scope out the Iraqi defenses. When they received small arms fire, the Apaches responded by firing rockets and a Hellfire missile at the Iraqi force. Immediately, white flags were raised and six hundred Iraqis tried to surrender to the Apaches. An infantry battalion was sent forward to accept the surrender and the Iraqi battalion was transported by Chinook aircraft to the POW camp we had already established on our side of the border. They paraded past me into the barbed wire compound, obviously scared. The last six off the aircraft were the Iraqi officers. They were very solemn as they went past, afraid of their fate. I looked at them and said, "*as-Salâm Alaikum,*" (God's peace be with you) and their faces lit up as they responded, "*Wa-laikum as-Salâm,*" (and God's peace be with you).

A short while later the translator informed us that the six officers had asked to be put to death. Saddam had told the officers that if they betrayed him or they were captured, he would have their families killed. We assured them that Saddam's reign was about to end and he would not have time to think about retribution for quite a while.

The night before the invasion, we had all our helicopters spread out across the desert floor. I stood on a small sand dune near the command post we had set up, and looked out over the desert floor where hundreds of Black Hawks were prepositioned. The crews and troops that would make the assault were sleeping (as best they could) next to their aircraft in preparation for a predawn liftoff. I walked down among the troops and crews. There was a palpable feeling of confidence, along with some nervous anticipation about the mission they were about to undertake.

I was barraged with questions from the troops: "General, you've been in combat, what's it like?"; "You've been shot at. How does it feel?" I tried to reassure them that they were trained and ready, that we were a far superior force, and enjoined them to just take care of themselves and their buddies and the rest would take care of itself. At that moment it became obvious to me why the week before, the division chaplains had performed sixty-five baptisms. Obviously there were many who wanted to "get right with God."

In the predawn hours of G-day—February 24, 1991—we lifted off and flew across the border, heading ninety-five miles deep into Iraq. Tensions were high. I was going in with an assault command post that would become our division forward until we could bring the main command post forward from the rear area.

We had an exceptional operational-readiness rate for the aircraft and for the Division's equipment. At the same time, we launched long ground convoys that would follow the air assault. The convoys were led by the lieutenant colonels and battalion executive officers into the forward areas with the logistical tail (fuel, ammunition, and other supplies) that was going to be required, and that exceeded our capability to airlift early on with the Chinooks.

We were on listening silence (meaning no radio transmissions unless an emergency arose), so the headset was silent. We flew north at about a hundred knots. As the sun arose, I looked out across the desert floor and saw hundreds of "rooster tails" made by the armored vehicles of the 24th Mechanized Division attacking on our right. Behind the armored vehicles, a five-ton supply vehicle followed. A large American flag was flying from an expedient flagpole rigged to the truck, showing the ingenuity and innovation of the American soldier. I thought, *Saddam, I hope you realize*

*what you've done because here comes the best that America has to offer
and we will prevail.*

By midafternoon, combat elements had established massive refueling
and rearming points at the FOB for the division's helicopters, and the 3rd
Brigade prepared to pass through the forward operating base and land in
the Euphrates valley.

It was a carefully orchestrated, well-rehearsed plan that came off almost
without a hitch. Our 1st Brigade encountered some initial resistance up in
the forward area, but that was handled rather expeditiously when one of
our Apache gunships put a Hellfire missile right on the guys shooting and
that was the end of that. Once again, a whole battalion surrendered.

Soon, we were almost overrun with prisoners. CH-47s brought supplies forward and hauled prisoners back to the rear. Everyone knew what
his or her role was, and everyone executed to perfection. It was incredible
to watch it in action—a truly amazing sight. I was proud to be a part of it.

———

We had handily defeated the Iraqis in an unbelievable four days and I had
repositioned back to our headquarters at the airfield, having finally arranged for a space in the water-treatment plant that I could use as an
office—a space barely large enough to squeeze two desks into if you put
them side by side. You could scarcely get two people in the room, and the
fact that one of those two was six foot five did not make it any easier.
Sharing this cubbyhole with me was General Ron Adams, the Assistant
Division Commander for Support. We were in the office early one morning, planning the move back to Fort Campbell, when a clerk came in and
excitedly said, "Lieutenant Colonel Steve Smith from General Officer
Management Branch in the Pentagon is on the line for you."

"Great," I said, since I had been trying to connect with Steve back in the
States, but with the time difference that was often difficult. Steve (now a good
friend, who is chief of human resources for Duke University) ran the General
Officer Management Office for the Chief of Staff of the Army at the time,
so I knew he would be aware of where my next assignment would be.

"I hate to bother you, Steve, but as you know I've been on the promotion list for major general since before we left Fort Campbell and I'm assuming that as soon as I touch base back at Campbell you will have
another assignment for me, right? I'm confident it couldn't top this one
but could you please give me a hint about the timeline at least? We're
coming up on the end of a school year and I'd like to make some plans
about Mark's schooling."

"Oh, God, General," he said. "You haven't been told?"

"Been told what, Steve?"

"That the chief has selected you to command a division."

My heart almost stopped. Now the other shoe would drop in terms of *which* division. "Outstanding. Command *what*?"

"You're going to command the 82nd Airborne," he said. "You mean General Luck hasn't told you that yet?"

"Steve, I haven't seen General Luck for at least a week and a half, but no, I knew nothing about it."

"General Sullivan says you're the one for the 82nd and we're to move you over to Fort Bragg within a month after you get back—probably around late June for you to take over the command." Gordon R. Sullivan was the highly respected Chief of Staff of the Army, well known for leading the Army's transition from its Cold War posture.

And that was how I found out about my next assignment. Hell of a way to run a railroad, but I wasn't complaining.

---

There's probably still an imprint in the twelve-foot ceiling of that room where I was talking from where I jumped up and hit my head. I was elated. The brigade-command experience at the 82nd had been terrific, and I had deep respect for their NCO corps and the can-do attitude of the troops in the "All-American" division. Anyone who would follow his or her leader out of an airplane in the middle of the night without knowing what is waiting for him down below is a special breed, and there is something special about leading troops like this—I was really looking forward to rejoining their ranks. Ironically, about two or three months before that, General Peay had told me, "General Vuono [then Army Chief of Staff] is coming over tomorrow and he's going to meet with us. You'll get a chance to see him out in the desert but I'm sure one of the things he's going to ask about is what the future holds for you and where I think you ought to go. Being candid here, I'd like for you to command *this* division [the 101st] and you could take over command as soon as you get back. On the other hand, he may look at you for the 82nd instead. The question is, which division would you rather command?"

I was floored. Imagine responding to *that*—particularly since I was being asked by the current commander of the division that I had just fought with—and a division with great capabilities and one that I thought a great deal of. But I looked at General Peay and said, "I love this division like a brother and what you've asked me is akin to asking me to choose between two children, so to speak, or between two brothers—but I will answer, if you let me tell you why." I paused for a moment and considered how to explain. "I would choose the 82nd because it is so highly deployable and so well resourced—and because they get to jump out of airplanes. You might find this hard to believe but I really love jumping out of airplanes. Both divisions have outstanding NCO corps and both are great divisions overall—and while I would happily take either one, if asked to choose, I would prefer the 82nd and would be honored to have been asked."

As a division commander I would be responsible for leading a cadre of more than sixteen thousand dedicated Americans; and while my overall philosophy on leadership would remain consistent, my approach would continue to evolve in keeping with the scope of responsibility.

When you're a battalion commander (lieutenant colonel), you're generally overseeing young, first-time commanders—so in many cases you've got to be a little more directive, more of a hands-on leader. But as you move up, you find yourself being less hands-on and more of a manager.

At the brigade level I had three superb battalion commanders working for me. There was Buck Kernan (retired four-star General William F. Kernan), Jack Hood (a retired colonel who should have been a general), and Keith Kellogg (who went on to become a three-star and should have been a four-star). All three were just outstanding, so at this level I spent far less time hands-on and more gently tweaking on the reins, if you will. I compare it to a stagecoach: at this point, I don't have to flog the horses to get them to run; instead I'm just sitting up there on that coach and gently pulling on the reins to keep them steering in the right direction. The energy and the horsepower are there even without me, and even though we're moving fast across rough terrain, I don't have to worry because I know these three horses will pull us through.

As you move up to division command (as a two-star, the position I was about to assume with the 82nd) you have two assistant division commanders to help you, and you normally have a great command sergeant major (which I had at brigade level, as well)—so what you have is all these high-powered future general officers who are commanding your brigades for you, so it just gets better and better.

Although the responsibilities are greater, the pressures of command are less.

The real key is to focus on the same overall philosophies that should guide you throughout your career—and for me those have always been *mission readiness* and *taking care of people*. You must ensure a constant state of readiness all the way on up through Chairman, and you must take care of your people. If you are effective with both of these, the odds are that you will have a successful command—and that's exactly what I was looking forward to doing as I headed to Fort Bragg.

The 82nd Airborne "All American" Division traces its roots all the way back to 1917, and both its nickname and the distinctive double A on the patch were adopted during World War I when it was realized that the Division was comprised of soldiers from every state across the country.

My new office in the headquarters building had a rather colorful history, too—it used to be the NCO club and was paid for 100 percent through the private donations of NCOs and their families. Later on I would kid Carolyn that I was moving up in the world since my last office (at the water-treatment plant) had been no bigger than a broom closet and here I was working out of what used to be a cocktail lounge. I could only imagine what my next office might be.

When I received my second star and moved from the 101st to the 82nd Airborne Division, General Gary Luck made the transition trouble-free and our relationship was one of mutual respect and great trust and confidence. We both shared those same overriding priorities of taking care of people and staying trained and ready, so he was very easy to work for. Of course, I had watched him in the desert and found him to be a great war fighter and a very smart, down-to-earth good old boy, and he became a great mentor to me. One night he called as I was taking off my bow tie following a formal dinner event.

"How fast can you get the 82nd ready to deploy to Miami for Hurricane Andrew relief?" he asked.

"Faster than the Air Force can get the planes to Green Ramp I can be there waiting for them."

I knew we had the Division Ready Brigade ready to go, and I knew I had two Division Ready Force battalions that could move instantaneously—particularly since they didn't have to go through ammunition issue or any other kind of special-equipment issue, with this being a humanitarian mission.

"It's midnight right now," he said. "And the Air Force says they can be there at seven o'clock in the morning."

"Tell them they're late," I said. With that we got the ball rolling, and by 7:00 A.M. we had five battalions standing by at Green Ramp, ready to get on the planes. By 9:00 A.M. we had four hundred vehicles in convoy ready to depart for Miami, even though we could not get support from the North Carolina Highway Patrol. It was a weekend and there was nobody in a position of authority to be found, and permits were required for a convoy such as this. Finally, around 10:00 A.M., I called the brigade commander over and told him to roll the convoys and "don't ask permission, ask for forgiveness. And if anyone in the highway patrol stops you, ignore them and keep rolling south. If somebody *does* insist on stopping you, give him or her my phone number and tell them to call here; I'll deal with that on my end." I never got one call.

We rolled four hundred vehicles from Fort Bragg to Miami, Florida—probably around nine hundred miles or so—and we had only one that broke down, and that happened as it pulled into the Homestead Air Force Base just outside Miami. It was a great mission for an important humanitarian cause, and we did not lose a vehicle en route. There were many stories of people standing on overpasses with yellow bows as the trucks roared on by, just showing their support. Only in America.

Jeff and Amy were married in the main post chapel during this assignment and we enjoyed having family and friends in our home for the outdoor reception. I counted myself lucky that I could be there that day.

May 1993 brought more good news, in the form of a third star and another new command. After I passed the colors of the 82nd to Mike Steel, both Carolyn and XVIII Airborne Corps commander Lieutenant General Gary Luck pinned the new stars on my collar, and my mother, siblings, sons, their spouses, and our first grandchild, Savannah, were present to share their pride and lend their support.

Life could not get much better than it was at that great moment.

"Guess where I'm calling you from?" I asked Carolyn over the phone in what had become something of a game between us, one that played out upon each of my two prior office moves, based on those offices' rather colorful histories.

"Nope, not even close. I'm calling you from a delivery room." Recognizing the tradition, she laughed, and I went on to explain that it was true. While my last office building a few blocks away at the 82nd used to be the NCO Club, the 1930s' style brick edifice that housed the XVIII ABC (Airborne Corps) headquarters was built in 1932 as the eighty-three-bed USA Station Hospital One, and my office was, in fact, where each and every baby on the base had been born until the hospital closed in 1941. I viewed this as a great omen, working out of the site where all those new lives had been brought into the world.

When I became a captain and was entrusted with the awesome responsibility of leading an A-Team of twelve soldiers back in the late 1960s, I assumed that responsibility with a conscious sense of duty to carry out my mission *and* an obligation to those eleven other families to do whatever was in my power to bring that team home safely. *I was humbled that the U.S. Army saw fit to entrust me with these twelve lives.* I wrote Carolyn that it was almost too much to imagine, and I know how proud of me she was at the time.

In June 1993, when I took over as commander of XVIII Airborne Corps, I would be entrusted with the well-being of 118,000 soldiers under my watch.

I was honored to be following General Gary Luck, who had had such great success as the corps commander and had led the corps through Desert Storm. When you look back at history, everything we had, from Urgent Fury (Grenada) to Just Cause (Panama) to Desert Storm, XVIII Airborne Corps had led the way—they are truly the tip of the spear for America's contingency forces.

I've said it over and over again, but as commander my primary responsibility was to ensure that we were trained and ready, and during this time period it became imperative to do so within the framework of the rapidly evolving joint environment. My priorities were to maintain the high level of readiness that Gary had built, and to fight to make sure that the corps' divisions were resourced to the maximum extent the army could afford. Not only was this grueling struggle for funds essential to the corps, but the skills, tactics, and strategies that I would use to garner those funds would become even more vital down the road, when I would lobby for substantially more capital on behalf of SOCOM (Special Operations Command) and then later as Chairman with astronomically higher stakes at the congressional and presidential levels, on behalf of the entire U.S. military. The experience I was receiving at the XVIII ABC was invaluable.

The XVIII Airborne was the Army's largest fighting force, referred to as "America's Contingency Force" and designed for rapid deployment anywhere in the world. Its 118,000 soldiers comprised the 101st Airborne Division (Air Assault) at Fort Campbell, Kentucky; the 10th Mountain Division (Light Infantry) at Fort Drum, New York; the 24th Infantry Division, later redesignated the 3rd Infantry Division (Mechanized) at Fort Stewart, Georgia; and of course the 82nd Airborne Division at Fort Bragg, North Carolina. In addition, there were a number of separate brigades stationed at Fort Polk, Louisiana, El Paso, Texas, and Fort Bragg.

I would always start by analyzing the readiness reports and then go out to meet with the subordinate commanders to make sure I clearly understood where they stood. I wanted to identify any shortcomings right at the start so that if we were called upon to do something that we weren't resourced to do, we wouldn't commit America's sons and daughters into battle in an unprepared state of readiness. My top priority remained the same, *training and readiness.*

* * *

On October 3 and 4, 1993, the devastating debacle that would later be known as Black Hawk Down occurred in Mogadishu, Somalia, leaving eighteen of our heroic Special Forces operators dead. The bulk of the participants fell under Task Force Ranger—the Special Operations entity—but the corps had contributed a small quick-reaction contingency force for the rescue operation under Task Force–10th Mountain Division. Led by Lieutenant Colonel Bill David, our force was comprised of a battalion (2nd Battalion, 14th Infantry Regiment) and a platoon (1st Platoon, C Company, 1st Battalion, 87th Infantry Regiment)—about 550 soldiers.

When the smoke settled after the event, I felt it was important that I fly to Mogadishu to see firsthand how our people were being employed and what kind of shape they were in—but before I did, I received a call from one of my division commanders.

"General, this is just not right," he began, continuing with an impassioned explanation of a deployment request he had received from CENT-COM, which had requested we put in an armored reaction force for the commander in Somalia. They wanted the force to consist of four Bradley companies. (To the untrained eye, a Bradley fighting vehicle may look somewhat like a tank, but at only twenty-eight tons and armed with TOW missiles and a 25-mm chain gun, although it serves an important function—it's no M1 Abrams tank.)

"We ought to be putting the M1s [tanks] in there because the Somalis have RPGs that will cut right through those Bradleys like butter, but the M1 will make a big difference. What we need right now is to make our troops impervious to their attacks, and to do that, we need armor. The Bradley just won't cut it." (At more than sixty tons and armed with a 105-mm rifled cannon or 120-mm smoothbore cannon plus a .50-caliber heavy machine gun, there's not much that can touch an M1 Abrams tank.)

"I'm on it," I assured the two-star making the plea, then turned to my aide-de-camp. "Get me General Reimer."

"FORSCOM's on the line, they're connecting General Reimer," I heard from the other room. (FORSCOM is the U.S. Army component that provides Army units for various contingency operations.)

"I need you to go to back to CENTCOM and tell them that we want to send two tank companies along with the two Bradley companies, but not just the Bradleys," I explained.

"It's really their call what they get, Hugh," General Reimer responded, as if I needed a lesson in Army chain of command.

"Sir, it may be their call but it is incumbent upon us to recommend the right forces—and four Bradleys is not it."

"I'll see what I can do," he said with a sigh.

If I didn't love the Army I sure as hell wouldn't have stayed in as long as I had up 'til then, but that didn't change the fact that sometimes I became very irritated. This was right up there at the top of the scale. It was just dumb and I was mad.

Some people find stress relief by resorting to liquor, others by inhaling burning tar and nicotine—for me, that five minutes of complete silence while drifting down from a perfectly good airplane beneath the protective nylon ripstock fabric of a parachute canopy is about as close to pure tranquillity as I can get. Fortunately, that night I had a jump scheduled, and I made it to Green Ramp at Pope just in time to make that jump. It helped.

A few hours later I returned to the office. It was just past midnight and Carolyn was probably sleeping soundly. Good for her, I thought. She had gone through a long day of her own, starting with getting Mark off to school, followed by a two-mile run and a walk with Charlie, our cocker spaniel. Then she hosted a Fort Bragg Community Foundation meeting. This was a group she had helped form in order to accept and disperse funds given to help soldiers' families. In the afternoon she chaired a Red Cross meeting as the senior adviser, then had dinner with Mark and attended a parent–teachers meeting at E. E. Smith, Mark's high school. This was a somewhat typical day in the life of a mother who also happened to be the corps commander's wife, so she needed the sleep.

I called Fort Stewart. "Has CENTCOM changed the order?"

"No, sir, it is still four Bradleys. We do have two tank companies we are preparing to load also, but we're running out of time. The ship is scheduled to depart in about four hours."

"Thank you." *Click.*

I glanced at the wall clock. Almost 12:20 A.M. and I couldn't think of a more perfect time to call and wake General Reimer. "Sir, this is important. We need to go to General Hoar [CINC CENTCOM] and tell him we are sending two tank companies along with the Bradleys. Let's be adamant about this. We have to have tank companies to supplement the Bradleys."

He almost grudgingly agreed to call General Hoar. I knew Joe Hoar—I had met him before and I knew he was a great guy. I also knew that he would be open at least to listening to Reimer. So I said, "I will be standing by right here, sir. As we speak I am rolling two tank companies down to the dock but I need an answer ASAP before we can load them up." About thirty minutes later I got the call authorizing the M1s.

---

When I landed in Mogadishu I visited JSOC and then went back to see our troops. I was very concerned that the command-and-control lash-up could potentially create unnecessary vulnerabilities. The chain of command in Somalia was very convoluted and I wanted to make sure that our commander on the ground, Lieutenant Colonel Bill David (commander of the JTF–10ᵗʰ Mountain, involved in the Black Hawk Down incident), knew unequivocally whom he was to respond to.

I asked Bill to talk me through how he would react if he had to respond to another Black Hawk Down incident today. I needed to see what he had learned and what steps he had taken to make sure history would not repeat itself on that front.

"Let me demonstrate, sir, because we've been out there practicing this all day," he said, striding out the door. "Follow me."

We boarded his Humvee, zigzagged through a maze of tiny residential blocks, and eventually arrived to find that they had already set up a typical Somali-type road block that our U.S. quick-reaction force might encounter in a Black Hawk Down–type scenario.

They had blocked the road with a huge stack of junk—tires, old refrigerators, burned-out car bodies, and such—stacked at least a half-story high, which made it impossible to get around it. It was very realistic. Colonel David gave a nod and a major cued the demonstration to begin. I expected to see the massive M1 respond, but instead a much smaller Bradley platoon rounded the corner and came screaming down the street toward the blockade. Instead of trying to confront it, the Bradley platoon diverted to an overwatch of this site, and the commander picked up the headset and called to his rear element with a report. Suddenly the ground started to rumble and wind carried the roar of the M1's fifteen-hundred-horsepower gas-turbine engine as it rounded the corner. Windows rattled with the grind of the hydrokinetic transmission as the tank kicked into gear, and instead of slowing down it lurched forward authoritatively toward the obstacle. Hundreds of Somalis had gathered to watch.

The rusty car bodies went flying through the air along with all the other rubble and it was a sight to behold. It made me feel great because I knew then that we had the right force to do the job with adequate protection for our troops. When I glanced over and saw the look on those Somalis' faces, I had no doubt that they had received the message loud and clear: *do NOT screw around with these guys.*

There were some important lessons we learned from Somalia. The first was the same one I had learned back in Vietnam during Project Delta, where we'd had our own dedicated aircrafts and the pilots lived with us. Whenever we went to a forward operating base, those gunships and those lift ships were right there with us; the pilots ate with us and we got to know them very well.

When we looked at Somalia, we saw that Bill David was doing his best to react effectively but he was unable to do so for a couple of reasons: number one, his mech force was provided by Pakistanis, and they were the force that he really needed to have instantly available to him on extremely short notice, but they were not under his control and he did not have the authority to require them to remain close at hand.

Second, Bill had not even been notified of the ranger operation that Major General Bill Garrison and his force were running that day, so he was unaware that there was a specific reason to demand that they remain on an especially short leash that day, as they should have been. *The mech force was the very unit that could have helped Garrison take care of the blockade that had prompted the calamity,* but they were not available. Instead they were spread all over the city, drinking tea or whatever they were doing, and their commander told Bill David that it would take hours to get all his guys together.

If you are going to have a rapid-reaction force, they need to understand that they're on a short tether so that they can go out on a moment's notice. Plus, you need a solid, integrated force *under one individual's control,* immediately ready to respond—almost like an air crew standing by on strip alert—and not a makeshift force like they had that would take hours to pull together.

Bottom line, I attribute all that to not having one individual in charge. The chain of command during that operation was horrendous, as history has proved, and there were no clear lines of responsibility. There must always be one person whose chest you can poke your finger on and say, "You are it and you are the one who is 100 percent responsible for this operation to go as smooth as silk."

A combat-ready force is one that trains as it will fight and is capable of functioning as a cohesive, integrated force under the direst circumstances—otherwise, the alternative can be devastating.

———

On my way back home I called the division commander who had insisted that the M1s supplement the Bradleys to personally thank him for his great read of what was required, and his perseverance in making sure that the requirement was met. It's a another example of the extraordinarily high caliber of personnel throughout the XVIII ABC (Airborne Corps).

The trip had reinforced the need to thoroughly integrate the concepts of joint warfare into the XVIII ABC in a practical way, on both the tactical and the strategic levels. I wanted us to train as a team; to make sure that as a corps our mission statement included the requirement to be able to fight as a joint task force—something that's taken for granted today but was totally new back in 1993.

To that end, I took over an old World War II area of Fort Bragg and turned it into a cutting-edge facility for joint warfare. We upgraded all the buildings, hardwired the electronics and communications suites, and came up with a first-class setup for operating as a joint task force that we could immediately fall in on if called upon—one that provided plenty of space for all the individual elements of that JTF.

We put together rehearsals and mock exercises to develop processes and to standardize our procedures (in a way, like those notebooks behind the DDO's desk had checklists to follow for every possible eventuality), and through these rehearsals we identified our shortfalls—and then rehearsed again after we corrected those shortfalls. My goal was to perfect the process so that if a real-life situation necessitated the activation of a joint task force, we could do so "at the push of a button"—and my gut told me that that button would have to be pushed in the very near future.

Admiral Paul David Miller (or PDM, as he was called), commander in chief of Atlantic Command (CINC USACOM) must have been reading my mind. It was a matter of only weeks before he announced that they wanted to run a big exercise testing the JTF concept using both the Marine forces at Camp Lejeune, North Carolina, and the 82nd Airborne Division at Fort Bragg. The Navy ships were operating off the coast of North Carolina. This was rather unusual in that it was a combination of both JTX (joint training exercise) and FTX (field training exercise), which meant that it was to be a large-scale, real-life exercise that used real planes, ships, soldiers, and sailors instead of electronic or tabletop simulations *and* it employed all the services' capabilities.

The scenario called for the joint task force to stand up at Camp Lejeune and the exercise would take place down in the Caribbean, with XVIII corps elements of the 101st and 82nd layered in. Under the command of General Bill Keyes (also commander of Fort Lejeune and now retired and CEO of Colt firearms), the Marine component would start off as the JTF commander and then halfway through the exercise I would come in with the XVIII Airborne Corps staff and seamlessly replace Bill Keyes's JTF headquarters with the XVIII ABC joint task force; demonstrating that both the Marine and Army joint task forces could effectively hand off command of the operation with perfect, uninterrupted continuity.

The deputy joint task force commander for the exercise was Rear Admiral Jay Johnson, who served in that capacity for both Bill Keyes and me to provide continuity of command and control. The exercise went off without a hitch.

This was really the first time that the Marines and Navy had the opportunity to observe the brilliance of the Army's School of Advanced Military Studies (SAMS) guys at work—and they were some of the brightest minds in the Army, the same think tank gurus the Chairman often called upon to draw up contingency planes for large-scale operations. They

were also exposed to the quality of our XVIII Airborne Corps plans officer and his remarkable shop; and their ability to keep generating plans,
branches, and sequels. It was just mind-boggling, and the Marine/Navy
guys seemed never to have seen anything like that. The planning process
was designed to take into account every possible eventuality so that there
would be no surprises on the battlefield. Right up front they defined specific courses of action to take according to each possible occurrence (the
branches) and various follow-ups depending on which of a multitude of
potential outcomes were to occur (the sequels). I could not have been
prouder of the corps.

Once again, the timing was almost uncanny. In less than a month I would
be called upon to command another joint task force, but this one would
not be an exercise, and its scope would be massive.

During this assignment we were blessed with five grandchildren. Jon and
Anne became the proud parents of Cassie, and twin girls, Heather and
Hannah; and Jeff and Amy added two sons to the family, Sam and Ben.

The family was growing.

**8:00 P.M., March 23, 2002, Walter Reed Intensive Care Unit**

My skin felt like it was on fire, and I could feel the effect almost immediately after the intravenous Neo-Synephrine fluid entered my bloodstream. It was a strange sensation as the medical team raised my blood pressure higher and higher, more uncomfortable than painful. In a way it reminded me of the rush I would feel every morning after my five-mile run, only without the accompanying accelerated heartbeat.

There were at least four doctors present the entire time—and their focused monitoring of my vitals was nonstop. While I was grateful for their attentiveness, I couldn't help feeling they were just waiting for that stroke or heart attack to kick in. The thought probably elevated my blood pressure every bit as much as the meds.

Fortunately, I didn't have a stroke or a heart attack, at least not yet. After being warned that the "extreme danger zone" would extend into the next two to three days, I actually drifted off to sleep for a few hours, satisfied that things were beginning to fall into place nicely.

# Chapter Ten ★★★

# THE GODFATHER— AIRBORNE

I was prepared for war.

I had led troops in both Vietnam and Desert Storm, but those were different. This time I was the commander, the one ultimately responsible for more than twenty thousand brave men and women who were about to follow me into battle.

September 18, 1994. After many months of rehearsals, the night of the invasion was at hand and I was ready to set in motion the forcible takeover of Haiti—a country controlled by the military of a ruthless dictator I had been ordered to remove from power so that its rightfully elected president could return to office. Upon President Clinton's authority, the Secretary of Defense had just signed the execute order and we were on our way.

Early on I had people on the ground—a low-profile team that painted a detailed portrait of exactly what we would encounter. These were soldiers, and even though they didn't come across as soldiers, they were. They told me who was guarding the palace at what hours, and who did so with vigilance, and who would sneak their Prestige Lagers and then doze off on their antiaircraft guns. They told me who was on which quad four and when they slipped out for Comme Il Fauts (Haitian cigarettes) and to relieve themselves. They observed the airfield and told me about the major who ran it; I knew him by name and the names of his entire company, and how they operated, and which habits they would repeat night after night. We had an electronic-eavesdropping capability on their communications that they were not aware of, and a dedicated satellite orbiting overhead to relay that and other mission communication. I had a phenomenal intell team and was confident that I was going into battle equipped with the most complete intelligence data possible. As the ancient warrior Sun Tzu said, "If you know the enemy . . . you need not fear the result of a hundred battles."

This information was vital since we were about to drop in seven battalions of infantry from the 82nd Airborne and insert teams of JSOC operators (elite commandos from Delta and SEAL Team Six) to execute violent seizures of strategic targets across the island. AC-130 Spectre gunships would circle the island overhead and take out key targets with their massive 105-mm howitzers and 20-mm Gatling guns, and for the first time two aircraft carriers anchored just over the horizon would be used as launching platforms for thousands of troops from both JSOC and the 10th Mountain Division.

Almost unbelievably, we had successfully pulled off a colossal deception that would allow us to take the country by surprise—otherwise, planes could be shot down and hundreds of paratroopers floating down in their harnesses could become nothing more than target practice for the Haitian military to pick off at will.

We were trained, ready, and well rehearsed; and I felt 100 percent cool, calm, collected, and confident—*Troy Aikman at the Super Bowl*—and I was about to utter the code word that would launch the largest U.S. airborne invasion since Operation Market Garden (Allied invasion of the Netherlands) in World War II. Little did I know that within minutes I'd be getting ten pounds of shit in a five-pound bag—news that would throw the entire OPLAN out the window and require me to call one of the biggest audibles in the history of the United States Army.

———

In February 1991 the charismatic Jean-Bertrand Aristide took office as President of Haiti after a landslide victory in a legitimate, democratic election; he was the overwhelming choice of the people in the first free election in the history of the country. Former president Jimmy Carter led an international team of observers to guarantee that the election was both legitimate and peaceful.

Only seven months later, Aristide was overthrown in a bloody coup and sent into exile by his own military chief, Lieutenant General Raoul Cedras. In what would become a revolving door of de facto presidents and prime ministers, Cedras emerged as the real ruler, even after he appointed Supreme Court Justice Emile Jonassaint to bear the title "president." The climate continued to deteriorate and more than seventy-thousand Haitians seeking refuge in the United States were intercepted at sea by the U.S. Coast Guard as they tried to flee the repression, torture, murders, and rapes that took place under the regime of Cedras and his FADH (Forces Armées d'Haiti) military and FRAPH (Front pour l'Avancement et le Progrès Haitien—Front for the Advancement and Progress of Haiti) paramilitary units.

The United Nations, the Organization of American States, and the United States supported the return of Aristide and sought to achieve this through diplomacy as well as economic sanctions and embargoes—but these served only to worsen the plight of the Haitians. Cedras remained unyielding, and what few concessions he did agree to were only manipulations for short-term relief, and he consistently reneged.

On July 31, 1994, by a vote of twelve to zero, the United Nations Security Council adopted Resolution 940, which authorized member states to use all necessary means to facilitate the departure of Haiti's military leadership and restore constitutional rule and Aristide's presidency. International support was key, but even long before the vote, President Clinton had ordered contingency planning to begin for Operation Uphold Democracy, which is where I came in.


In early January 1994, Admiral Paul David Miller (CINCACOM, commander in chief Atlantic Command) appointed me commander of Joint Task Force 180, its mission being to restore the legitimate government of Haiti (i.e., Aristide). In view of the in-country situation with Cedras and his military in power, it was designed as a forcible entry/combat operation. Under my direction, my planning staff would work in close conjunction with Admiral Miller's staff in Norfolk, Virginia.

I was fortunate enough to have a pair of spectacular plans officers—Major William "Burke" Garrett (who ultimately went on to become a major general and commander in chief of Southern European Task Force—U.S. Army Africa) and Major Kevin Benson—both "SAMs," advanced-military-planning graduates from Command and General Staff College, who originally presented me with the *existing* corps plan for Haiti. I looked down at it and almost laughed—it was the same sorry-ass three-page plan that had been on the shelf ten years prior when I was a brigade commander in the 82nd Airborne. It called for jumping one brigade of the 82nd into Port-au-Prince airfield to restore law and order to the entire country. I could not believe that in ten years virtually nothing had been done to revise a completely inadequate plan.

I worked with Burke and Kevin and issued some planning guidance, directing them toward a night operation that would involve a forcible entry—and one that would utilize a much larger force. Conceptually, our forces would descend on the country under the cover of darkness and take over critical targets throughout the island. When the Haitians awoke the next morning, they would find that the Americans "owned the island." The pair understood the concept and enthusiastically took off for a small office on the third floor to set up their planning base (which they would later identify as a supply closet) and began developing the plan, ultimately coming back to me with a detailed mission-analysis briefing, which was excellent.

What evolved was a plan to drop seven airborne battalions into Haiti—five into Port-au-Prince and two farther north—plus a Marine element that would land on the remote part of the island at Cap Haitien. My hope was that the island would be ours without ever firing a shot. Simultaneously, JSOC would be moving inland to secure the rest of the country while searching for weapons caches, and I would jump in with the headquarters element and set up a small tactical command post at an old baseball factory just outside Port-au-Prince. The XVIII ABC had a "bare base" capability (meaning that we didn't need infrastructure when we jumped in). We had the ability to set up our command post out of the equipment in our rucksacks—one reason why the rucksacks weighed between seventy and eighty pounds. Jumping in with the troops is the way paratroopers did it, and even though I was a three-star at the time, it goes right back to my motto of *leading from the front*.

That was the basic concept that we presented to Admiral Miller in Norfolk, with the understanding that we would come back with more once the details were fleshed out. He responded very favorably and we returned to Fort Bragg to take it to the next stop.

We then broke down the operation by command responsibility and met with each of those commands to lay out our concept and specify just what we expected them to do with it—namely, come back to us with particulars of how they would execute our objectives. I would meet with three-star Admiral Bill Keyes out of Camp Lejeune to cover the Marine component; my good friend Vice Admiral Jay Johnson (who had been my deputy on the recent training exercise) to cover the Navy elements; Major General Jim Record to go over the Air Force end of things; and Major General Bill Garrison to explore the JSOC/Special Operations piece.

Since I had selected JSOC to be the key element for the fast-hitting initial entry into the country (not to mention that both JSOC and my XVIII ABC headquarters were based at Fort Bragg), it made sense for me to take care of the JSOC briefing first. We had already chosen key strategic targets that included the National Palace, police stations (the Haitian police were not municipal policeman but soldiers under the direction of the brutal Cedras henchman, Colonel Michel François), Camp d'Application (where they kept their heavy weapons), the airfield, and air-defense systems (including two antiaircraft batteries and the security forces that guarded that airfield). There were additional sensitive down-town targets and a naval installation—twenty-six targets in all, each of which I wanted to hit hard and fast at H-hour, which I estimated to be around 11:00 P.M. Fast, efficient, professional, and synchronized, we would hit all twenty-six at the same instant and we would own that island, similar to what one of my mentors, General Carl Stiner, had done when he was a three-star commanding this same corps and had taken out the dictator Manuel Noriega during Operation Just Cause in Panama.

To pull this off I envisioned dropping approximately 500 rangers in an airdrop mode or an air-assault mode (whichever they preferred) from Guantanamo Bay into Dessalines to secure the barracks and another 250 rangers into Camp d'Application, where they would eliminate a major Fad'H force and weapons company; additional rangers would secure the U.S. embassy, as well as SEAL Team Six and Delta to be brought in by Army MH-60 choppers to take out the Haitian 4th Police Company and reinforce the rangers at the National Palace.

At H+20 minutes, an additional five-hundred-ranger element would parachute in just west of Port-au-Prince to establish Forward Operating Base Dallas. I also wanted to have Special Forces A-Teams—the Green Berets—all over the countryside by early the following morning, and the heavy firepower that SOF AC-130 Spectre gunships would provide from overhead. We would bring in multiple "Compass Call" electronic jamming aircraft to disrupt Haitian military command-and-control communications, as well as the marine contingent, which I purposely positioned on the remote part of the island at Cap Haitien.

By first light I wanted our presence strongly felt *all over the country,* not just in Port-au-Prince—so when Haitians got up and went to work they would be hit with a tremendous wow factor—meaning that almost everywhere they turned, they would find American troops. We would be peaceful, respectful, and fully abide by our very stringent rules of engagement, but we would be extremely visible all across the island. (This was in direct contrast to the approach taken by General Tommy Franks during Operation Iraqi Freedom, where he chose to "own Baghdad" rather than the entire country—and we have seen all the problems that choice created.)

I had already given JSOC a detailed overview of our objectives and asked them to come by and present their brief on the operational specifics once they had come up with a viable plan of execution. In short order, Colonel William "Jerry" Boykin contacted my office and said that he had done so, and he scheduled a time to present. (Jerry retired in 2007 as a lieutenant general amid a cloud of controversy for preaching anti-Islamic rhetoric from various pulpits while in uniform.)

He began his brief and I could tell within the first few minutes that it lacked any detail and was not well thought out; it appeared to have been thrown together in a very haphazard way. I started to stop him after the first two minutes, then thought, *It's got to get better.* I let him continue, but around the three-minute mark I couldn't take anymore.

"That's enough, Jerry," I said. "This is the most half-assed plan I've ever seen, so you go ahead and get the hell out of here and don't waste my time. When you get your act together you can come back and show me how you are *really* going to carry out what I have asked you to do."

He slithered out and I picked up the phone and called his boss, JSOC commander Major General Bill Garrison, who had recently returned from commanding the ill-fated Black Hawk Down mission in Somalia. "Bill, Jerry Boykin is on his way back and I was very disappointed in the plan I saw," I said. "You need to put some personal attention on this because it's a big deal and your guys are going to be the centerpiece of the takedown of Haiti."

I didn't have to remind the general that as my Special Ops commander, it was *his* responsibility to have presented me with a carefully conceived and well-constructed plan for this very important mission. "I'm on it, sir," was all he could muster, but my message was received.

To this day I can't imagine how Garrison could have let Boykin out that door with that original half-baked, piece-of-shit plan—whether he hadn't even listened to it or approached it as "just another planning drill." As Boykin left, I wondered what had happened to the *train as you fight, fight as you train* doctrine that we lived and breathed. As two-star general in charge of the entire command, Garrison should have listened to that plan and torn Boykin a new asshole before cutting him lose with it— especially with a presentation he was about to take to the three-star corps commander. Just a simple phone call would have been fine—something like, *General Shelton, we're not ready yet. Let's reschedule this.* Better yet, they should have looked at it two or three days before that and fixed it on the spot.

As it played out, Boykin called back the very next afternoon and tried to assure us that they had reworked it and come up with a solid plan—he wanted to come back in and rebrief that same day. "Are you sure you don't want to give this some more thought?" I asked, not wanting to waste even more of my time listening to his ramble.

"It's a good plan, sir," he said, and a few hours later he'd completed his rebrief and shut down his PowerPoint. I didn't have to think twice.

"Jerry, this is not a good plan," I said, looking into his eyes as he damn near shit a brick. "It's a *great* plan," I finally said. "Great job, we'll feather some details and I'll take it to Norfolk." In less than twenty-four hours they had come up with a smartly conceived battle plan that was well thought out, creative, and outlined a damn near perfect means to execute my objective of owning the island. Those guys can do wonders when they put the first team on it and when they take it seriously. (By the time the operation eventually played out, Garrison had retired and been replaced by General Pete Schoomaker as commander of the Joint Special Operations Command.)

I met with the other component commanders and the plan was taking shape nicely. It was time to update the CINC on where we stood.


My relationship with Admiral Paul David Miller was a great one and I looked forward to briefing him on how far we had taken the plan. He had a couple of dynamo guys working with him who went on to become three- and four-star flag officers whom I was also looking forward to seeing again: Admiral Tom Fargo, who went on to become commander in chief Pacific Command and was also the inspiration for the Captain Bart Mancuso character in the film *The Hunt for Red October*; and Vice Admiral Tom Wilson, his J2 (director of intelligence), who went on to become my J2 when I was Chairman. Admiral Miller had told me that these two young guys defied the old-salt mode of the Navy when he brought them in—both had great initiative and were adept at thinking outside the box. They would repeatedly demonstrate that he did not overstate their enormous value.

While Admiral Miller and his staff loved our overall plan, they did have one change: they did not want the corps jumping in, but instead insisted that my headquarters be based out on a ship. That was the Navy mentality, but in this case he was absolutely correct. I would be based on the USS *Mount Whitney,* about fifty miles out.

Today, the *Mount Whitney* serves as the command ship for the Commander Sixth Fleet, and she was the first U.S. Navy combatant to permanently accommodate women on board. With a complement of 150 enlisted personnel, 12 officers, and 150 civilian mariners from Military Sealift Command, the *Mount Whitney* carried enough food to feed the crew for ninety days and made one hundred thousand gallons of fresh water daily—so I felt more than comfortable that I would be in good hands even if the operation lasted significantly longer than we anticipated.

Most important, the ship's afloat-communications capability was second to none; being able to receive, process, and transmit vast amounts of secure data from any point on earth through HF, UHF, VHF, SHF, and EHF communications frequencies. This technology enabled the Joint Intelligence Center and Joint Operations Center—in essence my floating "war room"—to gather and process critical information with real-time satellite links to Admiral Miller, the Pentagon, and even the White House if necessary. The JOC (Joint Operations Center) was equipped with the most sophisticated floating command, control, communications, computer, and intelligence (C4I) ever commissioned, and I had no doubt that I would be taking full advantage of it to effectively command the widely dispersed air, ground, and maritime units that constituted our mission.

We were getting close, but there was still one element missing: we needed a platform from which to launch—one that was closer to Haiti than the United States, and even closer than Guantanamo Bay, Cuba. Without missing a beat, Admiral Miller proposed using aircraft carriers—a perfect solution that I had not thought of. We would put JSOC on the USS *America* and put the 10th Mountain Division on the USS *Enterprise* (the world's first nuclear-powered aircraft carrier). It turned out that the USS *America* was commanded by Benny Suggs, who happened to be a North Carolina State graduate from Whiteville, North Carolina and would go on to become Rear Admiral Suggs—Deputy Commander in Chief of U.S. Special Operations Command a year after I left the command—so I felt assured that we would be in great hands. We would also establish intermediate support bases at Guantanamo Bay and Great Inagua Island.

I walked out of there feeling confident that these innovative thinkers had taken a good plan and made it even better.

Using the Army methodology of sand-table drills, we set up a large-scale training drill at Fort Bragg, where, on March 23, 1994, I brought all the generals and admirals into a classified building—one that not many people know about—and we had a sand table built. I had twenty admirals and generals in the room that day. A big timeline wrapped all around the wall, starting at H minus forty-eight hours and documenting every event all the way up to when we transitioned into a new phase.

The "sand table" was an enormous model built on a forty-five-degree angle so that everybody sitting in the bleachers looked down on it, and I had two guys dressed in referee uniforms who used long sticks to point out whatever places the admirals or generals were describing as they talked through the details of their portion of the operation. This was a very comprehensive 3-D model of the whole island built by the J2 guys. On the far wall we had blow-up photos of key targets like Port-au-Prince, with the palace and gun fortifications identified, along with similar recon photos detailing specific areas of the other targets.

One of our key concerns was the airfield because we would be jumping two battalions onto it and the Haitians guarded the place with a twenty-five-man police force armed with AK-47s. You can only imagine what might have happened if the Haitians had been aware that we were coming, how easy it have been for them to pull out those AK-47s and pick off many of those paratroopers as they drifted down under parachutes.

Our recon revealed that this entire force normally went to bed at about 11:00 P.M., and they all slept in one small building adjacent to the airfield. Shortly before the jump we would intensify our eyes on the building, so if at any point the guards tried coming out of the structure during the jump, the AC-130 would hit it with one round and vaporize the building and that would be the end of that. Of course, the AC-130 would also be there to provide air support in the event that any other resistance was encountered.

We had a great plan and presented it hour by hour, with each flag officer presenting his own piece of the plan. It was an involved process that started around 8:00 A.M. and went straight through the day, but it was well worth it, and I could not have been more pleased with how it went. In a joint operation such as this, every admiral and general had to understand exactly how his piece had to take place in order for the plan to work. That was the only way to accomplish the mission and avoid fratricide.

I stood up to give my closing comments around 2:00 P.M. and that great day took a drastic 180. Colonel Dan McNeill, my G3 (recently retired as a four-star general who was in charge of Afghanistan), had entered the room and he looked horrified.

"Dan, is something wrong?" I asked.

"We've got an F-16 that just collided with a C-130 and so far over a hundred paratroopers are injured or killed."


I ran out, jumped into my Humvee, and raced off for the Pope Air Force Base Green Ramp, where I would arrive to find aircraft debris and bodies all over the place. It looked like a Civil War battlefield.

The two F-16 pilots had ejected, but the fighter aircraft had rocketed to the ground under full afterburner power and impacted a parked C-141. It resulted in a tremendous explosion and the fireball went right between two buildings where I had about two hundred paratroopers preparing for a jump. Between the impact, the pieces of airplane flying through the air, the original fireball, the secondary fires, and the exploding 20-mm F-16 ammunition, it was a horrible scene. Since Pope was adjacent to Bragg, the whole thing happened less than a mile from where we were having our meeting.

We continued to evacuate burn victims well into the night. We flew those who were at least somewhat stable to the Brooke Army Medical Center in San Antonio, Texas. Those who couldn't live long enough to make it to San Antonio or had more-severe problems were sent up to the University of North Carolina's Chapel Hill Burn Center, founded by John

Stackhouse to treat burn victims from his electrical-contracting business and who today is my neighbor, a World War II veteran and a great American. Others were treated at Duke University Medical Center in Durham, North Carolina. Three who were comatose and barely hanging on were taken to the intensive care ward on the top floor of Womack Army Medical Center at Fort Bragg. By the time it was over, we ended up with twenty-four dead, four traumatic amputations, more than twenty severely burned, and at least a hundred with other injuries.

The following night around seven o'clock I got a call that President Clinton would be coming to Fort Bragg to visit the injured troops in the hospital just as soon as he concluded his live TV press conference, which was due to start at seven thirty.

"Confirming that you said 'he's coming tonight'?" I asked, glancing down at my watch and running some quick calculations in my head. "Got it," I said after receiving the confirmation. "We look forward to his visit."

*Let's see*, I thought . . . *thirty minutes until his speech starts, maybe another thirty for the speech itself, fifteen-minute chopper ride to Andrews and forty-five-minute flight to Pope on Air Force One—tops.* That would put him at Fort Bragg in two hours.

I knew what a presidential entourage entailed, so we kicked into gear—we'd have to provide transportation for the press and staff that would inevitably be joining, so we got the word out to round up all our general-officer vans, then started contacting the drivers, coordinating with Womack, etc. It's funny—when word like that comes in, everyone becomes so energized that they just make things happen.

By nine or so we felt pretty good that we had everything covered—that's when the phone rang and we were told that President Clinton was not coming after all. Well, it was disappointing, but that's how these things go. *Stand down, everyone.*

Throughout the night I continued to get status reports on the injured troops and it wasn't pretty, particularly for those who had been transported out to the Burn Center.

The next morning I was on my way upstairs to pin the Audie Murphy awards on four outstanding NCOs when Marie Allen, my executive assistant and a truly great American, stopped me. "Sir, I just got a phone call from the White House. President Clinton's trip is back on, and he'll be arriving at Pope at noon."

"Okay, Marie," I responded calmly as I continued up the stairs. "Tell the chief, General Akers, and put the plan back in place. This one's easy: we just do exactly what we did last night."

"Got it, sir," Marie responded, somewhat surprised that I would go ahead with the awards ceremony so close to the President's arrival. As far as I was concerned, they could certainly handle the logistics without me, but the awards ceremony was an important event, too. It recognized extremely hard work on the part of exceptional noncommissioned officers. What's more, their families and friends would be there to share this great honor. Named after the most decorated soldier in World War II (and the one who coined my favorite phrase, *lead from the front*), the Sergeant Audie Murphy Club honored a select group of NCOs who had demonstrated outstanding performance and inherent leadership qualities.

Following the ceremony, I checked in at the office and headed out to meet the President.

I pulled up to Green Ramp and navigated my way around the security detail to park my Humvee. Good timing. It was only a few minutes before I saw the majestic aqua of *Air Force One* cutting through the North Carolina sky on its final approach into Pope. By that time, General Gordon Sullivan, Chief of Staff of the Army (a great leader and motivator), had arrived and joined us, as had Womack Commander Colonel Hal Timboe (later General Timboe, commander of Walter Reed), along with Major General Mike Steele (commander of the 82nd Airborne) and Major General Richard E. Davis, my outstanding deputy commander. We already had the red carpet rolled out, and the corps color guard and 82nd Airborne Division Band stood ready. As the main door popped open and the President stepped out, I snapped a tight salute and the 82nd band proudly began a perfect rendition of "Hail to the Chief."

By the time we had completed the rounds at Womack Army Medical Center, the President had visited every troop personally—and there had to have been a hundred of them. Colonel Hal Timboe and I accompanied him for each of them.

When we walked out of that last patient ward, the President looked at Hal and asked, "Is that all?"

Timboe replied, "Mr. President, that is all with the exception of three on the top floor that are in grave condition. We have done everything we can but it just doesn't appear that they're going to make it."

"I want to see those three," the President replied without hesitation. At this time it was just the three of us, without any press; they were all gathered outside the building.

We took the elevator to the top floor, where the isolation units were located. After donning the special attire that was required to enter those rooms, the President privately entered each of them—where he stood beside each man and gently put his hand on him, privately reflecting, then saying a prayer.

During the elevator ride down, Hal reached over and handed the President a piece of paper and said, "Mr. President, this is a copy of what George Washington said about being a commander in chief." I can't quote it exactly, but it read something like this: *there is no greater concern that a commander can show than to care for those who are seriously injured.*

I could see how greatly the President was affected when he read it, then said, "It's just something that I had to do." Outside, he met with the families who we were able to assemble out there. It was short notice and nobody knew he was coming, so these were the families who had already arrived to visit their loved ones. The Secret Service agents who flew in with the President commented on how impressed they were with the speed at which we responded, since they had no time to put in an advance team, as they almost always did. But we came to the rescue and had it covered.

As we arrived back at *Air Force One*, I told the President how very much his visit meant to the families and troops he just visited, and I personally thanked him for coming. He turned to me and said, "General, I had to come—and I should have come last night. Last night I had that press conference [regarding Whitewater] and all my handlers kept telling me, *Don't go to Fort Bragg—all the press will be there and fire questions about the press conference and it will totally detract from why you're going there.* . . . And they convinced me not to go. But last night I couldn't sleep, and around two A.M. I told myself that I didn't care who told me what, I had to come and visit those troops. This morning they still tried to dissuade me and I finally got fed up and said, *Read my lips. I am the President of the United States and I'm going to Fort Bragg, so get the plane ready to leave by eleven.* They understood that, so here I am." He said it with a kind of chuckle.

I thanked him again, telling him how much it meant to the injured soldiers and their families, and he departed.

———

As the situation in Haiti deteriorated, my involvement became even more active—it was really heating up and I was excited to be a part of such a cutting-edge joint operation. To be a joint-task-force commander took a different mind-set than being just an Army commander. One of the things the Army had done to prepare me to be a JTF commander was sending me to an Army course on joint war fighting, conducted at Maxwell Air Force Base. At the time I wondered why I was there, since I'd never thought I would use anything they were teaching. But it turned out to be a great learning experience and I was finally really putting those techniques into practice. General Bob Sennewald was one of the mentors who taught that course, and he contributed to making it a tremendous experience.

\* \* \*

My C-12 chalked up lots of flight hours as I made more and more trips to brief Admiral Miller on our status, usually accompanied by my great G3 Colonel Dan McNeill and Brigadier General Frank Akers, a brilliant U.S. Naval Academy graduate and my Chief of Staff. Finally we got the stamp of approval on the plan and an authorization to put together some exercises to see how the pieces worked in real time.

Once again, my SAMs guys did not disappoint, and over the course of the next few months we participated in three rather massive field training exercises that were extremely helpful, one of which was specifically intended as a rehearsal for Haiti, but we camouflaged it as best we could. Most flew under the radar screen, like Super Thrust I and Super Thrust II in April and June 1994 respectively, but word of Operation Agile Provider slipped out in May. It's no wonder, since more than forty-four thousand troops were involved. The following article, by David Usborne of *The Independent,* was rather typical:

## U.S. 'DRESS REHEARSAL' FOR HAITI INVASION: PENTAGON DENIES HUGE EXERCISE IS PRELUDE TO ATTACK
From DAVID USBORNE in Washington

*Sunday, 15 May 1994*

Speculation that President Clinton may be moving rapidly towards ordering a full-scale invasion of Haiti to reinstate ousted President Jean-Bertrand Aristide intensified yesterday after revelations of a massive military exercise in the Caribbean last week by U.S. Marines and Special Forces, writes David Usborne in Washington.

After initially denying reports of the maneuvers, the Pentagon later admitted that as many as 44,000 troops had been involved in exercises in Puerto Rico, the Bahamas and North Carolina. A mock invasion was staged of a fictitious state taken over in a coup by an "unfriendly leader." Officials denied that it had been launched with any actual country in mind.

Code-named 'Operation Agile Provider', the exercise involved amphibious vessels, warplanes and a submarine. In the course of the simulated invasions, Army Rangers penetrated 10 miles inland, took control of 'communications centers' and seized imaginary installations.

A military source told the Boston Globe that Agile Provider was pursued 'with Haiti in mind'.

They weren't too far off, since at the time we were already in the process of taking over a major portion of Great Inagua, the third-largest island of the Bahamas.

The question now became, once all the pieces were in place, how much notice would we need from the time the execute order was signed until we initiated H-hour, the time we would commence the invasion.

Once again putting pencil to paper, Burke and Kevin emerged from their supply-closet planning center (along with Dan McNeill, Brigadier General Akers, and a host of others) to report that forty-eight hours was the magic number. There were many things that would have to be done at the last minute, like positioning the C-130s we would have standing by packed with engineering equipment at MacDill Air Force Base in Tampa—just in case the Haitians blew the runway, these guys would be standing by to come in to repair it so that we could land follow-on forces.

————

At this point, tension really started mounting and Admiral Miller told me to get ready because this could go any day now. Excellent, I was ready.

We prepositioned our forces. We already had some intell guys in the country who had been reporting out, and we boosted this to increase their level of reporting. Everything was cranking ahead full speed, and the feeling that accompanied such complete preparedness was magnificent.

Then one day I got a call from Admiral Miller. "Hugh, slight change required. I want you to use Marines to take those targets in Port-au-Prince that you've presently got SEAL Team Six handling."

I couldn't believe what I was hearing and I had no idea where it was coming from. It could have had something to do with giving the Marines additional media exposure, or maybe the White House even pushed him to do it. I really don't know and that was not my concern. But fratricide is, and that's exactly what would be at risk if Marines were landed down in Port-au-Prince instead of isolated in Cap Haitien. What he was suggesting was positioning a Marine element going *crossways* to the flow of other traffic, just the same as if you drive down a street and somebody else decides to cross that street without slowing down.

"Admiral, I really do not want to do that. That really does interfere with the flow of this plan in a very serious way. It may even kill people."

"Got it, Hugh. But that's exactly what I want you do to—switch out SEAL Team Six with the Marines."

"I will get back with you on that, Admiral," I said, hanging up. I immediately called Bill Keyes for his take on it.

"Hugh, are you shitting me?" Keyes asked. "That is the dumbest fucking thing I have ever heard."

"Couldn't agree with you more, and thanks, Bill," I said, disconnecting to get Jay Johnson on the line to ask him the same question. What I was doing was finding out exactly what each of my component commanders thought, and every one of them was telling me, *No, that's not how we rehearsed it and it's absolutely not how it should be done.*

This was not right, and I had to get Admiral Miller to understand that.

"Sir, I really need to come and see you," I told him, and then had my J3 meet me at the plane. We climbed aboard the C-12 aircraft for the flight to Norfolk. My real reason for having him join me was that I needed him to be able to coordinate with his own counterparts while I was ironing out all this with the admiral.

I walked in and said, "Admiral, I have some very serious concerns about your directive for me to put the Marines down at Port-au-Prince. Let me show you on a map what the problem is." I unfolded my briefing maps and went through it step by step, showing him the flow to the point where it was obvious what the problem was. "I've gone over this with all the components," I told him as he gazed at the indications on the map. "And they all are very comfortable with that, and I can tell you right now that every one of them said absolutely do *not* put Marines in here, and once again I am *strongly* recommending that you don't make me change this plan."

He didn't speak a word, but his glare spoke volumes. Finally, almost threateningly, he said, "Are you telling me I will have to get a new JTF commander if I want to put Marines in there?"

I looked him dead in the eye and replied, "You got it, sir. That's exactly what I am telling you, because I've made it clear that in my mind you are going to create a safety-and-fratricide problem that I do not want to be a part of."

Admiral Miller is a good man and I really didn't know for sure what was going on, but he lightened up and said, "Okay, let me think about it."

"Okay," I said. "Anything else I can do for you?"

"No, Hugh, that will do it. Thanks very much for coming up."


Even though I was on great terms with him, I left there that day not knowing whether or not I would have a job the next day. But it didn't matter because I was going to stand up for what was right, and that was a *bad* decision any way you looked at it. I thought so and I had plenty of backup that concurred. So I got back in the plane and flew back to Fort Bragg. About an hour after I got back, the telephone rang and it was the admiral.

"I've looked at what you have proposed, and we will stick with your plan as you had it. And by the way, could you drop two battalions of paratroopers in up there at Cap Haitien so we don't have to keep the Marines floating around out there waiting for this plan? Let's just take the Marines out altogether."

"Admiral, I suppose I could do that since, as you know, I have a backup plan without them—the 82nd Airborne is more than capable of doing that, but I would highly recommend that you let the Marine Corps remain a part of what I think is going to be a highly successful and highly *visible* operation."

"Yeah, you're probably right. Just go ahead and leave it all the way you had it."

"Will do, sir. Thank you," I said. And that was that—basically two days wasted, but I'm quite certain we saved a number of lives in the process.

———

Someone once said it's better to be lucky than to be good. That was the case when the Army decided to send me to Harvard's Kennedy School of Government for professional-development training—and of all the times they could have picked for me to go, they selected the very week before we expected the Haiti operation to take place. It made no sense whatsoever and I was very concerned. I contacted General Reimer, my boss, at U.S. Army Forces Command, in an attempt to get out of the commitment since it was obvious that it must have been some mistake—nobody would purposely schedule the JTF commander to take some course when the order to invade was imminent.

General Reimer listened to my rationale, then he responded—and, much to my surprise, he was as calm and cool as ever. "Hugh, give yourself more credit—we are in *excellent* shape planning-wise thanks to all you've done, and there's very little more you can do until we get the word. So far there hasn't even been a date set for the invasion. Besides, I think you'd enjoy it."

A few days later, I reluctantly left for Cambridge, but with a STU-III–encrypted telephone packed into my suitcase. This allowed me to securely communicate with my chief of staff, Brigadier General Frank Akers, at Bragg. Each day after classes, I would run back to my room, break out the STU-III, and receive an update.

On about the third day it occurred to me that this was playing out as a perfect deception plan. I was sure by now that General Cedras's daily intelligence update must have included my location. Little did he know that while I was soaking up the superb courses at Harvard—one of which was "The Art of Negotiating," which I would put to good use *on him* with terrific results in a matter of days—the wheels of preparedness were continuing to turn across the joint task force. While I appeared to be laid back at Harvard, our readiness was improving by the day. Was I the only one who recognized the beauty of this deception, or was the scheduling of my attending the class not such a coincidence after all?

————

The operation was flowing like clockwork. Aboard the USS *Mount Whitney,* reports indicating the current status of the various pieces of the joint task force were flowing in nonstop—every step monitored and coordinated by the ops staff manning the bustling command center. Sixty-two aircraft carrying paratroopers of the 82nd Airborne Division and U.S. Army Rangers were already en route to their assigned drop zones. The Navy SEALs were in their "fast" boats, ready to launch from the USS *America* aircraft carrier to hit their assigned targets. AC-130 Spectre gunships for close air support—on the way. EH-130 electronic countermeasure and radio-jamming aircraft to disrupt enemy command and control communications—on the way. Direct satellite links to the Pentagon, White House Sit Room, and CINC USACOM—check. Black Hawks from the 82nd Airborne Division on the way—with Captain Jeff Shelton, my middle son, behind the stick of one of them.

H-hour was rapidly approaching and I was growing concerned. The day before, President Clinton had sent to Haiti a last-minute "negotiating" team consisting of former President Carter, Senator Sam Nunn, and former Chairman Colin Powell. The ground rules were clear: whichever direction the negotiations led them, they were to leave Cedras's bargaining table and be on their way out of the country no later than noon today, since their meeting would take place in one of our principal military targets.

I looked at my wristwatch—damn! It was already many hours past their "drop dead" departure time and I had just been informed that they were still meeting with Cedras; we were getting dangerously close to the point when I would not feel confident that all elements would get the word to stop if an agreement was reached.

Once again, one of our best sources of intell was CNN, so they were patched in to the monitors in the command center. I glanced up at one as former President Carter stepped up to the microphone, live. "We think we may be getting close to an agreement," he said.

I picked up my hotline to Admiral Miller, who answered immediately. "Hugh, I'm currently online with Secretary Perry and Shali (Chairman of the Joint Chiefs John Shalikashvili). They are in with the President; what do you have?"

"Sir, I need an immediate decision. The 82nd and rangers are already en route and the SEALs are preparing to launch. We have got to press them for a decision."

*Aboard the* Mount Whitney.

"Okay, stand by," he said.

"Tell them we've got to get Nunn, Powell, and Carter out of there now so they can get on that airplane and get the wheels rolling."

I found myself repeatedly glancing up at the red digital readout of the mission-countdown clock, which did as much good as does pounding on an elevator button to make it move faster.

He came back and said, "They are telling me they just need a few more minutes."

"Do they understand what we're dealing with here? Those minutes are critical. We have to get them on the airplane. We have to get them out of there. *Invasion forces are in the air.*" It was not one of my calmer moments.

"I'll get right back to you," he said. Wrong answer.


A few minutes later, and I mean right at the wire, Admiral Miller's hotline rang, and he reported, "They've got an agreement with General Cedras. I don't know what it is yet, but *stop your forces;* turn them around and stand by for further."

"I've got it," I said, then put the phone down and walked away, shaking my head as the ops team swiftly and professionally handled the incredibly involved logistics behind me.


A short while later, our new mission arrived in the form of an electronic transmission. I glanced down at the printout, which specified that we were to enter Haiti in *an atmosphere of cooperation and coordination* and prepare for the return of President Aristide. I am a military man who was commanding a military operation of more than twenty thousand individuals, and as such I had to reread the message. What in the hell was *an atmosphere of cooperation and coordination* in military terms? What were the *rules of engagement* given that scenario? What did that mean to the rifleman on the ground tomorrow morning? We needed a new plan, and fast. We only had eight hours before we were expected to take control of Haiti and there were no assurances that as we did so, the Haitians wouldn't resist. It was a real possibility that we had to anticipate.

No plan survives the first shot from the enemy. Our great well-rehearsed plan had just changed dramatically. I walked back to the *Mount Whitney*'s conference room and assembled a team along the way. "Come on with me," I said to General Frank Akers and Colonel Dan McNeill, and Bradley Graham of the *Washington Post* (who was embedded wih me) did not need me to invite him. He was enthralled; this was like a kid in a candy store for a fine reporter like Brad—soaking in every unbelievable twist and turn. We asked that Major General Dave Meade join us. General Meade was commander of the 10th Mountain Division. Fortunately, in anticipation that something like this might happen, we had asked Meade to accompany us on the *Mount Whitney* rather than remain on the aircraft carrier USS *Eisenhower,* where his 10th Mountain Division troops were assembled along with their UH-60 Black Hawks.

As we walked into the conference room, I said to Colonel McNeill, "This is it. It has been a great career and I have enjoyed every minute of it . . ." but I went on to reveal how I saw that moment as the end of that career because we had just been handed the aforementioned *ten pounds of shit in a five-pound bag.*

Trying to establish a safe and secure environment in an atmosphere like we were about to encounter with a rogue regime in charge was a tall order. But we had an alternate plan that the 10th Mountain Division had trained for. They were our peacekeeping force and as such were thoroughly trained in peacekeeping techniques and rules of engagement.

Within about an hour and a half we had totally revised the plan—the plan that had taken many months to develop and refine. Dan McNeill had made a number of phone calls and we had coordinated every piece of the new plan. I told Dan, "Get the helicopter ready to fly Dave back over to the USS *America* so he can brief the forces; they will have to hit the ground in about four hours from now."

So Meade left and went back to his ship. Later, Bradley Graham told me, "You know, I am still in awe of you guys. I have never seen anything work that smoothly in my life. I thought when the mission was turned around and you got a totally different type of mission—that there would be screaming and shouting and chaos. I have never seen anything click like that in my life. It was like a professional football team calling an audible from the line of scrimmage." I really appreciated his candid comments, especially considering the source. I thought, *Well, at least we are going to get credit for having a well-trained force regardless of how it turns out on the other end.*

———

Early on the morning of September 19, 1994, the heavily armored LCMs (landing craft, mechanized) hit the beaches, their huge ramps dropping down to discharge troops, vehicles, and tons of supplies. First off was Brigadier General Mike McDuffie, the XVIII ABC Corps Support Command commander who would later become my J4 once I became Chairman. They couldn't wait to get off those things because they all became seasick from the turbulent surf.

More than once our arrival was described as "a scene reminiscent of *Apocalypse Now*," as CNN cameras broadcast it live. At about the time McDuffie waded ashore, Dave Meade and his troops landed at Port-au-Prince and immediately started fanning out to take the city.

At the Port-au-Prince airport, a line of Black Hawks swooped down just ahead of me and off jumped hundreds more 10th Mountain Division soldiers, weapons at the ready. As we approached the airport I could see from the Black Hawk that there was an absolute mob down there.

Finding a secure spot, we made a slight loop, then touched down. The side doors were open and out jumped my SEAL Team Six security team, their specially modified MP-5Ns at the ready as they scanned the area through their wraparound Oakleys. When I stepped out in my BDU camouflage uniform and red beret, the SEALs literally had to use brute force to get me through the swarms of media, embassy officials, 10th Mountain soldiers, and senior-level Haitian military officials so that Dan and I could get inside the building where Major General Jerry Bates who had accompanied President Carter's detail into Haiti, gave me a quick briefing on what I was going to encounter when I met Cedras.

Then we got into our Humvees and caravanned over to Cedras's headquarters, which was only a ten-minute ride from the airport.

My first meeting with Cedras was another indication of the Army's wisdom of sending me to Harvard because at Harvard I had been put through an eight-hour practical exercise on negotiating. It was well done and I would put those skills to good use throughout my time in Haiti, beginning with the meeting I was about to have. Accompanying me was my translator, an extremely bright young captain (now a colonel) named Tony Ladouceur. Tony is a Haitian-born American and both his parents were from Haiti. He was a valuable member of my team and was at my side throughout this operation.

Cedras's office was outside the fence surrounding the National Palace. It resembled an old concrete barracks building, two stories tall and not that well kept. His office was on the second floor, and we entered it by climbing a steep flight of stairs at the very end of the building and walking down a porch-type walkway in front of the second-story offices. My four-person personal security team, headed by "Smitty" from SEAL Team Six, led the way. Their eyes concealed by dark sunglasses and carrying short automatic assault weapons, these were obviously guys you didn't want to screw with, unless you had a death wish.

We entered the room through a screen door and approached the long conference table that occupied most of the medium-size room. The overhead fans turned slowly but sure didn't seem to have much effect in offering relief from the sweltering heat.

The general was already present when we entered, and he extended his hand as we met for the first time. Pleasantries were exchanged through our translators, but I had no doubt that he was sizing me up as much as I was him. *Good luck with that,* I thought.

Cedras and his team sat on one side and I sat on the other, in the same basic arrangement we would take upon each of our subsequent meetings—Dave Meade sat directly next to me on one side, Captain Tony Ladouceur on the other. The rest of my entourage usually included my aide, Major John Campbell, (now Major General Campbell commanding the 101st Airborne Division [Air Assault]), Colonel Dan McNeill, my J3 (operations officer), and Colonel John Altenburg (now retired, Major General Altenburg handled the recent Guantanamo investigation). Later on, Ambassador Bill Swing would often join me, but he was not present for this first meeting.

I was about to commence negotiating the departure of a ruthless dictator and the first thing that came to my mind was that I felt like I was
about to bargain for a used car. But here I was sitting across the table
from General Cedras, knowing that I had to do this in an atmosphere of
cooperation and coordination. I had been struggling to put that in military terms, since those are the terms I knew he would best relate to. He
was youthful, slim, and looked like a good military leader. He spoke a bit
of English but not much—though I got the impression that he understood
everything I said even before Tony translated for him.

I had given prior thought to what I would say and I was fully aware
that my first words would set the tone for our entire relationship. "I appreciate the fact that you have decided to do this in an atmosphere of cooperation," I began. "I think that is the best for the Haitian people. I
think it is important that we understand my role and your role. My instructions are to carry out this operation to restore President Aristide to
his rightful place as president of this nation but to do it in a manner that
is best for the Haitian people and with the minimum amount of problems
and the minimum amount of fighting. My interpretation of cooperation
and coordination is that I am going to coordinate our activities with you
when we move in to take over places. When we want something turned in
or moved I will let you know and you will cooperate. As long as you cooperate I will continue to coordinate; but if you fail to cooperate I am going
to do it using whatever force is necessary to carry it out, and you do not
want that to happen because your forces will die. We will come out the
winner in this thing, but if you cooperate we will both be winners in the
sense that you will have carried out your lawful duty to restore your democratically elected president and I will have carried out the military mission
that I have been given by President Clinton. Do you understand that?"

He had been taking very finely printed notes the whole time I was
talking, and he finally looked up from those notes and simply said, "I
understand and I will cooperate."

I figured that was a major coup; I had let him know who was in charge
and that he was going to remain a player only for as long as he participated in what we planned to do. So far, so good—but I knew it was not
going to continue to be as easy as it had appeared.

I left and went directly to the embassy to introduce myself to Ambassador Bill Swing, a great North Carolinian whom I was looking forward
to meeting. He was an Africa specialist who had been sent to Haiti.

As soon as we met, I let the ambassador know that I clearly understood that he was responsible for the country and I was there to help coordinate everything for him. After our discussions, we decided that I
should put a liaison with him. I promised to brief him on a daily basis
about our planned activities and to meet with him frequently. If there was

something we were doing that he didn't agree with, we would immediately stop doing it and together figure out another solution. We established a great relationship right up front, one that was solidified by our common North Carolina upbringing. Beyond that, he viewed us as the savior of Haiti since he had watched it fall apart. He had become almost a nonplayer in Haiti with Cedras in charge.

We proceeded to move our forces ashore and seized the areas we had identified as being critical to having a presence in on the island. Special Forces teams spread throughout the remote areas and, just as planned, the U.S. presence was felt throughout the island; the Haitian military fully understood that they were no longer in charge.

Almost every day would bring with it another challenge. At one point a Special Forces A-Team in one of the villages encountered 150 Haitians under the command of a Haitian colonel. The young American captain approached the colonel and told him, "I am in charge; stand your people down and turn in your rifles." They did it without any questions or resistance. It was that way all over the island.

There was one major stronghold where they kept many of their heavy weapons, and we felt it was important to secure those weapons. I went to General Cedras the following day and looked him dead in the eye and said, "I want you to turn in every weapon you have—every howitzer, every mortar, any and everything you have stored there, and I want them immediately turned in to my Special Forces unit. All of that equipment will be transported to the airfield and inventoried there. While you may ultimately get it back, for now it is going to belong to us and we are going to put it under lock and key."

I knew this was a big decision on his part because it entailed his giving up his major force—his crown jewels, so to speak. As was his custom, he made some more notes, then looked up at me and simply said, "Okay."

I wanted to turn a backflip I was so happy with that, but instead I just nodded, said, "Thank you, good choice," and departed. That was the last real stronghold they had.

Overall, things were going very well, although we did have one incident where one of our Special Forces sergeants walked outside in the middle of the night and was shot. Our immediate response was to put a ranger company right on top of that place, and I demanded another meeting with General Cedras at six o'clock the following morning. While I was obviously relieved that the sergeant had sustained only a minor injury (from which he recovered), I was nonetheless irate that the incident had happened at all. For the first time Cedras saw another side of me because I was livid.

Towering over him, I said (through Tony), "You saw how fast those rangers got in there and they now own the place and I am not going to give control of it back to you. But hear me good: if that happens again we will kill everybody in sight, no questions asked. This is not going to be tolerated."

About three days later I had a young lieutenant from the Marine Corps out on a patrol up in Cap Haitien and he came under fire by a group of Haitian military. The lieutenant and his platoon returned fire and killed twelve of them. I met with General Cedras the next morning and again I was livid because that had been instigated by his forces. We came out the winner and did not have one man injured; yet we had twelve dead Haitian soldiers, whom he insisted on going up to visit.

The bodies were placed in body bags. Since some of the body parts were unidentifiable, there were thirteen bags for twelve human remains, the thirteenth bag filled with those unidentifiable parts.

When we arrived, Cedras approached the bags, knelt down and unzipped them, then pulled them open to reveal their contents. The heat in Haiti is tremendous, and there was no refrigeration out there, so it was not a very pleasant sight, nor was it a pleasant smell because decomposition was already setting in. It was a horrible scene.

As we walked away toward the helicopter, I put my hand on the general's shoulder. "You know, it is a pity that your soldiers had to die, because it was needless. I suggest you get the word out that they are going to be killed in masses if they fire at us anymore. They have to lay down their arms and accept the fact that they are no longer in charge." He looked up and without missing a beat he said, "I will get the word out." And he did.

Things continued to progress and the operation went very well. The joint force was magnificent, and the State Department had selected the day for President Aristide's return to Port-au-Prince: it was to be October 15, 1994. My job was to make sure that all semblance of the current junta was long gone before he set foot back on Haitian soil. It was time to tell Cedras and President Jonassaint that the time had come for them to vacate their offices.

I called Cedras to coordinate a meeting so that we all could discuss it. The meeting was set for 10:00 A.M. the following day, and he assured us that both he and the President would be there.

* * *

The following morning, Ambassador Swing and I arrived at the palace at the prearranged time, fully prepared for what could be a rather contentious "negotiation" to get Jonassaint out of the government offices well in advance of Aristide's arrival.

Smitty and the rest of my SEAL team led us into the facility, which strangely seemed not to have quite the usual level of security. We approached the president's office suite. "*Oui?*" said the unfamiliar colonel seated behind the desk in the outer office. Tony stepped up to translate for me and the two began an exchange in Creole. It was obvious that the colonel did not want to be bothered—at least not by us.

Tony looked at me and relayed, "He says the president is not in and there's nobody else available for us to see."

"Find out when the hell the president *is* going to be in today," I instructed. He did so, and even though I didn't speak a word of Creole I could tell that this guy was one obstinate, arrogant son of a bitch who had no intention of cooperating.

"He's not coming in today and I don't have any idea if he will be in tomorrow," echoed Tony, translating the colonel's brush-off. Ambassador Swing shot me a look, kind of *What are we going to do now?* But the Haitian hadn't even stopped talking—he was still rattling off something, and Captain Ladouceur was starting to respond.

I cut him off and turned for the door as my blood pressure skyrocketed. "Give it up, Tony. Way beneath our pay grade. Let's get the hell out of here."

On my instruction, the SEALs led us directly across the courtyard to Cedras's headquarters, the first time I had gone there without calling in advance for an appointment. "Keep up with me on this, Tony," I forewarned Captain Ladouceur as we charged down the second-floor outer walkway to Cedras's office, knowing full well that it was not going to be pleasant.

We barged in and I charged right up to the general and laid into him before he knew what had hit him, and I was mad—telling him what a sorry bastard he was for standing us up. Tony was trying his best to translate everything but I never slowed down to let him catch up, so basically what you had was me speaking loudly and forcefully and Tony trying to talk over me so that Cedras could hear the translation—and of course Cedras was still sitting there, not knowing which one to look at, the guy who was doing the yelling or the guy whom he could understand (even though I had no doubt that from day one he'd understood every word of English I said). It was ugly.

Cedras was very apologetic, in fact very effusive in his apologies—accepting full responsibility for the no-show. He claimed that his people

had failed to notify Jonassaint and it was entirely his fault. So we resched-
uled it for the following morning out at Jonassaint's home. *He will be
there,* the general emphatically assured us.


President Jonassaint's home was high in the mountains overlooking Port-
au-Prince. The building itself was a very modest ranch-style house, surrounded by a five-to-six-foot fence that was guarded by the Haitian
military when he was present. As was always the case, I had my SEAL
Team Six guys with us for protection, as well as Tony, to handle the translation. As we approached the house we were met by more than one hundred armed Haitians.

Ambassador Swing blanched and his eyes widened. "Boy, look at
that," he said. "They really have us."

I turned and replied, "Let's see. Four SEALs, one hundred fifty of
them; I'd say we have them outnumbered six to one." The ambassador
smiled nervously and I reassured him, "It's okay, we're going inside."

We entered through the gate and then through a side door that led into
what was like a mudroom, where we were greeted by a member of the
military who took us into the main room. Waiting for us inside were
President Jonassaint, their Secretary of Commerce, and their translator.

Ambassador Swing launched into a respectful explanation: "Mr. President, we are here to negotiate your departure from the buildings. As you
know, President Aristide is returning to take power again, and we must
make arrangements to move you out of the palace and out of the other government office buildings; and we want this to be done in a peaceful, orderly
manner to facilitate a smooth and orderly transition back in by President
Aristide. We would appreciate your support, and we would appreciate
your cooperation . . ." He continued for another ten minutes, presenting the
plan with a spirit of peaceful collaboration. The three Haitians listened
patiently, with no sign of emotion, and they remained silent even after the
ambassador had finished, as if contemplating how to respond.

Finally, President Jonassaint spoke up. "I still have affairs of state to
take care of and I need to remain in my offices. I cannot leave."

Their Secretary of Commerce, short, stocky, and belligerent, chimed in,
"We are the legitimate government of Haiti and you heard what our
president said, we cannot leave the buildings. We agreed with President
Carter, General Powell, and Senator Nunn [the three had been sent over
by President Clinton for the original negotiation] that we would leave
when Aristide returns, and, as the legitimate government, we will remain
in our buildings until such time as President Aristide touches down."

Ambassador Swing tried again: "We really need for you to reconsider
that and we need for you to move. We have to get the buildings in shape—
painting, signs, et cetera—and we need this interim period to do that."

The stocky guy cut him off. "You heard our president speak. We are the rightful government and we are not moving. We will stay until Aristide gets back and that is the way it is going to be."

Ambassador Swing was really getting frustrated and I was fighting-mad and ready to burst at the seams. Tony saw me clench my fists and sensed my tension. He put his hand on my leg—an implicit "down, boy." Swing turned to me and said, "General, do you have anything you would like to say?"

"Thank you, Mr. Ambassador," I said. "I do have something I would like to say." I turned to Tony and asked him to translate. "All of you just heard the United States ambassador tell you that you need to evacuate the buildings. Now let me put it in military terms for you: you are going to get your asses out of the buildings, and you are going to have them out by sunset tomorrow; and if you don't, we will throw your asses out of the buildings and we will take them over. President Jonassaint, I told you from the beginning, I want to do this peacefully, but you are refusing to do that, so let me tell you something else. As we speak, I have snipers covering every building. If we see you trying to leave the building with artifacts or trying to leave with papers—we will drop you in your tracks and then we will take the buildings. Now, tonight you are going to be observed through night-vision goggles, and we own the night, so if you try to take anything out at night, you will die." I paused. "Do all of you understand what I'm telling you?"

When I stopped, they were all staring at me. Jonassaint spoke first. "Why, General, of course we understand. We can be out by night without any problem whatsoever, and we will not take anything out of the buildings; the incoming government will need those records so we will leave everything just like it is."

I responded, "Thank you, Mr. President, for your cooperation, and I want to reinforce what I said, because I meant every word of it and I hope that you meant yours, as well."

Jonassaint said, "We are men of our word. We will be out of the buildings."

With that I stood up and looked at Bill Swing. "Well, Mr. Ambassador, I think that concludes our meeting." We shook hands and left the building.

We got back into the car and Ambassador Swing turned to me with a big grin on his face and said, "Now, General, that's what I call coercive diplomacy. I have never seen anybody turn as fast in my life."

"Mr. Ambassador," I said, "sometimes you can be nice and sometimes you have to be ruthless. It was obvious from this crowd that you had to be ruthless."

Before we even made it back to our car, my security contingent advised me that they had already received a report that the instant we left the room, Jonassaint had contacted General Cedras and warned him to vacate the government offices posthaste.

The entire group started evacuating within the next two hours.

———

There was another problem that had to be taken care of prior to Aristide's return, and that trouble was brewing in the form of Emmanuel "Toto" Constant, a high-profile anti-Aristide opposition leader with a broad underground web of supporters that was growing every day. Constant was the founder of FRAPH (Front pour l'Avancement et le Progrès Haitien), a paramilitary Haitian death squad responsible for multiple killings. Our concern was that as soon as we got Aristide back in office, Constant would unleash his rebellion and take over in yet another coup d'état. He was dynamic, outspoken, and persuasive, and he had to be quelled if we were to succeed in getting the rightfully elected president reinstated—but before we could contain him we had to find him.

Our first step was to raid his house, and that proved an absolute gold mine in the form of his computer. It didn't take long for our intell staff to crack the encryption and extract not only contact lists detailing every member of his resistance but an abundance of graphic e-mails between him and his partner, whom they suggested we utilize in a sting operation to locate and capture him. Their plan was to log on as the lover and set up a tryst to take place near their weapons camp, at which point we would snatch him from his vehicle.

It was a decent plan, but General Dave Meade (10th Mountain Division commander) and I decided that a more direct approach was less risky and most likely would work just as well. We e-mailed the individual identified as the leader's right-hand man and instructed him to have Constant at the airport the following day at 3:00 P.M., where he would personally meet with me—our rationale being that an egotistical "player" like Constant would not pass up the opportunity for a high-level photo op of such magnitude. Our instincts were correct and we received confirmation that Constant had agreed to the meeting.

The following day, General Meade ushered the well-dressed, confident resistance leader into a secluded office inside the airport, where he began to explain what the meeting was to be about. Not two minutes into the explanation, the door swung open and three SEAL Team Six operators burst into the room, guns at the ready, dark glasses scanning the room—and it scared the ever-living hell out of this guy. Seizing the moment, Meade turned to Constant and deadpanned, "Uh-oh, the Godfather is about to arrive. Have you ever met General Shelton?" Constant shook his head. "Well, you are about to see why we call him the Godfather. . . . If I can give you some friendly advice, listen very carefully to what he says, and do exactly what he instructs."

At this point the guy had almost lost control and asked permission to use the bathroom. Later on we would learn that his favorite movie was *The Godfather,* so I could just imagine what images were going through his head when three more SEALs stormed into the room and assumed their strategic positions.

When I entered, the cocky resistance leader stood and extended his hand, but by then he was sweating profusely. "General, I'm pleased to meet you," he said.

"Sit down," I commanded. "I don't shake hands." He took his seat and I continued. "Constant, I'm really disappointed in you. You appear to be a man of great intellect, but your actions are not in keeping with an intelligent man. You know so much about so many things, but what you don't know is that I have put a death sentence on your head, and that sentence has a timeline attached to it. Once that timeline begins, it cannot be stopped, and it begins the moment you refuse to cooperate with us. So, basically, you are getting ready to die."

"General, what is the problem? What can I do to help?" he implored in a panic.

"Let's start with this," I countered. "You are aware that we have your computer and have cracked your encryption so we know every member of your organization. As soon as we leave here, I want you to contact every one of them with clear instructions to cease and desist any activity directed against President Aristide, the Lavalas Party, or the American forces, and I want you to have that done by 2100 hours tonight. You are to become completely neutral, do you understand that?"

"Yes, I do, Mr. General, sir," he confirmed.

"Okay, the second point," I continued. "Tomorrow afternoon at two P.M., you are going on CNN television, live, and you are going to say that you welcome back President Aristide with open arms, and look forward to his return—and you can say any other nice things about him that you want, but you will say that as a minimum, do you understand that?"

"That is not a problem, Mr. General. I will do that."

We concluded the meeting and again Constant extended his hand. "I will shake your hand tomorrow afternoon only after you show that you deserve to have it shook," I said, and with that I led my SEAL team out the room.

I imagine that to some, stories like this may come across like movie scripts or action novels rather than real life—but in situations where the success of our mission literally determines the fate of thousands of lives (there were over more than five thousand Haitians killed in the dictatorship between 1991 and 1994), we will employ whatever legal tactics we believe offer the greatest chance of success with the lowest risk; and in this case General Meade's instinctive, spontaneous "Godfather" reference was spot-on to crack Constant. Within six hours he had contacted every member of the resistance, and the following day at exactly 2:00 P.M., live on CNN, he made an eloquent welcome-back speech to President Aristide—after which I approached him and shook his hand, as promised.

A year later, Emmanuel "Toto" Constant would resurface—in Queens, New York—after he had entered the United States through Puerto Rico on a tourist visa. He had allegedly changed professions from death-squad leader to crooked mortgage broker working with the mob in Brooklyn. Apparently having failed to learn his lesson about the dangers of associating with "The Godfather," in 2008 his alleged mob ties were a factor in his conviction for mortgage fraud, resulting in his being sentenced to twelve to thirty-seven years in prison.

More recently, in December 2009, it was reported that the Second Circuit Court of Appeals upheld a $19 million civil judgment against him, which awarded $15 million in punitive and $4 million in compensatory damages to three women who had survived rape, torture, and attempted killing by Haitian paramilitary forces under Constant's command.

———

Although it was the Department of State's job to coordinate the departure of General Cedras, Ambassador Swing asked that I take the lead since I had a working relationship with Cedras. I immediately called Cedras and we agreed to meet at his home.

Tony Ladouceur and I arrived at Cedras's palatial home and were met at the door by Yannick, his wife, who guided us into the expansive living room. As General Cedras emerged, Yannick excused herself and we got right down to business.

I informed the general that as soon as he changed command with interim commander Major General Jean-Claude Duperval the following day, I could no longer guarantee his safety, so I strongly suggested that it would be in his best interest—and that of his family—to leave Haiti immediately. We were prepared to offer him and his family transportation to the country of his choice and pay him for the loss of his home on the island.

"This is my home, it is my country. I can't leave, Yannick would kill me," he immediately shot back. This confirmed the intell I had received that he was terrified of his wife and deferred to her on most issues.

"Then you've got a real problem because I have firm intell that there is a plot among your own people to kill you," I said, looking him squarely in the eye so that there was no doubt I meant business. "Additionally, I can't assure you that there aren't elements of my own government that may be after you," I added, playing on his unfounded fears of our CIA. He started to perspire and looked nervously about the room.

"What am I to do? I can't leave, she would kill me," he repeated.

I reminded him of my concern for his life on multiple fronts but told him that the decision would ultimately be his to make, not mine. "Here's my phone number out on the *Mount Whitney*. You can call me at any time, but my suggestion is that you let your wife know that most likely you would not be the only member of the Cedras family to die, should you decide to stay in Haiti after tomorrow."

I gestured to Tony and we departed to backbrief Ambassador Swing, who, as always, was appreciative of my help. By that point, he and I had become quite a team.

I returned to my command ship and at 2:00 A.M. was awakened by the watch officer. "General, General Cedras is on the line and insists on talking with you right now."

Within a few short minutes I was in the command center, picking up the phone. "Shelton here."

In broken yet understandable English, General Cedras explained that he and his family would like to go to Venezuela—but he owned three properties and a boat, for which he expected remuneration. He described his beachfront residence, his main hillside villa where we had met, and his mother-in-law's private home. He gave a figure for their combined value, then suggested that the United States *lease* them from him for a combined five thousand dollars per month, with the first year's total of sixty thousand dollars paid 100 percent up front. It was this figure that I would communicate to Ambassador Swing, who would make the final decision in conjunction with the powers in Washington. Cedras also brought up the number of family members and associates he wanted transported off Haiti with him; it was obvious that we would need more than a Piper Cub.

I instructed him to start the family packing immediately, and I committed to get back with him after I received a response to the various points from Ambassador Swing.

By midmorning the following day, the State Department had a chartered aircraft en route to the island—but Cedras would not be going to Venezuela. They, along with a plethora of other countries, flatly refused to accept him. His options quickly narrowed to Panama. Additionally, the State

Department was willing to pay only fifty-five thousand dollars per year for the lease, which was five thousand less than the general had demanded. That decision sounded strange to me, but it wasn't my decision to make—so, as middleman I called Cedras back and relayed the information.

"Yes, Panama is no problem," he said without hesitation. But then he became upset, apparently insulted that the United States was trying to stiff him five thousand dollars. I just about fell off my chair. I had just agreed to provide him—free of charge—a private jet to whisk him and twenty-something relatives to a safe location, and, without a doubt in my mind, *saved his life* and those of his family—and he would rather play *Let's Make a Deal.*

"Are you understanding what I'm telling you, General Cedras?" I went on to relay that I had just received confirmation that his aircraft had arrived at Port-Au-Prince airfield. "We will even fly you out under the cover of darkness if you prefer—just to make this as smooth as possible for you. . . ."

I would love to take this guy with me the next time I negotiate a used-car purchase because there was *nothing* I could have said to get him to back down on that five-thousand-dollar difference. I called Bill Swing back again.


Ambassador Bill Swing worked with the State Department all day, but some idiot put a hold on the charter flight's departure until such time as Cedras would back down and accept five thousand dollars a year less. "Mr. Ambassador, would you please make it clear to these people that when a man does not feel *the combined value of his life and that of his family* is worth more than four hundred dollars a month, I can guarantee that we are not in the driver's seat in this particular negotiation." (I could have told him that even without my recent Harvard degree.)

Finally, as I considered bypassing the entire chain and calling Secretary of State Christopher directly, I stopped by Bill Swing's office to lay it out face-to-face. "Do those idiots realize that the charter—which is currently sitting on the runway guzzling outrageously expensive jet fuel while they haggle over five thousand dollars a year—is costing the American taxpayer five thousand dollars *per hour?*"


We had approval within the hour.


That night, General Cedras stepped into one of the heavily armed convoy vehicles wearing a dark blue suit instead of the traditional khaki uniform that had become his trademark. Joined by his chief of staff, Brigadier

*October 10, 1994. Couldn't ask for a better view as I watch General Cedras pass the flag to Haitian army Major General Jean-Claude Duperval.*

General Philippe Biamby, and both of their families, they were transported by the U.S. security forces in a roundabout route through the dark Haitian streets to the airport. Without fanfare of any kind, the entourage proceeded swiftly and directly from the motorcade up the stairs into the America Trans Air–chartered 757, whose royal-blue nose bore the name *Spirit of Indianapolis.*

Although I enjoyed participating in the return of a duly elected president to his rightful position, shortly before I left the island I had an experience that turned my stomach. Just a short distance from the airport, while driving through an area of "homes" that were in a poor state of repair—almost squalor—I noticed a secluded complex that was heavily guarded by Haitian forces.

"That's Aristide's personal residence," Tony pointed out.

"Let's take a look," I told my driver, realizing that this would probably be my only opportunity to see the place. We pulled into the compound and were met by the caretaker, who offered to give us a tour, since it was still being renovated and nobody had moved in yet.

When he opened the ornate front door and gestured for us to enter, I was sickened by the sight. The house was opulent throughout, with fine marble imported from Italy, beautiful crystal chandeliers, and exotic, hand-crafted fixtures. Amid such abject poverty, Aristide was spending millions of dollars to live like this.

I understood why it was so heavily guarded. It wasn't to protect Aristide but to prevent the Haitian people from taking back part of the wealth that was rightfully theirs.

A few days later, as I left Haiti, I worried about the future of the nation that had the president we had just reinstalled. Years later, my concerns would be shown to be fully justified.

Another chapter in the history of Haiti was closed and a new one was just beginning.

————

The lesson learned of Haiti, and of most other contingency operations in that decade, is that while military forces have excelled in achieving military tasks such as establishing order, separating combatants, and safeguarding relief supplies, they are less effective in solving nonmilitary problems rooted in persistent cultural, economic, and political strife. In cases like Haiti, military forces can help to create a secure environment in which to pursue lasting political and economic solutions—but they cannot achieve political outcomes themselves. The burden still remains on the statesman and the international community to rebuild the nation by pursuing integrated approaches that employ a broad range of policy tools and processes to ensure long-term success.

Former President Bill Clinton summarized it nicely in his autobiography, *My Life*:

> In 2004, after President Aristide resigned and flew into exile amidst renewed violence and strife, I thought back to what Hugh Shelton, the commander of the American forces, had told me: "The Haitians are good people and they deserve a chance." Aristide certainly made mistakes and was often his own worst enemy . . . Still, our intervention saved lives and gave Haitians their first taste of the democracy they had voted for. Even with Aristide's serious problems, the Haitians would have been far worse off under Cedras and his murderous coup. I remain glad that we gave Haiti a chance.

I completely agree.

\* \* \*

At the time of these incidents I had been commanding the XVIII Airborne as a three-star general for well over two years (with twenty-four months being the norm for such an assignment), so once again I faced the possibility that this could be the end of the line for my Army career. Congress limits the number of four-stars serving at any given time, and the Army's maximum allotment was nine. As I approached the thirty-three-month mark, there were two four-star commands opening up, and a lot more than two potential three-star candidates hoping to fill them. The nomination would be made by the President and confirmed by the Senate, with recommendations from the Army Chief of Staff (General Denny Reimer), the Chairman of the Joint Chiefs (General John Shalikashvili), and the Secretary of Defense, (Bill Cohen).

My experience in leading the XVIII Airborne would be highly regarded, but I was fully aware that there are never any guarantees. Even though my two predecessors (Jim Lindsay and Gary Luck) had gone on to receive their fourth stars, when I was promoted to lieutenant general I signed a contract that made it clear that I was serving at the pleasure of the Army Chief of Staff, and when he no longer had a need for me I would resign with no questions asked. Both Carolyn and I understood that and were prepared for that to happen at this time.

While there would be a four-star command opening at SOCOM (U.S. Special Operations Command), there was the perfect individual to fill it in my good friend Terry Scott, who was doing a great job commanding Army Special Ops at Fort Bragg. Not only would it have been a natural progression for Terry to slide right over to SOCOM, but there was a political piece of the puzzle rapidly heating up and leaning heavily in Terry's favor. General Wayne Downing was the current SOCOM commander and as such would have important (though unofficial) input into the recommendation of his successor. As a combatant commander he had the ears of the SecDef—most likely far more than did my biggest advocate, General Reimer. Not only was Downing good friends with Terry, but I had heard that he wasn't my biggest fan—allegedly because of some friction between him and my boss, General Luck, who had stepped on him a couple of times in years past. In Downing's mind I was part of the "Luck camp," so there was no doubt that I was not about to get his nod. So here I am, this apolitical officer just trying to do the very best job I can—but I'm stuck in the middle of this mounting political muck. Truth be told, as much as I would have relished receiving my fourth star and running SOCOM, I would never begrudge such an outstanding officer as Terry getting it instead.

There was, however, that second four-star opening—and it was one that General Reimer was lobbying heavily for me to get, since he concurred that most likely Terry had the SOCOM slot locked up. Reimer understood that if I didn't get either of these two four-star slots, I would be forced into mandatory retirement. That second opening was as commander of U.S. Forces Korea.

So there I was, after twenty-eight years in the service and never having been to Korea, weighing in my mind whether this was really somewhere I wanted to drag Carolyn, especially with a son still in high school and a mother who was rapidly aging. And I wasn't the only one who was questioning the choice. The new commander would be working very closely with the Korean Chief of Defense, who kept telling General Reimer and the rest of the Army leadership that he didn't want somebody who had never even been to his country.

As luck would have it, the Korean general was on his way to meet with Shalikashvili at the Pentagon, and Reimer's master plan was to fly him from D.C. down to Fort Bragg to "check out our contingency forces," where he would meet me and be convinced that I was the perfect individual to work with him and command the operation in Seoul. The problem was that he did not want to come. He wanted to meet with the Chairman and fly back home; a side trip to Fayetteville was high on the list of things this guy did *not* want to do. But Reimer kept pushing and insisting how important it was, and ultimately he wore down the poor guy; and I got a call that he was coming out to visit the next day. When he arrived, we gave him the VIP tour he rightfully deserved by virtue of his position, snapped a quick picture of the two of us shaking hands, put him back on his plane, and that was the end of it. He went home like he wanted to do in the first place, and I never heard another word from the man.

So I just kept on being the XVIII Airborne Corps commander and not really worrying about what was coming ahead, although I did start reading more and more of my fishing magazines, since it was becoming apparent that very soon my forced retirement would afford me plenty of time to fish.

Even so, in the back of my mind I knew that if that call *did* ever come in, I would have to decide whether to accept a fourth star and the Korean command or instead just hang it up and say, *I have had a great ride and enjoyed everything I've done, and I could not ask for a better high to go out on than commanding the XVIII Airborne Corps and a JTF.*

A few months later, that call from Denny Reimer finally came in, but you could have knocked me over with a feather when I heard what he had to say. "Hugh," he began, "get out that sunscreen, you're going to Tampa. The President has decided that you are the man to replace General Downing as SOCOM commander."

To this day I have no clue what played out behind the scenes, but suffice it to say that I was thrilled. I would be leaving one great command and taking over another. It was a dream come true. The only negative was how bad I felt for Terry and Carol Scott. In my opinion, Terry deserved to be promoted, and when the President nominated me instead, it basically slammed the door on Terry. I had not been a party to it and Terry understood that. He remained as Army Special Operations commander and was very supportive of me until he retired.

———

The 118,000 troops that comprised the XVIII Airborne Corps were spread out in units from New York to Florida, and representatives from each of those units packed the Fort Bragg Main Post Parade Field to observe the change-of-command ceremony between me and the XVIII ABC's next commander, Lieutenant General Jack Keane. Jack and his wife, Terry, had been our next-door neighbors at Fort Drum, so it made it all the more special that I would be passing the colors to such a good friend.

The day was truly cause for celebration in that not only would Jack be taking over the reins of this legendary corps, but I would be receiving my fourth star—the highest rank possible in today's Army. General John H. Tilelli Jr., the four-star Army Forces Command commander and my current boss, presided over both ceremonies as my family looked on with pride.

One reason I always enjoyed having these ceremonies at Fort Bragg was that our families lived close enough that they could attend. My and Carolyn's siblings and their spouses were part of my cheering section, and of course there was no way the boys (and their wives) would have missed it. What I've often thought about when I reflect on life's special occasions, such as this, is how incredibly fortunate I was to have had Mother there for each and every one of them—all the way through my retirement ceremony. When I say "there," I mean as vibrant and feisty and energetic as she was when she was sitting there with Daddy for my North Carolina State University graduation. And I know she felt as proud of me that day as she did when she looked down from that upper window of Speed Elementary School to see me beating the crap out of Arnold "the bully."

As soon as I passed the colors of the corps to Jack, Carolyn stepped up and took a place by my side. There I was, standing at attention with my eyes forward—certainly focused in the moment yet in a way just wanting to turn to Carolyn and burst out the same way I had wanted to when I became captain, and major, and colonel—just look at her and say, "Can you believe this?"—at which point we would both just crack up and shake our heads almost in disbelief. The funny thing is that we have always been so connected to each other that I didn't have to look down to know that she was thinking the exact same thing. But instead, I was pulled back into that very humbling moment as General Tilelli gave the command: "Publish the orders."

The adjutant stood slightly off to the side and declared in a booming voice that certainly didn't need the PA system that carried it across the huge parade grounds:

*"Attention to orders. Headquarters, Department of the Army, Washington, D.C. The President of the United States has reposed special trust and confidence in the patriotism, valor, fidelity, and abilities of Henry H. Shelton. In view of these qualities, and his demonstrated potential for increased responsibility, he is, therefore, promoted in the United States Army from Lieutenant General to General, by order of the Secretary of the Army."*

General Tilelli smiled broadly and ripped off the two cloth "three-star" patches that adorned the collar of my BDU camouflage shirt, and he pinned on the first of two black *metal* four-star pins. Carolyn reached up and pinned on the other, fumbling just a bit as even with her high-heel shoes it was quite a stretch for her. I was standing at attention, so I couldn't have bent down to help her out if I'd wanted to, but everybody in the crowd seemed to get a kick out if it. It was a wonderful—and very *meaningful*—ceremony.

I removed my helmet and Mark replaced it with my new maroon beret, which already had the four-stars pinned on. Carolyn was presented a dozen red roses in recognition of her contributions (and probably for finally getting those stars on) and there was rousing applause.

Once we made it to the reviewing stand, Tilelli spoke at length about the contributions I had made during my time at the XVIII, and I was touched by his sincerity. He was extremely complimentary, and it meant a great deal to me to hear that I had so impacted the lives of the great men and women of finest corps in the world. By the time he was finished, there seemed to be some tears flowing along with that vast sea of smiles. The following day I would depart for Tampa.

———

For the very last time I gazed out my office window at the home to almost 10 percent of the Army's active component forces, the largest airborne facility in the world—and I felt proud. Those five years were more than I ever could have asked for, a time that I will always consider a high point in my life in terms of being on the cutting edge with troops who were ready to go.

Being from North Carolina, I had always wanted to serve at Fort Bragg, and from the first time I was so inspired by those razor-sharp 82nd Airborne NCOs as an ROTC cadet, I had recognized that Fort Bragg was a great part of the Army in which to serve. It had been a great family assignment in a great community. Our son had gone to high school there for four years, so we were very much a part of that community. I had worked hard to make sure that the soldiers were integrating into the Fayetteville community and, in turn, the community gave them the support that they and their families were due. Carolyn was a big part of that, having been very involved in many Fort Bragg as well as Fayetteville activities. On post, as the corps commander's wife, she was the senior adviser to practically every program that supported military families, including the Red Cross, family support groups, community foundation, commissary, and post exchange, as well as the Officers Wives' Club, and was honorary adviser to the Enlisted Wives' Club. We frequently entertained not only military groups in our home but civilians from the local communities, and she volunteered in Mark's school.

It was with a tear in my eye that I was leaving the command and leaving those great troops behind, yet I had a great sense of satisfaction that I had taken care of the soldiers and their families, and I was parting with a good reputation as a commander who cared about them and who always led from the front—donning the parachutes right there with them and wanting to be the first out the door when that green Jump light popped on. I never understood those commanders who felt that they could effectively steer a battle from behind some desk. As Ulysses S. Grant said after the Battle of Shiloh, "The distant rear of an army engaged in battle is not the best place from which to judge correctly what is going on in front."

I was leaving behind a good, solid command that could go anywhere, anytime, and carry out the mission they had been assigned—and there is not much more that a commander can ask for.

An M1 Abrams tank weighs almost seventy tons, and I could not have been straining any harder had I been attempting to move one single-handed. But it wasn't an M-1 that I was exerting so much effort to budge, it was my right big toe—and it remained as rigid and unyielding as if it were disconnected. I still couldn't feel a thing, and the constant exertion was sapping what little energy I had.

"Now try the left one," prompted Jim Ecklund, the neurosurgeon, as beads of sweat ran off my forehead and soaked the white pillowcase beneath my head. Nothing. Then more doctors, and more requests: "Try pressing your knee against my hand," and, "Focus on your index finger— c'mon, you can move it." But I couldn't. Not yet. Nor could I brush my teeth, eat unassisted, shave, use the washroom—let's face it, I couldn't move, so there was not a thing I could do other than concentrate with all my being on getting those nerves to kick in and activate the muscles.

"You'll do it," Carolyn would say; not a psych-up—just a simple statement that she believed with all her heart.

"If anybody can, it's you," Anne would chime in. Their belief in me was inspirational and served as an additional motivator.


The second night in the hospital, Secretary Cohen and his wife, Janet, came by, along with Michael and Karen Ansari. I had started working for Michael as president of his International Operations division and he had assured me that I would not have to worry about any financial ramifications—my job would still be there and the paychecks would continue coming in. It was a generous offer.


The following day, the hospital issued their first statement, describing the fall and stating that I was "in serious condition but resting comfortably." That night, Jim Ecklund happened to be at my bedside when we noticed my picture pop onto the TV screen. It was a CNN report in which Bill Hemmer was discussing the details of my condition with CNN's medical specialist, Dr. Sanjay Gupta. While they were both extremely supportive in extending their good wishes, I was not at all comfortable with the information they were reporting—far more than was contained in the hospital's press release. "The fall most likely caused a swelling around the spinal column," Gupta reported, "and although sometimes it can lead to ongoing *paralysis or quadriplegia, that's probably not what we're talking about here. More likely, once the swelling goes down, the general will be able to walk and resume all the activities of normal living."*

*I didn't know whose case file he was reading, but at that moment I was just praying that the day would come when I could move my fingers enough to click the Off button on the TV remote.*

# Chapter Eleven ★★★★

# SPECIAL OPS

February 1996—September 1997

At ten below zero, exposed human skin can freeze within three minutes. At forty below, severe hypothermia can immobilize a body within two minutes—arresting breathing and heartbeat, and prompting seizures before coma and death.

It was two o'clock on a Sunday morning and where I was it was sixty below—yet I was pumped and experiencing a natural adrenaline high like you wouldn't believe. In a few seconds I'd be stepping from the rear ramp of a CASA 212 aircraft at twenty-four thousand feet and making my first night solo HALO jump—a unique "High Altitude / Low Opening" parachute technique that Special Forces use to elude enemy radar by jumping from very high altitudes and free-falling until they open their chutes quite close to the ground. It was dangerous but effective. I was a four-star general and back in school again—Special Ops military free-fall jump school, about to jump into a classified training area used by JSOC somewhere over the southwestern United States. (JSOC [Joint Special Operations Command—pronounced "jay-sock"] encompasses Delta Force, Navy SEAL Team Six, and other classified commando-type units.)

Double-checking the seal on my insulated F-16 helmet, I took a deep breath and made sure I had unrestricted oxygen flow, then confirmed the setting on my AAD (automatic actuation device), which hopefully would open my chute only 750 feet short of my smashing into the ground should I black out or for any other reason be unable to pull the rip cord myself. Fortunately, the polypropylene body suit I wore under my jumpsuit was protecting me from the extreme temperature.

I braced myself against the skin of the aircraft, moving into position as the wind crashed against my visor. I couldn't help but wonder what all the other four-stars were doing at that moment. The jump light changed from red to green, the jumpmaster yelled "GO," and I jumped into a black void, clear of the aircraft.

My downward speed was ever-increasing as I dropped like a lead ball with my arms and legs extended, my Special Ops modified M16 assault rifle strapped so tightly to my side it felt a part of me, the 60 pound rucksack between my legs making maintaining stability even more difficult. Just three seconds out the door I passed 60 MPH and five seconds later passed 110, rapidly approaching terminal velocity of just over 120 MPH. The light from my altimeter on my left wrist glowed in the dark and showed that I was losing altitude rapidly. In future jumps I would assume the "delta position," which would allow me to kick into aerodynamic overdrive and boost my vertical descent to over more than two hundred miles per hour. What a thrill.

———

I took over as commander in chief of U.S. Special Operations Command (CINCSOC) in February 1996, having just been promoted to four-star general, responsible for overseeing missions being carried out in 142 foreign countries by our Navy SEALs, Special Forces (Green Berets), Air Force Combat Control teams and Special Operations aircraft, Army rangers, and other highly classified "Special Mission Units"—a combination of both warrior and diplomat who often work under the cover of darkness.

Even though I had reached the highest Army rank possible, my motto was still the same: *lead from the front.* In this case, the front included jumping out of airplanes from more than twenty-four thousand feet, so I decided I'd better learn how to do that. Participating in night jumps with Delta and accompanying them on practice missions also gave me a great feel for what their precise capabilities were and could help me prevent others from confusing enthusiasm with capabilities.

As CINCSOC, you are the role model for all the Special Ops units. You set the tone, lead by example, fight for funds, write the doctrine, and provide the vision. While I did find it disappointing that as a four-star I was not out on the front lines, I took great satisfaction in contributing to the big picture.

It had been quite a while since I was a captain in Vietnam and served officially in Special Ops (where they called us the Snake Eaters), yet I had always proudly worn my 5th Special Forces combat patch on my right sleeve (rotating it along with the 173rd Airborne Brigade and 101st patches) since I held Special Operations in such high regard—and right off the bat that gave me some credibility with the troops.

That same degree of thought went into which beret I would wear—something that might not seem that significant to some, but to me it sent a very clear signal to the command of which I preferred. I was qualified to wear the black ranger beret, the red airborne one, and of course the prestigious Special Forces green beret. Since I'd left my airborne command back at Fort Bragg, I decided not to wear the red beret at this time. But SOCOM encompassed both rangers and Special Forces, so I opted to rotate the black and the green so that one group wouldn't get the impression that I favored one over another. I also found that wearing the patch and the beret created an instant bond with my troops; it said *I am one of you* instead of *I am the boss*. It was a subtle thing but one that was more in line with my style of leadership.

As an aside, during my tenure as Chairman, Army Chief of Staff General Eric Shinseki—a great guy who got the shaft by Rumsfeld after the two clashed—came up with an idea that almost started World War III in the ranger community. Hoping to instill that same sense of pride in the entire army that the black beret represented to the rangers, Ric announced, unexpectedly, at the annual Association of the United States Army gathering in Washington, D.C., that the black beret would no longer be unique to the rangers, but rather would encompass the entire U.S. Army. I was attending a meeting at the White House, unaware of what Ric had planned, but the second I walked into my office, one of my special assistants, Colonel Marty Dempsey, came in and said, almost in a state of disbelief, "Did you hear what the Army Chief of Staff just did?"

Both active and retired rangers were ready to burn him at the stake, and the Special Forces and airborne communities were not much happier. I thought Ric showed great courage in making the decision. Many other chiefs had toyed with idea but had not followed through with it. It was a worthwhile goal, but several of us who were qualified to wear all three berets wished that we had been in a better position to support his decision. For the next several weeks, a bitter battle was waged against his decision. Almost every day at our morning meeting, Secretary Rumsfeld would ask when I was going to get Shinseki under control. Meanwhile, since both Shinseki and I were Army and both our names started with an S, many were confused about who had made this unpopular decision. I was getting three hundred e-mails each day lambasting the decision, some even threatening. Ultimately, the Department of Defense decided to back Ric's plan, after the decision was made declaring "tan" the new official beret of the rangers.

---

While a well-rounded commander—a truly *effective* commander—must be knowledgeable of strategy and understand battlefield tactics, I think the greatest asset he can have are a few well-trained guys that can hit the enemy where he doesn't suspect it and use capabilities that the enemy may not even know exist. It is what I did back in the 3-60th Infantry when I infiltrated the enemy lines and attacked them from the rear—it's unconventional thinking—and I considered it to be my forte. This defines Special Ops, and it is one of the many reasons why I felt this command was a perfect fit for me.

The United States Special Operations Command (USSOCOM) operators have specialized skills, equipment, and tactics unique to SOCOM. They are structured with a regional focus to capitalize on specific language skills, political skills, and cultural-sensitivity training skewed to a specific area of operation (AO). Specialties include direct action (DA), psychological operations (PSYOPs), civil affairs (CA), combat controllers, combat weathermen, pararescue, rangers, SEALs (sea, air, land), Special Forces (SF), and Special Operations aviation (both Air Force and Army).

I came in to SOCOM on a real high, excited that I was about to serve with the finest, a very select group of elite individuals who are a premium national asset. That was my attitude as I went in, and they never disappointed me.

Carolyn and I were looking forward to the warm, subtropical climate that Tampa was known for, a welcome break from the freezing temperatures we would be leaving in Fayetteville—and a nice excuse for me to get out there in my twenty-one-foot Reinell inboard/outboard fishing boat all year round, since I had heard that redfish, grouper, and cobia were biting throughout the winter months—and I had a feeling that I would track down a twenty-pound jack crevalle, which would make a fine addition to our Sunday dinner table.

As I turned my red and grey Chevy K5 Blazer into the main gate of MacDill Air Force Base, an Air Force KC-135 took off overhead—an invaluable asset that provided the midair refueling piece that is so essential to our ability to conduct operations literally anywhere in the world. These guys are truly unsung heroes who are essential to America's arsenal of capabilities. Passing the modern "Welcome to MacDill AFB" sign, I smiled to myself; its digital readout framed perfectly by a pair of palm trees was in stark contrast to the rustic wooden Home of The Airborne and Special Operations Forces sign that welcomed visitors to Fort Bragg. Carolyn followed a short distance behind in my pride and joy, a jet-black 1986 Corvette. With its 230-horsepower tuned-port-injected V-8, it could take off like a rocket. After eleven years, I was glad to see that Corvette got wise and brought back the convertible—not that she would have wanted to put the top down on that frosty February morning. The Welcome sign blinked "33 degrees" and the skies unleashed a blustery downpour; it was one of the coldest Februarys in Tampa history. So much for the grouper.

Truth be told, at that moment fishing was the farthest thing from my mind. At 10:00 A.M. the following morning, General Wayne Downing would pass me the colors and I would become responsible for a command that was already becoming a dominant force in combating our rapidly escalating terrorist threat. During my last few weeks at Bragg I had given a great deal of thought to what I wanted to accomplish in my first four-star command, and I developed four highly ambitious goals.

First and foremost, I wanted to ensure that in every operational plan developed by the combatant commanders, those commanders felt comfortable that I was able to provide them with the Special Operations support they needed to carry out their plans. It was important for them to have confidence that my troops were fully trained and ready to provide that extra edge that has become synonymous with Special Operations, and I never wanted them to have to reject or compromise a plan because they questioned our capabilities. By the same token, I never wanted our enthusiasm to be confused with capabilities. Once again, *trained and ready* became my watch words.

My two immediate predecessors, Wayne Downing and Carl Stiner, had come up with a great plan to insert Special Operations elements directly into each of the combatant commanders' headquarters so that they had both a presence and a planning mechanism right there with them all the time. Not only did our presence reinforce our availability and enhance communication, but we all knew that a last-minute add-on was seldom effective anyway. My plan was to take their original plan to the next level by making sure that we had the *right* people in there. It was important that I visited each of these commanders to develop close personal relationships, and I made sure they had my private phone number and felt comfortable calling me at any hour of the day or night to ask for help.

Bearing in mind that SOCOM had forces deployed in more than seventy countries, on every continent, my next goal was to get to as many of these deployments as possible, to experience firsthand the challenges our operational forces were facing and make sure they had the equipment and resources they needed to carry out their mission.

Next, as commander I was responsible for the budget and acquisition-procurement program, so I had to hit the ground running and immediately get a handle on where we stood on that. Were we adequately funded, and if not, how much more did we need, and how were we going to get it? What kind of acquisitions and procurements were pending and what type of research and development were we currently pursuing that could give us some advanced technologies for the future?

Finally, I wanted to establish a strategic vision of the command. Where did I see this command going in the next fifteen to twenty years, and how far from there were we? Just exactly what would it take to get us there? Realizing that the budget cycle runs about five to seven years, this analysis had to be framed within a projection encompassing the next two or three budget cycles to determine if we were properly preparing for the future.

What started as a concept I called Joint Vision 2010 evolved into a strategy for the future that I would expand upon through my days as Chairman, eventually producing concepts of "full spectrum dominance" that would form the basis of military doctrine. We called this Special Operations Joint Vision 2020, and I signed the final draft on May 30, 2000.

Full-spectrum dominance refers to a force that is dominant across the full spectrum of military operations, "persuasive in peace, decisive in war, preeminent in any form of conflict." Although various military organizations had attempted *joint integration* in the past, for the most part it had been on a piecemeal basis. It was really Joint Vision 2020 that tied those pieces together and made it clear how essential such integration becomes in today's changing world. *Not only must we be able to win wars, but it is every bit as important that we actively contribute to peace.*

Joint Vision 2020 emphasized the importance of ongoing *transformation* of operational capabilities and reinforced the value of further experimentation, exercises, analysis, and conceptual thought, especially in the arenas of information operations, joint command and control, and multinational and interagency operations. Even though others (such as Donald Rumsfeld) would try to downplay the existence of a wide range of potential threats to our interests, Joint Vision 2020 acknowledged them and outlined five capabilities that were essential to the joint concept: "To build the most effective force for 2020, we must be fully joint: *intellectually, operationally, organizationally, doctrinally, and technically.*"

We stressed the importance of the centrality of information technology to the evolution of not only our own military but the capabilities of other players around the globe. Multinational and interagency partners had to be successfully integrated, and their processes, organizations, and systems had to be interoperable.

While this vision recognized the importance of technology and technical innovation to the U.S. military and its operations, at the same time it emphasized that technological innovation had to be accompanied by *intellectual innovation* leading to changes in organization and doctrine. I came up with a concept of what I called "decision superiority," which is *translating information superiority into better decisions arrived at and implemented faster than an enemy can react.*

Those were my goals when I went in, and I felt that they would be enough to keep me busy throughout my command. I was not disappointed.

———

Besides the climate, MacDill Air Force Base had an entirely different feel than Fort Bragg. Originally a WWII training and staging area for the B-17 Flying Fortress and B-26 Marauder, between 1979 and 1993 approximately half of all F-16 pilots were trained at MacDill. While a 1991 base-downsizing edict forced the cessation of all flight activity in 1993,

subsequent legislation overturned this and allowed me to use the flightline
as a temporary home for seventy-five C-130s during the Uphold Democracy Haiti operation. Today, the host wing has been redesignated for
military refueling missions, and besides SOCOM, the base is headquarters for the U.S. Central Command (CENTCOM), which oversees military operations throughout the Middle East.

Our home on the base was at 7701 Bayshore Drive, a beautiful two-
story house right on the water overlooking Tampa Bay. Just across Staff
Circle was the Officers' Club, which provided a picturesque venue for my
mid morning change-of-command ceremony and reception that was attended by more than four hundred military and civic leaders, despite the
unrelenting downpour that drenched our bodies but not our spirits. Secretary of Defense William Perry and Chairman John Shalikashvili presided over the pomp and pageantry of the tradition that dates back to
1775, when George Washington took over the Massachusetts militia from
General Artemas Ward. Ross Perot was on hand to show his strong support for Special Operations forces, and he seemed right at home as he enthusiastically introduced himself to my mother, brothers, sister, and other
members of the rapidly growing Shelton clan. Jon and Anne had blessed
us with three beautiful granddaughters by then, Cassie (two years old at
the time) and the twins (Heather and Hannah, only two months old), so
they decided that a trip and change-of-command ceremony wasn't the
right thing at the time. Jon was a Cobb County, Georgia police officer and
would be starting the U.S. Secret Service Special Agent Training Course
(SATC) the following month. Jeff and Amy drove down from Fort Bragg,
where he was stationed, flying UH-60 Black Hawks with the 82nd Airborne. With them were Samuel Hugh, two months old, and Savannah,
who was three and totally captivated by Kay Leonard (a SOCOM protocol officer) and her stories about her cat. That was much more interesting
than whatever Gramps was doing with the flag up in front of all those
people. Mark was back in Fayetteville, still in school. I can truly report
that a great time was had by all.

Following the ceremony, Carolyn flew back to Fayetteville to allow
Mark to finish his school year rather than move him to Tampa for the last
three months of the term. Since we had to vacate our home on Fort Bragg,
that meant we had to rent an apartment in downtown Fayetteville for them
to live in for three months—a sacrifice we felt was important to make for
Mark. Sacrifices like this are made every day by military families.

I went back to headquarters and late that afternoon met with the staff
in the conference room, just to let them all know that they were part of
my team and that I looked forward to working with them to ensure that
the readiness of our men and women in the field was always our first priority. I gave them a little of my command philosophy, which centered

around integrity, setting the example, taking care of our people, and maintaining our solid reputation as the "quiet professionals."

I had already been sent the equivalent of ten pounds of briefing papers, prepared by the staff as "read ahead" before I took command, so I had a good feel for what I was walking into. Still, the day before, I had met with General Wayne Downing (outgoing commander in chief, Special Operations Command) for about two hours in his office. We primarily discussed key personnel, strengths and weaknesses. His major concern was the deputy commander, Rear Admiral Chuck LeMoyne, a great Navy SEAL who had throat cancer and was near terminal. Our great friend Ross Perot had arranged for Chuck to fly to Texas to be treated by specialists as a last resort to save his life. Consequently, he was gone for weeks at a time and was very ineffective as the deputy but insisted on staying in his position. Wayne did not feel comfortable asking him to step down under those conditions but wanted me to know that it would increase my workload and be an issue I would have to deal with. Chuck gave it all he had until the very end, and he passed away on January 4, 1997.

———

At this time the unified Special Operations Command consisted of Army, Navy, and Air Force elements that all worked together seamlessly, like hand and glove. Rangers, Special Forces, PSYOPS (psychological operations), civil affairs, the 160th Aviation Regiment (Night Stalkers), and Delta Force fell under the Army umbrella, and the SEALS under the Navy. Air Force elements became vital participants in 1990, but the Marines were not yet a part of the command—although they would lead you to believe they were.

It takes only one glance at the famous Iwo Jima Memorial just outside the gates of Arlington National Cemetery to remind us of all the heroic contributions the Marines have made to our great country, and right off the top of my head I can rattle off the names of numerous Marines who are exceptional officers. But the Marines had elected to keep their forces outside the USSOCOM structure and formed Marine Expeditionary Forces, Special Operations Capable, units or MEUSOCs. I had observed that while the marines serving inside the MEUSOCs were fine individuals, they were not properly equipped or trained. They consisted of a small group of people who were supposed to have great capabilities—expert shooters who could free-fall and do SEAL-type work. But when you started talking to these individuals, you learned that some of them had not done a free fall in more than a year, and some of the shooters had not practiced their shooting skills in six months. It briefed well but was in essence the biggest bunch of bullshit I'd ever seen. These teams were not worthy of the name Special Operations.

The SOCOM Special Mission Units (SMUs consist of JSOC elements such as Delta Force and Navy SEAL Team Six) laboriously trained to off-the-chart standards, firing hundreds of rounds each week. Daily physical conditioning is performed to exhausting standards and their parachuting capabilities—conducted from extreme altitudes—ensure that they can penetrate a target area undetected with precision accuracy.

I used to caution the CINCS, *Don't fall victim into thinking that you are going to pull off some high-speed operation using a bunch of guys who haven't even used their equipment in six months to a year. Go to the pros, go to JSOC, go to Special Ops, if you really have first-class needs.* The Marine teams and in some cases "vanilla" Special Operations teams don't come close to the same standards as JSOC units—like Delta or SEAL Team Six—are trained to.

In addition to the MEUSOCs, the Marines assigned about fifty officers to SOCOM as liaison officers, the supposed intention being to streamline the communication between the Corps and SOCOM and provide us with additional high-level operational support. These were great officers, but the truth was that this, too, was a ruse. They were there to be spies for the Marine Corps, assigned to SOCOM to keep the Marine higher-ups informed on what SOCOM was up to and to enhance the illusion that the Marine Corps had Special Operations capabilities. I considered sending them back but instead I gave them an ultimatum: either you are a real part of my team or you're out; but you are not going to be in here just to see what we're doing. In the end, I decided to keep them because individually they were all great guys.

On the positive side, overall, the Marines have the greatest public affairs operation I had ever seen. For example, in some cases you may have only a handful of Marines on an Army or Navy operation, but you can easily be led to believe that it is a 100 percent Marine operation. I have never seen a better publicity operation in my life.

Secondly—and this is a great motivator—they instill in their people that if you have ever been a Marine, you will always be a Marine. I don't care if you're the chairman of the board of a giant corporation; the fact that you were a Marine comes first. If the other services could capture only 10 percent of that, it would help them immensely.

After I retired, the Marine component did eventually become an official part of SOCOM. Authorized in 2005, the unit was formed in 2006 and is based out of Camp Lejuene in North Carolina. The first unit to deploy, the 120-man MSOC Company Fox, became embroiled in an international incident about a month after their arrival in Afghanistan, when their convoy was ambushed and attacked by a suicide bomber. When the smoke settled, eight Afghans were dead and thirty-four were wounded along the highway. In an unprecedented move, following a complaint about the Marine company by Afghanistan President Hamid Karzi, they were expelled from the country pending an investigation surrounding claims by eyewitnesses that in response to the ambush, the Marines had started firing in all directions and their gunfire hit a number of civilians. The decision to remove the MSOC was made by Army Major General Frank Kearney, head of U.S. Special Operations Command-Central Command, based on his preliminary assessment of the Marines' actions. Probing even deeper, an investigation was launched into overall readiness issues encompassing the entire MSOC program.

———

My very first order of business consisted of briefs by my headquarters staff officers and their key people. I like to refer to that day as Death by PowerPoint, since every one of them used slide after slide to portray the current status of the command and the challenges they faced. This gave me a chance to meet each staff officer and his key people and hear firsthand, from them, the key issues they were dealing with.

You always inherit the existing staff, which provides for continuity. My J5 (logistics) was Brigadier General Doug Brown, who would go on to command JSOC and then become commander, USSOCOM, after General Charlie Holland. My J3 (operations) was USAF Major General Jim McCombs, an Air Force officer with almost forty years of duty—after Chuck LeMoyne was diagnosed as "terminal," I decided to move Jim up to take his place as my Deputy. Jim was superb. My J1 (personnel) was a great Army colonel named Tom Owens, whom I had known at Fort Bragg; and my aide-de-camp was also from Fort Bragg, Major (now Major General) Burke Garrett, an Army ranger and 82nd veteran. Colonel Harry Axson soon became my XO, and I've always kidded that if I ever decided to give this up to become an actor (not likely), I'd have the perfect stunt double in Harry—he was my exact height and build. He had been my G3 (ops officer) in the 82nd when I was the division commander.

My modus operandi has always been to hit the ground running, and with all the ops we had in progress when I stepped in (literally hundreds), this was no exception. My first real order of business was to analyze the individual-readiness reviews. These consist of reports submitted by the component commanders describing the current readiness status of their units in terms of personnel, training, and equipment. It's from these reports that I got my first snapshot of just how close we were to that all-important *trained and ready* position I keep going back to. Even before I made those base trips, the reports would give me a broad idea of what it was going to take to bring the operation up to par from a fiscal standpoint. In this case, as soon as I read the reports it became clear to me that I was going to need substantially more than the $3.2 billion that we had previously been allotted—but "needing" and receiving are two different animals, so I would have to get creative, and over the next few months I would give serious thought to how I would handle that vital budget testimony to the Senate Armed Services Committee.

In keeping with the goals I had established up front, early on I made it my business to pay personal visits to as many of our commanders as possible. I wanted to find out what those commanders needed from Special Ops, and then evaluate how well we could meet those needs. If the answer indicated anything less than 100 percent, I wanted quick answers to determine what I would have to do to raise that bar.

I already knew some of these commanders, like General Binnie Peay, my former boss in the 101st Airborne Division (Air Assault) during Desert Storm and now my next-door neighbor in Tampa, where he commanded Central Command; General George Joulwan, who was Wes Clark's predecessor as Supreme Allied Commander in Europe (SACEUR), General Gary Luck, my former boss at Fort Bragg and now U.S. Forces commander in Korea; and Admiral Joe Prueher (who subsequently became U.S. ambassador to China) in the Pacific. Others I would be meeting for the first time, like General Gene Harbinger at Strategic Command and General Jack Sheehan of Atlantic Command.

SOCOM had a 707 that was available to me for these trips. It was not kept at MacDill but rather at an off-site location since we used it for some rather unique missions when we needed a low visibility. It was a special plane capable of midair refueling, flown by a special crew. It was a flying command post that would allow me to function as commander no matter where I might be in the world at the time—very similar to how the President uses *Air Force One* as his office in the sky.

My first stop in theater was normally a courtesy call on the four-star commanders since I wanted to get their perspective on how SOF (Special Operations forces) was supporting them at that time and get their take on future challenges unique to their geographic theaters. What could I do to most effectively support their commands? After leaving the four-star headquarters I would try to visit three to five countries in the region, where I would meet with those countries' Chiefs of Defense and SOF commanders. An example would be a stop in Hawaii to visit the U.S. commander in charge of the Pacific, followed immediately by visits to Indonesia, East Timor, Singapore, and Thailand before returning to Tampa. I cannot overemphasize the importance of these relationships—both the original contact and then nurturing them. There are countless times when diplomatic channels might fail, yet a potentially devastating bullet would be dodged by my picking up the phone and seeking the quick personal intervention of one of these new friends.

The importance of this networking or "face time" cannot be overestimated in *any* field; it's all about *relationships*—sincere, well developed, and personal—as essential in the military as they are in business, politics, or even the home front. It wouldn't have mattered if we'd had Facebook, Twitter, or Skype in those days, although I might have fired off a quick tweet or SMS on occasion, I would never have sacrificed the value of face-to-face contact in the interest of convenience. I can honestly say that the close relationships I've been fortunate enough to have fostered are as important to my success, and to my being able to do my job effectively, as anything else.

It became a nice two-way street in that regard. My foreign hosts felt honored to be called on by a visiting American four-star. For example, when I would go to Jordan, King Hussein would want to see me even though I was really there to visit Major General Abdullah (head of the Jordanian armed forces), who would later become King Abdullah, with whom I struck up a great relationship that continued well into my days as Chairman, and still, today. Frequently these individuals would come back to the United States to visit us. I'd send them invitations and would host their visits, which often resulted in developing friendships that would serve us both well. I would go to international commanders' conferences and secretary of defense conferences where I would develop new friendships and nurture existing ones with my counterparts and peers.

During one of my visits to the Pacific, the Indonesian government invited Carolyn to join me as I met with their top officials. Indonesia, which is the fourth-largest nation in the world and has the world's largest Muslim population, was the site of a number of Special Operations training teams.

Landing in Jakarta, I was immediately taken to the office of the chief of defense for visits with him along with the heads of the Army and Navy.

Shortly thereafter, I visited with Lieutenant General Prabowo Subianto, the chief of the Indonesian Special Forces (who was married to President Suharto's daughter). Prabowo was a colorful character who later on would be accused of conducting operations that included torture, extortion, murder, kidnapping, and other mistreatment of his citizens (although he continues to deny the allegations). Had we known that at the time, I'm not sure Carolyn and I would have felt so comfortable when he escorted the two of us to a nearby field to witness a demonstration of his Special Forces capabilities.

The first demonstration involved skinning a boa constrictor. In a matter of seconds, two Indonesian Special Forces soldiers, using razor-sharp knives, skinned the snake from head to tail. To our disbelief, the boa, still very much alive, went slithering off minus his skin.

Next they demonstrated the mystic capabilities of three samurai-type soldiers. The first was blindfolded and, after I was allowed to inspect the blindfold to ensure that it was not transparent in any way, spun around until I was nearly drunk from watching him. He was handed a long sword while an apple was placed on the head of another soldier standing about thirty feet away. The blindfolded soldier, sword in hand, walked about the field, eventually ending up about five feet away from the individual with the apple, then suddenly he whirled about and in one clean swipe cut the apple in half, while Carolyn and I watched in amazement.

Then, a second soldier was blindfolded and spun about numerous times before being placed on a waiting motorcycle. Gunning the engine, he drove directly toward a formation of three hundred soldiers on the field in front of us, accelerating until the very end. I expected to see a disaster; but instead, the blindfolded soldier wove the motorcycle in and out among the troop formation at ever-increasing speed. The formation stood rock steady and the motorcycle avoided them all.

I asked Prabowo how they did it but he commented only that these troops were selected based on innate special abilities that only about one in every ten thousand individuals possessed. To this day, I can't imagine how they accomplished those feats.

The final station was a demonstration of how they lived off the land, and Carolyn was less than thrilled when they offered us a piece of snake, which was most likely prepared from the boa that had been skinned moments earlier. I must say that I was somewhat surprised that she managed to eat it.

After a long day we attended a dinner in our honor. Afterward, as was his custom, Lieutenant General Prabowo had arranged for musical entertainment in the form of karaoke—he loved to sing and appeared to consider himself right up there with Sinatra. Carolyn and I felt he was probably the worst singer we had heard in our lives, and about the best I could muster was a round of "Happy Birthday."

More meetings followed the next day before we lifted off in the 707 en route to Australia. Ironically, when I assumed my duties as CJCS (Chairman of the Joint Chiefs of Staff), the Indonesian Army chief, General Wiranto, would overthrow President Suharto in a military coup and I would become the only one in the U.S. government whom he would communicate with—*the sole link between President Clinton and General Wiranto.*

To me, this underscored the value of developing personal relationships, which often can be the key to resolving important issues.

————

As an aside, a variety of classified capabilities of my 707 made it the aircraft of choice for international terrorist-rendition missions. It could carry a rendition team comprised of FBI, CIA, doctors, and of course our own JSOC operators, who would provide security. If the mission was time-sensitive, we might have the plane standing by on two-hour strip alert, and once we got word the snatch was a go—bam. We were on the move.

Many times the only way top officials of certain countries would agree to cooperate with the CIA and FBI in capturing or turning over terrorists was if they were given guarantees that their own people would never know that they had been involved in the arrest or the extradition process. In these cases, it was imperative that the terrorist be brought to the United States for trial without fighting some international criminal court or international rule of law about extradition.

It's not uncommon for leaks to originate from the suspect's own country, which is what appeared to occur in the case of Mir Aimal Kasi, who was ultimately tried, convicted, and executed for the murders of two CIA employees outside CIA headquarters on January 25, 1993. In this instance, our task was to provide transportation and security for the FBI team that apprehended Kasi at 4:30 A.M. on June 15, 1997 from his room at the Shalimar Hotel in Dera Ghazi Khan, Pakistan. A C-141 was the aircraft of choice for this rendition, and unlike the usual quick in/quick out scenario that renditions often utilize, this C-141 remained at the Islamabad airport for forty-eight hours before the agents brought the prisoner on board for transport back to Andrews. Other countries were involved, as was a two-million-dollar reward, but we were not a part of whatever high-level negotiations were said to have occurred between Pakistan's prime minister Nawaz Sharif's government and our own.

Other high-profile renditions include Ramzi Yousef, mastermind of the 1993 World Trade Center bombing who was apprehended on February 7, 1995, by FBI and State Department DSS agents in Islamabad and flown to New York; Wali Khan Amin Shah, convicted of plotting to bomb eleven American commercial jumbo jets in a single day, who was arrested by the FBI in Malaysia on December 12, 1995; and Japanese Red Army member Tsutomu Shirosaki, who bombed the U.S. embassy in Jakarta in 1986 and was returned to the United States by the FBI on September 21, 1996.

There was a judge in New York that both the FBI and CIA loved to use for these renditions. For one thing, he respected the classified aspects of the case and made damn sure that nothing about it ever showed up in the press—which in many cases might have tipped off the citizens of those countries where we'd just made the snatch, that perhaps their leaders had been involved. That judge would make the initial rulings as to whether or not there was a valid case against the prisoner, how long he could be held, and whether or not he was going to be granted bail under law.

As soon as we landed, the FBI or CIA would take the prisoner and disappear—our role was complete. Our purpose was to provide the transportation and for our onboard JSOC operators to provide security for the air crew, the prisoner, and the medical staff (who would be on board in case the prisoner needed medical treatment).

We had a couple of these planes (as well as a couple of undercover planes that were available to us for other special missions where low profile was required), and the Air Force had a specially equipped C-141 we could use. Midair-refueling capability was essential since we didn't want to involve another country by virtue of just stopping there for a fill-up—not with our cargo.

———

Although I would continue to make these fact-finding and relationship-building trips throughout my tenure as commander in chief of Special Operation Command, after my first three or four months I felt comfortable that I had enough info to work with my staff to put pencil to paper and determine just how much it would cost to maintain our razor-sharp edge in a manner that would meet or exceed the requirements communicated to me by the combatant commanders, and correct some of the issues that were flagged in those readiness reviews. Working closely with my staff, we came up with a rather staggering $500 million add-on (in addition to the $3.2 billion that we were expecting)—substantially more than anyone had ever anticipated. Nonetheless, it's what I felt was required, and what I was determined to get.

The funding process for SOCOM is somewhat different from that of other commands in that so much of what we do is classified. Of course, it still requires congressional (and ultimately presidential) approval, but I felt a more creative Special Ops approach to that approval might be most effective in this instance.

My presentation to the Senate Armed Services Committee took place in a secure behind-the-scenes briefing area. I started by talking through some of the programs we had in the works and then went on to get into some ideas I had for the future, like an enhanced breaching capability for deep-underground targets or delivery of supplies behind enemy lines with pinpoint accuracy—couching them within the framework of how important they would be to combat our rapidly snowballing terrorism problem. But rather than take that immediately into the issue of cost, I arranged to bring in three "special guests."

The rear door popped open and in walked three special operators who had recently returned from Somalia, where they had participated in the operation that would be sanitized by Ridley Scott to become the movie *Black Hawk Down*, based on Mark Bowden's book.

I said, "Let me just take one second to introduce you to some of the brave heroes who participated in this operation . . ." and I introduced a master sergeant from the Air Force combat-control team, and a sergeant major from Delta Force, and an AH-6J Little Bird Night Stalker pilot from the Army 160th SOAR (Special Operations Aviation Regiment). "And let me tell you just a little bit about their background, and a little bit about what really happened over there. . . ."

Then, one by one, they described their experiences in vivid detail—how the copter had been downed behind enemy lines and their fellow operator killed. The senators were transfixed as the master sergeant recounted how he worked until dawn to retrieve the pilot's body, the melted wreckage and impenetrable titanium making it impossible to remove it intact and instead requiring him to hack it up and bring it back in pieces to be reassembled back at home for a dignified, proper burial—and how he had done this despite a constant barrage of enemy rocket-propelled grenades and small-arms fire throughout the night, rather than leave that body behind. I sat there as he told that story and I saw the entire row of senators in silent, rapt attention—senators who I was sure were fully prepared to grill me with tough arguments that suggested that what I was asking for was outrageous—and I watched as their eyes welled up, and by the time these three heroes were finished with their stories, the senators had tears streaming down their faces, and I thought, *Yes, here it comes. . . .*

They ended up giving me an additional half-billion-dollar add-on with virtually no questions asked. The reason why I knew the senators would react that way is that I knew how I had reacted when I heard that incredibly heroic story myself.

––––––––

That was a case where real-life drama almost exceeded anything the imagination could have created—*truth is stranger than fiction,* so to speak—but the fact is that we always seemed to have our hands full with seemingly impossible situations where, in the end, the courage, skill, and acumen of our operators made the impossible seem almost mundane with one triumph after another.

We had been notified by the CIA that a ship coming out of North Korea would be going through the Panama Canal with an illegal weapon on board, and we were greatly concerned that this weapon might get into either Iranian or Iraqi hands. The agent was not sure which of those two countries it was headed for. This was a case where he had everything else just right and we had confirmed that the ship was on the exact course he had predicted.

It was a very time-sensitive mission in which a specific SEAL Team Six component was called into action. While I cannot get into the tactical elements or operational details of the mission, what I can say is that our guys were able to "immobilize" the weapon system in a special way without leaving any trace.

It was a successful operation that went off without a hitch.

* * *

One potentially dangerous mission was successful because it precluded the event from happening.

CIA intell indicated that a key terrorist we had been hunting for a long time had been located. Their agents were on him and they were attempting to take a picture of him to give me the actionable intell I needed to green-light the mission. Until there was positive ID there was no way I would recommend to either the Chairman or the President that we should proceed, despite assurances from CIA higher-ups that they were certain that this was the guy.

The agent gave a detailed description that was a perfect match and said that the individual was carrying a large sum of money in a metal briefcase and had two henchmen at his side to protect both himself and the cash.

This was another SEAL Team operation since it called for them to board the ship in the middle of the night to capture or, if necessary, kill the guy.

It was one of those situations where to me, it just wasn't passing the sniff test—something didn't smell right about it despite the vivid details we were receiving. Finally we received the photo for identity confirmation, but by the time it was blown up it was so grainy that it could have been George Washington and we couldn't have told the difference. No way was it good enough that I would consider it *actionable* intelligence.

Despite strong pleas from the CIA to the contrary, we did NOT authorize the operation, but instead contacted a third party who boarded the ship when they arrived in the United Arab Emirates, and it was a damn good thing since it turned out that *this was a legitimate businessmen traveling with his wife.*

Had we gone in and killed this guy, it would've been a disaster. The CIA would most likely have tried to throw the blame in our direction, but, as is usually the case, the truth would most likely have eventually leaked anyway.

———

One of the more interesting facets of my time as CINCSOC involved our counterterrorist operations; and even though this was pre-9/11, we had an extensive counter terrorism (CT) force that was kept busy on a daily basis tracking terrorists throughout the world. My CT force had special intelligence that flowed into them and I made it my business to personally read these intell reports as they came in. Early on I picked up on one name that had not yet gained mass notoriety but had already blipped brightly on my internal radar screen: Usama bin Laden (referred to as "UBL" in Department of Defense and CIA circles). In spite of its name (al-Qaeda means "the base" in Arabic), it really consisted of a *web* of previously independent Islamist terrorists groups—or cells—that bin Laden and his minions had consolidated to form a deadly anti-Western and anti-Jewish force of fundamentalist Sunnis that called for global jihad (literally meaning "struggle," in this case it refers to a Muslim holy war).

My predecessors had been briefed on three terrorist-training camps in northern Sudan that were funded by bin Laden as early as January 1994, and by now these camps were drawing "students" from numerous countries. A year later, more camps popped up in Yemen not far from the Saudi border, around the same time as evidence was found linking UBL to Ramzi Yousef, the mastermind of the 1993 World Trade Center bombing. In November 1995, a car bomb killed five Americans and two Indians at a U.S.-operated military base in Riyadh, Saudi Arabia, and even though bin Laden denied responsibility for the attack, he was ultimately indicted for the crime on June 8, 1998. While this would be his first indictment in the United States, our sources also linked him to the June 1995 assassination attempt on Egypt's President Mubarak—and it was at that time that the prosecution charged that he ran a rapidly growing terrorist organization called al-Qaeda.

Bin Laden was obviously a figure to be dealt with, yet surprisingly until this point very little of any consequence had been done. I felt that this had to change, and I pushed hard to make him number one on our list to be hunted down and killed or captured.

In my second year at SOCOM, I directed my chief to pull together a group of really smart guys—Navy, Army, and Air Force "computer geeks"— to look at what I viewed as a mounting threat from al-Qaeda as an organization, with bin Laden at its head. The organization was expanding rapidly and already had cells in fifty-five to sixty countries spread throughout the world with no apparent pattern, so they were not easy to track, let alone shut down. How do you get a handle on something that is so large yet so incredibly elusive? To me, the money was the key: without it they would be unable to operate. My thought was that if we tracked it and worked backward, we could zero in on their location and then smoke them out.

We set up a dedicated office for this group and they utilized unclassified Internet sources to pick up the money trail—the flow of al-Qaeda funding. How were they getting their money, where was it coming from, how was it being laundered, and how was it channeled back into the system to support their operation?

In many respects, this was a computerized evolution of the transparent acetate-overlay technique I had developed when I was the S2 back in Vietnam. My team broke down the data into specific categories that would equate to the overlays: travel patterns of known or suspected terrorists;

hubs of communications with UBL cells; financial transactions carried out by the various cells located in sixty-plus countries (including the United States); etc. When these independent elements were merged together we found a tremendous geographic consistency—each built on the others and reinforced where the real action was—and *for the first time we had a handle on where al-Qaeda was operating from.*

When I saw what these guys had done it knocked my socks off—in a matter of months they had come up with great stuff. The data revealed two specific industries in which they were channeling the vast majority of their capital: the fishing and fertilizer industries throughout the world.

It showed the hot spots where all the traffic was flowing from, then the feeder organizations, and finally showed which countries had the biggest problems in terms of active cells. Afghanistan and Germany were major hubs, as we had expected. A few others came as more of a surprise, like the Philippines and Indonesia.


At around this time I got the call that took me into the Chairman's seat, but I felt great that I would be leaving my successor with an outstanding team and an excellent foundation upon which to build intelligence surrounding al-Qaeda and UBL.

As Chairman I would have an even greater role in our counterterrorism efforts in my direct dealings with the President and the National Security Counsel, and if I thought I was being bombarded with information at the CINCSOC level, I would be absolutely *inundated* when I became Chairman. But it was only information, not *true intelligence* and certainly not *actionable intelligence.* This provided the impetus for me to take these data-mining concepts—which were the very same concepts I had utilized back at the 173rd Airborne in Vietnam—and in October 1999 officially task General Pete Schoomaker (CINCSOC at that time) to develop a campaign plan that used these concepts to obtain detailed information on international terrorist organizations and identify terrorist leaders and their followers and their supporting institutions.

It was all about taking this massive amount of seemingly unrelated data and attempting to identify linkages and patterns (i.e., data mining); and, just as I had come up with the overlay-map mode of presentation, come up with a user-friendly visual display that intelligence analysts and ops planners could use to track these terrorists. Pete did a terrific job, and took it a step further by adding in a collaborative environment—a chat room, so to speak—wherein analysts could collaborate with one another on a real-time basis. His initial focus was al-Qaeda, but it subsequently went deeper than that.

Whereas my SOCOM data was entirely from open-source material, he added in government databases (from the various intelligence agencies) as well as the open-source material—and at this stage these six to eight computer experts were analyzing more then ten thousand Web pages per day, mostly news sources and the terrorist organizations' own Web sites (yes, they really had them). The program was called Able Danger.

In December 2001, just two months after my retirement, it was taken to the next level and expanded to an entire dedicated facility. Called SO-JICC (Special Operations Joint Interagency Collaboration Center), the system fuses data from both open-source and classified intelligence.

According to Doug Brown (Pete Schoomaker's successor as CINCSOC), SOJICC allows IT engineers, intelligence analysts, and Special Operations officers to integrate and use advanced software tools tailored to SOF mission sets. SOJICC is both a data-mining facility and a Skunk Works, a secretive effort to produce innovative designs quickly and efficiently.

The concept has mushroomed exponentially and has been used to support Special Operations Forces in Iraq and Afghanistan and a number of other classified missions. "SOJICC has successfully integrated complex data streams from the CIA, Defense Intelligence Agency, and National Security Agency," Brown revealed. "Additionally, thanks to collaboration on other efforts, SOJICC has data from most of the national laboratories and the Joint Warfare Analysis Center."

Besides data mining, the program now encompasses both pattern and speech recognition, machine learning/neural networking, audio and video capture, plus visualization and search optimization. It has become a valuable tool for combatant commanders to link and track terrorist personalities and events throughout the world. *Not a bad evolution from what started as a long, coffee-filled all-nighter by a twenty-five-year-old captain and his seasoned master sergeant on the outskirts of An Khe, Vietnam.*

---

During my twenty months as CINCSOC we supplied the trained, equipped, and ready forces to the combatant (theater) commanders so that they could conduct literally hundreds of missions that ran the gamut from large-scale humanitarian relief operations to low-profile infiltrations to capture or kill high-value targets. Some of these include the following:

## CT-43A RECOVERY OPERATION

April 3, 1996: search and rescue of CT-43A (military-modified Boeing 727) on official trade mission that crashed above Dubrovnik, Croatia. Rugged terrain, extreme cold. High-profile passengers including Secretary of Commerce Ron Brown, number of corporate executives, and *New*

*York Times* Frankfurt Bureau chief Nathaniel C. Nash, all killed in the crash.

## OPERATION ASSURED RESPONSE

April 13, 1996: combined SEAL, SF, and PSYOP forces respond to civil war in Liberia—Americans endangered. Rapid deployment, strike force, airlift, embassy protection, and evacuation of 436 Americans and 1,677 foreign nationals from sixty-eight countries. Hostile-fire environment, dozens of MH-53J evacuation flights protected by overhead fire-support sorties in AC-130H Spectre gunships and MC-130H electronics aircrafts. Missions vectored through rocket-propelled grenade and small-arms attacks.

## OPERATION JOINT GUARD

December 20, 1996: peacekeeping mission in Bosnia. Warring factions separated, land transferred, deter hostilities and reestablish civil authority. Later supplemented by three EC-130E Commando Solo (capable of transmitting AM, FM, HG, and TV broadcasts) aircraft to counter Serb radio and television broadcasts misrepresenting the Dayton Peace Accords.

## OPERATION SILVER WAKE

September 1996: open revolt in Albania prompts armed reconnaissance, intelligence, force protection, and embassy evacuation.

## OPERATION NOBLE OBELISK

May 25, 1997: JCET military training turns to force protection, HLZ reconnaissance, and embassy evacuation when rebel forces and military topple government in Sierra Leone.

## OPERATION FIRM RESPONSE

June 10, 1997: route reconnaissance, communications support, sensitive material retrieval/destruction, crucial assistance to U.S. ambassador when rebel forces attacked, and embassy security/evacuation of sixty-nine Americans after civil war breaks out in Congo's capital.

## MINE-CLEARING OPERATIONS

In 1997, President Clinton committed the United States to eliminating the threat of land mines to civilians by 2010. To that end, SOCOM demining effort greatly expands this humanitarian mission.

## AFRICAN CRISIS RESPONSE INITIATIVE (ACRI)

July 17 through August 30, 1996: Special Forces training of Rwanda military forces.

## Part II

# LIFE AT THE TOP

*There is at least one thing worse than fighting with allies—and that is to fight without them.*
—WINSTON CHURCHILL

*I*n Vietnam I had to deal with deadly fire and poisoned punji-stick booby traps, a sadistic team sergeant who tracked enemy kills by slicing off their ears and collecting them in a pickle jar, and a salivating Bengal tiger intent on ending my career at the rank of captain.

At Walter Reed, I was faced with Lieutenant Zack Solomon. Zack looked like a normal guy, a triathlete with a beautiful wife and adorable kids. He showed up around my fifth day in the hospital.

I was still without any feeling beneath my neck, so you can imagine what I thought when this guy showed up, introduced himself as my physical therapist, and informed me that it was time for me to stand up.

It was not a question, not a request, just a fact. Zack was incredibly demanding, unyielding, tough as nails—and, I would soon find out, deeply inspirational.

Needless to say, I was not able to magically stand, but that was the beginning of what would become a tight relationship. While I worked with Zack, nothing came easy. There was no build-up, no running start; he just dived right in like a walking Nike ad—"Just do it."

That first day he pushed me, and when I was still not able to feel anything and couldn't budge a muscle, he pushed even harder. Sweat rolled down my face as I struggled for some tiny success.

It didn't happen.

When I told him we'd given it our best shot, he responded with a coy smile, "Not yet you haven't."

This was my kind of guy.


You should have seen the look on his face when he saw it—more of a twitch than an actual movement—but for the first time since my accident, I had initiated the tiniest of contractions.

Between Zack and the doctors and nurses around the ICU, you'd have thought Babe Ruth had just hit a grand slam to clinch the seventh game of the World Series. At that moment, my first thought was how very much I wished that my first doctor—the one who'd been so positive that I would remain paralyzed for life—had been there to see it.

"Okay, enough for your first day," Zack said.

"Not so fast," I responded. "Two more for the Gipper."

## Chapter Twelve ★★★★

# INTERVIEW WITH THE PRESIDENT

July–September 1997

O ver the years I have been tracked down in some pretty remote places. Once I was standing near the open troop door of a C-130 about twelve hundred feet over Honduras just seconds before the green Jump light popped on to signal that we had reached our drop zone. As I started to stand in the door, I felt a hand grab my shoulder from behind. "Sir, I've got the XVIII Airborne Corps commander calling for you on SATCOM," shouted my aide through the deafening wind.

"Tell him I'll call back from the ground," I bellowed back, stepping into the humid air and sweltering heat.

A few years later, I was in Africa, this time with a Special Operations "A Detachment" training a battalion-size (six hundred soldiers) Namibian Defense Forces element in first aid, communications techniques, and battle drills. During this process the detachment also established friendships, learned more about the culture, practiced their language skills, etc. This was one of our many low-key missions that enabled us to punch well above our weight in terms of developing military relationships and supporting our allies. The U.S. ambassadors loved them.

Namibia is not the most modern country in the world, so when I was way out in the remote hillsides of the hinterlands like we were, a phone call from "home" was not high on my list of expectations. The team was demonstrating Battle Drill 4—how to react to ambush—while I was speaking one-on-one with the tribal chief about some concerns he had surrounding a destabilization along the northern border that threatened to intensify at any time, when my aide stepped in to interrupt. "Excuse me, sir. I have a priority call for you from the Pentagon," he announced, handing me the headset of our portable satellite radio.

I turned away and spoke into the encrypted device, "General Shelton."

"Sir, this is Brigadier General Stephens at the NMCC patching in Ms. Judy Miller from the Secretary's office." The digitized voice crackled at the other end, not even giving me time to respond before I heard Judy's firm, professional voice. I had never met her but I was well aware that as chief legal council to the Secretary of Defense, she was a trusted member of Secretary Cohen's team.

"General Shelton, it's Judy Miller. The Secretary has tasked me to ask you a series of questions, some of which are personal in nature. You are not required to answer them, but if you don't, then you will no longer be under consideration for the position of Chairman of the Joint Chiefs of Staff."

I knew that Shalikashvili was rapidly approaching the completion of his second two-year term as Chairman (the normal tour for a Chairman), so a replacement would have to be found, but we had all assumed that his Vice Chairman, General Joe Ralston, would get the nod. Under the Goldwater-Nichols Act, unless the President determines that it is in the national interest to do otherwise, he may appoint an officer as Chairman only if the officer has served as the Vice Chairman, a service chief, or the commander of a unified or combatant command—which narrows down the selection pool to thirteen officers. Putting aside the unusual setting in which Miller had tracked me down, I was taken aback that somehow I was under consideration for our country's top military position. Joe Ralston was an outstanding leader, a forward-thinking general, and to this day he remains a close friend of mine—he would have made an exceptional Chairman. Later on I would learn that even though he was the SecDef's first choice, Joe voluntarily withdrew his name when word leaked out that many years earlier he had had an extramarital affair while separated from his former wife, which left them scrambling to find a replacement—a replacement who was squeaky clean and could withstand the most intense background investigation. This concern was exacerbated when shortly thereafter yet another sexual scandal rocked the Pentagon.

First Lieutenant Kelly Flinn literally had become the poster child for the Air Force. Young, attractive, and highly intelligent, she had received the highest possible scores on all her evaluations and had become the first female to pilot the B-52 intercontinental bomber. Air Force Public Affairs capitalized on this by placing her in high-profile recruitment ads plus featured her in public appearances at air shows and other international events. Pentagon leadership couldn't have been more pleased with this consummate American military hero; she was just what they needed to bolster patriotism and boost the public's support of our armed forces. Little did they know that the shit was about to hit the fan, and it hit with a viral escalation that made front-page headlines and dragged Air Force Secretary Sheila Widnall and Chief of Staff Ron Fogleman on the mat before Congress. Word had leaked that the new Air Force poster child was having an affair with a soccer coach at Minot AFB who was married to one of her female enlisted subordinates. Even worse, she had denied the allegations and continued to lie about it afterward until the evidence was so overwhelming that she had no other choice but to come clean.

While ultimately Flinn was allowed to resign rather than face a court-martial, the country could ill afford another military scandal, which is where my call from Judy Miller came in. The scrutiny surrounding the Chairman selection would be intense—far more personal than any had ever been, which explains why Judy's questions probed so deeply.

"Let's see if I can tackle those questions, Judy," I said, as the Namibian chief looked quizzically in my direction, undoubtedly wondering what in the hell was so important that they had to call me from eight thousand miles away.

"Are you or have you ever been in substantial debt?" she began, systematically exploring every facet of my personal life—financial, lifestyle, morals, fidelity—you name it. When she finally got to the end she said, "Sounds good, General. Is there anything else that I should know that could embarrass you, the Secretary, the President, or the nation?"

"Yes, Judy, there is," I confided, waiting a beat before I continued. "To be completely open with you, I have a second wife."

It was one of those times where you thought the silence was deafening, and she had to have been wondering, *How in the hell did a bigamist make it all the way to four-star general?*

"Would you mind elaborating on that?" she finally asked.

"Many years ago I was given a Montagnard girl in Vietnam to be my wife. She was given to me by her father, the village chief, in appreciation for all I had done to protect his people . . ." and I went on to explain to her the buffalo ceremony and the betel-nut juice running down her chin and then finally how I had gracefully bowed out of it after explaining that I was already married.

"You don't expect that there will be any paternity suits, do you?" she asked, only halfway joking.

"No, Judy. I never saw that girl again," I said with a grin. "You've got nothing to worry about. I can't guarantee there won't be lawsuits, but if there are, they will be frivolous."

I returned to Tampa and about a week later I got another call from Secretary Cohen's office, this time from Bob Tyrer, the Secretary's tireless chief of staff. "General," he said, "we've made a number of cuts and you are now on the short list for consideration to be the Chairman, but before we go any further, the Secretary wants to know if you would accept that job."

The truth is that I really didn't want it, so I said, "Let me think about that overnight. I need to discuss it with my wife and I'll let you know." I figured a hesitation like that in Washington would be enough to turn him off, allowing me to stay in Tampa and serve out my Army career as the Special Operations commander. That's how I envisioned it when I took the position in the first place, and it still sounded good to me.

The following day I was surprised when Bob Tyrer called back, not to ask what I had decided but to take the bull by the horns on his end. "The Secretary understands your ambivalence but would like you to fly to Washington and speak with him in any event," he said.

Even though as commander I had the big plane at my disposal (an Air Force VC-137, a specially modified 707 that traveled with a crew of eighteen), I never used it for transport within the United States. Instead I utilized Air Force support and flew to Washington on the much more efficient C-21A, the military version of the Learjet 35 business jet.

I flew into Andrews AFB on the morning of Wednesday, July 16, 1997, where a car and driver were waiting to drive me to the Pentagon. Midmorning traffic wasn't too bad that day and we made it in about half an hour, passing the Jefferson Memorial out my right window before crossing over the George Mason Bridge and entering the Pentagon complex.

Secretary Cohen had called it an informal lunch and I suppose technically it was, since we met in his private dining room and his chef prepared what was probably an excellent meal, but I really wouldn't know about that since I didn't touch a thing. I did enjoy watching him, Bob Tyrer, and Jim Bodner (one of his special assistants and soon to become Principal Deputy Under Secretary of Defense for Policy, responsible for all U.S. international security policy) eat as they fired off one question after another. We had a good discussion. They were a good team and I thoroughly enjoyed the dialogue. While Judy Miller's questions were more personal and character related, these concentrated more on the issues—where I stood on various strategies and policies.

I have always respected Secretary Cohen and I liked him from the beginning. Just a few months earlier I had hosted him down in Tampa for the tenth anniversary of SOCOM since it was he and Senator Sam Nunn who had sponsored the bill and subsequent amendment to Goldwater-Nichols that set up SOCOM as we know it today. As such, we considered them the founding fathers of SOCOM and thought it only appropriate that they come down and celebrate with us by cutting the cake. Although Nunn was unable to attend, we were pleased that Secretary Cohen had made the trip.

The Cohen-Nunn amendment to the FY87 National Defense Authorization Act radically changed the way Special Operations forces (SOF) were managed. It established the Office of Assistant Secretary of Defense for Special Operations and Low Intensity Conflict and the U.S. Special Operations Command (SOCOM). It held the pursestrings with head-of-agency responsibility for the acquisition of SOF-unique materiel and a discrete funding line (Major Force Program 11 [MFP-11]). In Cohen-Nunn, Congress recognized that the things that make SOF different from conventional and strategic forces dictate a command structure that ensures cohesion and optimal use of limited resources. The essence of SOCOM is joint interoperability—and it was obvious by Cohen's sponsorship that he fully understood the importance of the *joint* concept—a cutting-edge philosophy that I shared.

The meeting seemed to go very well and as it turned out we had many similar views. But the fact still remained that I didn't want the job, so I just answered his questions in a very direct manner without regard for how the answers might affect his decision. He asked about my position surrounding our involvement in Bosnia, and I was blunt in my concern that to me it did not appear that the current Chairman, General John Shalikashvili, was offering President Clinton any clear-cut exit strategy to get us out of there. The Dayton Peace Accords had been signed on December 14, 1995, yet we were still heavily involved in an increasingly tumultuous situation. While I made it clear that I believed policy decisions should be left up to the Secretary (and ultimately the President), I did feel that it was important for the chairman to offer both individuals viable military options for us to leave the Balkans. By his reaction, it appeared that Secretary Cohen agreed.

He asked how I felt about base closures and again I was direct, explaining that while cognizant of the political volatility of my position, I believed that we had to close bases to come up with the funds necessary to procure new weapons and equipment that were essential to our state of readiness—and two more rounds of closures would generate more than twenty billion dollars.

We talked about gays in the military, my position on the role of NATO, the recurring theme of transitioning to a joint mode of warfare, and even a few more mundane matters such as my preference to start the day early and charge right into the day's agenda.

I was very candid with him—very open—and when I walked out of there to wait in the outer office I was fully aware that such outspoken candor was not particularly the smartest way to tackle an interview, but I've never been one for political correctness and I certainly wasn't about to start then, even if it meant not landing the top military position in our country.

I had just picked up the phone to call Tampa for messages when

Cohen's door popped open and Tyrer and Bodner departed in different directions, shaking hands and wishing me good luck on their way out. *Good luck?* What the hell did that mean?

Secretary Cohen was not far behind. "Why don't you ride over to Sandy Berger's office with me?" he asked without breaking stride, leading me out of the suite and down a flight of stairs to the Pentagon's River Entrance, where his limo was waiting to carry us over to the White House. It was more of a statement than a question, and I suppose it was his way of telling me that our interview had gone well.

Samuel Richard "Sandy" Berger had recently taken over as President Clinton's National Security Advisor after having been deputy under Tony Lake for Clinton's first term. Picture a sharp little ball of energy running around in the National Security Council and that's Sandy. With an undergrad degree from Cornell and a JD from Harvard Law, he was one of President Clinton's most trusted advisers—and it made sense that the President was using him to screen this round of candidates. I had no idea how many he had already seen or how many others would follow me. The fact that I was even going to the White House was a bombshell for me; I had fully expected to grab my lunch with the Secretary and then turn right around and head back to Tampa. Later on I would learn from the press that other strong contenders included General Charles Krulak, the Marine Corps Commandant, General Wesley Clark, the Commander of NATO, and General Dennis Reimer, the Army Chief of Staff. I had also learned that of all the people on the short list, I was the only one who did not have a political sponsor, meaning having a congressman or senator or other high-powered official calling the Secretary to encourage him to select their guy. Later, the Secretary kidded me about that, and I told him that the reason he had not gotten those calls about me was that when a certain congressman called me and said that he would like to sponsor me, I told him not only no, but *hell no,* because he had all the information he needed to either select me or eliminate me, and the last thing he needed was a bunch of phone calls to interrupt his day.

It is only a three-mile drive from the Pentagon to the White House and in no time at all the Secretary's armored Cadillac limo was cleared through the White House security gate. It was less than twenty-four hours earlier that I had indicated my ambivalence to Tyrer, and here I was pulling up to the portico, about to enter the West Wing. My gut said that this train was moving mighty fast. Even though I would be meeting only with Sandy Berger, there is still a tangible mystique that accompanies any meeting in the White House, let alone the West Wing, and Berger's office was just a few doors down from the Oval.

Sandy was expecting us and he greeted me warmly, asking about my flight as we veered right and proceeded to his corner office. Passing other offices along the way, we caught bits and pieces of breaking news on CNN: Whitewater independent counsel Kenneth Starr had just concluded that Vincent Foster's death had been a suicide. Foster had been Deputy White House Counsel during President Clinton's first term, and he had close personal ties with both the President and Mrs. Clinton. Although pundits would position this finding as politically favorable to the President, it resurrected a terrible personal episode that occurred some four years prior, and revisited the whole Clinton/Whitewater affair.

"What a horrible tragedy," Berger shared, gesturing for the Secretary and me to take seats on the sofa while he settled into a plush antique-looking chair across from his desk. "Vince was a good man, a family man. Ask me, it was the spotlight of Washington public life that killed him," he said, as if I needed another reason to question whether I really wanted the high-visibility Chairman job.

This was one of the few times I had seen the feisty fireplug so relaxed, as though all he had to do with his time was to sit and chat with me—and this was far from what I would call a slow news day. Besides the Foster announcement, the Senate campaign-financing investigation was heating up, U.N. Secretary General Kofi Annan had just presented a reorganization plan that would entail intense scrutiny by the President, and, of great concern to both Berger and the President, explosions in Bosnia indicated that the Serbs had begun a deadly retaliation against NATO for the recent arrest of Serbian war criminals. Just the day before, the President had warned the Serbs against such attacks. Still, Berger calmly sipped on his bottled water and asked if I had any questions for him.

"My understanding is that you are the one with the questions, Sandy," I replied, ready for him to commence with the next round of vetting questions.

"I don't have a one, but I'm sure the President will come up with a few," he said with a quick glance at his watch. "He should be ready to see you in about five minutes from now."

While I felt like snapping back, *It's a damn good thing I put on a clean shirt,* I just nodded and replied, "I look forward to that." And the truth is, I was looking forward to it. I had met President Clinton before and you can't help but like him. When he insisted on personally visiting those three dying soldiers at Womack Army Medical Center after the Pope AFB Green Ramp collision in 1994—with no cameras, no press, just him, me, and Hal Timboe—I knew that this was a compassionate, caring individual. A lot of guys in the military were prone to put him down. They were against his "don't ask, don't tell" policy being forced on the military—but I always found him to be a very engaging, witty individual—focused, listens attentively to everything you say, and of course he is smart as a whip—I mean extremely intelligent.

Both Berger and Cohen got up and Cohen extended his hand for a kind of good-luck handshake since he would be staying behind.

"You will have about fifteen minutes with the President, twenty tops," Berger shared. "Just be yourself and it will go just fine."

"That's all I know how to be," I answered honestly, as Berger led the way down the hall to the Oval Office.

Betty Currie (President Clinton's personal secretary) closed the door behind me as the President led me over to the two yellow chairs beneath the Rembrandt Peale portrait of George Washington at the north end of the Oval Office. Although there would be times when the President and I would sit on opposite sides of the ornate Resolute desk, for meetings such as this he seemed to prefer the comparative informality of the fireplace setting.

It began as a typical interview with the usual exchange of pleasantries, then the President seemed to focus in and there was no doubt that every one of my answers—and perhaps even the way in which I would answer— would have a direct bearing on whether I would serve out my time in uniform down in Tampa or side by side with the commander in chief, Secretary of Defense, and National Security Council. "Hugh, I've got a couple of items here that I would like to get your take on," he began.

We talked about everything from the fighting in Bosnia to the state of the Army. He asked what I thought of our Special Operations Command and I could tell that my running SOCOM was of particular interest to him: "I want to talk with you about some of their capabilities, and how we might use those capabilities in new ways," he continued, referring to the highly specialized equipment, procedures, and tactics of our Delta Force, Navy SEALs, and other top-tier Special Mission Units. Even though he didn't take a note, there was not a doubt in my mind that he was synthesizing every answer within the context of whether I would be of value to him in helping to solve whatever military challenges he was up against.

"If we were to find out who was responsible for Khobar Towers [the 1996 terrorist bombing of a Saudi Arabian housing complex in which twenty-one U.S. Air Force airmen were killed and hundreds of others seriously injured], what would be your recommendation if you were the chairman?"

That one was easy. "Mr. President," I responded, "I think that our national policy on terrorism has served us very well in the past, and therefore my recommendation to you would be that we make them pay a thousandfold for what they did to us."

"But what if we found out it was a country such as Iran that was responsible for it?" he followed up.

"Regardless of which country it was, if they are a nation-state or any kind of an organization that we can go after and have them pay a horrible penalty, my recommendation would be that we inflict the maximum degree of punishment on them." He just took it all in and nodded, and frankly I thought that would be the end of the interview; we had already gone ten minutes past the twenty-minute cap that Berger had warned me about. But instead he continued for at least an hour. And I'm sitting there thinking, *Gee whiz, I wonder who the next appointment is and I hope they don't mind waiting an hour to get in.* By this time a crowd had started to form outside the door, looking in the peephole and undoubtedly wondering what was going on in there. Finally, Betty knocked on the door, and that ended the interview.

I was escorted back to Sandy Berger's office and both he and Secretary Cohen perked up when I entered. "'S'bout time, General. How did it go?" Berger asked, clearly curious to know what we had been doing for the past hour and a half.

"Sandy, I don't have a clue," I responded honestly, shaking my head. "From my perspective I think it went well, you know he's great to talk to—and we talked about damn near everything there was to talk about—but seriously, you'll have to ask the President."

Cohen was about to chime in when the phone rang, the upper left blinking light indicating that it was one of the direct hotlines. "Yes, Mr. President," Berger said as he picked up the headset and listened for a quick beat. "Thank you, sir, I got it," he fired back as he hung up and looked back at me. "You've got the job."

Talk about a high-speed locomotive racing down the track at warp speed, it was one of those times when I felt almost bewildered and the reality had not yet set in.

"Let's go back to the Pentagon. We've got work to do," Secretary Cohen said, already halfway out the door.

"Not so fast," Berger cut in. "You're forgetting about the ceremony. The President will make the announcement at ten A.M. tomorrow in the Rose Garden, an official roll-out for the press and senior leadership. The President is looking forward to introducing you as the new Chairman."

We left the office and I mean my head is spinning as the Secretary led the way through the hallways like a man on a mission. "We've got to get your wife up here. How did you come?" he asked, rounding the corner toward the exit where his limo would be waiting.

"Well, I flew up in a plane," I answered, a blaring statement of the obvious.

"Not to worry, we'll send your plane back to get her," he said, climbing into the car while the driver held open the door.

I walked around and climbed in on the other side, glad that the driver had kept the air conditioner going on that humid, sweltering day. "You know, Mr. Secretary, we can't do that," I reminded him, knowing that using an official plane for Carolyn was against Department of Defense regulations, not to mention a very inefficient use of an airplane. "But I do need to call her so we can get her on a commercial flight."

As the car darted off down the long, circular White House driveway, the Secretary handed me the phone and I was relieved to find Carolyn at home. "You're going to have to scramble and be in Washington early tomorrow morning. President Clinton's going to have a Rose Garden roll-out and since you're married to the next Chairman, he thought it would be nice for you to be there."

"Is she excited?" asked the Secretary.

"Says she doesn't have anything to wear; has to run out and buy a new suit or whatever," I answered. I told Carolyn I would call her back with the details and turned the phone over to Secretary Cohen so that he could call General Jim Jones, his executive assistant.

"Jim, get a plane lined up to go pick up Mrs. Shelton in Tampa and bring her back here for tomorrow's ceremony," he said. "And iron out any conflicts we have with the Georgia delegation." He hung up and turned to me. "Okay, the plane's taken care of. As for tomorrow's schedule, I've got President Shevardnadze and his Minister of Foreign Affairs coming in, so I might have to slide them an hour or two since I really should be at your roll-out and check out Carolyn's new outfit." I knew that I was going to enjoy working with Secretary Cohen.

Just a few seconds later the phone rang and it was my "old friend" Judy Miller, the general counsel who had tracked me down in Namibia. The Secretary seemed surprised when he heard what Judy had to say, since she was calling to advise him that the request for Carolyn's airplane entailed an unauthorized and unlawful use of a military aircraft. We laughed about that later on, but I got the impression that the Secretary was somewhat embarrassed by it at the time. Even though I would have insisted that Carolyn fly commercial anyway, it was clear that he was trying to be nice and help me get her up there in a hurry. But it did serve as another great example of why those good lawyers are worth their weight in gold when they are trying to keep you out of trouble. As I had said for years, it's always best to have your legal advisor sitting with you at the defense table than sitting with the prosecution.

We were able to find Carolyn a last-minute commercial flight, and, through the persistence of Secretary Cohen and his staff, eventually we were even able to wend our way through the red tape and get reimbursed for the flight.

The great news is that Carolyn made it to D.C. in plenty of time, and her new outfit passed inspection with flying colors. The President was gracious enough to host Carolyn and me in a private Oval Office celebration just before we took our places in the Rose Garden for the official ceremony. Walking out the eastern door of the Oval Office, I leaned over to Carolyn and whispered the words we had jokingly reminded each other on so many occasions along the way: "We're a long way from Speed, North Carolina."

I chose to wear my black beret that morning, and as the President stepped up to the lectern to my immediate right, I felt proud, completely void of any semblance of doubt or ambivalence about taking the position. I understood that this was my destiny and I was energized. I had never expected to be Chairman, and until that moment never wanted to be Chairman; but when the President started to speak before the row of flags that served as our backdrop that windless morning, and when I glanced up to see the members of the Joint Chiefs seated in front of us, I was flushed with a sense of honor, duty, and responsibility. It was a post that would allow me the greatest opportunity to contribute, to make a difference, to institute strategies that would impact generations to come, and, every bit as important, would allow me to give back to a system that had been so very good to me throughout my career.

After a few informal remarks, the President made my nomination official:

> Over more than three decades of service to our nation, General Shelton has distinguished himself as a decorated solder, an innovative thinker, a superb commander. From Vietnam to Desert Storm he has proven his skill and courage in combat. And through long experiences in Special Operations he also brings to this job a unique perspective in addressing the broad range of challenges we face on the brink of a new century, from war fighting to peacekeeping, from conventional threats to newer threats, like the spread of weapons of mass destruction and terrorism.
>
> General Shelton's extensive experience in joint military operations and building coalitions with other nations gives him invaluable tools to serve as Chairman in our more interdependent world. I believe he is the right person for the job, the right person for our troops, for our

security, the right man for our country. I'm proud to nominate him to
help to lead our military into the twenty-first century. General?

I stepped up to the lectern and savored the moment as I waited for the
applause to subside. Secretary Cohen stood directly behind me and seemed
to be applauding the loudest. Finally, I began:

Thank you very much. With this honor comes the awesome responsibility of ensuring that our own forces remain trained, ready, and equipped
to deal with the threats and dangers of today, as well as an uncertain
future.
    This is a responsibility that I accept without hesitation or reserva-
tion, and I certainly look forward to continuing to serve on the side of
America's best, the great men and women of our armed forces who
serve proudly and selflessly. General Shalikashvili has done a magnificent job, and if confirmed by the Senate, I look forward to following in
his footsteps in the days ahead. Again, I'm deeply honored by my nomination, and I sincerely appreciate President Clinton's trust and confidence. Thank you.

Following the ceremony I went back to the Pentagon for a short discussion with Secretary Cohen and made plans to meet up with Carolyn later
in the day so we could fly back to Tampa together in preparation for my
return to Washington as Chairman. Glancing down at my wristwatch, I
smiled as I realized that less than twenty-four hours beforehand I'd been
on another flight, that one headed to the nation's capital to take a "preliminary" interview for a job I really hadn't wanted, and one that I considered an extreme long shot, at best. That's how fast it had all happened.
    I exited the Pentagon as the staff was setting up velvet ropes and vacu-
uming a red carpet that had just been rolled out near River Entrance. The
Georgian presidential entourage would be arriving shortly. The following
morning I would read in my "Early Bird" brief that those meetings had
culminated in the signing of an important document between our two nations entitled "Cooperation in the Area of Prevention of Proliferation of
Weapons of Mass Destruction and Promotion of Defense and Military
Relations." In just a few short months I would be a vital participant in the
forging of many similar alliances, and it was a responsibility that I would
never take lightly.

In today's post–9/11 environment it seems hard to recall a time when "September 11" brought to mind anything other than somber recollections of a

Daddy in his Sunday finest.

ROTC at North Carolina State.

One-year-old Hugh with Mother and Daddy.

Hugh as a 4-H Reserve Champion, 1955.

Seventeen-year-old Hugh with Carolyn and Woodie (1950 Ford wagon) on the Shelton farm near Speed, North Carolina, in 1959.

Special Forces Captain Shelton, Ha Thanh, Vietnam.

Montagnard villiage outside Ha Thanh, Vietnam.

Captain Shelton and A-104 Special Forces "A" Team, 5th Special Forces, RVN.

My young Montagnard friend, outside Ha Thanh, Vietnam.

Carolyn, Jeff, Jon, and me while a student at Air Command and Staff College, 1973.

*Top Left:* James and Annie Bell Johnson, Carolyn's parents.

New York ticker-tape parade upon return from Desert Storm, June 1991.

I've always loved our family gatherings at Emerald Isle, North Carolina, June 23, 1994.

Aboard the USS *Mount Whitney* coordinating the invasion of Haiti.

Commander Joint Task Force, Haiti.

Inside the Oval Office with Jon, Anne, the President, Carolyn, Amy, Jeff, and Mark, 1994.

Prepping for a jump in France, June 5, 1994.

Aviano Air Base, Italy.

NSC meeting in the White House Situation Room, August 1998.

Outside the Oval Office.

NSC meeting in the Cabinet Room, August 1998.

Formal affair at the White House.

Inside the Oval Office with the President, Secretary of State Madeleine Albright, and CIA Director George Tenet.

NATO conference with POTUS, Secretary of State Madeleine Albright, and Secretary of Defense William Cohen.

Discussing Iraq with the President at the Pentagon, February 17, 1998.

Secretary of Defense Cohen and I brief the press about Operation Desert Fox, December 16, 1998.

1999 Joint Chiefs in the Tank. (Left to right) Vice Chairman Joe Ralston, CJCS Shelton, CNO Admiral Jay Johnson, Air Force Chief of Staff General Mike Ryan, Army Chief of Staff General Eric Shinseki, Marine Corps Commandant General Jim Jones.

Press briefing on Operation Allied Force, June 10, 1999.

In Bosnia with Carolyn and the troops, 2000.

One of many great jumps with the Golden Knights while CINCSOC at McDill AFB, Florida, July 17, 1999.

Carolyn at the Yad Vashem Holocaust Memorial, Jerusalem, Israel, August 18, 1999.

White House Situation Room, May 2, 2000. Thanks for letting me sink your battleship, Mr. President.

Helo cockpit.

Carolyn, Hugh, and Mother Patsy beside a tasty chocolate Washington Monument at Quarters Six, Fort Myer, Virginia.

At the White House with President George W. Bush and Carolyn, 2001.

My son Jon of the United States Secret Service, on duty protecting President Bush at the Pentagon.

Secretary Rumsfeld and I meet with Uzbekistan Minister of Defense at NATO, June 2001.

NSC meeting in the White House Situation Room, 2001.

My final Oval Office meeting with President Bush, September 28, 2001.

On *This Week* with Sam Donaldson and Cokie Roberts.

General Dick Myers and Carolyn observe Secretary Rumsfeld pinning on a medal at my retirement ceremony, Fort Myer, Virginia, October 1, 2001.

Pulling out of the driveway of Quarters Six behind the wheel of my surprise retirement gift!
Fort Myer, Virginia, October 1, 2001.

It's all thumbs-up jumping with the Golden Knights.

Mark and Dad.

En route to becoming a master parachutist (over sixty-five jumps), 1st Lt. Jeff Shelton with Dad as LTG Commander XVIII Airborne, Fort Bragg, North Carolina, Green Ramp.

The entire family gathers at our home in Morehead City, North Carolina, for Fourth of July weekend, July 3, 2010.

barbaric act, but on September 11, 1997, I felt flattered when the Honorable Bob Etheridge (congressman for the second district of North Carolina) stood before the House of Representatives and commended the President for selecting me to be the next Chairman, urging the full Senate to affirm my confirmation as soon as possible. Here is a portion of what he said:

Mr. Speaker, I rise to praise President Clinton's appointment of Army General Hugh Shelton as Chairman of the Joint Chiefs of Staff and the U.S. Senate's Armed Services Committee's vote to confirm the nomination.

General Shelton's career is the embodiment of North Carolina values: hard work, service to country, respect, and commitment to excellence. He has earned the opportunity to service as the highest-ranking member of the U.S. military, Chairman of the Joint Chiefs of Staff.

General Shelton is a leader. His distinguished career of leadership and service to our nation began in 1963, when he joined the U.S. Army. He served with the 5th Special Forces Group from 1966 to 1967 and from 1969 to 1970 with the 173rd Airborne Brigade.

His service in the campaign against the Vietcong and Communist North Vietnamese in the highly volatile back country of Vietnam won him the respect of his colleagues for his personal sacrifice and service to our nation.

In the Persian Gulf War, our largest military confrontation since Vietnam, General Shelton served as assistant commander of the 101st Airborne Division (air assault) "when it made the largest, longest helicopter assault in history."

He has commanded Fort Bragg and the XVIII Airborne Corps and the 82nd Airborne Division at Fort Bragg, North Carolina. Currently, he serves as commander of U.S. Special Forces at MacDill Air Force Base in Tampa, Florida, which is home to the Army's Green Berets and the Navy's SEALs.

He has sacrificed, served, and fought to keep our nation free. God has blessed him with these great skills, which will serve him and the United States well as Chairman of the Joint Chiefs of Staff.

I commend the President for appointing General Shelton to this most important position, and I congratulate the general on this outstanding accomplishment. I urge the full Senate to complete his confirmation as soon as possible.

Things were looking pretty good and I had no reason to believe that there would appear a fly in the ointment, but *boy was I wrong.*

Two days earlier I had appeared before the Senate Armed Services

Committee feeling confident, well versed, and comfortable that I had a broad knowledge of the key military issues of the day, and reasonable, progressive ideas on how to deal with those issues. It was not surprising since about a week beforehand I had flown from Tampa to D.C. to be prepped by a bright group of officers with thousands of pages of paper covering every program in each branch of the military, and every issue the Chairman might be asked to comment on—ranging from gays in the military to the impact of submarines on the survival of the greatly endangered right-whale species.

This group of colonels was headed by Dave Petraeus (as of 2010 four-star commander of CENTCOM), a brilliant and highly energetic officer, who at the time was serving as the executive assistant to the Director of the Joint Staff, Vice Admiral Denny Blair. (Later, I would tell Denny that I had selected Petraeus as my executive assistant in lieu of the slate of officers who had been proposed. Denny had suspected that this might happen, and while he preferred to keep Dave, he knew the importance of the CJCS's executive assistant and he readily agreed. Denny himself was a brilliant individual and a team player of the first order.) I returned to Tampa with a number of three-ring binders filled with these papers and spent the entire week studying them to the point where I felt confident that I would walk into that Senate hearing room with a comprehensive understanding of the issues.

"Usually we don't go into things without an exit strategy, as you know, General," barked Arizona's Senator John McCain. "Does that concern you?"

It was September 9, 1997, and it served as a nice foreshadowing to the aggression I would witness on the part of Senator McCain over the next four years. I was being grilled by the Armed Services Committee and they were not happy with my previous answer.

To set the stage, we were heavily involved in the Balkans situation at the time, and just a short while back, General Shalikashvili had told the committee that he believed we would be out of the Balkans within the year. Of course, I recognized that the only way we could get out of there was to cut and run, in which case the whole place would go right back to the way we'd found it. So the reality was that we were *not* going to be out by the end of the year. Instead, my goal was to come up with a plan that would enable us to transition our forces out of there yet have a stable government in place, but until I became Chairman (if that's what their decision would ultimately lead to) I would not be in a position to develop such a plan, which would entail in-depth analysis and discussions with the Secretary and Joint Staff. So instead I acknowledged, "I am not aware of

exactly what our exit strategy is, but we have nine or ten months to go."
It was this statement that had inflamed McCain.

Others began to chime in, and it appeared that the hearing had turned into a forum for them to vent their displeasure with the present ambiguity surrounding our timetable for withdrawal.

Senator John W. Warner of Virginia warned that we were "on the brink of disaster" in Bosnia, citing recent attacks on American troops by mobs of rock-throwing Bosnian Serbs.

"Obviously in June of 1998 there may be a requirement for some kind of international effort in order to maintain the stability of the area," I responded, referring to potential U.S. involvement in a NATO peacekeeping force, "but it is too early to arrive at a decision as to what the appropriate U.S., if any, participation would be in a force of that nature."

I was asked about my position on using American troops to arrest indicted war criminals in Bosnia, and I admitted that I couldn't rule that out, but if that became the case, such a mission should involve our elite Special Mission Units rather than the ground troops we had as part of the NATO-led force.

Besides the Balkans, I had the opportunity to discuss my support of the Pentagon's target of a weapons-procurement budget of sixty billion dollars a year by the end of the century, my controversial position on the need for further military-base closings, and my opposition to buying any more B-2 bombers.

I was candid in my belief that recent adverse publicity would have a devastating impact on our recruitment endeavors, and that we would need to have major image rebuilding to counter this negativity and reestablish credibility.

As the grilling winded down, so too did the somewhat confrontational demeanor, and the committee members were unanimous in their praise— one by one, they verbalized their support of my nomination.

"I have no doubt that this committee and the full Senate will quickly confirm your nomination," Senator McCain concluded.

In spite of my frequent congressional testimonies as SOCOM commander, the truth is that I was a relatively unknown commodity in the Beltway— the new kid on the block—and as such neither the press nor the high-level national leadership with whom I would be interacting on a daily basis really knew what to expect. I have always preferred a low profile (something President Clinton would later poke fun at in relation to my height) and flying under the radar. As Elaine Sciolino and Steven Myers pointed out in *The New York Times,* while some maintained that I lacked the global view and NATO experience of Shalikashvili, others feared that I lacked the White House experience and political savvy of Powell (Colin Powell served as Chairman immediately prior to Shalikashvili). The reality is that time would tell, and I left the Senate committee room feeling confident and cautiously optimistic.

Two hours later, the senators had made their decision. By a vote of eleven to zero, the Senate Armed Services Committee had unanimously voted to endorse my nomination for Chairman. But it still had to be passed by the entire Senate, and it was there that the situation got ugly.

On November 22, 1996, an Air Force C-130 took off from Portland, Oregon, and plunged into the Pacific, killing ten Air Force reservists. For almost a year, family members had searched for answers, and their frustration with the Air Force over the lack of information was threatening to kill my nomination; at the very least it had put a halt to the process and was being used as a political bargaining piece to force the Air Force into action.

On behalf of the family members of the airmen, Oregon Senator Ron Wyden stood up before the full Senate as my confirmation vote was about to take place and announced that he was temporarily blocking the vote until he received a better explanation for the crash—something tangible that he could report back to the grieving families. Oregon's other senator, Gordon Smith, backed this ploy.

Although at first the Air Force wouldn't budge, eventually I made a few calls and convinced the powers that be that it was the right thing to do. I would have made those calls irrespective of the holdup on the vote, had I been asked.

Bottom line, a few days later, Wyden lifted his objection, pleased that the Air Force had responded so quickly and had reversed its prior decision and finally agreed to work with the National Transportation Safety Board in thoroughly investigating the crash.

A voice vote was taken and it was unanimous—I had been confirmed by the full Senate as the fourteenth Chairman of the Joint Chiefs of Staff.

———

I have always enjoyed Carolyn's perspective on my career:

> If you had told me that one day I was going to be the wife of a general, it would have scared me to death. If you would have told me I was going to be the wife of a four-star general and particularly the wife of the Chairman of the Joint Chiefs, I probably would have been too nervous to have married him at that point.

My own point of view is not much different because had I known all that when I got that telegram instructing me to report to Fort Bragg in

October 1966, I probably would have run in the other direction because it would have scared me to death.

The reality is that as I prepared to embark on this exciting new chapter of my life, I was psyched and both Carolyn and I couldn't have been happier.

Perhaps my brother, Benjamin Franklin Shelton III, a veterinarian, offered the most prophetic admonition: *"The snakes of Washington beware. The snake eater has arrived."*

O*n the top floor of the Heaton Pavilion at Walter Reed is a little-known, heavily protected facility known as Ward 72. With its bullet-proof windows, secured communications lines, and gold, entry-controlled, direct-access elevator, the suite of VIP rooms are replete with antiques and artifacts donated by leaders from all over the world. One room is reserved for the President, and adjoining it is another for the First Lady.*

*After a week in the ICU, the doctors determined that I was able to move up to the ward; and since the President was in excellent health, they moved me into the presidential suite. At the age of one hundred, Senator Strom Thurmond was happy to have the company; he was in the room directly next door. While on paper the amenities may appear extravagant, the truth is that I was still fighting to survive, and the private first-class dining room and such were of zero interest or benefit to me. The staff-to-patient ratio was exactly the same as the rest of the hospital, and with the steady stream of high-profile visitors I was about to receive, the security considerations were important.*

*Once the hospital issued its press release, the stream of well-wishers was overwhelming. Friends, co-workers, and individuals I didn't even know wanted to come by and express their good wishes. But Carolyn would have none of that; she was the perfect gatekeeper and made sure that what little energy I had was reserved for recovery, not visitation.*

*After a week of nearly sleepless nights in the bustling ICU, I was looking forward to the peace and quiet of the private ward—and within five minutes of their getting me settled up there, I drifted into a deep sleep. Unfortunately, not deep enough. Carolyn did her best to grab the phone before its loud ringer woke me up, but the calls were nonstop. "Hugh would love to see you, but he's just not strong enough for visitors quite yet," I would hear her say, over and over again. I awoke to one as she was saying, "I will most certainly pass along your message. . . . You're welcome, and we appreciate your call." She hung up and shook her head. "We have got to have them turn off this ringer, this is ridiculous . . . and President Bush sends his best."*

*Zack arrived at midafternoon, and he brought with him an impossibly ambitious agenda. "I hope you're ready to rumble, General, because today I'm going to have you up and walking."*

"Don't we wish," I said with a smile.

"Glad you're smiling now, because you won't be by the time I'm finished with you." He shot back a smile of his own, but one that strangely reminded me of Hannibal Lecter's expression before he devoured his victims. "The last thing you want is for those muscles to atrophy, or for a blood clot to develop. Getting you up will reduce the chance of that happening."

"I feel very light-headed, as if I'll faint if you stand me up," I said. "But let's get with it." I was 220 pounds of dead weight, so it took Zack and "King" Solomon—a physical therapist who looked like he could play middle linebacker for the Redskins—to "stand me up" (which really meant hold me in a vertical position), but as soon as they did, the room started to spin. I immediately said, "Better put me down, I'm going to faint."

"Just a little longer," Zack responded.


The last thing I remember before losing consciousness were frantic cries of "Code Blue!"—and even I knew that was hospital jargon for "cardiac arrest."

*Chapter Thirteen* ★ ★ ★ ★

# THE DRINKING
# DUCK SYNDROME

1997–1999

During the week between my departure from SOCOM and taking the oath as Chairman, I spent a great deal of time giving serious consideration to what I wanted to achieve in this awesome new post. If I'd thought I could make a difference when I became a general, I was absolutely *humbled* by the potential for worthwhile contributions I believed the Chairman position would afford me; and I was almost overtaken by the tremendous surge of responsibility I felt to make the very best of this opportunity.

What emerged first and foremost was a clear-cut agenda to remedy the terrible cuts that had been made to the military retirement system back in 1986. It was an abomination that now served as a deterrent to keeping good troops in the service and failed to recognize the sacrifices they made for our well-being—and I hoped that remedying this disgrace would become part of my legacy. I was also aware that such a repair would not be easy or cheap. Bringing the system up to snuff could take as much as *six billion dollars,* and I knew that Congress wasn't just sitting there waiting for my first day so they could cut me the check. What I would soon learn was that this would turn out to be only one of many pressing issues that were in dire need of attention.

I would be faced with installations in urgent need of repair and expansion; and worst of all, mounting evidence that our state of military readiness was highly *substandard*—some lieutenant colonels were actually reporting that their battalions were *not trained and not ready.* It was one after another, and it soon became clear to me that *I had taken over at a time when our military had severe readiness issues,* and it was with a sense of shock that I wondered, *Could it be that America is not fully protected?* How bad were these readiness issues? I was taking over a military that had *just trimmed seven hundred thousand people from its payroll* over the past seven years and *planned to cut at least sixty thousand more*. Now, with an increasing operational tempo, there were obvious readiness issues.

The moment was cathartic and it was crystal clear that whatever it took, *somehow it had to be fixed*.

────────

One would think that by the time they got around to the *fourteenth* Chairman they would have ironed out the kinks in the transition process, but we would soon find out that in Washington, very little actually ends up playing out as planned.

Carolyn and I left Tampa the last week of September and drove to D.C., stopping off to spend a few days with our family in Speed, North Carolina, on our way. We were driving two cars since I was towing the boat and Carolyn was towing a small trailer I had packed with about a thousand pounds of tools and woodworking equipment in order to reduce the household-goods weight to come in under the maximum that the Army would pay to move. No point in squandering funds if I could just as easily handle it myself. The only problem we encountered was that we had two flat tires on the small trailer before reaching Fort Myer. Thanks to my ranger training, I was traveling with not one but two spare tires, so we weren't delayed long either time.

We arrived in Speed and stayed at Mother's home—the same one we had stayed at before I deployed to Vietnam—and of course she was so excited to see us that at eighty-one years old she ran out to greet us with effusive hugs and help us unload our luggage—at least she offered to do so. It felt so good to be "home," and we would savor every minute of the two days we stayed there. My aunt Athlea (Henry Gray's wife), her daughter, Anne Boone Urquart (my cousin), and her husband, Billy, threw a big party for us on Mapleton Farm, and invited friends and family members from miles around. We dined in the same area Mammy Shelton had made short work of that rooster.

It was a great event, and to this day—as much as we have thoroughly enjoyed our world travels and black-tie affairs with presidents, kings, queens, princes, and prime ministers—those special family get-togethers in Speed are the ones that both Carolyn and I hold dearest to our hearts.

I remember looking over at Mother as she was so immersed in her element, flitting from one relative to another, always with this big smile that brightened everyone around her—and I thought how wonderful it was that she was still alive to enjoy the event, and how proud my father and Carolyn's parents would have been.

Those two days were both relaxing and invigorating, and we were now ready to embark upon the next exciting chapter in our lives, eager to move into our beautiful new quarters on Fort Myer and enjoy another celebration at the swearing-in ceremony on my first day as Chairman, October 1, 1997, easing into our new routine back in our nation's capital. I don't know who wrote that script, but it's far from how it actually played out.

We made it to the city less than five hours after leaving Mother's, and the first thing we were hit with upon arrival was that we would *not* be moving into the Chairman's designated quarters on Fort Myer as we were supposed to, since Shali had not yet moved out. In fact, he wasn't even planning to move until a couple of days after I assumed the position—a bit odd, I thought, but not worth all the criticism he would take since he knew that the CJCS had to hit the ground running and the Army service custom was for the outgoing to clear the quarters in time for the incoming "commander" to move in. What exacerbated the situation was that he wouldn't vacate for another two weeks. While it wasn't exactly as if Carolyn and I were forced to pitch a tent and live on the streets of downtown D.C. (the Army did provide us with temporary quarters until Quarters Six was available), it was a major distraction while I was trying to get up to speed.

As for my October 1 swearing-in ceremony? Not quite. On October 1, I would be meeting with Secretary Cohen and seventeen other heads of defense at the NATO Informal Defense Ministerial in Maastricht, the Netherlands. I would have to be sworn in a day before actually becoming Chairman since I would be halfway over the Atlantic in an Air Force C-32 (the military version of a Boeing 757, which was the plane utilized by the Chairman and his staff) when it became official at midnight.

And so it began—more reminiscent of the opening salvo of D-Day than the calm autumn breeze we had anticipated, but that's well and good. It was the beginning of the four most important years of my professional life, years in which I would challenge myself like never before, and have the opportunity to incorporate every lesson gleaned from all my great mentors—and forge them into a powerful, effective force for bringing about substantial, meaningful, and long-lasting improvements to our military and our great country.

* * *

On Monday, September 29, I spent the day getting up to speed by meeting with National Security Advisor Sandy Berger, outgoing Chairman General John "Shali" Shalikashvili, my friend Vice Chairman General Joe Ralston, and of course the one whom I would be working with closest, Secretary of Defense Bill Cohen.

It was a very productive meeting. The SecDef clearly wanted me to work the military lane while he would work the policy issues, but he really envisioned us working as a team. What a great way to start—and the truth is that it continued to work very well for the three-plus years we worked together.

I knew at our first meeting that Secretary Cohen was a leader with whom I would enjoy working. After serving three terms in the House and eighteen years in the Senate representing the state of Maine, he had been brought in by President Clinton as a Republican in a Democratic administration—which says a great deal for both the President and the SecDef. Having been on the prestigious Senate Armed Services Committee, he knew and understood the issues. On top of that, he was a great believer in Special Operations forces, having sponsored the Nunn-Cohen amendment to the 1987 congressional bill that created the Special Operations Command, as well as the office of the VCJCS (Vice Chairman of the Joint Chiefs of Staff)—and substantially upgraded the function of the CJCS to become the principal adviser to the President.

Every bit as important, Secretary Cohen was a man of great integrity and vision.

On the following day, which was still theoretically the day *before* I became Chairman, I was picked up in the black armored Cadillac that would become my primary transportation for the next four years, and used the ten minutes it would take to get from Fort Myer to the Pentagon to scan the the "Early Bird" to see what the hot topics would be for that day. Before I knew it, I was dropped off at the Pentagon River Entrance. As I walked past the guards, my office was just to the right, immediately beyond a display honoring General Omar Bradley, the first Chairman.

At this point it was still barren except for a few items that Shali had not yet removed, and the items I planned to use were still in storage with our household goods. Technically, I suppose the office was his for another sixteen hours anyway.

I had just enough time for a quick cup of coffee before going in to receive a thirty-minute morning update/intell briefing. This would be the same briefing the President would receive in his "President's Daily Brief."

Next I met with the VCJC (Vice Chairman of the Joint Chiefs) and DJS (director of the Joint Staff) prior to the VCJS and me heading upstairs to

meet with the Secretary of Defense and Deputy SecDef, John Hamre—
who had also only recently taken office.

The rest of that first day is somewhat of a blur in that Cohen would
be presiding over Shali's farewell ceremony on the parade grounds near
Quarters Six on Fort Myer, then come back to conduct my swearing in,
which we decided to keep private so as not to detract from Shali's big
day. Until then, my day would be packed with briefings to prepare me for
my first NATO Informal Defense Ministerial in Maastricht, the Netherlands, for which I would be leaving almost immediately after the swearing in.

Although the pomp and circumstance of my "welcome" would have to
wait for another two weeks, the official swearing-in could not, and this
was conducted in Cohen's office in front of a very small group. Joe
Ralston and his wife, DeDe, were there, as was Secretary Cohen's wife,
Janet. Mark was present, and of course Carolyn, who stood to my left,
holding the Bible, right between the SecDef and myself. Both Secretary
Cohen and I raised our right hands and I placed my left on the Bible. I
looked at him as he read the oath and I repeated it.

"Congratulations, Mr. Chairman," Cohen said, firmly shaking my
hand.

"Thank you, Mr. Secretary," I replied, really looking forward to working

*September 30, 1997 Secretary Cohen administers the oath as Carolyn looks on in-
side the SecDef's office.*

Air Force Two: *became my primary mode of travel for international trips.*

There's quite a history behind the fleet of aircraft used by the Chairman for international travel. The C-32 *(military modified Boeing 757 used as* Air Force Two*)* has its own encrypted computer local area network, plus secure worldwide-capable voice and data systems, including telephones, satellites, and fax and copy machines.

The private stateroom includes a changing area, lavatory, two first-class swivel seats at a worktable, and a convertible divan that seats three and folds out to a bed.

At times I flew on SAM-26000 or SAM-27000, the two VC-137 *(military modified Boeing 707) aircraft used as* Air Force One *from Presidents Kennedy through Bush.*

| SAM-27000 | SAM-26000 |
|---|---|
| **Aircraft type:** *VC-137C (Modified Boeing 707-353B)* | **Aircraft type:** *VC-137C (Modified Boeing 707-353B)* |
| **Primary** *Air Force One:* *Presidents Nixon, Ford, Carter, Reagan, George H. W. Bush* | **Primary** *Air Force One:* *Presidents Kennedy, Johnson, Nixon* |
| **Back-up** *Air Force One:* *Presidents George H. W. Bush, Clinton, George W. Bush* | **Back-up** *Air Force One:* *Presidents Ford, Carter, Reagan, George H. W. Bush, Clinton* |
| **Retired:** *August 29, 2001* | **Retired:** *March 24, 1998* |
| **Currently:** *Ronald Reagan Presidential Library* | **Currently:** *National Museum of the United States Air Force* |

with this inspirational leader. Following quick congratulations all around, both Cohen and I were off to Andrews Air Force Base, where we would take our own separate jets to the NATO conference, since he would continue on to Bulgaria, Bosnia, and France, whereas I would return to Washington for a few days before turning back around to meet with defense ministers in Germany, the UK, and France, and then continue on to Bosnia—returning to D.C. only long enough to attend my formal "welcome" ceremony and then get back on board for a quick trip to Miami to commemorate the SOUTHCOM (U.S. Southern Command) move from Panama.

Now that I think of it, maybe Shali stayed in that great Quarters Six residence those extra two weeks because that's the only time he got to see it in his four years as Chairman.

While the pace would never let up, I did become accustomed to it rather quickly, and between the amenities, the efficient on-board staff, and the cutting-edge communications suite, my time was just as productive at thirty-eight thousand feet as it was in my E Ring Pentagon office. (See inset)

———————

A few weeks later, Shali finally moved out and we were able to move into the beautiful Quarters Six, the official residence of the Chairman of the Joint Chiefs of Staff, located on the historic Fort Myer, Virginia, which is contiguous to Arlington National Cemetery. The Chairman's home is surrounded by the homes of the Air Force Chief of Staff, the Army Chief of Staff, and the Vice Chairman.

Fort Meyer is home to the "Old Guard," the soldiers who perform the ceremonial details for the White House, guard the Tomb of the Unknown Soldier, provide the caisson and riderless horse for dignitary funerals, etc.

The home was constructed in 1908, the year that Orville Wright made the world's first military test flight at Fort Myer. It was first occupied by General Omar Bradley, the first Chairman, and along the way was converted from two duplexes into a single ten-thousand-square-foot residence with ten bathrooms. It had three levels plus a full basement. The first level was the "official" entertainment area, which included a living room, dining room, sunroom, den, kitchen, and two bathrooms. On the second floor was the master bedroom with two separate bathrooms, a guest bedroom with bath, an office, a large dressing room where all my uniforms were kept and maintained by the enlisted aides, and a large sunroom that contained a desk for Carolyn and the treadmill and other exercise equipment. The third floor had three bedrooms and two baths, where our three

DEPARTMENT OF DEFENSE

*January 22, 1998. Prepping for Paris aboard SAM 27000.*

WHITE HOUSE

*November 22, 1963, Lyndon Johnson is sworn in as president aboard SAM 26000. The following day, President Kennedy's coffin would be flown from Dallas to Andrews AFB aboard the same plane.*

WHITE HOUSE

*President Ford on SAM 27000.*

*I flew on SAM 26000 for many of my overseas flights. This aircraft carried Presidents Kennedy, Johnson, Nixon, Ford, Carter, Reagan, George H.W. Bush, and Clinton. The stateroom was used to swear in President Johnson.*

*President Reagan on board SAM 27000.*

sons and their families stayed when they visited, as well as out-of-town guests.

The basement contained an office for the aides, a laundry room, a bath, a storage room, a large room that at the time contained a very large and antiquated boiler/furnace, and a room that I converted to a woodworking shop. There my large table saw, band saw, sander, joiner, and related equipment were kept. There was a large fenced-in backyard that we frequently used for entertaining. The front of the house overlooked a large parade field with a flagpole. The military police came every morning to raise the flag and back at dusk to lower it. The parade field overlooked the Washington monument and D.C. Every July Fourth the parade field was open to the public for viewing the fireworks on the National Mall. At my request, the Army, which bears the burden of maintaining all homes on Fort Myer, planned to renovate the quarters upon our departure, replacing the antiquated heating/AC systems, which, prior to the upgrade, took two days to change from AC to heat or vice versa, at a cost of $750,000. Two congressmen, including Congressman Hobson, chairman of the committee that oversees installations, came over to look at the quarters, and as they left, all they could say was, "Overdue." The request was approved within days and as Carolyn and I left, the renovation was under way.

———

Before I buckled down to the matters at hand, I fervently believed it was crucial to establish the ground rules and share what I expected from the Joint Chiefs. Previously I had read a book called *Dereliction of Duty*, by H. R. McMaster, then a young Army major—now a brigadier general and highly respected counterinsurgency specialist who is often called upon to consult with General Dave Petraeus. (Even though Brigadier General McMaster is a Tar Heel rather than a Wolfpack, I bear no grudge.) The book dealt with the deceit and deception that went on in Washington during the Johnson administration involving Secretary of Defense Robert McNamara and the Joint Chiefs, who failed to speak out even though they knew they were building a military campaign for Vietnam on lies.

I made the book required reading for every member of the Joint Chiefs and all the four-star combatant commanders. It is a valuable resource for leaders of any organization. In my case, I would not allow that type of politicizing and breakdown in integrity to happen under my watch. I insisted that all of them had the freedom, and obligation, to speak their minds and do what is right. As the principal military advisor to the President, I was duty-bound to tell it like it is, and I expected no less from either the Joint Chiefs or the commanders.

It seems to have made an impact, and it meant a great deal to me when

Tony Zinni (retired four-star general and Commander in Chief, CENT-COM), a valued friend and esteemed general, made note of this in his recent book, *Battle Ready*.

> I was blessed to serve under great leaders who allowed me to speak and welcomed and encouraged my input, even when it was contrary to their views. These men taught me more about courage than I learned on any battlefield—people like Hugh Shelton, who, as Chairman of the Joint Chiefs of Staff, required all of us four-star commanders to read (*Dereliction of Duty*) . . . At a breakfast meeting on January 29, 1998, the Chairman's message was clear [when he brought in the book's author, Major McMaster, to lead the breakfast]. [General Shelton] expected us to speak out.

———

The time had come for me to roll up my sleeves and get into coming up with a game plan to rectify the damage that been perpetrated against our servicemen and -women by the massive funding cuts of 1986, particularly in the area of retirement benefits and pay compression—which refers to the differential between pay in the officer corps and the noncommissioned officer corps.

I first learned of this problem as CINCSOC down in Tampa, but now in my position as Chairman I was finally in a position to do something about it. I contacted my J1 (Director of Manpower and Personnel) and had him investigate the situation and report back to me. I cannot overemphasize the mind-boggling talent we had in that joint staff, and my USAF brigadier general was no exception. Not only was his data far more revealing than I ever could have imagined, but he came in with a spectacular presentation called "Houston, we have a problem." I looked at it and it was dynamite. It verified and documented everything that I thought was going, and reaffirmed my original conviction to fix it.

Perhaps I was a bit naïve, but since this directly impacted the well-being of the men and women in all branches of the military, I naturally felt that all the Joint Chiefs of Staff would enthusiastically jump on board. So much for the predictability of Washington . . . not.

No sooner had I presented to the Joint Chiefs than I turned around and *the briefing leaked*—JOINT CHIEFS CONCERNED ABOUT PAY was the headline splashed across the front pages of all the *Times* military newspapers: the *Army Times, Navy Times,* and *Air Force Times.* They even had the name of the briefing, "Houston, we have a problem." This happened so fast that I had not even had a chance to talk to the Secretary of Defense about it, so this was bad—a complete 155-mm round blasting any semblance of a timely strategy to pull this thing off—so I told the J1 to put it on the back burner for now; there was no other choice. I had to obtain the SecDef's buy-in, then get presidential support on it, before asking Congress to buy into it—and at that point none of that was going to happen. Although I had to hold back on it temporarily, it remained my priority. I fully intended to get back to it.

In the meantime, we had anecdotal evidence that *readiness was slipping.* The newspapers had started reporting this, and I was also hearing it from members of Congress. In particular, Congressman Ike Skelton was very concerned about it and made it his business that I fully understood how bad it was. It was time to approach the service chiefs and find out directly what our state of readiness was from their perspective. If there truly was a problem, you certainly wouldn't want your adversaries to be aware of it, so I decided that the only place to discuss it was in the Tank, which is how we refer to the Joint Chiefs' Top-Secret conference room. The Tank is actually an SCIF (Sensitive Compartmentalized Information Facility)—the same type of facility that I mentioned during my DDO days—and it provides a secure venue for us to discuss classified information all the way up to the TS/SCI (Top-Secret/Sensitive Compartmentalized Information) classification level.

I assembled all the Joint Chiefs in the Tank and went down the line, one by one. I started with the Army Chief of Staff, my old boss, General Denny Reimer. "So tell me, Denny, what's your state of readiness? Got any problems?"

He didn't bat an eye. "Not a one, sir. We're fine."

"How about you?" I asked, looking directly at Jay Johnson (who had just started as Chief of Naval Operations), from the Navy.

Same exact answer: "Couldn't be better, sir."

I went down the line, to Chuck Krulak, Commandant of the Marine Corps, same thing. Air Force General Mike Ryan (who had really just taken over): identical. Every one of them told me that readiness was just fine.

*Strange*, I thought.

I waited another two weeks and I'm now hearing even more anecdotal evidence, so it's back into the Tank. *Tell me about your readiness.* And I get what I call "the drinking duck syndrome." Every one of the chiefs confidently confirmed that everything was just great, couldn't be better—nodding their heads like a row of bobbing ducks at a carnival.

Since readiness is really a function of operations, I had my J3 do something that Admiral Crowe actually had me do when I was a brigadier general working for him . . . I told the J3 to *poll the readiness reports.*

"I want to see twenty Army infantry battalions, and five Marine Corp battalions, and twelve Air Force squadrons, and nine Navy ship reports." There really wasn't any significance to the number of reports I was asking for—the point was just to get a random, representative sampling. "Let's see what the lieutenant colonels in charge of each of these organizations have said about their readiness."

When these random samples came back, I could not believe what I saw. It was horrible. An F-16 squadron commander said he had four F-16s sitting on the ramp with no engines. A Marine Corp battalion commander actually declared his unit *unfit for combat. We are not trained and ready.* It was one after the other.

So it was back to the Tank, and basically I hit them with it by projecting the reports themselves up onto the screen. As far as I'm concerned, this is a terrifying problem if you consider the implications of having a military that's not ready to fight. Every one of these guys should have been telling me that they needed help—readiness should be a top priority, but that wasn't the case. They were proud of their services and reluctant to admit the incredible problems that were starting to develop. Years of increased OPTEMPO (how frequently a unit deploys) on a force getting smaller by the year, combined with declining budgets, was taking its toll. It is the responsibility of the Congress to "raise and train armies," and that includes resourcing. But for Congress to fix it they obviously had to know about it and that is the job of the Chiefs. So I felt that the best way to wake them up was to embarrass the shit out of them, and that's what I did with the projections.

I turned around to them while the material was up on the board and said, "*Tell me now that we don't have a readiness problem.*" I was just that blunt. I said, "If this is not a readiness issue, I don't know what the hell is. So *now* do we all agree that we've got readiness issues?"

The bottom line is that they were embarrassed and they didn't have much to say, frankly. I had proven my point and said, *Guys, we have got to figure out in a hurry just what it will take to fix it and get it fixed. And oh, by the way, I know some of your installations are completely falling down—particular yours, Denny, since I've lived on a couple of those. So let's all get together, and* work *together, and figure out just exactly what it will take to fix it.*


We left that day with a consensus that we would work together to create a budget of exactly what it would take to fix the problems—both the readiness and the installation issues. I made it clear that this had to be done on an expedited basis. My real reason for this timing was that I was looking at the sequence of events for the upcoming budget—and I was also looking at the political races that were going to be developing over the next year or two. And I was looking at a big budget surplus at that time; so, between all of these, I was starting to see that there was a strategy that might allow us to actually pull this one off.

I went upstairs and spoke with John Hamre (Deputy Secretary of Defense) and Bill Cohen and we went over all the elements—the budget surplus, the political races, and I was really getting psyched that we could pull this thing off.

I went back into the Tank with a new presentation in which we had merged the original *Houston, we have a problem* pay issues with the readiness issues and the installation issues—and the magic number we came up with that would remedy the problem was a rather staggering $155 billion.

Almost as soon as I said it, Chuck Krulak, the Marine Corp Commandant, gave a huffy laugh and said, "There is no way I will support that. First of all, the number is outrageous and you're not going to get it—you'll be lucky if you get *one* billion dollars, and even if you do, that billion dollars will be taken out of something else, something else that I really need, like my modernization program—so what they will end up doing is in effect *breaking* my readiness. I am flying Vietnam-era helicopters and I need that Osprey and you know they'll just slide that money right on over from Osprey—so *hell no* I won't support this—no way."

"Okay, Chuck, got it, thanks," I said as I went around the table. "Jay, how about you?"

"I'm with you, sir. We've got to fix this stuff," Jay Johnson of the Navy responded.

"Denny?"

"How can I say no to reports like that? It's a lot of money, but yes—has to be done."

"Thanks, Denny," I said to Reimer, Army Chief of Staff. "Mike, what does the Air Force have to say?"

"You're kidding yourself if you think you'll get anywhere near that, but we might as well try for it. I can't have fighters sitting out there with no engines."

"Agree—they tend to fly better with them. You're up, Vice," I said to Joe Ralston, my number two.

"I think Chuck's right. If we go forward we'll get one billion—*if we're lucky*—most likely nowhere near that—and that will be spread over five years. Even worse, take a step back and look at it this way: no way you'll get it, and this will become your legacy. Colin Powell? Yeah, he was Chairman for Panama and Desert Storm. Bill Crowe? Sure, he was the first Chairman to benefit from Goldwater-Nichols. Hugh Shelton? He was the guy that tried to get $155 billion and failed. That, unfortunately, will become your legacy."

I had to chuckle at that—but only for an instant, because I thought about what he had said, and Joe is a bright guy and someone I have a great deal of respect for.

"You know what, Joe? I would rather go down as a failure trying to do the right thing than to go down as one who was successful in achieving the low standard that I set for myself. In my opinion, there's only one way to go on this, and that is to go forward and ask for what is right—to ask for the full amount of exactly what it would cost to take care of our men and women in uniform with their pay—to fix the pay compression, to fix the retirement system, to get the readiness and our installations back to the way they should be—and whether we like it or not, that figure is $155 billion. So my plan, gentlemen, is to go forward and ask for $155 billion.

"I just can't let them steal from my existing programs," the commandant rationalized.

"You know, Chuck, if I really thought that would happen, I would be concerned, too," I began, slowly working my way to the front of the room, toward the five flags adorning the wall. "But we have got some great lobbyists in this town and they work for Boeing; they work for Lockheed Martin; they work for General Dynamics; they work for Raytheon; they work for Northrop Grumman, and others. By now I am standing right in front of those flags and I turn around and look at the Chiefs. "And who in the hell have the *troops* got for lobbyists? They are sitting right here, gentlemen, *the six of us.* If *we* do not lobby for the troops, nobody does. And so why don't we do it as a team? Let's lobby for the troops and the lobbyists that work for the contractors will lobby to save the modernization program." I was fired up that day because I believed this so passionately.

One of the challenges in Washington is that sometimes you may get a big hand in public, a loud "great idea!" then before you turn around you get stabbed in the back as soon as you leave the room. However, I really felt that after that session, we would move as one body.

So then I went to see Cohen and told him all about the problem, and the study, and confided in him that the bill to fix it came to $155 billion, and to his credit he did not even flinch.

Cohen thought for a minute, then said, "We have to come up with a plan to get President Clinton on board with this." I said that I had the perfect way, then went on to remind him that in two weeks the Joint Chiefs had to appear before Congress with their posture hearings, where they had to declare their state of readiness—and of course they were legally bound to answer truthfully, and the truth is, they were flat-out hurting.

"Now," I said. "In about ten days we have the CINC conference, and that would be a great chance for us to ask the President to come over and let us lay out for him the challenges that we've got right now on readiness, and have the Joint Chiefs there, along with the combatant commanders as they normally would be, to talk a little bit about our testimony that is coming up. Then we would get a firsthand report from each of the combatant commanders on how they see readiness out in the field."

Cohen positively lit up; he thought that was a great idea.

I contacted the CINCs and filled them in, telling each one that he would have about three minutes to talk about readiness in his particular area.

The meeting itself was in the War College conference room at Fort McNair, because that was the only secure conference facility that was big enough to accommodate all these people. President Clinton accepted our invitation to come over and join us, so Cohen and I met him out front, explained to him a little bit about what he was about to walk into, and we went in for the show to begin.

It was completely aboveboard and all the CINCs were told was that they would be reporting to the President about readiness where we believed there to be serious issues . . . but I told them just to give their honest analysis. If they thought things were fine, that's what they should say. To the person, they were grateful to have been given that opportunity.

When the meeting was over, Clinton simply said, "Mr. Secretary, Mr. Chairman, when the Joint Chiefs appear before Congress next week, you tell the truth, and you tell them what you need to fix it. And on top of that, you tell them *I am behind you,* that I think you need to fix it and they need to give you the resources."

At that moment, I knew we were cleared in hot, as the fighter pilots say. We were ready to appear before Congress.

As a final bit of icing on the cake, I resorted back to a snake eater Special Ops type of ploy—a behind-the-scenes orchestration to achieve your desired results. This would all be played out during an administration that had a Democratic president and a Republican Congress; if played just right they could be positioned to play against each other to be viewed as being the most *pro defense*. To that end, I made the appropriate congressional visits, enlisted support from the key players on both sides, and, following our presentation, it was almost like flipping that switch on the cockpit to engage the autopilot—I just sat back and watched them try to convince their constituents that they were more pro defense than the opposition party. It was beautiful and I couldn't have scripted it more perfectly. We asked for $155 billion and walked out of there with $112 billion. Not bad against an initial prognosis of $1 billion or less. This was important. It was what it was all about.

I could not wait to get out of there and tell Carolyn how it had played out, and by now she's probably heard me repeat it a hundred times—but I will gladly repeat it a hundred more because it's a perfect example of exactly why I accepted the invitation to become Chairman. Unlike some who set their sights on seeing how high they can rise within the ranks, perhaps even motivated to a certain extent by the power and recognition—I had never set my sights on becoming Chairman. I'd never *wanted* to be Chairman. In order to be Chairman, I had to give up what I considered the best four-star job in the armed forces. But the impact our team, Secretary Cohen and the Joint Chiefs, was able to make on the lives of literally millions of great American servicemen and -women—improvements to their lives that in many cases will allow them to put their children through school, or take care of other necessities they might never otherwise have had the opportunity to do—is an awesome incentive to hold this position. When I walked out of that Senate chamber I felt inspired to get back to work and target the next area where I could generate substantial improvements that would help our great Americans long beyond my time. And the good news was that this was early 1998, and I had not even completed my first two-year term.

## A DAY IN THE LIFE
## OF THE CHAIRMAN

I am often asked to describe a typical day in the life of the Chairman. The truth is that every day was different, with new challenges based upon the ever-changing world situation. That's what made it so interesting. Following is an example of how one of those days might play out.

4:30 A.M. Time for PT, because there certainly wouldn't be any time to break away once I got to the Pentagon. I'd start with a five-mile run around Fort Myer, then follow that up with a daily regimen of pushups and sit-ups. On the weekends I'd occasionally utilize the post gym for a more extended workout.

There were four enlisted aides who were assigned to work at the house (two Army, one Navy, and one Marine), and they maintained the area we used for entertaining (living room, library, kitchen, and dining room). They also prepared the meals—particularly for our official formal dinners. (We would often host gatherings of approximately thirty invited guests in honor of the Chiefs of Defense and their wives from other countries; plus an annual New Year's party for four hundred invited guests, including members of Congress, Supreme Court justices, Cabinet members, etc.) The aides usually came in around 8:30 A.M. and left between 5:30 and 6:00 P.M., but we didn't allow them to come in on weekends unless we had to entertain guests. One of their functions was to maintain my uniforms, so before they left for the evening they would lay out the proper one for me to wear the following day.

Following a shower, I'd put on the uniform prepared by the aide and grab a quick breakfast before departing for the Pentagon.

5:45 A.M. About this time, one of my STU-III encrypted phones would generally start ringing, and I'd be provided with updates on key events that had taken place over the past twelve hours. These were timed to come in just after my run, and the main purpose was for me to be fully prepared should I bump into the SecDef or get a call from the President. The rule was to call and wake me during the night only if the call involved an issue I could do something about. If it was only advisory, my Vice would get the wake-up call, and I'd be advised of it during the 5:45 call. (After I retired and my Vice, Dick Myers, took over as Chairman, he told me how much joy it had given him to tell *his* Vice, Pete Pace, that *he* would now be getting those calls throughout the night.) High-profile events would be the exceptions, of course. If two airplanes ran together over the Pacific and killed fifty members of the Air Force, I'd be awakened for that, since it was very possible that the President would have been awakened and called me for an update. On the other hand, if a single airplane had a hard landing that damaged it in Afghanistan, they'd advise me of that in the morning call.

On extreme high-priority operations, such as the first strike of a big, four-day campaign to bomb the crap out of Saddam (as we did a few times), I'd often monitor those directly in the NMCC, regardless of the time. A CAT team (Crisis Action Team) would have been stood up, and I would usually monitor the op from a medium-size conference room I had

*Formal dining room where we would often host gatherings of foreign Chiefs of Defense and their wives.*

adjacent to the Crisis Action Center. It had secure video telecommunications as well as direct satellite links to the overhead reconnaissance platforms, so I was able to get a great hands-on feel for how everything was playing out.

On high-priority events that were somewhat smaller in scope—such as a Special Ops capture mission—I would not monitor it from the NMCC but instead would be notified of its outcome, no matter the time.

6:30 A.M. My armored Cadillac would pull into the driveway, and as soon as I entered the car, my driver would hand me a copy of the "Early Bird," a publication that highlighted all the military-related stories from the past twenty-four hours. I'd skim the hot topics on the short ride to the Pentagon and zero in on things like the public release of some topic that was not supposed to be leaked; and I knew we'd get into that in my early-morning meeting with the SecDef.

6:45 A.M. The Cadillac pulled up to the Pentagon's River Entrance, where one of my two officer aides would be waiting to take my briefcase and walk with me to my office, filling me in on late-breaking emergencies along the way. The executive officer, a sharp colonel, would go over the day's schedule. During my tenure I had three executive assistants. All three of them now serve as three- or four-star generals (Petraeus, Caldwell, and Lute).

**7:00 A.M.** I would walk across the hall into my conference room, where I received an update on the night's events—the J2 filled me in on intelligence developments, and the J3 on any operational updates on missions we had in progress or in the final stages of planning. Occasionally we would bring in the J4 (logistics officer) if there was something going on in his arena, and the Vice Chairman, the Director of the Joint Staff, the Special Assistant to the Chairman (a three-star), and all their aides would be present for this very quick, twenty- to thirty-minute briefing—the real purpose being to ensure that when I entered my 8:30 brief with the SecDef, I'd be doing so armed with the very latest information.

**7:30 A.M.** I would meet with my intell briefer (a civilian from the CIA) in a closed-door, Top-Secret session in which he would open his satchel and present me with the President's Daily Brief, a tightly controlled document read by the President, SecDef, and very few others. As soon as I read it, I would return it to him, and he would leave or I would ask for clarification: "Tell them I would like to know more about this event going on in Nairobi," or, "Who the hell is this guy?" He'd then take the questions back to George Tenet and tell him that the Chairman wanted to know more about this topic. Later that day I'd get the answer in the form of a highly classified message from the CIA, or occasionally George would pick up the STU-III red switch phone and call me with the details.

Hopefully, my J2 (Director of Intelligence) would have also received the information, although he would have received a more sanitized version. Only the PDB (President's Daily Brief) itself would list *actual sources* of the intell—where the other copies would only say "reliable sources," without naming them. To give an idea of the type of items covered in the PDB, here are a few hypothetical examples:

- The North Koreans are transporting a non-U.N.-compliant missile system to Libya and it's going to transit the Panama Canal on a given date.
- Syria's President al-Assad is attempting to buy enriched uranium from a particular country.
- A boatload of suspected Scud missiles that left Pyongyang is now approaching the Ivory Coast.
- A message from bin Laden has been intercepted en route to an agent in Yemen and we believe it to be a coded communication referring to a terrorist act to take place within the United States.

Much of the time it was extremely frustrating because they were bombarding us with so much data, it was almost like information overload, and the majority of the topics were things we couldn't do anything about anyway. When you analyze intelligence data, it's important to keep two things in mind. Number one: is the information accurate? Number two: if it's accurate, what can we do about it? A third consideration is more subjective, and that's what *should* we do about it, from a military perspective? It's important to verify that the intell has been corroborated—otherwise it could very easily be false info placed by individuals trying to use information warfare against us.

8:30 A.M. The Secretary of Defense's office was just up the escalator and immediately above mine, and each morning we'd meet at a round table to the left of his desk (it was right beside Rumsfeld's stand-up desk), along with the Vice Chairman (Joe Ralston, followed by Dick Myers) and the Deputy SecDef (John Hamre, followed by Rudy deLeon, who was followed by Paul Wolfowitz), and exchange information—often using the PDB as our springboard. The meeting would go anywhere from fifteen minutes to an hour, depending on whether or not it turned into war gaming. The SecDef would start things off: "What have you got, Hugh?"

I'd respond with whatever updates my J3 had just reported, such as, "The carrier battle group USS *Ronald Reagan* has arrived on station in the Persian Gulf and the *Constellation* redeployed and is headed back toward Japan. The 82nd Airborne lead elements just departed home station for Iraq this morning; they'll start closing in on Baghdad day after tomorrow." The Vice Chairman would add whatever seemed appropriate, then the Deputy SecDef would come in with issues he'd been working on—in the case of John Hamre or Rudy deLeon, generally congressional, Pentagon, or defense issues; but Wolfowitz inserted himself into operational details to a much greater extent, as tasked by Rumsfeld. That would kick off our priorities and we'd be off to jump-start our day.

9:00 A.M. During times of crisis, I often had meetings at the White House either to brief the President on the operations in progress or discuss the plans for upcoming missions. Throughout my four years, it seemed like we almost always had something going on that entailed the White House briefings. It made sense, since I was the President's principle military adviser.

I'd prep for these meetings from 9:00 to 9:45, and I'd bring in the appropriate members of my staff for the preparation. We would war-game the White House meeting, and after I was prepped, the staff would grill me on any potential questions I might be asked by the President—although once I got to the White House, I'd be the one doing the briefing. If the meeting took place in the Oval Office, I'd be flying solo—very rarely would any of my staff be included. The President would usually take one of the two seats in front of the fireplace and I would usually sit on the chair right beside him, or at the end of the sofa just next to him, so that I could easily show him any maps or charts I might have brought along with me.

```
┌─────────────────────────────────────────────────────────────┐
│  ┌──────────────────────────────────────────────────────┐   │
│  │ Tuesday, 16 June 1998                                 │   │
│  │ ┌──────────────┐      ℬ                               │   │
│  │ │Moscow, Russia│                                      │   │
│  │ └──────────────┘                                      │   │
│  │ Uniform: Day:     Class A w/ Garrison Cap             │   │
│  │         Eve:      Business Suit                       │   │
│  └──────────────────────────────────────────────────────┘   │
│                                                               │
│   0600          ⟨    PT/PDB/Breakfast    ⟩                   │
│                                                               │
│   0800          Dep enr Tushino Airfield                     │
│                 • Sedan #1: CJCS, XO, PSO                     │
│                 • Sedan #2: PAO, AIDE                         │
│                 • Van #1: AO2, INT, COMM2                     │
│                                                               │
│   0825          Arr Airfield dep enr Ryazan via Helo (FT 0 + 40) │
│                                                               │
│   0905          Arr Ryazan                                   │
│                 • Met by base Commander                      │
│                 • Tour of Airfield                           │
│                 • Long Range Aviation unit                   │
│                 • Gift exchange CJCS presents 3" Brass Medallion, │
└─────────────────────────────────────────────────────────────┘
```

*Entries in my trip book show that even in Moscow, my day starts with PT and the CIA "President's Daily Brief" (PDB).*

If the meeting took place in the White House Situation Room, I'd often take a staff member with me—perhaps the J3 if it dealt with an operation, or the J2 if it was intell related. The same was true when we met in the much larger Cabinet Room.

Either way, my driver would be waiting for me outside the Pentagon River Entrance, and we'd make the ten-minute drive to the White House, where the driver would roll down the tinted window at the main entry gate, and the Secret Service agent would admit us after a visual check of who was in the car. There'd be no need for checking ID, since the car, driver, and I were immediately recognizable to them. As we approached the gate at the West Wing entrance, occasionally we'd drive by photographers beside the driveway, trying to get a look at who was going in to the see President. They would strain to see who was in the car, but with the dark tinted windows I insisted on having on my limo, there was no way they'd see anyone.

Once we arrived at the West Wing, we'd walk past the Secret Service agent(s) and proceed a short distance to the Situation Room or walk directly to the waiting area just outside the Oval Office.

I'm often asked if I was nervous the first time I briefed the President in the Oval, and I'd have to say that despite a minor touch of anxiety I might have felt surrounding the President's potential reaction to what I had to say, I had this inner feeling that I knew the military piece of it so well, there was nothing to be nervous about. While I was conscious of the economic, political, diplomatic, and informational elements of whatever I'd be discussing (and fully aware that my recommendation could very well generate a potentially harsh political reaction), if I stuck to my job and restricted my comments to providing my best military advice, I'd be fine. That seems like a no-brainer, but you'd be surprised. My predecessor, for example (General John Shalikashvili), is a great guy, but on occasion he was known to be more worried about the political and diplomatic implications than the military side of the issue, and they didn't like that. I had been tipped off to this up front, so I was particularly sensitive to the importance of my staying within the military lane—but I did make it clear to the President that I fully understood that he had to consider those areas beyond just the military.

One of my most important responsibilities as Chairman was to stay in close contact with our allies, so I would try to call my foreign counterparts on those mornings that I did not have White House meetings. I did my best to call my French, German, and British, counterparts at least once a week—just to touch base and exchange our perspectives on various military issues that concerned all of us. These were one-on-one secure calls set up in advance by my assistant. They were *not* just PR calls, but rather important discussions about substantive issues. We developed a closeness that allowed us to cut through the political bullshit and get right to the point, military to military. These calls might be timed to precede an important NATO meeting, and I'd say, "I don't know what you think about this international criminal court but I'll tell you this: when we discuss it next week, the U.S. is going to be adamantly opposed to it for the following reasons . . ." and they might respond, "We don't see it that way, Hugh. We're going to support it." Then we would get into it. The forum was direct and unfiltered, the way it should be.

The four of us would meet as a group twice a year, and we'd rotate which country would host the get-together. It was a great combination of business and social, with our wives included; and we'd roll up our sleeves and foster close personal relationships, too. These were the times in which we shared why our politicians were leaning certain ways on issues that the others might not have been able to grasp, since we might have been coming from entirely different mind-sets—but by the time we left one another, we understood what was behind it all. I imagine there was some attempt to do similar things on the civilian side, but in many ways our military-to-military bond was unique—we had all pledged our lives to defending principles that we wholeheartedly believed, and we had all risen to the top of our militaries by doing so.

As you might imagine, these are often very strong individuals, and sometimes they had personalities we would not normally relate to, but we made it work. For example, the first Frenchman I dealt with, *Général d'armée aérienne* Jean-Philippe Douin, was not as easy to work with as his successor, Jean-Pierre Kelche, but we still did okay. I appreciated the political pressures he was under and we had a good relationship among the four of us.

Following those calls, I would often bring in one of my three speechwriters to go over an upcoming presentation. In my last year alone, I gave 232 speeches, and that doesn't include my daily press briefings. I'd be prepped for upcoming trips, as well, and these trips would usually encompass three or four countries. I would have to be completely brought up to speed on whatever issues could possibly arise—including what the U.S. position was and how that equated to that given country's position. That in itself was extremely time-consuming, and fluid—it changed from day to day.

**12:00 P.M.** Directly across the hall was the private Chairman's Dining Room, which was reserved for flag officers and key civilians. Most likely I'd just order lunch from there and eat at my desk while plowing through the mounds of paperwork, but sometimes I'd get to actually go over and enjoy the culinary work of our talented and creative chef.

**1:00 P.M.–4:00 P.M.** The afternoons were most often filled with briefings from various staff sections on upcoming issues, preparation for a briefing for the SecDef or the President, or an NSC (National Security Council) meeting at the White House. When I could find a few spare minutes, I would walk out to one of the staff sections, unannounced, to talk to the sergeants, petty officers, or more-junior officers who were laboring day in and day out to get the work done but had very little face time with the Chairman they were supporting.

**4:00 P.M.** Late afternoon would usually entail our Tank sessions, where the Joint Chiefs would assemble to discuss issues that were often going to the SecDef and the President. These were highly classified closed meetings and it was understood that unless someone was specifically invited into these meetings, they were not allowed to attend. The only people in that room were the six members of the Joint Chiefs, the Director of the Joint Staff, and my three-star assistant who normally traveled with the Secretary of State. Exceptions were made on a case-by-case basis. If the meeting surrounded a certain specialty—like the readiness issues I discussed earlier—then the J3 and his briefing officer might be invited to attend for that portion of the meeting, but that was it. The windows were blacked out, there were no phones of any kind (even the secure, encrypted phones were in a room off to the side), and the Tank was swept twice a week for bugs. Once that door closed, it was never opened from the outside. If they had to get some emergency message to us during a Tank session, a noncommissioned officer seated at the communications console in the anteroom just outside the entrance would send an e-mail or IM to the Director (a three-star), who would walk the message up to the appropriate person.

5:00 P.M. Normally, I would try to finish the paperwork that had come in during the day, especially the highly classified documents that I could not carry home to complete. The EA (executive assistant), whose office was positioned just outside my door in an area commonly referred to as "the bunker," would come in to fill me in on what had transpired during the day that I had missed while out of the office.

6:00 P.M. The Vice Chairman and I would meet to compare notes on the issues of the day. He might have attended an NSC meeting of the deputies from each department and have a feel for what the Department of State's position would be on a certain issue. Both Joe Ralston and Dick Myers were superb officers to work with. I never had to worry about protecting my "six o'clock" with either of them, to use a fighter-pilot expression for protecting one's back.

6:30 P.M. I collected the paperwork that I would need to have completed by the following morning and headed to the River Entrance, where the armored Cadillac and driver would be waiting to make the ten-minute drive back to Fort Myer and Quarters Six. Often, Carolyn and I would have to attend a social event, such as a reception at one of the embassies in D.C. Then it was time to finish the paperwork and hope the phone didn't ring while I attempted to catch a few hours of sleep.

———

There were a number of different issues that would cross my desk as Chairman—some of the more obvious were covered in the news or in my press briefings. Others were more obscure. I was quite honored that some of my personal achievements were recognized that year. In May I was especially privileged to be named National Father of the Year, and just a few months later presented with the 4-H Lifetime Achievement Award.

As Chairman, I tried to keep my sights set at one thousand feet and look at the big picture. How does this action impact our readiness today, and what effect might it have down the road? *I wanted to help shape the strategic environment and deter threats before they emerged.* I cautioned about complacency as the United States military shifted priorities nearly a decade after the end of the Cold War, and I criticized the claims by international observers that America faced a peaceful world and should thus *drastically demobilize.* I was concerned that we might lose our focus since we lacked a single enemy that we'd had for so many years, and warned that history had shown this to be common to prior interwar periods in this century.

Congress had recently issued a report based on the findings of an outside panel they had commissioned, and it concluded that the United States no longer faced the possibility of two regional conflicts, which was the standard upon which the Department of Defense evaluated readiness. I disagreed with that then as much as I do today, even though our focus has shifted to the proliferation of terrorism. Who's to say that while we're fighting wars in Iraq and Afghanistan, another might not draw us in involving Korea, or China, or a number of other places?

While I believed we could take comfort from the absence of a potential superpower, I was concerned that continued spurts of nationalism in some areas of the world, terrorism, and the growing pains of continued democratization still left us with many security-related concerns that were left unattended.

North Atlantic Treaty Organization (NATO) was going through some "interesting" ties on a number of fronts; one involving its primary function, another surrounding its expansion. I was a major advocate of a careful NATO expansion and the member nations' decision to give Russia a voice in NATO affairs—which was a hot issue at the summit I had just attended in the Netherlands, as well as the one I would be attending the following month. NATO had transformed from a military alliance designed to respond to crises into a political alliance designed to deter them before they escalate. I believed that NATO was no longer an alliance *against* anything . . . it had become an alliance *for* peace and stability.

I had just met with the new Russian Federation Minister of Defense, Army General Igor Dmitrievich Sergeyev, and after our discussions I believed that initial Russian reluctance to NATO expansion, seen as a threat to their borders and their strategic position in Europe, would diminish as the country recognized the advantages of having peaceful democratic neighbors.

"We are in the process of trying to replace the Iron Curtain with a picture window," I would say at speeches and press conferences.

The issue of land mines was a hot topic of the day, and we (along with China) were taking heat for not signing a fifty-nation treaty that banned all types of land mines. I believed that land mines were vital to the protection of U.S. interests in South Korea, where thousands of land mines were scattered throughout the demilitarized zone separating that country from North Korea. I also felt that antipersonnel mines, scattered among mines designed to destroy advancing tanks, were necessary implements of defense policy.

The controversy surrounding a U.S. ballistic-missile-defense system was all over the news, and I felt that *if we could afford it* and *if the technology was available,* I'd be a fan of that. But I was not a fan of deploying a half-baked solution that didn't work and that gave only a false perception of security at a cost of billions of taxpayer dollars.

––––––––

As Chairman of the Joint Chiefs, I was required every year to present a very in-depth military-posture presentation to Congress. I will never forget one of my very first ones before the Senate Armed Services Committee. It covered all aspects of the military, including personnel, readiness, modernization, base closures, operations, and global hot spots, among many other areas. The preparation for it was very extensive, the amount of backup data enormous. I brought along three solid catalog briefcases filled with data.

The night before the presentation, Secretary Cohen asked me how I felt about the hearing. I told him I felt great about our programs and my ability to articulate them, but I was concerned about John McCain, whom I had testified before on many occasions during my prior position of commander in chief of Special Operations Command.

It seemed that almost every time I would start to speak, he would take off like some rabid dog—screaming, shouting, getting all red in the face, using insulting language—explosive and on the attack—very seldom wanting to listen to what I had to say, preferring to make his points and be done with it. To be candid, I was convinced that he had a screw loose because normal people just didn't behave in that manner. I never had any problems with the other members of Congress, who behaved respectfully and appropriately.

"Don't worry about John," the Secretary told me, chuckling. "I was the best man at his wedding, and you won't have any problem with him as long as I'm seated next to you."

That was music to my ears.

The following morning, we headed to the Capitol. After the customary prehearing greetings and informal handshakes, the Secretary and I slipped into the leather seats at the green-felt-covered table in front of the lights and cameras. We both gave our opening statements, followed by those of Senators Warner and Levin.

Senator Levin turned the floor over to McCain, who gazed down upon Secretary Cohen from the elevated platform upon which the committee sat. The United States Senate seal affixed to the marble wall was visible above his right shoulder. He took a deep breath. Then, as we waited for him to ask Cohen his first question, McCain began to lambast him, a vicious attack replete with rude insults and personal invectives.

Eventually he would start to wind down, but just as we thought he had finished, he would launch into another fuming attack. This went on and on.

Finally I grabbed my pencil and scribbled a note to Cohen: "Mr. Secretary, I'm sure glad he's *your* friend and not mine."

The Secretary had to smile, even as his good friend continued ranting. Finally his time expired and the senator was cut off. Thanks to his ranting and raving, he did not have time to question me.

The next round went considerably better, as the various senators questioned both Cohen and me. Then it was McCain's turn again. This time he turned to me and directed his first question. When my answer did not fit with his political persuasions, he became visibly upset. Laying into me, he accused me of answering in a "politically correct" manner rather than answering truthfully.

Having heard about as much of this as he cared to, Secretary Cohen forcefully intervened. "Senator, you might call this man a lot of things, but I have never met a general who is more unpolitically correct in my life." It was probably the greatest on-the-record compliment I would receive in my four years as Chairman. It served to illustrate the great contrast in leadership styles: one man leading with trust and respect, the other with intimidation, aggression, and belligerence.

Fortunately, it did not become an issue with the ultimate outcome, but during the campaign leading up to the 2008 election I was extremely concerned about the possibility of someone as apparently unstable as McCain in the position of Commander in Chief, dealing with other countries and having responsibility over the nuclear welfare of ours. I could only imagine how some world leaders might react once they got to see the man I'd come to know—if John McCain launched into one of his episodes in the leader's presence: screaming, shouting, and flying off the chart out of the clear blue over some insignificant matter. Let's just say it's a damn good thing it never came down to that.

**11:35 A.M., April 1, 2002, Walter Reed, Ward 72**

I regained consciousness to a cacophony of questions being fired at me: "What's your name?" "Where are you?" "Why are you here?"

"I'm General Hugh Shelton, I'm here at Walter Reed, I think I just fainted, and apparently I'm doing better than you are at the moment," I said, indicating one of the twenty doctors hovered over me—this one drenched in sweat and panting heavily.

"I'm fine, too," she said. "I just sprinted up three flights of stairs when I heard the code alert." After a rigorous examination it was determined that I was correct, I had fainted—either a vasovagal neurocardiogenic syncope (overstimulation of the vagus nerve resulting in a dilation of my blood vessels) or an orthostatic hypotension (inadequate constriction of the blood vessels). Either way, my brain was not getting enough oxygen and I had passed out. By the looks of my burly physical therapist, it had scared Zack to the point of nearly having a heart attack of his own.

The good news was he wouldn't let up on me one bit. For a period after that, I had to wear an abdominal bind and compression stockings to help facilitate vascular constriction (similar principle to a fighter pilot's g-suit) and during my PT sessions a cardiologist would accompany us with a dose of atropine and a big cardio chair at the ready, just in case it happened again.

Zack continued with seemingly impossible demands, and I challenged myself to meet every one of them. By doing so, that tiny twitch became a real movement that I could control, and that led to greater movement, and eventually taking a step on my own. My left side was responding but not so my right, and that soon became Dr. Jim Ecklund's next challenge. There was a very real possibility that the progress I was making on my left side might never be duplicated on my right.

## Chapter Fourteen ★★★★

# BIN LADEN—CIA IS MIA

It was exactly 5:30 on the morning of August 7, 1998, and I had just lathered up and begun to shave when the earsplitting ringer of the STU-III sounded from the other room, a sure sign that some significant event had occurred the night before—a whirlwind I'd be swept into once I hit the office—but for now I would just be given a heads-up *Reader's Digest* version in case I would run into the Secretary of Defense prior to getting the full report during my 7:00 A.M. J2 and CIA intell briefs. At least I didn't have to worry about that ringer waking up the neighbors, since odds were that they'd be getting similar calls; directly next door was Air Force Chief of Staff Mike Ryan, and two doors down was my Vice Chairman, General Joe Ralston—who was about to become a vital participant in this episode.

Hustling to the blinking red light beside my bed, I wondered how Carolyn was able to sleep so soundly through all the commotion. Probably had something to do with her putting up with thirty-five years of the racket I made every morning at 4:30 sharp as I prepped for my PT—or maybe she was just getting back at me for days long gone by when the boys were babies and I'd be the one who wouldn't hear a thing when they cried in the middle of the night; yet, always the caring mother, Carolyn would instantly wake and be tuned in to their softest whimpers of distress.

"General Shelton," I said, noticing that once again I'd gotten shaving cream all over the red handset. Either it was time to adjust my schedule or switch to an electric razor.

"Sir, this is Brigadier General Shyken at the NMCC calling to inform you that at approximately 0730 hours Zulu, the United States embassies at Dar es Salaam, Tanzania, and Nairobi, Kenya were simultaneously attacked by truck bombs. Damage appears to be substantial. General Zinni requests a seven A.M. conference call for intell updates."

"Roger that, General. Thank you," I said, slamming down the phone and feeling sick. Bin Laden.


An hour earlier, as I'd jogged around the predawn still of Fort Myer, I'd been mulling over the multitude of threats that were challenging me as Chairman as I helped to guide our military into the new millennium.

Saddam Hussein was contained yet driving us nuts with his disregard of the U.N.-mandated WMD inspections, and in May 1998 UNSCOM (United Nations Special Commission) inspectors found stores of propellant specific to Scud missiles and compelling evidence of VX (a nerve agent) production. (Under the terms of the cease fire agreement that ended the Gulf War [U.N. Security Council Resolution 687], weapons of mass destruction [WMDs] of any kind were prohibited in Iraq, and all missiles with a range over 150 kilometers (93 miles), as well as all research and development, support, and manufacturing facilities, were to be dismantled; and Iraq was prohibited from using, developing, constructing, or otherwise acquiring ballistic missiles over that range in the future. In the case of VX, less than a single drop was deadly—and *more than enough could fit within a single Scud missile to take out all of Tel Aviv.*)

In the former Yugoslavia, Serbian President Slobodan Milosevic's genocide of Kosovar Albanians was a situation that could no longer be ignored. His "ethnic cleansing" would eventually drive a million from their homes and kill almost a quarter of them.

The conflict between Pakistan and India was teetering precipitously close to all-out nuclear war, and the mounting political instability within Pakistan was not making me feel any better about the situation.

In Africa, one could pick almost any country and the odds were that it was on the verge of anarchy. In June we deployed forces to Senegal in response to the deteriorating situation in Guinea-Bissau, and naval forces evacuated Americans from the strife in Eritrea. In just the prior few years, similar military evacuations had been conducted in Sierra Leone, Congo (formerly Zaire), Central African Republic, Liberia, and Rwanda.

We had large-scale force-protection issues going on in Saudi Arabia as we relocated from Dhahran and Riyadh to the remote Prince Sultan Air Base following the August 1996 terrorist bombing at the Khobar Towers (Saudi Arabia), which housed military personnel. (Nineteen U.S. servicemen and one Saudi were killed, hundreds more were seriously injured.)

Even though we still had more than thirty-seven thousand troops in South Korea, the brazen rhetoric of North Korea's "supreme leader" Kim Jong-il reinforced our concerns that he was secretly developing nuclear weapons despite his having signed the 1994 Agreed Framework document, which prohibited such development. (In 2002, Kim Jong-Il's government admitted the production of nuclear weapons, justifying such production as necessary for their own "security purposes." On October 9, 2006, North Korea announced the successful detonation of an underground nuclear test.)

I jogged past the Officers' Club on Jackson Avenue and could already see the post tennis courts that were just behind our quarters.

"Morning, General," the newspaper deliveryman smiled as he drove by, tossing morning editions of the *Washington Post* from his car onto the freshly mowed lawns along the row of two-story brick officers' residences. A bundle of happy-birthday balloons still fluttered from a mailbox in front of one, a child's tricycle left on the sidewalk of another. My run past that residential stretch had become a daily ritual—one that seemed to foster a nice sense of grounding amid the worldwide turmoil. A real Norman Rockwell moment—until you looked beyond the homes and saw the base security force with their M-16 rifles at the ready.

Turning left onto Grant Avenue, I passed Joe Ralston's house, which, unlike most mornings, was already lit up like a Christmas tree; at barely 5:00 A.M. it was a good indicator that Joe was tackling some crisis that would cross my desk by the time I got in. Winding down, I strode up my driveway and bounded up the steps onto my front porch, where I paused for a moment, the early-morning wind picking up just enough to give life to the flag that I had mounted on the porch's white pillar. Even before the sun rose the view across the Potomac was spectacular; and as I soaked in the magnificence of the softly lit Capitol and Washington Monument framed by the huge oak tree on my front lawn, I thought of another threat that scared the hell out of me—mainly because, unlike any enemy we had ever faced, this one had no real geographic base, infrastructure, equipment, or headquarters that we could target. And unlike the North Koreans or Milosevic or Saddam, this menace was determined to hit us right here at home. At that moment, all I could think of was Usama bin Laden and his al-Qaeda network.

Pundits contend that we could have done more to capture bin Laden, but was that the case? Were opportunities missed? Did we drop the ball? We had fourteen UBL (bin Laden) capture-or-kill-op plans on the shelf—specific, detailed, fleshed-out, preorchestrated scenarios, ranging anywhere from forces on the ground to armed Predator strikes to TLAMs (Tomahawk Land Attack Missile—BGM 109 cruise missile)—each ready to be executed instantly once we received actionable intelligence that confirmed his whereabouts—and we revised these plans at least once a month. Preprogrammed TLAM-equipped subs were kept at the ready in the Persian Gulf for years, just awaiting word that his location had been detected. It was like we were dealing with the Disappearing Man, and it was incredibly frustrating for all of us. I once told Madeleine Albright that my strong preference was to kill bin Laden, but if somehow we ended up capturing him instead, I wanted to bring him back to Fort Bragg to be an instructor for our special-warfare classes because every step he had taken seemed to be a perfect execution of the techniques we teach our Special Operations forces to avoid capture, which is why to this day we still have not caught him.

I arrived at the Pentagon about fifteen minutes earlier than usual, just to have a full half hour to get my operations and intelligence briefings and go over the "President's Daily Brief" prior to my call with Zinni. Later in the day the National Security Council would convene—most likely with President Clinton—and we would formulate a course of action. But if it did turn out to be al-Qaeda behind the bombings, it would prove to be an elusive target.

As was so often the case, the situation in Nairobi turned out to be even worse than our preliminary reports indicated. The blast left 212 dead (twelve Americans) and more than 4,000 injured.

As for Tanzania, as awful as it was (eleven killed, eighty-five wounded), it would have been worse had it not taken place on a national holiday, when the embassy was closed. Later we would learn that this embassy was somewhat of an afterthought, but the U.S. embassy in Uganda was also supposed to be hit.

It was a solemn meeting in the Oval Office that included the President, Berger, Secretary Cohen, Secretary Albright, Director George Tenet, and Ambassador Tom Pickering (Undersecretary of State and the number-three man at the State Department, previously ambassador to Russia, India, the U.N., Israel, El Salvador, Nigeria, and Jordan). It was not a long meeting. Once George communicated his solid belief that the bombings were the work of UBL and al-Qaeda, the President was swift in his decision to retaliate. He ordered George and me to put together lists of targets that were directly tied to bin Laden, and he gave us four days to do so.

My J2 staff had already collected tons of intelligence indicating that bin Laden and the UBL organization were using Afghani camps to train— we had photos of them, signal intelligence reports, and agent reports

(HUMINT); so those camps became the primary targets I would present to the SecDef and President on behalf of the Joint Chiefs. My recommendation would be to go with TLAMs, and I'd recommend that we do so when the camps were occupied so that we could kill the maximum number of terrorists being trained there.

There was one significant problem that would have to be overcome. In order to reach Afghanistan, the missiles would have to be fired over either Iran or Pakistan—and both options presented considerable challenges. We knew that if we were to launch the missiles over Iran, the Iranians would consider it an act of war and most probably would retaliate against our ongoing operations in the Gulf region.

The situation with Pakistan was not much better. The rhetoric between India and Pakistan was at an all-time high, and with both of them having a nuclear capability, our very real concern was that even though we believed our cruise missiles would *most likely* proceed undetected as they entered Pakistani airspace and traversed the country—if they *were* picked up by Pakistani early-warning radars, the intrusion of their airspace would almost certainly be construed as inbound Indian missiles carrying nuclear tips, which would probably prompt Pakistan to unleash a "retaliatory" nuclear strike on India.

One might think that the obvious solution would have been to inform or coordinate with Pakistan up front and let them know the missiles would be ours. Under normal circumstances, that might have worked. In this case, Pakistan's national intelligence agency, the ISI (Inter-Services Intelligence), was so connected with al-Qaeda, there was no doubt that such a forewarning would go right back to UBL and his minions, and in ten minutes those camps would be more deserted than an old Western ghost town, leaving our missiles to pound sand on empty tents and vacant training facilities.

So let's review our three potential options: we could overfly Iran and risk war with Iran; we could tip off Pakistan and waste our time, energy, and taxpayers' dollars on vacant camps; or we could roll the dice and run the risk of igniting a nuclear war between India and Pakistan.

What we came up with instead was a *great* plan that would blow them all away, and it came in the form of my Vice Chairman, Joe Ralston. Just as I have always understood the importance of creating close relationships with my counterparts all over the world, Joe had been aggressively doing the same, and in this case it was his friendship with Pakistan's Chief of Defense, General Jehangir Karamat, that would save the day.

We devised a plan whereby Joe would contact Karamat and request that they meet for dinner in Islamabad under the guise of whatever creative excuse Joe would fabricate, and—unknown to the Pakistani general—the dinner would be set to coincide with the night of our attack. As sixty-six

*I spoke with General Joe Ralston about his dining with Pakistan's Chief of Staff as our sixty-six cruise missiles flew by overhead.*

TLAMs rocketed by overhead (thirteen other missiles would be launched from the Red Sea and directed toward a secondary target in Sudan), Joe would be sharing beef karahi with his good friend Jehangir—and if by some chance the missiles were detected, then and only then would he advise the chief that those missiles were ours and not Indian nukes intended to delete Pakistan from the map.

It sounded great to me, and sounded just as good to the Secretary of Defense and the President, both of whom enthusiastically signed off on it.

* * *

While we were working out the details of getting Joe into Pakistan, about ten miles northwest, at the CIA's Langley headquarters, George Tenet and his team were developing a target list of their own—with particular emphasis on Sudan, since we'd learned it was an al-Qaeda cell inside Sudan that had helped carry out the embassy attacks. The president felt we needed to send a clear signal that we were not going to tolerate that. The CIA narrowed it down to two, and recommended that we hit both of them.

The first was a Sudanese hide-tanning factory that was theoretically owned by UBL, chosen because soil samples had picked up traces of a chemical that was used to make chemical-warfare weapons; the CIA intell report stated that it was a dual-use facility.

The second was the al-Shifa pharmaceutical factory, the largest in Khartoum, Sudan, and also dual-use. George reported that samples of O-ethyl methylphosphonothioic acid (EMPTA) were clandestinely taken outside the plant. EMPTA is the precursor for the toxic VX chemical agent.

All three of these targets (al-Qaeda training camps in Afghanistan and the two plants) were presented to the President for his consideration.

It's important to take a step back and look at the process that was involved here. These intelligence reports were provided by George Tenet, Director of Central Intelligence for the CIA, based on information given to him by his own analysts. I had to believe that George, as Director of the CIA, had in place some effective means of filtering the influx of data that came into his organization. When he presented that data to me, I was basically at his mercy as far as receiving *reliable* data, as was the President. A reasonable mind would assume that if the CIA saw fit to disseminate data considered *actionable intelligence* at the presidential level, it certainly should have been verified and vetted to be accurate, but then again, as they say, *assumptions are the mother of all screw-ups.*

As such, I challenged the intell on the hide-tanning factory. Something just didn't feel right about it. Before I took this concern to the White House, I took it into the Tank to solicit the Joint Chiefs' opinions.

Not only did they concur with my trepidation, but they were perplexed as to how something with a case that weak could ever have made it that far up the ladder. (If they thought that case was weak, they should have stuck around for six more years to see the case that the same outfit gave Colin Powell to take before the United Nations.)

In the Oval Office a short while later with Secretary Cohen, Secretary Albright, and Director Tenet, I expressed the concerns of the entire Joint Chiefs, stating that we did not feel comfortable with the *age* of the samples or the *locations* from which they had been taken. The Joint Chiefs were unanimous in the opinion that in a postmortem we would have trouble justifying why we'd destroyed the tannery. The President agreed and the tannery was taken off the list.

Later that week, the CIA received a gold mine that would dramatically ratchet up the priority of our strike. An electronic intercept revealed that bin Laden and his top henchmen would be meeting on August 20 at their compound in Khost, Afghanistan—a location that was already on our hit list, but now it would become the center of our attention. They were also overheard discussing another upcoming attack, this one involving chemical weapons. It was the first time we had solid, actionable intelligence that we truly believed might afford us an opportunity to take out bin Laden, and in this case we prayed it would be *before* the devastation a chemical attack would produce. The President was fired up, as were we all.

> *Indeed, I did have a relationship with Ms. Lewinsky that was not appropriate. In fact, it was wrong. It constituted a critical lapse in judgment and a personal failure on my part for which I am solely and completely responsible.*

It was only a few days after we received the bin Laden intercept that President Clinton spent the day testifying before Ken Starr's grand jury. On the night of August 17, he made a live speech to the nation. What amazed me was that the entire time this Starr investigation was going on, the President was deeply involved in the al-Qaeda situation and our upcoming missile strikes—yet he never lost focus and never appeared distracted in any way; it was always as if the absolute only thing on his mind was the successful execution of our operation. I had never seen anything like it.

———

On the morning of August 20, the President gave the order to execute, and the gyros on seventy-nine TLAMs started to spin. In six hours, give or take, each of their one-thousand-pound warheads would impact their targets.

———

On the night of the attack, Joe Ralston was thoroughly enjoying his dinner with General Karamat as those eighteen-feet-long TLAMs whizzed over Pakistani airspace at 550 miles per hour on their ninety-minute flight to the Afghanistan targets. Joe was fully prepared to intercede in the event that somebody came running in to inform his Pakistani host about the missiles—but that never happened. Our engineers had programmed those missiles to travel at such a low altitude, they were literally flying under the radar.

At around 10:30 P.M., Joe thanked the general profusely, told him how great it was to see him, and, along with his security team, departed. Most likely, by the time the warheads lit up the eastern Afghanistan night sky over Khost, Joe's Air Force 757 was already in the air and heading home.

---

--------
PAKISTAN
--------

8.    (C) IN THE WAKE OF REPORTS FROM A NUMBER OF SOURCES DURING
THE PAST TWO DAYS THAT VC JCS GEN JOHN RALSTON WAS IN PAKISTAN
MEETING SENIOR GOP MILITARY LEADERS DURING THE EVENING OF AUGUST
20, THE GOP MILITARY PRESS OFFICE (INTERSERVICES PUBLIC RELATIONS
DIRECTORATE) RELEASED ITS OWN OFFICIAL STATEMENT ON HIS PRESENCE
THE EVENING OF THE AIR STRIKES.  THE STATEMENT IS CLEARLY AIMED
AT ACCOUNTING FOR THE ALLEGED PRESENCE OF GEN RALSTON IN PAKISTAN
ON THE EVENING OF THE NIGHT IN QUESTION IN A WAY THAT SEEMS
PLAUSIBLE, YET MAKES CLEAR THAT THE PAKISTANI GOVERNMENT HAD NO
FOREKNOWLEDGE OF OR CONDONED IN ANY WAY THE U.S. ATTACK.

9.    (U) ACCORDING TO THE STATEMENT (TEXT REPORTED REFTEL) GEN
RALSTON REQUESTED PERMISSION TO MAKE A BRIEF STOPOVER AT
ISLAMABAD AIRPORT ON AUGUST 20 IN RESPONSE TO PAKISTANI INQUIRIES
TO CENTCOM ABOUT THE PRESENCE OF U.S. SHIPS IN INTERNATIONAL
WATERS OFF THE PAKISTAN COAST.  RALSTON ARRIVED AT 7:30 PM AND
DEPARTED AT 10:30 PM. GEN RALSTON REPORTEDLY TOLD HIS PAKISTANI
MILITARY INTERLOCUTOR, ARMY CHIEF OF STAFF KARAMAT, THAT THE
SHIPS IN QUESTION HAD NOTHING TO DO WITH PAKISTAN AND WERE
PROBABLY THERE FOR ACTION BEING CONTEMPLATED AGAINST TERRORIST
CAMPS IN AFGHANISTAN.  THE STATEMENT GOES ON TO SAY THAT GENERAL
KARAMAT BROUGHT THE MATTER IMMEDIATELY TO THE ATTENTION OF THE
                        CONFIDENTIAL

PAGE 04        ISLAMA  06448  02 OF 03  261517Z
PRIME MINISTER WHILE ALSO INDICATING TO GEN RALSTON THAT SUCH AN
ACTION BY THE U.S. WAS UNWARRANTED.  SINCE THE ATTACK CAME THAT
VERY NIGHT, THE STATEMENT CONCLUDES THAT GEN RALSTON HAD ARRANGED
TO BE IN PAKISTAN SO THAT, IF THE ATTACK WAS DETECTED BY
PAKISTANI AIR DEFENSES, HE WOULD BE IN A POSITION TO CLARIFY WHAT
WAS TAKING PLACE.

Current Class: CONFIDENTIAL

# UNCLASSIFIED

*August 26, 1998 Telex from U.S. Ambassador Islamabad to Secretary of State Albright regarding General Ralston's visit with Pakistan's General Karamat.*

* * *

Those attacks destroyed the camps and took out nearly fifty buildings plus a row of huts that apparently housed top al-Qaeda leaders, and they killed between thirty-five and forty terrorists in the camps. Later on we would learn that we had missed bin Laden by only about an hour, but to me a near miss was like being just a little bit pregnant—it's either yes or no, with nothing in between. It seemed like we were always barely missing him, but that did not keep us from trying—and for the first time, the public was really made aware of Usama bin Laden and the tremendous threat he posed.

That night, President Clinton made another live address to the nation.

### ADDRESS TO THE NATION BY THE PRESIDENT
[selected segments]
The Oval Office, August 20, 1998, 5:32pm EDT

THE PRESIDENT: Today I ordered our Armed Forces to strike at terrorist-related facilities in Afghanistan and Sudan because of the imminent threat they presented to our national security.

Our target was terror. Our mission was clear—to strike at the network of radical groups affiliated with and funded by Osama bin Laden, perhaps the preeminent organizer and financier of international terrorism in the world today.

A few months ago, and again this week, bin Laden publicly vowed to wage a terrorist war against America, saying—and I quote—"We do not differentiate between those dressed in military uniforms and civilians. They're all targets. Their mission is murder and their history is bloody."

With compelling evidence that the bin Laden network of terrorist groups was planning to mount further attacks against Americans and other freedom-loving people, I decided America must act.

Earlier today, the United States carried out simultaneous strikes against terrorist facilities and infrastructure in Afghanistan. Our forces targeted one of the most active terrorist bases in the world. It contained key elements of the bin Laden network's infrastructure and has served as a training camp for literally thousands of terrorists from around the globe. We have reason to believe that a gathering of key terrorist leaders was to take place there today, thus underscoring the urgency of our actions.

America is and will remain a target of terrorists precisely because we are leaders; because we act to advance peace, democracy and basic human values; because we're the most open society on Earth; and because, as we have shown yet again, we take an uncompromising stand against terrorism.

But of this I am also sure. The risks from inaction to America and the world would be far greater than action, for that would embolden our enemies, leaving their ability and their willingness to strike us intact. In this case, we knew before our attack that these groups already had planned further actions against us and others.

Let our actions today send this message loud and clear: There are no expendable American targets. There will be no sanctuary for terrorists. We will defend our people, our interests and our values. We will persist and we will prevail.

As for the al-Shifa pharmaceutical plant, it was a highly successful strike from a military perspective—we completely leveled it. But then the armchair quarterbacks started in with their criticism, including comments like how we had deprived those poor Sudanese babies and old people their aspirin and medicine, and how everyone except us "American baby killers" knew that that plant was never used for any kind of weapons manufacture. . . . The criticism was intense, but we brushed it off. America could not afford to stand idly by while terrorists planned and carried out attacks against America or its friends or allies.

Then the intell started to fade on us, and it turned out that this CIA intelligence had *not* really been collected at the pharmaceutical plant, but rather *three hundred yards away from it*. And now—by the way—the quarter teaspoon of soil sample turned out to have been collected *two years* earlier. Suddenly the whole thing just fell apart. It was not at all the type of solid intell that George had presented to us in the Situation Room or to the President in the Oval. It was a very weak case, and those "outrageous" comments about the aspirin and medicine didn't sound so outrageous anymore. What's the point of an overwhelming military success when the intelligence starts crumbling like that? It almost became counterproductive in that we did such a great job but in the end found ourselves having to ask, *What was it that we really destroyed?*

This is exactly what we always worried about, and why, ever since I was a captain in Vietnam, I always tended to err on the side of conservativism when it came to target selection, intelligence verification, and minimization of collateral damage—and I always stressed to those under my command that the three most important considerations before pulling that trigger were intelligence, intelligence, and intelligence. You have to consider how it will look in the postmortem, because they *will* go back and dissect every target of every operation. But more important, it's a matter of doing what's right. What sane person wants to take an innocent life or needlessly destroy property? However, unless we receive accurate, timely intelligence, that's exactly what we run the risk of doing.

* * *

This was a particularly busy time for me as I was deeply involved in preparing for the congressional budget hearings in which I would address our readiness deficits and present the case for the additional $155 billion. Throughout September I had strategic one-on-one meetings with the President, congressmen, and senators; plus I had many other unrelated testimonies before both the Senate and House Armed Services committees.

There were NATO Defense Ministerials to attend overseas and a handful of other summits for international Chiefs of Defense.

I tried my best to make appearances at major changes of command and other important ceremonies; and these could just as easily take place at EUCOM (U.S. European Command) in Stuttgart as they could on the Pentagon's parade ground outside my office.

I felt it essential to accommodate as many requests for press appearances as my schedule would allow, and during this period I frequently appeared on each of the networks' nightly news broadcasts, plus *Face the Nation, This Week with Sam Donaldson and Cokie Roberts, Meet the Press, Late Edition, Larry King Live*, and *Nightline.*

There were photo sessions for *Vanity Fair* and *Parade* magazine and newspaper interviews for hundreds of local and international publications.

During this short window, it seemed like I spent as much time shuttling back and forth on an Air Force 757 as I did on the ground, including trips to Australia, Bosnia, Jordan, Bahrain, Oman, Denmark, Norway, Portugal, Spain, Korea, Saudi Arabia, Thailand, Qatar, England, Belgium, and Poland. If only the Air Force awarded frequent-flier miles.

---

Fast forward to a Sunday afternoon in 2000 when Carolyn and I were about halfway down Interstate 95 on our way to the post exchange in Quantico, Virginia. I was driving myself since on weekends I'd prefer to use my personal car—against the advice of my Secret Service special agent son, Jon, and my security detail, who would constantly say I was just asking for trouble going out without my security team, and without my armored car. *You're the highest-ranking member of our military, which makes you a prime target,* they would warn me. The way I looked at it regarding security, if even I didn't know where I was going until I got ready to go, how was a terrorist going to track me? I was never going to follow any given patterns, and I was wearing my civilian clothes—so, in my mind, that small amount of privacy was well worth the risk.

Most likely Carolyn was making some comment about how nice it was to finally spend a day together when suddenly I got a call from the DDO (Deputy Director of Operations). "Sir, the CIA has notified me that they have just located Usama bin Laden."

I disconnected, then gave Carolyn fair warning as I swerved across three lanes to make the exit. "Hold on, now." You may have heard the term *burning rubber,* but it's true. I screeched to a quick stop at the top of the ramp and the acrid stench blasted in though the vents. "I know, I shoulda used my signal," I confided to Carolyn as I laid more tracks, spinning around to head back to the Pentagon. By the time the DDO connected me with General Zinni, I had to be going well over a hundred.

"Spin 'em up, Tony," I told him, referring to the cruise missiles I wanted to be ready to launch the split second the President gave the order. With each near miss, that adrenaline-fueled craving to *nail him next time* got stronger.

I fully understood that if they did have a real sighting, we'd have to move like greased lightning and jump-start those guys in the Persian Gulf who had the capabilities to hit him. I did *not* want this to be another tally in the close-call column. I pinned the accelerator to the floorboard, searching in vain for a policeman to provide an escort, and wishing that I *had* been driven in the armored Cadillac, since it was fully equipped with emergency lights and a siren.

At the Pentagon, I leaped from the car and darted inside. I had arranged to meet my driver, who would transport me to the White House in thirty minutes, plenty of time for my J2 and intell team to give me the full brief before I departed for Pennsylvania Avenue. Carolyn headed back to Fort Myer. So much for a quiet Sunday afternoon together.

By the time I stepped into the White House Situation Room, I had already reviewed the photos, been apprised of the source of the tip (which is generally the most highly classified of the data—in this case, it was a local tribesman), so I felt fully prepared when I entered to find that the rest of the team had arrived—Berger, Albright, Cohen, Tenet—although not the President. Unlike President Bush when he took office, President Clinton preferred to have his National Security Advisor, Sandy Berger, chair the NSC meetings and personally brief him upon their conclusion.

George started in with his brief and he was convinced that we finally had him—a confirmed report from a reliable source that two to three hours ago, UBL was under observation at his compound in Kandahar.

When George finished his accelerated presentation, both he and Albright looked at Secretary Cohen and me as if it went without saying that we had joined their bandwagon.

Secretary Cohen immediately challenged the reliability and timeliness of the information. George indicated that the source had been reliable in the past but because they'd had to move away to communicate with their CIA contact, the information was probably three hours old. Mentally I added ninety minutes, the approximate flight time of the TLAMs.

"I've gotta say I don't see it that way, George," I said, disappointed that I didn't share the elation in the room, yet nonetheless confident in my position. I told the group that I had just gotten off the phone with General Zinni and our concerns were the same. "Take a look at these photos. You've got a large number of families in there—women and children. What happens if by the time the TLAMs get there, the big guy is long gone and we end up killing a bunch of women and children? If that happens, as far as I'm concerned we have become terrorists ourselves. As you know, we've already started ramping up, but it's still another two hours before the missiles could strike, and if bin Laden follows his normal modus operandi, he'll be long gone."

"I agree," said Cohen. There was a brief discussion led by Sandy Berger, which ended with an obvious consensus that the risk was too high. UBL would live to see another day.

With that George closed his portfolio, obviously frustrated by the situation but in no way angry at any of us. "I'm going back to my son's lacrosse game," he said as he walked out the door.

Later, we would learn from the same source that if we had fired the TLAMs, we would have *missed* UBL by about an hour. That having been the case, the Monday-morning quarterbacking would still be going on today.

And that scenario continues to play out to this day. We kept TLAM-equipped submarines in the Persian Gulf through the day I retired, but that elusive son of a bitch continued to slip through our fingers. It was not for our lack of trying.

————

Every bureaucracy needs someone to shake things up, and in the case of both the Clinton and Bush administrations, Richard Clarke, later dubbed the "counterterrorism czar," did a great job of it. I have always had a great deal of respect for Dick, but frequently he would come in from watching a *Rambo* movie or something and present some wild-haired idea that would brief well—but when you looked at the reality of it, of what it would really take to pull it off, it was far better suited for an episode of *NCIS* than a real-life situation in which lives were on the line.

I can't count the number of times Dick would come up with bits of intell related to bin Laden combined with a wild idea of how we might get him. While I applauded his enthusiasm, he frequently failed to connect it to capability.

Dick did not want to be bothered with details, such as the fact that helicopters can fly for only two hours before they crash for lack of fuel,

notwithstanding the fact that in order to travel the route that he was proposing, the aircraft would have to make a nine-hour flight and would require two to three midair refuelings just to get there. What would happen
if one of them got shot down or crashed or had a mechanical problem?
Were we just supposed to forget their crews and leave them stranded?
These were standard considerations on each and every mission—call it War
Fighting 101—but details like that were miles beneath Dick's radar screen.

All too often, I was forced to add reality to Dick's ideas. "Dick, you're
failing to take into account that we're going to need a search-and-rescue
capability in case one of these pilots goes down, and what about those poor
guys on the ground? True, they're just a small element, but don't you think
you should have some kind of firepower that they can call on—like an AC-
130? Which, by the way, requires somehow getting into theater, and once it's
there it will require refueling of its own from the Combat Talons . . ." and a
whole host of other considerations that he had no interest in hearing about.

These would be very broad, very overall concepts—and creative ones
that I really wished we could utilize. He would take them to Sandy Berger
or give them to Cohen or me and ask, *Why can't you do this?* And, *Are
you sure you can't do that?*

We felt bad because these ideas briefed very well, and frankly you
knew some of them were going to catch the attention of the President, but
when you got into the details of what it would take to pull them off, they
were far more complicated than a military neophyte or wannabe understands. You cannot just snap your fingers and make it all happen, as many
times as I had wished it were that easy.

Another one of his ideas involved something about his knowing that UBL
was going to escape out of Afghanistan via a commercial aircraft that
would fly from Kabul to Chechnya. He had no idea when this would
happen—just that "at some point" it would. So his plan was for us to
maintain aircraft on strip alert in the region full-time that would be capable of quickly launching, intercepting, and shooting down the commercial aircraft that bin Laden might be on.

Could we do it? Of course. It was well within the realm of possibility
for us to keep somebody on strip alert on either a carrier or land base. But
who is going to sign the order that says shoot down a commercial carrier
in international airspace based on intell that bin Laden *might* be on that
plane? I can tell you somebody who would *not* ever give that order short
of receiving it in writing from the Secretary of Defense or the White
House, and his name is Shelton. Dick just took it as a *given* that we would
intentionally kill the crew and all those passengers since we would also be
killing bin Laden. We thought it was a harebrained scheme, since the
chance of our receiving reliable and timely info of this nature was nil.

As time went on I ended up just turning them over to my legal counsel for their analysis, because no operation goes forward without their blessing—and rightfully so. They would look at the legal implication of shooting down a commercial aircraft in international airspace, and let's not even go to the part about intentionally killing 150 innocent civilians just to get the one guy. But we always examined each idea in great detail. Dick was very proactive, aggressive, and insistent that UBL was going to do this or that. It wasted a lot of time that would have been better spent on realistic considerations.

My personal belief was that George Tenet was doing the best he could as Director of Intelligence for the CIA, especially considering the tremendous budget cuts the Agency was hit with in the midnineties. Still, many times I found that the enthusiasm of the Agency's paramilitary operators outweighed their actual capabilities.

There were multiple occasions in which the CIA would propose a combined operation consisting of their paramilitary forces working hand in hand with our counterterrorist (JSOC) teams. From my experience in those types of operations, I was always adamantly opposed to this arrangement. While I remained open to working with them, I would agree to do so only if we *segmented* the op in such a way that our operators could not be blamed for a failure that took place on their end. For the most part I found their people to be enthusiastic, patriotic, good Americans who certainly wanted to succeed, yet in many cases it seemed that they did not have the types of well-trained forces with *the right stuff* to actually carry it off.

Once, they came to me with intell indicating that at a given time, a white Nissan packed with high-value terrorists would be traveling from one place to another in Bosnia, and at some point they would stop their car at a river, board a ferry to get across it, then continue on through a rather mountainous region and head toward Sarajevo. It was presented as solid, confirmed intelligence (multiple sources/cross-verified) that we could take to the bank. This particular operation was so straightforward—so they said—that there wasn't a chance in the world anything could go wrong.

They proposed we combine our forces to form a single team to capture or kill these individuals, an idea that I rejected flat out. I countered that if we maintained the integrity of our own teams, I would consider working with them, but only if it was structured that their people carried out their assigned tasks and my operators would do ours. Of course, we would both be there to protect each other's back, that goes without saying—but operationally we would function separately. After a great deal of debate, they agreed, with the understanding that they would develop the plan.

What they came back with was that their team would capture or kill the suspects as they started to leave the river site, and at that point our forces would come in and pick them up. Their backup plan was that in the unlikely event that something went wrong and the CIA team was not successful at the river, our forces would intercept the terrorists farther up the road. It was really just presenting two different options for the capture or kill, the first being the total responsibility of the CIA, the second being entirely on our shoulders—both separate, both segmented, both fine with me, so I agreed.

Following a few rehearsals, we flew the Delta team from Fort Bragg to Tuzla, our main operating base in Bosnia, and we contacted the CIA to indicate that we were on scene and good to go. They confirmed that everything was set on their end.

The evening rolled around and our team deployed and moved into their hidden positions along the road leading to Sarajevo. Right on cue, our operators' radios came to life with the voice of the CIA-team leader. "Tango Blue, this is Anteater. The car is coming but our people are *not* in position. Repeat *not* in position." Needless to say, we executed as planned and it was a successful operation—one carload of terrorists that would not be blowing up any embassies. But the CIA never showed up. Hard to believe.

While I commend the Agency for coming through with excellent actionable intelligence in this case (the terrorists showed up where they were supposed to, when they were supposed to), it's hard to believe that the CIA paramilitary division could get away with that level of professional incompetence. These operations deal with matters of life and death and there's no room for ineptitude. Heads should have rolled right and left— and maybe they did. But I find it highly unlikely, since situations like that seemed the rule rather than the exception, which underscores why I insisted on operational segmentation.

Around the time of my retirement I noticed that the situation was starting to improve, and the Agency's Jawbreaker team in Afghanistan right after 9/11 did great work with the Northern Alliance, and in fact worked quite well with our teams. They certainly were huge assets to have, since they allowed our teams to hit the ground running with relationships they had already developed with the Northern Alliance, and you couldn't ask for anything better than that. It was a perfect scenario that demonstrated how we *could* work together, but I believe a great deal of that had to do with the caliber of that particular team—and hopefully the CIA has seen fit to raise the bar to that level overall. During my time, however, that was far from the case in snatch missions, ambushes, and such.

———

Many people wonder why at times the military does not take a certain action, or why when they do take action they hit the wrong target. The fact is, the military is entirely dependent upon the intelligence it receives in order to do its targeting, its strikes, its raids, and any other similar military action. One third of all the military working in the Washington area work for intell agencies. DIA, NSA, CIA—the list goes on. Army, Air Force, Navy—they all have their own intell centers and there is a great effort put into it—a worthwhile effort—but in the end, our operational military actions are only as good as the intelligence that supports them.

During the Kosovo operation, we had developed a list of *do not strike* targets—these are key positions that we do not want to hit either directly or with collateral damage. If our hitting a certain building would result in blowing out its windows and killing everybody in the embassy or hospital or orphanage next door, then we don't want to hit that building, and it should be on our do-not-strike list.

In the case of embassies, it was the responsibility of the U.S. State Department to provide the CIA and the military with lists of all the embassies in every country around the world; it was also their responsibility to keep that list current and to advise our military intelligence division of any updates or revisions. In the case of an ongoing conflict—a battle zone—we vetted these lists with the State Department prior to any attack, just to double-check that the information we were provided was both correct and current. Every no-strike target was identified on our maps with bright red circles, so once we were given the data, it was hard to miss.


During our operations in Belgrade, we had every embassy marked on a map, and each one that was indicated on the no-strike list had been circled. One of our strategic targets was the Yugoslav Federal Directorate of Supply and Procurement (FDSP)—basically it was a big military warehouse—but it housed and shipped missile parts to rogue nations such as Iraq and Libya and also served as the headquarters for Yugoslav Army procurement. It was an important target that we wanted to annihilate.

We were highly successful in that we hit the building we *thought* was the FDSP, but as it turned out, it was actually the Chinese embassy—and the bombing ended up killing three civilians and injuring twenty. Needless to say, it also created quite an international incident.

While watching CNN, we originally found out that we had mistakenly hit the wrong building and shortly thereafter confirmation came from a defense attaché who had just come back from Serbia and called in to the Pentagon to report that the CNN report was correct—the Chinese embassy had, in fact, moved from their old building (which was on our maps) into the one that we had hit. We had made a mistake in targeting because we were unaware that it was the embassy, although we did successfully hit the building we'd intended to hit.

The irony is that shortly thereafter, we sent the same list back to the

State Department and asked them to revalidate it and reconfirm where all the embassies were located, and the list we got back still indicated that the Chinese embassy was located in the old building they had long since moved out of, and it failed to indicate any problem whatsoever with our targeting the site that we had just struck. Still no entry that the Chinese embassy was located there. Once again, another indication of the deadly importance of accurate intelligence.

--------

So this all comes full circle, right back to the question of whether there was anything else we could have done to facilitate the capture of UBL and take down al-Qaeda. My answer is a resounding *yes*.

While I've expressed my frustration in dealing with an organization without a geographic base, the same *cannot* be said of the government that was harboring him—in this case the Taliban, the Sunni Islamist political movement that governed Afghanistan from 1996 until they were removed from power in late 2001 during Operation Enduring Freedom.

Under the leadership of Mullah Mohammed Omar, the Taliban were the controlling government in Afghanistan; and they were the ones who were providing sanctuary for Usama bin Laden and the al-Qaeda organization. They allowed them to train there, to live there, and basically they were part of each other's operations. Al-Qaeda–trained fighters were integrated with the Taliban army; and it was an al-Qaeda suicide bomber who, on September 9, 2001, solidified the Taliban's political position by assassinating their primary military opponent, Northern Alliance leader Ahmad Shah Massoud. In return, the Taliban provided bin Laden and his followers a safe haven, disregarding United States government requests for extradition.

Finding appropriate targets to bomb was *not* a problem in the case of the Taliban. Since they operated with an organized infrastructure, it was easy. They had buildings and government offices, and Omar operated right out of the official Capitol in downtown Kabul. We had specific coordinates for his Kandahar residence, too. By the time we did finally bomb it (after I retired in October 2001), he was long gone and has been in hiding ever since. The ten-million-dollar reward for information leading to his capture hasn't seemed to do any good, either. We had plenty of opportunities to get him, but a conscious choice was made not to do so. The obvious question becomes, *Why?* The answer is not one that can found on either the civilian or military floors of the Pentagon, but rather across the river in Foggy Bottom.

Following both the embassy bombings of 1998 and the subsequent bombing of the USS *Cole* in October 2000, Secretary Cohen and I made impassioned pleas to go after the Taliban—their headquarters, their infrastructure. We knew that we had the ability to totally take them out of business, so to speak. What we had was bin Laden and his terrorist organization, which the Taliban's ruling leadership (Mullah Omar) was allowing to operate at will—to live there, train there, and conduct terrorist operations there. The CIA confirmed that they were doing it, and everybody in the National Security Council knew it.

Both times that Secretary Cohen and I made our pleas, Secretary of State Albright pushed back and said, *No, the Taliban constitutes a legitimate sovereign government and we need to respect that—we need to démarche them first and give them a chance to correct their ways.*

I don't care what logo is embossed on the letterhead, as far as I'm concerned a démarche is basically a letter of reprimand, a slap on the wrist telling them that *we believe you are supporting terrorism and we are not going to put up with it any longer.* According to Albright, what Cohen and I were suggesting was declaring war on a nation-state, and her position was that despite Tenet's evidence to the contrary, the Taliban weren't the ones who were attacking us, that was bin Laden—and this all played out not ten seconds after George Tenet had tracked through exactly how bin Laden and the Taliban were working hand in hand.

I could not grasp how these diplomats could let these murderers off the hook with a letter from the principal's office. To my way of thinking, the démarche should have been delivered to Mullah Omar first class, up his ass, on the warhead of a TLAM missile.

Perhaps Josephus Daniels, a fellow North Carolinian, summed it up best when he was the Secretary of the Navy during World War I. Daniels defined an army as *a body of men assembled to rectify the mistakes of the diplomats.* My guess is that he had just left an NSC meeting in which his Secretary of State had threatened to démarche the Kaiser.

———

Since May 1998 it had seemed like every day would bring with it another crisis in Iraq, and Saddam was manipulating the UNSCOM weapons inspectors more effectively than Edgar Bergen did Charlie McCarthy. It was uncanny how he knew just how far he could push before President Clinton would take no more, but we all knew it would come to a head sooner rather than later. By the end of October, it had reached that point. The weapons inspectors could not do their jobs, so once again they prepared to leave the country.

The President had decided that rather than merely inflict punitive damage, our goal would be to achieve militarily what Richard Butler and the weapons inspectors had been unable to accomplish diplomatically—destroy Saddam's WMDs—a worthwhile objective, but one that was almost impossible to realize with air strikes alone; the WMDs were too

easy to hide. What we *could* do, however, was set back his WMD program a few years by destroying its infrastructure and means of delivery,
and this became our objective. We had solid intell on the location of his
delivery systems (missiles), research-and-development labs, manufacturing facilities (high-tolerance milling equipment and nuclear centrifuges),
intelligence and security forces, and Ba'ath party headquarters (center of
command-and-control elements).

Secretary Cohen and I discussed this at length and determined that it
was best to task General Zinni with developing two diverse plans of
attack—one a lighter option, the other much more intense.

As always, Tony Zinni, Commander in Chief, U.S. Central Command
(CINC CENTCOM) was on top of it and came up with two great plans.
There was little doubt that the larger option would inflict more damage,
*but* it was far more involved logistically and would take a great deal more
time to execute. To put things into perspective, neither plan was anywhere near the scale of the Gulf War, but our intention was to take out
Saddam's WMD program, not to remove him from power and take over
the whole country.

I invited Tony to fly to D.C. and join us for a Tank session so that he
could bounce both options off the Joint Chiefs, and he enthusiastically
did so on November 7, 1998.

Short, stocky, and tough as nails, Tony Zinni was never one to be subtle
about anything, and he didn't pull any punches on which option he preferred. The consummate marine stepped up to the seven flags just beyond
the head of the long conference table and turned to face the rows of generals and admirals. "While I can live with either plan, I'm certain you will
agree that *heavy* is the only way to go. If we're going to *hit* him, we should
*hit* him," he declared, capping the statement by pounding his fist on the
table.

He went on to track through each option, and when he was finished
with his presentation I called for a vote. The tally came in at four to
two . . . in favor of the *lighter* approach. Tony was surprised, and somewhat miffed that the vote was counter to his recommendation. The last
thing he'd expected when he flew up from Tampa was to find himself at
odds with the Joint Chiefs. While all parties were respectful, it was obvious that a discomfort fell over both sides of the room.

In addition to my responsibilities as military strategist, fiscal adminis-
trator, and guardian of the well-being of our troops, there were times
when I felt that it would be more appropriate to turn in my Army greens
for a striped referee shirt, and this was one of them. We adjourned and
Tony and I continued our conversation privately in my office.

"I understand they know their stuff but they were *out of line*," he began. "Nobody values their input more than I, you know that, General.
Hell, anything for a better plan . . . but in the end, *I'm* the commander

and push comes to shove it's *my* call, not theirs—and I was stabbed in the back with that damn vote."

While I've always been a staunch advocate of combatant commanders taking full advantage of the tremendous experience and knowledge of the Joint Chiefs (and how much better it might have played out had Tommy Franks "read that memo" instead of disregarding the Joint Chiefs and dealing directly with Rumsfeld), I was also a vigorous proponent of supporting the CINCs whenever I could. "Sounds to me like this one's best served by you presenting directly to the President and let him make the call," I suggested. "What do you think?" He agreed, and really appreciated the suggestion. His presentation was set for the following day at Camp David.

With Tony it was easy, and on those very few occasions when we've disagreed, we've respected each other and recognized that the eventual outcome of our battling it out would almost always be an *improved* plan anyway. The reality was that my position was that of *adviser,* and, per Title 10, the ultimate decision would be the President's, based on a recommendation from the CINC and the Secretary of Defense—although I never shied away from taking full advantage of my obligation to advise.

The Camp David meeting led to an exceedingly effective battle plan that was a combination of the two options. It would unfold as Operation Desert Viper. President Clinton signed the orders, and the assets began to move into the area.

In operations such as these, it was almost impossible to maintain the element of surprise, particularly when our plan entailed bringing 230 aircraft and an entire aircraft carrier battle group into the theater. (Fifteen ships would be deployed as part of the USS *Dwight Eisenhower* group.) Generally, by the time we had done so, Saddam had hidden most of the assets we'd targeted for destruction, and then eased them back to their operational locations in the weeks ahead.

This one played out only slightly differently. With the TLAMS preprogrammed and less than ten minutes to launch, Saddam backed down and agreed to let the inspectors back in—for the umpteenth time. The President called off the attack, and the cycle would continue. There was no doubt in my mind who was winning this game of three-card monte.

"Dammit, he did it again," I vented to Zinni over my secure hotline to his CENTCOM headquarters in Tampa, frustrated that irrespective of whether or not Saddam backed down, our intell confirmed that once again he had already moved his missiles and equipment out of harm's way. "It's getting old and there's got to be a better way."

"Couldn't agree with you more," the burly commander said. "Doesn't take The Amazing Kreskin to figure out that the ninety-thousand-ton carrier knockin' at your door is not dropping in to deliver take-out baba ghanoush."

We both laughed, but that in no way minimized the significance of our discussion. It was more a reflection of how our personal friendship allowed for a more informal interplay than most. "We need to catch him with his pants down. Lull him into a false sense of security, then blast his ass. I understand it's probably well beyond your tiny Semper Fi ability to comprehend," I chided him, "but think *Special Ops*. We've got to be sly, like a fox. In fact, we ought to call it Operation Desert Fox."

We went on to discuss specifics, and with Tony at the helm, Operation Desert Fox would become the most successful Iraqi operation since the Gulf War—but it would not be without extreme controversies.

Carolyn had moved into the adjoining First Lady's Room, and it's a good thing it was so spacious. Reminiscent of the scene in Miracle on 34th Street where the post office delivered sacks upon sacks of mail to "Santa Claus" in the courtroom, I was receiving literally thousands of get-well cards and letters from all over the world—and Carolyn's suite became her office to handle all that mail. Many were from kings, prime ministers, princes, and other heads of state; yet many more were hand-made cards drawn by elementary-school children. I was bowled over by the outpouring of concern and prayers for my recovery, and until that point I'd had no idea of the number of lives I had touched. It could not have been more humbling—or more motivating. I still feel bad that I was unable to answer the vast majority of those great wishes, but that in no way diminishes how much I appreciated them. I still meet people today who tell me they prayed for me.

While I continued to make strides, I found myself utterly exhausted after each of Zack's sessions; and Carolyn still had to restrict my visitation. There were some that we allowed to make short visits. These included Dick Myers, Eric Shinseki, Jack Keane, Jordan's King Abdullah, and our close friend Connie Stevens—who, coincidentally, arrived at the same time as President Clinton. This would be the second meeting with the President that I anticipated running only fifteen minutes, but before I knew it more than an hour had passed. (The first, of course, had resulted in my being selected as Chairman.)

All seemed to be progressing well—until the morning of April 7, when I experienced incredible abdominal pain. In keeping with my style, I did my best to tough it out, and lasted through the morning. By afternoon the pain was excruciating to the point where I was unable to breathe properly. A team of doctors and nurses was quick to respond. They surrounded me and fired off questions while performing various physical exams. Cutting through it all, I heard a brusque voice call out from the doorway, "Clear the way." Like the waters of the Red Sea, the gaggle of medical staff parted and in walked a tough, stocky firebrand who was chief of surgery, Colonel Mary Maniscalco-Theberge—or Dr. Mary, as we called her. "What's your pain level?" she asked.

*"About a seven point five," I answered.*

*"If he's telling you it's seven point five, it's probably more like twelve," one of the nurses chimed in. "The general doesn't complain about a thing." Dr. Mary nodded and continued her exam, then asked me a few more questions. Midway through one of them, I winced—it felt like I had just been stabbed.*

*"Get him to MRI, stat," she commanded. "The general has an aneurysm."*

*The diagnosis was like some special code that kicked everybody into hyperdrive. They could not get me onto a gurney fast enough—and I felt more like a NASCAR driver than a hospital patient as they sped me down that hallway. It's no wonder—if the aneurysm burst, most likely I would die.*

*There's a joke at Walter Reed that the last thing a patient sees before he dies is the row of flashing lights in the hallway outside surgery (since the ward staff would prefer the patient die in surgery instead of under their watch)—and it was that row of lights that I saw before I was overcome with the final stabbing pain.*

*Chapter Fifteen* ★★★★

# WAG THE DOG

December 1998

President Clinton's impeachment debate was set to take place on December 17, 1998. His only chance of political survival was in creating a distraction, an event of such magnitude that it would swing the spotlight away from the hearings—something like a war.

As if taking a page right out of Barry Levinson's 1997 film *Wag the Dog,* the President instructed Secretary Cohen and me to set the wheels in motion to bomb Iraq—massive strikes of such scope that TV networks would have no choice but to preempt the hearings with live feeds from Baghdad as the city was destroyed.

There was only one problem. Despite the torrent of conservatives' accusations that Clinton had orchestrated his own personal *Wag the Dog* by ordering the bombings to begin on Impeachment Day, *there was not one scrap of truth to it.*

In the movie *Wag the Dog,* Dustin Hoffman was hired to fabricate a war in order to divert attention from the sexual indiscretions of the President, and that's exactly what Secretary Cohen and I believed that President Clinton was about to be accused of orchestrating with our impending bombing of Iraq. Here's what really happened:

Throughout late November and early December 1998, Iraq continued to fire at our planes as we enforced the U.N.-mandated no-fly zone. We also had solid intelligence that the Iraqis were developing illegal missiles with parts supplied by both North Korea and Iran, missiles with a range greater than the 150-kilometer limit to which they were entitled, which posed direct threats to our friends in the region as well as our own troops in the south.

The U.N. inspectors had also just completed their work and found numerous red flags that demanded immediate attention.

Secretary Cohen and I worked with the Joint Staff to devise a plan to hit Iraq with 350 cruise missiles and 700 air sorties intended to take out their missile-milling plants, production facilities, delivery capabilities, and other key targets, including the Iraqi intelligence headquarters and Ministry of Defense.

As I packed for the White House to present the idea to Sandy Berger, Vice Admiral Scott Redd, my three-star J5 (Director of Strategic Plans and Policy—and a Fulbright scholar) felt compelled to laugh at my naïveté, warning me that I'd never get support for a strike anywhere near that big. Scott had been on the Joint Staff a lot longer than I had been Chairman, and he was a bright, sharp officer whose opinion I respected, but in this case I was confident that I could persuade the President to authorize far more than the ten to fifteen TLAMs Scott felt was all I could get.

When I returned from the White House a few hours later, my first stop was Scott's office. "You were right," I told him. "The President did not authorize the three hundred fifty TLAMs and seven hundred sorties that I suggested." Scott looked up with an I-told-you-so expression, which faded as I reported that the President had voluntarily *bumped up my request* to four hundred TLAMS and eight hundred sorties so that we could take out our alternate sites as well as the primary ones. Scott retired from the military a few days later, but after thirty-five years of great service to our country, I'm not suggesting that it had anything to do with his misread on this issue. His retirement had been planned long before this and he went on to head the National Counterterrorism Center seven years later.

My planners came back with specific dates, carefully chosen to maximize lighting conditions, a prime consideration when orchestrating air and missile strikes—and to conclude prior to Ramadan, since President Clinton had long since made it clear that he believed initiating any military action during Ramadan would be offensive to the Muslim world and damage relations with other Arab countries.

The ideal date fell just before Ramadan, on December 16. I reported this date to Secretary Cohen and together we went to the National Security Council, only to learn that the House had selected a date for the impeachment debate: December 17, the day after our strikes. What's important to note is that this impeachment date was announced *after* our planners had independently arrived at the most militarily advantageous date for the attacks, and the President had not even been briefed on that date yet.

Cohen and I couldn't believe it. If the strikes went forward as planned, we knew the President would be massacred by *Wag the Dog* accusations with potentially devastating political repercussions. Even though such political considerations were outside of my area of responsibility, Cohen and

I agreed that in this case it was both appropriate and our obligation to advise the White House of the concurrent dates (not that they couldn't have figured this out for themselves). Cohen went over to discuss it with Sandy Berger, assuming Sandy would pass along our concerns to the President—since it would be the President, of course, who would make the final decision as to the date for any attack.

Not much later we received word that the operation would proceed exactly as originally planned, the President insistent that we strike on whatever night would afford our pilots their greatest margin of safety. We confirmed that night to be December 16, the first night of the new moon.

The sixteenth arrived. Massive attacks began on two separate fields of battle, with the results playing out exactly as we had anticipated. In Iraq, our strikes were precise and highly effective, while in D.C., the President was being skewered by newspapers and television outlets across the globe. The air and missile strikes were over within seventy-two hours, while the *Wag the Dog* accusations continued to grow, until finally Congress demanded a full-scale official investigation, one in which Cohen and I would be the primary witnesses in a closed House session initiated by the departing House Speaker, Newt Gingrich. George Tenet was also present.

Between Cohen's reputation for complete integrity (not to mention the fact that he was a Republican in a Democratic administration), and mine as a nonpolitically correct, tell-it-like-it-is kind of a guy, our firm, sincere tracking of how the operation had played out seemed to douse the flames to a certain extent—at least until the majority whip, Tom DeLay, decided to add fuel to the fire by demanding to know whether Cohen believed that national security would be endangered if the House were to proceed with an impeachment vote the following day.

At first Secretary Cohen refused to answer, he did not think that was his decision to make—but DeLay pressed.

Finally, Cohen answered with an eloquent plea to support the troops:

> It's been the tradition throughout history that when we have people out there with the risk of dying, it's good to have good bipartisan support. Unity and bipartisan support is important for the morale of the troops.

The entire chamber broke out in applause and that was the end of it—at least in the House chamber that day. The following day's headlines would be mixed. The *Los Angeles Daily News* would ask, "Was it a coincidence of timing or the act of a man desperately trying to save his presidency?" They would conclude the former. Not so with the *Orange County Register*, which was more skeptical: "It is hard to believe the impeachment vote didn't figure in some way in the administration's latest military action." *The Washington Times* agreed: "If yesterday's American air strike on Iraq was not the act of a desperate man, it indisputably looked like one."

Even today, if one were to google "Clinton Wag the Dog"—almost twelve years after the impeachment hearings—the search would yield more than fifty thousand hits alleging that the President orchestrated his own personal *Wag the Dog*.

It may sound ironic when considering what prompted the impeachment in the first place, but the way I see it, President Clinton demonstrated exemplary leadership skills in his decision to strike on the sixteenth. He acted firmly, quickly, and with complete integrity, basing his decision totally and completely on what was best for the country and safest for our pilots, even though he was well aware that by making such a decision he would be personally battered by accusations. I gained a tremendous amount of respect for the President that day.

The MRI confirmed Dr. Mary's diagnosis—the aneurysm had traveled from my leg into my lung and the team was floored by how close it had come to bursting—probably only a matter of minutes. The medication they administered offered immediate relief, and once again, it seemed that I had cheated death.

Dr. Ecklund had hoped that we might have been approaching the time when I could undergo my neck surgery, but this episode put all that on hold. A setback, but one that I gratefully accepted, considering where I almost ended up.

That evening, I received two very special phone calls. The first was from Tom Brokaw, who called from an aircraft carrier in the Persian Gulf. Tom is not only one of the finest journalists ever to have hit the airwaves, but he's also one of the greatest individuals. Tom knew doctors at the Nick Buoniconti Spinal Cord Rehabilitation Center near Miami and he wanted to put one of them in touch with me.

Not long after Tom's call, Carolyn took a call from Ross Perot, who had always been a major supporter of the troops, and in particular our Special Forces. At one point, Ross had even offered to turn over the Magna Carta (which he owned) to the Chinese in exchange for the safe release of the U.S. aircrew they were holding prisoner. Carolyn held the phone up to my ear. "General, you have always taken care of the troops and never asked for anything in return, and I know you won't ask for help even now, so I'm calling to tell you that I want you to have the absolute finest medical treatment that money can buy, and I want you flown to the very finest facility to be seen by the very finest doctors. And you don't worry about the expenses. I've got that covered."

Such a call was the rule rather than the exception with Ross, and even though I did not accept his offer, it's just another example of his off-the-charts generosity and advocacy for our military. I thanked him profusely, and drifted off to sleep almost before I got off the line.

## Chapter Sixteen

# KING FOR A DAY

March 1999

Few leaders exemplified the "lead through intimidation" model better than Yugoslav president Slobodan Milosevic, who had no problem ordering mass murders, razing villages, forcing over a million Albanian refugees to flee the country, and perpetrating horrific crimes against humanity in an effort to exert Serbian control over Kosovo and rid the country of its ethnic Albanian majority. In response to these atrocities, on March 24, 1999, NATO authorized Operation Allied Force—air strikes directed against Serbian objectives inside the former Yugoslavia. The goal was to degrade the military and security structure that Milosevic had used to depopulate and destroy the Albanian majority in Kosovo. As Supreme Allied Commander Europe, General Wesley Clark was responsible for the operation. As Chairman of the Joint Chiefs, I was responsible for the day-to-day dealings with General Clark.

A few days into the bombing, it became abundantly clear to me that General Clark had developed a very weak battle plan, one without a strategic plan and corresponding targets. This concern was echoed by apprehensive calls I was getting from my counterparts in England, France, Germany, and Italy, plus General Mike Ryan (Air Force Chief of Staff) and NATO Air Component Commander in Europe. They were all infuriated by the prospect of conducting a war in such a haphazard manner, and expressing serious concerns about General Clark's ability to effectively command the NATO operation.

Something had to be done immediately. I quickly coordinated a session in my office that included my J2 (Director of Intelligence), J3 (Director of Operations), J5 (Director of Strategic Plans and Policy) and DJS (Director of Joint Staff)—and what I was about to ask of them bordered on the impossible.

"Gentleman, you are about to earn that massive paycheck Uncle Sam sends your wife to spend twice a month. If I told you the current Serbian strategic bombing plan was somewhat lacking, I'd be lying . . . because, basically—there isn't one. This is where you come in. We've got to develop a central theme—a strategy—and break it down into categories of targets specifically chosen to meet that theme."

I spent about an hour discussing the big picture with them, and providing guidance on how I thought we might achieve that overall objective. Whatever we ended up with was intended to persuade Milosevic to abide by the following five conditions:

- Ensure a verifiable stop to all military action and the immediate ending of violence and repression
- Ensure the withdrawal from Kosovo of the military, police, and paramilitary forces
- Agree to the stationing in Kosovo of an international military presence
- Agree to the unconditional and safe return of all refugees and displaced persons and unhindered access to them by humanitarian aid organizations
- Provide credible assurance of his willingness to work on the basis of the Rambouillet Accords in the establishment of a political framework agreement for Kosovo in conformity with international law and the Charter of the United Nations.

Under normal conditions, developing a plan like this would take a couple of months, or, in the case of an expedited situation, maybe a few weeks. Even though they would be working with some of the greatest minds in Washington—the Joint Staff—what I was about to ask bordered on insanity.

"By the way, you have twenty-four hours to meet back here and brief me on the completed plan," I said, without a doubt in my mind that they'd rise to the challenge and pull it off.

What they presented to me the following day was good—carefully thought out, as though they did have weeks to put it together. While Clark's bombing runs seemed random and haphazard, every one of these was designed in accordance with one of four categories—and the categories were intended initially to degrade Serbia's *military* capabilities, then their *economic*. Categories included:

1. Military infrastructure
2. Economic targets
3. Belgrade bridges and power grid (psychological demoralizers)
4. Tank-engine factory (employed thirty-two thousand workers)

I faxed the plan to General Clark "for his consideration," informing him that I would be flying to Mons, Belgium, where I would meet with my NATO counterparts. Together we would hear whatever revised plan he had come up with—but it had to have a specific, strategic plan to win the war. I suggested he check his fax machine ASAP for a document I thought might stimulate his thought process.

My counterparts and I had a brief premeeting in Brussels, then together we made the thirty-four-mile trip southwest to Casteau, a tiny village in the French-speaking region of Belgium where SHAPE (Supreme Headquarters Allied Powers Europe) was based, just a stone's throw north of Mons. Here, at the central command of NATO's military, we were to meet Wes and see what kind of plan he had come up with.

Not even two hours later, Wes was recapping the main points of his presentation and trying his best to read the faces on the five Chiefs of Defense seated around the small table. "If that doesn't bring Milosevic to his knees, I don't know what will," he said, as poised and polished as one would expect from a Rhodes scholar and West Point valedictorian—flipping between PowerPoint slides along the way. "I think you'll agree the escalation from military to economic targets—*if it gets that far*—makes perfect sense. Sustained attacks that will demoralize him. Of course we'll continue taking out their air defenses with F-15s, 16s, and 117s [F-15 Eagles, F-16 Fighting Falcons, F-117 Nighthawks] from Aviano [Aviano Air Base, about sixty miles north of Venice], bases all over Europe, and the USS *Theodore Roosevelt* in the Adriatic. The first category includes military headquarters, command-and-control sites, ordnance-storage sites, and such."

He was on a roll and had our full attention; it made sense. It should, as it was almost a word-for-word recitation of the plan we had sent over the day before. But it was a good plan and Wes had bought into it, which was a good thing since he was the one who would have to execute it.

"We'll launch the Tomahawks from both ships and subs to take out the highly defended targets in Pristina and Belgrade," he continued, flipping to the next category of target. "Next up, economic targets—we'll destroy his economic ability to wage war. Again, sustained attacks."

He flipped to a slide that read BRIDGES & UTILITIES. "Category Three . . . major bridges over the Danube, plus power plants, TV towers, water-treatment plants—all great *psychological* hits that will *demoralize* him." Well into the home stretch, the Supreme Allied Commander actually sounded like he knew what he was talking about. He would brief well in front of the cameras—although both Cohen and I thought he tended to be somewhat of a loose cannon at times, and absolutely in it for whatever was best for Wes. While I could be perfectly content trolling for Spanish mackerel or breaking into "Cripple Creek" on my Gibson Earl Scruggs Mastertone banjo, it was obvious that Wes had big aspirations, and he seemed very intent on making it to the top. So *why the hell didn't he come up with a plan like this in the first place?*

"Finally, dual-purpose facilities. We'll take out major industrial plants such as the Zastava auto plant, and Sloboda Vacuum Cleaner factory in Cacak—both are *also involved in tank manufacture and repairs.*" The dual-use aspect was very key to their being acceptable targets under the regulations of the Geneva convention. Our lawyers would review—and sign off on—each and every target before it was authorized. And they were very good.

Wes shut down the projector and flashed me a toothy grin. "That's it."

I glanced around the table and my four peers seemed happy. This was not just a courtesy but a necessity, since every NATO country—all nineteen of them—would have to approve every target, and Italy's chief had been the most vocal in his disapproval of Clark. He was providing not only resources but the Aviano Air Base, as well.

"Well done, Wes. As far as I'm concerned, you've got yourself a damn fine plan. Gentlemen?" I said, throwing it over to my four counterparts. They had a few specific questions, but overall they were pleased—probably as much because Clark took the time to answer their concerns as the plan itself. And Wes was basking in the glory of these four military heads responding so favorably to *his* plan. I've always been pleased with the way it all played out, and thought it was a great example of what the Packard Commission had in mind when they provided their input for what would eventually be passed as the Goldwater-Nichols Act of 1986—reworking the command structure of the military and increasing the powers of the Chairman.

There was a tremendous problem that needed an immediate solution, so I stepped in and assembled some of the finest military minds in Washington to turn around a well-constructed battle plan in the blink of an eye—and based on long-standing relationships (and friendships) with my international counterparts, we were able to cut through the clutter and get this thing back on track.

It was a solid plan, one I couldn't help feeling that General Clark should have come up with in the first place. Wes is an extremely intelligent guy, so perhaps he failed to utilize the talents of his terrific cadre of advisers—an essential tool in the repertoire of every great leader—to formulate a battle plan. But when a man's ego says "I don't need anyone's help," that's a pretty good time to start looking for a new leader. I was reminded of the old saying, "There is no limit to what a man can achieve if he doesn't mind who takes credit for it."

———————

"Mr. President, General Shelton owes you a *goddamn* explanation!" Vice President Gore exploded in the Oval Office on the morning of March 31, 1999. I'd never had any prior conflict with the Vice President, yet his reaction was so extreme, it almost seemed personal.

"Mr. President," he continued, "before you get an update on operations, I think you are owed an explanation as to how we could have three prisoners of war when you were explicitly told just yesterday that our troops had been pulled back five kilometers from that border, and now we find out that they apparently were not because we have three of them who have been picked up by the enemy. He owes you an answer."

I didn't know if the Vice President was having a bad week on the 2000 presidential campaign trail or what, but I felt like I was in the middle of a live-fire artillery exercise and I was the target. It was ugly, and the Vice President was clearly expecting President Clinton to pick up where he had left off and launch into me with an attack of his own.

This was the first of two Oval Office briefs I had that day, primarily to keep the President fully apprised on Operation Allied Force, which was just concluding its first week of NATO airstrikes. I had just advised them that three American soldiers had been captured along the rugged Macedonian border with Serbia, when only a few days earlier I had reported that General Clark created a buffer zone intended to minimize the possibility of such an event. Tensions were as high in that area (as they were in the Oval Office) and we had lots of troops manning observation positions and conducting patrols. Recently there had been some exchange of gunfire. There was no line on the ground that identified the border, and there was not even a good road through there—so it was easy to be off by hundreds of meters, which created the risk of inadvertently crossing the border.

Gazing at the Vice President as if reprimanding a five-year-old, the President calmly explained, "Well, Al, you know we are in a war over there, and sometimes in a war, things just don't play out the way we hope they would." It's what Sun Tzu called "the fog of war."

Turning to me, he continued. "Sorry for the interruption, Hugh. Carry on with your brief." I felt vindicated that the President had turned and fired that heat-seeker back into Gore's gut.

While President Clinton might have been less than perfect in certain areas, he was a highly effective leader who commanded respect with his laser focus on the issues at hand. He never stooped to egotistic power plays the way Gore had done.

Until about a month earlier, the soldiers had been participating in a United Nations mission to protect Macedonia called U.N. PREDEP (United Nations Preventive Deployment). When the U.N. failed to continue that mission, U.S. forces remained, but transferred to American control to protect the U.S. infrastructure at Camp Able Sentry at the Skopje airport—the base from which our soldiers had been operating for the past several years. In addition, they were supporting the withdrawal of the U.N. forces, coordinating with NATO forces in Macedonia for force protection, and continuing the observation patrols they had been conducting under the U.N. "blue helmets." These posts tended to be up in the hills, and often they involved a tower with a telescope and binoculars—some soldiers would stay in those towers, others would go out on patrol.

"Any word on CSAR?" asked the President, whose primary concern was whether combat search and rescue had achieved any success in locating the soldiers. With President Clinton, it always seemed that his first concern was about the well-being of our troops.

"Sir, Task Force Able Sentry sent out a Black Hawk the instant they got the word, and they were joined by two British choppers. French and Italian helos are on the way, plus we have an aircraft overhead with infrared capability—we want to locate that Humvee before the bad weather sets in."

Despite the best efforts of a well-executed search-and-rescue mission, they did not find them. In fact, we had no idea where they were—or even if they were still alive. In their last radio contact, the three soldiers talked about trying to escape, then being surrounded. That's when their signal cut out.

---

**Final Radio Transmission of captured soldiers**

**SOLDIERS:** *"We're in contact, we're taking direct fire."*

**HUMVEE 2:** *"You better not be bullshitting me, are you?"*

**SOLDIERS:** *"No, we're taking direct fire. We're trapped. They're all around us. We can't get out."*

End of transmission                    [Official Department of Defense transcript]

\* \* \*

The following day they did turn up—all beat up and battered, on Serbian television—clear violations of the Geneva Convention, but at least they were alive. We learned that fifty to sixty rounds of enemy small-arms fire peppered their vehicle as they tried to escape, but apparently they ended up stuck in some sort of road obstruction. Twenty or so Serb soldiers surrounded them, dragged them out of the Humvee, and really went to work on them—beating them bloody with rifle butts, kicks to the face and body, punches, et cetera. It was not a pretty picture, and we still had no idea where they were. The one thing we did know is that they needed medical attention.

More bad news came the following day, when the Belgrade-based news agency Tanjug announced that since they had *resisted arrest* and been *captured in Serb territory,* they would immediately be put on trial. The situation was going from bad to worse—a Serbian trial under the control of Slobodan Milosevic could have only one result.

Behind the scenes, CIA and military intelligence were working triple time to ascertain the whereabouts of the captives; but even if we'd had that information, a rescue operation would have been risky and most likely not without bloodshed. For now, the battle would be waged by three principals on the front lines—President Clinton, Secretary Cohen, and me—backed by our hardworking team of speechwriters and public affairs officers. Our battlefield would be the airwaves, our weapons TV cameras, microphones, and newspaper reports. Our message was clear and it went right to Milosevic: *Our soldiers must be released immediately or there would be dire consequences, and until they are released, they must be treated in full accordance with the Geneva Convention, including immediate access to medical attention.*

---

### Geneva Convention of 1949

**Partial prisoner-of-war provisions:**

- Prisoners must be kept in a place where their lives are not at risk.

- They are required only to give their name, rank, serial number and date of birth and may not be coerced into giving other information.

- They cannot be put on trial.

- They must be protected against insults and public curiosity.

- They may be imprisoned until the end of the conflict, but must be released immediately when it ends.

---

Secretary Cohen and I appeared on *Meet the Press, This Week with Sam Donaldson and Cokie Roberts,* FOX *News Sunday,* and *Late Edition,* plus we boosted the frequency of our Pentagon press briefings.

*March 28, 1999. Secretary Bill Cohen and me on* Meet the Press. *"We expect them to be treated humanely and in accordance with the Geneva Convention."*

"President Milosevic should make no mistake," Clinton said in one appearance. "We will hold him and his government responsible for their safety and for their well-being."

"These captive U.S. soldiers are prisoners of war and therefore should be covered by the protections of the Geneva Conventions . . ."

"No, this does not mean we are acknowledging being at war with Yugoslavia."

"By international law, the Geneva Convention applies to all periods of hostilities."

And Milosevic would counter with reasons why he did *not* consider the soldiers to be under the jurisdiction of the Geneva Convention . . . although he might think differently if NATO would release *his* captured soldier. . . .

It had been more than three weeks and we were no closer to getting our troops home, nor getting any assurances that they were being properly cared for. As luck would have it, I happened to be meeting with a friend who was Chief of the Bulgarian military, and the very next day he was leaving Washington to meet with Dragoljub Ojdani, the Chief of the General Staff of the Yugoslav Army. I've always said, *If you can't be good, be lucky,* so I asked him to take a very clear message back to Ojdani.

"You tell him that I said ultimately we are going to prevail, and he knows that. But I'm giving him a chance. Tell him I'm holding him *personally* responsible for the safety of these three guys, and on a military-to-military level I want him to press his president to release them in order to keep this on a level playing field of a war. Otherwise I will escalate it to a *personal vendetta* between the two of us because I have asked him on a personal level to release these innocent soldiers who were just trying to do their duty." We shook hands and he agreed.

Two days later he called me back from Sofia. "Hugh, I have delivered your message to General Ojdani. He said to assure you—general to general—your men are well cared for and your demand will be met."

Just a few days later they were released—although not in the manner I had anticipated.

Right in the middle of my back-channel contact, Jesse Jackson appeared on television and announced that he was flying to Belgrade to secure the prisoners' release—the release that was *already in the works* on my end. The very last thing we needed at that point was Jesse Jackson (*or anyone else*) getting in there to mess things up. But we were too late. Despite the U.S. State Department's lack of approval, Jackson showed up in Serbia and somehow talked himself into a personal meeting with President Milosevic. Following the meeting, he was all over the airwaves announcing how he had "successfully negotiated the soldiers' release"—which in his case included suggestions that we show good faith by *halting our bombing* and releasing the Yugoslav lieutenant we were holding in Tirana, Albania.

To us it was obvious that the Serbian leader was just playing the Reverend Mr. Jackson, notwithstanding Jackson's reports that he, Milosevic, and a few dozen of Jackson's religious enclave took time out of the negotiations to hold hands, bow their heads, and pray together. (We at the Pentagon and White House were less than convinced that the dictator's spiritual awakening was sincere, since only three days earlier his troops had committed one of the worst civilian massacres to date near the southwestern Kosovo village of Meja, which they burned down along with the surrounding villages, then systematically mowed down the entire adult-male population of those villages—the same day as 8,000 more refugees were forced to cross into Albania from Kosovo, joining the more than 370,000 who had already done so.)

\* \* \*

On Sunday, May 2, Jackson, along with his twenty-four followers and the three soldiers, crossed into neighboring Croatia chanting, "Free at last, free at last, thank God Almighty, free at last." As I saw the spectacle on TV, I picked up my phone and called my counterpart in Bulgaria to thank him. We both smiled at how persuasive "Jesse" was in negotiating the release.

As for Jackson's request that President Clinton and NATO view this as *a gesture that should not go ignored, the first step of peace and reconciliation . . . [and an] opportunity to choose peace with dignity,* we knew in whose court that "first step" would be, and I thought President Clinton expressed it quite well:

> As we welcome our soldiers home, our thoughts also turn to the over one million Kosovars who are unable to go home because of the policies of the regime in Belgrade. Today we reaffirm our resolve to persevere until they, too, can return—with security and self-government.

Secretary Cohen was even more specific:

> I don't believe that Milosevic acts out of any generosity. I think he's tried to act out of self-interest. As General Clark has indicated on many occasions before, Milosevic has miscalculated on virtually everything that he assumed would take place with respect to the West. I think he has miscalculated here, believing that by releasing these three soldiers that somehow would serve to undermine NATO unity and commitment to this campaign.
>
> So we're going to continue. It will not impede our intensification of the air campaign. We're going forward.

Along with the President, I was visiting our great troops at the Spangdahlem Air Base in Germany at the time—and it was their heroic efforts that I recognized.

> Milosevic expected dissension, and instead he's faced cohesion. And he's faced strength of purpose. The most powerful statement of this determination can be seen on the faces of our pilots and crews, like those here in Spangdahlem, as they climb into the cockpit for another mission over Yugoslavia.
>
> It can be seen in the eyes and hands of the great support teams in Aviano, aboard the Theodore Roosevelt, and across the region, as they fuel, arm, and prepare their aircraft for combat. And this determination

*is evident—it's evident in the efforts of our terrific soldiers, airmen, soldiers, sailors, marines, and they work in the mud, the heat, and the dust in Albania, both to care for the refugees that are streaming in from Kosovo and to prepare for military operations over Yugoslavia.*

*As you know, the great team in Albania includes the pilots and the crews that are flying the Apache helicopters like the ones that were involved in last night's incident. And I think this incident goes to show us that we must never lose sight of the fact that our military men and women operate in a very hazardous environment day in and day out in support of America's national security.*

*I've just returned from talking to some of those outstanding servicemen and women, and I can tell you that they understand their mission and that they will not fail in its execution.*

Following our broadcast, Jackson countered with another one of his own, in which he pressed President Clinton to recognize Milosevic's gesture by having NATO at least temporarily halt the bombing. He neglected to mention Milosevic's "gesture" of disregarding the Geneva Convention and forcing the captives to read anti-NATO propaganda under the threat of injury or death, nor did he mention the fractured ribs, nose, bruises, and other injuries they sustained immediately after their capture.

The gesture we chose to recognize was his refusal to meet the four NATO demands that would end his efforts to exterminate an entire ethnic population. We at the Pentagon were big believers that actions speak louder than words, so under the direction of President Clinton and with the full approval (and in many cases, participation) of the eighteen other NATO countries, that night we demonstrated some of that action.

The *New York Times* headline read NATO DARKENS BELGRADE AND AREA OF SERBIA, and Steven Erlanger filled in the details:

*All of Belgrade and parts of Serbia were plunged into darkness just after 10 o'clock Sunday, when NATO warplanes hit a major hydroelectric power station west of the capital...*

*As antiaircraft fire filled the skies over Belgrade, lights all over the city suddenly went dark, leaving the eerie sight of cars speeding across Belgrade bridges...*

*The attack on the power station seemed a clear rejection of the Rev. Jesse L. Jackson's request that the White House consider a halt to bombing after Mr. Milosevic released three captive American soldiers early Sunday.*

The three soldiers were taken to a military hospital and were examined, treated, and eventually returned home, where they were welcomed as heroes and presented medals by the President.

I can't overemphasize the extreme importance of these relationships with our international counterparts. In the case of Operation Allied Force, it's the Bulgarian Chief of Defense to whom we owe a tremendous debt of gratitude. Not only was he an integral part of securing the release of those three prisoners, but I give him credit for helping to pull out that final ace of spades that caused Milosevic's entire house of cards to tumble down.

It was early June and Milosevic was showing signs of crumbling, but it just was not happening. The way I saw it, things could play out one of two ways. Either the barbarian's military could stand behind him until the bitter end, in which case this could dwindle on for months, along with the ethnic atrocities—*or* they could turn against him, and without his military he would have no choice but to hoist the white flag.

I picked up the phone and called Bulgaria, once again reaching out to my counterpart to intercede by relaying yet another message to the Serbian Defense Chief. "This time I have an even more important message for him," I began. "He's got to understand that his boss is hanging on by the very thinnest of threads, and one day he is going to be carted off and hung for war crimes. I need you to tell him that if he and the rest of his military try to rally around Milosevic, and protect him in any way—then the United States and eighteen other nations would consider them to be vital elements of the Milosevic team, and they will be taken down just as quickly as he will go down. On the other hand, short of those who have committed war crimes [and would have to be dealt with accordingly], we would consider everybody else to have been honorable soldiers with none of the repercussions the others would most certainly be facing."

Again, my message was delivered, and three days later, Milosevic surrendered after his armed forces failed to support him. On June 9, NATO and Yugoslav military authorities signed the agreement stating that their forces would exit Kosovo, and the following day all air strikes ended.

———

The initial bombing runs included the first combat use of the B-2 Stealth bomber, an incredible asset in our strategic-bomber fleet. On March 24,

DEPARTMENT OF DEFENSE

1999, two B-2s flew sixteen hours from Whiteman Air Force base in Missouri to deliver their sixteen two-thousand-pound GBU-32 Joint Direct Attack Munitions (JDAM bombs) on Serbian targets to begin the air war—not only the first missions for the B-2s, but other than the original TLAM strikes, these B-2s executed the first bombing missions of the war.

In commemoration of this historic flight, the pilots and crew of aircraft 93-1087, the *Spirit of Pennsylvania,* sent me a Missouri flag they carried with them on the maiden bomb run, along with an engraved plaque recognizing the event. It was presented by Congressman Ike Skelton (Democrat, Missouri), a great supporter of our armed forces. To this day I have it displayed in my office at home.

———

I had high hopes that the new battle plan would turn things around, but it was not the case. The bombing was just not working, and if anything, Milosevic appeared almost emboldened. A big problem was that despite his eloquent presentation and apparent grasp of its importance, General Clark failed to completely act upon it. Sure, he was hitting *some* of the agreed-upon sites, but not all of them, and not in the organized progression he had briefed. Then the overseas calls started coming in again, and by the time my counterparts were finished venting, it all fell into place.

The initiation of a bomb run was not a simple process—and it wasn't one that could be accomplished instantaneously. Yet, according to these latest calls from the same four individuals, that's exactly what Wes was doing—somehow attempting to shoot from the hip with last-minute drops that failed to take into account the time I needed to run those targets by the President for his approval. The standard lead time was ninety-six hours to a week, but we streamlined this for Wes's benefit and whittled it down to forty-eight hours. That included other required clearances in addition to the time I needed to brief the President on what we had in store for the following day, and for him to give his nod of approval. This same process had to take place with the eighteen other NATO countries.

But Wes and his team were having real problems getting ahead of that power curve. The fact that a commander didn't know the planning cycle on air operations—particularly when *the entire mission is one big air operation*—is nothing short of terrifying. As I had learned while attending the Air Command and Staff Course as a major, air operations, just like ground plans, have many independent moving parts that must all move together in perfect orchestration; there really is an art to it. Between the munitions and intell radio codes and midair refuelers and electronic-warfare pieces, this is not a situation where someone can pick up a phone and call in a strike for that evening.

We ended up having to send someone out there to walk him through it, and finally, in time, things did progressively get better—but it was like pulling teeth to finally get there.

———

One thing that did *not* get any better was Wes's unfortunate inability to deal effectively with the press. To put it bluntly, for a smart guy he said some pretty dumb things. This was just over a month into the air strikes and I didn't know what he was thinking when he made a statement to the *Los Angeles Times* that was taken to indicate that the bombings were ineffective. This appeared to support the constant drumbeat we were hearing that Wes wanted a large ground plan to move into Serbia. This did not sit well with Secretary Cohen, who did not want to get into it with Wes directly, so instead he asked me to relay his message verbatim. I called Wes as requested: "The Secretary has asked me to deliver the following message, and I quote: *get your fucking face off the TV. No more briefings, period. That's it.*" I give Secretary Cohen a lot of credit for crafting a succinct instruction without a whole lot of ambiguity.

* * *

Only two days after NATO suspended air operations, Russian forces arrived in Kosovo in the predawn hours and were en route to Pristina Airport with the expectation of helping to police the area. General Clark, however, had other plans, and ordered British three-star general Michael Jackson, head of the Kosovo force, to block the Russians from entering the airfield. Jackson refused, saying, "No, I'm not going to do that. It's not worth starting World War III."

This whole thing apparently went all the way to the top in both London and D.C., and the next thing I knew, my phone was ringing at 3:00 A.M. and it was Sir Charles Guthrie, my British counterpart and also a very close friend (although by waking me at 3:00 A.M. he was treading dangerously close to losing that distinction). Sir Charles was doing everything in his power to persuade Wes to just let the Russians in, and go ahead with their police endeavors—but in the end, it was actually the White House that made the call and ended up abandoning their support for the Clark plan.

But the fact was that Lieutenant General Jackson did disregard a direct order from his superior, and in the ultimate coincidence, it was in the Senate hearing surrounding my nomination for second term as Chairman that it all hit the fan. Senator Warner left it that he planned to investigate NATO's command procedures and explore the matter further at some point down the road.

---

One afternoon in early June 1999, President Clinton pulled me aside and posed an interesting question. We were months into the war and the Serbs had still not quit, although I was seeing signs that they were beginning to teeter; the President's frustration was palpable. "Hugh, if you were king for a day, what would you do differently to win this war?"

I reminded him of the strategic importance of "Clark's" original battle plan, which hinged upon hitting those four vital target sets.

"Sir, after months of bombing we have still not been allowed to hit some of the more strategic targets near Belgrade," I reminded him. "I believe if we do so now, it would degrade Milosevic's infrastructure and have such a psychological impact that he would surrender, *if* he was ever going to quit based on air strikes alone."

"You think it would really have that big an impact?" the President asked.

"I do, sir. But our problem all along has been the French. They adamantly refuse to sign off on it."

This was not the first time the French had impeded crucial strikes, even after the UK, Germany, and Italy had proffered their support. It had

*Secretary Cohen looks on as French President Chirac and I greet each other.*

gotten to the point where their dissension was negatively impacting the big picture.

"In the morning I'll call President Chirac to bring him on board," the President promised.

The following day, he made the call. Less than forty-eight hours later, Milosevic hoisted the white flag and the war was over—the first time in history that a war was won by airpower alone.

President Clinton was unencumbered by any agendas surrounding the war, and his relationship with me was such that he felt safe enough to cut to the chase and pose his "king for a day" hypothetical. By virtue of his position and their prior encounters, he had Chirac's ear, so this one was easy: a strong leader using preestablished relationships to facilitate decisive action.

As I thought back about this encounter after leaving office, had Rumsfeld been Secretary of Defense then, rather than Cohen, the outcome

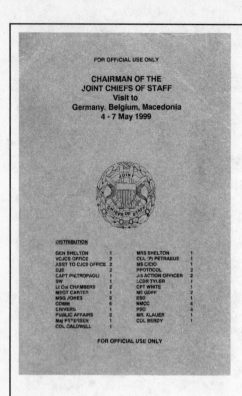

FOR OFFICIAL USE ONLY

**CHAIRMAN OF THE
JOINT CHIEFS OF STAFF
Visit to
Germany, Belgium, Macedonia
4 - 7 May 1999**

DISTRIBUTION

| | | | |
|---|---|---|---|
| GEN SHELTON | 1 | MRS SHELTON | 1 |
| VCJCS OFFICE | 2 | COL (P) PETRAEUS | 1 |
| ASST TO CJCS OFFICE | 2 | MS C/CIO | 1 |
| DJS | 2 | PROTOCOL | 2 |
| CAPT PIETROPAOLI | 1 | J-5 ACTION OFFICER | 2 |
| SW | 1 | LCDR TYLER | 1 |
| Lt Col CHAMBERS | 2 | CPT WHITE | 1 |
| MSGT CARTER | 1 | ME GOFF | 2 |
| MSG JONES | 2 | ESO | 1 |
| COMM | 6 | NMCC | 4 |
| DRIVERS | 1 | PSO | 4 |
| PUBLIC AFFAIRS | 2 | MR. KLAUER | 1 |
| Maj PETERSEN | 1 | COL BERDY | 1 |
| COL CALDWELL | 1 | | |

FOR OFFICIAL USE ONLY

---

As of 12:56 PM 5/4/99

FOR OFFICIAL USE ONLY

**Wednesday, 5 May 1999**
Brussels, BE to Spangdahlem, GE to Ramstein, GE
Uniform: Day:     Class A with Garrison Cap
       Tvl:     Class A with Garrison Cap

0630     Arr Brussels (Class A)

0645     Dep enr NATO HQ via motorcade

0700     Arr NATO HQ
*0100, Wed Wash, DC*     • Press Pool
        • Met by Secretary General Javier Solana

0705     Briefing to the President in Ambassador's office

0725     Meeting w/Sec Gen Solana

0805     Briefing on Operation Allied Force

0910     Greet US NATO staff

0930     Dep enr airport

0945     Arr airport VIP Lounge

0950     President meets w/PM Jean-Luc Dehaene

FOR OFFICIAL USE ONLY

---

As of 12:56 PM 5/4/99

FOR OFFICIAL USE ONLY

**Wednesday, 5 May 1999**
Brussels, BE to Spangdahlem, GE to Ramstein, GE
Uniform: Day:     Class A with Garrison Cap
       Tvl:     Class A with Garrison Cap

0630     Arr Brussels (Class A)

0645     Dep enr NATO HQ via motorcade

0700     Arr NATO HQ
*0100, Wed Wash, DC*     • Press Pool
        • Met by Secretary General Javier Solana

0705     Briefing to the President in Ambassador's office

0725     Meeting w/Sec Gen Solana

0805     Briefing on Operation Allied Force

0910     Greet US NATO staff

0930     Dep enr airport

0945     Arr airport VIP Lounge

0950     President meets w/PM Jean-Luc Dehaene

FOR OFFICIAL USE ONLY

---

As of 12:56 PM 5/4/99

FOR OFFICIAL USE ONLY

1025     Dep enr aircraft

1045     *CJCS aircraft arr Ramstein*

1045     Dep enr Spangdahlem via AF-1 (FT 0+40)

1125     Arr Spangdahlem
*0525, Wed Wash, DC*     • Met by: BGen and Mrs. Scott Van Cleef, CDR
        52nd Fighter Wing

1140     Dep enr TBD via motorcade

1145     Arr TBD

1155     Media availability

1220     Dep enr Flight Line

1225     Arr Flight Line
        • Greet F-16, A-10, and F-117 crews

1300     Dep enr Hangar One

1305     Arr Hangar One
        • Lunch Break

1340     Remarks to Base personnel and families
        • Wing Commander Remarks
        • **CJCS Remarks**

FOR OFFICIAL USE ONLY     9

*Chairman's Trip Book from May 1999 flight with President Clinton.*

might have ultimately played out with the same success. But the process would certainly have been more involved. Before even touching on the real issue—Chirac's holding up the strategic mission—Rumsfeld would most likely have zeroed in on two other areas first. Number one, why did the President pose the question to me instead of him? And number two, what was the President really trying to say when he asked me to think of myself as king? Until these were resolved to his satisfaction, we may never have gotten to the Chirac/bombing concern.

Cohen's hands-off leadership style yielded far better results than Rumsfeld's overanalyzing micromanagement style.

L*et me put it to you this way, there is no damn way you're going to get me to eat with that thing," I said, looking at the oversized fork they were trying to put in my hand. Captain Chuck Quick was a fine occupational therapist, and I'm sure at that moment he was thinking, Just what I need, a stubborn general to give me crap when I'm just trying to help him.*

*Chuck had come in to start me on an OT program that would allow me to undertake some of the everyday tasks that my injury had made impossible—things as seemingly second-nature as eating, or buttoning a shirt. Some tools of his trade were these oversized utensils, huge pencils, and such—that offered the patient a means to reacclimate the muscles to these skills. From my perspective, if I'm going to start writing, teach me how to do it with a regular pencil; I'm sure as hell not going to walk into my bank and whip out one of those big things to fill out my deposit slip.*

*What I didn't know at the time was that none of these individuals thought that I would ever reach the stage of being able to use "normal" paraphernalia again. But they eventually decided it was better to humor me than to resist, and they did their best to teach me using "real" props.*

*After the session, I took more calls, those from international counterparts— originally professional contacts, now friends. Again I was awed by how many of these close relationships I had forged.*

## Chapter Seventeen

# FULL PLATE

The beautiful tropical island of East Timor had become a complete bloodbath. Beatings were rampant, and more than a thousand innocent civilians had been murdered by the militia. Having proclaimed itself an independent state in 1975, shortly thereafter it had been invaded and occupied by Indonesia, which had declared it a province the following year. Now, with violence raging, the Indonesian military did nothing to stop it—in fact, they would become a part of the brutality.

President Clinton attempted to intercede, but Indonesia's president B. J. Habibie refused to take his calls. The U.S. ambassador was also unable to make contact.

British Prime Minister Tony Blair did reach Habibie, but all he got was lip service—a promise from Habibie that the violence would end; then, the following day, it intensified.

France agreed to send in international forces to supplement U.N. peacekeeping efforts; but that led to more rebuffs, and eventually the Indonesians attacked the U.N. officials.

President Clinton had had enough. He declared, "I am alarmed by reports I have just received of attacks on the U.N. compound in Dili. It is now clear that the Indonesian military is aiding and abetting the militia violence. This is simply unacceptable. *They must accept an international force.*" But the Indonesians still refused.

This had become a hot topic in our NSC meetings, and I shared with President Clinton that I had established some pretty solid relationships with my Indonesian counterpart, General Wiranto, the tough head of Indonesia's military.

"Think you could get through to him?" the President asked.

"I'd be surprised if he didn't take my call, Mr. President," I told him.

"Well, here's what I'd like you to tell him . . ." said the President, and he went on to outline what he wanted communicated to President Habibie, and what the consequences would be if the Indonesians continued the violence and refused to cooperate with international peacekeepers.

"I understand, Mr. President. I will call him this evening," I said, accounting for the time difference.


General Wiranto took my call immediately, just as if it were any good friend calling. He asked for two more days, then told me he was imposing martial law and was sure that that would settle things down and bring about peace.

We gave him those two days, but the terror continued. That's when I got angry, and he knew me well enough to know that you did not want to get me angry.

I called him back and it's a good thing there were no women or children within earshot of that call. Let's just say that I was "firm." "Why don't we start with the *billions* of dollars your country is expecting in from the International Monetary Fund? We will block those funds faster than shit goes through Moody's goose," I warned him.

"I will fly to the island immediately and assess the situation," he said.

"I think that is a great idea," I replied. "And by eight P.M. tomorrow night my time, I want to hear your voice on the phone reporting to me the results of that assessment."


The following night, he called. "Please tell President Clinton that we agree to allow the U.N. peacekeeping forces in," he reported.

"I will do that, and thank you. You made the right decision."


The final result was that Indonesia relinquished control of the island, and on May 20, 2002, East Timor became the first new sovereign state of the twenty-first century.


*The New York Times* ran this article [partial]:

## U.S. TO JAKARTA MESSENGER: CHAIRMAN OF THE JOINT CHIEFS
**By ELIZABETH BECKER, New York Times**

**WASHINGTON, Sept. 13, 1999**—As the violence in East Timor worsened, the Americans relied on one person to deliver a tough message to the Indonesian Government, senior Administration officials said today.

The go-between was the Chairman of the Joint Chiefs of Staff, Gen. Henry H. Shelton, who dealt on the telephone with his counterpart, Gen. Wiranto, the head of the powerful Indonesian military forces.

General Shelton spoke three times with General Wiranto, culminating on Friday with what senior officials called an "ugly message."

"It was a big plus to have someone who could call the Indonesian military," a senior Administration official said. "They were the ones calling the shots. We had a unique asset, and I don't see how our military could have done it without their past history with these generals."

———

Even in our post-Cold War environment, the safeguards that go into ensuring the integrity of our nuclear command-and-control systems are mindboggling, and it's all designed so that only our National Command Authority—the President and the Secretary of Defense or their duly deputized alternates or successors—have the ability to launch a nuclear strike, be it offensive or defensive.

```
W I R A N T O   (replaced Tanjung) (replaced by Widodo)      Feb98

General Wiranto
Commander in Chief of
  the Armed Forces
Jakarta, Republic of Indonesia
                                                  Hugh Shelton
Dear General Wiranto             sincerely        Henry H Shelton

26Feb98:  OBO men/women of Armed Forces, congrats on selection...worked to strength-
          en bonds of cooperation...w/b/w...important/challenging assignment.   JStaff
17Mar98:  Invite to NDU Intl Fellows, AY 98-99...                               JStaff
20Mar98:  Congrats on appointment as Def Minister....as well as CINC/Armed Forces
          will provide challenges/opportunities...military fortunate to have you
          in the lead...look forward to continuing relatoinship. w/b/w...       JStaff

 2Jul98:  t/y for ltr...pleased Col Arsyad attending NDU Intl fellows program
          in AY 98-99.  look forward to continued opportunities....w/b/w        JStaff

 8Oct98:  t/y for ltr re 1stAdm Dr Sapto J. Poerwowidagdo's attendance at Asia
          Foundation Forum on Civ-Mil Relations, 13-16Sep...his participation is a
          symbol of professional mil bond nations share...w/b/w                 JStaff
```

*Office card used by my secretary to track correspondence.*

The number of redundancies is staggering, and the entire operation is the ultimate responsibility of the Chairman. From my prior days as a DDO (Deputy Director of Operations), I was particularly sensitive to this area. Besides the NMCC (National Military Command Center), from which the DDO transmits the emergency action message that initiates the missile-launch process underground, there are backup sites, and backups for the backups—some under ground, others airborne. There's Looking Glass, the E6-B (modified 707) command-and-control backup to USSTRAT-COM's (U.S. Strategic Command) Global Operations Center, which used to remain aloft 24/7, but still remains on constant strip alert—with crews ready at a moment's notice to sprint to the cockpit and take off; and TACAMO, an E-6 airborne system capable of retransmitting emergency action messages completely encrypted on virtually any frequency.

The reason I mention the multitude of redundancy is because they are all dependent on one vital element without which there can be no launch; it's the one piece of the puzzle that is in essence the nuclear "deal breaker," and that's the Presidential authorization codes. Without those, it doesn't matter if we've got a thousand missiles verified inbound to the United States, we would be unable to launch a retaliatory strike. If our survival depended on launching a preemptive strike, without the President's having those authorization codes, such a strike would be impossible. That's how crucial it is to maintain the integrity of those nuclear-authorization codes—which are to remain within very close proximity to the President at all times. In the case of a change in administration, the incoming President actually receives the codes shortly before he assumes office. Prior to his inauguration, he has already been briefed and has already received his set of codes, so there is never even a one-second lapse after the inauguration.

As I mentioned during my time as DDO, even though movies may show the President wearing these codes around his neck, it's pretty standard that they are safeguarded by one of his aides, but that aide sticks with him like glue—and it's a position of extreme responsibility.

At one point during the Clinton administration—and until this day, to my knowledge this has never been released—the codes were actually missing for months. This is a big deal—a gargantuan deal—and we dodged a silver bullet. You may look at it and say, *Well, nothing happened,* and that's true—but it could have. As a Special Operator, I was taught that a plan should always avoid single-point failure—always have a backup. Well, this is the one point in the system where there is no backup, and it failed. So what happened, and how in the hell could we have lost the codes and not known it?

There's an entire department within the Department of Defense that handles all elements of the nuclear process, including creating the codes, safeguarding them, keeping them current, and making sure they are where they're supposed to be. That last part of the process is done by an individual whose responsibility it is to go to the White House every thirty days and physically view the codes to ensure that they are the correct, most current set; then, every four months he replaces them with an entirely new set.

At one point around the year 2000, this individual came back from the White House and reported that the President's aide said neither he nor the President had the codes—they had completely disappeared. Within minutes we issued replacement codes and implemented them throughout the system. But then an investigation was launched to determine what had happened and how long the codes had been missing.

Turns out that the individual whose job it was to verify the codes had gone to the White House as he was supposed to, approached the aides, and asked to see the codes for verification. The aide told him, *No problem, President Clinton has them personally, but if you'll wait here, I'll be right back with them.* He came back a minute later and said that the President was in an urgent meeting and could not be disturbed, but he assured him that the President took the codes very seriously and kept them close at hand. The guy was not thrilled, but he wasn't going to barge into the President's meeting, so he said, *Okay, we'll just check them next month.* But the following month, he was off, and it was another code checker who went in, and he heard the same thing: *Sorry, President Clinton is in a meeting, but he takes the codes very seriously and has them on his person—all is great with the codes.* This comedy of errors went on, without President Clinton's knowledge I'm sure, until it was finally time to collect the current set and replace them with the new edition. At this point we learned that the aide had no idea where the old ones were, because they had been missing for months. The President never did have them, but he assumed, I'm sure, that the aide had them like he was supposed to.

When I heard this, I flew up the escalator to the SecDef's office and told him, "You are not going to believe this . . ." We were both terrified that we might open up *The Washington Post* the next day to find the front-page headline, PRESIDENT LOSES KEY TO NUKES—LAUNCHES IMPOSSIBLE. It was exactly the type of event in Washington that provides the opposing party ammunition for attacking the other and diverts attention from other, more-pressing items of governance. Both Secretary Cohen and I were determined to fix the error immediately (it had already been "fixed" by issuing the current edition of codes) but, more important, also to fix the system that had allowed this to happen.

Fortunately, that story never broke. We learned a great lesson and changed the whole process, so that now they do have to physically see the codes, like they should have before. If the President is tied up in a meeting with another head of state and can't be disturbed at the moment, that's no problem—the checker's new instructions are to wait until he can physically see the codes—no exceptions allowed. You do whatever you can and think you have an infallible system, but somehow someone always seems to find a way to screw it up.

————

I seemed to be spending almost as much time overseas as I was at the Pentagon, but those trips paid dividends many times over. The truth is, the way our airplanes were equipped, it really did allow for as much productivity as if we were in the office. On some occasions, what played out on the plane was every bit as interesting as the destination itself. This was one of those times, and I was traveling with President Clinton.

We took off on *Air Force One* from Andrews Air Force Base around six o'clock in the evening and were due to arrive in Bosnia around seven the next morning, where President Clinton and I had a jammed day ahead of us consisting of very intense negotiations. Since the President and I would be heading in different directions following our initial meetings, most of my support staff (including aides, a doctor, security team, communications engineers, etc.) were transported separately in my own aircraft.

At about 3:00 A.M. I completed my prep in a private forward suite and could not wait to grab a few hours of sleep before we touched down—something the President had wisely chosen to do hours earlier. Mrs. Clinton entered the compartment and I stood.

"Trouble sleeping, General? Me, too," she said, as wide awake and energetic as if it were noon.

While that voice in my head said, *Can we please visit later? I have got to get some sleep,* what came out of my mouth was, "Just finishing up some last-minute prep."

"Are you sure I'm not keeping you up?" she asked, probably seeing the massive bags under my eyes.

"I'm fine, ma'am."

She smiled and took a seat and then, out of the clear blue, started to tell me that if it weren't for the ineptitude of some dumb-ass sergeant at a Marine Corps recruiting office (my words, not hers), she might very well have been a member of the armed forces at one point. It definitely got my attention.

"I was teaching law at the University of Arkansas and had become bored, so one day I decided to check on becoming a Marine," she began. "I found a local recruiting office and told the sergeant behind the desk that I wanted to enlist for two years of service. Without even looking up from his paperwork he asked what I was currently doing. When I told him I was teaching law, he responded that I would have to become an officer, which would entail at least a four-year stint. But I didn't want to be an *officer*, I just wanted to serve for two years and then get out.

"Finally, he looked up and snarled, 'Lady, with those Coke-bottle glasses you've got on, you probably couldn't make it into the Marines anyway.' And with that he left the room and I went home and cried for the rest of the day. So much for me becoming a Marine."

"Have you ever considered going back and asking that Marine, 'How am I doing now, Sergeant?'" I asked. We had a good laugh about it, but I think it says a lot about her desire to serve, not to mention the great strides we have made in recognizing the tremendous value of women in our military. The following day I believe I gave my speech in my sleep.

**C**arolyn *hung up the phone and was almost speechless. "You are not going to believe who just showed up to visit," she said in utter amazement, and I hadn't a clue. She had been unaffected when Presidents Clinton and Bush called, and she hadn't missed a beat during her chat with the King of Jordan. I could not conceive of who would prompt such a reaction. Then I heard a quick knock and my room door eased open. A full head of snow-white hair peeked inside.*

*"Mother?" I said. "How in the world did you get here?"*

*"It wasn't by horse," she said, still shaking from traversing downtown D.C. traffic right in the heart of rush hour. She came over and grabbed my hand, then gave me a quick kiss on the cheek. "Are you doing okay?"*

*"I was, but now I think I'm in a state of shock." To this day I can't imagine my eighty-five-year-old mother—who probably shouldn't even have been driving in the first place—driving her Chevy Caprice eight hours from the farm and somehow making it to the medical center.*

*"Mary Vanice wanted to come, but she was feeling a little under the weather," she said, referring to her younger sister, who was eighty-three at the time.*

*It goes without saying that as much as I appreciated my "high power" visitors, all of them combined couldn't top how loved I felt when Mother walked into that room. Years later, after she died, we found a three-by-five index card on which she had written out the directions given to her by the hospital. We still have that card.*

*Bright and early the following morning, Dr. Jim Ecklund came in to perform a series of strength tests to measure my progress, just as he had done every morning. "Okay, let's see you move the toes on your right foot," he would say, day after day, for weeks. I would strain and strain with all my might, but try as I might, nothing would happen.*

*This day began with the same ritual. "Let's say we make today the day, okay?" he began. "Go ahead and make that right toe move." As always, I gave it my all. "Come on," he encouraged.*

*"It moved!" he hollered, as excited as I'd ever seen him. It may seem*

*like a small thing, but it was a huge indicator that finally the nerves were connecting to that area of my body—an important factor in increasing my chances of recovery on my right side, as well as the left. It was a great day.*

*Chapter Eighteen*

# CHANGING OF THE
# GUARD—TEFLON DON

In January 2001, President Clinton attended his last National Security Council meeting in the White House Situation Room. This was just before the inauguration of President Bush, and in the course of the meeting he thanked everyone as a group and made some overall comments of appreciation. When he was finished, we all stood, and he started to leave through the main entry door immediately behind him, then turned back around and looked over at me standing about halfway down the table to his right.

"Hugh, I need to see you in private, please," he said, then passed behind Secretary Cohen and headed for the rear door, right behind me. Of course everyone in the room (including me) was wondering what was going on and why he wanted to see the Chairman in private.

"Let's go in here," he said as he opened the door and stepped into the Watch Center—the real hub of what we referred to as the Situation Room. Functionally somewhat similar to the Pentagon's NMCC, it served as the guts of the President's command-and-control center—monitoring and controlling intelligence, secure communications, and crisis management 24/7.

It was hard to tell who seemed more surprised, the President to find that the door led into such a raucous hive of activity, or the three duty officers, communications assistant, and intelligence analyst, whose realm had just been invaded by the President and the Chairman.

"No, this won't do," said the President, somewhat frazzled by the unfamiliar surroundings. "We've got to find somewhere quiet."

"Follow me, Mr. President," I said, leading him out through a back hallway toward the NSC secretariat section. I knew that the Deputy National

Security Advisor, Lieutenant General Donald Kerrick, was out of town, so I guided the President into Don's office. He stepped in and closed the door.

When I turned to face him I was surprised that he had come right over into my space, and again I was wondering, *What in the world is this all about?*

"I just wanted to take a moment to personally thank you," he said sincerely. "The men and women of the armed forces have done a tremendous job during my tenure as President . . . and . . ." He paused, really taking some time to formulate his thoughts, almost as if he was having trouble saying what was on his mind, yet knowing that he had to.

"Hugh, I know the last few years have put a tremendous strain on you based on my . . . activity. I know the principles for which you stand, and I know the *values,* and character, that our men and women in uniform expect—and possess—and in truthfulness, I have not lived up to those values; and yet, you have stuck by me. You have never wavered and you have never judged; you have just been the consummate professional about the whole thing. I just wanted to thank you for your service, your great leadership, and . . ."

Again he paused. I looked at him and tears were streaming down his face. "Hugh, you are an excellent role model for those great troops; and again, I want to personally thank you for your support during this difficult period. You have my greatest respect."

I was completely awed that the President of the United States had felt close enough to me to open up with such candor, thoughtful introspection, and raw emotion. He had turned away a bit to compose himself when I responded, "Thank you, Mr. President. It has been a pleasure working for you, and a great honor. You always had great focus from my standpoint, and you always had the best interests of our men and women in uniform at heart; I never doubted that for an instant. Working for you was easy, and I appreciate it."

With that he nodded "thank you," and we shook hands; then he turned and walked out. That was the last time I saw him as President.

While I waited a few moments for him to depart in private, I tried to imagine the depths of what he must have been feeling at that moment, as the book was about to be closed on any opportunities he had to achieve whatever goals he had set for himself eight years beforehand; and the jury was still out on how the hand of history would record his legacy. But from my standpoint, he was a brilliant individual with a keen understanding of the big picture, yet he could very quickly zero in and identify the weakest link in war plans. His focus was intense. If there was ever a question about which option gave our forces the best advantage, he never hesitated to approve that option. The changing of the guard was only a couple of days away, but I felt that as Commander in Chief, he would be hard to beat. His genuine concern was shown once again when he was one of the first to visit me as I lay paralyzed in Walter Reed.

———

January 20, 2001 was a cold and drizzly Inauguration Day, and the National Mall was a solid mass of expectant onlookers who had come to witness history unfold. Looking behind us at a sea of more than a million people, it was one of those times when Carolyn and I were thankful for our expedited entry. Our seats were on the Capitol's balcony, seven rows behind the incoming President; one couldn't have asked for a better view of Laura Bush holding out the very same King James Bible that George Washington used in his April 30, 1789 inauguration, and George W. Bush placing his left hand on it. Supreme Court Chief Justice William Rehnquist administered the oath of office, and Bush raised his right hand and repeated that oath. At the moment he finished, my loyalty immediately shifted to this new Commander in Chief.

Later, we joined the other Joint Chiefs and their wives at the presidential reviewing stand in front of the White House, where we would sit with members of the first family and the Cheneys to watch the parade coming down Pennsylvania Avenue.

During the parade, George H. W. Bush came over and talked with Carolyn and me at length, as proud a father as could be. It was not quite two years earlier that I'd had the pleasure of celebrating his seventy-fifth birthday with him in what was dubbed Operation Spring Colt, a parachute jump from twelve thousand feet with the parachuting team. What few people realize is that shortly after he jumped from the aircraft, the former President had trouble getting into position and began to tumble uncontrollably. It was only through the extraordinary aerial prowess of one of the Golden Knights, the Army's elite parachute team and a member of the U.S. Freefall Association that they were able to steady the guest of honor so that his parachute could properly deploy, and that happened only at the last possible moment. Once safely on the ground, the former President was aglow, joking with us on how much more pleasurable it was than the first time he'd jumped, which was over the Pacific after his bomber had been disabled by Japanese gunfire in World War II.

We had many invitations to attend inaugural balls and parties that night but declined the ones that were political gatherings, as I did my best to isolate myself from the political arena and walk squarely down the middle—not an easy task in a city where one's party affiliation seemed more significant than his blood type. While I do have personal opinions on the issues of the day (as every responsible citizen should), I am a registered independent and have always cast my vote based on the strengths of the individual and not his or her party. As Chairman (and every prior military position I held), it was crucial to leave politics at the door. The military advice I provided the President and the National Security Council was based on countless factors and variables, but politics was never one of them.

Carolyn and I rushed home from the parade. I changed from my military dress blue uniform into my mess dress uniform and Carolyn put on a long blue formal gown for the military inauguration party being held downtown. Catherine Bell, star of the popular TV series *JAG*, was the guest of honor; and we had a great time talking while I was eating and she was signing autographs. Before long the President and Mrs. Bush made a brief appearance and then Carolyn and I departed, since I wanted to prepare for the first day on the job with the new team.

At about that same time, another event was taking place in the Eisenhower Executive Office Building—this one on a much smaller scale than the afternoon's historic pomp and circumstance, but it was one that would rock the Pentagon's very foundation—not to mention age me twenty years during my remaining nine months as Chairman. Donald Rumsfeld, my new boss, was being sworn in as the twenty-first Secretary of Defense.

————

There are two kinds of relationships between a Chairman and a Secretary of Defense. There was the kind I had with Bill Cohen, where we worked together and protected each other's flanks. And there was the McNamara–Rumsfeld model, based on deception, deceit, working political agendas, and trying to get the Joint Chiefs to support an action that might not be the right thing to do for the country but would work well for the President from a political standpoint.

I have seen both.

Secretary Rumsfeld was more like the McNamara model. His nickname Teflon Don accurately referenced his dexterity at spinning a phrase in such a way that it deflected any negative implications. Nothing stuck to him.

In many ways, this style is set at the top from the very beginning.

Like Secretary Rumsfeld, Secretary Cohen is a Republican. Unlike Rumsfeld, Secretary Cohen was brought in by President Clinton as a

Republican in a Democratic administration, *an attempt to reach out and cross party lines.*

Such attempts at bipartisanship were not in the game plan of the George W. Bush administration.

Secretary Cohen is a man of great integrity and an easy man to talk to, one with a great feel for our armed forces. He stayed at the strategic level, a leader who had confidence that those he brought in to work for him would execute the details effectively. He was looking at policy, not tactical minutia. Secretary Cohen and I respected each other and had great confidence in each other. We trusted each other implicitly, working as hand in glove; he knew he could take my word to the bank.

Secretary Rumsfeld is also a man whom I personally like as an individual. When Cohen left and Secretary Rumsfeld came in, I wanted to have that same great relationship with him.

Unfortunately, from the first day I met with him, I started to become concerned. Although there was never any outward friction between us, I had the distinct impression that he mistrusted me because I had been assigned to him rather than having been his selection for Chairman.


On January 1, 2001, Secretary Cohen met privately with Secretary-elect Rumsfeld, an effort by Cohen to smooth the transition process by sharing some of the more important issues that Rumsfeld would inherit when he took over as SecDef in three weeks. Cohen had planned on covering Iraq, North Korea, Iran—but instead, his fellow Republican cut him off and wanted Cohen's take on how to control the admirals and generals, who, in Rumsfeld's opinion, had gained far too much power under Cohen's watch. Rumsfeld believed it was important for the Pentagon's *civilian* side to keep those dumb, uniformed warmongers in check.

Cohen disagreed and instead stressed his belief that it was *healthy* to have a strong military voice, just as it was healthy to have a strong *civilian* voice inside the Pentagon. Cohen believed justice was best served by a balance, and a strong leader was one who encouraged vigorous debate from all sides before making a decision. He understood that far more could be learned by analyzing the arguments of the opposition than by wasting time with hollow flattery from the sycophants; and far greater strides could be made than by strong-arm and domination.

Clearly Rumsfeld disagreed, reminding Cohen (as he would frequently remind all of us) that he had already been SecDef once (under Gerald Ford from 1975 to 1977), the implication being that his way was the right way and he didn't need anyone else's input—particularly if that input was counter to his predetermined position.

Harry Truman revealed his guiding philosophy with his famous desktop plaque: THE BUCK STOPS HERE. I often thought Donald Rumsfeld's should have said DON'T TELL ME, I ALREADY KNOW.

While I appreciated Secretary Cohen sharing with me his troublesome initial encounter with Rumsfeld, I had already experienced Rumsfeld's antimilitary bias on my own. A few months after I became Chairman, Rumsfeld was appointed to oversee the Commission to Assess the Ballistic Missile Threat to the United States, commonly called the Rumsfeld Commission. He had already held many government positions in the past (including congressman from 1963 to 1969, White House Chief of Staff, and Secretary of Defense), and at the time was chairman of the board of directors of Gilead Sciences. Joining him on the commission were Dr. Paul Wolfowitz and Dr. Stephen Cambone; both would become key players when he became SecDef.

The commission met from January through July 1998, with the finished report published on July 15, 1998. He interviewed a number of individuals throughout that time, including Secretary Cohen on June 17 and me on June 29.

The problem arose when my analysis of the immediate threat posed by various countries did not concur with his own, and he became confrontational. "How can you not believe that China poses an immediate and direct threat at this time?" he asked.

"Because I am directly quoting the National Intelligence Estimate," I responded. "I do not make this stuff up. Plus, just yesterday I verified the data with [CIA director] George Tenet and he confirmed that nothing has changed from that report. Is it something we should be paying attention to? Yes. Is it a top priority that we have to get done tomorrow? No, it's not—not unless the CIA and NIE come up with a different assessment."

The next thing I knew, I was called in to testify before a closed session of the Senate Armed Services Committee on the same issue, and this time it was Senator John McCain (Republican from Arizona) and Senator James Inhofe (Republican from Oklahoma) who asked the questions, and I gave them the same answer I had given Rumsfeld: "Because the National Intelligence Estimate, prepared by thousands of intelligence experts that we pay tons of money to prepare a thorough and accurate report, are telling us it is a nonissue right now, as is George Tenet."

McCain became agitated. "General, why don't you just jump on board and say they pose immediate threats?" he asked.

It sounded like a harmless enough question, but his demeanor indicated something quite different. He was referring to China and Iran. And even though he was well aware that the data backed my appraisal, he was visibly upset that my assessment did not comport with his.

*General,* he was basically saying to me, *I couldn't care less about the facts or what you think. Just give me the damn answer I want to hear and that supports my political position so we can get the hell out of here and have lunch.*

It was not the first time McCain had implied that I should twist the facts to support his position. And it wouldn't be the last. But I had never compromised my integrity by speaking anything short of the whole truth, and I sure as hell was not about to do so for him.

Instead, I went back to the facts at hand and just tracked through the whole thing once again.

He could have let it end there. Instead, McCain took off on yet another of his insulting tirades. It no longer surprised me. I often found it interesting how so many people were able to craft their ideal public persona and effectively present it when the cameras rolled, but behind the scenes they were entirely different—and McCain topped the list in this regard. I knew a different man from the one who came across as so affable and sensible in public. Behind the scenes, the man I—and many others in those private rooms with us—knew revealed himself as volatile and demeaning to those who did not share his views. The John McCain I knew was subject to wild mood swings and would break into erratic temper tantrums in the middle of a normal conversation. I know that tactic worked on a lot of people, but if anything, it was *counterproductive* for me. No way was I going to be baited into a verbal jousting match with him. Instead, I just listened to him and remained calm, and then responded with a straightforward analysis or description of the facts at hand. A few days ago, a friend called me, all excited that he had just found video streams of many of those hearings archived online—and he was amazed at how I could calmly sit there in the Senate hearing chamber as McCain attacked me with his explosive rants.

When the report came out, a good deal of Rumsfeld's recommendations were counter to my position, which prompted Inhofe to write me on behalf of the Senate:

> *Does this not contradict, if not undermine, your previously stated "confidence" that we will have at least three years' warning of any emerging long-range ballistic missile threat?*

Of course, I had to respond in an official manner that got entered into the Congressional Record, and it became a very big deal that took up an enormous amount of my time. Here is my response [emphasis added]:

Joint Chiefs of Staff,
Washington, DC, August 24, 1998.

Hon. James M. Inhofe,
U.S. Senate, Washington, DC.

**Dear Senator Inhofe:** Thank you for the opportunity to provide my views, together with those of the Joint Chiefs, on the Rumsfeld Commission Report and its relation to national missile defense. We welcome the contributions of this distinguished panel to our understanding of ballistic missile threat assessments. While we have had the opportunity to review only the Commission's pre-publication report, we can provide answers to your questions subject to review of the final report.

While the Chiefs and I, along with the Intelligence Community, agree with many of the Commission's findings, **we have some different perspectives on likely developmental timelines and associated warning times.** After carefully considering the portions of the report available to us, we remain confident that the Intelligence Community can provide the necessary warning of the indigenous development and deployment by a rogue state of an ICBM threat to the United States. For example, we believe that North Korea continues moving closer to the initiation of a Taepo Dong I Medium Range Ballistic Missile (MRBM) testing program. That program has been predicted and considered in the current examination. The Commission points out that through unconventional, high-risk development programs and foreign assistance, rogue nations could acquire an ICBM capability in a short time, and that the Intelligence Community may not detect it. We view this as an unlikely development. I would also point out that these rogue nations currently pose a threat to the United States, including a threat by weapons of mass destruction, through unconventional, terrorist-style delivery means. **The Chiefs and I believe all these threats must be addressed consistent with a balanced judgment of risks and resources.**

Based on these considerations, we reaffirm our support for the current NMD policy and deployment readiness program. **Our program represents an unprecedented level of effort to address the likely emergence of a rogue ICBM threat. It compresses what is normally a 6-12 year development program into 3 years with some additional development concurrent with a 3-year deployment**. This emphasis is indicative of our commitment to this vital national security objective. The tremendous effort devoted to this program is a prudent commitment to provide absolutely the best technology when a threat warrants deployment.

Given the present threat projections and the potential requirement to deploy an effective limited defense, **we continue to support the "three-plus-three" program.** It is our view that the development program should proceed through the integrated system testing scheduled to begin in late 1999, before the subsequent deployment decision consideration in the year 2000. While previous plus-ups have reduced the technical risk associated with this program, the risk remains high. Additional funding would not buy back any time in our already fast-paced schedule.

As to the Anti-Ballistic Missile (ABM) Treaty, the Chiefs and I believe that under current conditions continued adherence is still consistent with our national security interests. The Treaty contributes to our strategic stability with Russia and, for the immediate future, does not hinder our development program. Consistent with US policy that NMD development be consistent with the ABM Treaty, the Department has an ongoing process to review NMD tests for compliance. The integrated testing will precede a deployment decision [sic]. Although a final determination has not been made, we currently intend and project integrated system testing that will be both fully effective and treaty compliant. A deployment decision may well require treaty modification which would involve a variety of factors including the emerging ballistic missile threat to the United States (both capability and intent), and the technology to support an effective national missile defense.

Again, the Chiefs and I appreciate the opportunity to offer our views on the assessment of emerging ballistic missile threats and their relation to national missile defense.

Sincerely,
*Henry H. Shelton*

*Chairman*

---

Some had suggested that this ordeal might create a rocky working relationship since, as SecDef, Rumsfeld would be my new boss; but I was hopeful that an intelligent, experienced leader such as Rumsfeld would put all that behind him and forge ahead as a team to make great contributions and accomplishments, just as Cohen and I had done. That was certainly my plan, and I was 100 percent committed to President Bush and his new administration.

I had scheduled a meeting with Secretary Rumsfeld for the first day back at work following President Bush's inauguration, so that I could make it clear to him that I was glad to be a member of his team and looked forward to working with him.

The Joint Staff had been working long and hard for the past several months to properly prepare for the upcoming QDR (Quadrennial Defense Review), which is a legislatively mandated review of Department of Defense strategy and priorities that comes out every four years. It is a very detailed analysis that sets a long-term course for the DOD by assessing the threats and challenges the nation faces and rebalances strategies, capabilities, and forces to address current conflicts and future threats. (The February 2010 edition was 123 pages long.) It is a major undertaking that requires an enormous amount of work.

Since the QDR was the responsibility of the SecDef, we had gone to great lengths to provide him with the myriad of details that he and his staff would need to complete the QDR in a timely manner (since they would be working against a congressionally imposed milestone and knowing that many of his staff would not be confirmed by Congress for weeks). I wanted to use it as a tangible example of how my staff really looked forward to cooperating in the spirit of partnership and teamwork, and I hoped this meeting would set the stage for a great relationship between me and the Secretary and a tremendous coordinated working relationship between our two staffs.

* * *

When I walked into his huge office for the first of many such meetings, I was totally unaware of the volatile minefield I was about to breach. The Secretary rose from his large desk and gestured to a circular table where we would meet. "Have a seat, Hugh," he said with an inviting smile, his eyes becoming slits behind his wire-rimmed glasses. We took seats at the table where I had met with Cohen every morning for the past three years, and where Rumsfeld would convene his morning meetings from that day forward. (Joining the two of us for those morning meetings would be General Myers [my Vice], and Paul Wolfowitz [Secretary Rumsfeld's Deputy.])

"Mr. Secretary, I hope you understand I don't want to be viewed as a member of the old team," I began, speaking in a sincere, positive, upbeat manner. "Yesterday, when President Bush raised his hand and took the oath of office, my allegiance transferred immediately to you and him and the current administration. So please consider me a member of your team and not a member of the old team that's just hanging around, because that's certainly not the case." As I spoke, he showed no reaction whatsoever—not a nod, not a glimmer of recognition, nothing. It was odd, but I continued. "Anything I can do to help you in the transition, or anything you need at any time, all you have to do is just let me know."

I stopped, but still he was just frozen—then finally it hit me. He was in his own world and not particularly listening to a thing I was saying. Frankly, it got a little tense. Still, I went on. "A great example of this is the upcoming QDR. . . ."

At this point I stopped, since it was obvious that he had something he wanted to say. Finally he asked me, "How do you view your job?"

That was easy because it's specifically delineated by federal statute. "Mr. Secretary, I am the principal military adviser to you, the President, and the National Security Council, and also—"

"No, you are *not* the adviser to the National Security Council."

"Well, I beg your pardon, but according to Title Ten of the U.S. Code, it states very clearly that—"

"But not the staff, not the staff."

"No, sir," I answered, allowing him to save face when he realized that I had him by the balls since I knew exactly how the law defined my job. "I don't deal with staffs. I deal with the principals. It is you and the other principals of the NSC that I advise." Of course he wasn't worried about the staffs—it was his lame attempt to cover up his misguided power play, kind of like, *Oh, I must have misunderstood you, I thought you were talking about the staffs.* So I thought to myself, *We're going to need some heavy-duty cleaning supplies if all we're going to do is waste time having pissing contests like this.* I even made it easy for him by *volunteering* that

I was there to advise him, that I worked for him. Still, he was more concerned with marking his territory like a little bulldog than he was about getting down to the business of running the finest military force in the world. I could see why Cohen had become so frustrated when he went in on New Year's Day to discuss defending our country from Iran and China, yet all Rumsfeld wanted to discuss was defending his turf from the generals.

In the months ahead it would prove to be laborious. It wasn't that there was ever any actual antagonism between us, and it was not that I felt any tangible *friction* as much as I felt a sense of *distrust*—a sense of his not really wanting to ask my advice for fear that it would be viewed as his not being in charge—viewed as a weakness. *If I have to ask your advice, then you obviously know more about it than I do.*

Unlike Secretary Cohen, who understood military operations but respected the position of the principal military adviser and the Joint Chiefs and worked the policy issues, from the beginning it was obvious that Rumsfeld wanted to work both, in spite of the fact that his military experience was limited to dated experience at the junior-officer level in the Navy.

What I soon learned was that if I had the facts and pushed back with a strong position on issues that were important to me, Rumsfeld would back down every time. Just a short while into his term he called me into his office with a reorganization plan that most likely had been suggested to him by one of the many outside consultancy groups (some of whom were old, very outdated former administration personnel) brought in at great expense to dissect our operation. While he spoke, he thumbed through a spreadsheet. "Hugh, I've been scrutinizing assorted personnel issues and it seems evident we have some needless duplication here, particularly in the areas of your public affairs, legislative liaison, and protocol departments—so we should remedy this duplication by closing your shops down. I've got all three of those capabilities over here on my side, so I'm sure they can effectively serve us both very well." And that was that, end of discussion, the king had spoken—or so he thought when he closed the data sheet and started another topic: "Next, I want to—"

"Pardon me, Mr. Secretary, but Title Ten of the United States Code specifically says the Chairman provides *independent* military advice and that means you and I should not be drinking from the same bathwater. While it's true we both have our own departments, I can tell you that over the past three years I have seen them differ with each other far more than I have seen them agree, and I think it serves the Pentagon much better when you have two primary guys looking at an issue from a little different angle." Once again we were getting into this central philosophical difference. Both Cohen and I believed that discussion between conflicting perspectives was productive, while Rumsfeld and that entire group thought it was dangerous. I continued. "Your guy is looking at it from a *policy* standpoint and my guy is looking at it from an *operational* perspective. Together they help each other—yours helps mine focus on the *bigger* issue, and mine damn well better help yours track through the operational concerns."

He looked bored and was already looking through other files and signing various memos. "Go on, go on—or was that it?" he said, still not looking up.

"No, sir. Let's talk about my protocol department. If you want to take on handling my protocol issues over on your side, I can guarantee that you would need to substantially increase the size of your shop, there is no doubt in my mind." Then I took him through the legislative liaison concerns and closed in for the kill: "So I've got an idea of my own, and in the interest of efficiency I think you should give it some real consideration. If we add up all three of those shops on my side, I've got a total of nineteen people, and on your side those three shops total one hundred ninety people. I think it makes a great deal of sense to look at the big numbers first, and save those spaces on the side where the impact won't be felt as much, yet the savings would be far greater."

"Are there any updates on that situation in Uganda?" he asked, in the world's most flagrant non sequitur in the history of subject changes. But that was fine. I respected the fact that he backed down, and that would be the end of it—at least until I resigned and, predictably, he would hit my successor, Air Force General Dick Myers, for the same consolidation of the same three departments within three weeks of my departure—but since I had already forewarned Dick, he gave the Secretary the exact same response.

———

To get a handle on how the Chairman is able to ensure the personnel readiness, policy, planning, and training of an organization consisting of more than 2 million men and women (2010=1,425,000 active duty, 844,500 reserve) with an annual budget of more than $600 billion (FY 2010=$636.3 billion), plus serve as principal military adviser to the President and NSC, it's helpful to understand the basic structure of the Joint Chiefs.

Under the Chairman and Vice Chairman are the four service chiefs (each a four-star flag officer), who represent the various military branches:

| Service Chiefs |
|---|
| Chief of Staff of the United States Army |
| Chief of Naval Operations |
| Chief of Staff of the United States Air Force |
| Commandant of the Marine Corps |

Reporting directly to the Chairman and Vice Chairman are the directorates of the Joint Staff (each a three-star flag officer).

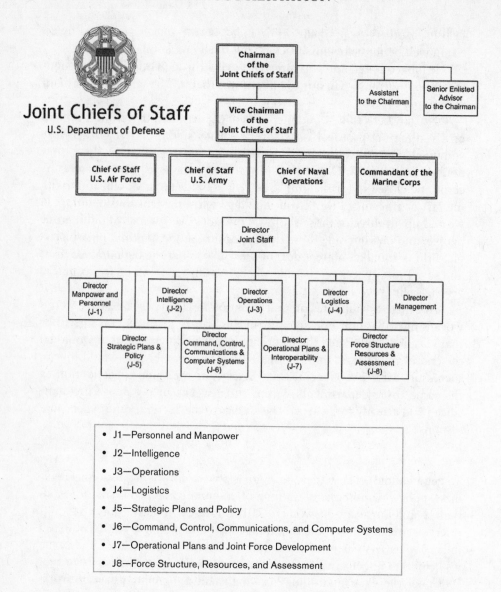

# Joint Chiefs of Staff
## U.S. Department of Defense

- J1—Personnel and Manpower
- J2—Intelligence
- J3—Operations
- J4—Logistics
- J5—Strategic Plans and Policy
- J6—Command, Control, Communications, and Computer Systems
- J7—Operational Plans and Joint Force Development
- J8—Force Structure, Resources, and Assessment

The Joint Staff is composed of about a thousand extremely bright officers from the Army, Navy, Air Force, and Marines—many of whom have PhDs from top universities, and, as I have said frequently, almost all have PhDs in war fighting—who assist the Chairman in accomplishing his responsibilities. The Director of the Joint Staff, a three-star flag officer, manages the Joint Staff much like a Chief of Staff for any organization.

My Director of the Joint Staff was an extremely bright young officer, Rear Admiral Scott Fry, who was very loyal, very supportive, and was bending over backward to meet Secretary Rumsfeld's needs in a timely manner from very early on. Like me, Scott very much wanted to be accepted as a valuable member of the new Bush/Rumsfeld team.

I had been hearing rumors that Rumsfeld was becoming increasingly dissatisfied with Scott, primarily because he was being brainwashed by his two henchmen, Doug Feith and Stephen Cambone, who were covering their own asses by blaming Scott for their failure to respond to Rumsfeld as quickly as he demanded. *We keep going to Admiral Fry for input from the Joint Staff, but he just won't cooperate,* they would say—and I know for a fact, firsthand, that Scott was breaking his ass to help these guys.

Scott got pulled into the middle of it when Rumsfeld was upset with *me* about something, as well. Concerned about the escalating unrest in Iran, Rumsfeld asked me to present our options, and when I did so he didn't like what he heard. To effectively take over that country—which is what he wanted—entailed an extremely large number of troops, most likely approaching half a million. This was the reality of the situation whether he liked it or not, and it was necessary because, as we had learned in Haiti, Bosnia, and Kosovo—the greatest demand for troops followed the actual war fighting, when the requirements turned to providing a safe and secure environment so that the new government, assisted by our government, turned to the "nation building" phase. The fact that Rumsfeld pared down—and in some cases disregarded—General Franks's original requests for heavy troops was one of the many reasons the situation in Iraq went to hell in a hand basket after the original military success. So, after my presentation to the Secretary, his response was basically, *General, you have got to be kidding. This is it?* My best guess is that he was thinking I had recently taken a magic course, because that was the only way to come up with a *realistic* plan to invade Iran in the manner he was after. "I need you to come back with some more nuanced plans," he said, giving me a few more days to pull them out of that hat.

I brought Scott in on it and he worked with the planners to come up with what we could, but the options were limited, and in my mind, the absolute worst thing we could have done was to start with the numbers that Rumsfeld was after and work backward to manufacture an unworkable plan just to justify and defend his end result. The process started with a mission analysis, and the troop requirements ultimately flowed from there—not a "wish" that we could do it with one-third of what the mission analysis showed the troop requirement was. But this gets into a fundamental difference between me and the new administration—the Rumsfeld, Cheney, Wolfowitz, Cambone, and Feith group, who operated exactly in that manner, which leads to very dangerous misinformation when it comes to matters of manipulating the American public regarding WMDs and many other things—but more on that later. For now, suffice it to say that I refused to do that and, to his credit, so did Scott.

Scott joined me for my next presentation to Rumsfeld, and when the

Secretary was once again dissatisfied with the plan that I presented, he looked to Scott, who presented a few minor changes but expressed the reality that the planners—and I'm referring to a group of the brightest brains in Washington who were resident on the Joint Staff—were no more adept at prestidigitation than was I, so Scott presented what he had, knowing full well up front he would be walking into that Rumsfeld ambush right along with me. "Admiral," Rumsfeld started, his temper obviously escalating, "sounds to me as if you are unable—or perhaps *unwilling*—to present specific options that the President and I have clearly requested." Then he turned to me. "Hugh, this is completely unacceptable."

And this takes us to April, when Rumsfeld's senior military adviser, Rear Admiral Ed Giambastiani (retired Joint Forces commander Admiral Edmund P. Giambastiani, Jr.) comes running into my office with a heads-up. "General, the boss has just heard from Feith and Cambone and he's about to fire Fry."

Ed is a good guy and I give him all the credit in the world for going out on that limb to tip me off, especially as close as he was with Rumsfeld. He had barely completed his sentence and I was out of my chair and halfway out my door before he could get his next word out: "Sir, sir . . . Please, you've got to let me get back out there, back to my desk—and please, just give it ten minutes or so, okay?"

He had done me such a great favor by coming down to me in the first place that of course I waited—but it wasn't easy and I didn't calm down any. I used the ten minutes to walk down to Scott Fry's office. Scott was seated as I walked in and immediately popped to attention. "Scott, how many snowflakes do we have outstanding?" I asked. *Snowflakes* referred to the notes that Rumsfeld used to request data or information. "Only three," Scott responded. "And all three are less than twenty-four hours old."

Scott had been working eighteen-hour days running the Joint Staff and going out of his way to support Rumsfeld's hollow staff, since many positions on the staff of the Secretary of Defense still had not been confirmed. Armed with that timely information, I charged into the hallway and up the escalator to the third floor. With my long legs, my guess is I was taking those steps about four at a time. Then I tore into his office without even knocking—I didn't have a clue whom he might have been meeting with at the time, and I understood full well that it could have been some foreign head of state or military head—it didn't matter and at that moment I couldn't have cared less. I barged in and there was Rumsfeld, all alone and standing at his stand-up desk. "Mr. Secretary, excuse me just one second, but I heard from a very reliable source that you are contemplating firing the Director of the Joint Staff," and for once, that got his attention. He raised his eyebrows and his glasses kind of popped up, and I knew he was wondering, *How in the hell did the Chairman find out about* that? I continued. "I just want you to know that if you do that, you are going to get two for the price of one. Because I will go right out with him. The guy works for me, and if you're not happy with him, you're not happy with me, and you haven't said a word to me about it."

"Mr. Chairman, I don't know where in the world you would've gotten that from. I've never thought about firing Admiral Fry. I think he is doing a fine job," he said, doing his best to stay afloat amidst the bullshit he was shoveling out.

"Well," I said, "I'm glad to hear that because I enjoy my job. And I can tell you that when it comes to supporting your staff, this guy is killing himself—in many cases being hit at three or four in the afternoon that they need volumes of information to answer some damn question and he will stay until all hours of the night to get that answer for them."

"Doesn't surprise me, he's a good man," Rumsfeld replied.

That seemed to be his pattern. We needlessly wasted a lot of time in this manner as he would try to diminish my authority or eliminate members of my staff. It was the worst style of leadership I witnessed in thirty-eight years of service or have witnessed at the highest levels of the corporate world since then.

————

I considered working for two presidents both an honor and a study in two contrasting styles. Both President Clinton and President Bush were very personable individuals and both highly intelligent. Clinton came across more intelligent than Bush, but I think to a large degree it was because that little smirk Bush had sometimes made him come across as more of a wiseass, a *look how cute I am* type of thing. It was too bad, because he had very good intuition and good judgment.

When we met, I found them both to be very attentive. They listened to you, they watched your eyes, they read your lips, they were willing to give you all the time you needed, and neither of them was the type that made you feel he was waiting for you to finish talking so that he could talk without really having heard what you were saying. Both of them had deep concern for our men and women in uniform, and both appeared genuinely concerned about the risks associated with the operations and about the potential loss of life: *What were the chances of success? What was the downside? What were the greatest risks? What end state were we looking at?* Both asked great questions, and they were not off three-by-five cards. They both listened to your brief and then came back with penetrating questions regarding military operations. They were always great exchanges, and after you had done that a few times, it became a natural thing.

Yes, he was the President, and yes, he was addressed as Mr. President—as well he should be, as the most powerful person in the world. But it became as comfortable talking to them as it was talking to one of Joint Chiefs.

They both really did make me feel like I was a part of their team, and it was a "Mr. President and Hugh" kind of a relationship with both of them.

But when it came to their styles, they could not have been more different.

President Clinton was noted for being late to a lot of meetings. The meetings were sometimes on the long side, but I can't say for sure if that was really his preference or that of his staff. It didn't seem to bother him, though. He seldom attended National Security Council meetings in the White House Situation Room, preferring instead to have Sandy Berger (his National Security Advisor) handle the meetings and report back to him. President Clinton preferred to meet with us in the Cabinet Room or the Oval Office.

Clinton was very much a night person. It was not uncommon to go to social events at the White House where the dancing and entertainment would continue long after midnight. On several occasions I remember sitting there almost squirming in my chair and commenting to Carolyn, *It's past midnight and I've got to be up in four hours to start my physical training in the morning. How long do you think this is going to last?* I'm sure she felt I was quite the barrel of fun. There we were in the White House State Dining Room, with Carolyn looking spectacular in her formal gowns, enjoying magnificent food presented by white-gloved servers in front of the famous George P. A. Healy painting of Lincoln over the fireplace, and thoroughly enjoying meeting the Clintons' diverse group of friends—from movie stars to foreign heads of state to business tycoons—with top entertainment often performed by the original composers or performers—and in spite of all this, once that clock struck ten I would start my whining. But she continued to put up with it, and *me*, and always with a smile.

When President Bush came in, there was an immediate difference in style.

President Bush would show up to meetings early. It was obvious that he liked the meetings to be well organized, crisp, and then get out of there. It was very organized, with little time for chitchat. Unlike President Clinton, President Bush attended almost all the NSC meetings, chairing them from the head of the table. Condoleezza Rice, his National Security Advisor, was very quiet in those meetings—seldom speaking at all, let alone chairing them. It wasn't for any lack of intellect, because she was extremely smart— and personable, too. I didn't think she really stepped into her own and flourished until she became Secretary of State; before that, she really took a backseat.

Early on you saw in President Bush a man who was going to be very loyal to those who worked for him—perhaps even too loyal at times. If you were on his team he would battle to the death for you. While this seems like a commendable attribute, when you're in a position of leadership, I don't believe one should allow loyalty to trump the necessity of satisfactory job performance. I'm not sure ex-President Bush would agree with that.

* * *

While I enjoyed working for President Bush, I never felt that I was considered a part of his team to the same degree as I had with President Clinton. One of the reasons was that I was forced to correct some inaccurate statements he had made during the campaign, and it put him in a rather embarrassing situation at the time. The incident started when the *Washington Post* leaked a classified document that said two of our ten divisions were in need of additional manpower, equipment, or training before being able to fight in a major regional war. But they did not report the full context in which this had been stated, so it really became great material for Republican Party sound bites as election time approached. With the exception of a few minor readiness details that were easily and quickly remedied, the report was in essence just stating the obvious: since these two divisions were occupied in Bosnia at the time, they were not able to meet their arrival dates called for in the war plans in a certain other area of the world (which was Korea, but that couldn't be released at the time).

Republican presidential candidate Bush was on the campaign trail gearing up for the biggest night of his entire political career—the last night of the 2000 Republican National Convention—when his staff discovered this readiness data. They must have been elated, perhaps even thinking it was the smoking gun that would lock up the whole election for them—and what a perfect way to attack the party in power.

So presidential candidate Bush stood at the convention, and at the very height of his speech—with more than fourteen million people hanging on his every word—he looked directly into the cameras and proclaimed, "If called on by the Commander in Chief today, two entire divisions of the Army would have to report, 'Not ready for duty, sir.'" And of course the crowds went crazy, but he had made what was considered a highly inflammatory comment that went right back to those two division commanders and their troops fighting the war in Bosnia, and it was something the Pentagon had to defend.

You can't really expect Condoleezza Rice (through whom this information was channeled) to have understood the intricacies of readiness issues, but their campaign military advisers should have, and they did not serve Bush well by allowing him to make such a statement that they had to have known was erroneous.

I was in California at the time, meeting with the Marines at Camp Pendleton followed by the sailors in San Diego, but on the day immediately following the convention I was in Los Angeles, making a speech at the Beverly Hills Hotel.

It was no surprise that as soon as I completed my speech, "Threats and Opportunities in the 21st Century," the reporters started firing off questions about candidate Bush's comment. "Was his statement correct?" they wanted to know.

"First of all," I began, knowing that the last thing I wanted to do was get enmeshed in the middle of a campaign issue—for *either* side, "I want to make it clear that I am neither paid nor in the position to comment on statements made by political candidates in the course of their campaigns—that is just not something I do—but for the record, those two division commanders are both honorable men and they both did exactly what we expect them to do. Nothing they said had anything to do with their *current* state of readiness the way it's being perceived—it only goes to the issue of their ability to meet the requirements of one particular operational plan [which I could not tell them was Korea], and they did the right thing and I am proud of them both for doing that. But believe me, their troops and their units are fully trained and ready divisions and are carrying out their missions in Bosnia even as we speak." I paused for a moment and then looked right into the camera that they had shoved up there. "I don't think I can make it any clearer than that, or be more direct than that. *Those divisions are trained and ready.*"

Then it became an even bigger deal, with Bush approached by CNN on his campaign train on the way to Ohio. *Would he concede the point after the Chairman had made it so clear that his point was wrong?*

"No, I would not concede that necessarily," he responded, going on to defend what he had said the night before. So the gloves were off, and I didn't even want to get into the ring. While acting only to right the record and restore the good names of my division commanders, I ended up rebutting Bush's big campaign statement, and the following day this was front-page-headline news in all the major papers, which, to paraphrase, read something to the effect of CHAIRMAN THINKS BUSH IS ALL WET, or some such thing that did not particularly endear me to the Bush camp, which was of course the same group that would be moving into the White House. But I did it because that's my style. I was not about to play politics or endear myself to anyone just to cover my ass in case they won, but I sure as hell *was* going to defend the good names of the division commanders and their great troops who were deployed and in harm's way—those are the ones I cared about, and that part was my job.

Between the time Bush was elected in November and started working in late January, I made private office calls on many of the incoming principals. During my visit with Condi Rice, she brought the issue up and basically apologized. She admitted to me that they had fed Bush the line, but then later she learned it was bum advice and they were wrong about it. We talked about how it had happened, and how readiness is calculated, but she just wanted to clear the air and apologize—and I respected her for stepping up to the plate with that. Still, I think it left a stigma in Bush's mind and precluded him from fully accepting me—although he was always a gentleman and treated me with great respect.

Getting back to comparing the two presidents, President Bush, like me, was more of a morning person. Early on, he invited all the combatant commanders (Rumsfeld had already changed their titles from "commander in chief" of their geographic command [which it had been since the creation of that command structure] to "combatant commander," since he believed the acronym CINC created the perception of too much power—i.e., diminished some of the perception of *his* power) and their wives to join him and Mrs. Bush for dinner at the White House. We were to confer with him first in the Cabinet Room and then meet our wives while he took an hour to freshen up—then he would join us later for dinner. We went to the Cabinet Room as our wives went upstairs, and after about a forty-five-minute meeting, instead of the President's taking that personal time, he concluded our meeting and said, "Okay, gentlemen. Let's go upstairs and see what the wives are doing." Then he led us all upstairs and we ended up starting dinner an hour earlier.

President Clinton always served excellent wines (not that I would really know the difference anyway since I preferred Bud Light), then started the meal with a toast.

It appeared to start the same way with President Bush, except when he clinked his glass with his spoon for attention and we all reached for our glasses, preparing for a toast, he bowed his head and said, "Let us pray. Heavenly Father . . ." It was substantially different and caught the Joint Chiefs and their wives off guard.

At dinner, I ended up sitting right across from President Bush and we had a very pleasant conversation about a variety of topics. He was very personable—and had a great sense of humor. You really had no choice but to like the man. Meanwhile, Carolyn was at another table, seated next to Vice President Cheney, and later she told me that he had no sense of humor at all and spoke very little. Somehow the President and I got on the topic of our personal schedules, and it turned out that we both enjoyed turning in quite early to get enough sleep so we could get up early and get our PT in the morning. The biggest surprise came about an hour later. We finished our delicious dinner, and sometime between eight thirty and nine, most of the group had downed their desserts and coffee and were getting ready for the entertainment portion of the evening to begin. As far as I was concerned, the President's next line provided better entertainment than I ever could have anticipated. He looked over at me and said, "Hugh, PT time will come early tomorrow. What do you say about calling it a night?"

I lit up and looked back at him. "Mr. President, I'm with you."

He stood up and said, "Ladies and gentlemen, it's been great meeting all of you and I look forward to serving with you. I hope you have a great evening." And with that he and Laura got up and exited the room. About ten seconds later, that room was empty. We were all out front, getting our transportation home. That sent a real signal to me that we were in for some real changes. Everybody loved it, and we had a good laugh about it on the way back to Wainwright Hall at Fort Myer, where most of the commanders were staying. Carolyn laughed as I reminded her of what I had said to Jon, Jeff, and Mark through the years: "Only drunks, criminals, and fools are out after midnight." We certainly wouldn't be in that category tonight.

On a more serious note, one of the major differences between the two presidents dealt with partisan politics. President Clinton had reached out to the Republican Party in an attempt to have bipartisan legislation and bipartisan views of the different issues that would be required. He further extended that hand by selecting Senator William Cohen, a Republican, to be his Secretary of Defense. Contrast that with the incoming administration of President Bush, which was filled with a number of neocons who had an intense distaste—and distrust—for anybody who was associated with either a prior administration or the Democratic Party in general, in spite of their high levels of expertise and experience. I'm talking about midlevel and low-level positions that required a nomination or an appointment to be made by the President. If they had touched the Democratic Party in any way or if they had worked in a prior Democratic administration, they could forget it because they just weren't going to be considered in any capacity. It's too bad because he lost a large number of top people who would have been loyal, dedicated workers—but it was not to be. From my standpoint, it was disruptive to good government. Long gone were the days of a bipartisan view of what was best for America, which made it a very distasteful environment.

With the Clinton administration, I always felt that I was free to express my honest opinions and they would be taken into consideration and either accepted or rejected, but I always seemed to get a fair shake. As I transitioned into the Bush administration, it felt more like some members of his team had a particular agenda—a direction they wanted things to go— and if you were going to be part of their team, you had better be willing to vote in that direction or you probably would be looking for another job—which made expressing honest opinions more challenging. If one did "jump on board" (to use the John McCain expression) and consistently vote the party way—*the Bush way*—then it was a pretty good bet you'd be granted Platinum Card access into that exclusive inner circle; and once there, Bush would defend you to the utmost—even in some cases if you were wrong. It was loyalty over everything else.

One of the most visible examples of this was Secretary Rumsfeld, who was coming under intense fire from many directions—and for good reason. Even a large number of staunch Republican Party members and senators were speaking out, saying that he was the worst Secretary of Defense in history and had to be fired—yet President Bush did not want to hear it, he did not want to see that there was validity to what they were saying. Instead, he blindly continued to support him, all in the name of loyalty. In other administrations, I believe such intense heat would at least have prompted a further investigation. If it turned out that where there's smoke, there's fire, then transition the person out—but we didn't see that. Not with Rumsfeld, and not with Karl Rove, and we know where that one led.

From a leadership standpoint—and from the perspective of what's best for the country in the long term, I find this ultraloyalty both disruptive and detrimental to good government. The obvious limitation is the sense of isolation it creates, since you're not having the benefit of dissenting views to stimulate a full understanding of key issues, but beyond that it can cut in the other direction, too. Some people were kept on after Bush had tendered his opinion and issued an instruction based on that opinion, yet certain strong-willed individuals seemed to disregard him and forge ahead with their own agendas, almost to the point of insubordination. A good example is Secretary Rumsfeld's deputy, Paul Wolfowitz. From 9/11 until they finally ended up pushing us to go into Iraq, the drumbeat was always the same: *the Iraqis are terrorists and they are the ones we ought to attack.*

The fact is that we had Iraq contained and *they were not a threat.* There was no evidence from the CIA or FBI connecting them to 9/11. And certainly if we were going to attack Iraq, there were a lot of other things that should have been taken into consideration, but were not. These were the types of individuals President Bush had selected, that was the type of advice that he got, and others were cast aside if they did not go along with this group of neocons that he brought in. One big exception was General Colin Powell.

————

They were calling it the Cowboy Summit, and Mexico's President Fox had just presented President Bush with an elaborate welcome-to-Mexico gift—an exotic pair of size-ten ostrich-skin cowboy boots emblazoned with the flags of both countries, the date, February 16, 2001, and the initials GWB embroidered in fine golden thread. The President had not even been in office a month, and he had chosen the beautiful city of San Cristobal as his first international destination—something he hoped would not be lost on twenty-one million Mexican Americans living back at home.

Somewhere around lunchtime, the President's private session with the Mexican leader was interrupted when an aide delivered an urgent notice: CNN had just interrupted their programming with a breaking news report. *The U.S. had just bombed Baghdad, where the shrill whine of air-raid sirens overpowered the day's final call to prayer and nonstop sweeps of antiaircraft tracer rounds cut aimlessly through the night sky in all directions.*

Excusing himself, the President contacted Rumsfeld, who had no idea what was going on, short of my unilaterally calling in the bombers to take out Baghdad (somewhat ironic in that immediately following 9/11, that's what he wanted to do instead of pursuing the real mastermind, UBL.)

While the shrapnel was about to hit the fan in the office of the Secretary of Defense, I was enjoying one of the few nonharried lunches I'd had since becoming Chairman—albeit a working lunch—and the slower pace was not a function of decreased workload but rather by virtue of its subject matter: I was meeting an Army chaplain to discuss the importance of faith and prayer and how we could most effectively meet the spiritual needs of our military community. It was an important topic, and as Chairman I knew it was my responsibility to ensure that guidance and support were as readily available to the nineteen-year-old infantryman who was the sole survivor of an IED blast near Kandahar, as it was to the sailor's wife, left home alone with four kids, no job, and the challenges of raising her children without her spouse. In my mind, our great men and women were sacrificing their blood to protect fundamental freedoms for their families and loved ones, and caring for the well-being of those families was as important to me as guns and tanks.

This was time well spent, although there would be no time for dessert. It was the SecDef calling, so I immediately returned to my office to take his call. "What the *hell* are you guys doing? Why are we attacking Iraq? Who approved this?"

Even though the bombing was not something I had to approve, I had been informed that it had taken place, so I was fully prepared when he called. The bombing was executed under the guidelines of what I called an "auto-response decision matrix," which was set up during the Clinton administration to protect our pilots, who were under constant bombardment as they flew to enforce both the northern and southern United Nations–mandated no-fly zones.

After the Gulf War, the United Nations set up two no-fly zones in which Iraqi aircraft were forbidden to fly. The southern zone was designed to protect the Shi'ite Muslim population, the northern one to protect the Kurdish—

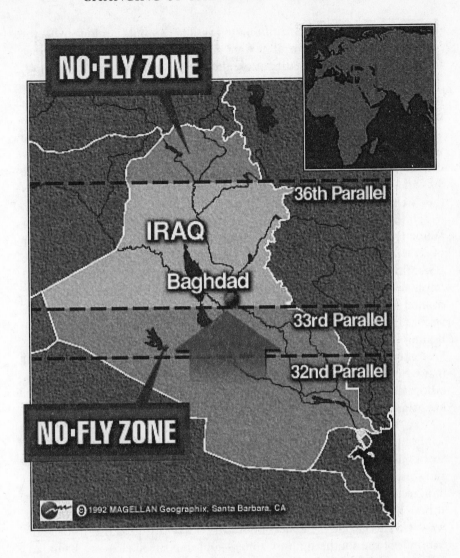

both of which Saddam would just as soon have eliminated. After our successful Operation Desert Fox, Saddam announced he would no longer respect these two zones; instead, he offered a huge award to anyone shooting down either American or British airplanes patrolling the zones.

As time went on, the situation worsened, and in 2000 there were 366 Iraqi attempts to shoot down the planes; by February 2001 there had been 51 antiaircraft artillery attempts and 14 surface-to-air missiles shot at our planes.

With the multitude of these attacks, General Tony Zinni (CINC CENTCOM at the time) and I created this matrix that listed various levels of aggression on the part of Saddam, with specific, predefined responses to those attacks on the part of our pilots. There would no longer be any "free lunches" for Saddam. If he fired at our pilots there would be a price to pay. There were five levels of escalating options, and each option required approval or authorization at different levels—with the highest one affording a very aggressive retaliation, so that was the only one that would require presidential approval. Others might require approval at the CINC level; lower ones the air mission commander could approve. The whole point of the concept was to have these retaliatory responses predefined and preauthorized, so that we didn't have to run and get the SecDef and President to sign off on each and every one, as frequently as they were occurring.

The attack that Rumsfeld was so bent out of shape about was one of these auto-responses. It was a fairly large-scale one, in which twenty-four strike aircraft (F-15s flying out of Kuwait and F-18s launched from the USS *Harry Truman* aircraft carrier) plus almost three dozen additional airplanes that provided command and control, jamming, electronic countermeasures, and enemy-air-support suppression, took out twenty different targets at five different locations in Iraq, using our very latest high-tech munitions, such as the AGM-130 optically guided missile.

Again, this had been going on for years (there were eighty days in 2000 that we made retaliatory strikes into Iraq), and since it was not at the highest option level of the auto-response matrix, there was no additional high-level sign-off required.


So I explained this to Rumsfeld on the phone, reminding him about the auto-response matrix and informing him that this was one of those preauthorized attacks. In fact, the only thing different about this attack was that although we fired the missiles from within the no-fly zone, four of the five *targets* were outside the zone—above the thirty-third parallel (the northern limit of the southern no-fly zone)—and thus much closer to Baghdad. This, combined with the heavy cloud cover at the time (which created an inversion that bounced the focused sound waves straight back to the desert floor with a tremendous amplification, instead of allowing them to dissipate as usual) got them all shaken up in Baghdad, and the Iraqis thought the city was under attack.

"General, the military is completely out of control and they have got to be reined in," Rumsfeld responded. Get up here to my office immediately and bring those so-called options with you. This situation is in dire need of urgent review."


I went to his office and tracked through the whole matrix with him once again. He was still upset and interested only in using the meeting to tell me all the reasons why it didn't work. "This is completely unsatisfactory," he finally said. "You will give the order to cease and desist immediately."

"I'll contact General Franks immediately, sir, but you realize we now will be putting our pilots in harm's way and not having Saddam pay any price for shooting at them. Don't you think that's just going to lead to more bold and aggressive measures on his part?"

"General, apparently it was *your* people who were not thinking when they tried to pull an end-around like this and institute such a plan without either my knowledge or approval, but I think you'll find things are going to run differently around here now."

"But, sir, with all due respect, you were briefed about it when—"

"General," he interrupted, "I will review it and get back to you on it at some point."

I left, but I was pissed. I really wanted to get him that DON'T TELL ME, I KNOW plaque. I felt like taking notes in case I ever decided to write a book on leadership—I was getting great material for the "what not to do" section. First of all, both he and the President were absolutely briefed on the *concept* (matrix) during transition and had accepted it. As for this strike, later on we found out that even though he was not *required* to have been notified, he *had been*; but a member of his senior staff had dropped the ball and failed to deliver the message.

Following the attack, the President's press secretary described the operation and took questions:

MR. FLEISCHER: Since 1991, coalition aircraft have been enforcing the no-fly zone in Iraq. Today allied armed forces conducted a routine strike associated with enforcement of the no-fly zone. Coalition aircraft struck targets that were instrumental in providing air defenses that threaten coalition aircraft that were on patrol in the southern no-fly zone.

The President authorized the strike because of the risk posed to our aircraft. All coalition aircraft have returned safely.

Question: Was this planned, Ari, or was this a spontaneous—

MR. FLEISCHER: The President authorized it yesterday.

Question: When did he authorize it?

MR. FLEISCHER: Yesterday.

Question: When was he informed today that it had happened?

MR. FLEISCHER: He authorized it yesterday morning and he was informed this afternoon.

An hour or so later, the President spoke to reporters. I found his statement somewhat confusing:

> The commanders on the ground, rightly, make the decision as to how to enforce the no-fly zone. I want to assure those who don't understand U.S. policy that this is a routine mission. Some of the missions require the commander in chief to be informed. This was such a mission. It is not the first time it has happened, regrettably so.

After leaving Rumsfeld's office, I called the CINC, General Franks. "Tommy, you are not going to believe this but . . ." and I went on to track through what had taken place, finally suggesting to him that we pull those pilots back and keep them out of harm's way. I did not want to set up those great pilots to die in the interest of some political pissing contest, and neither did Tommy. "Let's have them quit flying in those areas and back off until we see what I can do about this. Stand back to where they cannot get to them," I told him. I did not like it and I told the SecDef that. I thought it was an incredible regression from a creative, effective plan that had initially been approved by President Clinton and Secretary Cohen. But now it was Rumsfeld's call and he made it, allowing his ego to usurp common sense in order to set up a "Mother, may I?" situation. The flights were pulled back.

Eventually, I mentioned it to the President, which prompted Rumsfeld to suddenly come up with the perfect solution. He decided to send the plan back for my complete "top to bottom" review—so I could "get the kinks out. Fix the parts that were broken. Take the parts that were adequate and make them superior." Then, I was to present him with a new plan that was worthy of instituting. "Got, it, Mr. Secretary. Great idea," I said, taking back the plan.

We did review it, and found it perfect exactly the way it was. So it sat on my desk for about two weeks. Then we prepared a new cover page and renamed it the "Rumsfeld Auto-Response Matrix." After putting it into a nice presentation binding, we sent it back to him exactly the way it was—and of course he loved every word of it. The planes resumed patrolling the two designated zones and he was happy. But from my perspective, that little exercise cost us a month in which we were not carrying out our mission properly—a mission that included our responsibility to protect those on the ground, among many others. I found it very disappointing.

Before he took over as Chairman after I retired, I discussed with General Dick Myers the techniques I had found to be most effective in dealing with Rumsfeld (through holding firm to your position when you knew you were legally, morally, and ethically correct) and other things to beware of. Dick had already seen many as my Vice. Predictably, after his first week on the job, I received a call from him, telling me all the things Rumsfeld was already trying to pull regarding his staff.

Then, in October 2002, I heard that Rumsfeld had appointed General Nordy Schwartz as the new J3 (head of operations), one of the three most important directorate slots on the Joint Staff. Dick's choice had been Air Force Lieutenant General Ronald Keys. Nordy is a fine man and an excellent general with tremendous experience and exceptional ability—in fact he has since ascended to Air Force Chief of Staff—but I knew he was not Dick's choice. So, my assumption was that he must have been Rumsfeld's choice. I spoke with Dick and found that this was correct. When he first suggested Ron Keys, Rumsfeld had immediately pushed back and countered with Nordy. While Dick was able to hold his ground—and aggressively so—for two weeks, a shared escalator ride from Dick's second-floor Pentagon office to Rumsfeld's third would do him in.

"Dick, I know you feel pretty strongly about Ron for this job, and I can't tell you how much I respect that," Rumsfeld said as they slowly traveled between floors. "But in this one particular instance, I truly believe General Schwartz has exactly what we need in the operations area. You know what's coming up, and you know how crucial this is. This one is very important to me." By the time they stepped off at the third floor, they were ready to call Nordy with the great news.

(The truth of the matter is that neither was the ideal candidate for that position, and it had nothing to do with their capabilities. When selecting a J3, it's important to choose someone who will supplement your own area of specialty. Since very few knew more about the Air Force than Dick, it would have been in Rumsfeld's best interest to pick either an Army or a Navy officer for J3, rather than merely duplicate Dick's area of Air Force expertise, as was the case with Nordy.)

I asked Dick why in the hell he would allow the Secretary of Defense to override him like that, especially when it came down to an appointment as critical as J3. I again reminded him of my experience with Rumsfeld: that if you took a firm stand with him on issues that were important to you, he would back down every time.

Dick replied that the SecDef was pretty firm about Nordy being J3, and Dick didn't think this one was worth fighting about.

I love Dick Myers. He is a great guy; but I was very concerned that by acquiescing to Rumsfeld on an issue like this, the tone had been set for their entire relationship. And so it appears that Rumsfeld continued to disregard his advice, and in doing so he neutralized the Joint Chiefs. If the truth were known, that's probably the real reason Rumsfeld wanted Nordy in the first place. He knew that by appointing Nordy to that prestigious Joint Staff position, he would make Nordy "beholden" to him instead of Dick.

The stage was being set for marginalizing the Chairman and the Joint Chiefs.

This became enormously problematic in the Iraq planning process, when the SecDef's obvious agenda to bypass the Joint Chiefs and develop the war plan directly with General Tommy Franks led to a devastating chain of events.

Now just take that scenario, put it in a Xerox machine and hit the Copy button, and you've got the exact same thing happening at an even *higher* level in an appointment that would eventually lead to Chairman, the ultimate player Rumsfeld wanted to totally manipulate. Enter Marine Corps General Peter Pace, another extremely nice guy who was my J3 and is impossible not to like. Pete was a great J3 and would go on to become the first Chairman from the Marines. When Rumsfeld supported Dick Myers's recommendation to appoint Pete as his Vice (the natural progression to his becoming Chairman), Rumsfeld probably was ecstatic. Pete had a reputation for being a team player and an officer who was inclined to go along with what his boss wanted. That tied in exactly to what the SecDef liked. Somebody he could control. Somebody who would agree with every one of his suggestions. So now he's got his own man as J3 (who would shortly be moved up to Director of the Joint Staff, and then Chief of Staff of the Air Force), he's got his own man as Chairman, and he's about to lock in his *next* Chairman in Pete. Sadly, it was all about reducing the power provided to the Chairman by Goldwater-Nichols, reducing the power of the Joint Staff, and running the whole show himself. It caused me to cringe since this was *not* in the best interest of our Armed Forces or our nation, and was certainly not the intention of the Congress as spelled out in Goldwater-Nichols.

On a trip back to the Pentagon a few months after retiring, I witnessed Pete undercut Dick with Rumsfeld on two occasions when it was obvious what the SecDef wanted to hear—which was not the recommendation he was receiving from Dick. I felt bad for Dick in that he would not have the chance to serve as Chairman with a dedicated Vice who was as supportive of him and would work with him as a team—which is exactly what I had in both Joe Ralston and Dick Myers. I could not have asked for better

Vices than either of them and it was obvious to me that Dick would not have that experience.

The final straw was when the SecDef nominated his former military assistant, Admiral Ed Giambastiani, to be the Vice Chairman for General Pete Pace. Now all the pieces were in place for the SecDef to be given the advice he wanted to hear instead of the military advice he needed in terms of what was best for our men and women in uniform and what was best for our nation.

I get upset when I see the reemergence of the McNamara model, because it's not in the best interest of our great country to find ways around tried-and-true, established systems that may not be perfect but are far better than one individual trying to manipulate his way around an organization that offers hundreds of years of top military experience combined with the brightest young minds in the service—along with an appropriate system of checks and balances where everyone thrives on honest expression of thoughts. Perhaps if I had convinced the entire Joint Staff to send Rumsfeld copies of *Dereliction of Duty* for Christmas . . .

———

As for the Rumsfeld Commission findings, throughout his term as SecDef Donald Rumsfeld and Stephen Cambone committed much time and energy to developing a massive, space-based radar system—a technology that was astronomically expensive with questionable results. Almost immediately after Rumsfeld resigned, the program was canceled.

A*re you sure you're okay operating on my spine the day after Memorial Day?" I asked Jim Ecklund.*

*"Absolutely. I've always found that a six-pack or two tend to calm my nerves and steady my hands," he joked.*

*"Good answer, let's do it," I said, totally comfortable in his hands. While the strength of titanium proved problematic when our Delta team attempted to extract their comrade from his downed aircraft, I was most grateful for it when it came to the hardware Dr. Ecklund was about to use to rebuild my spine.*

*It was called a "laminectomy and instrumented fusion" and entailed removing pieces of four cervical vertebrae (C3, C4, C5, and C6) that had been compressed and rebuilding them with the help of titanium screws and rods. A friend had advised me against such a procedure, suggesting that instead I opt for a laminoplasty through a physician at Emory University. The procedure was supposedly somewhat less invasive. I did check it out, but my total confidence in Jim Ecklund steered me right back to Walter Reed.*

*The worst part of the surgery was that I had to ventilate myself. The thought of running that tube down my own throat caused great anxiety; however, the anesthesiologist explained that since they couldn't bend my head back because of the cervical collar, they were concerned that they might damage my throat. So they brought in a device that reminded me of a peace pipe and I breathed in fumes that were supposed to help numb my throat prior to my self-ventilation. After a few minutes, I looked up and saw the doctor approaching my neck with a huge lidocaine needle in the vicinity of my voice box.*

No way, *I thought, but as the needle was inserted I drifted off. Later they told me I did a great job of ventilating myself. I'll have to take their word for it as, thankfully, I don't recall doing it.*

*Inside the operating room, they had transferred me onto the operating table and taken great care to perfectly align my spine; maintaining this alignment was a crucial part of the procedure. "It's important that you* not move at all," they informed me before the operation began. "So you will only be conscious to the extent that you can respond to our instructions. And you are not going to be able to speak, so as we go from limb to limb, we'll have you squeeze our fingers to signal that the area is not causing you any pain."

During the procedure, the doctors made the rounds from limb to limb, and at each point I squeezed their fingers, signaling that it was okay—but all was not okay. I was in tremendous pain in the area of my neck, but since it wasn't on the checklist and I couldn't speak, I had no way of advising them of this pain. It was the worst of all worlds— something was terribly wrong and I had no way of letting them know about it. Suddenly, as if by magic, someone adjusted my head and the pain went away.

The next thing I knew, I was in the recovery room and Jim Ecklund was looking down at me. "It all went according to plan," he said, as calmly as if he had just finished his morning cup of coffee.

## Chapter Nineteen

# 9/11—INSIDE THE WAR ROOM

Carolyn, it's five thirty," I called upstairs as I headed out the door to retrieve the morning paper. It was September 11, 2001, and we would be heading for the NATO conference in Hungary. On the return trip, plans called for a stop in London, where I would be knighted by the Queen.

"Be right down," she called from the second floor.

Stepping out into the crisp morning air, I could see it was going to be a perfect day to fly—a few stars still visible through the clear early-morning sky, it would be another hour before sunrise. As I reached down for the paper, I spotted my next-door neighbor, who had the same idea. "Good morning, sir," he said with a spirit indicating that he, too, was already three hours into his day. We headed toward each other.

"Morning, Tim, how's it going?" At fifty-three, Lieutenant General Tim Maude was the Army's Deputy Chief of Staff for Personnel, and his current challenge was recruitment, which had become problematic in recent years. Tim's task was to turn it around.

"Things could not be finer, sir, although I'd be lying if I told you I wouldn't love to be on a golf course right now." Tim's passion was golf and we kept threatening to get out there and play someday.

"The only better way to spend a day like today involves a boat and trolling rods," I said, smiling back. "I'm hearing *a lot* about the Army of One campaign," I said, referring to the new ad campaign that replaced "Be All That You Can Be."

"It's only September and we've already exceeded our active-duty-recruitment goals for the year," he said with pride. Tim was instrumental in the campaign. Over his shoulder I could see my black armored Cadillac making the crisp turn onto Grant Avenue.

I started back for our house to tell Carolyn the car had arrived, then I turned back to Tim. "Teri and the girls doing well?"

"Just fine, sir. I'll pass along your regards."

But he never would. In exactly three hours, Tim would be killed when hijacked American Airlines flight 77 crashed into the new Pentagon office he had recently taken over; he would be the highest-ranking victim of the attack.

About forty minutes later we pulled up to the boarding ladder of *Speckled Trout*, a specially modified C-135 (the military version of a Boeing 707) generally reserved for the Air Force Chief of Staff. Besides VIP transport, *Speckled Trout* was used to test high-tech, futuristic systems under Air Force consideration. The executive suite was comfortable, despite the fact that other than the front windshield, the plane had no windows.

At around 7:30 we were wheels up, and the pilots had confirmed that the weather forecast called for perfectly clear skies all the way up the East Coast and across the Atlantic into Hungary.

Our suite occupied the rear of the aircraft and consisted of a round table with two oversized plush leather airline chairs facing each other with a sofa on the other wall and a pair of bunk beds at the rear with a small bathroom across from them. Carolyn was reading and I was editing my NATO comments when my executive assistant, Colonel Doug Lute, knocked at the door about an hour and a half into the flight. "Yes?" I called.

"Sir, just to advise you—the pilot has received word that a civilian aircraft has just struck the World Trade Center."

I looked at Carolyn. "You remember my speech last week? I sure hope that is not a terrorist attack." I was referring to a speech I had recently given at a conference on global terrorism. I had closed that speech with a warning to "be on your toes" since conditions were such that a domestic terrorist attack could occur at any time. This had the potential to play out exactly as I had warned.

Ten minutes later, Doug knocked once again. "Sir, it's a second plane, and it's hit the other tower of the World Trade Center."

"Doug, that's no coincidence. Have them turn us around, we're going back. Then I want General Myers on the line." He took off and Carolyn and I just looked at each other—no point in stating the obvious.

DEPARTMENT OF DEFENSE

Speckled Trout

Vice Chairman General Richard Myers was less than three weeks away from becoming the next Chairman, but at the moment he was acting Chairman—which is how the law reads whenever the Chairman is out of the country. Until I crossed back into United States airspace, all the decisions would be Dick's to make, in conjunction with Secretary Rumsfeld and the President.

Doug Lute was back, but it wasn't with word of General Myers on the line. "Sir, there's been some type of big explosion at the Pentagon, and what's more, we've been denied permission to return. All U.S. airspace has been shut down."

I sprang to my feet and headed out the cabin door en route to the communications console stretched along the aircraft skin just behind the cockpit. "Doug, tell the pilot we'll ask for forgiveness instead of permission, so have him turn us around. We're going home." I knew there was no way they were going to shoot down a 707 with UNITED STATES AIR FORCE emblazoned along the side.

The pilot followed orders very well, immediately making a steep 180-degree turn toward the west.

Meanwhile, Dick was on the phone, and the first report was that a *hand grenade* had just gone off in the Pentagon parking lot—a prime example of how first reports are almost always wrong. Since our connection was encrypted, he was able to give me a complete status report from the NMCC (National Military Command Center).

"We're still trying to determine what's going on but the hallways over here are filling up with smoke. That was no damn hand grenade in the parking lot. We've transitioned the SIEC [Significant Event Conference] into an Air Threat Conference Call, which is in progress as we speak. FAA has requested that NORAD take over control of U.S. airspace. Fighters have scrambled to escort *Air Force One,* and we're sending AWACS up to provide further monitoring. We've escalated to THREAT-CON Delta and are about to launch the NAOC. Bases around the world are locked tight, Wolfowitz has been relocated to Site-R—plus, Hadley has requested we implement full 'continuity of government measures' and we are proceeding along those lines. Hang on one . . ."

At that point I heard some commotion in the background, then Dick was back online. "Sorry, Chairman. Okay, we just got the word—the prior report was incorrect; it was *not* a hand grenade that exploded, it was another commercial airline that struck the Pentagon. No more on that, but continuing my prior, per the President we've gone Weapons Free in the event of a hijacked aircraft or one that threatens the White House."

Weapons Free—a more progressive rule of engagement whereby the Air Force is given the authority to shoot down any target not positively identified as friendly. "Got it. I need you to call Ed Eberhart (Ralph E. "Ed" Eberhart) at NORAD and let him know that we're coming back on *Speckled Trout,* and tell him that I would consider it a personal favor if he would see to it that the Chairman and his crew are not shot down on their way back to Andrews."

"Will do," replied General Myers.

Ten minutes later they called back with confirmation that we had been officially cleared to fly through the shutdown airspace. One of our pilots stuck his head out of the cockpit and announced, "Sir, our flight path will take us right over Manhattan, if you'd like to come up here about ten minutes from now." Carolyn joined me in the cockpit and it was a sight neither of us would ever forget.

We flew directly over what had been the Twin Towers, just a few minutes after they collapsed. Smoke was billowing up to about the ten- or fifteen-thousand-foot level—and even from our altitude you could tell there was a terrible mess down at the base. We vectored directly back to Andrews.

We landed to find the normally bustling Air Force base like a ghost town. Like so many government institutions, parts of the base had been evacuated. We were met by an entourage of three District of Columbia patrol cars

DEPARTMENT OF DEFENSE PHOTO MARK "RANGER" JONES

*We flew by just after the Towers collapsed, the only aircraft to fly over the devastation after the closure of U.S. airspace.*

and about a dozen motorcycle cops, who escorted us, lights flashing and sirens blaring, through the eerily deserted streets of the city all the way to the Pentagon, which was still ablaze and spewing plumes of thick gray smoke. We passed soldiers with automatic rifles in full battle dress. It felt like we were under siege.

Colonel Lute and I stepped out at the River Entrance and Ron drove Carolyn home. I went directly to my office, which was on the opposite side of the Pentagon from where the plane hit—still, the smoke was thick and the smell of cordite overwhelming. It permeated every sense like the battle zone it had become.

A quick update from Vice Admiral Scott Fry, Rear Admiral Lowell "Jake" Jacoby (my J2), and General Myers indicated that the CIA, DIA, and FBI were working feverishly to determine who was behind this heinous attack. My money was already on al-Qaeda.

Admiral T McCreary and Denny Klauer (my public affairs team) came by, along with Lieutenant Commander Suzanne Giesemann (my aide) and CW4 (Chief Warrant Officer) Marshall McCants (my personal security agent), and we took off for the site of the impact. The trek from one side of the Pentagon to the other was an experience in itself: the closer we got, the thicker the smoke. We passed through the center courtyard but instead of the lunch crowd relaxing on the park benches, there were teams of emer-

gency workers unloading body bags. We reentered at Corridor 5, which by that time had lost power, so the hallways were dark, and breathing was even more difficult. Those few who were in the corridor seemed to be rushing *opposite* our direction, trying to get away from the carnage. People were coughing, gagging, doing whatever they could to breathe—and a number wore surgical masks, but I have no idea where they came from.

Dick Myers had briefed me on the status of the command center—the NMCC—because that part of the building had taken a lot of smoke. Still, those in the center remained on duty, even though by then they had sent out alternate teams to activate the backup command site.

When we left the building and walked around to the area where the plane had hit, the firemen were still there along with rescue workers, still removing bodies from the carnage and looking for others. There was nothing I could do to help at that time.

I went back inside the building and up to Secretary Rumsfeld's office, where I met Senators Warner and Levin, along with the Secretary. We briefly discussed our current status, then went down to the main floor and over to the Pentagon Press Room for a briefing. At 6:42 P.M., we went live around the world. Our purpose was simple—to reassure the American people that the Pentagon was still intact and that our armed forces were ready for whatever was going to be required. It was really an impromptu briefing—but the feedback it generated has by far surpassed any other I have ever received. The nation was obviously shaken and looking for reassurance that their government was still functioning.

From there, I went back to my office and assembled the key members of the Joint Staff—the J2, J3, J5, etc., and went over what I wanted in terms of preparing me for the first NSC meeting, which, it would turn out, would follow the President's White House speech that very evening. It was to take place at 9:30 P.M. in the White House bunker, the PEOC (President's Emergency Operation Center), a location where I had never been before, and most likely never will be in again.

Prior to the PEOC meeting, I stayed at the Pentagon, working various options until around nine or so, when I headed over to the White House. I knew that evening's meeting would be very broad in scope, but I wasn't so sure that would be the case for the following morning NSC meeting. Before I went home that first night, I wanted to make damn sure I was well versed on all the potential terrorist groups, just to be prepared in the unlikely event that someone other than al-Qaeda was responsible. It was a very comprehensive review since at that point we did not know for sure whether the FBI and CIA would say that it was al-Qaeda, Hamas, Islamic Jihad, or any number of other possibilities.

The bunker can be described as functional yet very plain, with small, simple living accommodations off to one side, and the conference room in

DEPARTMENT OF DEFENSE

*September 11, 2001. Live Worldwide Broadcast. "We have watched the tragedy of an outrageous act of barbaric terrorism . . . but make no mistake about it,* your armed forces are ready."

which we met immediately next to it. Since I entered the White House facility at the West Wing, as usual, I was guided by the Secret Service past thick blast doors and through a long underground tunnel that terminated under the East Wing, where the bunker was located.

That very first meeting was short, general in nature, and involved participants somewhat expanded from our usual cast of players. It was more or less a damage assessment and preliminary inquiry in terms of who had done this. The President asked the typical questions: *Has anyone claimed responsibility? Do we have any intercepts? What kind of chatter was there beforehand?* George Tenet mentioned al-Qaeda reaching out into sixty countries, and the President responded that we would pick them off one at a time. Rumsfeld had already started suggesting we go after all the countries who provide any kind of support for these terrorist groups—Afghanistan, Sudan, Libya, Iran, and Iraq. "We must think broadly," he said.

Colin Powell took the opposite side, stressing a narrow approach. For public and international support, we had to keep it narrow—restrict it to al-Qaeda in Afghanistan. At this point there was very little sharing of information or divulging of information because both George Tenet (CIA) and Bob Mueller (FBI) were still scrambling and wanted their facts straight before they spoke to the President. We adjourned and agreed to reconvene the following morning.

* * *

There were actually two NSC meetings on Wednesday, the morning meeting in the Cabinet Room and the afternoon back in the Situation Room. We started with a rather large group, which is why it took place in the Cabinet Room. Needless to say, it was a very somber meeting—probably about as serious a meeting as I've ever seen. Andy Card was present, as was the Secretary of the Treasury, the Attorney General, Scooter Libby, Condoleezza and her deputy, Steve Hadley, and many more for the first part of the meeting. I was at the far end of the long table, immediately to the left of the Vice President, who had the President on his right side, next to Colin Powell.

I was one of the first to speak, reporting on two early-morning calls I had just completed in my office. The first was from Sir Michael, my British counterpart, pledging the full military support of his country. It was powerful, and another example of the unwavering support we consistently got from our friends across the pond.

The second call was also one of support, from a Middle East counterpart who asked that I keep the call private—which I certainly will. I have had lots of conversations with top Middle East leaders—many of whom I consider my friends—and while personally (and privately) they pledge military support (and mean it), the very next day you might see the same guy on television saying that he just told the Americans he would be no party to their request and would never grant that request. The bottom line is that they usually do come through as promised, but they have to say otherwise to protect their own asses on the home front.

As my term as Chairman was winding down, I felt blessed at the many friends I had made all over the world—and not even twenty-four hours after the barbaric acts, those friends were stepping up to the plate, completely unsolicited, to offer their personal and military support. The President was impressed—in fact he appeared to be emotionally touched—that I was getting these calls from our international friends. Later, others would start receiving similar calls, but these two were the first.

Not long into the meeting, they opened the doors for the press to come in and of course they all swarmed in and took over the room. It was a prescheduled photo op that the President felt was important to show the American people that all was under control and although the ship was damaged, it was not nearly to the point of sinking and was still steaming powerfully ahead and on course. We all stopped and posed as best we could (that's when the photo of me right under the painting of President Eisenhower was taken), and a few minutes later the handlers came

*September 12, 2001. NSC meeting in the Cabinet Room.*

in and cleared out everyone except the principals, and we got down to business.

First, George Tenet and Bob Mueller laid out everything they had. Tenet said that everything the CIA had clearly pointed to al-Qaeda. Bob Mueller started in and then made an off-the-cuff remark that there were a few other things that he couldn't share just yet because of evidentiary concerns. "If we ever capture these guys, we want to be able to take them to trial," he said.

That invoked a pretty strong rebuke from the President and the Attorney General. Ashcroft (Mueller's boss) was first to erupt, blurting out, "Get the damn stuff out on the table, Bob. We've got to catch these guys immediately and make damn sure this doesn't happen tomorrow, so whatever you've got, share it. Right now." *Welcome to the club, Bob,* I thought. He had started only about a week before (taking over as head of the FBI from Thomas Pickard on September 4, 2001).

Of course Bob Mueller was really just doing his job, being very concerned that he did not cross the line and end up with a guy like Usama bin Laden being captured, put on trial, and then released because the evidence would not be admissible because he had violated the procedures early on.

And then Ashcroft made a comment something to the effect of, *We hope that Shelton's people will get them anyway and then we don't have to worry about taking them to trial.*

But at any rate, Bob did share what he had, and 100 percent of it pointed to UBL. I was very concerned going into that meeting since terrorists do not have a lot of really great targets. They don't have a military, they don't have an infrastructure, and it's hard to find their leaders. Going after terrorists is more akin to fighting organized crime or thieves in the night. So my concern was that they were going to turn to the military—turn to me—like they had done so many times in the past and say, *Okay, Shelton, what targets do you have that we can go after?*

The truth is that we had lots of targets in plans that were on the shelf, but quantity does not equate with quality. What I brought with me were a couple of briefcases filled with books organized by type of terrorist organizations and targets that we had, plus those we already had programmed since we knew precisely where they were, and we knew exactly what it would take to hit them.

Let's take Afghanistan as an example: targets ranged all the way from what we called "jungle gym training camps," where they would train the terrorists—and there were approximately eight to ten of these. Then we had the drug-manufacturing facilities that they used to make the drugs that provide the funding for their operations. We had the Taliban leader's (Mohammed Omar) home and offices and different structures of theirs throughout the country. It was a large number of targets, but if you condensed it down to *good* targets we had probably less than a handful, and that was only if you went after the Taliban. The reality is that none was a particularly good target in terms of stopping a terrorist threat, and that's what this was really all about.

When Bob Mueller finished speaking, all heads turned to Rumsfeld and me, but before either one of us could say a word, the President spoke up. "We will get to the military options soon, but before we do, let's look at the political, economic, diplomatic, and all the other sources and tools that we've got and see what we can do with those as well. What can we do on the diplomatic side?" And there would be a discussion about that. "Okay, what about the political side?" and Condoleezza had some things to say about that. Then he turned to Paul O'Neill and asked about the economic options, which really got my attention since on two occasions in the past I had been in the Oval Office trying to get the President to allow us to put together plans to go after al-Qaeda finances because we knew where their money came from, and how they laundered it; but the previous two Secretaries of the Treasury had argued vehemently that we should not go after their funding because it might cause them to attack our financial institutions. My point was that if they *could* go after ours, wouldn't they do it anyway?

O'Neill started with the same argument on why it was a bad idea to hit their finances, but the President interceded immediately, as if he knew what was coming. He said, "We are going to use *every* tool that we have, to include economics; so let's start figuring out what we can do to destroy these guys economically."

Then they turned to me and Rumsfeld. I gave a brief synopsis of the types of targets that were available—probably talking for less than ten minutes in total. I elaborated on how these targets applied to al-Qaeda and then covered the forces we already had positioned in the Gulf.

We took a short break and I happened to be standing by George Tenet, and we struck up a private conversation.

"We ought to talk about the Northern Alliance," George began. "We're talking about deploying a team in there to work with them." The Northern Alliance was a consolidation of Afghan groups that were banded together to fight the Taliban. They included the Tajiks, Hazaras, Uzbeks, and Turkmen. Since the Taliban comprised the major backing of UBL, our working with the Northern Alliance could give us a great "jump start" in an offensive against the Taliban.

"Are you talking about augmenting their capabilities?" I asked.

"They'd have a long row to hoe without that support."

"What they really need is air support, laser designators, supplies, things that our Special Ops teams could be providing to specifically enhance their capabilities—*if* we were in there. It would be a great multiplier for them."

"It might make the difference," he agreed.

These were early first and second elements we were talking about, Special Ops and CIA forces that would go in to set the stage for whatever main attack we might have. The CIA team could establish and foster contacts with the various warlords—the Dostums, Karzais, etc.—and our Special Forces teams could supplement those relationships. George nodded as the meeting resumed; it was another tool for consideration in whatever plan would ultimately be chosen by the President.

At some point Rumsfeld and Wolfowitz started pushing hard to attack Iraq. In their minds, this disaster could be turned around into an ideal opportunity to end the problems we were having with Saddam Hussein—just blame the 9/11 attacks on him.

I did not agree with that because there was absolutely zero intelligence to indicate that Iraq was involved in the 9/11 attack. Nor was there intell linking either Saddam or anyone else in Iraq to Usama bin Laden. Both Mueller and Tenet had just made it clear that bin Laden and his organization were responsible for these terrorist acts. I wondered how Rumsfeld and Wolfowitz planned to blame this on Saddam, since neither the FBI nor the CIA had one shred of intell bringing Saddam into the picture.

Rumsfeld really didn't seem to care what Tenet and Mueller had briefed because this was a golden opportunity to go after Saddam Hussein. In his mind, everyone had to know that there were links between UBL, the al-Qaeda organization, and Saddam Hussein. *We gotta get this guy* was all we were hearing from Rumsfeld and Wolfowitz, referring to Saddam, not bin Laden. It was almost like paranoia.

Colin and I lobbied just as strongly in the other direction, based on the intelligence provided by the FBI and the CIA. It didn't stop.

Once we got back to the Pentagon, Wolfowitz was still insistent that we get our Iraq plans up to speed so that we were completely prepared to invade Iraq. We had General Tommy Franks dust off the Iraq plans and start taking a look at what would make the most sense from a planning perspective if the decision was made to take out Saddam at that time. We had a number of preexisting plans surrounding various Iraq operations, and we wanted Tommy prepared to present them, if required.

Early the following morning, as part of the same PT ritual I had been following for more than thirty-seven years, I made my five-mile run around the post. Not only was it something I wanted to do, it was something I *had* to do—my personal therapy, a time for my internal wheels to turn, where thoughts just seemed to gel.

But today was different. The air was stale. I wondered if it could be the acrid stench of burning carnage still adrift from the Pentagon. It was not like any other day since I'd been Chairman—the post was sealed tight. And that daily Norman Rockwell moment as I passed the newspaper guy was a thing of the past. In fact, since 9/11, I hadn't been getting a paper at all; I instructed my aides to follow up on that.

Carolyn had told me the news about Tim, and of course he came to mind as I ran past his house—one of the first times I had seen it completely dark. While I was terribly saddened to learn of his death and felt great sympathy for his family, just like at Fort Benning when the two aircraft in my platoon had run together, I had to remain focused on the mission. How were we going to settle the score and retaliate against those who had killed Tim Maude, my neighbor, in addition to thousands in the attacks on the Pentagon and the Twin Towers and the aircraft that had crashed in Pennsylvania? They and their families and loved ones deserved no less.

I had two weeks left as Chairman, and I sure as hell was going to make the best of them.

* * *

On September 13, George Tenet used the White House NSC meeting to officially present to the President the plan that he and I had discussed in our brief sidebar the day before. He brought Cofer Black (head of the CIA's counterterrorism center) with him for a follow-up presentation.

"What we're proposing is an aggressive covert-action plan directed primarily toward al-Qaeda and the Taliban, and to achieve this we will insert a CIA paramilitary team into Afghanistan to work closely with opposition forces—primarily the Northern Alliance—to prepare the way for Special Operations forces."

It was an aggressive plan, and Cofer presented it with a dynamic enthusiasm that completely captivated the President; he was totally on board. The plan would be refined in the days to come, but it would be the foundation of the CIA's Camp David presentation over the weekend.

Throughout that week we had National Security Council meetings, some with the President, others just the principals—but they all led up to the principals' weekend at Camp David. It was there that the President would decide which option to pursue.

In the interim, Congress would pass a significant joint resolution (signed into law by the President on September 18, 2001) authorizing the President "to use all necessary and appropriate force against those nations, organizations, or persons he determines planned, authorized, committed, or aided the terrorist attacks that occurred on September 11, 2001, or harbored such organizations or persons, in order to prevent any future acts of international terrorism against the United States by such nations, organizations or persons."

In theory I suppose Camp David was selected for our next round of discussions in order to lend a more informal feel to the proceedings. About seventy miles outside Washington in the Catoctin Mountains of Maryland, the setting certainly was rustic. Those meetings on Saturday, September 15, bore the distinction of being one of the very few times I would meet with the President in anything other than my Army uniform. Our official instructions specified casual attire, so an open-collar white shirt with fall jacket won out over the uniform. (For most weekend meetings at the White House [in either the Situation Room or the Oval Office], the Cabinet officials and POTUS came in very casual dress, and I would have been welcomed in civilian attire. Even so, I wore my uniform out of respect to the office. At one point President Clinton asked me if I owned any civilian clothes. "I think I've got an old suit hidden somewhere in my closet," I answered with a grin.)

In spite of the setting, it didn't take long for the meeting to turn ugly, with Cheney, Rumsfeld, and Wolfowitz pushing hard to invade Iraq, and Colin Powell and I countering that we should go after bin Laden at this time.

At one of the breaks, President Bush pulled me aside and asked, "What am I missing here, Hugh?"

"You've got it exactly right, Mr. President," I told him. "I have neither seen nor heard *anything* from either the CIA or the FBI that indicates any linkage whatsoever to Iraq. Stand firm, because it will destroy us in the eyes of the Arab world if we go after Iraq under the guise of Saddam somehow being tied to this when the facts show otherwise. What you'll have is the extremists and the fundamentalists painting it as the Americans are going after their Arab brothers just because they want to."

Earlier, both Colin and I had reiterated that there was *not one shred of evidence that Iraq was involved in the 9/11 attacks*—they had all the earmark of bin Laden but no link whatsoever to Saddam. By the time I was finished stating my case, the President seemed to have made his decision.

"We're going to get that guy [Saddam], but we're going to get him at a time and place of our own choosing," he said, nailing the lid on any further discussions about Iraq for the moment.

The meeting reconvened, and the President went around the table for opinions, much as he had in the Cabinet Room. "General, what have you come up with?" he asked when he came to me, referring to our plans to attack al-Qaeda in Afghanistan, as well as the Taliban. I presented three escalating options. The first entailed TLAM strikes, cruise missiles—which most likely would hit a few vacant training camps and cause some very expensive craters in the ground. The second option involved the TLAMs supplemented with manned bomber attacks on additional targets—an escalation from the first option, but still, most likely not of the intensity we were after at this point.

Before I could get to option three, a voice from behind the Secretary of Defense and me interrupted. It was Wolfowitz again. "But we really need to think broader than that right now; that's not big enough. We've got to make sure we go ahead and get Saddam out at the same time—it's a perfect opportunity."

The President became irate. "How many times do I have to tell you, we are *not* going after Iraq right this minute, we're going to go after the people we know did this to us. Do you understand me?" Colin and I just looked at each other and rolled our eyes.

I continued with my third option, which combined the first two and added boots on the ground, both Special Operators and traditional ground troops. Nothing was decided, although it was obvious that nobody would be backing options one or two.

It was another long day and it felt good to get home. As was so often the case, there were very few specifics I was able to share with Carolyn at the time, but I had one piece of info I had no problem revealing. "I can almost guarantee you we're going to invade Iraq before the end of President Bush's first term," I told her. "Between a comment he made to me and that constant drumbeat from Rumsfeld, Cheney, and Wolfowitz, it was obvious that here was a group intent on working backward to sell their case. And you know how much I want to get Saddam; I've spent four years of my life with that son of a bitch shooting at us every day, not to mention what he is doing to his own Iraqi people. But you don't take him out by lying to the American people and using 9/11 as an excuse to get him when he had nothing to do with it—that's just wrong."

"I found out something else that's not going to thrill you," she said, knowing that the last thing I needed was more bad news. "I've solved the mystery of the disappearing newspapers. Turns out after the attacks they heightened security on the post . . ."

THREATCON Delta, I said to myself.

". . . and the newspaper guy didn't have whatever security clearance is needed to get in for his deliveries. It's not just you; everybody is screaming that they want their morning papers."

"Would you please call . . ."

"Don't worry, I've already called whoever needed to be called, just give it a little time," she said, always three steps ahead of me.

About a year earlier, General Tony Zinni had left the position of CENT-COM commander, and General Tommy Franks had been the unanimous choice to move in as his replacement because he was very familiar with the Middle East AOR, where he had worked the past few years as commander of the Third Army. Tommy comes across as a good old country boy, the Texas cowboy with the Texas drawl. Smart guy. Thinks his way through things pretty logically. Had never been particularly egocentric, at least not that I had observed. He was just a good, solid, well-rounded guy. With Afghanistan being within the CENTCOM AOR (area of responsibility), our invasion plans would ultimately be Tommy's responsibility.

* * *

On September 20, along with his J3, Air Force Major General Gene Renuart, Tommy stepped into the Tank to present his plan to the Joint Chiefs, in preparation for the presentation to President Bush the following day. His aide passed out the briefing sheets as Major General Renuart headed to the front to find the six Joint Chiefs sitting there—the four service heads, the Vice Chairman, and me. Between the Army Chief of Staff, General Eric Shinseki; the Air Force Chief of Staff, General John Jumper (who had just taken over from General Mike Ryan a few weeks earlier); the Chief of Naval Operations, Admiral Vern Clark; and Commandant of the Marine Corps, General Jim Jones—not to mention me and General Myers—together, he was looking at more than two hundred years of experience, much of it in hands-on war fighting—like F-16 pilots with thousands of hours of combat air time, and Army division or corps commanders, or submarine or aircraft-carrier commanders, Special Ops commanders— an enormous wealth of experience that was at his disposal to work with him to hone his plan. The SecDef and Paul Wolfowitz were also seated at the long, shiny conference table.

Tommy watched intently as Major General Renuart presented his war plan. It appeared solid—not great by any means, but certainly not full of holes, either, especially given the short time he'd had to put it together.

His war plan consisted of the following four phases:

**Phase 1**: Set Conditions and Build Forces to Provide the National command Authority Credible Military Options;
**Phase 2**: Conduct Initial Combat Operations and Continue to set Conditions for Follow-on Operations;
**Phase 3**: Conduct Decisive Combat Operations in Afghanistan, Continue to Build the Coalition, and Conduct Operations AOR Wide;
**Phase 4**: Establish Capability of Coalition Partners to Prevent the Re-Emergence of Terrorism and Provide Support for Humanitarian Assistance Efforts.

There were a lot of questions about the details that he was unable to answer, but that's not uncommon—and it's nothing to look down upon. In those cases, the CINC would just say they didn't have the answers at that moment but would get back with them shortly. It was no big deal.

Tom's predecessor, Tony Zinni, would be the first to tell you that it didn't always feel great to be hit with all those questions; but, by the time you walked out of there—if you had listened to what the service chiefs— each one an expert in the capabilities of his services—were suggesting, ultimately you would end up with a far superior plan. After all, it was this group that would have to make sure the plan was supportable, and frequently offer the combatant commander resources he didn't even know existed. Unfortunately, Tommy didn't see it like that. He took those questions personally.

He and I spoke after the briefing and he never mentioned a word about being upset about how it had gone, and that didn't surprise me because I found all the questions to be both respectful and constructive. What *did* surprise me was years later (after his book came out), when I learned that Tommy felt like he had been completely torn up in there, extremely upset about how he had been treated. The following day, he had berated two of the Joint Chiefs, telling them, "Yesterday in the Tank, you guys came across like a mob of Title Ten motherfuckers, not like the Joint Chiefs of Staff."

What I had begun to see—and this became a very significant factor when, later on, the Iraq War was playing out—as soon as Tommy was promoted to four-star, he had developed a hell of an ego. It was not evident until he became the CENTCOM commander, then it started coming out in spades. I think ego was what that whole smear campaign against the Joint Chiefs was all about. He considered it a grave insult that other four-stars had the nerve to challenge him in there, yet what I saw firsthand was not one bit of disrespect, nor were there any unwarranted challenges. Our whole point was to work with the commanders and challenge all the elements so that they could walk out of there with a rock-solid plan that would achieve the desired end result with the minimum loss of life, property, and capital. In hearing how Tommy had viewed that meeting, I have to believe that anything short of a rousing round of applause for his perfect plan would have been more than his ego could handle.

After we both had retired, I was sitting on the board of the Anheuser-Busch Companies, when Tommy made a presentation at a Busch sales meeting in San Diego.

Throughout his talk he referred to the President as "George Bush" and the SecDef as "Don Rumsfeld" or "Rummy," again showing an ego that was unbelievable. After the presentation, several directors remarked to me that it was the worst presentation they had ever seen. One commented, "Who the hell does this guy think he is?"

The meeting with the President took place the following afternoon on the second floor of the White House, in a study within the President's living quarters. In addition to the SecDef, the Vice President was there, as were Tom and Gene from Tampa, and of course I had Dick Myers join us, and Major General Dell Dailey also flew up for the brief, since he would be commanding the secret JSOC part of the operation—which was a big part of the plan. By this time his lead elements had already gone in to meet up with George Tenet's CIA teams.

We had been allotted two hours, but it wasn't as if we were rushed in any way. The President seemed focused—but more relaxed than I had seen him since the attacks.

Tom went through each phase, much like he had with us the day before, with the President periodically stopping him for clarification. Like President Clinton, President Bush had a solid grasp of the tactical, operational specifics as well as the overall strategic concerns. He quickly "got it." We went over the timeline, talked about where we were on (overfly and basing rights), and we utilized a big matrix we'd created to show the President how all these many pieces had to come together.

When the issue of SOF (Special Operations forces) troop levels came up, I shot Dell a glance. This was an area where Rumsfeld was convinced that the force level should be a lot lighter, and he had repeatedly tried to get SOCOM and JSOC to cut back. So far, they remained firm, but I had little confidence that strength would hold up after I retired. Too many times I had seen Rumsfeld keep digging away like a little pit bull until he got his way.

As soon as we stepped out of the West Wing, I pulled Dell aside in the parking lot. "Look, I'm leaving in another few days, and whatever you do—do *not* let them browbeat you into trying to do something without the right-size force to make it successful, because ultimately it will all come back to you for having failed militarily to achieve your goals. You can't let them cut you to the bone and not have sufficient backup in case things don't go exactly as you thought they would. It's that redundancy that is going to save lives. Nobody will remember—or *care*—about the force level you *wanted* before they cut you back." Without the reductions, I thought, his plan was fine—he did have sufficient redundancies built in—but if Rumsfeld got his way, it could quickly turn into a disaster.

"I understand," he said. "I know what I need and I'll stick with it." To the best of my knowledge, that's exactly what he did.

———

It was a strange feeling, knowing that my morning run was one of my last at Fort Myer—one of my last as Chairman, or as a soldier. As I cooled down, I stopped beside the parade field just in front of our home. It was a magnificent postcard vantage point of the Washington, D.C. skyline that would be the envy of any photographer. The rising sun cast silhouette cutouts of the Capitol and the Washington Monument. Although we were doing our best to get things back on track, how the world had changed in my four years as Chairman. But still I was upbeat and optimistic about our great country and the brave men and women who were protecting it.

"Good morning, General," said a familiar voice behind me. I turned to see a man walking up Grant Avenue with a bag stuffed under his arm. He, too, was in silhouette and I couldn't make out who he was, but he sure knew me. "I brought your newspaper," he said with pride.

Sure enough, it was the paper guy. "Great," I said. "I understand you had some trouble with those security clearances. Glad to see you got them worked out."

"Where there's a will, there's a way, General. Not exactly worked out, but I wanted to be sure you got your news."

"Dare I ask?" I smiled, my curiosity getting the best of me.

"There was no way they were letting me drive on through the main gate, so I found this hole in the perimeter fencing. It was almost big enough for me to squeeze through, and with a little help—let's just say now I *can* fit through that hole."

*So much for THREATCON Delta,* I thought to myself, and thanked him profusely for his above-and-beyond efforts to do his job on my behalf.

———

Earlier in the year, I had attended my final Senate Armed Services Committee hearing. It was through four years of prior testimonies (many fiery and some even contentious) to both this and the House Committee that sweeping improvements and long-lasting strides were made for our great armed forces. Many of the comments spoken that day—on the record and entered into the United States Congressional Record—meant a great deal to me, especially considering the stature of the great statesmen making those comments. Here is one from Senator Levin, the committee chairman:

> "This may be the final time that General Shelton will be appearing before this committee to present his views on a defense budget before his term ends.

> "General Shelton, you have always put one cause above all others, and that's the well-being of America's armed forces and their families. History will record you as an outstanding Chairman of the Joint Chiefs who left the U.S. military more capable than you found it. And on behalf of all of us, I want to take this opportunity to express our gratitude for the tremendous service that you have given to this nation."

I wanted it on the record how very much I personally appreciated their stepping up to the plate on behalf of our servicemen and -women, yet also remind them that there was still work to be done:

> "It's been my great honor to serve the men and women of our armed forces. And I want to once again thank this committee—each and

every one—for your very strong and staunch support of our men and women in uniform.

"I'd like to focus for just a second on the decisive edge of our force, the men and women in uniform. President Bush stated that a voluntary military has only two paths. It can lower its standards to fill its ranks or it can inspire the best and the brightest to join and to stay. This starts with better pay, better treatment and better training. The president, I believe, had it exactly right. We must continue to close the significant pay gap that still exists between the military and the private sector, and we must make continued investments in health care, housing and other quality-of-life programs that are essential to sustain our force.

"Regarding health care, I want to thank the members of this committee for the great support that you gave our men and women in uniform, as well as our retirees; you made it happen, and it is reflected in everything that I see now in terms of morale, in terms of attitude, in terms of a recognition of the appreciation of their great efforts. There is still a concern as we look at health care, and that it is an entitlement basically that still competes with ammunition, with planes and ships, et cetera. We need to try to figure out a way to get that out of the O&M account and get that into a category of funding that recognizes it for what it is, a must pay that we pay up front, and not put it in the same category that we have precision munitions.

"We are a global power, the only one in the world, and sometimes that gets to be lonely also. But we have worldwide responsibilities and it is the great strength of America and the men and women in uniform that are out there daily carrying out, protecting our national interests, that I think certainly help provide for the peace and prosperity that we have today. And it's quite an investment—three cents on the dollar; that's what our armed forces provide for us today.

"Ultimately, I think we have to make sure that if we want to continue to enjoy that peace and prosperity, that if we want to continue to be recognized as a leading power in the world and to provide for the peace and stability for the rest of the world that also helps our own prosperity, we have to make an investment in that force. And that may mean that three cents on the dollar will not be sufficient in order to modernize this great force we've got and to keep us with the leading technology in the hands of the greatest force in the world."

Other complimentary comments were shared by Senator Warner:

> "I thank you and your family for . . . a lifetime contribution to freedom and to service in this country."

Senator Jean Carnahan:

> "I'd like to certainly express my gratefulness for your—the patriotism that you have shown, and for all you have done in the interest of peace around the world. Certainly the American people owe you a great debt of gratitude. And I thank you very much for that."

One by one, they had great things to say—until Senator John McCain took the floor. *General Shelton, last September twenty-seventh—I have your testimony—you said, "It's a real success story . . ."* and then, perhaps not so surprisingly, he used his time to attack. As always, I answered him calmly and directly. It had come full circle.

———

One question I'm frequently asked is how my career has affected my children, and in looking back, I have to say that at times it's made things pretty difficult for them. By the time I got to be Chairman, Jon and Jeff were married with kids, and Mark was in college; however, he decided to enlist in the Army, and as such would be starting out as a private. While on one hand we would have preferred that he stay in school and obtain a degree, we were fully supportive and proud of his decision to serve his country. I thought it would be special for both of us if I would actually swear him in, so I took a day of leave and drove up to Baltimore with Carolyn, where I administered his oath at the MEPS (Military Enlistment Processing Station) Center. It was poignant but quick, and following the swearing-in, Carolyn and I turned right back around and returned to Fort Myer.

After the ceremony, they put all these new recruits onto buses and transported them to Atlanta, where they arrived around 2:00 A.M. to meet up with other new recruits who had flown in from all over the country. They proceeded on to Fort Benning, Georgia, and dismounted the buses. There were hundreds of long-haired new recruits in jeans, cut-offs, and whatever other civilian clothes they happened to be wearing, milling about in a large, open area, waiting to be processed in so that they could begin their basic training. Mark—at six feet seven inches at this point—was right in the middle of the pack, just waiting with the rest of them to see what was supposed to happen next. Suddenly, the sergeant hollered out, "Mark Shelton, front and center."

Mark filtered through the throng and stepped to the front, not having any idea why the sergeant had selected him out of all the others. After turning Mark around to face all the others, the sergeant got on his mega-phone and announced, "If you don't know who this guy is, you better learn. This is the son of the Chairman of the Joint Chiefs of Staff, the highest-ranking general in our entire military. You *will* treat him accord-ingly." When I heard that, it broke my heart. Can you imagine the embar-rassment something like that caused this poor kid? Fortunately—and I suppose it was battle by fire—he made it through it all, becoming a mem-ber of the elite Army Ranger Regiment, and subsequently turned out to be a smart, well-rounded young man who now has a great job working for a top high-tech firm; not to mention being a devoted husband and spectacu-lar dad.

Mark was glad that I ended up *not* taking any action against that ser-geant; I did that for fear that it might embarrass him further. Truth be told, the real reason I didn't do anything was that I was so upset with that sorry-ass first sergeant that I didn't want to say or do something that might cause Mark even more issues, and he seemed to have handled it well.

Things weren't much better for my middle son, Jeff. When he was a young lieutenant in flight training at Fort Rucker, a major called him over and said, "Lieutenant, you've been here six weeks now and I notice your last name is Shelton. You're not related to the general who is commanding Fort Bragg, are you?"

"Yes, sir, he's my father," Jeff replied.

"What?" the major shouted back. "Your father is a *general* and you didn't report that to me? Don't you know there is a regulation that says you have to tell us if your dad is a general? What's the matter with you?"

Of course there was no regulation; this major was just being a total horse's ass, and I was livid. I picked up the phone and called the two-star commander of the aviation center, who also happened to have been my bunkmate in Desert Storm, Major General Ron Adams (retired as three-star general after commanding the stabilization force in Bosnia and Her-zegovina and commanding U.S. Army elements, NATO).

"Ron," I told him, "let me tell you what happened. One of your in-structors reamed my son's ass after he found out he was my son. That major was just a dumb son of a bitch and he's not what I'm calling about. I'm looking at the big picture and I think you've got a situation there you would want to be aware of. When I commanded the 82nd, on any given day I had *fifty* sons of general officers in my division and I *couldn't have cared less* that they were generals' sons or daughters. My goal was to treat people right, and I know you well enough to know that you feel the same way; so you might want to get that word out to those under your command so they stop the bullshit that major pulled out there."

Ron Adams is a great guy and I could feel him flushing all the way over the telephone line, but that was a situation he had to be made aware of.

"I got it, sir, and I will take care of this," he said. "Thank you very much for your call."

Jeff did just fine in spite of that ignorant major's comment. In fact, he did so well, he decided he wanted to become a Night Stalker—a member of the elite 160th Special Operations Aviation Regiment. Knowing how dangerous their missions were (among other things, the 160th insert and extract Delta Force, Navy SEAL Team Six, and other classified Special Mission Units), I encouraged him to get into some other aviation element, but Jeff was insistent—he wanted to be a Night Stalker.

The 160th is a very competitive unit, and a difficult one to get into. Only the very top pilots make the cut. So, on his own and having absolutely nothing to do with me, Jeff went through an incredibly rigorous assessment-and-selection process, and not only did he get selected for the intensive training, but he made it all the way through to the final cut; he was only one day away from being selected, and everything rode on the final interview process, in which all but a select few would be eliminated.

The night before the interview, he called Carolyn. "Mom, tomorrow is the big day when I go before the board and find out if I made it or not. The thing I'm most worried about is embarrassing you and Dad."

"Jeff, you are not going to embarrass us. It's your life and you're going to do whatever you want to do; and whatever that is, you're still our son and we love you," Carolyn assured him.

I imagine some might think that nepotism plays a big role in selections such as this, and my response to that is, "It better not"—especially in situations where there are lives on the line. The 160th is involved in many nearly impossible missions that only the very top pilots could pull off, usually conducted at night at high speeds and low altitudes with only night-vision goggles to provide the visibility. At this level, any attempt to shortcut the high standards would prove deadly.

During my discussion of Desert Storm I mentioned Lieutenant Colonel Dick Cody, who was commanding the Apache battalion at that time. By this time, Dick had become commander of the Night Stalkers and he was the one who would conduct the final interviews. When I heard that, I felt completely relieved. There was no way Dick would give Jeff or anyone else special treatment. This is the man who was sometimes introduced as "Dick Cody, before Cody dicks you."

*  *  *

Shortly after the interviews were completed, Cody flew down to Tampa to see me (I was commander of SOCOM at the time).

"General, I had to tell you in person how things played out in Jeff's interview," he said. "When Jeff stepped before the board, we put him through the wringer. I asked him, 'Why the hell do you think that we would ever want the commander in chief of Special Operations' son in this unit?' And he looked me in the eye and said with total confidence, 'Because I'm the damn best aviator that you could put in this unit, Colonel.' And, General, I have to tell you—in his case, he was speaking one hundred percent the truth. He is one of the best aviators I have ever seen come through here."

"Dick, as soon as I heard you were conducting that board, I felt great because I knew you would have eliminated him on the spot if he didn't measure up, because there are too many lives at stake for you to do otherwise." Then I thanked him for taking the time to come down and reinforce how it had played out, another example of an exceptional leader taking time to do the right thing.


One thing I always wanted to do was fly with Jeff, and with my retirement rapidly approaching, I realized that in just a few months I would lose that opportunity. With my hectic schedule as Chairman, those four years had flown by without my having flown with him even once. So I called Lieutenant General Doug Brown to set it up. At that time, Doug was U.S. Army Special Ops commander, and he went on to become the first member of the Army aviation branch to attain the rank of four-star general when he took over the entire U.S. Special Operations Command. Doug had also commanded the 160th, as well as JSOC (Joint Special Operations Command).

"Doug, I'm giving a speech to the 101st at Fort Campbell in a few days and I'd like to fly with Jeff. If this thing breaks up to your level, I do not want anything special out of it, I want a completely vanilla flight, just so I can say that I have flown with him."

"Sir," Doug replied, "don't you worry about it, you are welcome to fly with him anytime you like."


I then called Colonel Dell Dailey (retired lieutenant general who headed JSOC and later was appointed ambassador in charge of the State Department's counterterrorism efforts), who at that time was commander of 160th. Dell is the one I spoke with in the White House parking lot after presenting the Afghanistan war plan to President Bush in the White House living quarters.

"Dell, I want this to be very low-key and I don't want any special treatment when I'm out there. This is not the Chairman showing up for an official visit with all the bells and whistles, I just want a quick vanilla flight with Jeff."

"Sir, I think that would be great," Dell responded.

"I will just arrive at the unit and get into the aircraft for a very brief flight around the installation and come back and land."

"No problem," he said. "We'll keep it nice and simple."

When I arrived, they had a flight suit ready for me, and I suited up. Jeff walked me to the MH-6 Little Bird helicopter that he would be piloting. This is the same type of chopper that took out the *Iran Ajr* minelaying vessel in Operation Prime Chance, when it approached from the rear in the black of night, dropped down to eight hundred feet, and let loose with 2.75-inch rockets and Gatling-like machine-gun fire at four thousand rounds per minute.

Jeff did his walk-around check, then we boarded the tiny aircraft—so small, in fact, that once strapped in, you really felt like you were a part of it. He rotated the cyclic to ensure there were no obstructions, then completed his preflight check, confirming that all systems were good to go. While we stood by for our takeoff clearance, I told him that I insisted on one important ground rule.

"Now listen, Jeff, I want you to keep this son of a bitch at a good safe altitude and a good safe speed; I know what you're capable of, but that's not what this flight is about. Are we in sync on that?"

He smiled and said, "Yes, sir," but I had a feeling it was more of a "you better hold on tight, Dad" than a captain ready to follow an order. So he eased back on the collective, and the ground beneath the glass bubble fell away by about five feet; then he feathered the cyclic forward and we pitched down slightly and took off, gaining forward speed while flying about ten feet off the ground before initiating a more substantial ascent. As we climbed through about five hundred feet, he made a smooth 180-degree arc and we crossed over Interstate 24 and we were off. It turned out that he did exactly as promised, perfectly executing a professional flight—without the hotdogging I knew full well he could do if he chose.

After about a half hour, he turned around to head back to Fort Campbell, then asked me the sixty-four-thousand-dollar question: "Think you can handle this thing, Dad?"

While I am not a rated pilot, I did have the opportunity to fly a Huey quite a bit during Desert Shield/Storm, and I had also flown the UH-60 Black Hawk a time or two—just enough that I felt mildly comfortable behind the stick of a helicopter.

*Ready to fly with Night Stalker pilot son, Jeff.*

"You don't have to ask twice on that one, you bet I can handle her," I answered. "But before I do, I want you to get some more altitude, just in case. I want you to have plenty of time to take over the controls if necessary." He nodded, and took her up to about two thousand feet.

"Are you ready, Dad?" he asked.

"Yes, I've got the controls," I said.

"Okay, you've got the controls," he replied, following standard aviation parlance whatever aircraft you're flying. Then he took his hands off the controls, and as soon as he did, we started wobbling, then dipping as I overcorrected—not horribly, but enough to show that I had never flown a bird as responsive as this. It had a mind of its own and did *not* want to stay in trim. Every time I thought I had it straight and level, we'd dip in another direction, and I was sure Jeff was having a *great* time watching his big-shot four-star dad trying so hard to pull off what *looked* so easy but in reality was far from it—I could not get that tiny bird to stop its little Irish jig in the sky. I stuck it out for about a minute or so, and it was a workout—enough fun for one day.

"Jeff, you take the controls," I said.

"Are you sure you want me to? There's no rush, Dad, if you want . . ."

"Jeff, you're not funny; I said, *you take the controls*. And by the way, yes—you've proven your point."

Of course he immediately took over, and the second he did, the Little Bird stopped the erratic movement and seemed to purr with contentment. We both got a great laugh out of it. "And I have to admit, you got Dad on this one, I can't handle it—and you are one hell of a pilot," I told him.

About halfway back, he pointed out a large, open field and said, "Dad, I'm going to land down there." As we got closer, I saw that we would be landing beside another MH-6, which was already down there.

We landed and Jeff powered down. We got out and approached the second helo. "Dad, I'd like you to meet CW5 Karl Maier, one of our very best."

Maier snapped to a sharp salute, which I returned, then I extended my hand. "It's a pleasure to meet you, Karl."

"Sir, it's an honor to meet you," he said as we shook hands.

"Dad, you're going to transfer over to Karl's aircraft so he can show you a couple of things on how we train. I'll meet you back at Fort Campbell."

"Sounds great, Jeff, see you back there," I said, then I followed Maier into his aircraft and we both strapped ourselves in. A minute later, we were zipping over the treetops at breakneck speed.

"The first thing I'm going to show you is a shipboard landing, and we will use that tower to simulate the flight deck of a Navy ship," he said, pointing to a forty-foot tower up ahead. "I'm going to show you how we come right over the water—high speed, low altitude of about ten feet up—and how we put these guys right there on the deck." He dropped down to the deck with airspeed to the point of redline—we were rocketing toward that tower and to me it looked like we were only inches above the creek below, and with trees on both sides.

As we approached the tower, he said, "We're coming up to the ship," and somehow he immediately slammed it down atop the tower, then took off again. "We've dumped our guys off. . . ." Then we seemed to fall sideways off the tower, toward the grass, but it was an intentional maneuver, and he kicked in the speed and uprighted the bird, which was once again skimming the treetops.

"Now we're back in a ravine and have a bridge up ahead, and I've got two more guys that I've got to put down on the bridge because they're going to blow it and then disappear."

"Okay, good," I said, clinging to the side of my seat.

"And now we're at water level, and the trees are on both sides and there is the bridge in front of us coming up fast," and again, before I could see what was happening, he plopped down atop our "bridge," then fell sideways off it, and we were off again. As we headed back to Fort Campbell, I was thinking how that was the last thing I would ever want to do, but I had to admit it had been pretty damn exciting.

"And, sir, there is one thing that I have to tell you about your son, and I'm going to be very honest about this," he said, ready to share something that seemed to be weighing heavily on his mind.

"I appreciate that—go ahead."

"Sir, everything I just did with you, Jeff can do. The only difference is he does it *better*. He's one of the best damn pilots we've got; in fact, one of the best I have ever seen. I realize he couldn't show you this stuff today—they wouldn't allow it—but he can do all of this and a helluva lot more." My head just about popped a hole through that glass bubble, I was so proud—but I was glad that Jeff had shown professional restraint and given me the vanilla flight I'd requested. All we needed was to crash that thing and become the next day's front-page headline of the *Washington Post*.

I returned to D.C., and that night I called Jeff and thanked him for a great time, then shared with him all the great words Karl Maier shared with me. Besides the fact that Maier was an aviation hero in the 160th, for a CW5 to say that about a commissioned officer spoke volumes. "You are *very* well thought of over there, Jeff, and both your mother and I are very proud of you."

My final days as Chairman were consumed with post-9/11 planning for the war, along with preparations to turn over the controls to the expert piloting of General Dick Myers.

As much as we relished our time at the stately Quarters Six, the fact was that it was severely in need of upgrading to meet the demands of the twenty-first-century Chairman. At my request, an evaluation was initiated to determine if funds should be allocated for the renovation—things like installing fiber-optic communications links throughout the house, and replacing the antiquated heating/AC systems, which took two days to change from AC to heat or vice versa. The renovation would cost $750,000 and take six months. After hearing this "outrageous" amount, two congressmen from the Congressional Oversight Committee, including the longtime chairman from Ohio, Congressman Dave Hobson, came over to take a look. In under fifteen minutes they had seen enough. They shook their heads as they left, and said, "Long overdue." The request was approved within days.

* * *

Secretary Rumsfeld and his wife hosted a farewell dinner in our honor at their home. It was a delightful evening, with Joyce Rumsfeld being the consummate hostess. They presented me with a personal gift—a bronze statue of a bull with calf by Robert MacLeod—which we have prominently displayed in our home. Engraved on the bottom is *To Gen. Hugh Shelton with my respect and appreciation for your outstanding service to our nation. Donald Rumsfeld, October 1, 2001.*

————

"And joining us now is General Hugh Shelton, Chairman of the Joint Chiefs of Staff. Your last day in that role, General Shelton."

"My last day, Cokie. And delighted to be spending it here with you this morning."

It was the morning of September 30, 2001, and I was under the bright lights of ABC Television's Washington, D.C. studio. In spite of the 110 countries I had traveled to, meeting hundreds of world leaders—not to mention the multitude of times I'd been rushed to the White House for advisory sessions with our chief executive—it seemed like just yesterday that I'd sat in the Oval Office being "interviewed" by President Clinton for the job. It didn't seem much before that time that I arrived at Fort Benning for Infantry Officer Basic; it was hard to believe how those thirty-eight years had flown past.

As I got up that morning I knew it would be my final one as Chairman. I was scheduled to appear on *This Week* so I quickly read the "Early Bird" to see what the hot topics might be, so that I would be fully prepared if Cokie Roberts asked me about them. I was told that Sam Donaldson was off "on assignment," so today's interview would be just Cokie and me.

I missed the early-morning teleconferences that had been a routine in the Clinton administration so that all the Sunday-morning talk-show participants would at least know how the other participants would respond to a certain question. Those sessions proved invaluable at keeping the team on the same field. We would go over the hot tickets for that day. What was on the front page of the *Los Angeles Times* or *The New York Times* or the *Washington Post*? What were they going to be taking us to task for on that day, and what was the administration's position on it? National Security Advisor Sandy Berger ran those calls and coordinated the message. "Secretary Cohen, the last time you were on *Meet the Press* you stressed the importance of bilateral talks, so we anticipate Russert bringing that up again with you and General Shelton. Let's stick with that message. Is everyone else on board with that?" Berger's instructions were focused and clear, and, most important, they established a consistent message—one that minimized the chances of Albright's saying one thing and Tenet saying the opposite.

Each Sunday morning at six o'clock, my public affairs officer, Admiral T McCreary, would knock at my door, ready to join me at my kitchen table for a cup of coffee and those carefully orchestrated conference calls. One of the first items of business on the Bush agenda was to eliminate those weekly calls. T wouldn't get his coffee, and the interviews could be all over the board. You saw it from the very start, but it was really after 9/11 that you repeatedly saw that the left hand had no idea what the right one was doing.

Instead, on this morning I had my own teleconference with T, along with Denny Klauer. Together they were a dynamite team and could prepare me to walk into withering machine-gun fire and not flinch.

My driver, Ron, arrived right on time in the armored Cadillac, and transported me to ABC, where I knew that my interview with Cokie would focus on our deployment to Afghanistan. As usual, I would be walking the fine line about what I could say without giving away secrets that could endanger lives. At least I knew that Cokie was fair, and while she would push, she knew that certain restrictions applied to what I could and could not say.


"This morning's papers said that twenty-eight thousand troops, two dozen warships, and three hundred warplanes are in the area around Iraq and Afghanistan. Are we positioning ourselves, if necessary, to get in?" Cokie asked.

"As you know, for fifty years we've maintained a sizable force in the Middle East in support of our allies in the region, as well as to protect America's national interests," I responded. "But commenting on what types of forces we may have deployed or when we might commence a certain operation is something that I think serves only to aid and abet the terrorist organizations that are the target of our efforts in this war on terrorism."


It went well and I enjoyed it. On the ride home, I reflected on the number of press "opportunities" I had been exposed to in my four years as Chairman, along with the Senate and House Armed Services Committee hearings, which were carried live on C-SPAN. I was fortunate to have had the assistance of Admirals Steve Pietropoli and T McCreary, supported by Denny Klauer, to help prepare me for each of them. One wrong choice of words could make the national news or dig a hole that would take months to get out of. There were even recent cases of admirals or generals being fired because of how they had answered. It was always high adventure.

Arriving back home, Carolyn met me with the proverbial, "How did it go?"

"I was hoping you would tell me," I said, smiling back at her in another of our ongoing jokes, knowing that she couldn't since the show would not air for another couple of hours.

After coffee, we both set about preparing for the move. There were hundreds of details to be sorted out. Carolyn and the enlisted aides had already done a lot of preparation. Since much of the furniture on the main floor was furnished by the government, that had to be marked so it wouldn't be picked up by the movers. Although we could not have managed without those wonderful aides throughout my four years as Chairman of the Joint Chiefs of Staff, we were looking forward to our lives as *normal* people. Our move back to the Fairfax house we had owned for twenty-four years would be only an interim stop; the Army would authorize storage for up to five years before making our "final" move at government expense. That meant we would move about half of the items in our home and store the other half.

Throughout the day, I talked to Dick Myers regarding the Afghanistan deployment—a rather typical day. But when I went to sleep that night, I knew that the witching hour of midnight was rapidly approaching, and then Dick Myers would instantly be the new Chairman. For a job I had never aspired to, it had turned out to be the opportunity of a lifetime. Working together with Secretary Cohen and the Joint Chiefs, we had achieved the largest pay raise for the troops in eighteen years. We had fixed a badly broken HMO for both the active and retired soldiers by getting TRICARE for Life enacted into law. Both had been accomplished with great support from President Clinton and Senate Majority Leader Trent Lott, along with Senators John Warner and Carl Levin from the Senate Armed Services Committee. The $112 billion the Joint Chiefs had fought for was now reflected in the readiness of our forces that were deploying to Afghanistan to defeat the Taliban and al-Qaeda. Most recently, I had succeeded in helping keep President Bush from attacking Iraq under the pretense that it was somehow a part of the 9/11 attack, even though both the FBI and the CIA had categorically insisted that there was not a linkage.

Carolyn and I had met so many wonderful people whom we would never have had the opportunity to meet otherwise, some of whom had become fast friends. But tomorrow started a new chapter in life, one that Carolyn and I were excited about as I accepted new challenges with my new title, Former Chairman, Joint Chiefs of Staff.

---

That night we had a big barbecue in the Quarters Six backyard. It was a great family reunion with our children, grandchildren, brothers, sisters, and their spouses and children. It was the last of many dinners hosted there, and by far the most fun.

---

Between our children, grandchildren, and siblings staying with us the night before the retirement ceremony, Quarters Six felt more like Motel Six—albeit an upscale one. I should have known something was going on, but Carolyn's straight face was worthy of the most skilled Special Operator—she didn't reveal a thing. As I opened the door to lead the family to the retirement ceremony, Mike Lallier, the Cadillac Chevrolet dealer from Fayetteville, North Carolina, was standing in the driveway beside a brand-new magnetic-red Corvette convertible. "It's all yours, General. Congratulations," he said as he tossed me the keys.

I was floored, completely taken aback. "Had I known this was waiting for me, I would have retired eighteen years ago," I kidded Mike.

---

The ceremony itself was both grand and touching, with the highlight, once again, being that my mother and the rest of my family were there to share it with me. The joint-service color guard advanced the colors and the Old Guard played "The Ballad of the Green Berets." It was a great show of support from my friends and colleagues, including Secretary of State Colin Powell; CIA Director George Tenet; Senator Helms; Senator Edwards; members of Congress; Generals Myers and Pace, the secretaries of the armed services; combatant commanders, past and present; senior enlisted advisers; command sergeants major; Deputy Secretary of Defense Paul Wolfowitz; former Deputy Secretary of Defense Rudy de Leon; and, of course, Secretary Rumsfeld was at the helm, emceeing the event and delivering the official remarks. Carolyn was by my side, presenting me with the Defense Distinguished Service Medal.

That night, I appeared on *Larry King Live*.

Cutting right to the chase, Larry opened with a tough one: "Does it feel funny to be out?"

"Thanks, Larry. It does feel different," I answered. "And, it has been humbling. I have been very honored to have the opportunity to serve, and to lead, and be the representative of our great soldiers, sailors, airman, and marines here in Washington. It has been the greatest honor of my life."

"Is it a time when you say to yourself, at all, 'I wish I wasn't retiring'? In view of the events?"

"Larry, I use the analogy of a football player, a quarterback on a world-class team—he is in the first quarter, the team trailing by six points; he knows he has got a great team and he knows he can win. But the coach sends a runner out and says, 'Your eligibility has just expired.'

"But as I look over at the bench I see a couple of great all-Americans over there getting ready to come in. One is General Dick Myers, a great warrior, a visionary, a great leader. So I feel very good. Dick will lead the team to victory and he will be backed up by another great general, General Charlie Holland, who leads our Special Operations Command. We've got a tremendous team."

Sometimes Larry's way with words makes it somewhat difficult to keep a straight face when discussing the most serious of topics (especially when his crew starts laughing in the background), which was the case when he asked me, "Could you order a shooting down of a commercial aircraft? It would be you doing it, well—I mean it would be *the former you*."

"Larry, we . . ." I started, trying to compose myself. "That is a very serious issue. The *rules of engagement,* which is what we call the rules that our pilots go by, and the chain of command, which goes from the individual pilots all the way to our Commander in Chief, President Bush, are very carefully thought through, and laid out. And we are satisfied that we have the decision at the appropriate level to take the action that would be necessary to preserve the preponderance of life."

Larry is a great guy, and I have always enjoyed spending time with him on his show.

———

We actually completed the move out on October 15. Since the Myers were already in quarters just down the street and the Quarters Six renovations weren't due to start for a few weeks, we decided to move *after* the retirement ceremony, which greatly simplified our lives and allowed me to concentrate on the job 100 percent until the very end, without any move-related distractions.

———

Located in the Westminster area of central London just off the river Thames, Chelsea Barracks and Royal Hospital bear a rich legacy in British military history. Since their founding by King Charles II in 1681, there has only been one time that an *American* flag has flown over its storied walls, and that was in October 2001, in honor of me and Carolyn. By order of Queen Elizabeth II and Phillip, the Duke of Edinburgh, I was to be knighted into the Order of the British Empire.

I've always felt a unique bond with the UK since my family originated in England and Scotland, and throughout my time as Chairman our staunch British allies were the first to step forward with military support. Combine that with my great circle of close British friends and you can see why my being chosen for this honor meant so much to me.

Jerry MacKenzie (my ranger buddy, who by then had also been knighted, General Sir John Jeremy MacKenzie, past Deputy SACEUR) was governor of the Chelsea facility, so it was a perfect choice of venue for the ceremony, and his wife, Liz, was right by his side. Mike Jackson (General Sir Michael David Jackson, former Chief of the General Staff) was present, as was Sir Charles Guthrie (General Charles Ronald Llewelyn Guthrie, Baron Guthrie of Craigiebank), my British counterpart and friend, whom I sat next to at all the NATO meetings, along with his wife, Lady Kate Guthrie.

Just as I arrived for the ceremony, the escort officer handed me a handwritten note from Geoff Hoon, the British Secretary of State for Defence. Geoff was supposed to have been there but was called away at the last minute by Prime Minister Blair. His note was a real tearjerker; it spoke of the genuine warmth he felt for America—and the respect and admiration he had for me. It clearly came from the heart and I was greatly touched when I read it.

The ceremony was deep with British tradition yet at the same time very personal. After the speeches and tributes, I was presented with my medals and a big certificate signed by Queen Elizabeth and Prince Phillip. Then I rose to speak, and I did so from the depths of my heart. About halfway into it, I was talking about what a great nation England was and how much I valued them, when I looked up and saw that Sir Charles Guthrie and Lady Kate had broken down in tears, which just about forced me to tears. I took a deep breath and told myself, *I can't break up here and be remembered as this big bad American general who can't even get through his own speech without crying.* As it was, I got teary when I saw the Stars and Stripes flying overhead. Can you imagine a country actually flying another sovereign nation's flag above their homes in your honor? It was quite an experience, and a great way to begin my "retirement."

## Part III
# AFTER THE FALL

*Never interrupt your enemy when he is making a mistake.*
—NAPOLEON BONAPARTE

## *Chapter Twenty* ★★★★

# THE GAME FAVORS
# THE BOLD

10:15 A.M., June 13, 2002, Walter Reed Army Medical Center

On the morning of June 13, exactly eighty-three days after the fall, I walked out of Walter Reed under my own power, even though they attempted to take me out in a wheelchair. It was a goal I had set for myself, to walk out unassisted. There would still be more rehabilitative work to be done, but my recovery was nothing short of a miracle. I was headed home.

The timing could not have been better since I arrived just in time to join the family for our annual get-together at the beach on Emerald Isle, North Carolina, where Carolyn, Mother, and all our children, grandchildren, and siblings would laugh and experience the joy of life.

Looking back on that period of my life, I continue to be amazed at how strong Carolyn was in the face of such adversity. She took charge and showed a strength I had never seen before. Of course, I was usually deployed when she'd had to handle life's challenges in the past, so this was one of the first times I had the opportunity to really experience it firsthand.

Likewise, Jon and Anne, who lived nearby, were extraordinarily supportive, and the frequent visits by Cassie, Heather, and Hannah were always morale boosters.

Mary "Cissie" Patton, wife of Colonel David Patton, who had been a friend for years, stepped in and provided comfort and encouragement for Carolyn. Frequently they would go out to a local restaurant at night, giving Carolyn a much-needed break from the hospital setting she lived in throughout the eighty-three-day ordeal.

The concern, generosity, and care shown by Ross Perot, Tom Brokaw, and Michael Ansari, whom I had been working for at the time of the fall, was truly above and beyond. Each, in his own way, supported me in ways that mark them all as true friends, to whom I shall forever be indebted.

Since my birth, I had never spent a night in the hospital. During my eighty-three days in Walter Reed, I'd had the chance to see firsthand what a national treasure Walter Reed is. The quality of care, the doctors and nurses, the support staff—all first-rate. Today, when I return to Walter Reed, instead of a flashback to a dark period in my life, I am thankful to see that the individuals evacuated from the battlefields of Afghanistan and Iraq have access to this great facility. I pray that as Walter Reed closes in 2011 and the transfer to Bethesda is complete, the quality of care I experienced remains intact.

## CONGRESSIONAL MEDAL

Besides being able to fulfill a packed schedule of speaking commitments that would require me to stand up for hours on end, I had another incentive not to let up a bit with my intensive recovery program—on September 19, 2002, I was to receive the Congressional Gold Medal, the highest civilian award in the United States.

The process entailed a bill being approved by both houses of Congress and then signed into law by the President. For the medal itself, officials of the United States Mint met with the sponsors of the legislation and our family to discuss a number of possible designs for the medal—and they ended up actually conducting a contest to select the design. The winner not only received tremendous recognition but was present for the ceremony, as well. His designs were ultimately approved by the Secretary of the Treasury. The design was then sculptured, a die was made, and the medal was struck at the Philadelphia Mint.

The ceremony itself was held in the Rotunda of the Capitol, which made for a very impressive venue. Congressman and Speaker of the House Denny Hastert presided over the ceremony, and speakers included Senator Tom

*The medal—so pure in gold that it requires anyone who handles it to wear soft cotton gloves to preclude body oil from staining it or leaving their fingerprints embedded—is magnificent.*

Daschle, John Edwards, Secretary Bill Cohen, and Congressman Bob Etheridge, who had sponsored the bill that awarded the medal.

A large number of senators and congressmen, most of whom I had worked with during my tenure as CJCS, were in attendance, as were most of the Joint Chiefs of Staff.

It was one of my first public outings since my release from Walter Reed but I was determined to stand straight and tall, and to move as naturally as my injured body would permit. Obviously, having defied the odds, I was on display.

The event was attended by my entire family, most of Carolyn's, and a number of friends and relatives who drove up from the Tarboro, Speed, and Raleigh areas of North Carolina. Dr. Jim Ecklund, the chief of neurosurgery at Walter Reed who made my presence possible, and his wife attended, as did a great many people I had worked with through the years.

After the event, there were lots of photos taken in the Rotunda with family and friends. With the adrenaline pumping, I was able to stand on my feet and enjoy the activities far longer than I would have thought possible at that point.

## USS *NEW ORLEANS*

On March 21, 2009, the amphibious transport dock ship USS *New Orleans* collided with the Los Angeles–class attack submarine USS *Hartford* in the Strait of Hormuz. Under normal circumstances, this would not necessarily be something I'd include in this book, but as it turns out, the USS *New Orleans* is Carolyn's ship—well, sort of.

*My mother looks on as Carolyn christens the USS* New Orleans. *Northrop Grumman VP George R. Yount checks out her technique.*

Among the many activities that have kept us busy since retirement, one of the more interesting ones for Carolyn was her being awarded the great honor of christening the ship; and she did so at the Northrop Grumman Ship Systems port of New Orleans on November 20, 2004. My mother was standing beside Carolyn as a thousand guests shared in the celebration. "Bless this ship and all who sail in her," Carolyn proclaimed, just before she shattered the champagne bottle against the hull.

My personal opinion is that there's absolutely no truth to the rumor that her mighty blow actually damaged the submarine-detection system on the vessel. The great news is that repairs were swift, and she's gearing up for her next deployment.

## Chapter Twenty-one

# YOU BREAK IT,
# YOU OWN IT—IRAQ

I am the first to admit that the world is a better place without Saddam, but that does not change the fact that there was absolutely no link between him and 9/11, as some tried to lead us to believe. The United States had almost destroyed Iraq's capacity with our prior attacks and we had Saddam contained, yet all we were hearing was that escalating drumbeat from the civilian Pentagon leadership that Iraq was the crux of our terrorist issues. I believe it was that drumbeat that encouraged President Bush to walk out on a limb beyond the point of no return.

I would challenge anybody to show us a very serious terrorist threat against the United States that was coming out of Iraq. Did Iraq have an al-Qaeda cell? I suspect they did, just like the United States has al-Qaeda cells. They are everywhere, in more than fifty-five nations, but there was nothing that linked Saddam to a serious attack on the United States. Taking out Saddam as a key element of the U.S. war on terrorism was a fallacious argument, and our doing so would result in the loss of support from many nations that, immediately after 9/11, were clearly in our camp. Additionally, "breaking it," by taking out their government, meant "we owned it" and would require us to replace Saddam immediately with a leader for the Iraqis, clearly a task for which we were ill prepared going in.

But the Bush administration had their own agenda, and that agenda was taking out Saddam Hussein, whatever it took. Most Americans ultimately came to understand what I saw early on—that President Bush and his team got us enmeshed in Iraq based on extraordinarily poor intelligence and a series of lies purporting that we had to protect America from Saddam's evil empire because it posed such a threat to our national security. This chapter reveals the behind-the-scenes orchestrations that allowed all this to occur.

But first of all, some self-imposed ground rules: I do not want to get into either an analysis or a critique of whether the actions of my successors were right or wrong. It is hard to second-guess someone in that environment without knowing all the facts, and the decision-making process after I left is the business of Generals Myers and Pace. To try to insert myself into that process at this time would be the worst form of Monday-morning quarterbacking, and I have no interest in going there.

On the other hand, I can—and *will*—make judgments based on the outcome and the facts that I know, and those facts alone expose enough areas of conflict, manipulation, and egotistical megalomania to source the scripts of Hollywood melodramas for years. But this melodrama wasn't fiction. It was a real-life scenario that cost the U.S. citizens more than $900 billion and, far worse, thousands of lives.

————

I attended a Pentagon briefing in the Tank about two months before the invasion in which the Chairman at that time, General Myers, shared with me and other retired Chairmen the plan of attack, and while each one of us believed the plan would succeed militarily, some of us expressed our serious concerns about the aftermath.

During my tenure as Chairman, I had met with, and become friends with, many Middle East leaders—Chiefs of Defense, kings, crowned princes, presidents—and to a person each had consistently expressed the same concern whenever I would broach the subject of a counter-Iraq operation: *If you take out Saddam, who is going to replace him?* Without someone strong, the Kurds, the Sunnis, and the Shia would immediately be at one another's throats and the place would turn into a rabble; it would break out into civil war. They all agreed that Saddam was a horrible person who ruled with sadistic strong-arm tactics, but they also knew that his strength was the glue that held that country together. He was the common enemy who bonded the three groups instead of setting them against one another.

So I asked that day in the Tank, "Once you get in there, what's your plan? Taking them out will be a piece of cake, but then what?" I knew we had a great armed forces and that Saddam's diminished capabilities would make the military takeover easy. But my concern went beyond that. "After you remove Saddam, or after he flees the country, who is going to take over then, and who is going to keep these three diverse religious groups who hate one another apart?"

"Good questions and we've got that covered," was the answer. "We're going to carry Civil Affairs and Psychological Operations troops in with us, and they're going to be coming behind in numbers. We also believe the Iraqi people will welcome us with open arms; let's face it, they'll be thrilled that we helped them by taking out the dictator who's been terrorizing them for decades." That echoed Dick Cheney's public comment that he believed we would be *welcomed as liberators*.

"What about the old saying, 'If you break it, you own it'?" I asked, and then expressed my concern about the monumental task we'd have since by taking out Saddam, we were in essence going to own Iraq. We needed a plan for nation building—a plan that encompassed the political, economical, diplomatic, information, and military aspects of rebuilding a country. A plan that contemplated getting their power grids back online and getting their oil flowing again so that we could recoup some of the many billions of dollars this operation would cost the American people. And such a nation-building plan would take a large number of troops. Where were they?

Finally, I asked, "Where are our allies? If America invades Iraq by itself we will be viewed as the infidels from the West that have taken over Iraq solely for their oil and we'll be painted that way by all the extremists and radicals." We really needed the international community involved in the effort to rebuild Iraq. That rhetorical question was met with silence.

———

About a month later (when the war seemed inevitable) I was sitting on the board of directors of Anheuser-Busch and was asked by August Busch III, the chairman of the board, to give my fellow board members my impressions of how the war might play out. As I flew from Washington, D.C., to Chesterfield, Missouri's Spirit of St. Louis Airport on one of Busch's plush, Falcon 50EX private jets, that phrase just kept playing in my mind: *If you break it, you own it.* . . .

Before the official board business started, August III turned the floor of the elegant Anheuser-Busch boardroom, located in the sprawling South St. Louis complex, over to me for my prediction. "The war itself will be very short—and very decisive," I began. "But then it's going to get ugly. Saddam will either be captured or flee the country, and then I predict the place will turn into chaos since I do not believe we are going in with anywhere near sufficient forces to rebuild a nation that is larger than the state of Maryland.

Since we will be taking out the one unifying force that is keeping them apart, who is going to keep these three religious factions who hate one another from killing one another? Who is going to stop the looting? Who is going to make sure the black-market element doesn't run rampant, with killing and stealing and carrying out the vendettas they've wanted to for so long, but now finally can since there is no government? Who is going to keep it from turning into a civil war?

"Next, if the place does end up falling apart, I think the predominantly Shia Iran will attempt to link up with the Shia portion of Iraq by completely annexing the country. Either way, I imagine al-Qaeda will enter the fray, giving them a country that is somewhat analogous to Afghanistan; and lawless voids that America and Great Britain could not patrol will create a fertile breeding ground for terrorists and an even greater hatred of America."

That's how I told them I thought it would play out—and with the exception of the part about Iran annexing Iraq, I am sad to say I was right.

You may ask how I was able to get it so right when the powers making the decisions got it so wrong. Am I that much smarter than all of them? Not at all, but I do listen to the advice of those more experienced than I am in certain areas—in this case, the network of Middle East leaders. But just as important is learning from history, because inevitably history will always repeat itself. My experience in Haiti had taught me that when we went in, we were going to "break it," so I damn well better have enough troops on the ground to fix it—to maintain law and order so that there was no looting and violence. In Haiti it was bringing in Special Forces teams and positioning them out in the forested countryside, and doing what the conventional troops were doing in Port-au-Prince—maintaining control so that the people felt secure—otherwise, Haiti, like Iraq (or any other country in a similar position) would have broken out in civil war, with lawlessness throughout the country.

But you have to listen to your experts and learn from your history. *Totally ignoring it and creating your unique template that slashes troop strength and disregards tried-and-true military tactics and doctrine is not innovative and transformational, it's just stupid and asking for trouble.* Yet, this is exactly what Donald Rumsfeld did, and why the war in Iraq turned into such an explosive debacle—many years later we're still heavily involved, experiencing loss of life, off-the-charts financial strains in the billions, and terrorism continuing to grow. It did not have to play out that way.

———

To understand the depth of the problem, we must flash back to 1985, when President Reagan tasked the Packard Commission to conduct a sweeping review of the Department of Defense pursuant to Presidential Executive Order 12526. Since World War II, there had been thirty-five prior independent panels and reviews of the Pentagon process; and while few had trouble pointing out a multitude of problems, until Packard, none came up with workable solutions.

Those were the days of the four-hundred-dollar hammers and six-hundred-dollar toilet seats, and it didn't take a rocket scientist to see that something was rotten in Denmark; it did take David Packard (multimillionaire of Hewlitt-Packard and former Deputy Secretary of Defense) and his Blue Ribbon Commission on Defense Management to offer specific, sweeping recommendations for substantial reforms that would remedy the situation. The commission identified problems in the areas of budget and acquisition; ethics, conduct, and accountability; lines of command; and interservice rivalries.

The solutions would be instituted in what eventually became the Goldwater-Nichols act of 1986, which redefined the role of combat-theater commanders and the Joint Chiefs of Staff, establishing the Chairman as the principal military adviser to the President, Secretary of Defense, and NSC; and setting up the Joint Chiefs as the primary sounding board and valuable resource for the commanders in the development of their war plans. Goldwater-Nichols cut out the abuse, and, for the most part, it worked.

The problem comes in when you take a proven system that works and do everything in your power to bypass that great system for the sole purpose of advancing your own agenda, and that's exactly what Donald Rumsfeld pulled off. He greatly preferred the pre–Goldwater-Nichols structure (in spite of all the abuses that system fostered), which had given him far more power since he didn't have to worry about a Chairman who was now legally given the responsibility of principal military adviser to the President and NSC. If somehow Rumsfeld could pull off a means for his combatant commanders to *bypass the Joint Chiefs and not even seek their opinions,* it would be almost as good as the old days for him. Exit CENTCOM commander General Tony Zinni (who would never have played into Rumsfeld's hand) and enter his successor, General Tommy Franks, whose responsibility it would be to develop war plans and conduct operations in the Central Command area of responsibility (AOR). Both Afghanistan and Iraq are within that AOR. Tommy Franks's gigantic ego was a perfect fit for Rumsfeld's master plan; he would consider it empowering to deal solely with the Secretary of Defense (particularly considering the way he felt he was treated during the Afghanistan Tank presentation to the Joint Chiefs), yet from Rumsfeld's perspective, the quid pro quo would be General Franks's rather easy acquiescing to do things his way.

* * *

Rumsfeld's stage was set. The 2001 Afghanistan operation was a success, and I knew that President Bush had already determined that he was going to take out Saddam before the end of his first term; he had so much as indicated that to me during our Camp David sidebar conversation. Rumsfeld, Cheney, and Wolfowitz were certainly on board, so all that was necessary was to get the American people behind it, and come up with a great war plan. The first would be successful in the form of an incredible deception; the second, a fiasco.

## SLEIGHT OF HAND

In 2002 the buzz words were still *terrorism* and *WMD*—and for good reason. They were tremendous threats, as they still are today. What was bogus was the link that was created between Saddam and any terrorist threat to the United States, but it presented the best opportunity to garner support for an Iraq invasion.

I believe we were suffering from what lawyers would call "fruit of the poison tree." The fact is that Iraq was contained and we had no linkages of Iraq to any terrorist organizations at that time. Yes, I believed that they had weapons of mass destruction, because that is what the intell community had been pitching for years, and we had seen them use those weapons against the Kurds at one point. I have no reason to believe that President Bush did not believe the same thing. But the real question was, if they had them, what would they do with them and how could they deliver them?

Our 1999 attacks (more than four hundred cruise missiles and eight hundred air strikes) took out about 80 percent of their delivery capabilities, and subsequently, every time they fired at us, we struck back and *further* reduced their capabilities. It's true that they had saved a small percentage of some heavy-duty milling equipment by moving it out of the places we originally thought it would be, but they lost the vast majority. What this means is that Iraq in the 2002 to 2003 timeframe had a greatly diminished capability and was in a complete state of containment.

Even so, you still heard a steady drumbeat coming out of the Pentagon civilian leadership (Rumsfeld and Wolfowitz) as well as the Vice President that we needed to attack Iraq since Iraq was the crux of all the terrorist issues we were facing. It was that Rumsfeld/Wolfowitz/Cheney drumbeat that finally had President Bush walk out on a limb to the point where he was convinced that we needed to deploy troops even as he started to increase the rhetoric about how we were going to take Saddam out and attack Iraq. By then it was too late. It was take out Saddam or face embarrassment in the eyes of the world. And any good Texan is not going to back down once he has challenged his foe to a gunfight.

## THE WAR PLAN—TROOP LEVELS AND SUCH

Early on in the Bush administration, when I was Chairman, Secretary Rumsfeld had looked at the existing war plans for Iraq and basically said they were all obsolete because they used the same number of troops as were used in Desert Storm; and if you looked only at the major plan, it did approximate that number (about four hundred thousand to five hundred thousand troops). But there were much smaller plans, as well. Rumsfeld's contention was that over the years we had severely degraded the Iraqi army and we no longer needed anywhere near that number of troops; he believed that all we had to do was move in there and we would almost immediately own the place. I know for a fact that CENTCOM commander General Tommy Franks, the one who would be charged with executing the war plan, was under severe pressure from Secretary Rumsfeld to hold down the number of troops.

Secretary Rumsfeld believed it would take very few troops to overrun the Iraqi army, and for that first military stage he was right. But he failed to take into account the all-important second part of the equation: what size force would be necessary to maintain the safe and secure environment for the Iraqi people once the leadership had been taken out, and what was the plan to do this? Once again, it made sense to call upon the experts, the ones who had already done this and were willing to share this valuable experience with them.

If you look at Haiti as an example, we had a plan that was developed in Washington well before we even went in. We had fifty-one specific nation-building objectives that needed to be accomplished, and every agency in Washington, D.C. knew that they had to sign up for the ones that were applicable to their organizations. For example, somebody had to come in and revamp or realign the justice system. Who was best to do that? Clearly, the Justice Department. Someone had to vet the police and retrain them to our standards, and this was also the Justice Department. They sent Ray Kelly, the current police chief of New York City, and Ray did a fantastic job. Someone had to fix the transportation system, and this was the Department of Transportation. In theory, each organization had committed its piece of the puzzle to the Atlantic Command, and they all signed on for their part of the nation building. The problem was, in spite of our best intentions, it didn't happen. It fell apart, and didn't work.

The Justice Department did a great job, but it went downhill from there. The problem was that in Washington, people generally focus on one thing at a time, and it tends to be whatever is on the front page of the *Washington Post* or other newspapers at that moment, and that is what drives their agenda in many cases. Once we went in to Haiti and "owned the island," the various departments (with the exception of Justice) got busy doing other things that were more important to them at the time, despite their prior commitment. So it started to fall apart, forcing the military to take up the slack. Many of the skills necessary to do this type of nation building are found in the Army's Civil-Affairs units, which are frequently in high demand.

The good news is that as a result of this failure, a study was commissioned to learn from the mistakes and to lay out specifically what was necessary for a successful nation-building operation. It ended up being defined in President Clinton's PDD 56 (Presidential Decision Directive 56), "Managing Complex Contingency Operations." So, at the time of Iraq, *it was already on the shelf and just waiting to be instituted.* But, since it had been prepared under a Democratic administration, no one at the upper echelons of the Iraq planning circle ever bothered to refer to it, let alone institute its carefully organized steps to get the invaded country's vital services back online.

Rumsfeld and Franks apparently made the conscious decision to ignore PDD 56, and instead they decided to fight the last war—the one in Afghanistan—a totally different scenario because there was *nothing* in Iraq to equate to a fundamental strategic piece of the Afghanistan plan—that being the Afghanistan Northern Alliance, a built-in resistance movement supported by the CIA, which was already on the ground and had been for years. The Northern Alliance was perfect for the U.S. Special Forces to link up with to combat the Taliban and al-Qaeda. Special Forces were able to call in air strikes and provide vital reconnaissance data. That association became a major part of the Afghanistan war plan.

But Iraq had no similar resistance movement, and no one to serve a similar function, so how could Afghanistan possibly have been used as the model to create the Iraq battle plan?

The answer, according to Rumsfeld, Cheney, and Wolfowitz, was an Iraqi politician by the name of Ahmed Chalabi, who had long since convinced them that he and his INC (Iraqi National Congress) party were capable of overthrowing Saddam and unifying Iraqi public sentiment against him. They believed Chalabi was going to be the Northern Alliance, which proved to be dead wrong. The Northern Alliance was on the ground fighting and dying every day. Chalabi and his forces were wining and dining their fat asses in elite London hotels, funded by big bucks they had received throughout the years from the United States. The United States had been paying Chalibi's INC $340,000 a month for intelligence gathering, in part surrounding the existence of large stockpiles of weapons of mass destruction he promised existed, but were never found. The payments, according to Wolfowitz, were discontinued in May 2004. Around the same time, Fox News reported that U.S. officials had "rock solid" evidence that Chalabi spied for Iran, an accusation that Chalabi subsequently denied.

Rumsfeld was further emboldened and encouraged by the success of the Afghanistan plan and decided to go with it despite the vast differences—a tremendous mistake—and *one that would have been avoided had they followed the intended procedure and utilized that treasure chest of knowledge, the Joint Chiefs.*

## RUMSFELD AND FRANKS CONSPIRE TO BYPASS THE JOINT CHIEFS

In 2001, CENTCOM commander General Tommy Franks presented his Afghanistan war plan to the Joint Chiefs, and although I thought it was a productive give-and-take exchange in which the Chiefs posed realistic questions, Tommy's ego couldn't take it. He was highly perturbed. His ego apparently had grown out of sight, and he believed that he knew best and didn't need anybody else's opinion.

When the initial Afghanistan operation went well, Franks became even more isolated and cocky; and the Secretary of Defense took full advantage of it, to his own benefit, of course. He questioned why the general even bothered going through the Joint Chiefs, what with all his experience and expertise . . . he was always welcome to just pick up the phone and deal directly with the SecDef. And that offer of direct access inflated Tommy's head about ten hat sizes, because in his mind, he was now "above" the Joint Chiefs and working directly for "the man"—Secretary Rumsfeld—which is just exactly how Rumsfeld wanted it to be.

Franks was subsequently tasked to prepare a war plan for Iraq, and he came back with a plan based on overwhelming the Iraqis and also having enough to deal with the aftermath of what would be involved—it was a decent plan with realistic numbers, and the Chairman of the Joint Chiefs, General Dick Myers, was strongly in favor of that plan. Rumsfeld was not, and he wanted it slashed.

\* \* \*

From day one Rumsfeld clearly resented the Chairman's newfound responsibilities and authorities under Title Ten, all new since the last time he'd been Secretary of Defense. He liked it the old way, which he felt gave him much more power.

The new dynamic Rumsfeld created between himself and Franks diminished the role of the Joint Chiefs, for all intents and purposes, and gave Rumsfeld almost total control. When Rumsfeld slashed General Franks's troop estimates, who was there to lobby on his behalf? Nobody, because the SecDef had basically cut out his team of four-star advocates—the Joint Chiefs—by suggesting that Franks deal directly with him rather than keep the Joint Chiefs in the loop. (Although Title Ten chain of command goes directly from the CINC to the SecDef, historically the CINCs present their plans to the Joint Chiefs for review before presenting them to the SecDef—for obvious reasons.) Neglecting the input from the senior members of each service would, in the end, prove very costly.

When the SecDef decided to micromanage the war plan by excising tried-and-true methods of planning such as a failsafe mechanism called "branches and sequels," along with RFFs (Requests for Future Forces) and TPFDDs (Time-Phased Force and Deployment Data/Documents) nobody was on Tommy's team to push back with him to convince the SecDef that such modifications were ill-advised. When Rumsfeld made logistic decisions many levels beneath his pay grade, like "borrowing" tanks from Kuwait for the 3rd Infantry Division to use instead of allowing them to use equipment they were familiar with, about all Tommy could do was roll his eyes and say, "Great idea, sir," because he decided to go it alone. Eventually, Tommy Franks acquiesced to almost everything because he had completely isolated himself, and he ended up with the *Rumsfeld* plan of battle, which was incredibly flawed and insufficient—and one that still has us positioned today—more than seven years later—trying to dig ourselves out of the crap they spread all over the Iraqi countryside.

Amid all this, there was one man who heeded the great message contained in H. R. McMaster's *Dereliction of Duty*, and at great professional risk to himself, he decided to speak the truth. Army Chief of Staff General Eric Shinseki realized that the very lives of our great servicemen and -women depended on his doing so.

General Shinseki had been in charge of our stabilization force in Bosnia and he was probably the world's foremost authority on what it took to rebuild a nation and provide that all-important safe and secure postwar environment. As one of the Joint Chiefs, Ric's expertise was there for the asking—and, per Goldwater-Nichols, he was supposed to have been consulted. He understood the numbers of troops it would take, and he was ready to point out that it wouldn't be just the number you put out on the street, it's three times that number because you have three eight-hour shifts—so, in February 2003, Shinseki spoke out and stated that it would take at least one hundred sixty thousand to two hundred thousand troops.

"Preposterous," stated Rumsfeld, who then turned his deputy, Paul Wolfowitz, loose on Shinseki.

"Way off the mark," said Wolfowitz. "By August of 2003, around thirty-four thousand is a much more realistic figure of what we will need." Then, Wolfowitz went on to denigrate the Army Chief of Staff for having given such a ludicrous number in the first place. Wolfowitz testified before Congress on February 27, 2003, and said, "It's hard to conceive that it would take more forces to provide stability in post-Saddam Iraq than it would take to conduct the war itself and to secure the surrender of Saddam's security forces and his army." With no experience, little did he understand.

Of course, in retrospect, Ric Shinseki was 100 percent right. As I write this today (in 2010), the Associated Press morning headline read "U.S. MAY SLOW PACE OF IRAQ TROOP PULLOUT." More than *seven years* after the invasion, we still have *ninety-six thousand* troops in Iraq, and months after the Iraqi election, internal bickering and ballot challenges have precluded the formation of an Iraqi government. Quoting today's AP report, ". . . partnership between al-Maliki's State of Law coalition and the religious Shiite Iraqi National Alliance threatens to anger Sunnis who heavily backed al-Maliki's main rival, Iraqiya. If Sunnis continue to feel sidelined, that in turn could fuel sectarian tensions and raise fears of new violence." Yesterday's bombings and shootings marked 119 deaths, the bloodiest day of 2010.

Shinseki went on to retire and today continues to serve our nation as the Secretary of Veterans Affairs, but his last months of military service were not very pleasant ones for him because he had spoken up and told the truth. Unlike the team that Rumsfeld preferred as his inner circle, Ric was not a yes man. Unfortunately, because his opinion did not support what Rumsfeld and Franks wanted to do, he was viewed as the enemy. It's almost a shame that Ric was too much of a soldier to drop Rumsfeld a note asking, *Now whose numbers were "preposterous"?* and another to Wolfowitz asking, *Now who was "way off the mark"?*

## PRESIDENTIAL RHETORIC

By this time, Bush was publicly bragging to the international community that "we're going to take this guy out of there whether you are with us or

against us (although we want you with us)," so between that and the fact
that he had already deployed in the region, Bush had walked too far out
on that limb to turn back. I also believe this big-bad-cowboy Bush mentality completely turned off the international community—and of course
that was compounded by the xenophobic comments Rumsfeld was making,
calling the *old* NATO irrelevant. He had them all angered to start with, and
then continued to make inappropriate remarks, like this one from January 2003: "Germany has been a problem and France has been a problem,"
he told the foreign press. "You're thinking of Europe as Germany and
France. I don't. I think that's *old Europe*." Not surprisingly, the response
was both instant and harsh, and the United States was labeled as "arrogant."
Roselyne Bachelot, the French Environment Minister, told reporters, "If
you knew what I felt like telling Mr. Rumsfeld . . ." but then she stopped herself, saying she couldn't use such an offensive word in public.

## WMDS

And then the WMD intell started falling apart. Even so, I will admit that
I believed—and still believe—it's possible that somewhere in Syria or buried underground or somewhere else, Saddam had chemical and biological weapons—artillery pieces and maybe Scud warheads. Where I draw
the line is that they ever posed any strategic threat to the United States—
that contention was always utter bullshit and every one of them knew it,
or should have known it. That's where the intentional deception of the
American people took place, not in the contention that the WMDs were
there to begin with—because we did honestly believe that part. The only
part of the United States that was directly threatened by the WMDs were
the troops that we deployed in the region for the war, and by the way—the
more troops we put in the region, the more Americans became threatened
by the WMDs.

   Add to that the fact that without a doubt the Iraq operation took major resources away from other areas that *did* pose real threats on the terrorism front, and you have another element of the invasion that actually
escalated our terrorist threat rather than reduced it.

After the Afghanistan operation went so well, the President started speaking more and more about this madman Saddam Hussein. He stated publicly that Saddam had to go, insinuating that it was for the safety of
the American people, even though he still had little evidence to that effect. Having had Rumsfeld deploy troops into the region, the President
started walking out on that limb, as his public comments got bolder
and bolder.

I had learned during my tenure as Chairman that if you let your mouth overload your ass, you've got to back it up or you look weak as hell. That's exactly where Bush was headed.

Colin, meanwhile, rhetorically asked me, "What the hell are we doing? [The President] knows there's no linkage." He and I had agreed on that from the start. We also agreed that whatever we did needed to be done as part of a multinational effort.

Meanwhile, Cheney kept going back to the CIA over and over, trying to beat George Tenet into coming up with *anything* that tied 9/11 to Saddam. Tenet, a good guy who isn't easily steamrolled, was doing the best he could to come up with something. That something came in the form of a defector code-named Curveball, who was feeding U.S. intelligence hundreds of pages of fabricated data outlining Saddam's profusion of WMDs. Those famous "mobile biological weapons labs"—completely fabricated. The documents verifying Saddam Hussein's attempts to purchase uranium powder from Niger for nuclear WMDs—complete forgeries. Did Colin have any clue that they were less than authentic? Hell no. He spent countless hours challenging the CIA's data and seeking assurances before he spoke before the U.N. Security Council. Armed with the intelligence and data provided by the CIA, Colin appeared before the United Nations and stated his case, really the President's case, but one he believed was true at the time.

Many months later, when Colin and I discussed it, he confided in me that the most disappointing thing in his entire career of public service was that U.N. briefing. I told him that given what he had to work with at that time, nobody could have done a better job. I still believe that. But the ones who provided that bad intell should have been nailed, because their intelligence was flat-out wrong. Heads should have rolled left and right, but nobody was held accountable. People were kept on in the name of loyalty. Figures lie and liars figure, and in this case the liars were allowed to walk, while Colin Powell had to take all the heat.

Finally, Colin convinced the President that we needed multinational support to invade Iraq, but by the time he went to brief the U.N. we had already deployed and the other countries knew we were going to attack, either with them or not—so why would they sacrifice the lives of soldiers or funds when they knew we were going in anyway? (This is all with the exception of our great British friends, who stood right by our side anyway. Some other nations elected to send a handful of troops, some as "observers"—but these were, in essence, liabilities rather than assets.)

\* \* \*

At the time I was working with General Tony Zinni, who by then had retired. When Tony and I learned that we were going to invade without sufficient troops, and without multinational participation, all we could do was look at each other, roll our eyes, and say, "You have got to be kidding." It was so obvious that they would win the battle but then be in big trouble.

Tony went vocal on this early on. It was good for him. I felt I could not do that because Dick Myers had shared much of this information with me in confidence, and I certainly would never have betrayed that confidence. Also, Tony was getting the word out anyway, should anyone have wanted to listen.

## INTELL

One frustration that was shared by all of us (on a number of fronts besides Iraq)—was the lack of sufficient intell, and you have to go back at least fifteen years to fully understand what George Tenet was dealing with. It was a time of severe budget reductions, and Congress emasculated the CIA—withdrew their funding and forced them to get rid of many of their really in-depth covert programs. Human-intelligence assets were reduced, and to a great degree the United States was left with only technical means of intelligence against the major countries—wiretaps, radio intercepts, and such—and those are just not the same thing. With third- and fourth-tier countries like Iraq, Bosnia, Haiti, Kosovo, and, to a lesser degree, Iran, and all of South America, the situation was even worse and our ability to receive timely, actionable intelligence was severely impaired. It's why it took so long to find Saddam, and of course even longer to locate UBL. In the case of Iraq, about all we were getting were occasional electronic intercepts or sporadic HUMINT reports coming in from a few who were still on the CIA payroll, and even those just about always came in late or inaccurate and most of the time both. It severely tied our hands.

When you're dealing with intelligence data, there is an incredible amount of information that comes in—it is not "intelligence," it's just information. It is staggering what the analysts have to ferret through. Maybe 95 percent of it will be obvious garbage, 4 percent falls in the middle, .0001 percent is good solid actionable intell (if there is any at all), and the rest of it could be something that if you took out of context might look like you're exactly right. Since in this case there was no real factual intell, what Wolfowitz and this group did was go for the out-of-context piece that looked good, and make their case from that. Those were the pieces they were searching for—that one tiny iota of information they could spin a story around and try to build a case on that.

## EYE OFF THE BALL—
## FIRST WAR DISINTEGRATES

One of the unintended consequences of the Iraq invasion of 2003 (and something that the Joint Chiefs most likely would have forewarned) was that as troops and equipment were pulled from Afghanistan to invade Iraq, the Afghanistan commander found himself stretched for resources; and once that happened, the tremendous gains that had been made started to recede. He first noticed a Taliban resurgence in the remote areas and then they began to rebuild their entire "empire," with the common goal of fighting the Americans. Al-Qaeda was still operating along Pakistan's border, and as the commander lost more and more of his resources to Iraq, these al-Qaeda cells flourished and the whole Afghanistan operation started to deteriorate. Now, nine years later, we're getting those resources back in there in an attempt to tamp them down, along with the situation in its nuclear-armed neighbor, Pakistan.

---

Spinning the possible possession of WMDs as a threat to the United States in the way they did it is, in my opinion, tantamount to intentionally deceiving the American people and justifying the necessity of war. The cost of this endeavor is measured in thousands of our great American military men and women who have been killed or severely injured, and spending the hard-earned treasure of our citizens on something that was just not true. As of September 2010, more than forty-four hundred U.S. soldiers have been killed and more than thirty-two thousand seriously wounded in the Iraq War, and about $900 billion has been spent. We owe every one of these brave men and women our respect, gratitude, and honor—that point is unchallenged.

What I find revolting is that their sacrifices are based on the devious deception at the top that manipulated the system in order to satisfy personal agendas.

## Chapter Twenty-Two ★★★★

# FEED THE GORILLA

I love the press, but like any beast you have to water and feed them, and let them out every so often. . . . I fed them stories . . . and it kept them happy and satisfied and not wandering off in search of anecdotal episodes that might not be reflective of the operation but nonetheless would produce sound bites for the evening news or headlines for the newspapers.

Many of us who grew up in the Vietnam era harbored a deep distrust—bordering on disdain—of the media. Perhaps it was the reporting on the Vietnam War, which tended to mix the military and the political processes rather than portray the military as an extension of the political process, as it should have been. To the soldiers fighting the war, being painted as the scapegoat for the political process in Washington seemed terribly unfair. The reporting seemed biased, unbalanced, and, in many cases, prejudicial.

In retrospect, after reading H. R. McMaster's book, *Dereliction of Duty*—which chronicles the deceit and deception taking place in Washington during that period and the lack of cohesion and moral courage among the Joint Chiefs, each of whom was fighting to place his own service in the best light—maybe their reporting was deserved.

There was also a concern that any time a member of the military spoke with the media, the message could be taken out of context, blown out of proportion, or misquoted—resulting in censure or even firing.

In the years following Vietnam, there seemed to be a greater understanding by the media for the role they played in keeping Americans informed and perhaps even a greater understanding of their responsibility to report accurately and fairly. My opinion first started to change as I attended a joint officer war-fighting course at Maxwell Air Force Base shortly after

being promoted to brigadier general. Network news correspondents David
Martin (CBS) and Pete Williams (NBC) were guest speakers, and their ex-
planations of the press's crucial function in a free society, plus their own
obligation to report the news with a sense of *truth* and *responsibility,* really drilled home how important it was for us to work together in the interest of timely and honest reporting.

Even so (and irrespective of the 1960s era paranoia), there are legitimate
questions to consider. *Are there certain times when national security must
trump the fundamental right of freedom of the press, guaranteed in the First
Amendment?* If so, who gets to make that call? These are the types of issues
I faced every day.


When I was Chairman, one of my responsibilities encompassed taking a
short stroll down the E Ring, often accompanied by either Secretary Cohen or Secretary Rumsfeld, and stepping beneath the bright row of TV
lights in the Pentagon's press briefing room to handle the daily press conferences. In many respects I think that's what I'm best known for to the
general public. I can't tell you how many times people have stopped me
and asked, "Aren't you the guy who's always talking to reporters in front
of that blue curtain and Pentagon seal?"

While they call it a briefing room, it's really more like a state-of-the-art
TV studio—with near-perfect acoustics, top-of-the-line microphones and

studio lights, full control room with video switcher and audio board, plus direct network feeds and links to facilitate live broadcasts around the world.

On 9/11, when Secretary Rumsfeld and I, along with Senators Warner and Levin, were first to brief the nation that our military was functioning full throttle in spite of the physical damage to the Pentagon—I wouldn't be surprised if our worldwide audience exceeded 100 million viewers. Representing our military—and our country—as spokesman to an audience of that scope was a massive responsibility, and one that I always took on with deference and respect.

In March 1991, General Tom Kelly, one of my mentors, announced his retirement from the Army. Like me, General Kelly spent many mornings dodging verbal bullets fired his way by the Pentagon press corps, and at times his tough Irish demeanor blasted back some pretty effective rounds of his own. Many of the reporters, and perhaps even the viewers, assumed that he viewed the relationship as adversarial. His final briefing proved otherwise, when he signed off with an unsolicited sharp *defense* of the news media and the First Amendment. He said:

> "Believe it or not, I've enjoyed this little interlude. Got a lot of letters from people who really don't understand the hurly-burly and give-and-take of a press briefing and at no time were you ever impolite to me and at no time did I ever become offended; and as you know, I hold a lot of you in great respect. . . . Having a free press has served the United States well for 215 years. It is a crucial element in our democracy. And if anybody needs a contrast, all they have to do is look at a country that doesn't have a free press and see what happens there."

The room erupted in a standing ovation, and rightfully so. I wholeheartedly agree with General Kelly's analysis.

———

Over the years I've had so many great experiences with the press, some of which served to dissipate whatever skepticism may have lingered from the Vietnam days. Perhaps the greatest example of this occurred in Haiti in 1991 when I was commander of Joint Task Force 180, and I was seriously concerned that this one might have resulted in my being thrown out of the Army for divulging Top-Secret mission plans to more than 150 members of the media.

Just a few days out from D-Day I received a call from ACOM informing me that the White House had decided I would be required to carry about 150 members of the media with us into Haiti, and they were to be embedded into every element of our operation. They would accompany the troops during the invasion, aboard the airplanes, ships, and ground vehicles—and remain embedded with that unit throughout the operation.

I was told that they would fly into Pope Air Force Base, where we would pick them up and escort them to Fort Bragg, where I had been ordered to brief them in great detail about the Top Secret invasion that was about to commence—with the firm understanding that they would not reveal any of this classified information until *after* the invasion had occurred. At least that was the "understanding."

Under normal circumstances, the procedure involved in securing a Top-Secret security clearance that would be required to receive such a briefing is both intense and time consuming. It involves a thorough examination by the Defense Security Service (DSS) (at the time, Defense Investigative Service, DIS) investigators who scrutinize all aspects of the last ten years of an applicant's life, including FBI background check, financial review (credit record), and criminal history; plus field surveys where investigators personally interview co-workers, employers, friends, educators, and neighbors, at the same time analyzing records held by employers, courts, and rental offices. The process usually takes anywhere from four to eight months, although it's not uncommon for backlogs to extend this to more than a year. To my knowledge, none of these reporters had been cleared, except for whatever peripheral screening the Department of Defense public affairs department may have undertaken; so what we had were 150 noncleared individuals whose very jobs were to disseminate information in as expedient a manner as possible so as to scoop the competition. From my perspective, the very lives of the 22,000 troops who would be part of the invasion depended on operational secrecy.

From the moment I was given this order, I had nightmares that I would brief the plan, then wake the following morning to find it splashed across the front pages of all the major newspapers, and leaked as "breaking news" on all the network news shows.

While this was all coming to a head, I received a call from the Army Chief of Staff, General Gordon Sullivan. "Hugh, I know you're on top of this media embedding, but I've got a guy from the *Washington Post* that we want to embed with your headquarters," he said, as I was about ready to throw up at the thought of some reporter shadowing my every move when I was trying to run the invasion.

"What's his name?" I asked, not even trying to cover up the disdain in my voice.

"He's a good man, one of the best," General Sullivan volunteered. "Bradley Graham."

I almost laughed out loud because I had just returned from an executives' course at Harvard University and in one of my seminars I'd been teamed up with Brad and seven others. He and I got to know each other very well and cemented our friendship over early-morning jogs. I couldn't have thought of anyone I could feel more comfortable with as my "shadow" than Brad.

"Good choice, sir," I told the Chief of Staff. Bradley joined the group and throughout the operation he was very unintrusive and I was very comfortable with his presence.

I proceded with my classified brief (although *not* getting into those areas that exceeded the Top-Secret level and went into TS-SCI, such as the JSOC specifics), and we adjourned to go our separate ways—the reporters to their assigned units, and Brad and I to Guantanamo Bay, Cuba, where we would catch the *Mount Whitney* and sail to Haiti.

As it turned out, my fears were unfounded; to my knowledge, not one reporter leaked a word of information before the agreed-upon time, and at that moment I gained a great deal of respect for the press, and this confidence has never been betrayed.

In addition to the 150 reporters who were embedded with our various units, when I arrived in Haiti we had 450 members of the media on the ground, including every major broadcast network in the world. We could have handled it the same way so many others have in the past, which is just allowing them to do their own thing and inserting a staff of public-affairs officers to serve as "filters"; or, you could do as we did, which was stop and ask the question, *What are they here for?* Of course the answer seems simple: *they are here to report news on what is going on.* Their jobs depended on feeding timely information back to their parent organizations.

Early on in our planning stage we took this assumption to the next step and developed an entire public affairs strategy around it. If from their perspective they needed newsworthy stories, and from ours we might prefer that they cover certain key events over others, the logical solution was for us to provide them with exciting, important, newsworthy stories for them to cover on a daily basis. We even provided transportation for them to get to those stories if they happened to be in outlying areas, such as with the marines up in Cap-Haitien or Special Forces in other remote locations. But we had to have a plan because without a plan, this gorilla does not get fed, and a hungry gorilla almost inevitably will wander off into the wilderness and feed on isolated stories of their own that are not indicative of an overall situation yet could be spun in such a way as to do real damage to the operation. They may find the one soldier whose poncho liner was stolen and now he is getting cold at night, and the next day's headline becomes "U.S. ARMY MISTREATING ITS TROOPS" rather than the thousands of other valid, worthwhile stories that would constitute *real* news of the great humanitarian work we are doing, or the removal of the sadistic police chief who was beating his own innocent citizens just for fun.

My primate experts (aka public affairs officers) did an awesome job of keeping that gorilla fed by giving them a story a day; understanding, of course, that they could cover that story or any other of their choosing—but at least we were offering them something valuable to report. By the time we landed on that island, Lieutenant Colonel Tim Vane and Colonel Barry Willy had already become public affairs gurus, and every day from then on they had something. From day one we had a great relationship with the press. We felt like the journalists were reporting fairly, and the press felt like we were respectful of their needs and desirous of accommodating those needs.

The Haiti operation was a forum for another great example of exceptional reporting—one that almost rivaled the effectiveness of our entire military-intelligence effort. CNN's Christiane Amanpour's investigative prowess was as good as I have ever seen, and about as good as it can get. It was almost like she had advance warning that a sensitive operation was about to take place at a given location, because CNN typically would be on the scene either prior to our arrival or within seconds afterward. Our operators would arrive to find Christiane already on the scene with microphone in hand and camera at the ready—standing by to scoop the other networks. She had a tremendous intell system that was somehow figuring out how our operations were going to play out.

Throughout my time in Haiti, the snake eater in me was curious to know just how Christiane was consistently pulling off this excellent reconnaissance—to the point that in my waning days on the island, I just had to know. My deputy (Admiral Jay Johnson, the future Chief of Naval Operations but now my naval component commander for the task force) and I invited Christiane to be our guest for a working lunch out on the *Mount Whitney*. Not only would it be a great opportunity for her to see the Navy's most advanced C4 command-and-control JOC (joint operations center), but I promised to share some inside information that she had been unable to secure on her own—just on background—but even so it would allow her to gain a broader education of how all the pieces of the Cedras/Aristide puzzle came together at the very last moment.

She eagerly accepted and we sent a helicopter to pick her up and shuttle her from Port-au-Prince to the *Mount Whitney*, still operating about five miles offshore.

Following a relaxing lunch inside the captain's mess, Jay and I escorted her off to a small, private conference room and we sat down over coffee and tea to commence our exchange. I briefed her on what had transpired when Cedras refused to leave due to the financial conflict with the State Department, and she shared with us how it was that she was able to remain one step ahead of us day in, day out.

It turned out that she just had a massive network of contacts spread all over the island, locals whom she had "recruited" to keep her fully apprised of whatever they heard—classic HUMINT that was very well executed. I never did ask her how much she had to pay them, if she paid them anything at all—but in hindsight that would have been interesting to know.

It was a great exchange for both of us, and it left me wondering if we wouldn't be best served by firing half the intell community in Washington and just contracting those services over to CNN.

Around the time of my final days in Haiti, another event so impacted our public affairs effort that I almost felt like writing a thank-you note to its participants. The O. J. Simpson trial was rapidly gaining traction up in Los Angeles and 450 reporters suddenly boarded airplanes and left the "old news" of Haiti to capture their next headline, which would be found in Judge Lance Ito's courtroom in downtown Los Angeles. It provided the opportunity for me to leave the island by turning the operation over to Major General Dave Meade and returning to my corps headquarters to start focusing on my next mission.

It's impossible for me to talk about responsible, extraordinary reporting without mentioning Tom Brokaw—a multitalented journalist and author with a heart of gold.

In the interest of full disclosure, I did briefly work for NBC shortly after I retired—but only for a six-month trial period (beginning in December 2001) to see how I would like it. I insisted that my contract have a number of caveats stating that (a) I would not do anything that would undermine the administration—and that would apply to whatever administration was in office at the time; (b) I would not do anything that would divulge information that would hurt the troops; and (c) I would not be critical of the job that the troops were doing. I probably ended up turning down more assignments than I accepted, concerned that many would be construed as criticism of the troops, and I had said up front that I refused to do that. Shortly thereafter I had my fall, effectively eliminating any prospect of history recording my name alongside those of Walter Cronkite and Edward R. Murrow in the Broadcasters Hall of Fame.

* * *

While I was Chairman, NBC did a special called "A Day in the Life of the Chairman," and it consisted of Tom accompanying me throughout the day, all the while cameras rolling for them to edit however they saw fit. I couldn't believe it when I opened up the front door of my Fort Myer residence, ready to step out for my daily 4:30 A.M. five-mile jog—and there was Tom and his crew waiting for me beside their van, packed with TV equipment, standing by to follow me on this run to get footage of it. I think if I had pushed a little harder, I probably could have persuaded Tom to get out there and run with me, but instead I completed my run on my own as the cameraman recorded it all—then I turned around and came back, all hot and sweaty and ready to collapse over my first cup of morning coffee.

I opened the door and, once again, there stood Tom, grinning broadly and ready to visit with me in the kitchen over a cup of coffee—where apparently they had set up their cameras during my jog. (After seeing the footage shot in the kitchen that night on the news, Carolyn berated me because it showed that I had left the pantry door open and coffee spilled on the countertop.) That continued throughout the day—just me, Tom, and the crew, which was always a few steps in front. I even took them inside the NMCC and allowed Tom to join me for a Top-Secret briefing (although neither the crew nor the cameras were allowed in for that).

I think Tom would agree that it was a very special day—and one in which we really bonded on a personal level. It turned out that we had a great deal in common, both being from small towns—Tom from Webster, South Dakota, and of course I'm from Speed, North Carolina.

What really put all this in perspective happened immediately after my fall, in March 2002. While very few people even knew about the fall in those first few days, even fewer made it through my unyielding security force (i.e., Carolyn) and were allowed to speak with me; I was still fighting total paralysis and needed all the energy I could muster for that.

"Hugh, I'm going to let you take this one, if you're up for it," Carolyn said, preparing to hold the phone up to my ear. "It's Tom Brokaw calling from an aircraft carrier in the middle of the Persian Gulf." That was Tom, and it did bring a smile to my face.

"Hugh, I'm very close with one of the top specialists in spinal-cord injuries and I want to get you up to see him right away. You let me know what I can do to make that happen." While I was incredibly grateful, I was already in top hands where I was—but the generosity Tom demonstrated at that moment just reinforced how I've always felt about him—he's just a wonderful, down-to-earth human being.

Once I did finally get out, he contacted me again.

"Hugh, what you have done is beyond belief. I've been told that your battling back from an injury like that almost defied the realm of medical possibility—I've got to do a special about your recovery." And he did, right in front of the Arlington House at Arlington National Cemetery.

———

Jack McWethy (ABC News defense correspondent who died in a ski accident in 2008) was another real gentleman who was a tribute to his profession. He was well respected and well connected—and had just shared some interesting information with Captain (later Rear Admiral) Steve Pietropaoli, my Public Affairs officer. A very excited Steve came running into my office to fill me in.

"McWethy is onto tonight's Bosnian snatch," Steve revealed, speaking a mile a minute about a classified terrorist apprehension we had planned to execute in just a few hours. "Sounds like it's going to be ABC's lead story on the evening news; Jack wants to know if we have a comment." I knew it was time to get the first team together, which meant adding Denny Klauer. There are none better at coming up with the optimum plan for handling issues related to the media than Steve and Denny and later T McCreary (retired Rear Admiral). It was people like this whom I referred to whenever I accepted any recognition "on behalf of the men and women of the armed services."

"Ask him to come on down to my office and I most certainly will have a comment for him," I told Steve, knowing that Jack would be right down the hall in the press briefing room.

Jack's a great guy and he and I respected each other. When he came in we shook hands and I closed the door behind him, motioning for him to take a seat in one of the guest chairs at the opposite end of the office from my desk. I leaned against the back of the other chair, still standing, but looking down at Jack.

"I understand that you have picked up on some information that we're getting ready to do some type of an operation against either terrorists or insurgents in Bosnia, and I want to make a deal with you," I said, and there was no doubt that I had his undivided attention. "The information you've got is one hundred percent wrong unless we give the *execute* command, and I can guarantee you that if you get on the air and leak it, that command will never be given because you will have put my operators in harm's way, so that op will be canceled. In essence, you will have just reported on an event that will never occur—bad for you, and bad for us. On the other hand, if you keep this to yourself and do not make that broadcast—if and when we ever execute that operation, I will give you a call within minutes, you will come to my office, and I will brief you at a great level of detail on what we did so you will not only have an exclusive but you will have an exclusive knowing far more about what played out behind the scenes than you ever would otherwise."

That was a no-brainer. Jack didn't even have to think about it. He stood, extended his hand, and said, "General, you've got a deal." We shook hands and he left.

Around three or four in the morning, the DDO notified me that the operation had been successful, and I had my J3 contact Jack with all the details. Our operation had played out safely and effectively, and Jack got his exclusive. I always viewed that as a great example of a responsible press—and both the institution and Jack personally gained a great deal of respect in my eyes.

———

Some interactions are not so positive, although I do consider myself fortunate that in my entire career there has been only one show that I have cut off, and that's *60 Minutes*. I have no use for their occasional disregard for the truth and twisting of facts to advance their own agenda. Perhaps it's different today now that Mike Wallace is no longer with the program, but I always felt it was problematic when he was.

My one and only encounter with them occurred when I was at Fort Campbell and they were trying to make a case that the night-vision goggles we were using were ineffective and resulted in troops being killed. They wanted to document this on tape, and requested to come out and fly with us in order to do so.

At the time, I was the Assistant Division Commander for the 101st Airborne (Air Assault). First of all, I knew the goggles worked—in fact, they worked so well that it was almost magic the way they lit up even the darkest of nights; and the troops absolutely loved them. But even if that hadn't been the case, I would have wanted them to cover it because they would be doing us a great service by exposing an ongoing systemic problem that was endangering our great men and women in uniform (even though that was not in any way the case in this event).

We gave them an open-ended invitation to come up on any night of their choosing and join the air crew for an actual mission in which the goggles would be used. *They* chose the night and we set it up for them to fly in UH-60 Black Hawks so that they could experience the entire capability of the light-enhancement system.

As they boarded the aircraft we fitted them with the night-vision devices—the very same models as the pilot and flight crew were wearing—and after takeoff it was clear that they were quite impressed by how the goggles completely illuminated what had been the darkest of nights. Naturally, the pilot wanted to demonstrate just how much could be accomplished with this great technology, so he really put on a show for them by descending to near-treetop level and then cranking up the throttle, so they ended up on a high-speed run right along the contour of the land beneath them, up and down the hills and valleys and easily avoiding obstructions in their path. These are gifted aviators and they left no holds barred. They landed and the TV crew seemed more than satisfied, in fact *excited* by what they had just experienced.

As they prepared to leave, they took the names and contact information for the aircrew, just so that they could be properly identified on the telecast—or so the pilots were told. No sooner had the pilots gone home and gotten to sleep than their phones began to ring; it was the *60 Minutes* representative inquiring as to the "real story" since they assumed that everything the pilots said during the flight was merely mimicking the party line and that, in fact, they hated the goggles.

The warrant officers who received these calls were livid, and the following day they came back and reported that they had shown the CBS TV crew everything they had, told them the truth, and *shown* them how great the goggles worked, but the *60 Minutes* crew didn't believe any of it and accused them of lying.

As if that disrespectful behavior wasn't bad enough, to add insult to injury, they ran the report on the night-vision goggles but used *none* of the footage or interviews or facts that they had gathered that night; instead, they had gathered anything they could find that would back their preconceived negative opinion of the goggles.

You would think that by now they would get the message that I have no use for that type of so-called reporting, but it must go over their heads, because as recently as two weeks ago they called me to go on the show and talk about various military issues—this most recent being to give my opinion of the current "don't ask, don't tell" policy.

Another questionable situation arose surrounding Charles Gibson when he was hosting *Good Morning America* and I was commanding the JTF-180 in Haiti. I like Charlie but I think it was dirty pool the way he ambushed me on network television by setting me up under false pretenses and then turning the tables once the cameras went live.

The afternoon before the interview, I was meeting with Ambassador Swing when I happened to glance out the window of his second-story office at the U.S. embassy in Port-au-Prince and saw a little Toyota pickup truck flying down the street with a load of Haitian police on board. They screeched to a stop, jumped out of the truck, and ran over to an old man who was just walking down the street—then, for no apparent reason, they took out their batons and beat him until he fell to the ground, at which point they laughed, climbed back into the truck, and took off.

I turned to the ambassador and said *we have got to stop that*—and I immediately got Cedras on the phone and demanded he meet with us early the following morning to get into this—and we did so just a short while before I was scheduled to do live interviews with all three morning network-TV shows.

When Cedras and I met the following morning, I was very tough on him and told him what would happen to both him and his vicious police chief, Lieutenant Colonel Michel Francois (who was instrumental in the original coup that removed Aristide from power), if such brutality continued to occur. He pledged to take care of it posthaste.

I quickly moved to the building where they had set up the lights and camera for my interview, and I took a seat in front of the camera. A technician fitted me with a microphone, clipping it to my collar and running the wire under my jacket and around to the back, where he also somehow connected the earpiece in which I would hear the various hosts back in New York.

First up was Charlie Gibson, and the technician informed me that we were about a minute away from going live. "Can you give us a sound check, General?" he said, somewhat frantically trying to eliminate some static he was getting with the connection.

"Check one, check two, check check," I repeated.

"Okay, we're good to go, sir," he said with a sense of relief. "You should have New York in your earpiece."

"General Shelton? Charlie Gibson speaking. Can you hear me?"

"Loud and clear, Charlie. How's everything in New York?"

"Just great, General. And I hear things are going well in Haiti," he said.

"Charlie, I've got great troops, things are going like clockwork, I could not ask for it to be going any better."

"That's exactly what it looks like from here; great job." And then I heard the *Good Morning America* theme song playing in my earpiece.

"Stand by, everyone," some new garbled voice cut in. "We're live in five, four, three, two . . ."

I pretty much just sat there looking at the camera with a smile on my face, waiting to be cued, when the red camera light popped on and I heard Charlie introduce me. "This is Charles Gibson and this morning we are speaking live with Lieutenant General Hugh Shelton in Port-au-Prince, Haiti. General Shelton is the joint task force commander who is commanding our forces there. Good morning, General."

"Good morning, Charlie," I said, trying to smile cheerfully, even though it was still just the camera lens I was speaking to; they hadn't even provided me with a monitor on which to see Charlie.

Suddenly Charlie's tone seemed to change, and instead of the nice, cheerful "great to talk with you" voice I had conversed with before going on the air, now he was hard-line and aggressive. "General, just yesterday we watched here in America as Haitian police brutally beat innocent Haitian civilians with clubs and nightsticks. How long are you and your troops going to idly stand by and allow that to take place? Is that why you're there, to stand by and watch vicious attacks such as that?"

I felt like I had just walked into an L-shaped ambush all alone and been subjected to withering gunfire. But I responded, "Well, Charlie, as you know, the troops are doing a great job, and one of the challenges that we had early on was the fact that the Haitian police had been beating their own people, and that resulted in a meeting early this morning with General Cedras in which I told him unequivocally that it will stop today or we will take out those police every time they do it, and disarm them if that's what it is going to take. I was extremely firm with General Cedras and he has assured me that that will not take place again, but you can trust me, we're going to be watching that with a jaundiced eye."

I was about to die.

At that moment, I had actually changed American policy because our goal going in had been that we *not* get into police work, that it was not our job. Our position was that if we were going to leave a police force in place over there, they were going to have to do the job on their own.

Charlie cut back in and immediately switched to another subject. And from that point on, the rest of his questions were softballs. I don't think I had ever been set up like that in my life—but it happens. To be frank, I'm actually fine with Charlie. That was the only time he pulled a stunt like that with me, but it certainly reinforced my feeling that when dealing with the press, you do have to stay on your toes.

———

I've been fortunate to have had so many great experiences with other individuals including Tim Russert, Larry King, Jim Lehrer, Lou Dobbs, Ted

Koppel, David Martin, Bob Woodward, Bradley Graham, Bill Friday, Barbara Starr, Jamie McIntyre, Tom Ricks, Martha Raddatz, Dan Rather, Elaine Sciolino, George Wilson, Bob Schieffer, Tom Philpott, and Thomas Friedman; and I thank them for the respect and cooperation that we've shared throughout the years.

In today's society we have many names for the organized process of publicly disseminating information, but they all have to play by the same set of rules. Whether you call it public affairs, strategic communication, information operations, or a myriad of other names—the mission must be founded on truth or you're in for real trouble.

I often end my speaking engagements with Q and A sessions, and I'm frequently asked if (in the interest of national security) I have ever lied to the press. My answer: *no.* They often follow up by asking if there is ever an occasion when it might be necessary to do so. My answer: *I sure can't think of any at the moment.* And that same answer applies to a major automaker accepting responsibility for a stuck accelerator, or a government spinning a story about prisoner abuse in an American-run prison in Cuba, or the hunt for weapons of mass destruction in a Middle East country.

Today, there is a great deal of concern about information operations. I can tell you that from a military perspective—and I hope from the perspective of other areas of government—it is never about lying to the U.S. press or the U.S. people, but rather it is about coordinating all the elements of our government so that the picture we are painting is the same. This can get very complicated in some cases if you are trying to influence people like the North Koreans or even to mislead them to a degree, while at the same time you can never mislead or lie to the American people. Consequently, it is a very fine line that you must walk. It was one of the toughest issues I had to deal with as Chairman—getting that effective information-ops program going effectively.

After I retired, it appeared that the program took a dramatic turn for the worse. As a recently retired Chairman I would receive three or four e-mails a day from the Department of Defense that were also distributed to analysts and news organizations; but the obvious, biased, one-sided spin being put on everything made me want to vomit. Not only was it sickening, but it was so obvious that it was just hype that there was no way it could have been effective. The capper for me was when something as obvious as the mistakes at Abu Ghraib were painted in such a positive light, as if almost justifying the "few isolated incidents of misconduct" within the context of the total number of prisoners there. Well, guess what? There is *no* positive light, so in a major screw-up like this, just admit what happened and deal with it, but don't play games with numbers to try to cover up reality. *One* incident would have been too many. Figures lie and liars figure. After that, I ended up just deleting those e-mails. I spoke with Secretary Cohen and Colin Powell about this a few years later and learned that they had quit reading them even before I had, for the very same reason.

On one of my appearances on the Larry King show, Larry asked me to describe the *fine line* between what the military does and does not want covered. I took issue with that overall premise because I believe it's essential to our great system of democracy that the citizens be given all the facts in a straightforward manner without bias or spin—with only two exceptions. Here's how I answered:

"I don't think the line is too thin, Larry. What the military would not like to have covered is, first of all, on the operational side, anything that would aid, abet, assist, support, or in any other way help the enemy to know what the intent of our forces are; such as their location, direction of movement, et cetera. That's one."

"(The second would be) anything that would be in violation of the Geneva convention or that would cause undue stress and anxiety on the part of those family members of those that were serving."

I still stand behind that statement. The public has the right to know the full truth, and we have the obligation to tell it.


In the words of George Washington: *If the freedom of speech is taken away, then dumb and silent we may be led, like sheep to the slaughter.*

# Chapter Twenty-Three

# FUTURE CONCERNS

Just a few years ago, America was engaged in a war for survival, much like our current war to prevail against terrorism. The war I'm referring to is the Cold War, a war that America was engaged in for more than forty years—a war we finally won in 1989 with the fall of the Berlin Wall.

This victory was followed by an immediate demand to reduce our armed forces as America had done after every major conflict in our history—WW I, WW II, Korea, Vietnam. And so we set out on the same course—reducing the Army from 785,000 to today's 480,000, the Air force from thirty-six to twenty tactical fighter wings, and the Navy from six hundred ships to approximately three hundred. Desert Storm caused a pause in downsizing, but as soon as it was over we continued at an even faster pace. All in all, *we took more troops out than the entire armed forces of the UK, Germany, Denmark, and the Netherlands combined.*

Worse yet, we continued to dismantle our human-intelligence network, placing an overreliance on technology to provide the intelligence we'd need to fight in what are commonly referred to as tier-three and tier-four countries—countries like Haiti, Bosnia, Kosovo, Afghanistan, and Iraq, where our ability to collect was severely hampered by a lack of the application of technology. Much evidence of this has been revealed by the 9/11 Commission Report.

But without the two superpowers to hold everyone in check, we saw ethnic, religious, and tribal warfare erupt around the globe; and when you combine that with the "CNN effect" of bringing the violence right into our living rooms and Americans being "better angels of mercy," as Abraham Lincoln put it, there was an almost instantaneous demand for our military intervention. America has many tools in our kit bag—political, diplomatic, economic, informational, and military—with the military being the hammer and the last tool we should consider using. But because the military can move fast and produce highly visible results, it often becomes the tool of first choice.

In the decade following Desert Storm, that demand led to a 300 percent increase in the use of our armed forces, at a cost of many billions of dollars per year, plus a fraying of our forces. That trend continues today, with the new fuel being the "war on terrorism" and the ongoing operations in Afghanistan and Iraq.

Today we are still dealing with the aftermath of the Iraq operation to ensure that chaos does not reign and that a bitter civil war among the Sunnis, Shi'ites, and Kurds does not end up providing Iran the excuse it's looking for to enter Iraq due to the threat at its border. That's exactly what the Middle East leaders in the countries throughout the region have feared since Desert Shield and Desert Storm, and many have expressed those concerns to me personally on multiple occasions.

But other challenges are developing with even greater long-term consequences for America's national security.

## CHINA

Nine years ago the Chinese government conducted the largest military exercise they had shown to a Westerner, and they did so in my honor. Through the help of our intelligence community, we witnessed them preparing for weeks prior to my arrival. Their standard, my Chinese counterpart told me, was the United States military—and they were trying hard to meet that standard. Their live-fire demonstration was massive, involving thousands of troops in intricately orchestrated maneuvers—no surprise since our intell reveals that they are pouring more and more of their national resources into their armed forces, and much of it now is going into *offensive*-weapon systems. They are equipping their ships with missiles that can take out U.S. ships anytime they come within range of that ship. It's a very real concern, and one we should not take lightly.

In addition to some basic ideology differences, economically, both the United States and China are competing for resources in the Pacific, and many economists believe the Pacific economy will be more important to the United States in the next ten years than the European economy has been for the last forty years. Whether or not that comes to fruition, only time will tell. But China—a country with population of 1.3 billion—wants the United States out of the Pacific; it's a market they prefer to keep for themselves.

In spite of all this, the impressions I brought back with me from the San Jie site outside Nanjing were not all the ones the Chinese had hoped for. While I found their troops to be physically fit and well trained, their equipment was old and about twenty years behind that of the United States. At first glance, it might appear that we are in an excellent position; after all, how can their antiquated hardware compete against our cutting-edge technology? But the truth is that there are many countries, including some of our allies, who will sell them the technology—technology that is *almost* as good as the United States has today. And if you throw in the tremendous size advantage their force has over ours, maybe that technology is even "good enough." It certainly closes the technology gap. And if their economy starts perking the way most analysts predict, I believe in another five to ten years we will have a major competitor—and something to be very concerned about downstream.

One question becomes how this gets communicated to the American people. We would all like to bring down the size of our armed forces, as we've done following every war. What I'm concerned about is that once we do eventually pull out of Iraq and Afghanistan, we will downsize even more. Today's budget deficits could cause a downturn in the economy, prompting much tighter budgets and allowing the technology gap to be closed at an alarming rate. At the same time, China will continue going in the other direction. Reversing that trend would cost billions, and rebuilding our armed forces is measured in decades, not just years. It's a concern that the President will have to deal with, and one that rests within the current Chairman's ballpark to bring to the forefront from the military perspective.

At the same time, we have a golden opportunity to nip this in the bud with the Chinese. Their economy is not yet perking at full speed; and we have a window of opportunity to develop a better relationship with them. We should take advantage of it, while we still have that chance, unless we want to enter another Cold War. Using our diplomatic and political tools, we should do everything within our power to develop an atmosphere of cooperation and coordination rather than allow an adversarial relationship to develop. Multinational corporations and an intertwining of our economies will advance this cause significantly. In this regard, fostering support for multinational cooperation, exchanges between their students and ours, and programs that provide exchanges between their military officers and ours are examples of programs that might foster improved relations between our countries and lower the threshold for potential military conflict.

## RUSSIA

If you visited Russia anytime since the Berlin Wall came down, you would know that they still consider themselves a superpower—a great nation they believe is still on a par with the United States. Unfortunately, they have fallen on hard times. It's a broken economy combined with an antiquated economic system, and reform of the old communist/socialist system has been extraordinarily slow. Both their infrastructure and defense systems have decayed, and their nuclear devices are in a sad state of disrepair. When you add to this environment basic ideological differences and conflicting economic interests, you end up with tremendous challenges for the United States in the years ahead, and a potentially volatile situation in the present.

Russia is a country eleven time zones in size and teeming with natural resources. If they ever get their act together economically with a free-enterprise system, they will be awesome—a real competitor. At the moment, they are still very distrustful of America because of the Cold War, but in my mind, to a large extent that's our fault.

While inducting former members of the Soviet empire into the North Atlantic Treaty Organization (NATO) was the right thing to do, this increased their distrust of the United States. Placing elements of our National Missile Defense System in Poland, right on their border, was another stick in their eye. Wisely, in my opinion, the current administration has remedied that mistake.

But the fact remains, in my opinion, that we simply have not done nearly as much as we should to convince them that we can be a friend. We did not successfully reach out to them in the way that I had wanted when I was Chairman, despite my best efforts. There were still too many Washington egos that felt that subordinating our own interest, to a degree, in order to work with the Russians in a partnership that could be mutually beneficial to both countries, was a bridge too far. Perhaps over time this will change.

However, as with China, today's political and economic climate affords us a prime opportunity to reach out and forge strong allies, which would be in the best interest of all. I believe the Obama administration, along with Secretary of State Clinton, will reach out to both China and Russia to foster a fluid dialogue and at least take the first step toward bringing them both on board. I certainly hope so.

## NORTH KOREA

The year 2013 marks a half century since the Korean War ended and we still have twenty-five thousand servicemen and -women in South Korea who, along with their South Korean counterparts, are standing guard to protect against the million-man North Korean army, who are just across the demilitarized zone.

In Seoul, Korea, there are thousands of Americans whose lives would be at stake if the North Koreans were to attack. The North Koreans have artillery that can easily range Seoul, but it's on railroad tracks and rolls in and out of caves, so it's very hard to get to it, even with some of the best bombs we've got. Dramatically upping the stakes, North Korea is now a nuclear threat, and its leader, Kim Jong Il, could wake up one morning with a toothache and decide he's going to launch a nuke against South Korea. What do we do there? How do we reach out to North Korea? Can we get any kind of a new peace? In the past we've tried by instituting the Agreed Framework and Six-Party Talks, but once North Korea conducted their nuclear tests, those efforts were shut down.

## KOREAN AGREED FRAMEWORK AND SIX-PARTY TALKS

The Agreed Framework is the protocol whereby we were trying to keep the North Koreans from manufacturing nuclear weapons. They now have that capability, and on May 25, 2009, they conducted their second nuclear-test explosion, after which President Obama had a strong statement that called for an immediate response from the international community. He called it a "blatant defiance of the United Nations Security Council" and a "matter

---

**NORTH KOREAN NUCLEAR SITUATION**

**Oct 2006** - North Korea conducts an underground nuclear test

**Feb 2007** - North Korea agrees to shut down its main nuclear reactor in exchange for fuel aid

**June 2007** - North Korea shuts its reactor in Yongbyon

**June 2008** - North Korea makes public declaration of its nuclear assets

**Oct 2008** - The U.S. removes North Korea from its list of countries which sponsor terrorism

**Dec 2008** - The U.S. suspends energy aid and Pyongyang slows dismantling of its nuclear program

**April 2009** - Pyongyang launches rocket they contend carries a communications satellite

**May 25, 2009** - North Korea conducts its second nuclear test

**August 5, 2009** - Former President Clinton visits North Korea to secure the release of two detained U.S. journalists

**October 6, 2009** - North Korea tells China it may be willing to return to Six-Party Talks

**November 19, 2009** - President Obama, along with South Korean counterpart Lee Myung-bak, urges North Korea to return to international nuclear negotiations

of grave concern to all nations." The President suggested working through the Six-Party Talks to address the issue. In addition to the United States, other participants are North and South Korea, Russia, Japan, and China.

North Korea is a very poor nation. Many people are starving. Most of their revenues are spent buying as much military hardware as they can, while the poor people starve. The Agreed Framework set up the system in which the six signatories provided North Korea with foodstuffs, heavy fuel oil, and two light water reactors for energy, in exchange for North Korea's agreeing to discontinue further activity on their nuclear-weapons program. It was a relatively cheap way to keep them from building their deadly WMD program, but since their test, the program is at a standstill, for obvious reasons. It's time to get them back on track.

## INDONESIA

As the fourth largest nation in the world and the world's largest Muslim population, Indonesia is on the verge of disintegrating. It is a nation consisting of seventeen thousand islands, about six thousand of them inhabited.

Ruled for years by a corrupt regime that oppressed its own people (while at the same time being supported by the United States), it became a fertile field for the radical extremists to incite discontent, riots, and revolution. Earlier I mentioned the brutality on their island of East Timor; and in December 2004, their island of Ache was facing the same challenge when they were struck by the calamitous tsunami disaster that killed 230,000 people and left more than 500,000 homeless. The disintegration of Indonesia has tremendous implications for our friends and allies—Australia, New Zealand, Malaysia, Singapore, etc. It weighs heavily on peace and stability throughout the region and consequently on the economic future of the United States. The United States is engaged, but the question is: can we stop the disintegration in progress, and if so, how?

## AFGHANISTAN

On September 15, 2001, when the decision was made to conduct the Afghanistan operation, a prophetic CIA director George Tenet told the President in no uncertain terms that wresting power away from the warlords would be the greatest challenge America would face in Afghanistan. We knew going in it would be tough.

The Afghanistan operation started out going great, but then in 2003, when President Bush decided to invade Iraq, we diverted our attention and our

resources to Iraq. Afghanistan became second-page news. In the interven-
ing years, we witnessed a resurgence of both the Taliban and al-Qaeda,
and the lack of central government control. In fact, as Tenet predicted, the
warlords have maintained control of their areas. Drug trafficking has increased significantly since we entered the country in 2001. One estimate
is that Afghan poppy production has risen from 12 percent when we entered to 90 percent today. Karzai and his government have failed to get their
arms around the country in the way that it was envisioned, and corruption
is still rampant.

Afghanistan, a nation still ruled by tribal and Islamic law, is the fifth-
poorest nation in the world. It ranks second only to Somalia in corruption.
It is a nation without infrastructure, a judicial system as we know it, or any
semblance of a governance system below their recently elected bicameral
legislature at the national level. It is estimated that more than five million
land mines are scattered about the landscape, left there from endless civil
wars in addition to the occupation by Russians and the United Kingdom.
More than two hundred thousands Afghans have suffered debilitating
injuries.

While our initial efforts were highly successful, teaming up our Special Operations Forces with the Northern Alliance, an internal resistance
group, as the effort became a NATO-led operation that focused on nation
building, progress slowed, as predicted. The Taliban and al-Qaeda forces
reemerged and started to exert their influence and control over the remote
areas initially; then, emboldened by their successes, they started to expand
their sphere of influence. Still back in Washington, we remained focused
on Iraq, as was shown in the 2009 administration's supplemental budget
request, which reflected spending almost three times the amount in Iraq as
we were spending in Afghanistan. Our military leadership was not without fault. Some of our generals in Afghanistan were not steeped in the ways
of the Pentagon or how the interagency works inside the Beltway. They also
knew that the Army and Marine Corps, which were bearing the brunt of the
fighting in both Iraq and Afghanistan, were stretched almost to the breaking point. Rather than be the squeaky wheel and get grease in the form of
more troops to match the mission they had been given, they suffered in
silence.

All that changed in 2009 when Secretary of Defense Gates relieved
General McKiernan and put a war fighter by the name of General Stan
McChrystal in charge. Teamed up with General Dave Petraeus (Commander
Central Command and responsible for the entire region), America now
has two generals who understand how to fight on the battlefield, as well
as in Washington for resources.

Stan McChrystal made an assessment of the situation he inherited and
immediately saw the mission/resource mismatch. His request for thirty-

thousand additional troops, while not a political bestseller in Washington, came at a critical time to reverse the trend he found in Afghanistan—a growing insurgency, a reemerging Taliban, and a loss of confidence by the Afghan people, which undermines the confidence the international community has in Karzai.

Today, it appears that Generals Petraeus and McChrystal (commander U.S. Forces Afghanistan) are starting to turn things around. Only time will tell if the U.S. effort, as a part of NATO, will be able to leave behind a stable Afghanistan with an elected government, a nation governed by the rule of law and a nation with a more sophisticated infrastructure and systems resembling today's more modern nations. For sure, it won't be easy or fast. But if we remember the conditions that led to 9/11 and take into consideration the possible outcome of an al-Qaeda–controlled Afghanistan that already has a toehold in Afghanistan's next-door, nuclear-armed neighbor, Pakistan, we just might conclude that the effort will be well worth it.

## WMDS

Today, more than ever before, we have to be concerned about the proliferation of weapons of mass destruction. We know too well that these indiscriminate killers are not only in the hands of unfriendly nation-states but are in the inventories of nonstate actors as well. al-Qaeda, among many other terrorist organizations, represents a threat that doesn't respect national borders, and it doesn't discriminate between military and civilian targets. Terrorists are not bound by the international rules of armed conflict, nor are they bound by any type of international treaties. We have to be prepared to deal with and defeat an enemy that doesn't have a conscience. Because of the growing potential of these threats, homeland defense is a topic that the entire national community must continue to focus on during the early part of this century. The threat to Americans is no longer confined to the superpower showdown that we lived with over the last five decades; since 9/11, it's been a whole new ballgame.

## CYBER SECURITY

In addition to these types of asymmetric threats, we also have to be concerned about cyber attacks against our information systems. We are more and more becoming dependent upon our information systems in both our civilian communities and the military. In fact, the two are so intertwined, an attack on our civil infrastructure could also have a major impact on our military capabilities.

Cyber attacks, of course, can be disproportionate to the size of the force that is coming against you. When a nuclear scientist in Russia earns less than a hotel doorman in New York, it's a pretty good bet that top technical minds more than qualified to hack into highly secured systems can be hired on the cheap for nefarious purposes.

When I was Chairman we established a joint task force for computer-network defense. We met great resistance from many quarters that were concerned that the Department of Defense would impact on the privacy of others. We had wanted to explore using the Internet as an offensive tool but decided to delay that until we had at least protected our own systems. But we did utilize this same technical talent and spin them off into an offensive capability—something that would allow us to bankrupt an entire country at the push of a button. And before I retired, we were there. It goes without saying that any action of this type would be undertaken only under presidential directive. But it should cause us all concern because if we can do it now, it won't be long before our enemies can do the same thing to us, and that's why we've got to be focused on preventing that now, before it's too late. To date, our secret-level systems have not been penetrated; the challenge is to keep it that way.

But are our greatest vulnerabilities really inside the classified Pentagon systems? Not in my mind. I contend that they are all around us, encompassing our banking, our power grids, our water supplies, virtually every aspect of our twenty-first-century lifestyle. Major strides were made after 9/11, but the systems still aren't protected to the extent that they must be. For instance, there's one cable in a major metropolitan area that if hacked into could shut down the entire segment of our air-traffic-control system. And as long as you are in that position, you are not that well protected, and that act of sabotage could occur tonight.

## INTERNATIONAL CRIMINAL COURT

Secretary Cohen and I fought a two-man battle for three years and four months to keep President Clinton from signing the International Criminal Court accords, because we felt that America's men and women in uniform should never be submitted to a criminal court that is political in nature—one in which the judges are political appointees from other countries who are responding to their own governments and making judgments in accordance with those governments' agendas. Here's an example: during the time we were bombing Kosovo, we had the good fortune to have one of the greatest F-16 pilots who has ever flown the airplane. He was flying out of Aviano Air Base, Italy, where he and his family had been assigned prior to the war. There, an armada of NATO aircraft would depart every day, or night, dropping bombs on the Serbs who had invaded Kosovo. He was scheduled to join the elite Thunderbirds as soon as the war was over. One of his missions required him to take out a key bridge that was used by the Serbs to transport Serbian troops and troop supplies from the Belgrade area down to the front lines. It was a key strategic target.

The pilot released his smart bomb from about thirty thousand feet and followed its progress on a small cockpit-mounted monitor, since the bomb was equipped with a nose-mounted TV camera. He watched closely as the bomb dropped through the clouds, his finger on a toggle switch, just so that he could deactivate it if something went wrong. The bomb was on a perfect path, heading right for the bridge, avoiding rows of houses that we knew were on both sides of the bridge yet were outside the bomb's destructive blast radius. He continued to watch as the bomb got closer and closer, and the bridge got bigger and bigger on his TV monitor until it almost filled the entire screen. Finally, at the very last second, after it became physically impossible for him to activate the switch, a train entered the right-hand side of frame, then the whole screen went blank. The bomb took out the bridge and the train. We hadn't meant to hit the train, although in my mind there was nothing wrong with that, except it turned out, based on Serb reports, that there had been civilians on the train. And of course that was painted by the Serbs as a war crime; so in their eyes, the pilot was now a war criminal. I visited Aviano AFB a couple of days after the mission. The unit was having a family day near the Air Force housing located nearby and I joined them for a hot dog. It provided me with the perfect opportunity to thank them for their service and the great manner in which they were prosecuting the war.

As I arrived, the squadron commander, a great pilot in his own right and obviously a fine leader, told me that the F-16 pilot had taken the hit pretty hard, especially now that they had been informed that General Clark, the Supreme Allied Commander, had ordered an investigation into the incident. He not only felt terrible about the civilians who had been killed but saw a great career opportunity—and potentially his entire career—being ended because of the incident. He was a tall officer who probably had squeaked past the maximum sitting-height requirement to be an F-16 pilot.

I walked over to the pilot and introduced myself to him and his wife. I said, "I understand you're the pilot who took out that key strategic bridge for us?" I could see the sudden look of apprehension in his face. "Great job," I said. "Too bad they put those civilians on board—I'm sure they learned a lesson from that. Don't worry about General Clark's investigation. I assure you no one is going to touch you. You're one of my heroes and you did exactly what we asked you to do." His wife's hand went up to catch her tears as I saw tears well in his eyes. I reached out to shake his hand as he broke into tears. The emotions that had built in him since the event were released as I stood there feeling helpless, but so glad that I had arrived at the time I did. As soon as he regained control, he thanked me. I reassured him again how proud I was to have a great pilot like him on my team and to have a great couple like them serving their country.

At the time, one of the judges on the international court was from Serbia, and it was a Serbian train that had been bombed, and the Serbs who had issued the international-war-crimes warrant. So picture this great pilot three years later, after he's been assigned to Frankfurt, Germany. He's sitting outside a small local restaurant, enjoying dinner with his wife and two young sons, when suddenly the German police surround the table and arrest him, immediately whisking him off to The Hague to be tried as a war criminal because the Serbs had declared him one. Of course, this is just a fictional example, but I didn't ever want to put our men and women in uniform in a position like that; but that's exactly what we would be leaving ourselves open to if we became signatories to the International Criminal Court.

President Clinton called me on December 31, 2000—the last day countries could become parties to the treaty without ratifying it—and he said, "Hugh, I wanted to tell you personally that today I made a decision to sign it. I figured that we're better off having our nose under the tent, where maybe we can influence the way it'll be carried out, than we would be to be on the outside with Iran, North Korea, et cetera."

I said, "Mr. President, you've got a lot of things on your plate and a lot to consider. While I recommend that from a military perspective you not sign it, I understand why you did." And he signed it—but he did not send it on for Senate ratification. On May 6, 2002, President Bush sent a note to the U.N. suspending the prior signature. The jury is still out as far as where we go from here, but I believe that our signing off on that program as currently proposed would be dangerous indeed.

## TRIALS FOR "ENEMY COMBATANTS"

One of the great things about the United States is a judicial system that provides due process for those accused of a crime. It is a model that we tout throughout the world as the "gold standard." To hold individuals—even those accused of heinous terrorist acts anywhere, including Guantanamo—without due process and the right to a speedy trial is wrong and reflects poorly on our judicial system and on us as a nation. This, by the way, is the same judicial system that we point to as the reason why our troops should not be subjected to the International Criminal Court System, and you can't have it both ways.

Placing individuals in Guantanamo and holding them for years without due process makes us look like a third-world country and damages our reputation immensely. The detainees should be placed in federal prisons, tried in an expeditious manner, and executed, imprisoned, or released in a fair and impartial manner—just as we did with Ted Bundy and the likes. *Close Guantanamo* or use it as a holding area for large numbers of detainees until we can sort out where they should go, and this process should be capped at a maximum of thirty days.

The men and women in our armed forces are a tremendous group who are safeguarding America's interests around the world. They serve in the finest traditions of those who have gone before them, and they're keeping peace in a very dangerous and very complex world. We owe it to those great troops, and to the great American public, to maintain that fine tradition by ensuring that we hold our commanders (all the way to the top) accountable and responsible for conducting themselves with the utmost character and integrity, and to speak out in the spirit of McMaster's *Dereliction of Duty*, when they see situations in which these principles are being violated. Intelligence can no longer be manipulated to justify an agenda. Prisoner abuse and withholding of due process can no longer be tolerated.

General Dave Petraeus was working as my executive officer when I required all the Joint Chiefs to read *Dereliction of Duty,* and from the way he is leading his own troops, it is obvious to me that he took those words to heart. Here's a letter he sent them when the issue of "questionable" interrogation techniques was exposed, and it's something we should all take to heart.

> What sets us apart from our enemies in this fight . . . is how we behave. In everything we do, we must observe the standards and values that dictate that we treat noncombatants and detainees with dignity and respect . . . Some may argue that we would be more effective if we sanctioned torture or other expedient methods to obtain information from the enemy. They would be wrong.
>
> Beyond the basic fact that such actions are illegal, history shows that they also are frequently neither useful nor necessary. Certainly, extreme physical action can make someone "talk"; however, what the individual says may be of questionable value. In fact, our experience in applying the interrogation standards laid out in the Army Field Manual (2-22.3) on *Human Intelligence Collector Operations* that was published last year shows that the techniques in the manual work effectively and humanely in eliciting information from detainees.

\*   \*   \*

The years ahead present some significant challenges to America. They will test more than our armed forces; they will test America's *mettle,* our *values,* our *will,* our ability to *persevere* in the face of these global threats— and our willingness to continue to work together to harness the power of an international effort to face these threats to our way of life.

Perhaps my greatest concern is that we hold fast to maintaining the incredibly high standards that have made us the greatest country in the world. In doing so, I am confident that through hard work and diligence, we will meet any challenge and triumph over any enemy or obstacle in our path.

# *Afterword* ★★★★

AAR

**A**fter every military operation we conduct an after-action review—an AAR—in which we evaluate what went right, what went wrong, and what could have been done differently to achieve a more successful outcome.

During my months of recovery at Walter Reed, I found myself conducting my own personal AAR of my life—evaluating which of my accomplishments I was proudest of, and which of my choices seemed better at the moment than they ultimately turned out to be.

Putting aside the question of whether or not that damn oak tree really needed to be trimmed that morning, I can honestly say that I could not come up with one regret; I have always been grateful for the hand that God dealt me. I put my family first and firmly believe that our people and their families are our nation's most precious asset; and if we treat them with care and dignity there is nothing we may not ask of them.

We take pride in all our sons' accomplishments and the hard work it took to achieve them. They did this in spite of the many times they had to move, leave friends behind, and start over. They are good citizens of this great country.

We are also fortunate to be the grandparents of seven wonderful grandchildren—each of them unique and special, and each brings great pride and joy to our lives. Our very favorite time is summer, when they and their parents all come to visit, and swimsuits are standard attire for those trips. If we're not out there swimming or sailing or kayaking, chances are we'll be found with fishing rod in hand . . . unless they've "borrowed" our golf cart for jaunts through the neighborhood.

* * *

Jon, who became a United States Secret Service agent on President Clinton's and Bush's details (and is now with the Service in Charlotte), along with his wife, Anne, have blessed us with three fantastic granddaughters as accomplished in the classroom as they are on the playing field. Cassie, sixteen, has excelled in many sports through the years (soccer, softball, basketball, swimming); but now, as a junior, she concentrates on volleyball and plays in cities from Atlanta to Baltimore. Her fourteen-year-old twin sisters, Heather and Hannah, are also skilled volleyball players who somehow find time to add discus and shot put into their repertoire.

Jeff not only passed that aviator's test but became a pilot for the Night Stalkers, the Army's most elite aviation unit. After serving in Afghanistan, he left the Army and today works for one of America's top defense contractors; and he remains a member of the U.S. Army Reserve. His daughter Savannah is our oldest grandchild. An adept gymnast and cheerleader (easy to spot since she is the "flier" at the top of the pyramid), she just graduated from high school and now begins an exciting new chapter in her life. Her brothers, Sam and Ben, are fourteen and thirteen, respectively, and are constantly involved in sports, with football and lacrosse their current favorites. Ben is our golfer and frequently plays with his dad. Sam carries on a family tradition I started many years ago—and one that he shares with his dad and Uncle Jon—he loves to play the guitar.

Mark, our youngest son, works for one of America's largest information-technology firms in Research Triangle Park, North Carolina. He and his wife, Aylan, have blessed us with our seventh grandchild, Henry Hugh Shelton II, who will celebrate his first birthday right around the date of this publication. His proud Gran (Carolyn) is not shy about announcing that he holds multiple degrees in "being cute." Although I completely agree, I prefer to point out that one of his very first outfits was a Wolfpack uniform, lest there be no doubt about his allegiance. (He was only a few weeks old at the time.)

I am fortunate to have received a number of awards in my life—from being knighted by Queen Elizabeth II to the U.S. Congressional Gold Medal—but none made me prouder than Mark and Aylan's naming Henry after me.

About a month after Henry was born, we attended the homecoming service in Speed Baptist Church—the same church where Carolyn and I were married—and where only three years earlier we buried Mother beside

my daddy. Following the services, we drove about a mile up Highway 122 and pulled over beside a North Carolina highway sign identifying the roadway as the General Henry Hugh Shelton Highway, which had been named in my honor a few years earlier.

Cradling little Henry in my arms on that spectacular Sunday morning, I stood beside the sign for a photo; and I thought about how blessed I had been throughout my life, and what this wonderful part of North Carolina had meant to me. Now, I held the youngest of the next generation. It was almost overwhelming.

———

Serving my country has been both an honor and a privilege, and when I finally was able to walk out of Walter Reed, it was with a determination to pass along what I could to the next generation of great Americans, through speeches on values-based leadership and by serving as executive director at the General H. Hugh Shelton Leadership Center at my alma mater, North Carolina State University, and establishing the Hugh and Carolyn Shelton Military Neurotrauma Foundation.

I was raised in a home by parents who instilled positive leadership traits and attributes early on. These same values were reinforced both in Speed Baptist Church and in the small Speed elementary school I attended. This was followed by serving in a values-based leadership organization for most of my adult life. Leadership traits were stressed in each professional-development school I attended and were reinforced daily by most senior leaders. Integrity, as an example, could never be compromised. Still, I had witnessed leadership failures even in an organization that made values-based-leadership training one of its highest priorities.

As I was retiring, we witnessed the debacle at Enron, which impacted thousands of lives as a result of leadership failures at the highest levels. This was followed closely by Global Crossing, Tyco, and numerous others. At this same time, North Carolina State University reached out to me and asked that I return to the university, after I retired, to be a part of a leadership initiative they wanted to pursue, and to name in my honor. I seized on this as an opportunity to make a difference by contributing my experiences and expertise developed over thirty-eight years in the armed forces.

After several meetings, we settled on an arrangement whereby they would establish The General H. Hugh Shelton Leadership Initiative and I would serve as executive director. Shortly thereafter, very generous contributions by Mr. Ross Perot, Mr. and Mrs. Ed Gore, and the Anheuser-Busch Companies, Inc., got the programs off to a flying start. A few years later it was designated a center, and today it is thriving and clearly *making a difference in the lives that we touch*, at high school, university, and corporate levels.

On a personal note, I'm thrilled that Heather and Hannah will be attending the institute this summer; and Cassie, who attended last year, will return—but this time as a peer leader. They are already great young ladies and I'm sure will be even stronger and more confident in their abilities with this experience. Hannah has already determined that not only will she attend North Carolina State but that she will play volleyball for them. We're still working on the other grandchildren.


Recently I was approached by a parent in the local hardware store; I had never seen this person before. "General," said the parent, "your program has changed my son's life—totally turned it around. Thank you."

It doesn't get any better than that.

———

Many have asked me at what point in my life I targeted being the Chairman. The truth is, never. I always felt fortunate to be where I was at the time, yet I was diligent in discussing with Carolyn what I should do to prepare for the next job—the next rank—never more than that. I had no ambition to be a general, and frankly I never thought that would happen. I loved what I was doing and savored the moments. Being commander-in-chief of SOCOM was a blast, and I went on from that to accept the Chairman

position with a sense of service and responsibility—not jubilation. As Chairman, my focus remained on doing the best I could, while preparing myself for whatever challenges the future might bring.

A year after I left Walter Reed I bumped into Colonel Michael Rosner, chief of neurosurgery at the hospital. What he said to me that day really made an impact on me: "General, we see a lot of these spinal-cord injuries and almost every one of them goes into a deep depression, not believing that they will ever regain use of their limbs. Until you, we could never tell them that anyone had recovered, but what you have done will provide that glimmer of hope to all the patients that we see. . . . You will really make a difference."

If that is true and my recovery inspires others to do the same, then maybe getting out there to trim that old oak tree wasn't such a bad choice after all.

———

Just before Christmas 1994, President Clinton invited my entire family into the White House Rose Garden to present me with the U.S. Army Distinguished Service Medal. While I greatly valued the medal and all it stood for, it paled in comparison to the divine appreciation I felt that my mother was alive to hear the President of the United States utter the following words about her son.

### THE WHITE HOUSE

**December 20, 1994**

**REMARKS BY THE PRESIDENT
IN AWARDS CEREMONY FOR LIEUTENANT GENERAL SHELTON
AND THE FORCES OF OPERATION UPHOLD DEMOCRACY**
**The Rose Garden**

**2:47 P.M. EST**

THE PRESIDENT: Secretary Perry, Admiral Owens, members of the Joint Chiefs; to General Shelton and Mrs. Shelton, members of the Shelton family; to the representatives of each of our military services who served in Haiti and their families; all the other distinguished guests here, welcome to the Rose Garden.

We gather today to honor General Shelton and members of our Armed Forces for their service to our nation in Operation Uphold Democracy. All those who have served and all those who still serve in Haiti have served with extraordinary skill, courage and dedication.

For three years the United States and other countries throughout the world tried everything short of force to remove Haiti's illegal military regime and to restore its democratically elected government. It wasn't until the regime's leaders knew our Armed Forces were on the way that they agreed to step down peacefully.

Think for a moment where we would be today had we not acted and had General Shelton and the other members of our Armed Forces not performed their mission so admirably. The military regime would still be in power in Haiti, terrorizing the people there. Tens of thousands of refugees would continue to pose a threat to our region's stability. The march of democracy in the Americas would have suffered a severe setback. And the commitments of the United States in the international community would have proved empty.

Instead, we kept our word. President Aristide, Haiti's freely elected leader, has returned to office. The parliament is functioning. A sense of security and hope has replaced the climate of fear. The private sector is beginning the job of getting back on its feet. The rebuilding process has begun. And clearly our region is more stable and secure.

At the Summit of the Americas last week when we had 34 democratically-elected leaders from our hemisphere, I think no one would dispute the fact that the emotional highlight of the weekend was President Aristide's speech in three languages, expressing his gratitude to those who supported freedom and democracy in Haiti.

General Shelton, your careful planning and your ability to adapt to a fast-changing situation were at the heart of our success in Haiti. The strong personal leadership, the steady hand, and the real determination that you, personally, conveyed to the military leaders of Haiti in the first days, from the first moment of your action there, were, I know, absolutely critical to the success of this operation and to its peacefulness.

"Let our history recall that you answered the call of duty, you did your job, you advanced America's mission. Freedom and democracy are better as a result."

First, we asked you to prepare an innovative, integrated invasion force, drawing on the special capabilities of each of our services. Then, when the regime agreed at the 11th hour to leave, you had to switch gears immediately, and to ready our troops for a soft entry into Haiti.

On the ground, you have done a magnificent job of laying a secure foundation for the future. This has allowed 800 international police monitors from all around the world to work with an interim police force that is gaining the respect of the Haitian people. As a result, we've been able to draw down our own forces from 20,000 to about 6,000 at Christmastime. This number will soon decrease further as we transfer our mission in Haiti to the United Nations.

Through your efforts, General, Haiti today is democratic and free and much more secure. The Haitian people themselves, of course, must meet the difficult challenges ahead. It will take time for rebuilding and progress, but now at least all Haitians have a chance to work for a better future for themselves and their children.

The hand painted signs we see in Haiti today say it all: Thank you, America. Today America says: Thank you, General. And thanks to the men and women of our military who served so well in Haiti.

In a few moments I will be honored to award General Shelton the Army Distinguished Service Medal. But first I want to recognize the exceptional concern the General has also shown for the men and women under his command. I know that their safety and their well-being were always his first priority. And for that our nation is also grateful to General Shelton.

General, you requested that enlisted members from all our military branches join you today to receive the Armed Forces Expeditionary Medal on behalf of their respective services. The soldiers who stand before us are the finest of America's finest. Each also will be awarded an individual commendation for meritorious service in Haiti.

I'd like to recognize them now. From the Coast Guard, Radioman 1st Class, Charles Brown. From the Air Force, Staff Sergeant John McCormick. From the Navy, Senior Chief Operations Specialist Samuel Wood. From the Marine Corps, Sergeant Paul Panici. From the Army, Staff Sergeant Morris Jones. And from the Special Forces, Sergeant 1st Class Shannon Davis. Each of you has helped to prove once again that our military is the best prepared, the best equipped, the best trained, the most devoted and highly motivated military in the entire world. [Applause.]

It is now my privilege to present all of you and General Shelton with your awards. Let our history recall that you answered the call of duty, you did your job, you advanced America's mission. Freedom and democracy are better as a result. Haiti's long night of fear has given way to a new day of hope. [Applause.]

[The awards are presented.] [Applause.]                    END2:55 P.M. EST

I thought it was a great example of what a leader can achieve by holding steadfast to his or her principles and values. Having Carolyn, the boys, and Mother there to share it with me was about the best Christmas gift I could ever receive.

**The General H. Hugh Shelton Leadership Center** develops values-based leaders who are committed to personal integrity, professional ethics, and selfless service. Center outreach programs focus on leadership development within corporate, governmental, educational, nonprofit, and youth-development organizations. The program offers scholarships and international leadership-enrichment experiences and conducts an annual forum that features nationally recognized speakers. Finally, leadership institutes for high school students focus on the principles of honesty, integrity, compassion, diversity, and social responsibility, and are conducted across North Carolina and other states each summer.

Please visit http://www.ncsu.edu/extension/sheltonleadership or call 919-513-0148 for more details.

### Hugh and Carolyn Shelton Military Neurotrauma Foundation

The Shelton Foundation was established as a 501(c)(3) charitable organization to enable innovative research initiatives for the early diagnosis and management of neurotrauma in a military environment. The Foundation will sponsor sustained research and development of far-forward diagnostics, data-collection systems, and new techniques and treatments designed to restore and repair neural injury.

Please visit http://www.sheltonfoundation.org/ for more details.

# Glossary

1LT – First lieutenant

2LT – Second lieutenant

AC-130 – Spectre four-engine turboprop gunship

ADM – Admiral

AH-6 – Little Bird Special Operations helicopter gunship

AH-64 – Apache helicopter gunship

AIT – Advanced Individual Training (Brigade)

AOR – Area of Responsibility

ARVN – Army of the Republic of Vietnam

AWACS – Airborne Warning and Control System

AWOL – Absent without leave

B-1 – Lancer strategic bomber

B-2 – Stealth bomber

B-52 – Stratofortress strategic bomber

BDA – Battle damage assessment

BDE – Brigade

BDU – Battle dress uniform

BG – Brigadier general

Black Hawk – UH-60 utility helicopter

BLUFOR – Blue force

BN – Battalion

BMEW – Ballistic Missile Early Warning

Bradley – M-2 infantry fighting vehicle or M-3 cavalry fighting vehicle

**C-17** – Four-engine jet USAF Cargo plane

**CA** – Civil affairs

**CAT** – Crisis Action Team

**CAV** – Cavalry

**CCIR** – Commander critical information requirement

**CD** – Cavalry division

**CENTAF** – Central Command, Air Force

**CENTCOM** – Central Command; one of America's Unified/Joint Commands

**CG** – Commanding general

**CG** – Coast Guard

**Chinook** – CH-47 helicopter

**CIA** – Central Intelligence Agency

**CIDG** – Civilian Irregular Defense Group(s)

**CINC USCENTCOM** – Commander in Chief, Central Command

**CINC** – Commander in Chief, the President. Formerly referred to combatant commanders, as well

**CJCS** – Chairman Joint Chiefs of Staff

**COL** – Colonel

**COMM** – Communications

**CONPLAN** – Contingency plan

**CONUS** – Continental United States

**CP** – Command post

**CPL** – Corporal

**CPT** – Captain

**CSAR** – Combat search and rescue

**CWO** – Chief warrant officer

**DAIG** – Deputy assistant inspector general

**DCSPER** – Deputy Chief of Staff of the Army in Charge of Personnel

**D-Day** – Beginning of hostilities

**DDO** – Deputy Director of Operations

**DEPORD** – Deployment order

**DIA** – Defense Intelligence Agency

**DOD** – Department of Defense

**DZ** – Drop zone

**EAC** – Emergency action cell

**F-16** – Falcon fighter bomber

**F-117** – Night Hawk Stealth bomber

**F/A-18** – Naval/Marine fighter bomber

**FAC** – Forward air controller

**FBI** – Federal Bureau of Investigation

**FLIR** – Forward-looking infrared

**FOB** – Forward operating base

**FORSCOM** – U.S. Army Forces Command

**FRAGO** – Fragmentary order

**FRAPH** – Front for the Advancement and Progress of Haiti, a far-right anti-Aristide Haitian paramilitary group

**FTX** – Field exercise

**G1** – Personnel staff officer/section, corps or division level

**G2** – Intelligence staff officer/section, corps or division level

**G3** – Operations staff officer/section, corps or division level

**G4** - Logistics staff officer/section, corps or division level

**GBU** – Guided bomb unit

**GCCS** – Global Command Control System

**G-Day** – Beginning of ground phase of a campaign

**GEN** – General

**GI(s)** – Military personnel

**GOMO** – General Officer Management Office

**GPS** – Global Positioning System

**Hellfire** – Laser-guided antitank missile

**H-Hour** – The specific hour at which a particular operation commences

**Howitzer** – An indirect fire cannon

**HQ** – Headquarters

**HTLD** – High Technology Light Division

**Huey** – UH-1 Iroquois utility helicopter

**HUMINT** – Human intelligence (as opposed to electronic or signals intelligence)

**Humvee** – High-mobility, multipurpose wheeled vehicle

**IADS** – Integrated Air Defense System

**ICAF** – Industrial College of the Armed Forces

**ICBM** – Intercontinental ballistic missile

**ID** – Infantry division

**IED** – Improvised explosive device

**IOAC** – Infantry Officer Advanced Course

**IOBC** – Infantry Officer Basic Course

**J1** – Personnel staff officer/section, joint headquarters

**J2** – Intelligence staff officer/section, joint headquarters

**J3** – Operations staff officer/section, joint headquarters

**J33** – Current operations staff officer/section, joint headquarters

**J4** - Logistics staff officer/section, joint headquarters

**J5** - Strategic plans & policy staff officer/section, joint headquarters

**J6** - Communications staff officer/section, joint headquarters

**JCS** – Joint Chiefs of Staff

**JDAM** – Joint direct attack munition

**JIC** – Joint Intelligence Center

**JOC** – Joint Operations Center

**JRSC** – Jam-resistant secure communications

**JSOC** – Joint Special Operations Command

**JSOTF** – Joint Special Operations Task Force

**JSTARS** – Joint Surveillance Target Attack Radar System

**JTF** – Joint Task Force

**Klick** – GI slang for kilometer

**KM** – Kilometers

**LLDB** – Vietnamese Special Forces

**LNO** – Liaison officer

**LT** – Lieutenant

**LTC** – Lieutenant colonel

**LTG** – Lieutenant general

**LZ** – Landing zone

**M1A1** – Abrams tank

**M-14** – 7.62 mm Infantry rifle

**M-16** – 5.56 mm Infantry rifle

**M-60** – 7.62 mm machinegun

**M-26** – U.S. fragmentation grenade

**M-109** – Paladin 155 mm self-propelled howitzer

**MACV** – (U.S.) Military Assistance Command, Vietnam

**MAJ** – Major

**MANPADS** – Man Portable Air Defense System—a shoulder-fired missile

**Mech** – Mechanized

**MEDEVAC** – Medical evacuation helicopter

**MEUSOCs** – Marine Expeditionary Forces, Special Operations Capable

**MG** – Major general

**MI** – Military intelligence

**MILPERCEN** – Army Military Personnel Center

**MOS** – Military occupation specialty

**MRE** – Meals, ready to eat

**MSG** – Master Sergeant

**NATO** – North Atlantic Treaty Organization

**NBC** – Nuclear, biological, chemical

**NCO** – Noncommissioned officer—corporal or sergeant

**NEO** – Noncombatant evacuation operations

**NGO** – Nongovernmental organization

**NMCC** – National Military Command Center

**NORAD** – North American Aerospace Defense Command

**Northern Alliance** – An organization that fought the Tabliban governemnt in Afghanistan.

**NSA** – National Security Agency

**NSC** – National Security Council

**NTC** – National Training Center, Fort Irwin, California

**NVA** – North Vietnamese Army

**OCS** – Officer Candidates School

**OER** – Officer Efficiency Report

**OPFOR** – Opposing force

**OPLAN** – Operation plan

**OPORDS** – Operation orders

**PDB** – President's Daily Brief

**POW** – Prisoner of war

**Predator** – Unmanned Aerial Vehicle used for surveillance and capable of delivering missiles

**PSYOPS** – Psychological operations

**PT** – Physical training

**PVT** – Private

**RADM** – Rear admiral (upper half)

**RDML** – Rear admiral (lower half)

**RDJTF** – Rapid Deployment Joint Task Force

**Rendition** – Practice of moving criminals and terrorists from one country to another, often for interrogation

**ROK** – Republic of Korea

**ROTC** – Reserve Officer Training Corps

**RPG** – Rocket-propelled grenade

**RTO** – Radio telephone operator

**S1** – Personnel staff officer/section, brigade or battalion level

**S2** – Intelligence staff officer/section, brigade or battalion level

**S3** – Operations staff officer/section, brigade or battalion level

**S4** – Logistics staff officer/section, brigade or battalion level

**Sapper** – A military engineer; Viet Cong saboteur

**SATCOM** – Satellite communications

**SCIF** – Sensitive Compartmented Information Facility

**Scud** – Soviet-design ballistic missile

**SECDEF** – Secretary of Defense

**SF** – Special Forces

**SFC** – Sergeant First Class

**SGM** – Sergeant Major

**SGT** – Sergeant

**SIGINT** – Signals intelligence

**SMU** – Special Mission Unit

**SOCCENT** – Special Operations Command Central Command

**SOCOM** – Special Operations Command

**SOF** – Special Operations forces

**Spectre** – AC-130 aircraft

**SSG** – Staff Sergeant

**STRATCOM** – U.S. Strategic Command

**TAC** – Tactical (officer) or tactical command post

**TF** – Task Force

**TLAM** – Tomahawk land-attack missile (cruise missile)

**TOC** – Tactical operations center

**TOT** – Time on target

**TOW** – Tube-launched, optically tracked, wire-guided antitank missile

**TRADOC** – U.S. Army Training and Doctrine Command

**UAE** – United Arab Emirates

**UAV** – Unmanned aerial vehicle; remotely piloted vehicle (RPV)

**UBL** – Usama bin Laden (this spelling and acronym preferred by most government organizations)

**UDT** – Underwater detonation team

**UK** – United Kingdom

**UN** – United Nations

**USAF** – United States Air Force

**USSOCOM** – United States Special Operations Command

**VADM** – Vice Admiral

**VC** – Vietcong

**VTC** – Video teleconference

**WMD** – Weapon(s) of mass destruction

**WO** – Warrant Officer

**WWMCCS** – Worldwide Military Command and Control System

**XO** – Executive Officer

**XVIII ABC** – Eighteenth Airborne Corps

**Yellowcake** – Milled uranium oxide that can be enriched to produce uranium suitable for use in reactors and weapons

**Promotions**

| | |
|---|---|
| | Second Lieutenant, 19 September 1964* |
| | First Lieutenant, 07 January 1965 |
| | Captain, 19 March 1967 |
| | Major, 07 February 1974 |
| | Lieutenant, Colonel, 06 November 1978 |
| | Colonel, 01 October 1983 |
| | Brigadier General, 01 August 1988 |
| | Major General, 01 October 1991 |
| | Lieutenant General, 07 June 1993 |
| | General, 01 March 1996 |

*Date of rank adjusted for time not spent on active duty.

# Index

## About the Authors

**GENERAL (RET.) HUGH SHELTON** served two terms as Chairman of the Joint Chiefs of Staff under Presidents Bill Clinton and George W. Bush. Shelton was the chief architect of the military response to the September 11 attacks, and has served in the U.S. Army for thirty-eight years as a specialist in airborne strategies and special operation tactics. He has been awarded the Congressional Gold Medal, the Purple Heart, six Distinguished Service Medals, and knighted by Queen Elizabeth. He lives in Morehead City, North Carolina, with his wife, Carolyn.

**RON LEVINSON** is a veteran film and television producer, director, writer, and studio executive. A past board member of the U.S. Air Force Public Advisory Counsel (where he counseled the Office of the Secretary of the Air Force on motion picture and television production), he currently lives in Los Angeles.

**MALCOLM McCONNELL** is the author or co-author of thirty books, including the *New York Times* #1 bestseller *American Soldier* with General Tommy Franks. McConnell lives in Queenstown, Maryland.